Robust Portfolio Optimization and Management

THE FRANK J. FABOZZI SERIES

Robust Portfolio Optimization and Management

FRANK J. FABOZZI
PETTER N. KOLM
DESSISLAVA A. PACHAMANOVA
SERGIO M. FOCARDI

John Wiley & Sons, Inc.

FJF
To my wife Donna and my children,
Francesco, Patricia, and Karly

PNK
To Åke and Gunilla, my parents, and to John and Carmen,
my wife's parents, for their unending love and support

DAP
To my husband, Christian Hicks,
and in memory of my grandfather, Georgyi Milyankov

SMF
To the memory of Bertrand Russell to whom I owe
the foundation of my intellectual development

Contents

Preface

In the past few years, there has been a notable increase in the use of financial modeling and optimization tools in equity portfolio management. In addition to the pressure on asset management firms to reduce costs and maintain a more stable and predictable performance in the aftermath of the downturn in the U.S. equity markets in 2002, three other general trends have contributed to this increase. First, there has been a revived interest in predictive models for asset returns. Predictive models assume that it is possible to make conditional forecasts of future returns—an objective that was previously considered not achievable by classical financial theory. Second, the wide availability of sophisticated and specialized software packages has enabled generating and exploiting these forecasts in portfolio management, often in combination with optimization and simulation techniques. Third, the continuous increase in computer speed and the simultaneous decrease in hardware costs have made the necessary computing power affordable even to small firms.

As the use of modeling techniques has become widespread among portfolio managers, however, the issue of how much confidence practitioners can have in theoretical models and data has grown in importance. Consequently, there is an increased level of interest in the subject of robust estimation and optimization in modern portfolio management. For years, robustness has been a crucial ingredient in the engineering, statistics, and operations research fields. Today, these fields provide a rich source of ideas to finance professionals. While robust portfolio management undoubtedly demands much more than the robust application of quantitative techniques, there is now a widespread recognition for the need of a disciplined approach to the analysis and management of investments.

In this book we bring together concepts from finance, economic theory, robust statistics, econometrics, and robust optimization, and illustrate that they are part of the same theoretical and practical environment—in a way that even a nonspecialized audience can understand and appreciate. At the same time, we emphasize a practical treatment of the subject, and translate complex concepts into real-world applications for robust return forecasting and asset allocation optimization. Thereby, we address a number of issues in portfolio allocation and rebalancing. In particular, we discuss how to make portfolio management robust with respect to model risk, long-term views of the market, and market frictions such as trading costs.

The book is divided into four parts. Part I covers classical portfolio theory and its modern extensions. We provide an up-to-date treatment of methods for advanced risk management, nonnormal distributions for asset returns, transaction costs, and multiaccount portfolio management. Part II introduces traditional and modern frameworks for robust estimation of returns. We address a number of topics that include dimensionality reduction, robust covariance matrix estimation, shrinkage estimators, and the Black-Litterman framework for incorporating investors' views in an equilibrium framework. Part III provides readers with the necessary background for handling the optimization part of portfolio management. It covers major issues in numerical optimization, introduces widely used optimization software packages and modeling platforms, and discusses methods for handling uncertainty in optimization models such as stochastic programming, dynamic programming, and robust optimization. Part IV focuses on applications of the robust estimation and optimization methods described in the previous parts, and outlines recent trends and new directions in robust portfolio management and in the investment management industry in general. We cover a range of topics from portfolio resampling, robust formulations of the classical portfolio optimization framework under modeling uncertainty, robust use of factor models, and multiperiod portfolio allocation models—to the use of derivatives in portfolio management, currency management, benchmark selection, modern quantitative trading strategies, model risk mitigation, as well as optimal execution and algorithmic trading.

We believe that practitioners and analysts who have to develop and use portfolio management applications will find these themes—along with the numerous examples of applications and sample computer code—useful. At the same time, we address the topics in this book in a theoretically rigorous way, and provide references to the original works, so the book should be of interest to academics, students, and researchers who need an updated and integrated view of the theory and practice of portfolio management.

TEACHING USING THIS BOOK

This book can be used in teaching courses in advanced econometrics, financial engineering, quantitative investments and portfolio management, as the main course book, as supplemental reading on advanced topics, and/or for student projects. The material in Chapters 2 through 11 of the book is appropriate for undergraduate advanced electives on investment management, and all topics in the book are accessible to graduate students in finance, economics or in the mathematical and physical sciences. The material is also appropriate for use in advanced graduate electives in the decision sciences and operations research that focus on applications of quantitative techniques in finance.

For a typical course, it is natural to start with Chapters 2, 5, and 6 where modern portfolio and asset pricing theory and standard estimation techniques are covered. Basic practical considerations are presented in Chapters 4 and 11. Chapters 3, 7, 8, 10, 12, and 13 are more advanced and do not have to be covered in full. A possibility is to focus on the most common techniques used in portfolio management today, such as Value-at-Risk (VaR) and Conditional Value-at-Risk (CVaR) (in Chapter 3), shrinkage estimators and the Black-Litterman model (in Chapter 8), robust optimization (in Chapters 10 and 12), and transaction costs and portfolio rebalancing (in Chapter 13). Student projects can be based on specialized topics such as multiaccount optimization (in Chapter 4), numerical optimization techniques (in Chapter 9), modern trading strategies, optimal execution, and algorithmic trading (in Chapter 14).

ACKNOWLEDGMENTS

In writing a book that covers a wide range of topics in portfolio management theory and practice, applied mathematics, statistics, and operations research, we were fortunate to have received valuable comments and suggestions from the following individuals (listed below in alphabetical order):

- Sebastian Ceria and Robert Stubbs of Axioma, Inc. reviewed Chapter 12.
- Eranda Dragoti-Cela of Siemens—Fin4Cast reviewed Chapter 12.
- Dashan Huang of Kyoto University reviewed Chapters 10, 12, and 13.
- Ivana Ljubic of the University of Vienna reviewed Chapter 12.
- John M. Manoyan of CYMALEX Advisors reviewed Chapter 14.
- Jeff Miller of Millennium Partners reviewed Chapters 13 and 14.
- Bernd Scherer of Morgan Stanley reviewed Chapter 4.
- Melvyn Sim of the National University of Singapore Business School reviewed Chapter 12.

■ Reha Tütüncü of Goldman Sachs Asset Management reviewed Chapters 10 and 12.

We thank Morgan Stanley Capital International, Inc., http://www.msci.com, for providing us with the MSCI World Index data set used in some of the computational examples throughout the book. In particular, we are indebted to Nicholas G. Keyes for answering all of our questions in regards to the data set.

Megan Orem typeset the book and provided editorial assistance. We appreciate her patience and understanding in working through numerous revisions of the chapters and several reorganizations of the table of contents.

Frank J. Fabozzi
Petter N. Kolm
Dessislava A. Pachamanova
Sergio M. Focardi

Frank J. Fabozzi is Professor in the Practice of Finance in the School of Management at Yale University. Prior to joining the Yale faculty, he was a Visiting Professor of Finance in the Sloan School at MIT. Frank is a Fellow of the International Center for Finance at Yale University and on the Advisory Council for the Department of Operations Research and Financial Engineering at Princeton University. He is the editor of the *Journal of Portfolio Management* and an associate editor of the *Journal of Fixed Income*. He earned a doctorate in economics from the City University of New York in 1972. In 2002 was inducted into the Fixed Income Analysts Society's Hall of Fame and is the 2007 recipient of the C. Stewart Sheppard Award given by the CFA Institute. He earned the designation of Chartered Financial Analyst and Certified Public Accountant. He has authored and edited numerous books in finance.

Petter N. Kolm is a doctoral student in Finance at the School of Management, Yale University, a financial consultant in New York City, and a member of the editorial board of the *Journal of Portfolio Management*. Previously, he worked in the Quantitative Strategies Group at Goldman Sachs Asset Management where his responsibilities included researching and developing new quantitative investment strategies for the group's hedge fund. Petter coauthored the books *Financial Modeling of the Equity Market: From CAPM to Cointegration* and *Trends in Quantitative Finance*. His research interests include various topics in finance, such as equity and fixed income modeling, delegated portfolio management, financial econometrics, risk management, and optimal portfolio strategies. Petter received a doctorate in mathematics from Yale University in 2000. He also holds an M.Phil. in applied mathematics from the Royal Institute of Technology in Stockholm and an M.S. in mathematics from ETH Zürich.

Dessislava A. Pachamanova is an Assistant Professor of Operations Research at Babson College where she holds the Zwerling Term Chair. Her research interests lie in the areas of robust optimization, portfolio risk management, simulation, and financial engineering. Dessislava's academic research is supplemented by consulting and previous work in the financial industry, including projects with quantitative strategy groups at WestLB and Goldman Sachs. She holds an A.B. in Mathematics from Princeton University and a Ph.D. in Operations Research from the Sloan School of Management at MIT.

Sergio Focardi is a founding partner of the Paris-based consulting firm The Intertek Group and consults and trains on quantitative methods in equity portfolio management. Sergio is a member of the Editorial Board of the *Journal of Portfolio Management*, co-author of the CFA Institute's monograph *Trends in Quantitative Finance* (Fabozzi, Focardi and Kolm, 2006) of the books *Financial Econometrics* (Rachev, Mittnik, Fabozzi, Focardi, Jasic, Wiley, 2007), *Financial Modeling of the Equity Market* (Fabozzi, Focardi and Kolm, Wiley, 2006), *The Mathematics of Financial Modeling and Investment Management* (Focardi and Fabozzi, Wiley, 2004), *Risk Management: Framework, Methods and Practice* (Focardi and Jonas, Wiley, 1998), and *Modeling the Markets: New Theories and Techniques* (Focardi and Jonas, Wiley, 1997). Sergio has implemented long-short equity portfolio selection applications based on dynamic factor analysis. His research interests include the econometrics of large equity portfolios and the modeling of regime changes. Sergio holds a degree in Electronic Engineering from the University of Genoa and a postgraduate degree in Communications from the Galileo Ferraris Electrotechnical Institute (Turin).

CHAPTER 1

Introduction

A s the use of quantitative techniques has become more widespread in the financial industry, the issues of how to apply financial models most effectively and how to mitigate model and estimation errors have grown in importance. This book discusses some of the major trends and innovations in the management of financial portfolios today, focusing on state-of-the-art robust methodologies for portfolio risk and return estimation, optimization, trading, and general management.

In this chapter, we give an overview of the main topics in the book. We begin by providing a historical outlook of the adoption of quantitative techniques in the financial industry and the factors that have contributed to its growth. We then discuss the central themes of the book in more detail, and give a description of the structure and content of its remaining chapters.

QUANTITATIVE TECHNIQUES IN THE INVESTMENT MANAGEMENT INDUSTRY

Over the last 20 years there has been a tremendous increase in the use of quantitative techniques in the investment management industry. The first applications were in risk management, with models measuring the risk exposure to different sources of risk. Nowadays, quantitative models are considered to be invaluable in all the major areas of investment management, and the list of applications continues to grow: option pricing models for the valuation of complicated derivatives and structured products, econometric techniques for forecasting market returns, automated execution algorithms for efficient trading and transaction cost management, portfolio optimization for asset allocation and financial planning, and statistical techniques for performance measurement and attribution, to name a few.

Today, quantitative finance has evolved into its own discipline—an example thereof is the many university programs and courses being offered in the area in parallel to the "more traditional" finance and MBA programs. Naturally, many different factors have contributed to the tremendous development of the quantitative areas of finance, and it is impossible to list them all. However, the following influences and contributions are especially noteworthy:

- The development of modern financial economics, and the advances in the mathematical and physical sciences.
- The remarkable expansion in computer technology and the invention of the Internet.
- The maturing and growth of the capital markets.

Below, we highlight a few topics from each one of these areas and discuss their impact upon quantitative finance and investment management in general.

Modern Financial Economics and the Mathematical and Physical Sciences

The concepts of portfolio optimization and diversification have been instrumental in the development and understanding of financial markets and financial decision making. The major breakthrough came in 1952 with the publication of Harry Markowitz's theory of portfolio selection.[1] The theory, popularly referred to as *modern portfolio theory*, provided an answer to the fundamental question: How should an investor allocate funds among the possible investment choices? Markowitz suggested that investors should consider *risk and return* together and determine the allocation of funds among investment alternatives on the basis of the trade-off between them. Before Markowitz's seminal article, the finance literature had treated the interplay between risk and return in a casual manner.

The idea that sound financial decision making is a quantitative trade-off between risk and return was revolutionary for two reasons. First, it posited that one could make a quantitative evaluation of risk

---

[1] Harry M. Markowitz, "Portfolio Selection," *Journal of Finance* 7, no. 1 (March 1952), pp. 77–91. The principles in Markowitz's article were later expanded upon in his book *Portfolio Selection*, Cowles Foundation Monograph 16 (New York: John Wiley & Sons, 1959). Markowitz was awarded the Nobel Prize in Economic Sciences in 1990 for his work.

and return *jointly* by considering portfolio returns and their comovements. An important principle at work here is that of portfolio diversification. It is based on the idea that a portfolio's riskiness depends on the covariances of its constituents, not only on the average riskiness of its separate holdings. This concept was foreign to classical financial analysis, which revolved around the notion of the value of single investments, that is, the belief that investors should invest in those assets that offer the highest future value given their current price. Second, it formulated the financial decision-making process as an optimization problem. In particular, the so-called mean-variance principle formulated by Markowitz suggests that among the infinite number of portfolios that achieve a particular return objective, the investor should choose the portfolio that has the smallest variance. All other portfolios are "inefficient" because they have a higher variance and, therefore, higher risk.

Building on Markowitz's work, William Sharpe,[2] John Lintner,[3] and Jan Mossin[4] introduced the first asset pricing theory, the capital asset pricing model—CAPM in short—between 1962 and 1964. The CAPM became the foundation and the standard on which risk-adjusted performance of professional portfolio managers is measured.

Modern portfolio theory and diversification provide a theoretical justification for mutual funds and index funds, that have experienced a tremendous growth since the 1980s. A simple classification of fund management is into active and passive management, based upon the *efficient market hypotheses* introduced by Eugene Fama[5] and Paul Samuelson[6] in 1965. The efficient market hypothesis implies that it is not possible to outperform the market consistently on a risk-adjusted basis after accounting for transaction costs by using available information. In active management, it is assumed that markets are not fully efficient and that a fund manager can outperform a market index by using specific information, knowledge, and experience. Passive management, in con-

---

[2] William F. Sharpe, "Capital Asset Prices," *Journal of Finance* 19, no. 3 (September 1964), pp. 425–442. Sharpe received the Nobel Prize in Economic Sciences in 1990 for his work.

[3] John Lintner, "The Valuation of Risk Assets and the Selection of Risky Investments in Stock Portfolio and Capital Budgets," *Review of Economics and Statistics* 47 (February 1965), pp. 13–37.

[4] Jan Mossin, "Equilibrium in a Capital Asset Market," *Econometrica* 34, no. 4 (October 1966), pp. 768–783.

[5] Eugene F. Fama, "The Behavior of Stock Market Prices," *Journal of Business* 38 (January 1965), pp. 34–105.

[6] Paul A. Samuelson, "Proof that Properly Anticipated Prices Fluctuate Randomly," *Industrial Management Review* 6, no. 2 (Spring 1965), pp. 41–49. Samuelson was honored with the Nobel Prize in Economic Sciences in 1970.

trast, relies on the assumption that financial markets are efficient and that return and risk are fully reflected in asset prices. In this case, an investor should invest in a portfolio that mimics the market. John Bogle used this basic idea when he proposed to the board of directors of the newly formed Vanguard Group to create the first index fund in 1975. The goal was not to outperform the S&P 500 index, but instead to track the index as closely as possible by buying each of the stocks in the S&P 500 in amounts equal to the weights in the index itself.

Despite the great influence and theoretical impact of modern portfolio theory, today—more than 50 years after Markowitz's seminal work—full risk-return optimization at the asset level is primarily done only at the more quantitatively oriented firms. In the investment management business at large, portfolio management is frequently a purely judgmental process based on qualitative, not quantitative, assessments. The availability of quantitative tools is not the issue—today's optimization technology is mature and much more user-friendly than it was at the time Markowitz first proposed the theory of portfolio selection—yet many asset managers avoid using the quantitative portfolio allocation framework altogether.

A major reason for the reluctance of investment managers to apply quantitative risk-return optimization is that they have observed that it may be unreliable in practice. Specifically, risk-return optimization is very sensitive to changes in the inputs (in the case of mean-variance optimization, such inputs include the expected return of each asset and the asset covariances). While it can be difficult to make accurate estimates of these inputs, estimation errors in the forecasts significantly impact the resulting portfolio weights. It is well-known, for instance, that in practical applications equally weighted portfolios often outperform mean-variance portfolios, mean-variance portfolios are not necessarily well-diversified, and mean-variance optimization can produce extreme or non-intuitive weights for some of the assets in the portfolio. Such examples, however, are not necessarily a sign that the *theory* of risk-return optimization is flawed; rather, that when used *in practice*, the classical framework has to be modified in order to achieve reliability, stability, and robustness with respect to model and estimation errors.

It goes without saying that advances in the mathematical and physical sciences have had a major impact upon finance. In particular, mathematical areas such as probability theory, statistics, econometrics, operations research, and mathematical analysis have provided the necessary tools and discipline for the development of modern financial economics. Substantial advances in the areas of robust estimation and robust optimization were made during the 1990s, and have proven to be of great importance for the practical applicability and reliability of portfolio management and optimization.

Any statistical estimate is subject to error—estimation error. A robust estimator is a statistical estimation technique that is less sensitive to outliers in the data. For example, in practice, it is undesirable that one or a few extreme returns have a large impact on the estimation of the average return of a stock. Nowadays, Bayesian techniques and robust statistics are commonplace in financial applications. Taking it one step further, practitioners are starting to incorporate the uncertainty introduced by estimation errors directly into the optimization process. This is very different from the classical approach, where one solves the portfolio optimization problem as a problem with deterministic inputs, without taking the estimation errors into account. In particular, the statistical precision of individual estimates is explicitly incorporated in the portfolio allocation process. Providing this benefit is the underlying goal of *robust portfolio optimization*.

First introduced by El Ghaoui and Lebret[7] and by Ben-Tal and Nemirovski,[8] modern robust optimization techniques allow a portfolio manager to solve the robust version of the portfolio optimization problem in about the same time as needed for the classical portfolio optimization problem. The robust approach explicitly uses the distribution from the estimation process to find a robust portfolio in *one single* optimization, thereby directly incorporating uncertainty about inputs in the optimization process. As a result, robust portfolios are less sensitive to estimation errors than other portfolios, and often perform better than classical mean–variance portfolios. Moreover, the robust optimization framework offers great flexibility and many new interesting applications. For instance, robust portfolio optimization can exploit the notion of statistically equivalent portfolios. This concept is important in large-scale portfolio management involving many complex constraints such as transaction costs, turnover, or market impact. Specifically, with robust optimization, a manager can find the best portfolio that (1) minimizes trading costs with respect to the current holdings and (2) has an expected portfolio return and variance that are statistically equivalent to those of the classical mean-variance portfolio.

An important area of quantitative finance is that of modeling asset price behavior, and pricing options and other derivatives. This field can

[7] Laurent El Ghaoui, and Herve Lebret, "Robust Solutions to Least-Squares Problems with Uncertain Data," *SIAM Journal on Matrix Analysis and Applications* 18 (October 1997), pp. 1035–1064.

[8] Aharon Ben-Tal, and Arkadi S. Nemirovski, "Robust Convex Optimization," *Mathematics of Operations Research* 23, no. 4 (1998), pp. 769–805; and Aharon Ben-Tal, and Arkadi S. Nemirovski, "Robust Solutions to Uncertain Linear Programs," *Operations Research Letters* 25, no. 1 (1999), pp. 1–13.

be traced back to the early works of Thorvald Thiele[9] in 1880, Louis Bachelier[10] in 1900, and Albert Einstein[11] in 1905, who knew nothing about each other's research and independently developed the mathematics of Brownian motion. Interestingly, while the models by Thiele and Bachelier had little influence for a long time, Einstein's contribution had an immediate impact on the physical sciences. Historically, Bachelier's doctoral thesis is the first published work that uses advanced mathematics in the study of finance. Therefore, he is by many considered to be the pioneer of financial mathematics—the first "quant."[12]

The first listed options began trading in April 1973 on the Chicago Board Options Exchange (CBOE), only one and four months, respectively, before the papers by Black and Scholes[13] and by Merton[14] on option pricing were published. Although often criticized in the general press, and misunderstood by the public at large, options opened the door to a new era in investment and risk management, and influenced the introduction and popularization of a range of other financial products including interest rate swaptions, mortgage-backed securities, callable bonds, structured products, and credit derivatives. New derivative products were made possible as a solid pricing theory was available. Without the models developed by Black, Scholes, and Merton and many others following in their footsteps, it is likely that the rapid expansion

---

[9] Thorvald N. Theile, "Sur la Compensation de Quelques Erreurs Quasi-Systématiques par la Méthodes de Moindre Carrés [On the Compensation of Some Quasi-Systematic Errors by the Least Square Method]," *Vidensk. Selsk. Skr. 5* (1880), pp. 381–408.

[10] Louis Bachelier, "Théorie de la Speculation [Theory of Speculation]," *Annales Scientifiques de l'École Normale Supérieure Sér.*, 3, 17 (1900), pp. 21–86

[11] Albert Einstein, "On the Movement of Small Particles Suspended in Stationary Liquid Demanded by the Molecular-Kinetic Theory of Heat," in R. Fürth (ed.), *Investigations of the Theory of Brownian Movement* (New York: Dover Publications, 1956).

[12] The term "quant" which is short for *quantitative analyst* (someone who works in the financial markets developing mathematical models) was popularized, among other things, by Emanuel Derman in his book *My Life as a Quant* (Hoboken, NJ: John Wiley & Sons, 2004). On a lighter note, a T-shirt with the words "Quants Do It with Models" circulated among some quantitative analysts on Wall Street a few years ago.

[13] Fischer S. Black and Myron S. Scholes, "The Pricing of Options and Corporate Liabilities," *Journal of Political Economy* 81, no. 3 (1973), pp. 637–659. Scholes received the Nobel Prize of Economic Science in 1997 for his work on option pricing theory. At that time, sadly, Fischer Black had passed away, but he received an honorable mention in the award.

[14] Robert C. Merton, "Theory of Rational Option Pricing," *Bell Journal of Economics and Management Science* 4, no. 1 (Spring 1973), pp. 141–183. Merton received the Nobel Prize of Economic Science in 1997 for his work on option pricing theory.

of derivative products would never have happened. These modern instruments and the concepts of portfolio theory, CAPM, arbitrage and equilibrium pricing, and market predictability form the foundation not only for modern financial economics but for the general understanding and development of today's financial markets. As Peter Bernstein so adequately puts it in his book *Capital Ideas*: "Every time an institution uses these instruments, a corporation issues them, or a homeowner takes out a mortgage, they are paying their respects, not just to Black, Scholes, and Merton, but to Bachelier, Samuelson, Fama, Markowitz, Tobin, Treynor, and Sharpe as well."[15]

Computer Technology and the Internet

The appearance of the first personal computers in the late 1970s and early 1980s forever changed the world of computing. It put computational resources within the reach of most people. In a few years every trading desk on Wall Street was equipped with a PC. From that point on, computing costs have declined at the significant pace of about a factor of 2 every year. For example, the cost per gigaflops[16] is about $1 today, to be compared to about $50,000 about 10 years ago.[17] At the same time, computer speed increased in a similar fashion: today's fastest computers are able to perform an amazing 300 trillion calculations per second.[18] This remarkable development of computing technology has allowed finance professionals to deploy more sophisticated algorithms used, for instance, for derivative and asset pricing, market forecasting, portfolio allocation, and computerized execution and trading. With state-of-the-art optimization software, a portfolio manager is able to calculate the optimal allocation for a portfolio of thousands of assets in no more than a few seconds—on the manager's desktop computer!

---

[15] Peter L. Bernstein, *Capital Ideas* (New York: Free Press,1993).

[16] Flops is an abbreviation for *floating point operations per second* and is used as a measure of a computer's performance. 1 gigaflops = 10^9 flops.

[17] See Michael S. Warren, John K. Salmon, Donald J. Becker, M. Patrick Goda, Thomas Sterling, and Grégoire S. Winckelmans, "Pentium Pro Inside: I. A Treecode at 430 Gigaflops on ASCI Red. II. Price/Performance of $50/Mflop on Loki and Hyglac," *Supercomputing '97*, Los Alamitos, 1997, IEEE Computer Society; and Wikipedia contributors, "FLOPS," *Wikipedia, The Free Encyclopedia*, http://en.wikipedia.org/w/index.php?title=FLOPS&oldid=90585825 (accessed December 1, 2006).

[18] As of November 2006, the IBM BlueGene/L system with 131072 processor units held the so-called Linpack record with a remarkable performance of 280.6 teraflops (that is, 280.6 trillions of floating-point operations per second). See TOP500, www.top500.org.

But computational power alone is not sufficient for financial applications. It is crucial to obtain market data and other financial information efficiently and expediently, often in real time. The Internet and the World Wide Web have proven invaluable for this purpose. The World Wide Web, or simply the "Web," first created by Tim Berners-Lee working at CERN in Geneva, Switzerland around 1990, is an arrangement of interlinked, hypertext documents available over the Internet. With a simple browser, anybody can view webpages that may contain anything from text and pictures, to other multimedia based information, and jump from page to page by a simple mouse click.[19] Berners-Lee's major contribution was to combine the concept of hypertext with the Internet, born out of the NSFNet developed by the National Science Foundation in the early 1980s. The Web as we know it today allows for expedient exchange of financial information. Many market participants—from individuals to investment houses and hedge funds—use the Internet to follow financial markets as they move tick by tick and to trade many different kinds of assets such as stocks, bonds, futures, and other derivatives simultaneously across the globe. In today's world, gathering, processing, and analyzing the vast amount of information is only possible through the use of computer algorithms and sophisticated quantitative techniques.

Capital Markets

The development of the capital markets has of course had a significant impact on quantitative finance and the investment management industry as a whole. Investors today have a vast number of assets available in the capital markets, from more traditional assets such as stocks, bonds, commodities (precious metals, etc.) and real estate to derivative instruments such as options, futures, swaps, credit linked securities, mortgage-backed securities and other structured products, and specialized financial insurance products. These securities and products allow market participants to get exposure to, or to hedge risks—sometimes very specific risks. For example, a corporate bond portfolio manager may decide to hedge specific credit risks in his portfolio using a credit default swap, or a proprietary trader can short equity volatility by selling a volatility swap.

However, the number of assets available alone is not enough to guarantee success, if the assets are only traded infrequently and in small volumes. Successful capital markets have to be liquid, allowing market participants to trade their positions quickly and at low cost. An asset is

---

[19] A recent study concluded that as of January 2005 there are over 11.5 billion public webpages available on the Internet, see Antonio Gulli and Alessio Signorini, "The Indexable Web is More than 11.5 billion pages," 2005, Dipartimento di Informatica at Universita' di Pisa and Department of Computer Science at University of Iowa.

said to be liquid if it can be converted to cash quickly at a price close to fair market value. The U.S. capital markets are the most liquid in the world with Japan and the United Kingdom following. Cash, being the basic liquid asset, does not fluctuate in value—it itself defines price. All other assets can change in value and have an uncertain future price, making them risky assets. Naturally, informed investors will only hold less liquid and risky assets if they can expect to earn a premium, a risk premium.

With the tremendous increase in the number of assets—and with it, the amount of investment opportunities—it is hard, even for larger investment houses, to track and evaluate the different markets. Quantitative techniques lend themselves for automatic monitoring and analysis of the full multitude of securities. These tools give quantitative analysts, portfolio managers, and other decision makers the opportunity to summarize the vast amount of information available, and to present it in a cohesive manner. Modern financial and the econometric models rely on the access to accurate data, often with as long history as possible. It is typically much easier to obtain clean and trustworthy financial data from mature and liquid markets. In fact, the lack of reliable data is one of the inherent problems in applying sophisticated quantitative models to more illiquid markets. In these cases, practitioners are forced to rely on simulated data, make stronger assumptions in their models, or use less data-intensive models.

CENTRAL THEMES OF THIS BOOK

The purpose of this book is to provide a comprehensive introduction and overview of the state-of-the-art of portfolio management and optimization for practitioners, academics, and students alike. We attempt to bridge the gap from classical portfolio theory, as developed in the early 1950s, to modern portfolio optimization applications used in practice today. In particular, we provide an up-to-date review of robust estimation and optimization methods deployed in modern portfolio management, and discuss different techniques used in order to overcome the common pitfalls associated with classical mean-variance optimization. We discuss recent developments in quantitative trading strategies, trade execution, and operations research. While we focus on real world practical usability, and emphasize intuition and fundamental understanding, we try not to sacrifice mathematical rigor whenever possible.

We note that the concept of robustness in investment science extends beyond statistical and modeling methods. It suggests a new approach to financial forecasting, asset allocation, portfolio management, and trading. As a matter of fact, the concept of a *robust quantitative investment framework* seems to be gaining ground in the quantitative investment community, and is loosely defined by the following four stages:

1. Estimate reliable asset forecasts along with a measure of their confidence.
2. Deploy a robust model for portfolio allocation and risk management.
3. Manage portfolio rebalancing and trading costs efficiently as market conditions change.
4. Monitor and review the entire investment process on a regular basis.

The last stage includes the ability to evaluate past performance, as well as to measure and analyze portfolio risk. The role of quantitative models for econometric forecasting and optimization at each of these stages is very important, especially in large-scale investment management applications that require allocating, rebalancing, and monitoring of thousands of assets and portfolios.

From a broad perspective, the topics in this book can be categorized in the following four main areas: robust estimation, robust portfolio allocation, portfolio rebalancing, and management of model risk.

Robust Estimation

Models to predict expected returns of assets are routinely used by major asset management firms. In most cases, these models are straightforward and based on factors or other forecasting variables. Since parameter estimation in these financial models is data-driven, they are inevitably subject to estimation error. What makes matters worse, however, is that different estimation errors are accumulated across the different stages in the portfolio management process. As a result, the compounding of small errors from the different stages may result in large aggregate errors at the final stage. It is therefore important that parameters estimated at the different stages are reliable and robust so that the aggregate impact of estimation errors is minimized.

Given the existing plethora of financial forecasting models, the entire topic of robust statistical estimation is too extensive to cover in this book.[20] We will, however, touch upon several major topics. In particular, we review some fundamental statistical techniques for forecasting returns, show how robust statistical estimators for important inputs in the portfolio optimization process can be obtained, and how a robust

---

[20] For an overview of equity forecasting models, see Frank J. Fabozzi, Sergio M. Focardi, and Petter N. Kolm, *Financial Modeling of the Equity Market: From CAPM to Cointegration* (Hoboken, NJ: John Wiley & Sons, 2006).

portfolio allocation framework minimizes the impact of estimation and model errors. We describe robust frameworks for incorporating the investor's views such as shrinkage techniques and the Black-Litterman model to produce informed forecasts about the behavior of asset returns.

Robust Portfolio Allocation

Robust asset allocation is one of the most important parts of the investment management process, and the decision making is frequently based on the recommendations of risk-return optimization routines. Several major themes deserve attention. First, it is important to carefully consider how portfolio risk and return are defined, and whether these definitions are appropriate given observed or forecasted asset return distributions and underlying investor preferences. These concerns give rise to alternative theories of risk measures and asset allocation frameworks beyond classical mean-variance optimization. Second, the issue of how the optimization problem is formulated and solved in practice is crucial, especially for larger portfolios. A working knowledge of the state-of-the-art capabilities of quantitative software for portfolio management is critical. Third, it is imperative to evaluate the sensitivity of portfolio optimization models to inaccuracies in input estimates. We cover the major approaches for optimization under uncertainty in input parameters, including a recently developed area in optimization—*robust optimization*—that has shown a great potential and usability for portfolio management and optimization applications.

Portfolio Rebalancing

While asset allocation is one of the major strategic decisions, the decision of how to achieve this allocation in a cost-effective manner is no less important in obtaining good and consistent performance. Furthermore, given existing holdings, portfolio managers need to decide how to rebalance their portfolios efficiently to incorporate new views on expected returns and risk as the economic environment and the asset mix change. There are two basic aspects of the problem of optimal portfolio rebalancing. The first one is the robust management of the trading and transaction costs in the rebalancing process. The second is successfully combining both long-term and short-term views on the future direction and changes in the markets. The latter aspect is particularly important when taxes or liabilities have to be taken into account. The two aspects are not distinct, and in practice have to be considered simultaneously. By incorporating long-term views on asset behavior, portfolio managers may be able to reduce their overall transaction costs, as their portfolios do not have to be rebalanced as often. Although the interplay between the different aspects is complex to evaluate and model, disciplined portfolio rebalancing using an optimizer provides portfolio managers with new opportunities.

Managing Model Risk

Quantitative approaches to portfolio management introduce a new source of risk—model risk—and an inescapable dependence on historical data as their raw material. Financial models are typically predictive—they are used to forecast unknown or future values on the basis of current or known values using specified equations or sets of rules. Their predictive or forecasting power, however, is limited by the appropriateness of the inputs and basic model assumptions. Incorrect assumptions, model identification and specification errors, or inappropriate estimation procedures inevitably lead to model risk, as does using models without sufficient out-of-sample testing. It is important to be cautious in how we use models, and to make sure that we fully understand their weaknesses and limitations. In order to identify the various sources of model risk, we need to take a critical look at our models, review them on a regular basis, and avoid their use beyond the purpose or application for which they were originally designed.

OVERVIEW OF THIS BOOK

We have organized the book as follows. Part I (Chapters 2, 3, and 4) introduces the underpinnings of modern portfolio theory. Part II (Chapters 5, 6, 7, and 8) summarizes important developments in the estimation of parameters such as expected asset returns and their covariances that serve as inputs to the classical portfolio optimization framework. Part III (Chapters 9, 10, and 11) describes the tools necessary to handle the optimization step of the process. Part IV (Chapters 12, 13, and 14) focuses on applications of the methods described in the previous parts, and outlines new directions in robust portfolio optimization and investment management as a whole.

We start out by describing the classical portfolio theory and the concepts of diversification in Chapter 2. We introduce the concepts of efficient sets and efficient frontiers, and discuss the effect of long-only constraints. We also present an alternative framework for optimal decision making in investment—expected utility optimization—and explain its relationship to classical mean-variance optimization.

Chapter 3 extends classical portfolio theory to a more general mean-risk setting. We cover the most common alternative measures of risk that, in some cases, are better suited than variance in describing investor preferences when it comes to skewed and/or fat-tailed asset return distributions. We also show how to incorporate investor preferences for higher moments in the expected utility maximization framework, and discuss polynomial goal programming. Finally, we introduce a new approach to portfolio selection with higher moments proposed by Malevergne and Sornette, and illustrate the approach with examples.

Chapter 4 provides an overview of practical considerations in implementing portfolio optimization. We review constraints that are most commonly faced by portfolio managers, and show how to formulate them as part of the optimization problem. We also show how the classical framework for portfolio allocation can be extended to include transaction costs, and discuss the issue of optimizing trading impact costs across multiple client accounts simultaneously.

Chapter 5 introduces a number of price and return models that are used in portfolio management. We examine different types of random walks, present their key properties, and compare them to other trend-stationary processes. We also discuss standard financial models for explaining and modeling asset returns that are widely used in practice—the Capital Asset Pricing Model (CAPM), Arbitrage Pricing Theory (APT), and factor models,

The estimation of asset expected returns and covariances is essential for classical portfolio management. Chapter 6 covers the standard approaches for estimating parameters in portfolio optimization models. We discuss methods for estimating expected returns and covariance matrices, introduce dimensionality reduction techniques such as factor models, and use random matrix theory to illustrate how noisy the sample covariance matrix can be. In Chapter 7, we provide an introduction to the theory of robust statistical estimation.

Chapter 8 presents recent developments in asset return forecasting models, focusing on new frameworks for robust estimation of important parameters. In particular, we discuss shrinkage methods and the Black-Litterman approach for expected return estimation. Such methods allow for combining statistical estimates with investors' views of the market.

The subject of Chapter 9 is practical numerical optimization, our goal being to introduce readers to the concept of "difficult" versus "easy" optimization problems. We discuss the types of optimization techniques encountered in portfolio management problems—linear and quadratic programming, as well as the more advanced areas of convex programming, conic optimization, and integer programming. We explain the concept of optimization duality and describe intuitively how optimization algorithms work. Illustrations of the various techniques are provided, from the classical simplex method for solving linear programming problems to state-of-the-art barrier- and interior-point methods.

Classical optimization methods treat the parameters in optimization problems as deterministic and fully accurate. In practice, however, these parameters are typically estimated from error-prone statistical procedures or based on subjective evaluation, resulting in estimates with significant estimation errors. The output of optimization routines based on poorly estimated inputs can be seriously misleading and often useless. This is a reason why optimizers are sometimes cynically referred to as "error maximizers." It is important to know how to treat uncertainty in the estimates of input parameters in optimization problems. Chapter 10 provides a taxonomy of methods for optimization under uncertainty. We review the main ideas behind stochastic programming, dynamic programming, and robust optimization, and illustrate the methods with examples.

Chapter 11 contains practical suggestions for formulating and solving optimization problems in real-world applications. We review publicly and commercially available software for different types of optimization problems and portfolio optimization in particular, and provide examples of implementation of portfolio optimization problems in AMPL (an optimization modeling language) and MATLAB (a popular modeling environment).

Chapter 12 focuses on the application of robust optimization and resampling techniques for treating uncertainty in the parameters of classical mean-variance portfolio optimization. We present robust counterparts of the classical portfolio optimization problem under a variety of assumptions on the asset return distributions and different forms of estimation errors in expected returns and risk.

In Chapter 13, we describe recent trends and new directions in the area of robust portfolio management, and elaborate on extensions and refinements of some of the techniques described elsewhere in this book. In particular, we provide an overview of more advanced topics such as handling the underestimation of risk in factor models, robust applications of alternative risk measures, portfolio rebalancing with transaction and trading costs, and multiperiod portfolio optimization.

The last chapter of the book, Chapter 14, provides an outlook of some important aspects of quantitative investment management. We address the use of derivatives in portfolio management, currency management in international portfolios, and benchmark selection. We examine the most widespread quantitative and model-based trading strategies used in quantitative trading today, and discuss model risk including data snooping and overfitting. The chapter closes with an introduction to optimal execution and algorithmic trading.

The appendix at the end of the book contains a description of the data used in illustrations in several of the chapters.

One

Portfolio Allocation: Classical Theory and Extensions

CHAPTER **2**

Mean-Variance Analysis and
Modern Portfolio Theory

A major step in the direction of the quantitative management of portfolios was made by Harry Markowitz in his paper "Portfolio Selection" published in 1952 in the *Journal of Finance*. The ideas introduced in this article have come to build the foundations of what is now popularly referred to as *mean-variance analysis, mean-variance optimization*, and *Modern Portfolio Theory* (MPT). Initially, mean-variance analysis generated relatively little interest, but with time, the financial community adopted the thesis. Today, financial models based on those very same principles are constantly being reinvented to incorporate new findings. In 1990, Harry Markowitz, Merton Miller, and William Sharpe were awarded the Nobel prize for their pioneering work in the theory of financial economics.[1]

Though widely applicable, mean-variance analysis has had the most influence in the practice of portfolio management. In its simplest form, mean-variance analysis provides a framework to construct and select portfolios, based on the expected performance of the investments and the risk appetite of the investor. Mean-variance analysis also introduced a whole new terminology, which now has become the norm in the area of investment management. However, more than 50 years after Markowitz's seminal work, it appears that mean-variance portfolio optimization is utilized only at the more quantitative firms, where processes for automated forecast generation and risk control are already in place. At many firms, portfolio management remains a purely judgmen-

---

[1] Markowitz was awarded the prize for having developed the theory of portfolio choice, Sharpe for his contributions to the theory of price formation for financial assets and the development of the Capital Asset Pricing Model, and Miller for his work in the theory of corporate finance.

tal process based on qualitative, not quantitative, assessments. The quantitative efforts at most firms appear to be focused on providing risk measures to portfolio managers. These measures offer asset managers a view of the level of risk in a particular portfolio, where risk is defined as underperformance relative to a mandate.

It may be useful to note here that the theory of portfolio selection is a normative theory. A *normative theory* is one that describes a standard or norm of behavior that investors should pursue in constructing a portfolio, in contrast to a theory that is actually followed. Asset pricing theory goes on to formalize the relationship that should exist between asset returns and risk if investors construct and select portfolios according to mean-variance analysis. In contrast to a normative theory, asset pricing theory is a *positive theory*—a theory that derives the implications of hypothesized investor behavior. An example of a positive theory is the *capital asset pricing model* (CAPM), discussed in more detail in Chapter 5. It seeks to explain and measure the excess return of an asset relative to the market. Specifically, as we will see, the CAPM states that an asset's excess return is proportional to the market's excess return, where the constant of proportionality is the covariance between the asset return and the market return divided by the variance of the market return. It is important to bear in mind that, like other financial theories, CAPM is a *model*. A model relies on a number of basic assumptions. Therefore, a model should be viewed as only an idealized description of the phenomenon or phenomena under study.

In this chapter, we begin with a general discussion of the benefits of diversification before we introduce the classical mean-variance framework. We derive the mean-variance portfolio for equality constraints and then illustrate some of its basic properties through practical examples. In particular, we show how the shape of the so-called efficient frontier changes with the addition of other assets (risky as well as risk-free) and with the introduction of short-selling constraints. In the presence of only risky assets, the mean-variance efficient frontier has a parabolic shape. However, with the inclusion of a risk-free asset, the efficient frontier becomes linear, forming the so-called Capital Market Line. We close the chapter with a discussion of utility functions and a general framework for portfolio choice.

THE BENEFITS OF DIVERSIFICATION

Conventional wisdom has always dictated "not putting all your eggs into one basket." In more technical terms, this old adage is addressing the benefits of diversification. Markowitz quantified the concept of diversification through the statistical notion of covariance between individual securities, and the overall standard deviation of a portfolio. In essence, the old adage is saying that investing all your money in assets that may all perform poorly at the same time—that is, whose returns are highly correlated—is not a very prudent investment strategy no matter how small the chance that any one asset will perform poorly. This is because if any one single asset performs poorly, it is likely, due to its high correlation with the other assets, that these other assets are also going to perform poorly, leading to the poor performance of the portfolio.

Diversification is related to the *Central Limit Theorem,* which states that the sum of identical and independent random variables with bounded variance is asymptotically Gaussian.[2] In its simplest form, we can formally state this as follows: if $X_1, X_2, ..., X_N$ are N independent random variables, each X_i with an arbitrary probability distribution, with finite mean μ and variance σ^2, then

$$\lim_{N \to \infty} P\left(\frac{1}{\sigma \sqrt{N}} \sum_{i=1}^{N} (X_i - \mu) \leq y \right) = \frac{1}{\sqrt{2\pi}} \int_{-\infty}^{y} e^{-\frac{1}{2}s^2} ds$$

For a portfolio of N identically and independently distributed assets with returns $R_1, R_2, ..., R_N$, in each of which we invest an equal amount, the portfolio return

$$R_p = \frac{1}{N} \sum_{i=1}^{N} R_i$$

is a random variable that will be distributed approximately Gaussian when N is sufficiently large. The Central Limit Theorem implies that the variance of this portfolio is

$$\text{var}(R_p) = \frac{1}{N^2} \sum_{i=1}^{N} \text{var}(R_i)$$

$$= \frac{1}{N^2} N \cdot \sigma^2$$

$$= \frac{\sigma^2}{N} \xrightarrow[N \to \infty]{} 0$$

---

[2] This notion of diversification can be extended to more general random variables by the concept of *mixing.* Mixing is a weaker form of independence that can be defined for quite general stochastic processes. Under certain so-called *mixing conditions,* a Central Limit Theorem can be shown to hold for quite general random variables and processes. See for example, James Davidson, *Stochastic Limit Theory* (Oxford: Oxford University Press, 1995).

where σ^2 is the variance of the assets. In particular, we conclude that in this setting as the number of assets increase the portfolio variance decreases towards zero. This is, of course, a rather idealistic situation. For real-world portfolios—even with a large number of assets—we cannot expect a portfolio variance of zero due to nonvanishing correlations.

It is well known that asset returns are not normal, and often exhibit fat tails. There is also certain evidence that the variances of some asset returns are not bounded (i.e., they are infinite and therefore do not exist). This calls to question the principle of diversification. In particular, it can be shown that if asset returns behave like certain so-called stable Paretian distributions, diversification may no longer be a meaningful economic activity.[3] In general, however, most practitioners agree that a certain level of diversification is achievable in the markets.

The first study of its kind performed by Evans and Archer in 1968 suggests that the major benefits of diversification can be obtained with as few as 10 to 20 individual equities.[4] More recent studies by Campbell et al.[5] and Malkiel[6] show that the volatility of individual stocks has increased over the period from the 1960s to the 1990s. On the other hand, the correlation between individual stocks has decreased over the same time period. Together, these two effects have canceled each other out, leaving the overall market volatility unchanged. However, Malkiel's study suggests that due to a general increase in idiosyncratic risk (firm specific) it now takes almost 200 individual equities to obtain the same amount of diversification that historically was possible with as few as 20 individual equities.

In these studies, the standard deviation of the portfolio was used to measure portfolio risk. With a different measure of risk the results will be different. For example, Vardharaj, Fabozzi, and Jones show that if portfolio risk is measured by the tracking error of the portfolio to a benchmark, more than 300 assets may be necessary in order to provide for sufficient diversification.[7]

The concept of diversification is so intuitive and so powerful that it has been continuously applied to different areas within finance. Indeed,

---

[3] Eugene F. Fama, "Portfolio Analysis In a Stable Paretian Market," *Management Science* 11, no. 3 (1965), pp. 404–419.

[4] John L. Evans, and Stephen H. Archer, "Diversification and the Reduction of Dispersion: An Empirical Analysis," *Journal of Finance* 23, no. 5 (December 1968), pp. 761–767.

[5] John Y. Campbell, Martin Lettau, Burton G. Malkiel, and Yexiao Xu, "Have Individual Stocks Become More Volatile? An Empirical Exploration of Idiosyncratic Risk," *Journal of Finance* 56, no. 1 (February 2001), pp. 1–43.

[6] Burton G. Malkiel, "How Much Diversification Is Enough?" Proceedings of the AIMR seminar "The Future of Equity Portfolio Construction," March 2002, pp. 26–27.

[7] Raman Vardharaj, Frank J. Fabozzi, and Frank J. Jones, "Determinants of Tracking Error for Equity Portfolios," *Journal of Investing* 13, no. 2 (Summer 2004), pp. 37–47.

a vast number of the innovations surrounding finance have either been in the application of the concept of diversification, or the introduction of new methods for obtaining improved estimates of the variances and covariances, thereby allowing for a more precise measure of diversification and consequently, for a more precise measure of risk. However, overall portfolio risk goes beyond just the standard deviation of a portfolio. Unfortunately, a portfolio with low expected standard deviation can still perform very poorly. There are many other dimensions to risk that are important to consider when devising an investment policy. Chapters 3, 6 and 8 are is dedicated to a more detailed discussion of different risk models, their measurement, and forecasting.

MEAN-VARIANCE ANALYSIS: OVERVIEW

Markowitz's starting point is that of a rational investor who, at time t, decides what portfolio of investments to hold for a time horizon of Δt. The investor makes decisions on the gains and losses he will make at time $t + \Delta t$, without considering eventual gains and losses either during or after the period Δt. At time $t + \Delta t$, the investor will reconsider the situation and decide anew. This one-period framework is often referred to as *myopic* (or "short-sighted") behavior. In general, a myopic investor's behavior is suboptimal in comparison to an investor who takes a broader approach and makes investment decisions based upon a multiperiod framework. For example, nonmyopic investment strategies are adopted when it is necessary to make trade-offs at future dates between consumption and investment or when significant trading costs related to specific subsets of investments are incurred throughout the holding period.

Markowitz reasoned that investors should decide on the basis of a trade-off between risk and expected return. Expected return of a security is defined as the expected price change plus any additional income over the time horizon considered, such as dividend payments, divided by the beginning price of the security. He suggested that risk should be measured by the variance of returns—the average squared deviation around the expected return.

We note that it is a common misunderstanding that Markowitz's mean-variance framework relies on joint normality of security returns. Markowitz's mean-variance framework does not assume joint normality of security returns. However, later in this chapter we show that the mean-variance approach is consistent with two different frameworks: (1) expected utility maximization under certain assumptions; or (2) the assumption that security returns are jointly normally distributed.

Moreover, Markowitz argued that for any given level of expected return, a rational investor would choose the portfolio with minimum variance from amongst the set of all possible portfolios. The set of all possible portfolios that can be constructed is called the *feasible set*. *Minimum variance portfolios* are called *mean-variance efficient portfolios*. The set of all mean-variance efficient portfolios, for different desired levels of expected return, is called the *efficient frontier*. Exhibit 2.1 provides a graphical illustration of the efficient frontier of risky assets. In particular, notice that the feasible set is bounded by the curve I-II-III. All portfolios on the curve II-III are efficient portfolios for different levels of risk. These portfolios offer the lowest level of standard deviation for a given level of expected return. Or equivalently, they constitute the portfolios that maximize expected return for a given level of risk. Therefore, the efficient frontier provides the best possible trade-off between expected return and risk—portfolios below it, such as portfolio IV, are inefficient and portfolios above it are unobtainable. The portfolio at point II is often referred to as the *global minimum variance port-*

EXHIBIT 2.1   Feasible and Markowitz Efficient Portfolios[a]

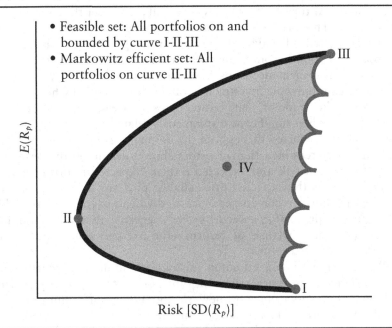

[a] The picture is for illustrative purposes only. The actual shape of the feasible region depends on the returns and risks of the assets chosen and the correlation among them.

folio (GMV), as it is the portfolio on the efficient frontier with the smallest variance.

Exhibit 2.2 shows a schematic view of the investment process as seen from the perspective of modern portfolio theory. This process is often also referred to as *mean-variance optimization* or *theory of portfolio selection*. The inputs to the process are estimates of the expected returns, volatilities and correlations of all the assets together with various portfolio constraints. For example, constraints can be as straightforward as not allowing the short-selling of any assets, or as complicated as limiting assets to be traded only in round lots. An optimization software package is then used to solve a series of optimization problems in order to generate the efficient frontier. Depending upon the complexity of the portfolio, the optimizations can be solved either with a spreadsheet or with more specialized optimization software. After the efficient frontier has been calculated, an optimal portfolio is chosen based on the investor's objectives such as his degree of aversion to various kinds of risk. Later in this chapter, we describe what is meant by an investor's optimal portfolio.

Though the implementation of this process can get quite involved, the theory is relatively straightforward. In the next section we will begin by presenting Markowitz's classical framework. Our focus is on providing an intuitive and practical approach to modern portfolio theory as opposed to giving a complete theoretical treatment. In Chapter 4, we discuss some natural generalizations and extensions to this framework used by practitioners in the financial markets today. Furthermore, the incorporation of alternative risk measures and estimation/model risk are covered in Chapters 3, 8, and 12.

EXHIBIT 2.2   The MPT Investment Process

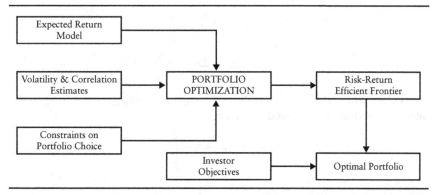

Source: Exhibit 2 in Frank J. Fabozzi, Francis Gupta, and Harry M. Markowitz, "The Legacy of Modern Portfolio Theory," *Journal of Investing* 11, no. 3 (Fall 2002), p. 8.

CLASSICAL FRAMEWORK FOR MEAN-VARIANCE OPTIMIZATION

In this section we place the intuitive discussion thus far into a more formal mathematical context and develop the theory of mean-variance optimization. Suppose first that an investor has to choose a portfolio comprised of N risky assets.[8] The investor's choice is embodied in an N-vector $\mathbf{w} = (w_1, w_2, ..., w_N)'$ of weights, where each weight i represents the percentage of the i-th asset held in the portfolio, and

$$\sum_{i=1}^{N} w_i = 1$$

For now, we permit short selling, which means that weights can be negative. Later on in this chapter we will discuss no short-selling and in Chapter 4 we consider more general constraints.

Suppose the assets' returns $\mathbf{R} = (R_1, R_2, ..., R_N)'$ have expected returns $\boldsymbol{\mu} = (\mu_1, \mu_2, ..., \mu_N)'$ and an $N \times N$ covariance matrix given by

$$\boldsymbol{\Sigma} = \begin{bmatrix} \sigma_{11} & \cdots & \sigma_{1N} \\ \vdots & & \vdots \\ \sigma_{N1} & \cdots & \sigma_{NN} \end{bmatrix}$$

where σ_{ij} denotes the covariance between asset i and asset j such that $\sigma_{ii} = \sigma_i^2$, $\sigma_{ij} = \rho_{ij}\sigma_i\sigma_j$ and ρ_{ij} is the correlation between asset i and asset j. Under these assumptions, the return of a portfolio with weights $\mathbf{w} = (w_1, w_2, ..., w_N)'$ is a random variable $R_p = \mathbf{w}'\mathbf{R}$ with expected return and variance given by[9]

$$\mu_p = \mathbf{w}'\boldsymbol{\mu}$$

$$\sigma_p^2 = \mathbf{w}'\boldsymbol{\Sigma}\mathbf{w}$$

For instance, if there are only two assets with weights $\mathbf{w} = (w_1, w_2)'$, then the portfolio's expected return is

$$\mu_p = w_1\mu_1 + w_2\mu_2$$

---

[8] Throughout this book we denote by $\mathbf{x}'$ the transpose of a vector $\mathbf{x}$.
[9] Subsequently, we will use $E(R_p)$, where R_p is the return on a portfolio, and μ_p interchangeably.

and its variance is

$$\sigma_p^2 = \begin{bmatrix} w_1 & w_2 \end{bmatrix} \begin{bmatrix} \sigma_{11} & \sigma_{12} \\ \sigma_{21} & \sigma_{22} \end{bmatrix} \begin{bmatrix} w_1 \\ w_2 \end{bmatrix}$$

$$= \begin{bmatrix} w_1\sigma_{11} + w_2\sigma_{21} & w_1\sigma_{12} + w_2\sigma_{22} \end{bmatrix} \begin{bmatrix} w_1 \\ w_2 \end{bmatrix}$$

$$= w_1^2\sigma_{11} + w_2^2\sigma_{22} + 2w_1w_2\sigma_{12}$$

In this chapter, we simply assume that expected returns, μ, and their covariance matrix, Σ, are given. Naturally, in practice these quantities have to be estimated. We describe different techniques for this purpose in Chapters 6, 7 and 8.

By choosing the portfolio's weights, an investor chooses among the available mean-variance pairs. To calculate the weights for one possible pair, we choose a target mean return, μ_0. Following Markowitz, the investor's problem is a constrained minimization problem in the sense that the investor must seek

$$\min_{\mathbf{w}} \mathbf{w}'\Sigma\mathbf{w}$$

subject to the constraints[10]

$$\mu_0 = \mathbf{w}'\mu$$

$$\mathbf{w}'\iota = 1, \iota' = [1, 1, ..., 1]$$

We will refer to this version of the classical mean-variance optimization problem as the *risk minimization formulation*. This problem is a quadratic optimization problem with equality constraints, with the solution given by[11]

$$\mathbf{w} = \mathbf{g} + \mathbf{h}\mu_0$$

---

[10] It is common in many practical applications to replace the targeted expected portfolio return constraint with $\mu_0 \leq \mathbf{w}'\mu$, expressing the fact that the expected return should not be below a minimum value. However, with the introduction of inequality constraints, the portfolio optimization problem no longer becomes analytically tractable, but has to be solved by numerical optimization techniques.

[11] This problem can be solved by the method of Lagrange multipliers. See Chapter 7 in Sergio M. Focardi and Frank J. Fabozzi, *The Mathematics of Financial Modeling and Investment Management* (Hoboken, NJ: John Wiley & Sons, 2004).

where **g** and **h** are the two vectors

$$\mathbf{g} = \frac{1}{ac - b^2} \cdot \Sigma^{-1}[c\iota - b\mu]$$

$$\mathbf{h} = \frac{1}{ac - b^2} \cdot \Sigma^{-1}[a\mu - b\iota]$$

and

$$a = \iota'\Sigma^{-1}\iota$$
$$b = \iota'\Sigma^{-1}\mu$$
$$c = \mu'\Sigma^{-1}\mu$$

Consider a two-dimensional Cartesian plane whose x and y coordinates are the portfolio standard deviation and expected return, respectively. In this plane, each feasible portfolio is represented by a point. Consider now the set of all efficient portfolios with all possible efficient portfolio pairs. This set is what we referred to earlier as the *efficient frontier*. Each portfolio on the efficient frontier is obtained by solving the optimization problem above for different choices of μ_0.

In this section we have described the classical formulation of the mean-variance optimization problem as one of minimizing portfolio risk subject to a targeted expected portfolio return. However, there are many other possible and equivalent formulations to this problem. For example, for a particular level of risk we can find a combination of assets that is going to give the highest expected return. We discuss this and other alternatives later in this chapter.

Mathematically, the mean-variance problem as described above is an optimization problem referred to as a *quadratic program*. In the simple form presented, the problem can be solved analytically. In extensions involving only so-called equality constraints,[12] finding the optimum portfolio reduces to solving a set of linear equations. However, in more complex cases, analytical solutions are often not available and numerical optimization techniques must be used. Chapter 9 provides an overview of different optimization techniques for solving the mean-variance optimization problem and its generalizations.

Now that we know how to calculate the optimal portfolio weights for a targeted level of expected portfolio return, we look at an example. First, we use only four assets and later we will see how these results

---

[12] Constraints of the form $\mathbf{Aw} - \mathbf{b}$ and $\mathbf{Aw} \leq \mathbf{b}$ are referred to as equality and inequality constraints, respectively.

change as more assets are included. For this purpose, we use the four country equity indices in the MSCI World Index for Australia, Austria, Belgium, and Canada.[13]

Let us assume that we are given the annualized expected returns, standard deviations, and correlations between these countries according to Exhibit 2.3. The expected returns vary from 7.1% to 9%, whereas the standard deviations range from 16.5% to 19.5%. Furthermore, we observe that the four country indices are not highly correlated with each other—the highest correlation, 0.47, is between Austria and Belgium. Therefore, we expect to see some benefits of portfolio diversification in this case.

Next, we compute the efficient frontier using the formulas presented above. By varying the targeted expected portfolio return over the window [5%, 12%], and for each increment solving the portfolio optimization problem described above, we calculate the weights. In Exhibit 2.4 we can now see explicitly what we derived theoretically: the weights vary linearly as we change the targeted expected return. Substituting the weights into the formulas of the portfolio expected return and standard deviation above, we can trace out the resulting efficient frontier as in Exhibit 2.5.

We observe that the four assets in Exhibit 2.5 (represented by the diamond-shaped marks) are all below the efficient frontier. This means that for a targeted expected portfolio return, the mean-variance portfolio has a lower standard deviation. A utility maximizing investor, measuring utility as the trade-off between expected return and standard deviation, will prefer a portfolio over any of the individual assets. As a matter of fact, by construction, we know that the portfolios along the efficient frontier minimize the standard deviation of the portfolio for a given expected portfolio return.

The portfolio at the leftmost end of the efficient frontier (marked with a circle in Exhibit 2.5) is the portfolio with the smallest obtainable

EXHIBIT 2.3 Annualized Expected Returns, Standard Deviations, and Correlations between the Four Country Equity Indices: Australia, Austria, Belgium, and Canada

Expected Returns	Standard Deviation	Correlations		1	2	3	4
7.9%	19.5%	Australia	1	1			
7.9%	18.2%	Austria	2	0.24	1		
9.0%	18.3%	Belgium	3	0.25	0.47	1	
7.1%	16.5%	Canada	4	0.22	0.14	0.25	1

---

[13] For details on the MSCI World Index and its individual constituents, refer to Appendix A of this book.

EXHIBIT 2.4 Weights of the Efficient Portfolios of Australia, Austria, Belgium, and Canada for Different Levels of Expected Return

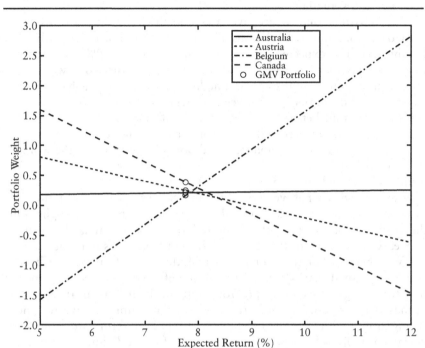

Note: The weights of the *global minimum variance portfolio* (GMV) are marked with circles.

standard deviation. This portfolio is the global minimum variance portfolio (GMV). It can be computed directly by solving the optimization problem

$$\min_{\mathbf{w}} \mathbf{w}'\Sigma\mathbf{w}$$

subject to

$$\mathbf{w}'\iota = 1 , \iota' = [1, 1, ..., 1]$$

which has the solution[14]

---

[14] This problem can also be solved by the method of Lagrange multipliers. See Chapter 7 in Focardi and Fabozzi, *The Mathematics of Financial Modeling and Investment Management.*

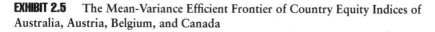

EXHIBIT 2.5   The Mean-Variance Efficient Frontier of Country Equity Indices of Australia, Austria, Belgium, and Canada

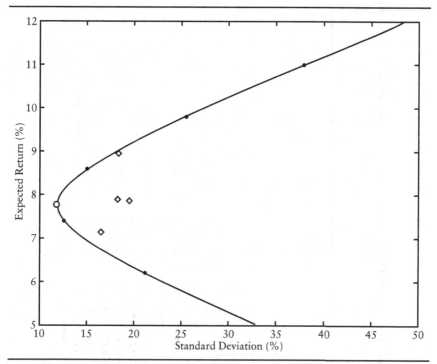

Note: Constructed from the data in Exhibit 2.3. The expected return and standard deviation combination of each country index is represented by a diamond-shaped mark. The GMV is represented by a circle.

$$w = \frac{1}{\iota'\Sigma^{-1}\iota} \cdot \Sigma^{-1}\iota$$

Increasing the Asset Universe

From theory we know that by introducing more (low-correlating) assets, for a targeted expected portfolio return, we should be able to decrease the standard deviation of the portfolio. In Exhibit 2.6 the assumed expected returns, standard deviations, and correlations of 18 countries in the MSCI World Index are presented.

Exhibit 2.7 illustrates how the efficient frontier widens as we go from 4 to 12 assets and then to 18 assets. By increasing the number of investment opportunities we increase our level of possible diversification.

EXHIBIT 2.6 Annualized Expected Returns, Standard Deviations, and Correlations between 18 Countries in the MSCI World Index

Expected Returns	Standard Deviation	Correlations		1	2	3	4	5	6	7	8	9	10	11	12	13	14	15	16	17	18
7.9%	19.5%	Australia	1	1																	
7.9%	18.2%	Austria	2	0.24	1																
9.0%	18.3%	Belgium	3	0.25	0.47	1															
7.1%	16.5%	Canada	4	0.22	0.14	0.25	1														
12.0%	18.4%	Denmark	5	0.24	0.44	0.48	0.21	1													
10.3%	20.4%	France	6	0.22	0.41	0.56	0.35	0.45	1												
9.5%	21.8%	Germany	7	0.26	0.48	0.57	0.35	0.48	0.65	1											
12.0%	28.9%	Hong Kong	8	0.31	0.17	0.17	0.19	0.18	0.22	0.24	1										
11.6%	23.3%	Italy	9	0.20	0.36	0.42	0.22	0.38	0.47	0.47	0.16	1									
9.5%	22.1%	Japan	10	0.32	0.28	0.28	0.18	0.28	0.27	0.29	0.24	0.21	1								
10.9%	19.7%	Netherlands	11	0.26	0.38	0.57	0.39	0.45	0.67	0.67	0.24	0.44	0.28	1							
7.9%	22.7%	Norway	12	0.33	0.37	0.41	0.27	0.41	0.45	0.47	0.21	0.32	0.28	0.50	1						
7.6%	21.5%	Singapore	13	0.34	0.22	0.23	0.20	0.22	0.22	0.26	0.44	0.19	0.34	0.24	0.28	1					
9.9%	20.8%	Spain	14	0.26	0.42	0.50	0.27	0.43	0.57	0.54	0.20	0.48	0.25	0.51	0.39	0.25	1				
16.2%	23.5%	Sweden	15	0.27	0.34	0.42	0.31	0.42	0.53	0.53	0.23	0.41	0.27	0.51	0.43	0.27	0.49	1			
10.7%	17.9%	Switzerland	16	0.26	0.47	0.59	0.32	0.49	0.64	0.69	0.23	0.45	0.32	0.67	0.48	0.25	0.53	0.51	1		
9.8%	18.5%	United Kingdom	17	0.25	0.34	0.47	0.38	0.40	0.58	0.53	0.22	0.40	0.28	0.68	0.43	0.24	0.46	0.45	0.57	1	
10.5%	16.5%	United States	18	0.05	0.05	0.21	0.62	0.11	0.29	0.29	0.13	0.17	0.08	0.32	0.15	0.12	0.21	0.22	0.26	0.31	1

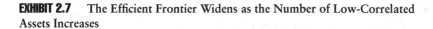

EXHIBIT 2.7 The Efficient Frontier Widens as the Number of Low-Correlated Assets Increases

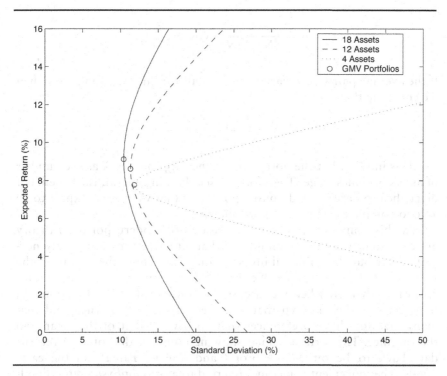

Note: The efficient frontiers have been constructed with 4, 12, and 18 countries (from the innermost to the outermost frontier) from the MSCI World Index.

We now ask whether it is possible in general to decrease portfolio risk (and keeping the expected portfolio return constant) by increasing the asset universe. To answer this question, we first observe that the portfolio variance can be bounded by

$$\mathrm{var}(R_p) = \mathbf{w}'\mathbf{\Sigma}\mathbf{w}$$

$$= \frac{1}{N^2}\sum_{i=1}^{N}\mathrm{var}(R_i) + \frac{1}{N^2}\sum_{i \neq j}\mathrm{cov}(R_i, R_j)$$

$$\leq \frac{1}{N^2}N\sigma_{\max}^2 + \frac{1}{N^2}(N-1)N \cdot A$$

$$= \frac{\sigma_{\max}^2}{N} + \frac{N-1}{N} \cdot A$$

where σ_{max}^2 is the largest variance of all individual assets and A is the average pairwise asset covariance,

$$A = \frac{1}{(N-1)N} \sum_{i \neq j} \text{cov}(R_i, R_j)$$

If the average pairwise covariance A and all variances are bounded, then we conclude that

$$\text{var}(R_p) \xrightarrow[N \to \infty]{} A$$

This implies that the portfolio variance approaches A as the number of assets becomes large. Therefore we see that, in general, the benefits of diversification are limited up to a point and that we cannot expect to be able to completely eliminate portfolio risk.

At this point, we note that the results of modern portfolio theory are consistent with the assumptions that either returns are jointly normally distributed, or that all investors only care about the mean and the variance of their portfolios. We make this statement more precise later on in this chapter, when we discuss the concept of utility functions. In practice, it is well known that asset returns are not normal and that many investors have preferences that go beyond that of the mean and the variance. The earliest studies showing nonnormality of asset returns date back to Benoit Mandelbrot[15] and Eugene Fama[16] in the early 1960s. The movement sometimes referred to as *econophysics*[17] has developed methods for the accurate empirical analysis of the distribution of asset returns that show significant deviations from the normal distribution.[18,19] In particular, there is evidence that the variances of some asset

---

[15] Benoit Mandelbrot, "The Variation in Certain Speculative Prices," *Journal of Business* 36, no. 3 (October 1963), pp. 394–419.

[16] Eugene F. Fama, "The Behavior of Stock Market Prices," *Journal of Business* 38, no. 1 (January 1965), pp. 34–105.

[17] Rosario N. Mantegna and H. Eugene Stanley, *An Introduction to Econophysics* (Cambridge: Cambridge University Press, 2000).

[18] Ulrich A. Mueller, Michel M. Dacorogna, and Olivier V. Pictet, "Heavy Tails in High-Frequency Financial Data, in Robert J. Adler, Raya E. Feldman, and Murad S. Taqqu (eds.), *A Practical Guide to Heavy Tails* (Boston, MA: Birkhaeuser, 1998), pp. 55–77.

[19] For recent empirical evidence on the distribution of asset returns and portfolio selection when distributions are nonnormal, see Svetlozar T. Rachev, and Stefan Mittnik, *Stable Paretian Models in Finance* (Chichester: John Wiley & Sons, 2000); and Svetlozar T. Rachev (ed.), *Handbook of Heavy Tailed Distributions in Finance* (New York: Elsevier/North Holland, 2001).

returns are not bounded, but rather that they are infinite. Moreover, one can show that in specific cases where variances are unbounded and asset returns behave like certain stable Paretian distributions, diversification may no longer be possible.[20]

Adding Short-Selling Constraints

In our theoretical derivations above, we imposed no restrictions on the portfolio weights other than having them add up to one. In particular, we allowed the portfolio weights to take on both positive and negative values; that is, we did not restrict short selling. In practice, many portfolio managers cannot sell assets short. This could be for investment policy or legal reasons, or sometimes just because particular asset classes are difficult to sell short, such as real estate. In Exhibit 2.8 we see the

EXHIBIT 2.8 The Effect of Restricting Short Selling: Constrained versus Unconstrained Efficient Frontiers Constructed from 18 Countries from the MSCI World Index

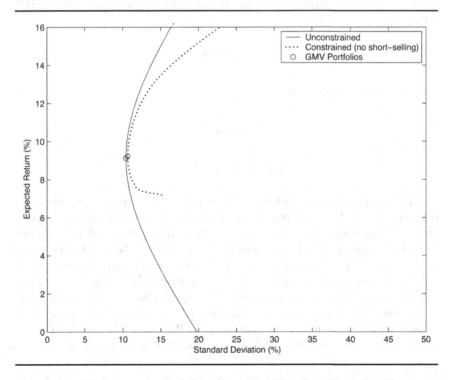

---

[20] Eugene F. Fama, "Portfolio Analysis In a Stable Paretian Market," *Management Science* 11, no. 3 (October 1965), pp. 404–419.

effect of not allowing for short selling. Since we are restricting the opportunity set by constraining all the weights to be positive, the resulting efficient frontier is inside the unconstrained efficient frontier.

Alternative Formulations of Classical Mean-Variance Optimization

The mean-variance optimization problem has several alternative but equivalent formulations that are very useful in practical applications. These formulations are equivalent in the sense that they all lead to the same efficient frontier as they trade expected portfolio return versus portfolio risk in a similar way. We review two of these formulations here.

Expected Return Maximization Formulation

We previously formulated the mean-variance optimization problem as one of minimizing the risk of the portfolio for a certain level of targeted expected return μ_0. However, we could also begin by choosing a certain level of targeted portfolio risk, say σ_0, and then maximize the expected return of the portfolio:

$$\max_{\mathbf{w}} \mathbf{w}'\mathbf{\mu}$$

subject to the constraints[21]

$$\mathbf{w}'\mathbf{\Sigma}\mathbf{w} = \sigma_0^2$$

$$\mathbf{w}'\iota = 1, \iota' = [1, 1, ..., 1]$$

This formulation, which we will refer to as the *expected return maximization formulation* of the classical mean-variance optimization problem, is often used by portfolio managers that are required to not take more risk, as measured by the standard deviation of the portfolio return, than a certain prespecified volatility. For example, portfolios managed relative to a benchmark can be modeled in this fashion. Here the objective is to maximize the excess return of the portfolio over the benchmark and at the same time make sure that the risks in so doing do not exceed a given tracking error over the benchmark. We come back to this particular problem later in Chapter 4 when we discuss index tracking.

---

[21] It is common in many practical applications that the equal sign in the risk constraint is replaced by a weak inequality, that is, $\mathbf{w}'\mathbf{\Sigma}\mathbf{w} \leq \sigma_0^2$, expressing the fact that the risk is not allowed to be above a maximum value.

Risk Aversion Formulation

Another alternative is to explicitly model the trade-off between risk and return in the objective function using a risk-aversion coefficient λ. We refer to the following formulation as the *risk aversion formulation* of the classical mean-variance optimization problem:

$$\max_{w} (w'\mu - \lambda w'\Sigma w)$$

subject to

$$w'\iota = 1, \iota' = [1, 1, ..., 1]$$

The risk aversion coefficient is also referred to as the *Arrow-Pratt risk aversion index*. When λ is small (i.e., the aversion to risk is low), the penalty from the contribution of the portfolio risk is also small, leading to more risky portfolios. Conversely, when λ is large, portfolios with more exposures to risk become more highly penalized. If we gradually increase λ from zero and for each instance solve the optimization problem, we end up calculating each portfolio along the efficient frontier. It is a common practice to calibrate λ such that a particular portfolio has the desired risk profile. The calibration is often performed via backtests with historical data. For most portfolio allocation decisions in investment management applications, the risk aversion is somewhere between 2 and 4.

THE CAPITAL MARKET LINE

As demonstrated by William Sharpe,[22] James Tobin,[23] and John Lintner[24] the efficient set of portfolios available to investors who employ mean-variance analysis in the absence of a risk-free asset is inferior to that available when there is a risk-free asset. We present this formulation in this section.[25]

---

[22] William F. Sharpe, "Capital Asset Prices: A Theory of Market Equilibrium Under Conditions of Risk," *Journal of Finance* 19, no. 3 (September 1964), pp. 425–442.
[23] James Tobin, "Liquidity Preference as a Behavior Towards Risk," *Review of Economic Studies* 67 (February 1958), pp. 65–86.
[24] John Lintner, "The Valuation of Risk Assets and the Selection of Risky Investments in Stock Portfolios and Capital Budgets," *Review of Economics and Statistics* 47 (February 1965), pp. 13–37.
[25] For a comprehensive discussion of these models and computational issues, see Harry M. Markowitz (with a chapter and program by Peter Todd), *Mean-Variance Analysis in Portfolio Choice and Capital Markets* (Hoboken, NJ: John Wiley & Sons, 2000).

Assume that there is a risk-free asset, with a risk-free return denoted by R_f and that the investor is able to borrow and lend at this rate.[26] The investor has to choose a combination of the N risky assets plus the risk-free asset. The weights $\mathbf{w}'_R = (w_{R1}, w_{R2}, ..., w_{RN})$ do not have to sum to 1 as the remaining part $(1 - \mathbf{w}'_R \iota)$ can be invested in the risk-free asset. Note also that this portion of the investment can be positive or negative if we allow risk-free borrowing and lending. In this case, the portfolio's expected return and variance are

$$\mu_p = \mathbf{w}'_R \mu + (1 - \mathbf{w}'_R \iota) R_f$$

$$\sigma_p^2 = \mathbf{w}'_R \Sigma \mathbf{w}_R$$

because the risk-free asset has zero variance and is uncorrelated with the risky assets.

The investor's objective is again for a targeted level of expected portfolio return, μ_o, to choose allocations by solving a quadratic optimization problem

$$\min_{\mathbf{w}_R} \mathbf{w}'_R \Sigma \mathbf{w}_R$$

subject to the constraint

$$\mu_0 = \mathbf{w}'_R \mu + (1 - \mathbf{w}'_R \iota) R_f$$

The optimal portfolio weights are given by

$$w_R = C \Sigma^{-1} (\mu - R_f \iota)$$

where

---

[26] We remark that, in practice, this assumption is not valid for most investors. Specifically, an investor may not be able to borrow and lend at the *same* interest rate, or may *only* be permitted to lend. If there are no short-selling restrictions on the risky assets, similar theoretical results to the ones presented in this section are obtained also for these cases. See, Fischer Black, "Capital Market Equilibrium with Restricted Borrowings," *Journal of Business* 45, no. 3 (July 1972) pp. 444–455; and Jonathan E. Ingersoll, Jr., *Theory of Financial Decision Making* (Savage, MD: Rowan & Littlefield Publishers, Inc., 1987).

$$C = \frac{\mu_0 - R_f}{(\mu - R_f \iota)' \Sigma^{-1} (\mu - R_f \iota)}$$

The above formula shows that the weights of the risky assets of any minimum variance portfolio are proportional to the vector $\Sigma^{-1}(\mu - R_f\iota)$, with the proportionality constant C, defined above. Therefore, with a risk-free asset, all minimum variance portfolios are a combination of the risk-free asset and a given risky portfolio. This risky portfolio is called the *tangency portfolio*. Fama demonstrated that under certain assumptions the tangency portfolio must consist of all assets available to investors, and each asset must be held in proportion to its market value relative to the total market value of all assets.[27] Therefore, the tangency portfolio is often referred to as the "market portfolio," or simply the "market."[28]

We know that for a particular choice of weights, w_R^0, such that $(w_R^0)'\iota = 0$, the portfolio only consists of the risk-free asset. On the other hand, for the choice of weights, w_R^M, such that $(w_R^M)'\iota = 1$, the portfolio consists of only risky assets and must therefore be the market portfolio. Because

$$w_R^M = C^M \Sigma^{-1} (\mu - R_f \iota)$$

for some C^M, we have by using $(w_R^M)'\iota = 1$ that the weights of the market portfolio are given by

$$w_R^M = \frac{1}{\iota' \Sigma (\mu - R_f \iota)} \cdot \Sigma^{-1} (\mu - R_f \iota)$$

It is also easy to verify that the market portfolio can be calculated directly from the *maximal Sharpe ratio optimization problem*:

$$\max_{w} \frac{w'\mu - R_f}{\sqrt{w'\Sigma w}}$$

subject to $w'\iota = 1$.

---

[27] Eugene F. Fama, "Efficient Capital Markets: A Review of Theory and Empirical Work," *Journal of Finance* 25, no. 2 (May 1970), pp. 383–417.

[28] Although strictly speaking it is not fully correct, we will use the terms "market portfolio" and "tangency portfolio" interchangeably throughout this book.

In Exhibit 2.9 every combination of the risk-free asset and the market portfolio M is shown on the line drawn from the vertical axis at the risk-free rate tangent to the Markowitz efficient frontier. All the portfolios on the line are feasible for the investor to construct. The line from the risk-free rate that is tangent to the efficient frontier of risky assets is called the *Capital Market Line* (CML).

We observe that with the exception of the market portfolio, the minimum variance portfolios that are a combination of the market portfolio and the risk-free asset are superior to the portfolio on the Markowitz efficient frontier for the same level of risk. For example, compare portfolio P_A, which is on the Markowitz efficient frontier, with portfolio P_B, which is on the CML and therefore some combination of the risk-free asset and the market portfolio M. Notice that for the same level of risk, the expected return is greater for P_B than for P_A. A risk-averse investor will prefer P_B to P_A.

With the introduction of the risk-free asset, we can now say that an investor will select a portfolio on the CML that represents a combination of borrowing or lending at the risk-free rate and the market portfo-

EXHIBIT 2.9   Capital Market Line and the Markowitz Efficient Frontier

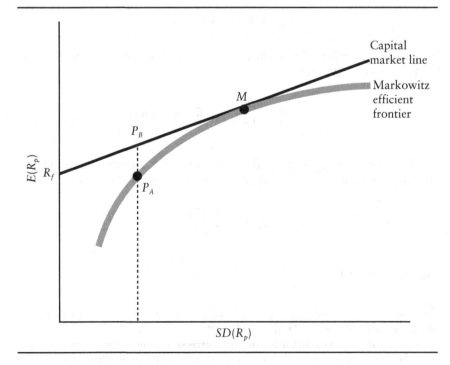

lio.[29] This important property is called *separation*. Portfolios to the left of the market portfolio represent combinations of risky assets and the risk-free asset. Portfolios to the right of the market portfolio include purchases of risky assets made with funds borrowed at the risk-free rate. Such a portfolio is called a *leveraged portfolio* because it involves the use of borrowed funds.

The separation property also has important implications in practice. Specifically, practical portfolio construction is normally broken down into at least the following two steps:

1. Asset allocation: Decide how to allocate the investor's wealth between the risk-free security and the set of risky securities.
2. Risky portfolio construction: Decide how to distribute the risky portion of the investment among the set of risky securities.

The first point is an integral part in devising an investment plan and policy for a particular investor. This is closely linked to an investor's strategic goals and general risk profile as well as his liquidity requirements. In this book the focus is more on the second point. In later chapters we will discuss various kinds of forecasting techniques that can be used in order to maximize different investment objectives and controlling the risk of the risky portion of the portfolio.

Deriving the Capital Market Line

To derive the CML, we begin with the efficient frontier. As we have seen above, in the absence of a risk-free asset, Markowitz efficient portfolios can be constructed by solving a constrained optimization problem that finds an optimal trade-off between return and variance, with the optimal portfolio being the one portfolio selected based on the investor's preference (which we see later is quantified by the investor's utility function). However, the efficient frontier changes once a risk-free asset is introduced and we assume that investors can borrow and lend at the risk-free rate.

We can derive a formula for the CML algebraically. Based on the assumption of homogeneous expectations regarding the inputs in the portfolio construction process, all investors can create an efficient portfolio consisting of w_f placed in the risk-free asset and w_M in the market portfolio, where w represents the corresponding percentage (weight) of the portfolio allocated to each asset. Thus, $w_f + w_M = 1$. As the expected

---

[29] Today it is normal practice to use standard deviation rather than variance as the risk measure because with the inclusion of a risk-free asset the efficient frontier in the expected return/standard deviation coordinate system is linear.

return of the portfolio, $E(R_p)$, is equal to the weighted average of the expected returns of the two assets, we have

$$E(R_p) = w_f R_f + w_M E(R_M)$$

Since we know that $w_f = 1 - w_M$, we can rewrite $E(R_p)$ as

$$E(R_p) = (1 - w_M) R_f + w_M E(R_M)$$

which can be simplified to

$$E(R_p) = R_f + w_M [E(R_M) - R_f]$$

Since the return of the risk-free asset and the return of the market portfolio are uncorrelated and the variance of the risk-free asset is equal to zero, the variance of the portfolio consisting of the risk-free asset and the market portfolio is given by

$$
\begin{aligned}
\sigma_p^2 = \text{var}(R_p) &= w_f^2 \text{var}(R_f) + w_M^2 \text{var}(R_M) + 2 w_f w_M (R_f, R_M) \\
&= w_M^2 \text{var}(R_M) \\
&= w_M^2 \sigma_M^2
\end{aligned}
$$

In other words, the variance of the portfolio is represented by the weighted variance of the market portfolio.

Since the standard deviation is the square root of the variance, we can write

$$w_M = \frac{\sigma_p}{\sigma_M}$$

If we substitute the above result and rearrange terms, we get the explicit expression for the CML

$$E(R_p) = R_f + \left[\frac{E(R_M) - R_f}{\sigma_M} \right] \sigma_p$$

Equilibrium Market Price of Risk

The bracketed portion of the second term in the equation for the CML

$$\left[\frac{E(R_M) - R_f}{\sigma_M} \right]$$

is often referred to as the *risk premium*.

Let us examine the economic meaning of this risk premium. The numerator of the bracketed expression is the expected return from investing in the market beyond the risk-free return. It is a measure of the reward for holding the risky market portfolio rather than the risk-free asset. The denominator is the market risk of the market portfolio. Thus, the first factor, or the slope of the CML, measures the reward per unit of market risk. Since the CML represents the return offered to compensate for a perceived level of risk, each point on the CML is a balanced market condition, or equilibrium. The slope of the CML determines the additional return needed to compensate for a unit change in risk, which is why it is also referred to as the *equilibrium market price of risk*.

In other words, the CML says that the expected return on a portfolio is equal to the risk-free rate plus a risk premium, where the risk premium is equal to the market price of risk (as measured by the reward per unit of market risk) times the quantity of risk for the portfolio (as measured by the standard deviation of the portfolio). Summarizing, we can write

$$E(R_p) = R_f + \text{Market price of risk} \times \text{Quantity of risk}$$

SELECTION OF THE OPTIMAL PORTFOLIO WHEN THERE IS A RISK-FREE ASSET

Given the Markowitz efficient frontier or the CML (which replaces the efficient frontier when a risk-free asset is included), how does one select the optimal portfolio? That is, how does one determine the optimal point on the efficient frontier or the optimal combination of the market portfolio and the risk-free asset in which to invest? Investors have different preferences and tolerances for risk. In order to formalize these concepts, we first introduce the notion of utility functions and indifference curves. Thereafter, we show how the optimal portfolio is chosen within this framework.

Utility Functions and Indifference Curves

There are many situations where entities (i.e., individuals and firms) face two or more choices. The economic "theory of choice" uses the concept of a utility function to describe the way entities make decisions when faced with a set of choices. A *utility function*[30] assigns a (numeric) value to all possible choices faced by the entity. These values, often referred to as the *utility index*, have the property that *a* is preferred to *b*, if and only if, the utility of *a* is higher than that of *b*. The higher the value of a particular choice, the greater the utility derived from that choice. The choice that is selected is the one that results in the maximum utility given a set of constraints faced by the entity.

The assumption that an investor's decision-making process can be represented as optimization of a utility function goes back to Pareto in the 18th century. However, it was not until 1944 that utility theory was mathematically formalized by von Neumann and Morgenstern.[31] Utility functions can represent a broad set of preference orderings. The precise conditions under which a preference ordering can be expressed through a utility function have been widely explored in the literature.[32]

In portfolio theory, entities are faced with a set of choices. Different portfolios have different levels of expected return and risk—the higher the level of expected return, the larger the risk. Entities are faced with the decision of choosing a portfolio from the set of all possible risk/ return combinations. Whereas they like return, they dislike risk. Therefore, entities obtain different levels of utility from different risk/return combinations. The utility obtained from any possible risk/return combination is expressed by the utility function, expressing the preferences of entities over perceived risk and expected return combinations.

A utility function can be presented in graphical form by a set of indifference curves. Exhibit 2.10 shows indifference curves labeled u_1, u_2, and u_3. By convention, the horizontal axis measures risk and the vertical axis measures expected return. Each curve represents a set of portfolios with different combinations of risk and return. All the points on a given indifference curve indicate combinations of risk and expected return that will give the same level of utility to a given investor. For example, on utility curve u_1 there are two points u and u', with u having a higher expected return than u', but also having a higher risk.

Because the two points lie on the same indifference curve, the investor has an equal preference for (or is indifferent between) the two

---

[30] Strictly speaking, a utility function is a twice continuously differentiable function u from the set of all choices to the real line with the requirements that $u' > 0$ and $u'' \leq 0$.

[31] John von Neumann and Oskar Morgenstern, *Theory of Games and Economic Behavior* (Princeton, NJ: Princeton University Press, 1944).

[32] See, for example, Akira Takayama, *Mathematical Economics* (Cambridge: Cambridge University Press, 1985).

EXHIBIT 2.10   Indifference Curves

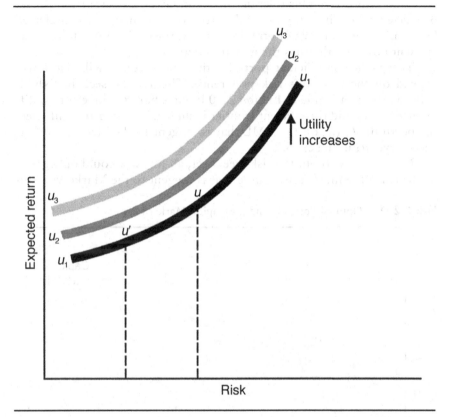

points, or, for that matter, any point on the curve. The positive slope of an indifference curve reflects that, to obtain the same level of utility, the investor requires a higher expected return in order to accept higher risk. For the three indifference curves shown in Exhibit 2.10, the utility the investor receives is greater the further the indifference curve is from the horizontal axis, because that curve represents a higher level of return at every level of risk. Thus, among the three indifference curves shown in the exhibit, u_3 has the highest utility and u_1 the lowest.

The Optimal Portfolio

A reasonable assumption is that investors are risk averse. A risk averse investor is an investor who, when faced with choosing between two investments with the same expected return but two different risks, prefers the one with the lower risk.

In selecting portfolios, an investor seeks to maximize the expected portfolio return given his tolerance for risk. Given a choice from the set of efficient portfolios, the optimal portfolio is the one that is preferred by the investor. In terms of utility functions, the optimal portfolio is the efficient portfolio that has the maximum utility.

The particular efficient portfolio that the investor will select will depend on the investor's risk preference. This can be seen in Exhibit 2.11, which is the same as Exhibit 2.10 but has both the investor's indifference curves and the efficient frontier included. The investor will select the portfolio P^*_{CML} on the CML that is tangent to the highest indifference curve, u_3 in the exhibit.

Notice that without the risk-free asset, an investor could only get to u_2, which is the indifference curve that is tangent to the Markowitz effi-

EXHIBIT 2.11   Optimal Portfolio and the Capital Market Line

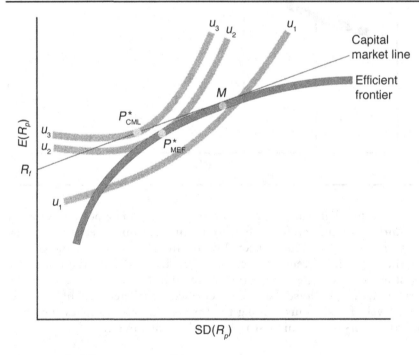

u_1, u_2, u_3 = Indifference curves with $u_1 < u_2 < u_3$
M = Market portfolio
R_f = Risk-free rate
P^*_{CML} = Optimal portfolio on capital market line
P^*_{MEF} = Optimal portfolio on efficient frontier

cient frontier. This portfolio is denoted by P^*_{MEF} in the exhibit. Thus, the opportunity to borrow or lend at the risk-free rate results in a capital market where risk-averse investors will prefer to hold portfolios consisting of combinations of the risk-free asset and the tangency portfolio M on the Markowitz efficient frontier.

MORE ON UTILITY FUNCTIONS: A GENERAL FRAMEWORK FOR PORTFOLIO CHOICE

In the classical Markowitz framework an investor chooses a certain desired trade-off between risk and return. As we saw above, this preference relation can also be expressed by utility functions. Utility functions allow us to generalize the mean-variance framework into a much wider class of problems, *expected utility maximization problems.*

This general framework is based upon the idea that a rational investor with utility u and initial wealth W_0 chooses his portfolio **w** as to maximize his expected utility one period ahead,

$$\max_{\mathbf{w}} E\left[u(W_0(1 + \mathbf{w}'\mathbf{R}))\right]$$

subject to

$$\mathbf{w}'\iota = 1, \iota' = [1, 1, ...,1]$$

where **R** is the vector of the individual asset returns.

To get comfortable with this framework, let us consider two special cases. First, let us assume that asset returns are jointly normally distributed (that is, fully described by the mean and the variance). Then for any utility function u, $Eu(\mathbf{w}'\mathbf{R})$ is just a function of the portfolio mean and standard deviation. Therefore, this special case resembles classical portfolio theory.

Second, we make an assumption about the investor's utility function, namely, we assume that an investor's utility function is given by the *quadratic utility*

$$u(x) = x - \frac{b}{2}x^2, \quad b > 0$$

so that

$$E\left[u(W_0(1 + \mathbf{w}'R))\right] = E\left[W_0(1 + \mathbf{w}'R) - \frac{b}{2}W_0^2(1 + \mathbf{w}'R)^2\right]$$

$$= u(W_0) + W_0 E(\mathbf{w}'R) - \frac{b}{2}W_0^2\left[2E(\mathbf{w}'R) + E\left[(\mathbf{w}'R)^2\right]\right]$$

$$= u(W_0) + W_0\mu_p(1 - bW_0) - \frac{b}{2}W_0^2(\sigma_p^2 - \mu_p^2)$$

where μ_p and σ_p are the expected return and standard deviation of the portfolio, respectively. Consequently, we see that also in this case the objective function only depends on the mean and the variance of the portfolio. Thus, this special case is equivalent to mean-variance analysis.

For a general utility function, the optimization problem described above will no longer be equivalent to the classical mean-variance analysis, but often leads to more complex formulations. For a utility function it is common to require that $u' > 0$ and $u'' \le 0$. This means that an investor always prefers more to less utility, but that marginal utility decreases with increasing wealth. In this setting, an investor's aversion to risk is measured by his *absolute* and *relative risk aversion*, given by

$$r_A(x) = -\frac{u''(x)}{u'(x)}$$

and

$$r_R(x) = -\frac{xu''(x)}{u'(x)}$$

These measures express the intuitive fact that the "more curved" the utility function is, the more risk-averse the investor is. Some of the commonly used utility functions are listed below, and depicted in Exhibit 2.12:

■ *Linear utility function*

$$u(x) = a + bx, \qquad r_A(x) = r_R(x) = 0$$

The risk aversions are zero and therefore the linear utility function is referred to as risk-neutral.

EXHIBIT 2.12   Different Utility Functions

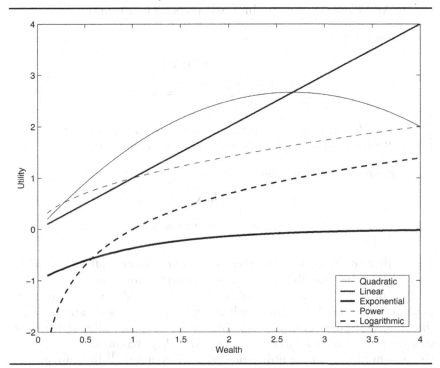

■ *Quadratic utility function*[33]

$$u(x) = x - \frac{b}{2}x^2, \quad b > 0$$

$$r_A(x) = \frac{b}{1-bx}, \quad r_R(x) = \frac{bx}{1-bx}$$

■ *Exponential utility function*

$$u(x) = -\frac{1}{\lambda}e^{-\lambda x}, \quad \lambda = 0$$

$$r_A(x) = \lambda, \quad r_R(x) = \lambda x$$

---

[33] This utility function satisfies $u' > 0$ only when $x < 1/b$, which implies that there are certain states where the investor would choose less wealth over more. This is a problem with the quadratic utility function.

This utility function is often referred to as *constant absolute risk aversion* (CARA) because the absolute risk aversion is constant.

■ *Power utility function*

$$u(x) = x^{\alpha}, \quad 0 < \alpha < 1$$

$$r_A(x) = \frac{1-\alpha}{x}, \quad r_R(x) = 1 - \alpha$$

This utility function is often referred to as *constant relative risk aversion* (CRRA) because the relative risk aversion is constant.

■ *Logarithmic utility function*

$$u(x) = \ln(x)$$

$$r_A(x) = \frac{1}{x}, \quad r_R(x) = 1$$

This utility function is often referred to as *constant relative risk aversion* (CRRA) because the relative risk aversion is constant.[34]

In practice, the choice of utility function depends on the particular application at hand, together with computational considerations. With the computational resources available today it is possible, at least for smaller portfolios, to solve the expected utility maximization through simulation for any of the utility functions given above.[35] In many practical portfolio management applications, there is a trade-off: computational convenience and speed versus modeling error and accuracy.

Levy and Markowitz showed how to approximate power utility functions using quadratic utility and compared their performance with the approximations on a sample of mutual fund returns.[36] They concluded that mean-variance approximations to power utility functions do well for returns from –30% to about 60%. Several other studies (e.g.,

---

[34] As a matter of fact, the logarithmic utility function provides an extension of the power utility function for $\alpha = 0$ by the nature of the equality

$$\lim_{\alpha \to 0} \frac{x^{\alpha} - 1}{\alpha} = \ln(x)$$

[35] See for example, Paul Samuelson, "When and Why Mean-variance Analysis Generically Fails," forthcoming in the *American Economic Review*; Andrew Ang and Geert Bekaert, "International Asset Allocation With Regime Shifts," *Review of Financial Studies* 15, no. 4 (2002), pp. 1137–1187.

[36] Haim Levy and Harry Markowitz, "Approximating Expected Utility by a Function of Mean and Variance," *American Economic Review* 69, no. 3 (1979), pp. 308–318.

Pulley,[37] Kroll et al.,[38] and Cremers et al.[39]) compare portfolio allocation using more general utility functions along with the empirical return
distribution to mean-variance optimization, and conclude that the
approximation error and the resulting performance differences from
only using means and variances are very small.

Kallberg and Ziemba compared different utility functions and how
they affect the optimal composition of portfolios.[40] Their study provides
empirical support for portfolio allocations using utility functions that
have different functional forms and parameter values but similar absolute risk aversion result in similar optimal portfolios. Their findings suggest that the portfolio optimization problem is relatively robust with
respect to changes of utility function, provided that the level of absolute
risk aversion remains the same.

These results show that in many practical applications, we can
choose the utility function that allows for the most efficient numerical
solution. Being the computationally most easily tractable utility function, it is not a surprise that quadratic utility is by far the most commonly used in practice today.

We note, however, that most of the studies above were performed
using assets exhibiting return distributions not too far away from normality. For so-called elliptical distributions such as the normal, Student-
t, and Levy distributions, it has been demonstrated that the mean-variance approximation of the expected utility is exact for all utility functions.[41] This offers a possible explanation for the good performance of
the classical mean-variance formulation in the studies. Furthermore, it
was pointed out by Cremers, et al. that higher moments do not seem to
matter very much for investors with power utility.

When asset returns in a particular portfolio exhibit skew, fat tails, and
high correlation—such as is the case with some stocks and many deriva-

---

[37] Lawrence M. Pulley, "A General Mean-Variance Approximation to Expected Utility for Short Holding Periods," *Journal of Financial and Quantitative Analysis* 16
(September 1981), pp. 361–373.
[38] Yoram Kroll, Haim Levy, and Harry M. Markowitz, "Mean-Variance Versus Direct Utility Maximization," *Journal of Finance* 39, no. 1 (1984), pp. 47–61.
[39] Jan-Hein Cremers, Mark Kritzman, and Sebastien Page, "Portfolio Formation
with Higher Moments and Plausible Utility," Revere Street Working Papers 272–12,
undated.
[40] Jerry G. Kallberg and William T. Ziemba, "Comparison of Alternative Utility
Functions in Portfolio Selection Problems," *Management Science* 29, no. 11 (November 1983), pp. 1257–1276.
[41] Guy Chamberlain, "A Characterization of the Distributions That Imply Mean-
Variance Utility Functions," *Journal of Economic Theory* 29, no. 1 (1983), pp. 185–
201.

tive securities—higher moments do matter. We discuss risk measures that take higher moments into account in more detail in Chapter 3.

SUMMARY

- Markowitz quantified the concept of diversification through the statistical notion of covariance between individual securities, and the overall standard deviation of a portfolio.
- The basic assumption behind modern portfolio theory is that an investor's preferences can be represented by a function (utility function) of the expected return and the variance of a portfolio.
- The basic principle underlying modern portfolio theory is that for a given level of expected return a rational investor would choose the portfolio with minimum variance from amongst the set of all possible portfolios. We presented three equivalent formulations: (1) the minimum variance formulation; (2) the expected return maximization formulation; and (3) the risk aversion formulation.
- Minimum variance portfolios are called mean-variance efficient portfolios. The set of all mean-variance efficient portfolios is called the *efficient frontier*. The efficient frontier with only risky assets has a parabolic shape in the expected return/standard deviation coordinate system.
- The portfolio on the efficient frontier with the smallest variance is called the global minimum variance portfolio.
- The mean-variance problem results in an optimization problem referred to as a quadratic program.
- The efficient frontier widens as the number of (not perfectly correlated) securities increases. The efficient frontier shrinks as constraints are imposed upon the portfolio.
- With the addition of a risk-free asset, the efficient frontier becomes a straight line in the expected return/standard deviation coordinate system. This line is called the *capital market line*.
- The tangency point of the efficient frontier with only risky assets and the capital market line is called the *tangency portfolio*.
- The *market portfolio* is the portfolio that consists of all assets available to investors in the same proportion as each security's market value divided by the total market value of all securities. Under certain assumptions it can be shown that the tangency portfolio is the same as the market portfolio.
- The excess expected return of the market portfolio (the expected return of the market portfolio minus the risk-free rate) divided by the stan-

dard deviation of the market portfolio is referred to as the *equilibrium market price of risk*.

■ The capital market line expresses that the expected return on a portfolio is equal to the risk-free rate plus a portfolio specific risk premium. The portfolio specific risk premium is the market price of risk multiplied by the risk (standard deviation) of the portfolio.

■ A utility function is a numerical function that assigns a value to all possible choices faced by an entity. A *utility function* is a preference ordering that allows us to rank different choices from most to least preferred. The concept of utility functions allows us to consider a more general framework for portfolio choice, beyond that of just the mean and the variance.

■ The quadratic utility function provides a good approximation for many of the standard utility functions such as exponential, power, and logarithmic utility.

CHAPTER 3

Advances in the Theory of Portfolio Risk Measures

The portfolio manager may use his or her experience in stock picking or rely upon quantitative modeling techniques in the portfolio selection process. However, generally speaking, the main objective of portfolio selection is the construction of portfolios that maximize expected returns at a certain level of risk. For example, in the classical mean-variance framework, discussed in Chapter 2, estimates of the expected returns and the covariance matrix of the assets were used to calculate the optimal portfolio.

It is now well known that asset returns are not normal and, therefore, the mean and the variance alone do not fully describe the characteristics of the joint asset return distribution. Indeed, many risks and undesirable scenarios faced by a portfolio manager cannot be captured solely by the variance of the portfolio. Consequently, especially in cases of significant nonnormality, the classical mean-variance approach will not be a satisfactory portfolio allocation model.

Since about the mid-1990s, considerable thought and innovation in the financial industry have been directed towards creating a better understanding of risk and its measurement, and towards improving the management of risk in financial portfolios. From the statistical point of view, a key innovation is the attention paid to the ratio between the bulk of the risk and the risk of the tails. The latter has become a critical statistical determinant of risk management policies. Changing situations and different portfolios may require alternative and new risk measures. The "race" for inventing the best risk measure for a given situation or portfolio is still ongoing. It is possible that we will never find a completely satisfactory answer to the question of which risk measure to use, and the choice to some extent remains an art.

We mention in passing, that one reason for highly nonnormal asset return distributions with fat tails and nonnegligible higher moments is regime changes. Commonly, these are modeled by regime and Markov switching techniques.[1] These types of models are often data-hungry and computationally intensive, as they have to be solved by simulation and dynamic programming techniques. Although they are typically out of reach for practical portfolio management situations, they provide an alternative to the models discussed in this chapter and show promise for the modeling of dynamic portfolio allocation and time-varying investment opportunities sets.[2]

In this chapter, we examine some of the most common alternative portfolio risk measures used in practice for asset allocation. We begin by discussing dispersion and downside measures. Then, we turn to modifications to the generalized utility based framework. In particular, we study techniques based upon expansions of the utility function in higher moments such as its mean, variance, skew, and kurtosis.

The empirical estimation of higher moments and other alternative risk measures is often very sensitive to estimation errors. We discuss and illustrate some of the most common pitfalls.

One possibility that helps circumvent, to some extent, the error-prone measurement of higher moments and sensitive risk measures is to make stronger assumptions on the multivariate distribution of the asset returns. We conclude the chapter by describing a novel technique developed by Malevergne and Sornette that relies upon this idea.[3]

DISPERSION AND DOWNSIDE MEASURES

Simplistically speaking, we distinguish between two different types of risk measures: (1) dispersion and (2) downside measures. In this section

[1] See, for example, Chapter 16 in Frank J. Fabozzi, Sergio Focardi and Petter N. Kolm, *Financial Modeling of the Equity Market* (Hoboken, NJ: John Wiley & Sons, 2006).

[2] See, for example, Andrew Ang and Geert Bekaert, "International Asset Allocation with the Regime Shifts," Working Paper, Columbia University and NBER, 2001.

[3] Yannick Malevergne and Didier Sornette, "High-Order Moments and Cumulants of Multivariate Weibull Asset Returns Distributions: Analytical Theory and Empirical Tests: II," *Finance Letters* [Special Issue: Modeling of the Equity Market] 3, no. 1 (2005), pp. 54–63; and "Higher-Moment Portfolio Theory: Capitalizing on Behavioral Anomalies of Stock Markets," *Journal of Portfolio Management* 31, no. 4 (Summer 2005), pp. 49–55.

we provide a brief overview of the most common dispersion and down-side measures and their usage.[4]

Dispersion Measures

Dispersion measures are measures of uncertainty. Uncertainty, however, does not necessarily quantify risk. Dispersion measures consider *both* positive and negative deviations from the mean, and treat those deviations as equally risky. In other words, overperformance relative to the mean is penalized as much as underperformance. In this section, we review the most popular and important portfolio dispersion measures such as mean-standard deviation, mean-absolute deviation, and mean-absolute moment.

Mean-Standard Deviation and the Mean-Variance Approach

For historical reasons, portfolio standard deviation (or portfolio variance) is probably the most well-known dispersion measure. The mean-variance framework, also referred to as classical portfolio theory, which we covered in Chapter 2, was pioneered by Markowitz in the 1950s.

Mean-Absolute Deviation

Konno[5] introduced the *mean-absolute deviation* (MAD) approach in 1988. Rather than using squared deviations as in the mean-variance approach, here the dispersion measure is based on the absolution deviations from the mean; that is, it is defined as

$$MAD(R_p) = E\left(\left|\sum_{i=1}^{N} w_i R_i - \sum_{i=1}^{N} w_i \mu_i\right|\right)$$

where

$$R_p = \sum_{i=1}^{N} w_i R_i$$

---

[4] For a further discussion, see Sergio Ortobelli, Svetlozar T. Rachev, Stoyan Stoyanov, Frank J. Fabozzi, and Almira Biglova, "The Correct Use of Risk Measures in Portfolio Theory," *International Journal of Theoretical and Applied Finance* 8, no. 8 (December 2005), pp. 1–27.

[5] Hiroshi Konno, "Portfolio Optimization Using L1 Risk Function," IHSS Report 88-9, Institute of Human and Social Sciences, Tokyo Institute of Technology, 1988. See, also, Hiroshi Konno, "Piecewise Linear Risk Functions and Portfolio Optimization," *Journal of the Operations Research Society of Japan* 33, no. 2 (1990), pp. 139–156.

R_i and μ_i are the portfolio return, the return on asset i, and the expected return on asset i, respectively.

The computation of optimal portfolios in the case of the mean-absolute deviation approach is significantly simplified, as the resulting optimization problem is linear and can be solved by standard linear programming routines.

We note that it can be shown that under the assumption that the individual asset returns are multivariate normally distributed,

$$MAD(R_p) = \sqrt{\frac{2}{\pi}}\sigma_p$$

where σ_p is the standard deviation of the portfolio.[6] That is, when asset returns are normally distributed, the mean-absolute deviation and the mean-variance approaches are equivalent.

Mean-Absolute Moment

The mean-absolute moment (MAM_q) of order q is defined by

$$MAM_q(R_p) = (E(|R_p - E(R_p)|^q))^{1/q}, q \geq 1$$

and is a straightforward generalization of the mean-standard deviation ($q = 2$) and the mean-absolute deviation ($q = 1$) approaches.

Downside Measures

The objective in downside risk measure portfolio allocation models is the maximization of the probability that the portfolio return is above a certain minimal acceptable level, often also referred to as the *benchmark level* or *disaster level*.

Despite their theoretical appeal, downside or safety-first risk measures are often computationally more complicated to use in a portfolio context. Downside risk measures of individual securities cannot be easily aggregated into portfolio downside risk measures, as their computation requires knowledge of the entire joint distribution of security returns. Often, one has to resort to computationally intensive nonparametric estimation, simulation, and optimization techniques. Furthermore, the estimation risk of downside measures is usually higher than

---

[6] Hiroshi Konno and Hiroaki Yamazaki, "Mean-Absolute Deviation Portfolio Optimization Model and its Application to Tokyo Stock Market," *Management Science* 37, no. 5 (May 1991), pp. 519–531.

for standard mean-variance approaches. By the estimation of downside risk measures, we only use a portion of the original data—maybe even just the tail of the empirical distribution—and hence the estimation error increases.[7] Nevertheless, these risk measures are very useful in assessing the risk for securities with asymmetric return distributions, such as call and put options, as well as other derivative contracts.

We discuss some of the most common safety-first and downside risk measures such as Roy's safety-first, semivariance, lower partial moment, Value-at-Risk, and conditional Value-at-Risk.

Roy's Safety-First

Two very important papers on portfolio selection were published in 1952: first, Markowitz's[8] paper on portfolio selection and classical portfolio theory; second, Roy's[9] paper on *safety first*, which laid the seed for the development of downside risk measures.[10]

Let us first understand the difference between these two approaches.[11] According to classical portfolio theory, an investor constructs a portfolio that represents a trade-off between risk and return. The trade-off between risk and return and the portfolio allocation depend upon the investor's utility function. It can be hard, or even impossible, to determine an investor's actual utility function.

Roy argued that an investor, rather than thinking in terms of utility functions, first wants to make sure that a certain amount of the principal is preserved. Thereafter, he decides on some minimal acceptable return that achieves this principal preservation. In essence, the investor chooses his portfolio by solving the following optimization problem

$$\min_{\mathbf{w}} P(R_p \leq R_0)$$

---

[7] For further discussion of these issues, see Henk Grootveld and Winfried G. Hallerbach, "Variance Versus Downside Risk: Is There Really That Much Difference?" *European Journal of Operational Research* 114, no. 2 (1999), pp. 304–319.

[8] Harry M. Markowitz, "Portfolio Selection," *Journal of Finance* 7, no. 1 (1952), pp. 77–91.

[9] Andrew D. Roy, "Safety-First and the Holding of Assets," *Econometrica* 20, no. 3 (July 1952), pp. 431–449.

[10] See, for example, Vijay S. Bawa, "Optimal Rules for Ordering Uncertain Prospects," *Journal of Financial Economics* 2, no. 1 (1975), pp. 95–121; and Vijay S. Bawa, "Safety-First Stochastic Dominance and Portfolio Choice," *Journal of Financial and Quantitative Analysis* 13, no. 2 (June 1978), pp. 255–271.

[11] For a more detailed description of these historical events, we refer the reader to David Nawrocki, "A Brief History of Downside Risk Measures," College of Commerce and Finance, Villanova University, Faculty Research, Fall 2003.

subject to

$$\mathbf{w}'\iota = 1 \,,\, \iota' = [1, 1, ..., 1]$$

where P is the probability function and

$$R_p = \sum_{i=1}^{N} w_i R_i$$

is the portfolio return. Most likely, the investor will not know the true probability function. However, by using Tchebycheff's inequality, we obtain[12]

$$P(R_p \leq R_0) \leq \frac{\sigma_p^2}{(\mu_p - R_0)^2}$$

where μ_p and σ_p denote the expected return and the variance of the portfolio, respectively. Therefore, not knowing the probability function, the investor will end up solving the approximation

$$\min_{\mathbf{w}} \frac{\sigma_p}{\mu_p - R_0}$$

subject to

$$\mathbf{w}'\iota = 1 \,,\, \iota' = [1, 1, ..., 1]$$

---

[12] For a random variable x with expected value μ and variance σ_x^2, Tchebycheff's inequality states that for any positive real number c, it holds that

$$P(|x - \mu| > c) \leq \frac{\sigma_x^2}{c^2}$$

Applying Tchebycheff's inequality, we get

$$P(R_p \leq R_0) = P(\mu_p - R_p \geq \mu_p - R_0)$$
$$\leq \frac{\sigma_p^2}{(\mu_p - R_0)^2}$$

We note that if R_0 is equal to the risk-free rate, then this optimization problem is equivalent to maximizing a portfolio's Sharpe ratio.

Semivariance

In his original book, Markowitz proposed the usage of *semivariance* to correct for the fact that variance penalizes overperformance and underperformance equally.[13] When receiving his Nobel Prize in Economic Science, Markowitz stated that ". . . it can further help evaluate the adequacy of mean and variance, or alternative practical measures, as criteria." Furthermore, he added "Perhaps some other measure of portfolio risk will serve in a two parameter analysis. . . . Semivariance seems more plausible than variance as a measure of risk, since it is concerned only with adverse deviations."[14]

The portfolio semivariance is defined as

$$\sigma_{p,\,min}^2 = E\left(min\left(\sum_{i=1}^{N} w_i R_i - \sum_{i=1}^{N} w_i \mu_i, 0 \right) \right)^2$$

where

$$R_p = \sum_{i=1}^{N} w_i R_i,$$

R_i and μ_i are the portfolio return, the return on asset i, and the expected return on asset i, respectively. Jin, Markowitz, and Zhou provide some of the theoretical properties of the mean-semivariance approach both in the single-period as well as in the continuous-time setting.[15] A generalization to the semivariance is provided by the lower partial moment risk measure that we discuss in the next subsection.

Lower Partial Moment

The *lower partial moment risk measure* provides a natural generalization of semivariance that we described above (see, for example, Bawa[16]

---

[13] Harry Markowitz, *Portfolio Selection—Efficient Diversification of Investment* (New York: Wiley, 1959).

[14] Harry Markowitz, "Foundations of Portfolio Theory," *Journal of Finance* 46, no. 2 (June 1991), pp. 469–477.

[15] Hanqing Jin, Harry Markowitz, and Xunyu Zhou, "A Note on Semivariance," Forthcoming in *Mathematical Finance*.

[16] Vijay S. Bawa, "Admissible Portfolio for All Individuals," *Journal of Finance* 31, no. 4 (September 1976), pp. 1169–1183.

and Fishburn[17]). The lower partial moment with *power index* q and the *target rate of return* R_0 is given by

$$\sigma_{R_p, q, R_0} = (E(\min(R_p - R_0, 0)^q))^{1/q}$$

where

$$R_p = \sum_{i=1}^{N} w_i R_i$$

is the portfolio return. The target rate of return R_0 is what Roy termed the *disaster level*.[18] We recognize that by setting $q = 2$ and R_0 equal to the expected return, the semivariance is obtained. Fishburn demonstrated that $q = 1$ represents a risk neutral investor, whereas $0 < q \leq 1$ and $q > 1$ correspond to a risk seeking and a risk-averse investor, respectively.

Value-at-Risk (VaR)

Probably the most well-known downside risk measure is *Value-at-Risk* (VaR), first developed by JP Morgan, and made available through the RiskMetrics™ software in October 1994.[19] VaR is related to the percentiles of loss distributions, and measures the predicted maximum loss at a specified probability level (for example, 95%) over a certain time horizon (for example, 10 days). In April 1993, the Basel Committee proposed several amendments to the original so-called 1988 Basel Accord that regulates the minimal capital requirements for banks. While previously the Basel Accord had covered only credit risk (deposits and lending), the new proposal that took effect in 1998 also covers market risk, including organization-wide commodities exposures (measured by 10 day 95% VaR).[20] Today VaR is used by most financial institutions to both track and report the market risk exposure of their trading portfolios.

Formally, VaR is defined as

---

[17] Peter C. Fishburn, "Mean-Risk Analysis with Risk Associated with Below-Target Returns," *American Economic Review* 67, no. 2 (March 1977), pp. 116–126.

[18] Roy, "Safety-First and the Holding of Assets."

[19] JP Morgan/Reuters, *RiskMetrics™—Technical Document*, 4th ed. (New York: Morgan Guaranty Trust Company of New York, 1996). See also http://www.risk-metrics.com.

[20] Basel Committee on Banking Supervision, "Amendment to the Capital Accord to Incorporate Market Risks," 1996.

$$VaR_{1-\varepsilon}(R_p) = \min \{R\,|\,P(-R_p \geq R) \leq \varepsilon\}$$

where P denotes the probability function. Typical values for $(1-\varepsilon)$ are 90%, 95%, and 99%.[21] Some of the practical and computational issues related to using VaR are discussed in Alexander and Baptista,[22] Gaivoronski and Pflug,[23] and Mittnik, Rachev, and Schwartz.[24] Chow and Kritzman discuss the usage of VaR in formulating risk budgets, and provide an intuitive method for converting efficient portfolio allocations into value-at-risk assignments.[25] In a subsequent article, they discuss some of the problems with the simplest approach for computing the

---

[21] There are several equivalent ways to define VaR mathematically. In this book, we generally use ε to denote small numbers, so the expression

$$VaR_{1-\varepsilon}(R_p) = \min \{R\,|\,P(-R_p \geq R) \leq \varepsilon\}$$

emphasizes the fact that the $(1-\varepsilon)$-VaR is the value R such that the probability that the possible portfolio loss $(-R_p)$ exceeds R is at most some small number ε such as 1%, 5%, or 10%. For example, the 95% VaR for a portfolio is the value R such that the probability that the possible portfolio loss exceeds R is less than $\varepsilon = 5\%$.

An alternative, and equivalent way to define $(1-\varepsilon)$-VaR is as the value R such that the probability that the maximum portfolio loss $(-R_p)$ is at most R is at least some large number $(1-\varepsilon)$ such as 99%, 95%, or 90%. Mathematically, this can be expressed as

$$VaR_{1-\varepsilon}(R_p) = \min \{R\,|\,P(-R_p \leq R) \geq 1-\varepsilon\}$$

In some standard references, the parameter α is used to denote the "large" probability in the VaR definition, such as 99%, 95% or 90%. VaR is referred to as α-VaR, and is defined as

$$VaR_{\alpha}(R_p) = \min \{R\,|\,P(-R_p \leq R) \geq \alpha\}$$

Notice that there is no mathematical difference between the VaR definitions that involve α or ε, because α is in fact $(1-\varepsilon)$. In this book, we prefer using ε instead of α in the VaR definition so as to avoid confusion with the term "alpha" used in asset return estimation (see Part II of the book, e.g., Chapters 6 and 8).

[22] Gordon J. Alexander and Alexandre M. Baptista, "Economic Implications of Using a Mean-VaR Model for Portfolio Selection: A Comparison with Mean-Variance Analysis," *Journal of Economic Dynamics & Control* 26, no. 7 (2002), pp. 1159–1193.

[23] Alexei A. Gaivoronski, and Georg Pflug, "Value-at-Risk in Portfolio Optimization: Properties and Computational Approach," *Journal of Risk* 7, no. 2 (2005), pp. 1–31.

[24] Stefan Mittnik, Svetlotzar Rachev, and Eduardo Schwartz, "Value At-Risk and Asset Allocation with Stable Return Distributions," *Allgemeines Statistisches Archiv* 86 (2003), pp. 53–67.

[25] George Chow and Mark Kritzman, "Risk Budgets—Converting Mean-Variance Optimization into VaR Assignments," *Journal of Portfolio Management* 27, no. 2 (Fall 2001), pp. 56-60.

VaR of a portfolio.[26] In particular, the common assumption that the portfolio itself is lognormally distributed can be somewhat problematic, especially for portfolios that contain both long and short positions.

VaR also has several undesirable properties as a risk measure.[27] First, it is not subadditive, so the risk as measured by the VaR of a portfolio of two funds may be higher than the sum of the risks of the two individual portfolios. In other words, for VaR it *does not* hold that $\rho(R_1 + R_2) \le \rho(R_1) + \rho(R_2)$ for all returns R_1, R_2. The subadditivity property is the mathematical description of the diversification effect. It is unreasonable to think that a more diversified portfolio would have higher risk, so non-subadditive risk measures are considered unnatural and undesirable. Second, when VaR is calculated from generated scenarios, it is a nonsmooth and nonconvex function of the portfolio holdings. As a consequence, the VaR function has multiple stationary points, making it computationally both difficult and time-consuming to find the global optimal point in the optimization process for portfolio allocation.[28] Third, VaR does not take the *magnitude* of the losses beyond the VaR value into account. For example, it is very unlikely that an investor will be indifferent between two portfolios with identical expected return and VaR when the return distribution of one portfolio has a short left tail and the other has a long left tail. These undesirable features motivated the development of Conditional Value-at-Risk that we discuss next.

Conditional Value-at-Risk

The deficiencies of Value-at-Risk led Artzner et al. to propose a set of desirable properties for a risk measure.[29] They called risk measures satisfying these properties *coherent risk measures*.[30] *Conditional Value-at-Risk* (CVaR) is a coherent risk measure defined by the formula

$$CVaR_{1-\varepsilon}(R_p) = E(-R_p | -R_p \ge VaR_{1-\varepsilon}(R_p))$$

---

[26] George Chow and Mark Kritzman, "Value at Risk for Portfolios with Short Positions," *Journal of Portfolio Management* 28, no. 3 (Spring 2002), pp. 73–81.

[27] Hans Rau-Bredow, "Value-at-Risk, Expected Shortfall and Marginal Risk Contribution," in Giorgio Szegö (ed.) *Risk Measures for the 21st Century* (Chichester: John Wiley & Sons, 2004), pp. 61–68.

[28] For some possible remedies and fixes to this problem see, Henk Grootveld and Winfried G. Hallerbach, "Upgrading Value-at-Risk from Diagnostic Metric to Decision Variable: A Wise Thing to Do?" in *Risk Measures for the 21st Century*, pp. 33–50. We will discuss computational issues with portfolio VaR optimization in more detail in Chapters 13 and 19.

[29] Philippe Artzner, Freddy Delhaen, Jean-Marc Eber, and David Heath, "Coherent Measures of Risk," *Mathematical Finance* 9 (November 1999), pp. 203–228.

Therefore, CVaR measures the expected amount of losses in the tail of the distribution of possible portfolio losses, beyond the portfolio VaR. In the literature, this risk measure is also referred to as *expected shortfall*,[31] *expected tail loss* (ETL), and *tail VaR*. As with VaR, the most commonly considered values for $(1 - \varepsilon)$ are 90%, 95%, and 99%.

Before we formulate the mean-CVaR optimization problem, we discuss some mathematical properties of the CVaR measure. To this end, let us denote by **w** the N-dimensional portfolio vector such that each component w_i equals the number of shares held in asset i. Furthermore, we denote by **y** a random vector describing the uncertain outcomes (also referred to as *market variables*) of the economy. We let the function $f(\mathbf{w},\mathbf{y})$ (also referred to as the *loss function*) represent the loss associated with the portfolio vector **w**. Note that for each **w** the loss function $f(\mathbf{w},\mathbf{y})$ is a one-dimensional random variable. We let $p(\mathbf{y})$ be the probability associated with scenario **y**.

Now, assuming that all random values are discrete, the probability that the loss function does not exceed a certain value γ is given by the cumulative probability

$$\Psi(\mathbf{w}, \gamma) = \sum_{\{\mathbf{y}|f(\mathbf{w},\mathbf{y}) \leq \gamma\}} p(\mathbf{y})$$

---

[30] A risk measure ρ is called a *coherent measure of risk* if it satisfies the following properties:

1. *Monotonicity.* If $X \geq 0$, then $\rho(X) \leq 0$
2. *Subadditivity.* $\rho(X + Y) \leq \rho(X) + \rho(Y)$
3. *Positive homogeneity.* For any *positive* real number c, $\rho(cX) = c\rho(X)$
4. *Translational invariance.* For any real number c, $\rho(X + c) \leq \rho(X) - c$

where X and Y are random variables. In words, these properties can be interpreted as: (1) If there are only positive returns, then the risk should be non-positive; (2) the risk of a portfolio of two assets should be less than or equal to the sum of the risks of the individual assets; (3) if the portfolio is increased c times, the risk becomes c times larger; and (4) cash or another risk-free asset does not contribute to portfolio risk.

Interestingly, standard deviation, a very popular risk measure, is not coherent—it violates the monotonicity property. It does, however, satisfy subadditivity, which is considered one of the most important properties. The four properties required for coherence are actually quite restrictive: when taken together, they rule out a number of other popular risk measures as well. For example, semideviation-type risk measures violate the subadditivity condition.

[31] Strictly speaking, expected shortfall is defined in a different way, but is shown to be equivalent to CVaR (see, Carlo Acerbi and Dirk Tasche, "On the Coherence of Expected Shortfall," *Journal of Banking and Finance* 26, no. 7 (2002), pp. 1487–1503).

Using this cumulative probability, we see that

$$\text{VaR}_{1-\varepsilon}(\mathbf{w}) = \min\{\gamma | \Psi(\mathbf{w}, \gamma) \geq 1 - \varepsilon\}$$

Since CVaR of the losses of portfolio $\mathbf{w}$ is the expected value of the losses conditioned on the losses being in excess of VaR, we have that

$$\text{CVaR}_{1-\varepsilon}(\mathbf{w}) = E(f(\mathbf{w}, \mathbf{y}) | f(\mathbf{w}, \mathbf{y}) > \text{VaR}_{1-\varepsilon}(\mathbf{w}))$$

$$= \frac{\displaystyle\sum_{\{\mathbf{y} | f(\mathbf{w}, \mathbf{y}) > \text{VaR}_{1-\varepsilon}(\mathbf{w})\}} p(\mathbf{y})f(\mathbf{w}, \mathbf{y})}{\displaystyle\sum_{\{\mathbf{y} | f(\mathbf{w}, \mathbf{y}) > \text{VaR}_{1-\varepsilon}(\mathbf{w})\}} p(\mathbf{y})}$$

The continuous equivalents of these formulas are

$$\Psi(\mathbf{w}, \mathbf{y}) = \int_{f(\mathbf{w}, \mathbf{y}) \leq \gamma} p(\mathbf{y}) dy$$

$$\text{VaR}_{1-\varepsilon}(\mathbf{w}) = \min\{\gamma | \Psi(\mathbf{w}, \gamma) \geq 1 - \varepsilon\}$$

$$\text{CVaR}_{1-\varepsilon}(\mathbf{w}) = E(f(\mathbf{w}, \mathbf{y}) | f(\mathbf{w}, \mathbf{y}) \geq \text{VaR}_{1-\varepsilon}(\mathbf{w}))$$

$$= \varepsilon^{-1} \int_{f(\mathbf{w}, \mathbf{y}) \geq \text{VaR}_{1-\varepsilon}(\mathbf{w})} f(\mathbf{w}, \mathbf{y})p(\mathbf{y}) dy$$

We note that in the continuous case it holds that $\Psi(\mathbf{w}, \gamma) = 1 - \varepsilon$ and therefore the denominator

$$\sum_{\{\mathbf{y} | f(\mathbf{w}, \mathbf{y}) > \text{VaR}_{1-\varepsilon}(\mathbf{w})\}} p(\mathbf{y})$$

in the discrete version of CVaR becomes ε in the continuous case.

Moreover, we see that

$$\text{CVaR}_{1-\varepsilon}(\mathbf{w}) = \varepsilon^{-1} \int_{f(\mathbf{w}, \mathbf{y}) \geq \text{VaR}_{1-\varepsilon}(\mathbf{w})} f(\mathbf{w}, \mathbf{y})p(\mathbf{y}) dy$$

$$\geq \varepsilon^{-1} \int_{f(\mathbf{w}, \mathbf{y}) \geq \text{VaR}_{1-\varepsilon}(\mathbf{w})} \text{VaR}_{1-\varepsilon}(\mathbf{w})p(\mathbf{y}) dy$$

$$= \text{VaR}_{1-\varepsilon}(\mathbf{w})$$

because

$$\varepsilon^{-1} \int\limits_{f(\mathbf{w}, \mathbf{y}) \geq \mathrm{VaR}_{1-\varepsilon}(\mathbf{w})} p(\mathbf{y})dy = 1$$

In other words, CVaR is always at least as large as VaR, but as we mentioned above, CVaR is a coherent risk measure, whereas VaR is not. It can also be shown that CVaR is a concave function and, therefore, has a unique minimum. However, working directly with the above formulas turns out to be somewhat tricky in practice as they involve the VaR function (except for those rare cases when one has an analytical expression for VaR). Fortunately, a simpler approach was discovered by Rockefellar and Uryasev.[32]

Their idea is that the function

$$F_\varepsilon(\mathbf{w}, \xi) = \xi + \varepsilon^{-1} \int\limits_{f(\mathbf{w}, \mathbf{y}) \geq \gamma} (f(\mathbf{w}, \mathbf{y}) - \xi)p(\mathbf{y})dy$$

can be used instead of CVaR. Specifically, they proved the following three important properties:

Property 1. $F_\varepsilon(\mathbf{w}, \xi)$ is a convex and continuously differentiable function in ξ.

Property 2. $\mathrm{VaR}_{1-\varepsilon}(\mathbf{w})$ is a minimizer of $F_\varepsilon(\mathbf{w}, \xi)$.

Property 3. The minimum value of $F_\varepsilon(\mathbf{w}, \xi)$ is $\mathrm{CVaR}_{1-\varepsilon}(\mathbf{w})$.

In particular, we can find the optimal value of $\mathrm{CVaR}_{1-\varepsilon}(\mathbf{w})$ by solving the optimization problem

$$\min_{\mathbf{w}, \xi} F_\varepsilon(\mathbf{w}, \xi)$$

Consequently, if we denote by $(\mathbf{w}^*, \xi^*)$ the solution to this optimization problem, then $F_\varepsilon(\mathbf{w}^*, \xi^*)$ is the optimal CVaR. In addition, the optimal portfolio is given by $\mathbf{w}^*$ and the corresponding VaR is given by ξ^*. In other words, in this fashion we can compute the optimal CVaR *without* first calculating VaR.

In practice, the probability density function $p(\mathbf{y})$ is often not available, or is very difficult to estimate. Instead, we might have T different scenarios $Y = \{\mathbf{y}_1, ..., \mathbf{y}_T\}$ that are sampled from the probability distribu-

---

[32] See, Stanislav Uryasev, "Conditional Value-at-Risk: Optimization Algorithms and Applications," *Financial Engineering News*, no. 14 (February 2000), pp. 1–5; and R. Tyrrell Rockefellar and Stanislav Uryasev, "Optimization of Conditional Value-at-Risk," *Journal of Risk* 2, no. 3 (2000), pp. 21–41.

tion or that have been obtained from computer simulations. Evaluating the auxiliary function $F_\varepsilon(\mathbf{w}, \xi)$ using the scenarios Y, we obtain

$$F_\varepsilon^Y(\mathbf{w}, \xi) = \xi + \varepsilon^{-1} T^{-1} \sum_{i=1}^{T} \max\left(f(\mathbf{w}, \mathbf{y}_i) - \xi, 0\right)$$

Therefore, in this case the optimization problem

$$\min_{\mathbf{w}} \text{CVaR}_{1-\varepsilon}(\mathbf{w})$$

takes the form

$$\min_{\mathbf{w}, \xi} \xi + \varepsilon^{-1} T^{-1} \sum_{i=1}^{T} \max\left(f(\mathbf{w}, \mathbf{y}_i) - \xi, 0\right)$$

Replacing $\max(f(\mathbf{w}, \mathbf{y}_i) - \xi, 0)$ by the auxiliary variables z_i along with appropriate constraints, we obtain the equivalent optimization problem

$$\min \xi + \varepsilon^{-1} T^{-1} \sum_{i=1}^{T} z_i$$

subject to

$$z_i \geq 0, \, i = 1, \ldots, T$$

$$z_i \geq f(\mathbf{w}, \mathbf{y}_i) - \xi, \, i = 1, \ldots, T$$

along with any other constraints on $\mathbf{w}$, such as no short-selling constraints or any of the constraints we will discuss in Chapter 4. Under the assumption that $f(\mathbf{w}, \mathbf{y})$ is linear in $\mathbf{w}$,[33] the above optimization problem

---

[33] This is typically the case as the loss function in the discrete case is chosen to be

$$f(\mathbf{w}, \mathbf{y}) = -\sum_{i=1}^{N} w_i(y_i - x_i)$$

where x_i is the current price of security i.

is linear and can therefore be solved very efficiently by standard linear programming techniques.[34]

The formulation discussed above can be seen as an extension of calculating the *global minimum variance portfolio* (GMV) (see Chapter 2) and can be used as an alternative when the underlying asset return distribution is asymmetric and exhibits fat tails.

Moreover, the representation of CVaR given by the auxiliary function $F_\varepsilon(\mathbf{w},\xi)$ can be used in the construction of other portfolio optimization problems. For example, the mean-CVaR optimization problem

$$\max_{\mathbf{w}} \; \boldsymbol{\mu}'\mathbf{w}$$

subject to

$$\mathrm{CVaR}_{1-\varepsilon}(\mathbf{w}) \le c_0$$

along with any other constraints on $\mathbf{w}$ (represented by $\mathbf{w} \in C_{\mathbf{w}}$), where $\boldsymbol{\mu}$ represents the vector of expected returns, and c_0 is a constant denoting the required level of risk, would result in the following approximation

$$\max_{\mathbf{w}} \; \boldsymbol{\mu}'\mathbf{w}$$

subject to

$$\xi + \varepsilon^{-1}T^{-1}\sum_{i=1}^{T} z_i \le c_0$$
$$z_i \ge 0, \; 0 = 1, \ldots, T$$
$$z_i \ge f(\mathbf{w}, \mathbf{y}_i) - \xi, \; 0 = 1, \ldots, T$$
$$\mathbf{w} \in C_{\mathbf{w}}$$

To illustrate the mean-CVaR optimization approach, we discuss an example from Palmquist, Uryasev, and Krokhmal.[35] They considered two-week returns for all the stocks in the S&P 100 Index over the period July 1, 1997 to July 8, 1999 for scenario generation. Optimal portfolios were constructed by solving the mean-CVaR optimization problem above for a two-week horizon for different levels of confidence.

---

[34] See Chapter 9 for further discussion of numerical optimization.

[35] Pavlo Krokhmal, Jonas Palmquist, and Stanislav Uryasev, "Portfolio Optimization with Conditional Value-At-Risk Objective and Constraints," *Journal of Risk* 4, no. 2 (2002), pp. 11–27.

EXHIBIT 3.1   Efficient Frontiers of Different Mean-CVaR Portfolios

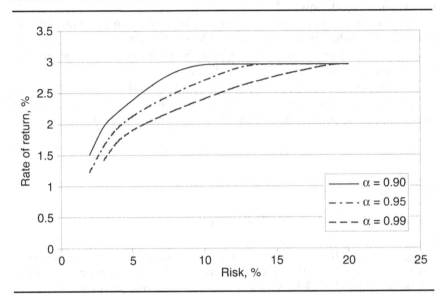

Source: Pavlo Krokhmal, Jonas Palmquist, and Stanislav Uryasev, "Portfolio Optimization with Conditional Value-At-Risk Objective and Constraints," *The Journal of Risk* 4, no. 2 (2002), p. 21. This copyrighted material is reprinted with permission from Incisive Media Plc, Haymarket House, 28-29 Haymarket, London, SW1Y 4RX, United Kingdom.

In Exhibit 3.1 we see three different mean-CVaR efficient frontiers corresponding to $(1 - \varepsilon) = 90\%$, 95%, and 99%. The two-week rate of return is calculated as the ratio of the optimized portfolio value divided by the initial value, and the risk is calculated as the percentage of the initial portfolio value that is allowed to be put at risk. In other words, when the risk is 7% and $(1 - \varepsilon)$ is 95%, this means that we allow for no more than a 7% loss of the initial value of the portfolio with a probability of 5%. We observe from the exhibit that as the CVaR constraint decreases (i.e., the probability increases) the rate of return increases.

It can be shown that for a normally distributed loss function, the mean-variance and the mean-CVaR frameworks generate the same efficient frontier. However, when distributions are nonnormal these two approaches are significantly different. On the one hand, in the mean-variance approach risk is defined by the variance of the loss distribution, and because the variance incorporates information from both the left as well as the right tail of the distribution, both the gains and losses are contributing equally to the risk. On the other hand, the mean-CVaR

EXHIBIT 3.2   Comparison Mean-CVaR95% and Mean-Variance Efficient Portfolios

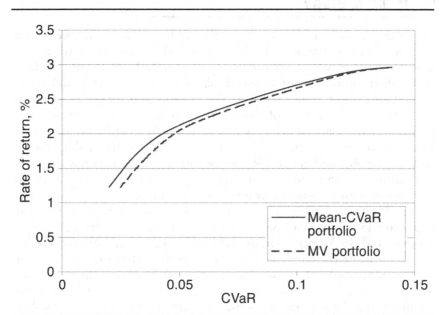

Source: Pavlo Krokhmal, Jonas Palmquist, and Stanislav Uryasev, "Portfolio Optimization with Conditional Value-At-Risk Objective and Constraints," *The Journal of Risk* 4, no. 2 (2002), p. 23. This copyrighted material is reprinted with permission from Incisive Media Plc, Haymarket House, 28-29 Haymarket, London, SW1Y 4RX, United Kingdom.

methodology only involves the part of the tail of the distribution that contributes to high losses.

In Exhibit 3.2 we can see a comparison between the two approaches for $(1 - \varepsilon) = 95\%$. The same data set is used as in the illustration above. We note that in return/CVaR coordinates, as expected, the mean-CVaR efficient frontier lies above the mean-variance efficient frontier. In this particular example, the two efficient frontiers are close to each other and are similarly shaped. Yet with the inclusion of derivative assets such as options and credit derivatives, this will no longer be the case.[36]

---

[36] Nicklas Larsen, Helmut Mausser, and Stanislav Uryasev, "Algorithms for Optimization of Value-at-Risk," on P. Pardalos and V. K. Tsitsiringos (eds.), *Financial Engineering, e-commerce and Supply Chain* (Boston: Kluwer Academic Publishers, 2002), pp. 129–157.

PORTFOLIO SELECTION WITH HIGHER MOMENTS THROUGH EXPANSIONS OF UTILITY

As we saw in Chapter 2, the mean-variance framework is a special case of general utility maximization that arises when investors have a quadratic utility or when asset returns are normally distributed. Many return distributions in the financial markets exhibit fat tails and asymmetry that cannot be described by their means and variances alone. In many instances, the tails of the return distribution significantly affect portfolio performance.[37] Harvey and Siddique have shown that skew in stock returns is relevant to portfolio selection.[38] In particular, if asset returns exhibit nondiversifiable coskew, investors must be rewarded for it, resulting in increased expected returns. They also showed that in the presence of positive skew, investors may be willing to accept a negative expected return. Several other studies have shown that skew is an important factor in asset pricing (see for example, Arditti and Levy,[39] Jondeau and Rockinger,[40] Kraus and Litzenberger,[41] and Nummelin[42]).

To illustrate the effect of skew and kurtosis in the portfolio selection process, we consider three two-asset portfolios: Australia/Singapore, Australia/United Kingdom, and Australia/United States. For each portfolio, the mean, standard deviation, skew, and kurtosis are computed based on the empirical return distribution over the period January 1980 through May 2004 and depicted in Exhibit 3.3. First, we observe that while the return is a linear function of the weight, w, of the first asset,[43] and the standard deviation is convex, the qualitative behavior of the skew and the kurtosis is very different for the three portfolios. Clearly, the skew and kurtosis are highly nonlinear functions that can exhibit multiple maxima and minima. Second, we see that in the case of Australia/Singapore, the

---

[37] Norbert J. Jobst and Stavros A. Zenios, "The Tail That Wags the Dog: Integrating Credit Risk in Asset Portfolios," *Journal of Risk Finance* 3, no. 1 (Fall 2001), pp. 31–44.

[38] Campbell R. Harvey and Akhtar Siddique, "Conditional Skewness in Asset Pricing Tests," *Journal of Finance* 55, no. 3 (June 2000), pp. 1263–1295.

[39] Fred Arditti and Haim Levy, "Portfolio Efficiency Analysis in Three Moments: The Multi Period Case," *Journal of Finance* 30, no. 3 (June 1975), pp. 797–809.

[40] Eric Jondeau and Michael Rockinger, "Conditional Volatility, Skewness, and Kurtosis: Existence, Persistence, and Comovements," *Journal of Economic Dynamics and Control* 27, no. 10 (August 2003), pp. 1699–1737.

[41] Alan Kraus and Robert Litzenberger, "Skewness Preference and the Valuation of Risk Assets," *Journal of Finance* 31, no. 4 (1976), pp. 1085–1100.

[42] Kim Nummelin, "Global Coskewness and the Pricing of Finnish Stocks: Empirical Tests," *Journal of International Financial Markets, Institutions and Money* 7, no. 2 (1997), pp. 137–155.

[43] The weight of the second asset is $1 - w$ such that the portfolio weights add up to 1.

EXHIBIT 3.3   The Effect of Skew and Kurtosis on the Three Two-Asset Portfolios: Australia/Singapore, Australia/United Kingdom, and Australia/United States

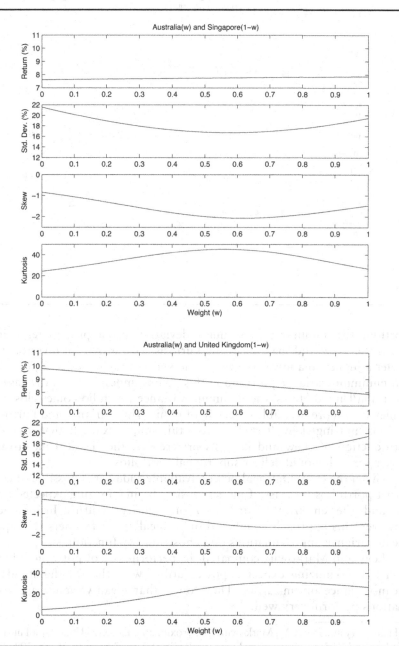

EXHIBIT 3.3   (Continued)

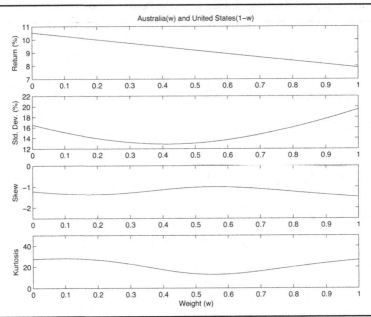

portfolio that minimizes the standard deviation also approximately minimizes the skew and maximizes the kurtosis. Given that an investor will prefer a higher to a lower skew and a lower to a higher kurtosis, the global minimum variance portfolio in this case is undesirable. In the case of Australia/United States, the minimum-variance portfolio comes closer to achieving a more desirable objective of minimizing variance and kurtosis, and maximizing skew. It is clear from this simple example that with the introduction of skew and kurtosis preferences, the classical mean-variance approach would deliver suboptimal portfolios.

Given the computational power available today, it is possible to construct portfolios (at least of moderate size) by maximizing expected utility and the empirical distribution of security returns. In practice, however, this approach is unheard of. Typically, practitioners rely upon mean-variance approximations of a chosen utility function.

Levy and Markowitz compared the performance of portfolio allocation by maximizing expected power utility with that of the standard mean-variance optimization. They found that mean-variance approximations perform very well.[44]

---

[44] Haim Levy and Harry M. Markowitz, "Approximating Expected Utility by a Function of Mean and Variance," *American Economic Review* 69, no. 3 (June 1979), pp. 308–317.

Cremers, Kritzman, and Page[45] show empirically that the log and power utility functions are fairly insensitive to higher moments and, therefore, mean-variance optimization performs very well for investors with log or power utility. However, for discontinuous or S-shaped utility functions,[46] this result no longer holds, and mean-variance optimization shows significant loss in utility compared to an optimization of the full utility function. Of course, in these cases the loss of utility depends on the exact form of the utility function. It is to be expected that in the future it will become more common to use more realistic ("real-world") utility functions in making portfolio allocation decisions.

In this section, we derive a generalization of the mean-variance framework that incorporates higher moments such as skew and kurtosis, but that is significantly easier than solving the general expected utility maximization problem. The first attempt to extend the classical mean-variance optimization to higher moments was made by Jean in the early 1970s.[47] Later, more general and rigorous treatments have been presented by several authors (see for example, Athayde and Flôres[48] and Harvey et al.[49]). We provide a review of these approaches.

By expanding the expected utility of the end of period wealth

$$W = W_0(1 + \mathbf{w'R}) = W_0(1 + R_p)$$

in a Taylor series around the expected end of period wealth

---

[45] Jan-Hein Cremers, Mark Kritzman, and Sebastien Page, "Portfolio Formation with Higher Moments and Plausible Utility," 272-12 Revere Street Working Papers, November 22, 2003; and Jan-Hein Cremers, Mark Kritzman, and Sebastien Page, "Optimal Hedge Fund Allocations—Do Higher Moments Matter?" *Journal of Portfolio Management* 31, no. 3 (Spring 2005), pp. 70–81.

[46] Daniel Kahneman and Amos Tversky, "Prospect Theory: An Analysis of Decision under Risk," *Econometrica* 47, no. 2 (March 1979), pp. 263–290.

[47] William H. Jean, "The Extension of Portfolio Analysis to Three or More Parameters," *Journal of Financial and Quantitative Analysis* 6, no. 1 (1971), pp. 505–515; and "More on Multidimensional Portfolio Analysis," *Journal of Financial and Quantitative Analysis* 8, no. 3 (June 1973), pp. 475–490.

[48] See Gustavo M. Athayde and Renato G. Flôres Jr., "Finding a Maximum Skewness Portfolio—A General Solution to Three-Moments Portfolio Choice," *Journal of Economic Dynamics and Control* 28, no. 7 (2004), pp. 1335–1352; "The Portfolio Frontier with Higher Moments: The Undiscovered Country," *Computing in Economics and Finance 2002*, Society for Computational Economics, 2002, and "Certain Geometric Aspects of Portfolio Optimization with Higher Moments," EPGE/ Fundaçao Getulio Vargas, 2002.

[49] Campbell R. Harvey, John C. Liechty, Merril W. Liechty, and Peter Mueller, "Portfolio Selection with Higher Moments, Working Paper, Duke University, 2003.

$$\overline{W} = W_0(1 + \mathbf{w}'\boldsymbol{\mu}) = W_0(1 + \mu_p)$$

where $\mu = E(\mathbf{R})$, we get

$$E[u(W)] = u(\overline{W}) + u'(\overline{W})E[W - \overline{W}] + \frac{1}{2}u''(\overline{W})E[(W - \overline{W})^2]$$

$$+ \frac{1}{3!}u^{(3)}(\overline{W})E[(W - \overline{W})^3] + \frac{1}{4!}u^{(4)}(\overline{W})E[(W - \overline{W})^4] + O(W^5)$$

$$= u(\overline{W}) + \frac{1}{2}u''(\overline{W})E[(W - \overline{W})^2] + \frac{1}{3!}u^{(3)}(\overline{W})E[(W - \overline{W})^3]$$

$$+ \frac{1}{4!}u^{(4)}(\overline{W})E[(W - \overline{W})^4] + O(W^5)$$

where the second equality follows from $E[W - \overline{W}] = 0$. The functions $E[(W - \overline{W})^k]$, $k = 2, 3, \ldots$ are called the central moments of the random variable W. In particular, we recognize that the second central moment is just the variance of W. Further, the third and fourth central moments are referred to as the *skew* and *kurtosis* of W.[50]

Using the following notation,

$$\mu_p = E(R_p)$$
$$\sigma_p^2 = E[(R_p - \mu_p)^2] = E[(W - \overline{W})^2]$$
$$s_p^3 = E[(R_p - \mu_p)^3] = E[(W - \overline{W})^3]$$
$$\kappa_p^4 = E[(R_p - \mu_p)^4] = E[(W - \overline{W})^4]$$

where $R_p = \mathbf{w}'\mathbf{R}$, we have

$$E[u(W)] = u(\overline{W}) + \frac{1}{2}u''(\overline{W})\sigma_p^2 + \frac{1}{3!}u^{(3)}(\overline{W})s_p^3 + \frac{1}{4!}u^{(4)}(\overline{W})\kappa_p^4 + O((W - \overline{W})^5)$$

For example, for logarithmic utility $u(x) = \ln(x)$ (a CRRA investor, see Chapter 2) we have

---

[50] This is slightly different from the standard definition of skew and kurtosis that are given by the *standardized third and fourth central moments*

$$E\left[\left(\frac{W - \overline{W}}{\sigma_p}\right)^3\right] \text{ and } E\left[\left(\frac{W - \overline{W}}{\sigma_p}\right)^4\right]$$

$$E\left[\ln(W)\right] = \ln(\overline{W}) - \frac{1}{2\overline{W}^2}\sigma_p^2 + \frac{1}{3\overline{W}^3}s_p^3 - \frac{1}{4\overline{W}^4}\kappa_p^4 + O((W - \overline{W})^5)$$

$$\approx \ln(\overline{W}) - \frac{1}{2\overline{W}^2}\sigma_p^2 + \frac{1}{3\overline{W}^3}s_p^3 - \frac{1}{4\overline{W}^4}\kappa_p^4$$

The portfolio choice problem for this investor could be formulated as the optimization problem

$$\max_{\mathbf{w}} \left(\ln(\overline{W}) - \frac{1}{2\overline{W}^2}\sigma_p^2 + \frac{1}{3\overline{W}^3}s_p^3 - \frac{1}{4\overline{W}^4}\kappa_p^4 \right)$$

subject to

$$\mathbf{w}'\iota = 1, \iota' = [1, 1, ..., 1]$$

where $\overline{W} = W_0(1 + \mathbf{w}'\mu)$.

Similarly, we note that the "generic" optimization problem for investors with preferences described by the first four moments takes the form

$$\max_{\mathbf{w}} \mathbf{w}'\mu - \lambda_1\sigma_p^2 + \lambda_2 s_p^3 - \lambda_3\kappa_p^4$$

subject to

$$\mathbf{w}'\iota = 1$$
$$\iota' = [1, 1, ..., 1]$$

The parameters λ_1, λ_2, and λ_3 are determined by the choice of utility function (as in the example with the logarithmic utility function above) or simply by the level of risk aversion or risk preference an investor has for each individual moment. For example, one can calibrate the parameters λ_1, λ_2, and λ_3 using historical data so that portfolio backtests with historical data meet the desired investment goals.

The formulation above involving higher moments of the underlying asset returns provides more freedom in describing investors' preferences than the classical mean-variance framework. A rational investor's preference is high odd moments, as this would decrease extreme values on the side of losses and increase them on the side of gains. Similarly, the investor prefers low even moments, as this implies decreased dispersion and therefore less uncertainty of returns.[51]

The Mathematics of Portfolio Selection with Higher Moments

Dealing with the third and higher portfolio moments quickly becomes cumbersome algebraically and can also be computationally inefficient unless caution is used. It is convenient to have similar formulas for the skew and kurtosis as for the portfolio mean and standard deviation

$$r_p = \mathbf{w}'\boldsymbol{\mu}$$
$$\sigma_p^2 = \mathbf{w}'\boldsymbol{\Sigma}\mathbf{w}$$

where $\boldsymbol{\mu}$ and $\boldsymbol{\Sigma}$ are the vector of expected returns and the covariance matrix of returns of the assets. In full generality, each moment of a random vector can be mathematically represented as a *tensor*. In the case of the second moment, the second moment tensor is the familiar $N \times N$ covariance matrix, whereas the third moment tensor, the so-called *skew tensor*, can intuitively be seen as a three-dimensional cube with height, width, and depth of N. The fourth moment tensor, the *kurtosis tensor*, can similarly be visualized as a four-dimensional cube.

When dealing with higher moments in the portfolio choice problem, it is convenient to "slice" the higher moment tensors and create one big matrix out of the slices. For example, the skew tensor (a three-dimensional cube) with N^3 elements and the kurtosis tensor (a fourth-dimensional cube) with N^4 elements, can each be represented by an $N \times N^2$ and an $N \times N^3$ matrix, respectively. Formally, we denote the $N \times N^2$ and $N \times N^3$ skew and kurtosis matrices by[52]

$$\mathbf{M}_3 = (s_{ijk}) = E[(\mathbf{R}-\boldsymbol{\mu})(\mathbf{R}-\boldsymbol{\mu})' \otimes (\mathbf{R}-\boldsymbol{\mu})']$$
$$\mathbf{M}_4 = (\kappa_{ijkl}) = E[(\mathbf{R}-\boldsymbol{\mu})(\mathbf{R}-\boldsymbol{\mu})' \otimes (\mathbf{R}-\boldsymbol{\mu})' \otimes (\mathbf{R}-\boldsymbol{\mu})']$$

where each element is defined by the formulas

$$s_{ijk} = E[(R_i-\mu_i)(R_j-\mu_j)(R_k-\mu_k)], i, j, k = 1, \ldots, N$$

$$\kappa_{ijk} = E[(R_i-\mu_i)(R_j-\mu_j)(R_k-\mu_k)(R_l-\mu_l)], i, j, k, l = 1, \ldots, N$$

---

[51] For a theoretical formalization and justification of this result, see Robert C. Scott and Philip A. Horvath, "On the Direction of Preference for Moments of Higher Order Than Variance," *Journal of Finance* 35, no. 4 (September 1980), pp. 915–919.
[52] The expression A ⊗ B is referred to as the *Kronecker product of A and B*.

For example, when $N = 3$, the skew matrix takes the form

$$
\mathbf{M}_3 = \begin{bmatrix}
s_{111}\ s_{112}\ s_{113} & s_{211}\ s_{212}\ s_{213} & s_{311}\ s_{312}\ s_{313} \\
s_{121}\ s_{122}\ s_{123} & s_{221}\ s_{222}\ s_{223} & s_{321}\ s_{322}\ s_{323} \\
s_{131}\ s_{132}\ s_{133} & s_{231}\ s_{232}\ s_{233} & s_{331}\ s_{332}\ s_{333}
\end{bmatrix}
$$

Just like the covariance matrix, the third and fourth moment tensors are symmetric. In fact, out of the N^3 and N^4 elements the number of different skew and kurtosis components in each tensor are given by[53]

$$
\binom{N+2}{3} \text{ and } \binom{N+3}{4}
$$

For example, if the number of assets considered is three, then the covariance matrix has six different elements, the skew matrix has 10 different elements, and the kurtosis matrix has 15 different elements. Taking the symmetries into account is important in practical applications involving many securities, as it significantly speeds up numerical computations and simulations.

Using the tensor notation we can restate the generic four-moment optimization problem in the form

$$
\max_{\mathbf{w}} \mathbf{w}'\boldsymbol{\mu} - \lambda_1 \mathbf{w}'\boldsymbol{\Sigma}\mathbf{w} + \lambda_2 \mathbf{w}'\mathbf{M}_3(\mathbf{w} \otimes \mathbf{w}) - \lambda_3 \mathbf{w}'\mathbf{M}_4(\mathbf{w} \otimes \mathbf{w} \otimes \mathbf{w})
$$

subject to

$$
\boldsymbol{\iota}'\mathbf{w} = 1, \boldsymbol{\iota}' = [1, 1, ..., 1]
$$

This formulation can be efficiently solved by nonlinear programming packages.[54] In general, as the objective function is a polynomial of fourth order in the portfolio weights, the problem is no longer convex and may therefore exhibit multiple local optima. A geometric characterization of the efficient set of the above portfolio choice problem involving the first three moments has been provided by Athayde and Flôres.[55]

---

[53] This fact follows from the symmetry relationships $s_{ijk} = s_{jik} = s_{kji} = s_{ikj}$ and $\kappa_{ijkl} = \kappa_{jikl} = \kappa_{kjil} = \kappa_{ljki} = \kappa_{ikjl} = \kappa_{ilkj} = \kappa_{ijlk}$.

[54] We discuss nonlinear optimization further in Chapter 9.

[55] Athayde and Flôres, "Finding a Maximum Skewness Portfolio—A General Solution to Three-Moments Portfolio Choice."

POLYNOMIAL GOAL PROGRAMMING FOR PORTFOLIO OPTIMIZATION WITH HIGHER MOMENTS

In this section we discuss an approach to the portfolio optimization problem with higher moments that is referred to as the *polynomial goal programming* (PGP) approach.[56] We suggested in the previous section that investors have a preference for positive odd moments, but strive to minimize their exposure to even moments. For example, an investor may attempt to, on the one hand, maximize expected portfolio return and skewness, while on the other, minimize portfolio variance and kurtosis. Mathematically, we can express this by the multiobjective optimization problem:

$$\max_{\mathbf{w}} O_1(\mathbf{w}) = \mathbf{w}'\boldsymbol{\mu}$$

$$\min_{\mathbf{w}} O_2(\mathbf{w}) = \mathbf{w}'\boldsymbol{\Sigma}\mathbf{w}$$

$$\max_{\mathbf{w}} O_3(\mathbf{w}) = \mathbf{w}'\mathbf{M}_3(\mathbf{w} \otimes \mathbf{w})$$

$$\min_{\mathbf{w}} O_4(\mathbf{w}) = \mathbf{w}'\mathbf{M}_4(\mathbf{w} \otimes \mathbf{w} \otimes \mathbf{w})$$

subject to desired constraints. The notation used in this formulation was introduced in the previous section. This type of problem, which addresses the trade-off between competing objectives, is referred to as a *goal programming* (GP) problem. The basic idea behind goal programming is to break the overall problem into smaller solvable elements and then iteratively attempt to find solutions that preserve, as closely as possible, the individual goals.

Because the choice of the relative percentage invested in each asset is the main concern in the portfolio allocation decision, the portfolio weights can be rescaled and restricted to the unit variance space $\{\mathbf{w} \mid \mathbf{w}'\boldsymbol{\Sigma}\mathbf{w} = 1\}$. This observation allows us to formulate the multiobjective optimization problem as follows:

---

[56] See, for example, Pornchai Chunhachinda, Krishnan Dandapani, Shahid Hamid, and Arun J. Prakash, "Portfolio Selection and Skewness: Evidence from International Stock Markets," *Journal of Banking and Finance* 21, no. 2 (1997), pp. 143–167; Qian Sun and Yuxing Yan, "Skewness Persistence with Optimal Portfolio Selection," *Journal of Banking and Finance* 27, no. 6 (2003), pp. 1111–1121; Arun J. Prakash, Chun-Hao Chang, and Therese E. Pactwa, "Selecting a Portfolio with Skewness: Recent Evidence from U.S., European, and Latin American Equity Markets," *Journal of Banking and Finance* 27, no.7 (2003), pp. 1375–1390; and Ryan J. Davies, Harry M. Kat, and Sa Lu, "Fund of Hedge Funds Portfolio Selection: A Multiple Objective Approach," Working Paper, ISMA Centre, University of Reading, 2004.

$$\max_{\mathbf{w}} O_1(\mathbf{w}) = \mathbf{w}'\mu$$

$$\max_{\mathbf{w}} O_3(\mathbf{w}) = \mathbf{w}'M_3(\mathbf{w} \otimes \mathbf{w})$$

$$\min_{\mathbf{w}} O_4(\mathbf{w}) = \mathbf{w}'M_4(\mathbf{w} \otimes \mathbf{w} \otimes \mathbf{w})$$

subject to

$$\iota'\mathbf{w} = 1, \iota' = [1, 1, ..., 1]$$
$$\mathbf{w}'\Sigma\mathbf{w} = 1$$

In general, there will not be a single solution of this problem that can maximize both $O_1(\mathbf{w})$ and $O_3(\mathbf{w})$, and minimize $O_4(\mathbf{w})$. Instead, the solution to the multiobjective optimization problem has to be obtained in a two-step procedure. First, optimal values of each individual objective are calculated separately, that is, we maximize $O_1(\mathbf{w})$ and $O_3(\mathbf{w})$, and minimize $O_4(\mathbf{w})$ subject to the constraints. Let us denote the optimal values so obtained by O_1^*, O_3^*, and O_4^*. In the second step, the optimization problem that has to be solved is one that attempts to simultaneously minimize the deviations of each individual objective from its optimal value

$$\min_{\mathbf{w}} O(\mathbf{w}) = (d_1(\mathbf{w}))^{p_1} + (d_3(\mathbf{w}))^{p_3} + (d_4(\mathbf{w}))^{p_4}$$

subject to the constraints

$$\iota'\mathbf{w} = 1, \iota' = [1, 1, ..., 1]$$

$$\mathbf{w}'\Sigma\mathbf{w} = 1$$

where $d_i(\mathbf{w}) = O_i^* - O_i(\mathbf{w})$ for $i = 1, 3, 4$ and p_1, p_3, p_4 are chosen parameters expressing the investor's preference for each moment.[57]

Trivially, this optimization problem collapses to a standard mean-variance optimization problem if we give no weight to the skew and kurtosis terms. The preference parameters p_1, p_3, p_4 have an explicit economic interpretation in that they are directly associated with the *marginal rate of substitution* (MRS),

---

[57] Alternatively, from a computational perspective it is sometimes more convenient to use the objective function $O_{(\mathbf{w})} = d_1(\mathbf{w}) + \lambda_3 d_3(\mathbf{w}) + \lambda_4 d_4(\mathbf{w})$.

$$MRS_{ij} = \frac{\partial O}{\partial d_i} \Big/ \frac{\partial O}{\partial d_j} = \frac{p_i}{p_j} \frac{d_i(\mathbf{w})^{p_i - 1}}{d_j(\mathbf{w})^{p_j - 1}}$$

which measures the desirability of foregoing objective O_i in order to gain from objective O_j.

SOME REMARKS ON THE ESTIMATION OF HIGHER MOMENTS

From a practical point of view, when models involve estimated quantities, it is important to understand how accurate these estimates really are. It is well known that the sample mean and variance, computed via averaging, are very sensitive to outliers. The measures of skew and kurtosis of returns,

$$\hat{s}^3 = \frac{1}{N} \sum_{i=1}^{N} \left(R_i - \hat{R} \right)^3$$

$$\hat{k}^4 = \frac{1}{N} \sum_{i=1}^{N} \left(R_i - \hat{R} \right)^4$$

where

$$\hat{R} = \frac{1}{N} \sum_{i=1}^{N} R_i$$

are also based upon averages. These measures are therefore also very sensitive to outliers. Moreover, it is well known that the standard error of estimated moments of order n is proportional to the square root of the moment of order $2n$.[58] Consequently, the accuracy of moments beyond $n = 4$ is often too low for practical purposes.

As a matter of fact, the impact of outliers is magnified in the above measures of skew and kurtosis due to the fact that observations are raised to the third and fourth powers. Therefore, we have to use these measures with tremendous caution. For example, in the data set of MSCI

---

[58] Maurice G. Kendall, Alan Stuart, J. Keith Ord, Steven F. Arnold, and Anthony O'Hagan, *Kendall's Advanced Theory of Statistics: Volume 1: Distribution Theory* (London: Arnold Publishers, 1998).

World Index and United States returns from January 1980 through May 2004, the skews are -0.37 and -1.22, respectively. Similarly, the kurtosis for the same period is 9.91 for the MSCI World Index and 27.55 for the United States. However, recomputing these measures after removing the single observation corresponding to the October 19, 1987 stock market crash, the skews are -0.09 and -0.04, while the kurtosis are 6.78 and 5.07, for the MSCI World Index and the United States indices, respectively. That is a dramatic change, especially in the U.S. market, after removing a single observation. This simple example illustrates how sensitive higher moments are to outliers. The problem of estimating the higher moments (and even the variance) gets worse in the presence of heavy tails, which is not uncommon in financial data. In practice, it is desirable to use more robust measures of these moments.

In the statistics literature, several robust substitutes for mean and variance are available. However, robust counterparts for skew and kurtosis have been given little attention. Many practitioners eliminate or filter out large outliers from the data. The problem with this approach is that it is done on an *ad hoc* basis, often by hand, without relying upon methods of statistical inference. Several robust measures of skew and kurtosis are surveyed and compared through Monte Carlo simulations in a paper by Kim and White.[59] Kim and White's conclusion is that the conventional measures have to be viewed with skepticism. We recommend that in applications involving higher moments, robust measures should at least be computed for comparison along with traditional estimates.

THE APPROACH OF MALEVERGNE AND SORNETTE[80]

The mean-variance approach and the generalized formulation with higher moments described earlier in this chapter rely upon empirical estimates of expected returns and risk, that is, centered moments or cumulants. In principle, these could all be estimated empirically. However, the estimation errors of higher moments quickly get very large. In

---

[59] Tae-Hwan Kim and Halbert White, "On More Robust Estimation of Skewness and Kurtosis," *Finance Research Letters* 1, no. 1 (2004), pp. 56–73.

[60] For the remaining part of this section, we will use the notation of Malevergne and Sornette. Yannick Malevergne and Didier Sornette, "High-Order Moments and Cumulants of Multivariate Weibull Asset Returns Distributions: Analytical Theory and Empirical Tests: II," *Finance Letters, Special Issue: Modeling of the Equity Market* 3, no. 1 (2005), pp. 54–63. In particular, we denote security returns by r in the one-dimensional case, and r in the N-dimensional case. Similarly, we write q in the one-dimensional case and q in the N-dimensional case, for the transformed variable and vector, respectively.

particular, the standard error of the estimated moment of order n is proportional to the square root of the moment of order $2n$, so that for daily historical times series of returns, which with a decent length amount to about a few thousand observations, moments of order greater than six often become unreasonable to empirically estimate.[61] One way to proceed is to make stronger assumptions on the multivariate distribution of the asset returns. We describe a technique developed by Malevergne and Sornette for this particular problem.[62]

First, we recall from statistical theory that the dependence between random variables is completely described by their joint distribution. Therefore, for a complete description of the returns and risks associated with a portfolio of N assets we would need the knowledge of the multivariate distribution of the returns. For example, assume that the joint distribution of returns is Gaussian, that is,

$$p(\mathbf{r}) = \frac{1}{(2\pi)^{N/2}\sqrt{\det(\boldsymbol{\Sigma})}} \exp\left(-\frac{1}{2}(\mathbf{r}-\boldsymbol{\mu})'\boldsymbol{\Sigma}^{-1}(\mathbf{r}-\boldsymbol{\mu})\right)$$

with $\boldsymbol{\mu}$ and $\boldsymbol{\Sigma}$ being the mean and the covariance of the returns $\mathbf{r}$. Then we would be back in the mean-variance world described in Chapter 2, because in the Gaussian case the joint distribution is completely described by the mean and the covariance matrix of returns.

In general, the joint distribution of asset returns is not normal. We attempt to represent their multivariate distribution by

$$p(\mathbf{r}) = F((\mathbf{r}-\boldsymbol{\mu})'\boldsymbol{\Sigma}(\mathbf{r}-\boldsymbol{\mu}))$$

where F is an arbitrary function. We see immediately that if we chose $F(x) = \exp(x)$, we would retrieve the Gaussian distribution. Malevergne and Sornette suggest constructing the function F in such a way that each return r_i is transformed into a Gaussian variable q_i.

The One-Dimensional Case

Let us assume that the probability density function of an asset's return r is given by $p(r)$. The transformation $q(r)$ that produces a normal variable q from r is determined by the conservation of probability:

---

[61] See, for example, Maurice G. Kendall, Alan Stuart, J. Keith Ord, Steven F. Arnold, and Anthony O'Hagan, *Kendall's Advanced Theory of Statistics: Volume 1: Distribution Theory* (London: Arnold Publishers, 1998).

[62] Malevergne and Sornette, "High-Order Moments and Cumulants of Multivariate Weibull Asset Returns Distributions: Analytical Theory and Empirical Tests: II."

$$p(r)dr = \frac{1}{\sqrt{2\pi}} e^{-\frac{q^2}{2}} dq$$

If we integrate this equation from minus infinity up to r, we get

$$F(r) = \frac{1}{2}\left[1 + \mathrm{erf}\left(\frac{q}{\sqrt{2}}\right)\right]$$

where $F(r)$ is defined by

$$F(r) = \int_{-\infty}^{r} p(r')dr'$$

and erf is the so-called *error function* given by

$$\mathrm{erf}(x) = \frac{2}{\sqrt{\pi}} \int_0^x e^{-t^2} dt$$

If we solve for q, we obtain

$$q(r) = \sqrt{2}\,\mathrm{erf}^{-1}(2F(r) - 1)$$

In the case where the probability density function of r only has one maximum, it can be shown that there exists a function $f(x)$ such that the above change of variables takes the form[63]

$$q(r) = \mathrm{sgn}(r)\sqrt{|f(r)|}$$

---

[63] $f(x)$ is defined by the so-called Von Mises variables

$$p(r)dr = C\frac{f'(r)}{\sqrt{|f(r)|}} e^{-\frac{f(r)}{2}} dr$$

where C is a normalizing constant. This representation is valid if the pdf of r has a single maximum, that is, the pdf is so-called unimodal. (See Paul Embrechts, Claudia Kluppelberg, Thomas Mikosh, "Modelling Extremal Events for Insurance and Finance," *Applications of Mathematics*, vol. 33 (Berlin and Heidelberg: Springer, 1997).

By construction, the new variable q is standard normal (i.e., $q(r) \sim N(0,1)$). Let us now see how we would use this transformation in the multidimensional case.

The Multidimensional Case

By virtue of the transformation described earlier, we can map each component r_i of the random vector $\mathbf{r}$ (representing asset returns) into a standard normal variable q_i. If these variables were all independent, we could simply calculate the joint distribution as the product of the marginal distributions. Of course, in practice the components will not be independent, and it becomes important to describe their dependence. We can do this by calculating the covariance matrix $\mathbf{\Sigma_q}$ of $\mathbf{q}$ by standard techniques (see Chapter 6).

Given the covariance matrix $\mathbf{\Sigma_q}$, using a classical result of information theory[64] the best joint distribution of $\mathbf{q}$ in the sense of entropy maximization is given by

$$p(\mathbf{q}) = \frac{1}{(2\pi)^{N/2}\sqrt{\det(\mathbf{\Sigma_q})}} \exp\left(-\frac{1}{2}\mathbf{q}'\mathbf{\Sigma_q^{-1}}\mathbf{q}\right)$$

By a transformation of variables, we obtain the joint distribution of $\mathbf{r}$,

$$p(\mathbf{r}) = p(\mathbf{q})\left|\frac{\partial \mathbf{q}}{\partial \mathbf{r}'}\right|$$

where

$$\left|\frac{\partial \mathbf{q}}{\partial \mathbf{r}'}\right|$$

denotes the determinant of the Jacobian. Observing that[65]

$$\left|\frac{\partial q_i}{\partial r_j}\right| = \sqrt{2\pi}p_j(r_j)e^{\frac{1}{2}q_i^2}\gamma_{ij}$$

---

[64] C. Radhakrishna Rao, *Linear Statistical Inference and Its Applications* (New York: John Wiley & Sons, 2002).
[65] Here, δ_{ij} is the Dirac delta function defined by

$$\delta_{ij} = \begin{cases} 1, i = j \\ 0, i \neq j \end{cases}$$

we immediately obtain

$$\left|\frac{\partial q}{\partial r'}\right| = (2\pi)^{\frac{N}{2}} \prod_{i=1}^{N} p_i(r_i) e^{\frac{1}{2}q_i^2}$$

Therefore, the joint distribution of r becomes

$$p(\mathbf{r}) = \frac{1}{\sqrt{\det(\Sigma_q)}} \exp\left(-\frac{1}{2}q(\mathbf{r})'(\Sigma_q^{-1} - I)q(\mathbf{r})\right) \prod_{i=1}^{N} p_i(r_i)$$

where $p_i(r_i)$ is the marginal density function of r_i. We note that if all the components of **q** were independent, then $\Sigma_q = I$, and $p(\mathbf{r})$ would simply be the product of the marginal distributions of r_i.

It can also be shown that in this framework, where the arbitrary random variables **r** are transformed into the standard normal variables **q**, the new transformed variables conserve the structure of correlation of the original ones as measured by copula functions. In particular, we have that

$$p(r_1, ..., r_N) = c(F_1(r_1), ..., F_N(r_N)) \prod_{i=1}^{N} p_i(r_i)$$

where

$$c(x_1, ..., x_N) = \frac{1}{\det(\Sigma_q)} \exp\left(-\frac{1}{2}q(x)'(\Sigma_q^{-1} - I)q(x)\right)$$

and $F_i(r_i)$ are the marginal distribution functions of F. The function c: $R^N \to R$ is the density of the Gaussian copula[66] function C, that is,

$$c(x_1, ..., x_N) = \frac{\partial C(x_1, ..., x_N)}{\partial x_1, ..., \partial x_N}$$

This property shows that this approach is based on the assumption of arbitrary marginal distributions with a Gaussian copula. We obtained the Gaussian copula from the transformation of the arbitrary marginal

---

[66] For an introduction to copulas, see Appendix B in Fabozzi, Focardi, and Kolm, *Financial Modeling of the Equity Market: From CAPM to Cointegration.*

distributions to Gaussian marginal distributions under the assumption that the covariance matrix is constant. Finally, we remark that Malevergne and Sornette tested the Gaussian copula hypothesis for financial assets and found that it holds well for equities.[67]

SUMMARY

- The mean-variance framework only takes the first two moments, the mean and the variance, into account. When investors have preferences beyond the first two moments, it is desirable to extend the mean-variance framework to include higher moments.
- Two different types of risk measures can be distinguished: dispersion and downside measures.
- Dispersion measures are measures of uncertainty. In contrast to downside measures, dispersion measures consider both positive and negative deviations from the mean, and treat those deviations as equally risky.
- Some common portfolio dispersion approaches are mean standard deviation, mean-variance, mean-absolute deviation, and mean-absolute moment.
- Some common portfolio downside measures are Roy's safety-first, semivariance, lower partial moment, Value-at-Risk, and Conditional Value-at-Risk.
- In principle, optimal portfolio allocations—at least for moderately sized portfolios—can be calculated by maximizing expected utility under the empirical distribution of security returns.
- Approximations to the expected utility framework can be derived by expanding the utility function in a Taylor series. In this fashion, portfolio optimization problems can be formulated that include moments of desirable order. Typically, the mean, variance, skew, and kurtosis are considered.
- Higher-order moments are very sensitive to estimation error.
- The approach by Malevergne and Sornette is based on the idea of transforming an arbitrary marginal distribution function to a Gaussian marginal distribution function (under the assumption of a Gaussian copula).

---

[67] Yannick Malevergne and Didier Sornette, "Testing the Gaussian Copula Hypothesis for Financial Assets Dependences," *Quantitative Finance* 3, no. 5 (October 2003), pp. 231–250.

CHAPTER 4

Portfolio Selection in Practice

Markowitz's seminal paper on portfolio selection has undoubtedly had a major impact not only on academic research, but also on the financial industry as a whole. It shifted the focus of investment analysis away from individual security selection and toward the concept of diversification and the impact of individual securities on a portfolio's risk-return characteristics. In the mean-variance optimization framework, efficient portfolios are formed by choosing an asset based upon its interaction with other assets in the portfolio as well as on its contribution to the overall portfolio, and not only on the basis of its standalone performance.

Nevertheless, for portfolio management in practice, the classical mean-variance framework only serves as a starting point. The original approach proposed by Markowitz is often extended in several different directions. It is common to amend the mean-variance framework with various types of constraints that take specific investment guidelines and institutional features into account. In this chapter, we provide a simple classification of the most common portfolio constraints used in practice. In particular, we discuss linear, quadratic and integer/combinatorial constraints along with two illustrations. The first one shows how an index tracking portfolio can be constructed by minimizing its tracking error relative to the index. The second one illustrates the use of more complicated combinatorial restrictions such as so-called minimal holdings and cardinality constraints.

The inclusion of transaction costs in the portfolio selection problem may present a challenge to the portfolio manager, but is an important practical consideration. We explain how to extend traditional asset allocation models to incorporate transaction costs. For a detailed discussion of transaction cost measurement and modeling, we refer the interested reader to Chapter 3 in Fabozzi, Focardi, and Kolm.[1]

---

[1] Frank J. Fabozzi, Sergio M. Focardi, and Petter N. Kolm, *Financial Modeling of the Equity Market: From CAPM to Cointegration* (Hoboken, NJ: John Wiley & Sons, 2006).

Yet another level of difficulty in creating asset allocation models that take transaction costs into consideration is optimizing these costs across multiple client accounts. We discuss the topic of multiaccount optimization in the final section of this chapter.

Capital gains taxes can make a strategy that is profitable on a pretax basis into a losing one on an after-tax basis. Therefore, it is important for the portfolio manager to factor tax consequences into the investment decision. Because of the way capital gains and losses from trading can be used to cancel each other for tax purposes, incorporating taxes properly necessitates a multiperiod view of the market. Unfortunately, this also makes quantitative modeling of portfolio allocation with taxes very complex. The problem is further complicated by the fact that different investors are in different tax brackets, and therefore have different effective tax rates. We will briefly discuss the subject of taxes in Chapter 13. The after-tax allocation problem is a large topic by itself, and a comprehensive treatment of the subject is beyond the scope of this book.[2]

PORTFOLIO CONSTRAINTS COMMONLY USED IN PRACTICE

Institutional features and investment policy decisions often lead to more complicated constraints and portfolio management objectives than those present in the original formulation of the mean-variance problem. For example, many mutual funds are managed relative to a particular benchmark or asset universe (e.g., S&P 500, Russell 1000) so that their tracking error relative to the benchmark is kept small.[3] A portfolio manager might also be restricted on how concentrated the investment portfolio can be in a particular industry or sector. These restrictions, and many more, can be modeled by adding constraints to the original formulation.

In this section, we describe constraints that are often used in combination with the mean-variance problem in practical applications. Specifically, we distinguish between linear, quadratic, nonlinear, and combinatorial/integer constraints.

Throughout this section, we denote the current portfolio weights by w_0 and the targeted portfolio weights by w, so that the amount to be traded is $x = w - w_0$.

---

[2] A good starting point for this topic is in the following papers by Don Mulvihill appearing in Bob Litterman and the Quantitative Resources Group of Goldman Sachs Asset Management, *Modern Investment Management: An Equilibrium Approach* (Hoboken, NJ: John Wiley & Sons, 2003): "Investing for Real After-Tax Results" (Chapter 29); "Asset Allocation and Location" (Chapter 31); and "Equity Portfolio Structure" (Chapter 32).

[3] We will discuss selecting a benchmark in Chapter 14.

Linear and Quadratic Constraints

Some of the more commonly used linear and quadratic constraints are described below.

Long-Only Constraints

When short-selling is not allowed, we require that $\mathbf{w} \geq 0$. This is a frequently used constraint, as many funds and institutional investors are prohibited from selling stocks short.

Turnover Constraints

High portfolio turnover can result in large transaction costs that make portfolio rebalancing inefficient. One possibility is to limit the amount of turnover allowed when performing portfolio optimization. The most common turnover constraints limit turnover on each individual asset

$$|x_i| \leq U_i$$

or on the whole portfolio

$$\sum_{i \in I} |x_i| \leq U_{\text{portfolio}}$$

where I denotes the available investment universe. Turnover constraints are often imposed relative to the *average daily volume* (ADV) of a stock. For example, we might want to restrict turnover to be no more than 5% of average daily volume. Modifications of these constraints, such as limiting turnover in a specific industry or sector, are also frequently applied.

Holding Constraints

A well-diversified portfolio should not exhibit large concentrations in any specific assets, industries, sectors, or countries. Maximal holdings in an individual asset can be controlled by the constraint

$$L_i \leq w_i \leq U_i$$

where L_i and U_i are vectors representing the lower and upper bounds of the holdings of asset i. To constrain the exposure to a specific set I_i (e.g., industry or country) of the available investment universe I, we can introduce constraints of the form

$$L_i \le \sum_{j \in I_i} w_j \le U_i$$

where L_i and U_i denote the minimum and maximum exposures to I_i.

Risk Factor Constraints

In practice, it is very common for portfolio managers to use factor models to control for different risk exposures to risk factors such as market, size, and style.[4] Let us assume that security returns have a factor structure with K risk factors, that is

$$R_i = \alpha_i + \sum_{k=1}^{K} \beta_{ik} F_k + \varepsilon_i$$

where F_k, $k = 1, \ldots, K$ are the K factors common to all the securities, β_{ik} is the sensitivity of the i-th security to the k-th factor, and ε_i is the non-systematic return for the i-th security.

To limit a portfolio's exposure to the k-th risk factor, we can impose the constraint

$$\sum_{i=1}^{N} \beta_{ik} w_i \le U_k$$

where U_k denotes maximum exposure allowed. To construct a portfolio that is neutral to the k-th risk factor (for example, market neutral) we would use the constraint

$$\sum_{i=1}^{N} \beta_{ik} w_i = 0$$

Benchmark Exposure and Tracking Error Constraints

Many portfolio managers are faced with the objective of managing their portfolio relative to a benchmark. This is the typical situation for index fund managers and passive managers who are trying to deliver a small outperformance relative to a particular benchmark, such as the Russell 1000 or the S&P 500.

Let us denote by $\mathbf{w}_b$ the market capitalization weights (sometimes also referred to as the *benchmark weights*), and by $\mathbf{R}$ the vector of

---

[4] We discuss risk factors and factor models in more detail in Chapter 6.

returns of the individual assets, so that $R_b = \mathbf{w}_b' \cdot \mathbf{R}$ is the return on the benchmark. A portfolio manager might choose to limit the deviations of the portfolio weights from the benchmark weights by imposing

$$\|\mathbf{w} - \mathbf{w}_b\| \leq M$$

or, similarly, for a specific industry I_i require that

$$\sum_{j \in I_i} w_j - w_{bj} \leq M_i$$

However, the most commonly used metric to measure the deviation from the benchmark is the *tracking error*. The tracking error is defined as the variance of the difference between the return of the portfolio $R_p = \mathbf{w}' \cdot \mathbf{R}$ and the return of the benchmark $R_b = \mathbf{w}_b' \cdot \mathbf{R}$, that is, $\mathrm{TEV}_p = \mathrm{var}(R_p - R_b)$. Expanding this definition, we get

$$
\begin{aligned}
\mathrm{TEV}_p &= \mathrm{var}(R_p - R_b) \\
&= \mathrm{var}(\mathbf{w}'\mathbf{R} - \mathbf{w}_b'\mathbf{R}) \\
&= (\mathbf{w} - \mathbf{w}_b)'\mathrm{var}(\mathbf{R})(\mathbf{w} - \mathbf{w}_b) \\
&= (\mathbf{w} - \mathbf{w}_b)'\boldsymbol{\Sigma}(\mathbf{w} - \mathbf{w}_b)
\end{aligned}
$$

where $\boldsymbol{\Sigma}$ is the covariance matrix of the asset returns. In order to limit the tracking error, a constraint of the form

$$(\mathbf{w} - \mathbf{w}_b)'\boldsymbol{\Sigma}(\mathbf{w} - \mathbf{w}_b) \leq \sigma_{\mathrm{TE}}^2$$

can be added to the portfolio optimization formulation. In the next section, we provide an example that shows how the tracking error constraint formulation can be used for index tracking.

Note that a pure tracking-error constrained portfolio ignores total portfolio risk or *absolute* risk. In practice, this can result in very inefficient portfolios (in a mean-variance sense) unless additional constraints on total volatility are imposed.[5]

General Linear and Quadratic Constraints

The constraints described in this section are all linear or quadratic, i.e. they can be cast either as

---

[5] Philippe Jorion, "Portfolio Optimization with Tracking-Error Constraints," *Financial Analysts Journal* 59, no. 5 (September-October 2003), pp. 70–82.

$$\mathbf{A}_w \mathbf{w} \le \mathbf{d}_w$$
$$\mathbf{A}_x \mathbf{x} \le \mathbf{d}_x$$
$$\mathbf{A}_b (\mathbf{w} - \mathbf{w}_b) \le \mathbf{d}_b$$

or as

$$\mathbf{w}' \mathbf{Q}_w \mathbf{w} \le \mathbf{q}_w$$
$$\mathbf{x}' \mathbf{Q}_x \mathbf{x} \le \mathbf{q}_x$$
$$(\mathbf{w} - \mathbf{w}_b)' \mathbf{Q}_b (\mathbf{w} - \mathbf{w}_b) \le \mathbf{q}_b$$

These types of constraints can be dealt with directly within the quadratic programming framework, and there are very efficient algorithms available that are capable of solving practical portfolio optimization problems with thousands of assets in a matter of seconds. In Chapters 9 and 11, we provide a survey of some of the standard approaches and the software available for the solution of these optimization problems.

Example: Minimizing Index Tracking Error

The wide acceptance of portfolio theory has provided for the growth in the use of passive portfolio management techniques and the enormous popularity of index funds. A very simple classification of portfolio and fund management is into *active* and *passive* approaches. In active management, it is assumed that markets are not fully efficient and that a fund manager can outperform standard indices by using specific information, knowledge, and experience. Passive management, in contrast, relies on the assumption that financial markets are efficient and that return and risk are fully reflected in asset prices. In this case, an investor should invest in a portfolio that mimics the market.

John Bogle used this basic idea in 1975 when he proposed to the board of directors of the newly formed Vanguard Group to create the first index fund. The objective of the mutual fund that he suggested was not to try to beat the S&P 500 index, but instead to mirror the index as closely as possible by buying each of the index's 500 stocks in amounts equal to the weights in the index itself. Today, indexing is a very popular form of mutual fund investing.

The index tracking problem is the problem of reproducing or mimicking the performance of a stock market index, but without purchasing all of the stocks that make up the index. Here we construct a *tracking portfolio* of the MSCI World Index over the period January 1980 to May 2004 by minimizing the tracking error of a portfolio of some of the individual country equity indices to the index portfolio.[6] In other words, we solve the optimization problem

$$\min_{\mathbf{w}} (\mathbf{w} - \mathbf{w}_b)' \Sigma (\mathbf{w} - \mathbf{w}_b)$$

subject to the usual constraint that

$$\mathbf{w}' \iota = 1, \, \iota' = [1, 1, ..., 1]$$

where $\mathbf{w}_b$ are the market capitalization weights.

Each month, when we rebalance our portfolio, we use the historical covariances calculated from five years of daily data. The first five years of the sample, from January 1980 to December 1984, are used to construct the first estimates used in the simulation in January 1985. We consider three different portfolios, with 6, 13, and all countries in the MSCI World Index. The specific countries in the portfolios with 6 and 13 assets were drawn at random. The number of assets in the index varies over time (typically, between 23 to 26 countries) as the constitution of the MSCI World Index changes.

By the rebalancing at the end of each month, we calculate the realized tracking error. The results are depicted in Exhibits 4.1 and 4.2. In particular, we observe that as the number of assets in the tracking portfolio increases, the tracking error decreases, as expected. With only six assets we are able to track the index with an annualized tracking error of about 2.5%.

The reason why the tracking error is not equal to zero when we are using all the assets is that the weights in the tracking portfolio are constant throughout the month (they are only rebalanced monthly), whereas the market capitalization weights can change daily.

Combinatorial and Integer Constraints

The following binary decision variable is useful in describing some combinatorial and integer constraints:

$$\delta_i = \begin{cases} 1, & \text{if } w_i \neq 0 \\ 0, & \text{if } w_i = 0 \end{cases}$$

where w_i denotes the portfolio weight of the i-th asset.

---

[6] A description and basic statistical properties of this data set are provided in Appendix A.

EXHIBIT 4.1 Monthly Tracking Error of the Index Replicating Portfolio with 6, 13, and All Assets Rebalanced Monthly

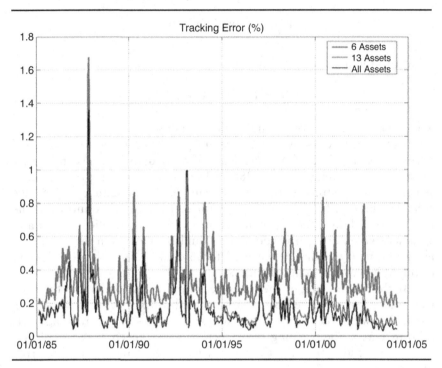

EXHIBIT 4.2 Average Yearly Tracking Error Over the Period January 1985 through May 2004 for a Tracking Portfolio of Different Numbers of Assets

Number of Assets	Average TE
1	5.44%
2	4.48%
3	3.68%
6	2.50%
12	2.29%
18	1.70%
25	0.15%

Minimum Holding and Transaction Size Constraints

The classical mean-variance optimization problem often results in a few large and many small positions. In practice, due to transaction costs and other ticket charges, small holdings are undesirable. In order to eliminate small holdings, threshold constraints of the following form are often used

$$|w_i| \geq L_{w_i} \delta_i \quad i = 1, \ldots, N$$

where L_{w_i} is the smallest holding size allowed for asset i.

Similarly, because of the fixed costs related to trading each individual security, it is desirable to avoid small trades. Therefore, a portfolio manager might also want to eliminate new trades, x, smaller than a pre-specified amount

$$|x_i| \geq L_{x_i} \delta_i \quad i = 1, \ldots, N$$

where L_{x_i} is the smallest transaction size permitted for asset i.

In practice, few portfolio managers go to the extent of including constraints of this type in their optimization framework. Instead, a standard mean-variance optimization problem is solved and then, in a "postoptimization" step, generated portfolio weights or trades that are smaller than a certain threshold are eliminated. This simplification leads to small, but often negligible, differences compared to a full optimization using the threshold constraints. Given that the mean-variance optimization problem with threshold constraints is much more complicated to solve from a numerical and computational point of view, this small discrepancy is often ignored by practitioners. In Chapter 9, we discuss the numerical optimization techniques used in solving these types of constraints, and address some of the computational difficulties.

Cardinality Constraints

A portfolio manager might want to restrict the number of assets allowed in a portfolio. This could be the case when, for example, he is attempting to construct a portfolio tracking a benchmark using a limited set of assets. The cardinality constraint takes the form

$$\sum_{i=1}^{N} \delta_i = K$$

where K is a positive integer significantly less than the number of assets in the investment universe, N.

Minimum holding and cardinality constraints are related. Both of them attempt to reduce the number of small trades and the number of portfolio positions. Therefore, it is not uncommon that both constraints are used simultaneously in the same portfolio optimization. There are situations in which imposing only cardinality constraints will lead to some small trades. Conversely, with only minimum holding constraints, the resulting portfolio might still contain too many positions, or result in too many trades. Portfolio managers often have the desire not to keep the number of assets too large, and at the same time make sure that all of their holdings are larger than a certain threshold.

Round Lot Constraints

For the most part, portfolio selection models proposed in the literature are based on the assumption of a perfect "fractionability" of the investments, in such a way that the portfolio weights for each security could be represented by real numbers. In reality, securities are transacted in multiples of a minimum transaction lots, or rounds (e.g., 100 or 500 shares). In order to model transaction round lots explicitly in the optimization problem, portfolio weights can be represented as

$$w_i = z_i \cdot f_i, \quad i = 1, ..., N$$

where f_i is a fraction of portfolio wealth and z_i is an integer number of round lots. For example, if the total portfolio wealth is \$10 million and stock i trades at \$86 in round lots of 100, then

$$f_i = \frac{86 \cdot 100}{10^7} = 8.6 \times 10^{-4}$$

In applying round lot constraints, the budget constraint

$$\sum_{i=1}^{N} w_i = 1$$

may not be exactly satisfied. To accommodate this situation, the budget constraint is relaxed with "undershoot" and "overshoot" variables, $\varepsilon^- \geq 0$ and $\varepsilon^+ \geq 0$, so that

$$\sum_{i=1}^{N} f_i z_i + \varepsilon^- - \varepsilon^+ = 1$$

This formula can be written in a more compact way as

$$z'\Lambda\iota + \varepsilon^- - \varepsilon^+ = 1, \quad \iota' = [1, 1, ..., 1]$$

where $\Lambda = \text{diag}(f_1, f_2, ..., f_N)$, that is, Λ equals the diagonal matrix of the fractions of portfolio wealth.

The undershoot and overshoot variables need to be as small as possible at the optimal point, and therefore, they are penalized in the objective function, yielding the following optimization problem:

$$\max_z z'\Lambda\mu - \lambda z'\Lambda\Sigma\Lambda z - \gamma(\varepsilon^- + \varepsilon^+)$$

subject to

$$z'\Lambda\iota + \varepsilon^- - \varepsilon^+ = 1, \quad \iota' = [1, 1, ..., 1]$$
$$\varepsilon^- \geq 0, \varepsilon^+ \geq 0$$

where λ and γ are parameters chosen by the portfolio manager.

Normally, the inclusion of round lot constraints to the mean-variance optimization problem only produces a small increase in risk for a prespecified expected return. Furthermore, the portfolios obtained in this manner cannot be obtained by simply rounding the portfolio weights from a standard mean-variance optimization to the nearest round lot.

In order to represent threshold and cardinality constraints we have to introduce binary (0/1) variables, and for round lots we need integer variables. In effect, the original *quadratic program* (QP) resulting from the mean-variance formulation becomes a *quadratic mixed integer program* (QMIP). Therefore, these combinatorial extensions require more sophisticated and specialized algorithms that often require significant computing time.

Example: A Combinatorial Problem in Asset Allocation

To illustrate the difficulty encountered in these combinatorial problems, we consider the four-asset example from Chang, et al.[7] with the expected returns, standard deviations, and correlation matrix given in Exhibit 4.3.

---

[7] T.-J. Chang, N. Meade, J. E. Beasley, and Y. M. Sharaiha, "Heuristics for Cardinality Constrained Portfolio Optimization," *Computers and Operations Research*, 27, no. 13 (November 2000), pp. 1271–1302. We are grateful to the authors for allowing us to use their examples here.

EXHIBIT 4.3 Expected Returns, Standard Deviations, and Correlations of Stock 1 through 4

Asset	Return (weekly)	Std. Dev. (weekly)	Correlation Matrix			
			1	2	3	4
1	0.48%	4.64%	1			
2	0.07%	3.06%	0.12	1		
3	0.32%	3.05%	0.14	0.16	1	
4	0.14%	0.04%	0.25	0.10	0.08	1

Source: T.-J. Chang, N. Meade, J. E. Beasley, and Y. M. Sharaiha, "Heuristics for Cardinality Constrained Portfolio Optimization," *Computers and Operations Research* 27, no. 13 (November 2000), p. 1279. Reprinted with permission.

EXHIBIT 4.4 Efficient Frontier with a Minimum Proportion of 0.24

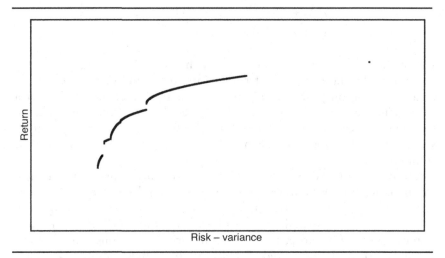

Source: T.-J. Chang, N. Meade, J. E. Beasley, and Y. M. Sharaiha, "Heuristics for Cardinality Constrained Portfolio Optimization," *Computers and Operations Research* 27, no. 13 (November 2000), p. 1282. Reprinted with permission.

First, we consider the problem of calculating the efficient frontier subject to no short-selling and proportional minimum holding constraints $L_{w_i} = 0.24$ for all i. The result is presented in Exhibit 4.4. We observe that the efficient frontier is discontinuous, unlike the classical mean-variance efficient frontier. This implies that there are certain expected portfolio returns that no rational investor would consider because there are portfolios available with less risk and greater return.

Next, let us consider the cardinality constrained problem and using the four stocks in Exhibit 4.3 calculate the efficient frontier of portfolios containing only two stocks. With only four stocks, we can proceed in the following way. First, we calculate the efficient frontier of all feasible combinations of two assets,

$$\binom{4}{2} = \frac{4!}{(4-2)!} = 6$$

In Exhibit 4.5, six line segments representing each a two-asset efficient frontier are shown. The exhibit depicts the complete universe of feasible two-asset portfolios. We observe that certain portfolios are dominated. For example, the portfolio consisting of assets 1 and 2, and the portfolio consisting of assets 1 and 4, are dominated by the portfolio consisting of assets 1 and 3. By eliminating all dominated portfolios, we obtain the efficient frontier consisting of the set of efficient portfolios of two assets, shown in Exhibit 4.6. As with the minimum holding constraints, the cardinality constrained efficient frontier is discontinuous.

In this four-asset case, the solution is obtained by enumeration. However, as the number of assets grows, simple enumeration techniques

EXHIBIT 4.5   Feasible Combinations of Two Assets

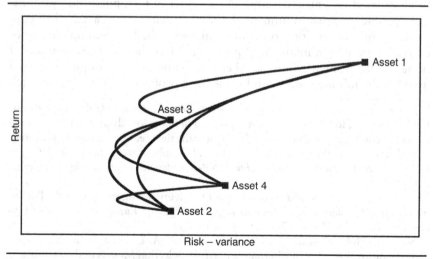

Source: T.-J. Chang, N. Meade, J. E. Beasley, and Y. M. Sharaiha, "Heuristics for Cardinality Constrained Portfolio Optimization," *Computers and Operations Research* 27, no. 13 (November 2000), p. 1279. Reprinted with permission.

EXHIBIT 4.6   Cardinality Constrained Efficient Frontier

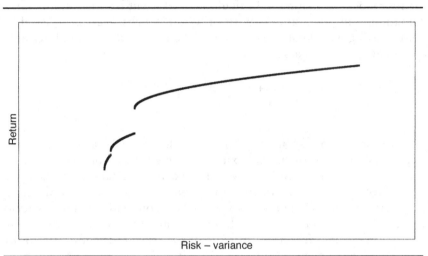

Source: T.-J. Chang, N. Meade, J. E. Beasley, and Y. M. Sharaiha, "Heuristics for Cardinality Constrained Portfolio Optimization," *Computers and Operations Research* 27, no. 13 (November 2000), p. 1280. Reprinted with permission.

become computationally unfeasible, as the number of combinations to be considered becomes too large. As a matter of fact, portfolio optimization problems with minimum holding constraints, cardinality constraints, or round lot constraints are so-called NP-complete (nondeterministic polynomial time)[8] problems.[9] For the practical solution of these problems, heuristics and other approximation techniques are often used.[10] Bartholomew-Biggs and Kane have proposed a penalty approach

---

[8] A formal definition of NP-completeness is technical and outside the scope of this book. However, for our purposes, it suffices to define it loosely as algorithms of exponential complexity, that is, algorithms where the time required grows exponentially with the size of the problem. For a formal definition, refer to Michael Garey, *Computers and Intractability: A Guide to NP-completeness* (New York: W. H. Freeman, 1979).

[9] Renata Mansini and Maria Grazia Speranza, "Heuristic Algorithms for the Portfolio Selection Problem with Minimum Transaction Lots," *European Journal of Operational Research* 114, no. 2 (1999), pp. 219–233.

[10] Norbert J. Jobst, Michael D. Horniman, Cormac A. Lucas, and Guatam Mitra, "Computational Aspects of Alternative Portfolio Selection Models in the Presence of Discrete Asset Choice Constraints," *Quantitative Finance* 1, no. 5 (2001), pp. 1–13; and Hans Kellerer, Renata Mansini, and Maria Grazia Speranza, "Selecting Portfolios with Fixed Costs and Minimum Transaction Lots," *Annals of Operations Research* 99, no. 3 (2000), pp. 287–304.

for solving the portfolio optimization problem with constraints for minimum holdings and round lots.[11] Their approach results in an objective function with multiple local optima. Therefore, a combination of local and global optimization techniques is used in order to find the global optima.[12] In general, this type of approach works for smaller problems where fewer assets are involved. However, when the number of assets increases, this technique becomes too burdensome computationally.

INCORPORATING TRANSACTION COSTS IN ASSET-ALLOCATION MODELS

Standard asset-allocation models generally ignore transaction costs and other costs related to portfolio and allocation revisions. However, the effect of transaction costs is far from insignificant. On the contrary, if transaction costs are not taken into consideration, they can eat into a significant part of the returns. Whether transaction costs are handled efficiently or not by the portfolio or fund manager can therefore make all the difference in attempting to outperform the peer group or a particular benchmark.

The typical asset-allocation model consists of one or several forecasting models for expected returns and risk. Small changes in these forecasts can result in reallocations which would not occur if transaction costs had been taken into account. Therefore, it is to be expected that the inclusion of transaction costs in asset-allocation models will result in a reduced amount of trading and rebalancing.

In this section we demonstrate how transaction costs models can be incorporated into standard asset-allocation models. For simplicity, we will use the mean-variance model to describe the basic approach. However, it is straightforward to extend this approach into other frameworks.

In 1970, Pogue gave one of the first descriptions of an extension of the mean-variance framework that included transaction costs.[13]

---

[11] Michael Bartholomew-Biggs and Stephen Kane, "A Global Optimization Problem in Portfolio Selection," School of Physics Astronomy and Mathematics, University of Hertfordshire, Technical Report, undated.

[12] Global optimization techniques as well as heuristics used in order to solve combinatorial and integer optimization problems do not guarantee that the global optimum is found. Typically, these algorithms set out to find the "best" local optimum. For practical purposes, however, this normally delivers a satisfactory solution at a reasonable computational cost.

[13] Gerry A. Pogue, "An Extension of the Markowitz Portfolio Selection Model to Include Variable Transactions' Costs, Short Sales, Leverage Policies and Taxes," *Journal of Finance* 25, no. 5 (1970), pp. 1005–1027.

Several other authors including, for example, Schreiner,[14] Adcock and Meade,[15] Lobo, Fazel, and Boyd,[16] Mitchell and Braun,[17] have provided further extensions and modifications to this basic approach. These formulations can be summarized by the mean-variance risk aversion formulation with transaction costs, given by

$$\max_{\mathbf{w}} \mathbf{w}'\boldsymbol{\mu} - \lambda \mathbf{w}'\boldsymbol{\Sigma}\mathbf{w} - \lambda_{TC} \cdot TC$$

subject to $\iota'\mathbf{w} = 1$, $\iota = [1,1,...,1]'$ where TC denotes a transaction cost penalty function and λ_{TC} a transaction cost aversion parameter. In other words, the objective is to maximize expected return less the cost of risk and transaction costs. The transaction costs term in the utility function introduces resistance or friction in the rebalancing process that makes it costly to reach the mean-variance portfolio, which would have been the result had transaction costs not been taken into account. We can imagine that as we increase the transaction costs, at some point it will be optimal to keep the current portfolio.

Transaction costs models can involve complicated nonlinear functions. Although there exists software for general nonlinear optimization problems, the computational time required for solving such problems is often too long for realistic investment management applications, and the quality of the solution is frequently not guaranteed. Very efficient and reliable software is available, however, for linear and quadratic optimization problems. It is therefore common in practice to approximate a complicated nonlinear optimization problem by simpler problems that can be solved quickly. In particular, portfolio managers frequently employ approximations of the transaction cost penalty function in the mean-variance framework.[18]

[14] John Schreiner, "Portfolio Revision: A Turnover-Constrained Approach," *Financial Management* 9, no. 1 (Spring 1980), pp. 67–75.

[15] Christopher J. Adcock and Nigel Meade, "A Simple Algorithm to Incorporate Transaction Costs in Quadratic Optimization," *European Journal of Operational Research* 79, no. 1 (1994), pp. 85–94.

[16] Miguel Sousa Lobo, Maryam Fazel, and Stephen Boyd, "Portfolio Optimization with Linear and Fixed Transaction Costs and Bounds on Risk," Information Systems, Technical Report, Stanford University, 2000.

[17] John E. Mitchell and Stephen Braun, "Rebalancing an Investment Portfolio in the Presence of Transaction Costs," Technical Report, Department of Mathematical Sciences, Rensselaer Polytechnic Institute, 2002.

[18] See for example, Andre F. Perold, "Large-Scale Portfolio Optimization," *Management Science* 30, no. 10 (1984), pp. 1143–1160; and Hiroshi Konno and Annista Wijayanayake, "Portfolio Optimization Problem under Concave Transaction Costs and Minimal Transaction Unit Constraints," *Mathematical Programming and Finance* 89, no. 2 (2001), pp. 233–250.

One of the most common simplifications to the transaction cost penalty function is to assume that it is a separable function dependent only on the portfolio weights $\mathbf{w}$, or more specifically on the portion to be traded $\mathbf{x} = \mathbf{w} - \mathbf{w}_0$, where $\mathbf{w}_0$ is the original portfolio and $\mathbf{w}$ is the new portfolio after rebalancing. Mathematically, we can express this as

$$TC(\mathbf{x}) = \sum_{i=1}^{N} TC_i(x_i)$$

where TC_i is the transaction cost function for security i and x_i is the portion of security i to be traded. The transaction cost function TC_i is often parameterized as a quadratic function of the form

$$TC_i(x_i) = \alpha_i \cdot \chi_{\{x_i \neq 0\}} + \beta_i |x_i| + \gamma_i |x_i|^2$$

where the coefficients α_i, β_i, and γ_i may be different for each asset, and $\chi_{\{x_i \neq 0\}}$ is the indicator function that is equal to one when $x_i \neq 0$ and zero otherwise.

When all $\alpha_i = 0$, the resulting optimization problem is a quadratic optimization problem of the form

$$\max_{\mathbf{w}} \; \mathbf{w}'\boldsymbol{\mu} - \lambda \mathbf{w}'\boldsymbol{\Sigma}\mathbf{w} - \lambda_{TC}(\boldsymbol{\beta}'|\mathbf{x}| + \boldsymbol{\Gamma}|\mathbf{x}|^2)$$

subject to the usual constraints, where $\boldsymbol{\beta}' = (\beta_1, ..., \beta_N)$ and

$$\boldsymbol{\Gamma} = \begin{bmatrix} \gamma_1 & 0 & \cdots & \cdots & 0 \\ 0 & \gamma_2 & \ddots & & \vdots \\ \vdots & \ddots & \ddots & \ddots & \vdots \\ \vdots & & \ddots & \ddots & 0 \\ 0 & \cdots & \cdots & 0 & \gamma_N \end{bmatrix}$$

In particular, as this is a quadratic optimization problem, it can be solved with exactly the same software that is capable of solving the classical mean-variance optimization problem.

Alternatively, piecewise-linear approximations to transaction cost function models can be used. An example of a piecewise-linear function of transaction costs for a trade of size t of a particular security is illustrated in Exhibit 4.7. The transaction cost function illustrated in the graph assumes that the rate of increase of transaction costs (reflected in the slope of the function) changes at certain threshold points. For example, it is smaller in the range 0% to 15% of daily volume than in the range 15% to 40% of

EXHIBIT 4.7   An Example of Modeling Transaction Costs (TC) as a Piecewise-Linear Function of Trade Size t

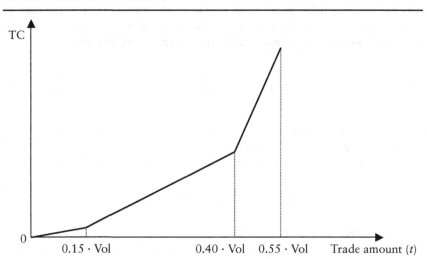

daily volume (or some other trading volume index). Mathematically, the transaction cost function in Exhibit 4.7 can be expressed as

$$TC(t)$$
$$= \begin{cases} s_1 t, & 0 \le t \le 0.15 \cdot \text{Vol} \\ s_1(0.15 \cdot \text{Vol}) + s_2(t - 0.15 \cdot \text{Vol}), & 0.15 \cdot \text{Vol} \le t \le 0.40 \cdot \text{Vol} \\ s_1(0.15 \cdot \text{Vol}) + s_2(0.25 \cdot \text{Vol}) + s_3(t - 0.40 \cdot \text{Vol}), & 0.40 \cdot \text{Vol} \le t \le 0.55 \cdot \text{Vol} \end{cases}$$

where s_1, s_2, s_3 are the slopes of the three linear segments on the graph.

Including piecewise-linear functions for transaction costs in the objective function of the mean-variance (or any general mean-risk) portfolio optimization problem is easy.[19] One simply introduces new decision variables that correspond to the number of pieces in the piecewise-linear approximation of the transaction cost function (in this case, there are three linear segments, so we introduce variables y_1, y_2, y_3), and writes the penalty term in the objective function for an individual asset as

$$\lambda_{TC}(s_1 \cdot y_1 + s_2 \cdot y_2 + s_3 \cdot y_3)$$

---

[19] See, for example, Dimitris Bertsimas, Christopher Darnell, and Robert Soucy, "Portfolio Construction through Mixed-Integer Programming at Grantham, Mayo, Van Otterloo and Company," *Interfaces* 29, no. 1 (1999), pp. 49–66.

If there are N assets in the portfolio, the total transaction cost will be the sum of the transaction costs for each individual asset. That is, the penalty term becomes

$$\lambda_{TC} \sum_{i=1}^{N} (s_{1,i} \cdot y_{1,i} + s_{2,i} \cdot y_{2,i} + s_{3,i} \cdot y_{3,i})$$

In addition, one needs to specify the following constraints on the new decision variables:

$$0 \le y_{1,i} \le 0.15 \cdot Vol_i$$
$$0 \le y_{2,i} \le 0.25 \cdot Vol_i$$
$$0 \le y_{3,i} \le 0.15 \cdot Vol_i$$

Note that because of the increasing slopes of the linear segments and the goal of minimizing that term in the objective function, the optimizer will never set the decision variable corresponding to the second segment, $y_{2,i}$, to a number greater than 0 unless the decision variable corresponding to the first segment, $y_{1,i}$, is at its upper bound. Similarly, the optimizer would never set $y_{3,i}$ to a number greater than 0 unless both $y_{1,i}$ and $y_{2,i}$ are at their upper bounds. So, this set of constraints allows us to compute the total traded amount of asset i as $y_{1,i} + y_{2,i} + y_{3,i}$.

Of course, one also needs to link the traded amount of asset i to the optimal portfolio allocation. This can be done by adding a few more variables and constraints. We would introduce variables z_i, one for each asset in the portfolio, that would represent the amount traded (but not the direction of the trade), and would be nonnegative. Then, we would require that

$$z_i = y_{1,i} + y_{2,i} + y_{3,i} \quad \text{for each asset } i$$

and also that z_i equals the change in the portfolio holdings of asset i. The latter condition can be imposed by writing the constraint

$$z_i = |w_i - w_{0,i}|$$

where $w_{0,i}$ and w_i are the initial and the final amount of asset i in the portfolio, respectively.[20]

Despite their apparent complexity, piecewise-linear approximations for transaction costs are very solver-friendly, and save time (relative to nonlinear models) in the actual portfolio optimization. Although modeling transaction costs this way requires introducing new decision variables and constraints, the increase in the dimension of the portfolio optimization problem does not affect significantly the running time or the performance of the optimization software, because the problem formulation is "easy". We will discuss numerical optimization and related issues further in Chapter 9.

MULTIACCOUNT OPTIMIZATION

Portfolio managers who handle multiple accounts face an important practical issue. When individual clients' portfolios are managed, portfolio managers incorporate their clients' preferences and constraints. However, on any given trading day, the necessary trades for multiple diverse accounts are pooled and executed simultaneously. Moreover, typically trades may not be crossed. That is, it is not simply permissible to transfer an asset that should be sold on behalf of one client into the account of another client for whom the asset should be bought.[21] The trades need be executed in the market. Thus, each client's trades implicitly impact the outcomes for the other clients: the *market impact* of the combined trades may be such that the benefits sought for individual accounts through trading are lost due to increased overall transaction costs. Any robust multiaccount management process, therefore, has to ensure accurate accounting and fair distribution of transaction costs among separate accounts.

One way to handle the effect of trading in multiple accounts is to use an iterative process, in which at each iteration the market impact of the trades in previous iterations is taken into account.[22] More precisely, single clients' accounts are optimized as usual, and once the optimal allocations are obtained, the portfolio manager aggregates the trades and computes the actual marginal transaction costs based on the aggregate level of trading. He then reoptimizes individual accounts using these marginal transaction costs, and aggregates the resulting trades again to compute new

---

[20] This constraint can be written in an equivalent, more optimization solver-friendly form, namely,

$$z_i \geq w_i - w_{0,i}$$
$$z_i \geq -(w_i - w_{0,i})$$

We will revisit this idea in a number of applications in Chapters 10, 12 and 13.

[21] Section 406(b)(3) of the Employee Retirement Income Security Act of 1974 (ERISA) forbids cross-trading.

[22] Arlen Khodadadi, Reha Tutuncu, and Peter Zangari, "Optimization and Quantitative Investment Management," *Journal of Asset Management* 7, no. 2 (July 2006), pp. 83–92.

marginal transaction costs, etc. The advantage of this approach is that little needs to be changed in the way individual accounts are typically handled, so the existing single-account optimization and management infrastructure can be maintained. The disadvantage is that most generally, this iterative approach does not guarantee a convergence (or its convergence may be slow) to a "fair equilibrium," in which clients' portfolios receive an unbiased treatment with respect to the size and the constraint structure of their accounts.[23] The latter equilibrium is the one that would be attained if all clients traded independently and competitively in the market for liquidity, and thus is the fair solution to the aggregate trading problem.

An alternative, more comprehensive approach is to optimize trades across all accounts simultaneously. O'Cinneide, et al.[24] describe such a model, and show that it attains the fair equilibrium we mentioned above.[25] Assume that client k's utility function is given by u_k, in the form of dollar return penalized for risk. Assume also that a transaction cost model τ gives the cost of trading in dollars, and that τ is a convex increasing function.[26] Its exact form will depend on the details of how trading is implemented. Let $\mathbf{t}$ be the vector of trades. It will typically have the form $(t_1^+, ..., t_N^+, t_1^-, ..., t_N^-)$, i.e., it will specify the aggregate buys t_i^+ and the aggregate sells t_i^- for each asset $i = 1,..., N$, but it may also incorporate information about how the trade could be carried out.

The multiaccount optimization problem can be formulated as

$$\max_{\mathbf{w}_1, ..., \mathbf{w}_K, \mathbf{t}} E[u_1(\mathbf{w}_1)] + ... + E[u_K(\mathbf{w}_K)] - \tau(\mathbf{t})$$
$$s.t. \quad \mathbf{w}_k \in C_k, k = 1, ..., K$$

where $\mathbf{w}_k$ is the N-dimensional vector of asset holdings of client k, and C_k is the collection of constraints on the portfolio structure of client k. The

---

[23] The iterative procedure is known to converge to the equilibrium, however, under special conditions, see Colm O'Cinneide, Bernd Scherer, Xiaodong Xu, "Pooling Trades in a Quantitative Investment Process," *Journal of Portfolio Management* 32, no. 4 (Summer 2006), pp. 33–43.

[24] Colm O'Cinneide, Bernd Scherer, Xiaodong Xu, "Pooling Trades in a Quantitative Investment Process."

[25] The issue of considering transaction costs in multiaccount optimization has been discussed by others as well. For example, see Dimitris Bertsimas, Christopher Darnell, and Robert Soucy, "Portfolio Construction Through Integer Programming at Grantham, Mayo, Van Otterloo, and Company." We will come back to Bertsimas et al.'s model when we discuss portfolio rebalancing in Chapter 13.

[26] As we mentioned in the previous section, realistic transaction costs are in fact described by nonlinear functions, because costs per share traded typically increase with the size of the trade due to market impact.

objective can be interpreted as maximization of net expected utility. That is, as maximization of the expected dollar return penalized for risk and net of transaction costs. In the above optimization problem, t is most generally a vector of independent decision variables, as there may be several ways in which the desired trades can be implemented. For example, if under the client account guidelines a euro-pound forward could also be implemented as a euro-dollar forward plus a dollar-pound forward, then t is a vector of decision variables capturing this possibility. However, if there is only one way to trade from $\mathbf{w}_k^0$ to $\mathbf{w}_k$ for all clients k, then t is uniquely determined by the difference between the optimal holdings $\mathbf{w}_k$ and the initial holdings $\mathbf{w}_k^0$.

The problem can be significantly simplified by making some reasonable assumptions. For example, it can be assumed that the transaction cost function τ is additive across *different* assets, that is, that trades in one asset do not influence trading costs in another. In such a case, the trading cost function becomes additive:

$$\tau(\mathbf{t}) = \sum_{i=1}^{N} \tau_i(t_i^+, t_i^-)$$

where $\tau_i(t_i^+, t_i^-)$ is the cost of trading asset i as a function of the aggregate buys and sells of that asset. Splitting the terms $\tau_i(t_i^+, t_i^-)$ further into separate costs of buying and selling, however, is not a reasonable assumption, because simultaneous buying and selling of an asset tends to have an offsetting effect on its price.

To formulate the problem completely, let $\mathbf{w}_k^0$ be the vector of original holdings of client k's portfolio, $\mathbf{w}_k$ be the vector of decision variables for the optimal holdings of client k's portfolio, and $\eta_{k,i}$ be constants that convert the holdings of each asset i in client k's portfolio $w_{k,i}$ to dollars, that is, $\eta_{k,i} w_{k,i}$ is client k's dollar holdings of asset i.[27] We also introduce new variables $w_{k,i}^+$ to represent the upper bound on the amount of each asset client k will buy

$$w_{k,i} - w_{k,i}^0 \le w_{k,i}^+, \quad i = 1, ..., N, \quad k = 1, ..., K$$

The aggregate amount of asset i bought for all clients can then be computed as

---

[27] Note that $\eta_{k,i}$ equals 1 if $w_{k,i}$ is the actual dollar holdings.

$$t_i^+ = \sum_{k=1}^{K} \eta_{k,i} w_{k,i}^+$$

The aggregate amount of asset i sold for all clients can be easily expressed by noticing that the difference between the amounts bought and sold of each asset is exactly equal to the total amount of trades needed to get from the original position $w_{k,i}^0$ to the final position $w_{k,i}$ of that asset;[28] in fact

$$t_i^+ - t_i^- = \sum_{k=1}^{K} \eta_{k,i}(w_{k,i} - w_{k,i}^0)$$

Here t_i^+ and t_i^- are nonnegative variables. The multiaccount optimization problem then takes the form

$$\max_{\mathbf{w}_1,\,...,\,\mathbf{w}_K,\,\mathbf{t}^+,\,\mathbf{t}^-} E[u_1(\mathbf{w}_1)] + ... + E[u_K(\mathbf{w}_K)] - \sum_{i=1}^{N} \tau_i(t_i^+, t_i^-)$$

$$s.t. \quad \mathbf{w}_k \in C_k, k = 1, ..., K$$

$$w_{k,i} - w_{k,i}^0 \le w_{k,i}^+, \quad i = 1, ..., N, \quad k = 1, ..., K$$

$$t_i^+ = \sum_{k=1}^{K} \eta_{k,i} w_{k,i}^+, \quad i = 1, ..., N$$

$$t_i^+ - t_i^- = \sum_{k=1}^{K} \eta_{k,i}(w_{k,i} - w_{k,i}^0), \quad i = 1, ..., N$$

$$t_i^+ \ge 0, \quad t_i^- \ge 0, \quad w_{k,i}^+ \ge 0, \quad i = 1, ..., N, \quad k = 1, ..., K$$

O'Cinneide, Scherer, and Xu studied the behavior of the model in simulated experiments assuming that all clients have linear utility, and that the transaction cost function has the form

$$\tau(t) = \theta |t|^\gamma$$

---

[28] Note that, similarly to $\mathbf{w}_k^+$, we could introduce additional sell variables $\mathbf{w}_k^-$, but this is not necessary. By expressing aggregate sales through aggregate buys and total trades, we reduce the dimension of the optimization problem, because there are fewer decision variables. This would make a difference for the speed of obtaining a solution, especially in the case of large portfolios and complicated representation of transaction costs. We discuss numerical optimization issues in Chapter 9.

where t is the trade size, and θ and γ are constants satisfying $\theta \geq 0$ and $\gamma \geq 1$.[29] The parameters θ and γ are specified in advance and calibrated to fit observed trading costs in the market. The transaction costs for each client k can therefore be expressed as

$$\tau_k = \theta \sum_{i=1}^{N} \left| w_{k,i} - w_{k,i}^0 \right|^{\gamma}$$

O'Cinneide, Scherer, and Xu observed that key portfolio performance measures, such as information ratio (IR),[30] turnover, and total transaction costs, change under this model relative to the traditional approach. Not surprisingly, the turnover and the net information ratios of the portfolios obtained with multiaccount optimization are lower than those obtained with single-account optimization under the assumption that accounts are traded separately, while transaction costs are higher. These results are in fact more realistic, and are a better representation of the post-optimization performance of multiple client accounts in practice.

As a final remark, we point out that multiaccount optimization is fundamentally different from traditional portfolio optimization. Its purpose is not simply to make the best choice for each individual client, but, rather, to make the best choice for each client while ensuring fairness in the allocation of liquidity across accounts. In fact, it can be shown that in this model (1) total welfare of all clients is maximized, and (2) the allocation of trading resources is Pareto optimal so that no reallocation of liquidity among the clients will improve the outcome of one without worsening the outcome of another.[31] More specifically, each client's portfolio is optimal given the prices of liquidity resulting from the aggregate trades, and there is no advantage for any client in doing any further trading for his own account.

---

[29] Note that $\gamma = 1$ defines linear transaction costs. For linear transaction costs, multiaccount optimization produces the same allocation as single-account optimization, because linear transaction costs assume that an increased aggregate amount of trading does not have an impact on prices.

[30] The information ratio is the ratio of (annualized) portfolio residual return (alpha) to (annualized) portfolio residual risk, where risk is defined as standard deviation.

[31] An outcome is Pareto optimal if there is no other outcome that makes every participant in the economy at least as well off and at least one participant strictly better off. In other words, a Pareto optimal outcome cannot be improved upon without hurting at least one participant in the economy.

SUMMARY

■ Some of the most common constraints used in practice are no short-selling constraints, turnover constraints, maximum holding constraints, and tracking error constraints. These constraints can be handled in a straightforward way by the same type of optimization algorithms used for solving the mean-variance problem.

■ Integer constraints or constraints of combinatorial nature are more difficult to handle and require more specialized optimization algorithms. Some examples of these type of constraints are minimum holding constraints, transaction size constraints, cardinality constraints (number of securities permitted in the portfolio), and round lot constraints.

■ Transaction and trading costs can be incorporated in standard asset-allocation models such as the mean-variance framework, and will most often significantly influence the optimal portfolio allocation decision.

■ For investment managers who handle multiple accounts, increased transaction costs because of the market impact of simultaneous trades can be an important practical issue, and should be taken into consideration when individual clients' portfolio allocation decisions are made to ensure fairness across accounts.

Robust Parameter Estimation

CHAPTER 5

Classical Asset Pricing

This chapter introduces a number of models for asset returns, considering time series in discrete time. The objective of the chapter is to introduce basic concepts in time series analysis and to develop some intuition for time series models, in particular random walk models and trend stationary models, describing some of their key properties.

DEFINITIONS

We begin our discussion of equity price models by introducing some definitions and fixing some notations. A financial *time series in discrete time* is a sequence of financial variables such as asset prices or returns observed at discrete points in time, for example, the end of a trading day or the last trading day of a month. Most models that we will consider in this book assume that the spacing between points is fixed, for example, models of daily returns assume that returns are observed between consecutive trading days. In order to recover fixed spacing between time points due to weekends, holidays, or periods when trading is suspended, a sequence of trading days different from the sequence of calendar days is typically introduced. When dealing with international markets, special care is required as holidays and periods of suspension of trading might be different in different markets.

Not all financial variables can be represented with the fixed periodicity described here. For instance, in most markets intraday trades are randomly spaced as trading occurs when the correct match between buy and sell orders is found. When considering high-frequency data (i.e., data related to individual trades) the assumption of periodic, fixed discrete time points must be abandoned.

Consider a time series of prices P_t of a financial asset, where t is a discrete sequence of points. Assume that there are no dividend payouts. The *simple net return* of an asset between periods $t - 1$ and t is defined as the percentage change of its price:

$$R_t = \frac{P_t - P_{t-1}}{P_{t-1}} = \frac{P_t}{P_{t-1}} - 1$$

The *gross return* is defined as

$$1 + R_t = \frac{P_t}{P_{t-1}}$$

For example, if the closing price of a stock at the end of a given trading day is \$10.00 and goes to \$11.00 at the end of the following trading day, the simple net return of that stock in that day is 0.1 or 10%. The gross return is the ratio of prices in subsequent periods, equal to 1.1 in the above example.

From this definition it is clear that the *compound return* $R_t(k)$ over k periods is

$$R_t(k) = \frac{P_t}{P_{t-k}} - 1 = \frac{P_t}{P_{t-1}}\frac{P_{t-1}}{P_{t-2}}\cdots\frac{P_{t-k+1}}{P_{t-k}} - 1 = \prod_{i=0}^{k-1}(R_{t-i} + 1) - 1$$

or

$$R_t(k) + 1 = \prod_{i=0}^{k-1}(R_{t-i} + 1)$$

If there are dividend payouts, they must be added to the price change. For example, suppose that there is a dividend payout D_t made just prior to the moment when the price P_t is observed. The simple net return then becomes

$$R_t = \frac{P_t + D_t}{P_{t-1}} - 1$$

Note that the moment in which prices are observed is critical: Asset prices change after dividends are paid. All other returns can be computed accordingly.

Now consider the logarithms of prices and returns:

$$p_t = \log P_t$$

The *log return* is defined as the natural logarithm of the gross return:

$$r_t = \log (1 + R_t)$$

Following standard usage, we denote prices and returns with upper case letters and their logarithms with lower case letters. As the logarithm of a product is the sum of the logarithms, we can write

$$r_t = \log(1 + R_t) = \log\frac{P_t}{P_{t-1}} = p_t - p_{t-1}$$

$$r_t(k) = \log(1 + R_t(k)) = r_t + \dots + r_{t-k+1}$$

Note that for real-world price time series, if the time interval is small, the numerical value of returns will also be small. Therefore, as a first approximation, we can write

$$r_t = \log (1 + R_t) \approx R_t$$

THEORETICAL AND ECONOMETRIC MODELS

A model of returns is a mathematical representation of returns. In finance theory, different types of models are considered. There are models that represent the time evolution of returns and models that represent relationships between the returns of different assets at any given moment. The former is exemplified by a random walk model, the latter by conditions of no-arbitrage. The distinction is important because models that represent the time evolution of assets can be used to make probabilistic forecasts starting from initial conditions.

Financial models are *approximate* models, not only in the sense that they are probabilistic models but also in the sense that the probability distributions assumed in the models are idealizations of reality and therefore never completely accurate. As a consequence, many different models might compete to describe the same phenomena. Consider also that financial time series have only one realization. This fact poses severe restrictions on selecting and testing financial models in practice.

There might be a trade-off between accuracy and the span of life of a model insofar as different models, or the same model but with different parameters, might apply to the same variables in different periods. When estimating time-varying models, typically an appropriate time window is chosen based on some statistical criteria.[1]

We can also make a distinction between (1) models that are based on theoretical economic considerations and (2) models that are econometric hypotheses. Theoretical models include the *General Equilibrium Theories* (GET), the *Capital Asset Pricing Model* (CAPM), and the *Arbitrage Pricing Theory* (APT); econometric models include the random walk and multifactor models.

While it can be said that econometric models lack a theoretical basis, some qualification is required. In principle, an econometric hypothesis has the status of an economic theory; however, with a sufficient number of parameters, an econometric hypothesis can fit any data set with arbitrary accuracy. This is the major potential weakness. Because econometric models contain an arbitrary number of parameters (and, therefore, can fit any finite set of data), complementary principles from the theory of learning are required to constrain these models. In the next section, we introduce a basic and fundamental model, the random walk.

RANDOM WALK MODELS

The *random walk model* is a basic model of stock prices based on the assumption of market efficiency. The basic idea is that returns can be represented as unforecastable fluctuations around some mean return. This assumption implies that the distribution of the returns at time t is independent from, or at least uncorrelated with, the distribution of returns in previous moments.

There are several different random walk models which we describe below.[2]

---

[1] For more on advanced estimation and model selection, see for example, Frank J. Fabozzi, Sergio M. Focardi, Petter N. Kolm, *Financial Modeling of the Equity Market: From CAPM to Cointegration* (Hoboken, NJ: John Wiley & Sons, Inc., 2006).
[2] The random walk model applies to many phenomena in economics as well as the social and physical sciences. We restrict our discussion to random walk models of asset prices.

Simple Random Walk Model

To gain an understanding of the random walk, let us first consider one type of random walk. Suppose that a sequence of discrete, equally spaced instants of time is given. Suppose that at every instant a stock price can only go up or down by a fixed amount Δ with probability ½ independent of previous steps. The price movement is an idealized representation of a pure random path. This type of random walk model is called *a simple random walk*.

Arithmetic Random Walk Model

The up or down price movement at each step can be represented as a *Bernoulli variable*. A Bernoulli variable is a random variable that can assume only two values, which we represent conventionally as 0 and 1, with probabilities p and $q = 1 - p$. The two values can represent outcomes such as success or failure, up and down, and so on. Consider a sample of n trials of a Bernoulli variable. The distribution of 0s and 1s follows a binomial distribution:

$$P(k \text{ zeros in } n \text{ trials}) = \binom{n}{k}p^k q^{n-k} = \frac{n!}{k!(n-k)!}p^k q^{n-k}$$

For large n, the binomial distribution can be approximated by a normal distribution.

Call P_t the price after t steps; P_0 is the initial price where the random walk starts. The difference $P_t - P_0$ is the sum of t independent Bernoulli variables. It can assume discrete values:

$$P_t - P_0 = -t\Delta + 2m\Delta; \quad m = 0, 1, ..., t$$

in the range $[-t\Delta, +t\Delta]$. For example, at time $t = 1$ the price can assume only one of two values $P_0 - \Delta$, $P_0 + \Delta$; at time $t = 2$ the price can assume only one of three values $P_0 - 2\Delta$, P_0, $P_0 + 2\Delta$, and so on. Note that the price P_t can be equal to the starting price P_0 only at even numbers of steps: 0, 2, 4, ... The distribution of the sum of independent Bernoulli variables is called a *binomial distribution*. The probability of a Bernoulli variable takes the form

$$P(P_t - P_0 = -t\Delta + 2m\Delta) = \binom{t}{m}; \quad m = 0, 1, ..., t$$

After a sufficiently large number of steps, the Bernoulli distribution is well approximated by a normal distribution. Therefore, we can now generalize the simple random walk assuming that at each time step an asset price P_t moves up or down by an amount that follows a normal probability distribution with mean μ. The movement of the price P_t is called an *arithmetic random walk with drift*. Under this model, prices move up or down at each time step according to a normal distribution, independent from previous prices:

$$P_t - P_{t-1} = \mu + \eta_t$$

where η_t is a normal white noise term.

Strict white noise or *strong white noise* is defined as a sequence of *independent and identically distributed* (IID) random variables with zero mean and finite variance. A weaker definition of white noise is often given. According to this weaker definition, weak white noise is a sequence of zero-mean, finite-variance uncorrelated variables. Weak white noise is often called white noise. Note, however, that if noise is normally distributed the above distinction is useless. In fact, two normal variables are uncorrelated if and only if they are independent.

Suppose that noise is distributed as an IID sequence of zero-mean normal variables with variance σ^2. It is convenient to write the random walk model as follows:

$$\Delta P_t = P_t - P_{t-1} = \mu + \sigma\varepsilon_t$$

where ε_t is a sequence of IID normal variables with zero mean and unitary variance. The term μ is called the *drift*, the term σ is called the *volatility*.

We can see, therefore, that there are different possible definitions of random walks. An arithmetic random walk with normal increments is a model where the value of the price variable at time t is equal to the value at time $t-1$ plus a constant (the drift) plus a totally unforecastable (i.e., independent from the past) normally distributed noise term. However, we can also define a random walk with nonnormal, uncorrelated increments. This type of random walk is not completely unforecastable. In fact, white noise with nonnormal uncorrelated terms exhibits some residual forecastability.[3]

Consider an arithmetic random walk with normal increments. From the above formulas we can immediately write

---

[3] See Clive Granger and Paul Newbold, *Forecasting Economic Time Series: Second Edition* (New York: Academic Press, 1986).

$$P_t = P_0 + t\mu + \sum_{i=1}^{t} \eta_i$$

From the same formula, we see that a realization of an arithmetic random walk can be thought of as being formed by the sum of two terms: a deterministic straight line $P_t = P_0 + t\mu$ plus the sum of all past noise terms, that is,

$$\sum_{i=1}^{t} \eta_i$$

Every realization of a linear model can be thought of as the sum of a deterministic model which is the solution of the deterministic linear model plus the weighted sum of past noise. In the case of arithmetic random walks, the noise weights are all equal to one. Exhibit 5.1 provides

EXHIBIT 5.1 One Realization of an Arithmetic Random Walk with $\mu = 0.00027$ and $\sigma = 0.022$ over 10,000 Days

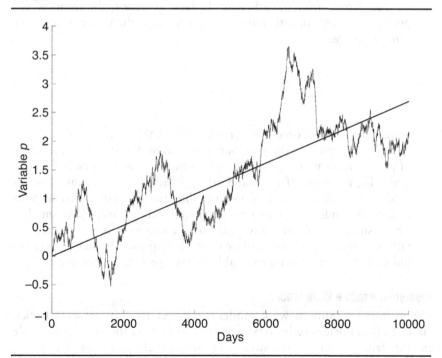

a graphical illustration of one realization of an arithmetic random walk p with daily drift σ = 0.00027 and daily volatility σ = 0.022. Assuming that the variable p is the logarithm of a stock price process P, the daily drift and volatility correspond to a 7% yearly return and a 35% yearly volatility for the stock price process P.

A number of observations are in order:

- In the arithmetic random walk random shocks (i.e., the noise terms) never decay, as in every moment the price level is affected by the sum of all past shocks, each with weight 1.
- Prices make "excursions" around the straight line $P_t = P_0 + t\mu$. This means that they depart from the straight line, meander, and then cross it again.
- These excursions are not periodic. They have neither a mean finite length nor a mean finite height. In other words, although a random walk crosses the straight line $P_t = P_0 + t\mu$ with probability one, the average time for crossing is infinite.
- Over a sufficiently long period of time, any parallel to the line $P_t = P_0 + t\mu$, however distant, will be crossed.
- In the arithmetic random walk model of prices, both the mean and the variance grow linearly with time. In fact, at time t, the mean of the prices is the deterministic term $P_t = P_0 + t\mu$ while the variance σ_t^2 is the sum of t terms:

$$\sum_{i=1}^{t} \varepsilon_i$$

whose variance is t times the variance of each term, $\sigma_t^2 = t\sigma^2$.

- As a consequence of the previous observation, the standard deviation of prices grows with the square root of time. In the presence of a positive drift, the ratio of the standard deviation and the mean of prices tend to zero. In the limit of infinite time, the risk associated with an arithmetic random walk process for prices becomes arbitrarily small.
- The assumption of normally distributed increments is not fundamentally a restriction as long as noise is an IID sequence. In fact, the sum of finite-mean, finite-variance variables is asymptotically normal.

Geometric Random Walk Model

The arithmetic random walk model for prices has several drawbacks. First, it allows prices to become negative. In fact, as the normal variable extends from $-\infty$ to $+\infty$, the sum of random shocks can assume any real value. By appropriately choosing the drift and the volatility, the probability of negative prices can be made arbitrarily small. However, the probability of negative prices will never be zero. Negative prices could be prevented by setting "absorbing barriers" in the random walk models. An absorbing barrier in a time-series model is a straight line placed at a given value such that the model stops if it crosses the barriers. In price models, these barriers can represent bankruptcies. However, in this way the random walk model looses its simplicity.

Second, the arithmetic random walk model conflicts with the empirical fact that the average size of price fluctuations grows with time. Over long periods of time, asset prices grow but so do fluctuations. Only price percentage changes seem to remain stationary. We could therefore assume that simple net returns are an IID sequence. Under this assumption, we can therefore write the following equation:

$$R_t = \frac{P_t - P_{t-1}}{P_{t-1}} = \mu + \eta_t$$

where η_t is a white-noise term. If noise is distributed as a zero-mean normal variable with variance σ^2, we can write

$$R_t = \frac{P_t - P_{t-1}}{P_{t-1}} = \mu + \sigma \varepsilon_t$$

where ε_t is a sequence of independent normal variables with zero-mean and unitary variance.

The above random walk is called a *geometric random walk with drift*. It is a nonlinear model of prices as the noise term multiplies the price variable. In the geometric random walk, noise terms feed back into the process multiplicatively. Using the expression for the gross compound return we can represent prices as the product of gross returns:

$$P_t = \left(\frac{P_t}{P_{t-1}} \frac{P_{t-1}}{P_{t-2}} \cdots \frac{P_1}{P_0} \right) P_0 = \left(\prod_{i=0}^{t-1} (R_{t-i} + 1) \right) P_0$$

Exhibit 5.2 represents 10 realizations of a geometric random walk with $\mu = 0.00027$ and $\sigma = 0.022$ over 2,500 days that correspond approximately to 10 years.

EXHIBIT 5.2   Ten Independent Realizations of a Geometric Random Walk with μ = 0.00027 and σ = 0.022 over 2,500 Days[a]

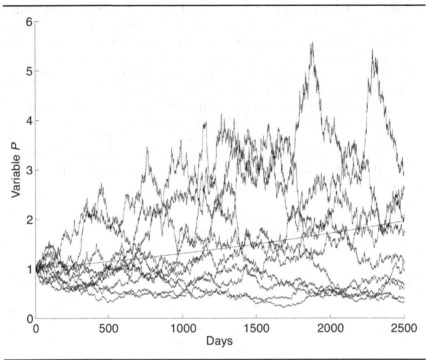

[a] The exponential line represents the process mean.

Lognormal Model

The distribution of prices is a product of normal distributions; it is not a normal distribution itself. This is a major drawback of the geometric random walk model in discrete time. To avoid this problem, let us consider the logarithm of prices. Recall from the definitions given above that the log returns are the differences of log prices. Now assume that log returns can be represented as an arithmetic random walk:

$$r_t = p_t - p_{t-1} = \mu + \varepsilon_t$$

If noise is distributed as a zero-mean normal variable with variance σ^2, we can also write

$$r_t = p_t - p_{t-1} = \sigma\varepsilon_t, \, \varepsilon_t \sim N_t(0, 1), \, E(\varepsilon_t\varepsilon_s) = 0 \text{ for } t \neq s$$

As $r_t = \log (1 + R_t)$, if log returns are normally distributed, simple gross returns are lognormally distributed. A random variable z is called lognormal if its logarithm $x = \log z$ is normally distributed. It can be demonstrated that if (μ, σ^2) are, respectively, the mean and the variance of x then the mean and the variance of z are, respectively,

$$\left(e^{\left(\mu + \frac{\sigma^2}{2}\right)}, e^{(2\mu + \sigma^2)}(e^{\sigma^2} - 1) \right)$$

If log returns are independent normal variables, log prices evolve as an arithmetic random walk. The prices themselves evolve as a geometric random walk but with lognormal increments. The mean of prices is an exponential

$$P_t = P_0 e^{\left(\mu + \frac{\sigma^2}{2}\right)t}$$

Exhibits 5.3a and 5.3b represent 10 realizations of an arithmetic random walk for log prices and the corresponding ten realizations of prices.

The effect of compounding of returns over very long periods is illustrated in Exhibits 5.4a and 5.4b; these represent respectively 10 realizations of an arithmetic random walk for log returns and the corresponding ten realizations of the price process over 10,000 time steps.

The assumption of normality of log returns is not required to justify the lognormal model. In fact, if the distribution of log returns is a nonnormal distribution but independent and with bounded variance, the sum of log returns is asymptotically normal. As we saw in Chapter 2, this is a key result of probability theory known as the *Central Limit Theorem* (CLT). Stated differently, the log return process is approximately normal if we consider log returns on sufficiently long time intervals.

It should be clearly stated that the above does not imply that price processes are always asymptotically random walks. First, the CLT can be generalized to *independently distributed* (ID) processes (i.e., processes that have bounded but time-varying means and variances); however, additional conditions are required. Second, if the sequence X_t shows autocorrelation, the asymptotic validity of the CLT hinges on whether correlations decay sufficiently fast. If autocorrelations exhibit slow decay, the CLT does not hold. Ultimately, if the X_t variables have infinite variance, the CLT holds in a totally different form. In a nutshell,

EXHIBIT 5.3a   Ten Realizations of an Arithmetic Random Walk for the Log Price Process[a]

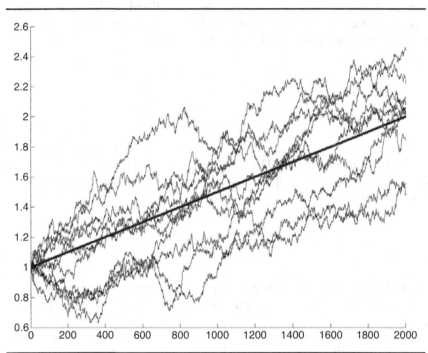

[a] As in Exhibit 5.2, if one time period corresponds to a day, the exhibit represents approximately eight years.

if log returns are either correlated or time-varying, two phenomena occur: (1) There can be short-term deviations from the lognormal behavior which might result in profit opportunities; and (2) the asymptotic behavior of the X_t sequence depends on the asymptotic behavior of the autocorrelations and the time-dependence of means and variances.

In all these random walk models, the lack of forecastability means that the past does not influence the future. This statement should not be confused with the statement that the random walk model does not convey information. Actually, the information conveyed by a random walk model within a given time horizon can be arbitrarily high if the volatility is arbitrarily small.[4] However, the assumption of normally distributed noise terms entails fundamental simplifications when dealing with financial portfolios.

---

[4] This statement can be made more precise within the theory of information.

EXHIBIT 5.3b Ten Realizations of the Price Process Corresponding to the Log Price Process of Exhibit 5.3a[a]

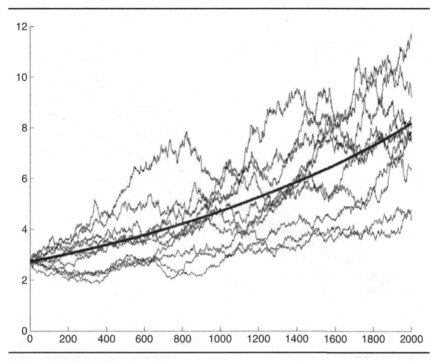

[a] Note the effect of compounding.

Multivariate Random Walk

The models discussed so far are models of univariate price series, that is, they model any given individual price series independently from other price series. A model of this type is too simple to be empirically acceptable. If asset price series were independent random walks, then large portfolios would be fully diversified and therefore nearly deterministic. Empirically, this is not the case. Even large aggregates of stock prices, for example the S&P 500, exhibit random behavior.

This fact entails that there are mutual dependencies between returns or between log returns. If returns or log returns are jointly normally distributed, then dependencies can be fully accounted for by linear correlation coefficients.

This is not to say that the covariance matrix is able to capture *in full generality* the dependencies in a return process. First, correlations at lagged times (i.e., correlations of a dynamic nature) are not captured by

EXHIBIT 5.4a   Ten Realizations of an Arithmetic Random Walk for Log Return over 10,000 Steps

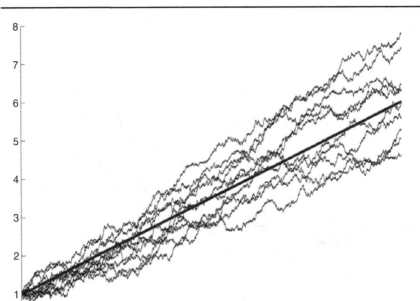

the static covariance or correlation matrices. Second, there are forms of nonlinear dependency that are not captured by covariances and correlations. Alternative tools include *copula functions* and *transfer entropies*.[5] Here we simply state that in the restricted case of a normal multivariate random walk, the probability distribution is fully described by a vector of means and the covariance matrix.

Multivariate random walk models are fully described by a vector of means and by the variance-covariance matrix. Consider, for instance, a multivariate random walk model for log prices. Suppose there are n log price processes. In this case, log returns are a sequence of independent multivariate normal variables. In vector-matrix notation, the model is written as

---

[5] See, for example, Chapter 17 and Appendix B in Frank J. Fabozzi, Sergio M. Focardi, Petter N. Kolm, *Financial Modeling of the Equity Market: From CAPM to Cointegration* (Hoboken, New Jersey: John Wiley & Sons, 2006).

EXHIBIT 5.4b   Ten Realizations of a Price Process Corresponding to the Log Price Processes in Exhibit 5.4a

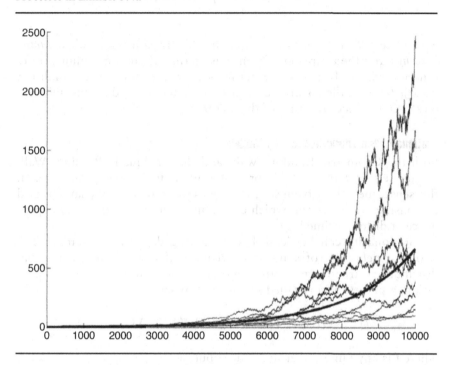

$$r_t = p_t - p_{t-1} = \mu + \varepsilon_t$$

where r_t is the n-vector of log returns, p_t is the n-vector of prices, $\mu = (\mu, ..., \mu_n)$ is the n-vector of mean returns, and ε_t is a sequence of independent zero-mean, normal n-vectors with covariance matrix $[\sigma_{ij}]$.

If we consider a large number of assets—for example, all the assets in a universe such as the S&P 500 or the MSCI—the variance-covariance matrix has a huge number of entries. In order to reduce the dimensionality of multivariate random walk models, simplifications are called for, and factor models are an effective way to reduce the complexity. Model complexity has to be reduced to make estimates robust, not for computational reasons. A multifactor model of returns can be written in the following general form:

$$r_i(t) = \mu_i + \sum_{i=1}^{N} \beta_{i,j} f_j(t) + \varepsilon_i(t)$$

where the $f_j(t)$ are the factors and the $\beta_{i,j}$ are constants called *factor loadings* and the ε_i are zero-mean noise terms. Factors are multivariate random walks. If the noise terms satisfy the additional condition $E[\varepsilon_i(t)\varepsilon_j(t)] = 0$, the covariance structure of the model depends uniquely on the covariance structure of the factors.

Stationary and Trend-Stationary Models

Both the Geometric Random Walk and the Arithmetic Random Walk are models of *unpredictable* processes with time-varying variance. In this sense, they differ from stationary processes, which are characterized by constant variance and which can exhibit autocorrelation and dependence at different time lags.

Stationarity can be defined with varying degrees of strength. The strongest definition of stationarity requires that all finite dimensional distributions are invariant after time translation. According to this definition, a process $x(t)$ is called *strictly stationary* if

$$f(t_1, ..., t_n) = f(t_1 + \tau, ..., t_n + \tau), \forall \tau, \forall n, \forall (t_1, ..., t_n)$$

where f is any finite-dimensional distribution.

This definition is often too strong and is replaced by the weaker definition of *covariance stationarity*.[6] A process $x(t)$ is said to be covariance-stationary if

$$\text{mean}(x(t)) = \mu = \text{constant}, \forall t$$
$$\text{var}(x(t)) = \sigma^2 = \text{constant}, \forall t$$
$$\text{cov}(x(t), x(t+\tau)) = \lambda(\tau), \forall t$$

We remark that the last condition means that the covariance between different observations is just a function of the time difference (τ) between observations.

---

[6] In the econometric literature a strictly stationary process is sometimes called a *strongly stationary process* and a covariance stationary process is sometimes called a *weakly stationary process* or simply a *stationary process*. A covariance stationary process is sometimes also called a *second order stationary process* because second order moments are involved. It is possible to define a *l-th order stationary process* if all the joint *l*-th order moments are time invariant.

Consider a process $x(t)$ of the following form:

$$x(t) = \mu + \eta(t)$$

where $\eta(t)$ is a zero-mean stationary process. A process of this type is mean-reverting. Suppose that at time t the process assumes the value $x(t) \neq \mu$. The expectation at time $t + 1$ is μ. Simply stated, this means that a stationary process tends to revert to its mean. This is the case even if the process $\eta(t)$ is formed by a sequence of IID variables. This property is called the *regression effect*. Note that the regression effect of returns cannot in itself be exploited to earn a profit.[7] The ability to earn a profit would require true forecastability (i.e., conditional dependence) and not simply the regression effect. However, if *prices* were subject to a regression effect, returns would be forecastable; as a result excess gains could be realized.

A trend stationary process is a process of the following form:

$$x(t) = \mu(t) + \eta(t)$$

where $\mu(t)$ is a deterministic function and $\eta(t)$ is a zero-mean stationary process.

Returns are assumed to be stationary processes. While individual asset prices are not (in general) stationary, portfolios might have stationary values.

GENERAL EQUILIBRIUM THEORIES

General Equilibrium Theories[8] (GETs) are global mathematical models of an economy. They are based on two key principles:

---

[7] This statement needs qualification. The knowledge of the mean would indeed allow one to earn a profit if the mean is sufficiently high (or low if short selling is allowed). However, asset pricing theories constrain the mean to assume values that do not allow excess profit after adjusting for risk.

[8] The empirical adequacy of GETs has been questioned repeatedly. There are two key issues: (1) It was demonstrated by Harrison and Kreps that, in absence of arbitrage, any price process can be rationalized as a GET and (2) there is scant empirical evidence that GETs work in practice when specific utility functions are assumed. These questions are beyond the scope of this book. See Michael Harrison and David M. Kreps, "Martingale and Arbitrage in Multiperiod Securities Markets," *Journal of Economic Theory* 20, no. 2 (June 1979), pp. 381–408.

■ Supply/demand equilibrium
■ Agent optimality

Let's consider the application of GETs to the problem of asset pricing. Consider an economy formed by agents that, at each time step, decide, within their budget constraints, the composition of their investment portfolio and the amount they consume. Suppose that agents are able to make a probabilistic forecast of dividends and prices, that is, we assume that each agent knows the joint probability distribution of prices for all future moments and all assets. Agents can order their preferences of consumption through a utility function. We consider a utility function as a numerical function of consumption. In Chapter 2 we defined the concept in more detail.

Each agent is characterized by a utility function. As prices are random variables, the utility function is a random variable. Agent decision making is characterized by the principle that each agent maximizes the expected value of his or her utility, choosing the portfolio that maximizes the expected utility derived by the stream of consumption. GETs apply to both finite and infinite time horizons. In the finite case, final wealth coincides with final consumption; in the infinite case, utility is defined over an infinite stream of consumption. The maximization of expected final wealth without intermediate consumption is a special case of maximizing a stream of consumption.

The quantity demanded and supplied depends on the price and dividend processes. In equilibrium, asset supply and demand originated by different agents must match. GETs seeks the price process that maximizes agent utility under equilibrium constraints.

The mathematical details of GETs are complex. The existence and uniqueness of the equilibrium solution is a delicate mathematical problem. A full treatment of GETs is well beyond the scope of this book. In the next section, however, we will discuss CAPM, the simplest example of GET.

CAPITAL ASSET PRICING MODEL (CAPM)

In Chapter 2 we introduced mean-variance portfolio selection. The Capital Asset Pricing Model is an equilibrium asset pricing model that was developed from mean-variance portfolio selection. The CAPM is an abstraction of the real-world capital markets based on the following assumptions:

■ Investors make investment decisions based on the expected return and variance of returns.
■ Investors are rational and risk-averse.

■ Investors subscribe to the Markowitz method of portfolio diversification.
■ Investors all invest for the same period of time.
■ Investors have the same expectations about the expected return and variance of all assets.
■ There is a risk-free asset and investors can borrow or lend any amount at the risk-free rate.
■ Capital markets are (perfectly) competitive and frictionless.

The first five assumptions deal with the way investors make decisions. The last two assumptions relate to characteristics of the capital market. All investors are assumed to make investment decisions over some single-period investment horizon. The CAPM is essentially a static relationship which, per se, does not imply any dynamics. Asset price dynamics must be added. The usual assumption is that returns are serially independent, that is, prices are random walks.

A risk-averse investor who makes decisions based on expected return and variance should construct an efficient portfolio using a combination of the market portfolio and the risk-free rate. The combinations are identified by the Capital Market Line (CML). Based on this result, Sharpe derived an asset pricing model that shows how a risky asset should be priced.[9] A powerful implication is that the appropriate risk that investors should be compensated for accepting is not the variance of an asset's return but some other quantity. Now we determine this risk measure.

First, we need to introduce the notion of *systematic* and *unsystematic risk*. Suppose asset returns are multivariate normal. We can leave undecided whether returns are simple net returns or log returns. Consider a portfolio P consisting of N assets; call w_i the weight of asset i in portfolio P. As w_i is the percentage of asset i in P,

$$\sum_{i=1}^{N} w_i = 1$$

The variance of portfolio P is

---

[9] William F. Sharpe, "Capital Asset Prices: A Theory of Market Equilibrium Under Conditions of Risk," *Journal of Finance* 19, no. 3 (September 1964), pp. 425–442. Closely related work was also done by Tobin and Lintner, see James Tobin, "Liquidity Preference as a Behavior Towards Risk," *Review of Economic Studies* 25, no. 2 (February 1958), pp. 65–86; and John Lintner, "The Valuation of Risk Assets and the Selection of Risky Investments in Stock Portfolios and Capital Budgets," *Review of Economics and Statistics* 47, no. 1 (February 1965), pp. 13–37.

$$\text{var}(R_P) = \sum_{i=1}^{N} \sum_{j=1}^{N} w_i w_j \text{cov}(R_i, R_j)$$

If we substitute M (market portfolio) for P and denote by w_{iM} and w_{jM} the proportion invested in asset i and j in the market portfolio, then the above equation can be rewritten as

$$\text{var}(R_M) = \sum_{i=1}^{N} \sum_{j=1}^{N} w_{iM} w_{jM} \text{cov}(R_i, R_j)$$

Collecting terms, the above equation can be expressed as follows:

$$\text{var}(R_M) = w_{1M} \sum_{j=1}^{N} w_{jM} \text{cov}(R_1, R_j) + w_{2M} \sum_{j=1}^{N} w_{jM} \text{cov}(R_2, R_j)$$
$$+ \dots + w_{NM} \sum_{j=1}^{N} w_{NM} \text{cov}(R_N, R_j)$$

Given the linearity of the covariance, the covariance of asset i with the market portfolio is expressed as follows:

$$\text{cov}(R_i, R_M) = \sum_{j=1}^{N} w_{jM} \text{cov}(R_i, R_j)$$

Substituting the right-hand side of the left-hand side of the equation into the prior equation gives

$$\text{var}(R_M) = w_{1M} \text{cov}(R_1, R_M) + w_{2M} \text{cov}(R_2, R_M)$$
$$+ \dots + w_{NM} \sum_{j=1}^{N} w_{jM} \text{cov}(R_N, R_j)$$

Notice how the market portfolio variance can be represented as a function solely of the covariances of each asset with the market portfolio. Sharpe defines the degree to which an asset covaries with the market portfolio as the asset's *systematic risk*. More specifically, he defines systematic risk as the portion of an asset's variability that can be attributed to a common factor. Systematic risk is the minimum level of market risk that can be obtained for a portfolio by means of diversification across a large number of randomly chosen assets. As such, systematic risk is the risk that results from general market and economic conditions that cannot be diversified away. Sharpe defines the portion of an asset's variability that can be diversified away as *nonsystematic risk*. It is also sometimes called *unsystematic risk, diversifiable risk, unique risk, residual risk,* and *company-specific risk*. This is the risk that is unique to an asset.

Consequently, total risk (as measured by the variance) can be partitioned into systematic risk as measured by the covariance of asset i's return with the market portfolio's return and nonsystematic risk. The relevant risk is the systematic risk. The portfolio size needed to achieve diversification depends on market conditions. For example, during the TMT bubble this number significantly increased. The existence of systematic and unsystematic risk is a general property of large portfolios of assets subject to long-range correlations. In the absence of long-range correlations, there would not be any systematic risk and the Central Limit Theorem would hold.

Let us now suppose that the market is in equilibrium. As we have seen in Chapter 2, the CML represents an equilibrium condition in which the expected return on a portfolio of assets is a linear function of the expected return on the market portfolio. Individual assets do not fall on the CML. Instead, it can be demonstrated that the following relationship holds for individual assets:

$$E[R_i] = R_f + \frac{[E[R_M] - R_f]}{\text{var}(R_M)} \text{cov}(R_i, R_M)$$

This equation is called the *security market line* (SML). In equilibrium, the expected return of individual securities will lie on the SML and *not* on the CML. This is true because of the high degree of nonsystematic risk that remains in individual assets that can be diversified out of portfolios. In equilibrium, only efficient portfolios will lie on both the CML and the SML.

The ratio

$$\frac{\text{cov}(R_i, R_M)}{\text{var}(R_M)}$$

can be estimated empirically using return data for the market portfolio and the return on the asset. The empirical analogue for the above equation is the following linear regression, called the *characteristic line*:

$$R_{it} - R_{ft} = \beta_i [R_{Mt} - R_{ft}] + \varepsilon_{it}$$

where ε_{it} is the error term.

The beta term β_i in the above regression is the estimate of the ratio

$$\frac{\text{cov}(R_i, R_M)}{\text{var}(R_M)}$$

in the SML. Substituting β_i in the SML equation gives the beta-version of the SML

$$E[R_i] = R_f + \beta_i[E[R_M] - R_f]$$

This is the CAPM. It states that, given the assumptions above, the expected return on an individual asset is a positive linear function of its index of systematic risk as measured by beta. The higher the beta, the higher the expected return.[10]

ARBITRAGE PRICING THEORY (APT)

The arbitrage principle is perhaps the most fundamental principle in modern finance theory. Essentially it states that it is not possible to earn a risk-free return without investment. The *Arbitrage Pricing Theory* is a particular formulation of relative pricing theory based on the principle of absence of arbitrage. The APT places restrictions on the prices of a set of assets.[11]

In the previous sections we introduced two families of models that we can consider benchmark models: the family of unpredictable random walks and the family of predictable trend-stationary models. We then discussed the conceptual rationalization of price processes in terms of GETs. In terms of predictability, realistic models are somewhere in between these extremes. We now briefly discuss the implications of GETs on price and return models.

Let's start with CAPM and APT models. These models are not dynamic models, but static models that place restrictions on the cross

---

[10] The conditional CAPM is a version of CAPM where the CAPM regression equation at time t is conditional upon an information set known at time $t - 1$. A problem with Conditional CAPM, proposed by Jagannathan and Wang, is the difficulty of identifying the information set. (See Ravi Jagannathan and Zhenyu Wang, "The Conditional CAPM and the Cross-Section of Expected Returns," *Journal of Finance* 51, no. 1 (March 1996) pp. 3–53.)

[11] We cover the APT in more detail in Chapter 6.

sections of returns. Both CAPM and APT are compatible with random walk models. They are also compatible with other models, but their typical implementation is based on the random walk model. Much of classical quantitative financial analysis is based on multivariate random walk models with restrictions dictated by either the CAPM or by linear factor models such as the APT model. Hence the fundamental importance of random walk models.

Dynamic models used in asset management are rarely the product of GETs; rather they are for the most part econometric models supported by theoretical insight. There is no evidence, empirical or theoretical, that the return process of individual securities can be represented as trend-stationary models. We say that a group of securities are cointegrated if there is a nontrivial linear combination of the securities that is stationary.[12] Due to cointegration a portfolio may be trend-stationary. In addition, there are predictors for equity return processes. This implies that it is possible to model trend stationarity by coupling return and price processes with exogenous variables.

Note that these considerations do not offer a free path to profitability. The profitability of dynamic strategies is, in fact, eroded by transaction costs. Only those strategies that generate profit well in excess of transaction costs can be considered truly profitable.

SUMMARY

- The arithmetic random walk is the basic model of unpredictable (i.e., random) processes. An *arithmetic* random-walk model is a linear model; this implies that it is formed by the addition of its stochastic and random parts.
- The stochastic part of an arithmetic random-walk model is such that random innovations never decay.
- An arithmetic random walk makes excursions that are not periodic and have infinite mean height and length. In other words, there is no reversion to the mean and it might take an unbounded time to recover losses.

---

[12] A formal definition of cointegration and its wider use in portfolio management is outside the scope of this book. The interested reader may consult the original paper by Granger were cointegration was first introduced, Clive W.J. Granger, "Some Properties of Time Series Data and Their Use in Econometric Model Specification," *Journal of Econometrics* 16, no. 1 (1981), pp. 121–130; and Chapter 12 in Fabozzi, Focardi, Kolm, *Financial Modeling of the Equity Market: From CAPM to Cointegration*.

- Though an arithmetic random walk model is not a realistic model of equity prices, it can be a realistic model of the logarithms of prices (i.e., logprices).
- If log prices follow an arithmetic random walk, then prices follow (at least approximately) a lognormal model.
- A *geometric* random walk model is a nonlinear model that approximates a lognormal model.
- A number of economic theories have been proposed to explain asset price processes, the most popular being the Capital Asset Pricing Model (CAPM) and Arbitrage Pricing Theory (APT).
- CAPM is the simplest General Equilibrium Theory (GET); APT and factor models are econometric models.
- All three—CAPM, APT, and factor models—are compatible with multivariate random walks.
- While trend-stationary models are not a realistic representation of single stock price processes, they might well be a realistic representation of portfolios.

CHAPTER 6

Forecasting Expected Return
and Risk

In this chapter, we discuss the estimation of the inputs required for portfolio asset allocation models. Our major focus will be on estimating expected asset returns and their covariances using classical and practically well probed techniques. Modern techniques using dynamic models and hidden variable models are covered in Fabozzi, Focardi, and Kolm.[1]

In the classical mean-variance framework, an investor's objective is to choose a portfolio of securities that has the largest expected return for a given level of risk, as measured by the portfolio volatility. By return (or expected return) of a security we mean the change (or expected change) in a security's price over the period, plus any dividends paid, divided by the starting price. Of course, since we do not know the true values of the securities' expected returns and covariance, these must be estimated or forecasted.

Historical data are often used for this purpose. For example, an analyst might proceed in the following way: observing weekly or monthly returns, he might use the past five years of historical data to estimate the expected return and the covariance matrix by the sample mean and sample covariance matrix. He would then use these as inputs to the mean-variance optimization, along with any ad hoc adjustments to reflect his views about expected returns on future performance. Unfortunately this historical approach most often leads to counter-intuitive, unstable, or merely "wrong" portfolios. Better forecasts are necessary.

---

[1] See Chapters 14, 15, and 16 in Frank J. Fabozzi, Sergio M. Focardi, and Petter N. Kolm, *Financial Modeling of the Equity Market: From CAPM to Cointegration* (Hoboken, NJ: John Wiley & Sons, 2006).

Statistical estimates can be very noisy and do typically depend on the quality of the data and the particular statistical techniques used. In general, it is desirable that an estimator of expected return and risk have the following properties:

- It provides a forward-looking forecast with some predictive power, not just a backward-looking historical summary of past performance.
- The estimate can be produced at a reasonable computational cost.
- The technique used does not amplify errors already present in the inputs used in the process of estimation.
- The forecast should be intuitive, that is, the portfolio manager or the analyst should be able to explain and justify them in a comprehensible manner.

The outline of this chapter is as follows. We begin by discussing techniques from traditional fundamental analysis that can be used for the estimation of expected returns. Specifically, our coverage includes dividend discount and residual income models.

Thereafter, we turn to the usage of the sample mean and covariance as a forecast of expected returns and future risk. The forecasting power of these estimators is typically poor, and for practical applications, modifications and extensions are necessary. We focus on some of the most common and widely used modifications.

Random matrix theory provides an explanation for the poor behavior of the sample covariance matrix: only a few "factors" carry real information about how different securities interact. This result suggests that security returns should be modeled with a small set of factors. We provide a overview of factor models and their use in practice.

Other approaches to volatility estimation and forecasting have been suggested. We provide a survey of forecasting techniques based upon implied volatilities, clustering techniques, and GARCH models.

We close the chapter by considering a few applications of the techniques and approaches to investment strategies and proprietary trading.

DIVIDEND DISCOUNT AND RESIDUAL INCOME VALUATION MODELS

By buying common stock, an investor receives an ownership interest in the corporation. Common stock is a perpetual security. The owner of the shares has the right to receive a certain portion of any cash flow from the company paid out in terms of dividends. The value of one share should equal the present value of all future cash flow (dividends) the owner of the stock expects to receive from that share. In turn, to value one share, the investor must project or forecast future dividends. This approach to the valuation of common stock is referred to as the *discounted cash flow approach*. In this section we will discuss the *dividend discount model* (DDM), and an extension, the *residual income valuation model* (RIM).

If for each time period we are given the expected dividends D_1, D_2, D_3, ..., for one share of stock, and the appropriate interest or discount rates R_1, R_2, R_3, ..., then the *dividend discount model price* of the stock (also referred to as *fair value* or *theoretical value*) is

$$P = \sum_{t=1}^{\infty} \frac{D_t}{(1 + R_t)^t}$$

Future dividends are not certain however, and whether or not a corporation will pay dividends is decided by its board of directors. Yet for a company that does not pay dividends (for example, a company that retains earnings), the same principle applies, as retained earnings should eventually turn into dividends. In this case, the fair value of a security is defined to be the present value of the discounted free cash flow stream FCF_1, FCF_2, FCF_3, ...

$$P = \sum_{t=1}^{\infty} \frac{FCF_t}{(1 + R_t)^t}$$

Historically, this was the form of the first dividend discount model as originated by John B. Williams in his book *The Theory of Investment Value* published in the 1930s.[2] After a decade of irrational exuberance and accounting scandals, his model was an attempt to bring more science to investing.

There are many variations on the above two basic DDMs such as two-stage, three-stage growth models, and stochastic DDMs that are beyond the scope of this book.[3] Instead, we are going to discuss how this basic framework can be used to construct estimates of the expected return (ER) on a security that can then be used as an input in mean-variance analysis.

---

[2] John B. Williams, *The Theory of Investment Value* (Cambridge, MA: Harvard University Press, 1938).

[3] See for example, Pamela P. Peterson and Frank J. Fabozzi, "Traditional Fundamental Analysis III: Earnings Analysis, Cash Analysis, Dividends, and Dividend Discount Models," Chapter 11 in Frank J. Fabozzi and Harry M. Markowitz (eds.), *The Theory and Practice of Investment Management* (Hoboken, NJ: John Wiley & Sons, 2002).

First, if we assume the discount rate R is constant, and that the security would be sold after T periods for a price of P_T, the two formulas above would take the form

$$P = \sum_{t=1}^{T} \frac{D_t}{(1+R)^t} + \frac{P_T}{(1+R)^T}$$

and

$$P = \sum_{t=1}^{T} \frac{FCF_t}{(1+R)^t} + \frac{P_T}{(1+R)^T}$$

Now let us assume that the observed market price of a stock is P_A. Given the stock price after T periods and all dividends or free cash flows, we have

$$P_A = \sum_{t=1}^{T} \frac{D_t}{(1+ER)^t} + \frac{P_T}{(1+ER)^T}$$

and

$$P_A = \sum_{t=1}^{T} \frac{FCF_t}{(1+ER)^t} + \frac{P_T}{(1+ER)^T}$$

The price after T periods could come from an analyst's price expectations, or from any other pricing model. If all other inputs in the formulas above are known we can solve for the expected return, ER.

For example, consider the following inputs:

$D_1 = \$2.00 \quad D_2 = \$2.20 \quad D_3 = \$2.30 \quad D_4 = \$2.55 \quad D_5 = \$2.65$
$P_5 = \$26 \quad\quad T = 5$

and the market price to be $25.89. Then the expected return is found by solving the following equation for ER:

$$\$25.89 = \frac{\$2.00}{(1+ER)} + \frac{\$2.20}{(1+ER)^2} + \frac{\$2.30}{(1+ER)^3} + \frac{\$2.55}{(1+ER)^4}$$
$$+ \frac{\$2.65}{(1+ER)^5} + \frac{\$26.00}{(1+ER)^5}$$

By trial and error, it can be determined that the expected return is 9%.

The expected return is the discount rate that equates the present value of the expected future cash flows with the present value of the stock. This rate is also referred to as the *internal rate of return*. For a given set of future cash flows, the higher the expected return, the lower the current value. The relation between the market value of a stock and the expected return of a stock is shown in Exhibit 6.1.

Although the dividend discount model is a useful framework for the estimation of expected returns, it can be very sensitive to the quality of the inputs. The determination of future dividends is often very hard, and analysts normally have to make various assumptions. For example, often it is assumed that future dividends grow at a constant growth rate g so that

$$D_t = D_{t-1}(1+g) = D_1(1+g)^{t-1}$$

EXHIBIT 6.1   The Relation Between the Market Value of a Stock and the Stock's Expected Return

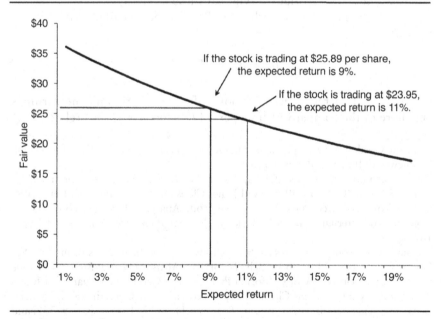

Source: Pamela P. Peterson and Frank J. Fabozzi, "Traditional Fundamental Analysis III: Earnings Analysis, Cash Analysis, Dividends, and Dividend Discount Models," Chapter 11 in Frank J. Fabozzi and Harry M. Markowitz (eds.), *The Theory and Practice of Investment Management* (Hoboken, NJ: John Wiley & Sons, 2002).

Under this assumption, the basic DDM takes the form

$$P = \frac{D_1}{ER - g}$$

which is referred to as the Gordon model.[4] Consequently, the expected return can be calculated as

$$ER = \frac{D_1}{P} + g$$

Several researchers have noted that the *residual income valuation model* (RIM) turns out to be much less sensitive to errors in the inputs than the basic DDM.[5] The residual income valuation model is also referred to as the *discounted abnormal earnings model* (DAEM) and the *Edwards-Bell-Ohlson model* (EBOM).[6] Due to their practical importance, we now give a brief overview of these models.[7]

The basic idea that underlies the RIM is the so-called *clean surplus relation*

$$B_t = B_{t-1} + E_t - D_t$$

where B_t and E_t represent the book value per share, and the earnings per share of the company at time period t, respectively. This relationship

---

[4] Myron Gordon, *The Investment, Financing, and Valuation of the Corporation* (Homewood, IL: Irwin Publishing, 1962).

[5] See, for example, Thomas K. Philips, "Estimating Expected Returns," *Journal of Investing 12* (Fall 2003), pp. 49–57; and James Claus and Jacob Thomas, "Equity Premia as Low as Three Percent? Evidence from Analysts' Earnings Forecasts for Domestic and International Stock Markets," *Journal of Finance 56*, no. 5 (2001), pp. 1629–1666.

[6] So named for some of the researchers who worked on these types of models. See Edgar O. Edwards and Philip W. Bell, *Theory and Measurement of Business Income* (Berkeley, CA: University of California Press, 1961); Gerald A. Feltham and James A. Ohlson, "Valuation and Clean Surplus Accounting for Operating and Financial Activities," *Contemporary Accounting Research 11*, no. 2 (1995), pp. 689–731; and James A. Ohlson, "Earnings, Book Values, and Dividends in Equity Valuation," *Contemporary Accounting Research 11*, no. 2 (1995), pp. 681–687.

[7] For more details on the residual income valuation model, we refer the reader to John D. Stowe, Thomas R. Robinson, Jerald E. Pinto, and Dennis W. McLeavey, *Analysis of Equity Investments: Valuation* (Charlottesville, VA: Association for Investment Management and Research, 2002).

reflects the fact that any item that enters onto a firm's balance sheet must first pass through its income statement. By recursively substituting this expression into the basic DDM above, we obtain the formula for the EBOM

$$P = B_0 + \sum_{t=1}^{\infty} \frac{E_t - ER \cdot B_{t-1}}{(1+ER)^t}$$

In other words, the value of a stock is equal to its book value per share, plus the present value of expected future per-share residual income.

As before, given all inputs, we can solve for the expected return of the stock from the above equation. Nevertheless, due to the infinite sum, this formula can be hard to work with for practical purposes, and often various growth rate assumptions are used.

Under the assumption that the *return on equity* (ROE) and the spread between return on capital and the cost of capital are time invariant, Philips derives three equivalent formulas from the EBOM equation above,

$$ER = \frac{B_0(ROE_1 - g)}{P} + g$$
$$= \frac{FCF_1}{P} + g$$
$$= \frac{E_1 - gB_0}{P} + g$$

where ROE_1 is the return on equity for the first period.[8] We note that these expressions are of similar form as the Gordon model presented earlier. For purposes of calculating the expected return on a stock, the last expression is often the most convenient one to use, as future earnings, current book-to-price, and the growth rate (often chosen to be the growth of nominal GDP) are readily available. As compared to the DDM, Claus and Thomas show that the residual income estimate of expected return is much less sensitive to errors under various growth rate assumptions.[9]

Of course, these "accounting valuation" techniques can also be used in cross-sectional rankings of stocks. For example, studies by Herzberg[10]

---

[8] Philips, "Estimating Expected Returns."
[9] Claus and Thomas, "Equity Premia as Low as Three Percent? Evidence from Analysts' Earnings Forecasts for Domestic and International Stock Markets."
[10] Martin M. Herzberg, "Implementing EBO/EVA® Analysis in Stock Selection," *Journal of Investing* 7 (Spring 1998), pp. 45–53.

and Frankel and Lee[11] show that these "accounting valuation" techniques have some merit in predicting cross-sectional stock returns. In the studies conducted by these researchers, they ranked their respective stock universes according to V/P, where V denotes the RIM fair value (using an appropriate discount rate) and P the current market value. They conclude that rankings based upon the V/P ratio perform better than the standard book-to-price ratio, and that these models perform best for holding periods of three to four years (although Herzberg reports that some superior performance is also found on horizons as short as three months).

THE SAMPLE MEAN AND COVARIANCE ESTIMATORS

The most commonly used approach for estimating security expected returns and covariances for portfolio allocation purposes is to calculate the sample analogues from historical data, the so-called sample mean and covariance estimators. It is important to remember that when we rely upon historical data for estimation purposes, we implicitly assume that the past provides a good estimate for the future.

However, it is well known that expected returns exhibit significant time variation (nonstationarity) and that realized returns are strongly influenced by changes in expected returns.[12] Consequently, extrapolated historical returns are in general poor forecasts of future returns, or as a typical disclaimer in any investment prospectus states: "Past performance is not an indication of future performance."

One problem of basing forecasts on historical performance is that markets and economic conditions change throughout time. For example, interest rates have varied substantially, all the way from the high double digits to the low interest rate environment in the early 2000s. Other factors that change over time, and that can significantly influence the markets, include the political environment within and across countries, monetary and fiscal policy, consumer confidence, and the business cycle of different industry sectors and regions.

Of course, there are reasons why we can place more faith in statistical estimates obtained from historical data for some assets as compared

---

[11] Richard Frankel and Charles M. C. Lee, "Accounting Valuation, Market Expectation, and Cross-Sectional Stock Returns," *Journal of Accounting and Economics* 25, no. 3 (June 1998), pp. 283–319.

[12] See Eugene F. Fama and Kenneth R. French, "The Equity Risk Premium," *Journal of Finance* 57, no. 2 (2002), pp. 637–659; and Thomas K. Philips, "Why Do Valuation Ratios Forecast Long-Run Equity Returns?" *Journal of Portfolio Management* 25, no. 3 (Spring 1999), pp. 39–44.

to others. Different asset classes have varying lengths of histories available. For example, not only do the United States and the European markets have longer histories, but their data also tends to be more accurate. For emerging markets, the situation is quite different. Sometimes only a few years of historical data are available. As a consequence, based upon the quality of the inputs, we expect that for some asset classes we should be able to construct more precise estimates than others.

In practice, if portfolio managers believe that the inputs that rely on the historical performance of an asset class are not a good reflection of the future expected performance of that asset class, they may alter the inputs objectively or subjectively. Obviously, different portfolio managers may have different beliefs and therefore their "corrections" will be different.

Given the historical returns of two securities i and j, $R_{i,t}$ and $R_{j,t}$, where $t = 1, \ldots, T$, the sample mean and covariance are given by

$$\overline{R}_i = \frac{1}{T} \sum_{t=1}^{T} R_{i,t}$$

$$\overline{R}_j = \frac{1}{T} \sum_{t=1}^{T} R_{j,t}$$

$$\sigma_{ij} = \frac{1}{T-1} \sum_{t=1}^{T} (R_{i,t} - \overline{R}_i)(R_{j,t} - \overline{R}_j)$$

In the case of N securities, the covariance matrix can be expressed directly in matrix form:

$$\Sigma = \frac{1}{N-1} \mathbf{X}\mathbf{X}'$$

where

$$\mathbf{X} = \begin{bmatrix} R_{11} & \cdots & R_{1T} \\ \vdots & \ddots & \vdots \\ R_{N1} & \cdots & R_{NT} \end{bmatrix} - \begin{bmatrix} \overline{R}_1 & \cdots & \overline{R}_1 \\ \vdots & \ddots & \vdots \\ \overline{R}_N & \cdots & \overline{R}_N \end{bmatrix}$$

Under the assumption that security returns are *independent and identically distributed* (IID), it can be demonstrated that Σ is the maximum-likelihood estimator of the population covariance matrix and that this matrix follows a Wishart distribution with $N - 1$ degrees of freedom.[13]

As mentioned before, the risk-free rate R_f does change significantly over time. Therefore, when using a longer history, it is common that historical security returns are first converted into excess returns, $R_{i,t} - R_{f,t}$, and thereafter the expected return is estimated from

$$\bar{R}_i = R_{f,T} + \frac{1}{T} \sum_{t=1}^{T} (R_{i,t} - R_{f,t})$$

Alternatively, the expected excess returns may be used directly in a mean-variance optimization framework.

Unfortunately, for financial return series, the sample mean is a poor estimator for the expected return. The sample mean is the *best linear unbiased estimator* (BLUE) of the population mean for distributions that are not heavy-tailed. In this case, the sample mean exhibits the important property that an increase in the sample size always improves its performance. However, these results are no longer valid under extreme thick-tailedness and caution has to be exercised.[14] Furthermore, financial time series are typically *not* stationary, so the mean is not a good forecast of expected return. Moreover, the resulting estimator has a large estimation error (as measured by the standard error), which significantly influences the mean-variance portfolio allocation process. For example:

- Equally-weighted portfolios often outperform mean-variance optimized portfolios.[15]

---

[13] Suppose $X_1, ..., X_N$ are independent and identically distributed random vectors, and that for each i it holds $\mathbf{X}_i \sim N_p(0, \mathbf{V})$ (that is, $E(\mathbf{X}_i) = 0$, where 0 is a p dimensional vector, and

$$\text{Var}(\mathbf{X}_i) = E(\mathbf{X}_i \mathbf{X}_i') = \mathbf{V}$$

where $\mathbf{V}$ is a $p \times p$ dimensional matrix). Then, the Wishart distribution with N degrees of freedom is the probability distribution of the $p \times p$ random matrix

$$S = \sum_{i=1}^{N} \mathbf{X}_i \mathbf{X}_i'$$

and we write $S \sim W_p(\mathbf{V}, N)$. In the case when $p = 1$ and $V = 1$, then this distribution reduces to a chi-square distribution.

[14] Rustam Ibragimov, "On Efficiency of Linear Estimators Under Heavy-Tailedness," Discussion Paper Number 2085, Harvard Institute of Economic Research, Harvard University, 2005.

[15] J. D. Jobson and B. M. Korkie, "Putting Markowitz Theory to Work," *Journal of Portfolio Management* 7 (Summer 1981), pp. 70–74.

■ Mean-variance optimized portfolios are not necessarily well diversified.[16]

■ Uncertainty of returns tends to have more influence than risk in mean-variance optimization.[17]

These problems must be addressed from different perspectives. First, more robust or stable (lower estimation error) estimates of expected return should be used. One approach is to impose more structure on the estimator. Most commonly, practitioners use some form of factor model to produce the expected return forecasts (covered later in this chapter). Another possibility is to use Bayesian (such as the Black-Litterman model) or shrinkage estimators. Both are discussed further in Chapter 8.

Second, mean-variance optimization is very sensitive to its inputs. Small changes in expected return inputs often lead to large changes in portfolio weights. To some extent this is mitigated by using better estimators. However, by taking the estimation errors (whether large or small) into account in the optimization, further improvements can be made. In a nutshell, the problem is related to the fact that the mean-variance optimizer "does not know" that the inputs are statistical estimates and not known with certainty. When we are using classical mean-variance optimization, we are implicitly assuming that inputs are deterministic, and available with great accuracy. In other words, bad inputs lead to even worse outputs, or "garbage in, garbage out."

We will now turn to the sample covariance matrix estimator. Several authors (for example, Gemmill;[18] Litterman and Winkelmann;[19] and Pafka, Potters, and Kondor[20]) suggest improvements to this estimator using weighted data. The reason behind using weighted data is that the market changes and it makes sense to give more importance to recent, rather than to long past, information. If we give the most recent observation a weight of one and subsequent observations weights of d, d^2, d^3, ... where $d < 1$, then

[16] Philippe Jorion, "International Portfolio Diversification with Estimation Risk," *Journal of Business* 58, no. 3 (July 1985), pp. 259–278.

[17] Vijay K. Chopra and William T. Ziemba, "The Effect of Errors in Means, Variances, and Covariances on Optimal Portfolio Choice," *Journal of Portfolio Management* 19, no. 2 (1993), pp. 6–11.

[18] Gordon Gemmill, *Options Pricing, An International Perspective* (London: McGraw-Hill, 1993).

[19] Robert Litterman and Kurt Winkelmann, "Estimating Covariance Matrices," *Risk Management Series*, Goldman Sachs, 1998.

[20] Szilard Pafka, Marc Potters, and Imre Kondor, "Exponential Weighting and Random-Matrix-Theory-Based Filtering of Financial Covariance Matrices for Portfolio Optimization," Working Paper, Science & Finance, Capital Fund Management, 2004.

$$\sigma_{ij} = \frac{\sum_{t=1}^{T} d^{T-t}(R_{i,t} - \bar{R}_i)(R_{j,t} - \bar{R}_j)}{\sum_{t=1}^{T} d^{T-t}}$$

$$= \frac{1-d}{1-d^T} \sum_{t=1}^{T} d^{T-t}(R_{i,t} - \bar{R}_i)(R_{j,t} - \bar{R}_j)$$

We observe that

$$\frac{1-d}{1-d^T} \approx 1 - d$$

when T is large enough. The weighting (decay) parameter d can be estimated by maximum likelihood estimation, or by minimizing the out-of-sample forecasting error.[21]

Nevertheless, just like the estimator for expected returns, the covariance estimator suffers from estimation errors, especially when the number of historical return observations is small relative to the number of securities. The sample mean and covariance matrix are poor estimators for anything but independent, identically distributed (IID) time series. In IID case, the sample mean and covariance estimator are the maximum likelihood estimators of the true mean and covariance.[22]

The sample covariance estimator often performs poorly in practice. For instance, Ledoit and Wolf[23] argue against using the sample covariance matrix for portfolio optimization purposes. They stress that the sample covariance matrix contains estimation errors that will very likely perturb and produce poor results in a mean-variance optimization. As a substitute, they suggest applying shrinkage techniques to covariance estimation. We discuss this technique in more detail in Chapter 8.

The sample covariance matrix is a nonparametric (unstructured) estimator. An alternative is to make assumptions on the structure of the covariance matrix during the estimation process. For example, one can include

---

[21] See Giorgio De Santis, Robert Litterman, Adrien Vesval, and Kurt Winkelmann, "Covariance Matrix Estimation," in Robert Litterman (ed.), *Modern Investment Management: An Equilibrium Approach* (Hoboken, NJ: John Wiley & Sons, 2003), pp. 224–248.

[22] See, for example, Fumio Hayashi, *Econometrics* (Princeton: Princeton University Press, 2000).

[23] Olivier Ledoit and Michael Wolf, "Honey, I Shrunk the Sample Covariance Matrix," *Journal of Portfolio Management* 30, no. 4 (Summer 2004), pp. 110–117.

information on the underlying economic variables or *factors* contributing to the movement of securities. This is the basic idea behind many asset pricing and factor models that we will describe in subsequent sections. Such models are intuitive and practical, and are very widely used.

It is important to remember, however, that introducing a structure for any statistical estimator comes at a price. Structured estimators can suffer from specification error, that is, the assumptions made may be too restrictive for accurate forecasting of reality. As a solution, Jagannathan and Ma[24] proposed using portfolios of covariance matrix estimators. Their idea was to "diversify away" the estimation and specification errors to which all covariance matrix estimators are subject. Portfolios of estimators are typically constructed in a simple fashion: they are equally weighted, and easier to compute than, say, shrinkage estimators.[25] For example, one of the portfolios of estimators suggested by Jagannathan and Ma and Bengtsson and Holst[26] consists of the average of the sample covariance matrix, a single-index matrix, and a matrix containing only the diagonal elements of the sample matrix. The latter matrix is more stable than a full asset-asset covariance matrix, as the sample covariance matrix is frequently noninvertible due to noisy data and in general may result in ill-conditioned mean-variance portfolio optimization.[27] The single-index matrix is a covariance matrix estimator obtained by assuming that returns are generated according to Sharpe's classical single-index factor model.[28] Other portfolios of estimators add the matrix of constant correlations (a highly structured covariance matrix that assumes that each pair of assets has the same correlation). Interestingly, a recent study of several portfolio and shrinkage covariance matrix estimators using historical data on stocks traded on the New

---

[24] Ravi Jagannathan and Tongshu Ma, "Three Methods for Improving the Precision in Covariance Matrix Estimators," Manuscript, Kellogg School of Management, Northwestern University, 2000.

[25] As we mentioned earlier, shrinkage estimators will be covered in detail in Chapter 8. In essence, they are sophisticated portfolios of estimators that are typically constructed using optimization. The weights of the estimators in the portfolio are computed so that the quadratic risk of error function of the combined estimator is minimized. The idea is that the proportions of the different estimators in the sophisticated portfolio should be such that the estimation error is reduced without creating too much specification error.

[26] Christoffer Bengtsson and Jan Holst, "On Portfolio Selection: Improved Covariance Matrix Estimation for Swedish Asset Returns," Working Paper, Lund University and Lund Institute of Technology.

[27] See Chapter 9 for a discussion of ill-conditioned optimization problems.

[28] William Sharpe, "A Simplified Model for Portfolio Analysis," *Management Science* 9 (January 1963), pp. 277–293. Sharpe suggested a single-factor model for returns, where the single factor is a market index. We will discuss factor models later in this chapter.

York Stock Exchange concluded that while portfolios of estimators and shrinkage estimators of the covariance matrix were indisputably better than the simple sample covariance matrix estimator, there were no statistically significant differences in portfolio performance over time between stock portfolios constructed using simple portfolios of covariance matrix estimators and stock portfolios constructed using shrinkage estimators of the covariance matrix, at least for this particular set of data.[29] As a general matter, it is always important to test any particular estimator of the covariance matrix for the specific asset classes and data with which a portfolio manager is dealing before adopting it for portfolio management purposes.

Further Practical Considerations

In this subsection, we consider some techniques that are important for a more successful implementation of the sample mean and covariance matrix estimators, as well as advanced estimators encountered in practice.

Heteroskedasticity and Autocorrelation Consistent Covariance Matrix Estimation

Financial return series exhibit serial correlation and heteroskedasticity.[30] *Serial correlation*, also referred to as *autocorrelation*, is the correlation of the return of a security with itself over successive time intervals. The presence of heteroskedasticity means that variances/covariances are not constant but time varying. These two effects introduce biases in the estimated covariance matrix. Fortunately, there are simple and straightforward techniques available that almost "automatically" correct for these biases.

Probably the most popular techniques include the approaches by Newey and West,[31] and its extension by Andrews,[32] often referred to as "Newey-West corrections" in the financial literature.[33]

[29] David Disatnik and Simon Benninga, "Shrinking the Covariance Matrix—Simpler Is Better," Working Paper, Tel Aviv University, Israel, June 2006.

[30] See John Y. Campbell, Andrew W. Lo, and A. Craig MacKinlay, *The Econometrics of Financial Markets* (Princeton, NJ: Princeton University Press, 1997).

[31] Whitney K. Newey and Kenneth D. West, "A Simple, Positive Semidefinite Heteroskedasticity and Autocorrelation Consistent Covariance Matrix," *Econometrica* 56, no. 3 (1987), pp. 203–208.

[32] Donald W.K. Andrews, "Heteroskedasticity and Autocorrelation Consistent Covariance Matrix Estimation," *Econometrica* 59, no. 3 (1991), pp. 817–858.

[33] However, these techniques can be traced back to work done by Jowett and Hannan in the 1950s. See G. H. Jowett, "The Comparison of Means of Sets of Observations from Sections of Independent Stochastic Series," *Journal of the Royal Statistical Society*, Series B, 17 (1955), pp. 208–227; and E.J. Hannan, "The Variance of the Mean of a Stationary Process," *Journal of the Royal Statistical Society*, Series B, 19 (1957), pp. 282–285.

Dealing with Missing and Truncated Data

In practice, we have to deal with the fact that no data series are perfect. There will be missing and errant observations, or just simply not enough data. If care is not taken, this can lead to poorly estimated models and inferior investment performance. Typically, it is tedious but very important work to clean data series for practical use. Some statistical techniques are available for dealing with missing observations; the so-called *expectation maximization* (EM) algorithm being among the most popular for financial applications.[34]

Longer daily return data series are often available from well-established companies in developed countries. However, if we turn to newer companies, or companies in emerging markets, this is often not the case. Say that we have a portfolio of 10 assets, of which five have a return history of 10 years, while the other five have only been around for three years. We could, for example, truncate the data series making all of them three years long and then calculate the sample covariance matrix. But by using the method proposed by Stambaugh,[35] we can do better than that. Simplistically speaking, starting from the truncated sample covariance matrix, this technique produces improvements to the covariance matrix that utilizes all the available data.

Data Frequency

Merton[36] shows that even if the expected returns are constant over time, a long history would still be required in order to estimate them accurately. The situation is very different for variances and covariances. Under reasonable assumptions, it can be shown that estimates of these quantities can be improved by *increasing the sampling frequency.*

However, not everyone has the luxury of having access to high-frequency or tick-by-tick data. An improved estimator of volatility can be achieved by using the daily high, low, opening, and closing prices, along with the transaction volume.[37] These types of estimators are typically referred to as *Garman-Klass estimators.*

---

[34] See Roderick J. A. Little and Donald B. Rubin, *Statistical Analysis with Missing Data* (New York: Wiley-Interscience, 2002); and Joe L. Schafer, *Analysis of Incomplete Multivariate Data* (Boca Raton, FL: Chapman & Hall/CRC, 1997).

[35] For a more detailed description of the technique, see Robert F. Stambaugh, "Analyzing Investments Whose Histories Differ in Length," *Journal of Financial Economics* 45, no. 3 (1997), pp. 285–331.

[36] Robert C. Merton, "On Estimating the Expected Return on the Market: An Exploratory Investigation," *Journal of Financial Economics* 8, no. 4 (1980), pp. 323–361.

[37] See, Mark B. Garman and Michael J. Klass, "On the Estimation of Security Price Volatilities from Historical Data," *Journal of Business* 53, no. 1 (1980), pp. 67–78; and Michael Parkinson, "The Extreme Value Method for Estimating the Variance of the Rate of Return," *Journal of Business* 53, no. 1 (1980), pp. 61–65.

Some guidance can also be gained from the option pricing literature. As suggested by Burghardt and Lane, when historical volatility is calculated for *option pricing purposes*, the time horizon for sampling should be equal to the time to maturity of the option.[38]

As Butler and Schachter point out, when historical data are used for volatility forecasting purposes, the bias found in the estimator tends to increase with the sample length.[39] However, it can be problematic to use information based on too short time periods. In this case, often the volatility estimator becomes highly sensitive to short-term regimes, such as over- and underreaction corrections.

An Argument Against Portfolio Variance

The most common critique levied against mean-variance optimization is the use of the portfolio variance as a measure of risk. Variance measures the dispersion of an asset's return from its expected return (or mean). As a result, by using the variance as a risk measure the returns, both above as well as below the expected return, are treated the same. However, an investor typically views returns that are higher than the expected return differently than the ones that are lower. On the one hand, an investor being long a particular asset obviously prefers returns above his expected return. On the other, an investor wants to avoid returns that are below his expected return.

Therefore, one can argue that risk measures should only consider unfavorable outcomes, or "downside" risk, and not outcomes where the return is above the expected return. For this purpose, Markowitz suggested the semivariance, calculated in a similar fashion as the variance but with the omission of returns above the expected return. Many other measures of downside risk are used by practitioners today, and we discussed some of the most common ones in Chapter 3.

The beauty of Markowitz's portfolio theory is its simplicity. Despite the abundance of empirical evidence that asset returns are not normally distributed, some practitioners feel that in many practical applications, return distributions are not too far away from normal to be of concern.

Chow, et al. introduced a novel yet simple idea to incorporate outlier information into the covariance estimation.[40] They suggest the esti-

---

[38] Galen Burghardt and Morton Lane, "How to Tell if Options Are Cheap," *Journal of Portfolio Management* 16, no. 2 (Winter 1990), pp. 72–78.

[39] John S. Butler, and Barry Schachter, "Unbiased Estimation of the Black-Scholes Formula," *Journal of Financial Economics* 15, no. 3 (March 1986), pp. 341–357.

[40] George Chow, Eric Jacquier, Mark Kritzman, and Kenneth Lowry, "Optimal Portfolios in Good Times and Bad," *Financial Analysts Journal* 55, no. 3 (May/June 1999), pp. 65–73.

mation of two separate covariance matrices. The first one computed from security returns during more quiet or less risky periods, and the second one calculated from outliers during more risky periods. They identify the two different regimes by examining the distance

$$d_t = (\mathbf{R}_t - \mathbf{\mu})\mathbf{\Sigma}^{-1}(\mathbf{R}_t - \mathbf{\mu})'$$

where $\mathbf{R}_t$, $\mathbf{\mu}$, and $\mathbf{\Sigma}^{-1}$ denote the vector of returns, the mean vector of the returns, and the standard sample covariance matrix of returns. Given a threshold parameter d_0, if $d_t < d_0$, the corresponding return vector is said to belong to the low-risk regime, and conversely, if $d_t \geq d_0$, it is said to belong to the high-risk regime. For each regime, a covariance matrix can be estimated, giving $\mathbf{\Sigma}_{\text{high}}$ and $\mathbf{\Sigma}_{\text{low}}$. The full sample covariance matrix is then defined to be

$$\mathbf{\Sigma} = p\mathbf{\Sigma}_{\text{low}} + (1 - p)\mathbf{\Sigma}_{\text{high}}$$

where p is the probability of falling within the low-risk regime and $1 - p$ is the probability of falling within the high-risk regime. The parameter p can be chosen by the portfolio manager, determined by estimation, or calibrated through historical backtests.

If the full sample covariance matrix is used, then in a period of higher or lower than normal volatility, the portfolio will be suboptimal. The blending of the two different covariance matrices mitigates this effect and gives the portfolio manager greater flexibility to control portfolio volatility.

In a subsequent paper, Kritzman, et al.[41] use a two-state Markov chain regime switching model to determine and forecast the probability parameter p_t (p is now time-dependent). In this setup, the resulting covariance matrix becomes

$$\mathbf{\Sigma}_t = p_t\mathbf{\Sigma}_{\text{low}} + (1 - p_t)\mathbf{\Sigma}_{\text{high}}$$

which can be used in the mean-variance framework to calculate regime-sensitive portfolios.

The Program Evaluation and Review Technique for Portfolio Management

The techniques for estimating forecasts discussed in this chapter are all based on the use of reliable financial times series. It can be difficult to

---

[41] Mark Kritzman, Kenneth Lowry, and Anne-Sophie Van Royen, "Risk, Regimes, and Overconfidence," *Journal of Derivatives* 8, no. 3 (Spring 2001), pp. 32–42.

estimate expected returns and variances from more qualitative assessments such as recommendations based on fundamental analysis. Even if a fundamental analyst might be able to provide a rough estimate of the expected target price of the security, it might be difficult for him to assess the associated risk. In this section we describe how the estimation techniques used in the so-called *Program Evaluation and Review Technique* (PERT) developed in the late 1950s by the U.S. Navy[42] can be applied in a portfolio management framework. This approach uses three estimates: an "optimistic," a "pessimistic," and a "most likely" estimate where the most likely estimate is weighted more heavily.

To better understand this approach, let us assume that the analyst has proposed a specific investment strategy and we want to assess its expected return and variance. We start by asking the analyst to provide us with the following information:

1. What is the time horizon over which you expect this investment strategy to be profitable?
2. Given the time horizon you provided in 1, please complete the following sentences:

   a. Most likely outcome: under normal circumstances expected return will be ___%.
   b. Most optimistic outcome: there is a 1 in 10 chance that the return will be greater than ___%.
   c. Most pessimistic outcome: there is a one in 10 chance that the return will be less than ___%.

We can now use PERT to estimate the analyst's implied expected return and variance by

$$\hat{\mu} = \frac{r(0.10) + 2r_m + r(0.90)}{4}$$

$$\hat{\sigma}^2 = \left(\frac{r(0.90) - r(0.10)}{2.65}\right)^2$$

where r_m and $r(p)$ denote the mode (as obtained by 2.a) and the pth percentile of the return distribution (as obtained by 2.b-c).[43] Question 1

---

[42] See, Special Projects Office, "Bureau of Naval Ordinance PERT Summary Report: Phase I and Phase II," Navy Department, 1958; and *DOD and NASA Guide to PERT/COST Systems Design*, Office of Secretary of Defense and National Aeronautics and Space Administration, 1962.

assesses the expected forecast horizon and can be used to rescale the forecasts of expected return and variance to another desirable time-frame (monthly or yearly, etc.)

While these types of approximations definitely do have their limitations, they allow us to incorporate qualitative investment strategy opinions into a quantitative framework.

RANDOM MATRICES

In order to better understand the reason for the poor behavior of the sample covariance matrix, we introduce an area that developed in the 1950s by quantum physicists, called *Random Matrix Theory* (RMT).[44]

First, let us take a look at an example that demonstrates the instability of the sample covariance matrix for a larger number of assets. A simple test is the computation of the variance-covariance matrix over a moving window. If one performs this computation on a broad set of equities, such as the S&P 500, the result is a matrix that fluctuates in a nearly random way, although the average correlation level is high. Exhibit 6.2 illustrates the amount of fluctuations in a correlation matrix estimated over a moving window. The plot represents the average when the sampling window moves.

An evaluation of the random nature of the covariance matrix security returns was first proposed by Laloux, Cizeau, Bouchaud, and Potters, using random matrix theory.[45] A random matrix is the covariance matrix of a set of independent random walks. As such, its entries are a set of zero-mean, independent, and identically distributed variables. The mean of the random correlation coefficients is zero, as these coefficients have a symmetrical distribution in the range [−1,+1].

Interesting results can be shown in the case when both the number of sample points T and the number of time series N tend to infinity. Suppose that both T and N tend to infinity with a fixed ratio:

---

[43] See L. B. Davidson and D. O. Cooper, "A Simple Way of Developing a Probability Distribution of Present Value," *Journal of Petroleum Technology* 28, no. 9 (September 1976), pp. 1069–1078; and D. L. Keefer and S. E. Bodily, "Three-Point Approximations for Continuous Random Variables," *Management Science* 29, no. 3 (May 1983), pp. 595–609. These two articles provide several other types of two and three-point approximations to the mean and variance, respectively.
[44] Madan L. Mehta, *Random Matrix Theory* (New York: Academic Press, 1995).
[45] Laurent Laloux, Pierre Cizeau, Jean-Philippe Bouchaud, and Marc Potters, "Noise Dressing of Financial Correlation Matrices," *Physics Review Letter* 83, no. 7 (1999), pp. 1467–1470.

EXHIBIT 6.2   Fluctuations of the Variance-Covariance Matrix

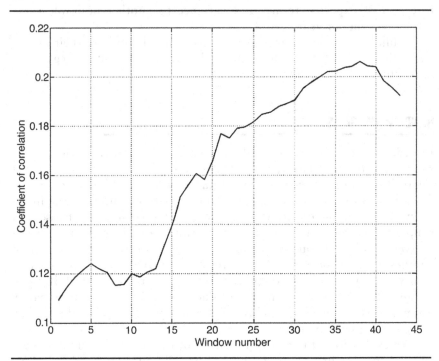

$$Q = T/N \geq 1$$

It can then be shown that the density of eigenvalues of the random matrix tends to

$$\rho(\lambda) = \frac{Q}{2\pi\sigma^2} \frac{\sqrt{(\lambda_{max} - \lambda)(\lambda_{min} - \lambda)}}{\lambda}$$

$$T, N \to \infty, Q = T/N \geq 1$$

$$\lambda_{max,\,min} = \sigma^2 \left[1 + \frac{1}{Q} \pm 2\sqrt{\frac{1}{Q}} \right]$$

where σ^2 is the average eigenvalue of the matrix. Exhibit 6.3 illustrates the theoretical function and a sample computed on 500 simulated inde-

EXHIBIT 6.3   Theoretical Distribution of the Eigenvalues in a Random Matrix and Distribution of the Eigenvalues in a Sample of 500 Simulated Independent Random Walks

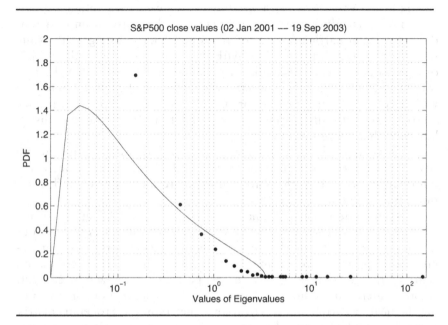

pendent random walks. The shape of the distribution of the eigenvalues is the signature of randomness.

If the covariance matrix entries do not have a zero mean, then the spectrum of the eigenvalues is considerably different. Malevergne and Sornette demonstrate that if the entries of the covariance matrix are all equal—with the obvious exception of the elements on the diagonal—then a very large eigenvalue appears, while all the others are equal to a single degenerate eigenvalue.[46] The eigenvector corresponding to the large eigenvalue has all components proportional to 1, that is, its components have equal weights.

If the entries of the covariance matrix are random but with nonzero average, it can be shown that a large eigenvalue still appears. Nevertheless, a small number of large eigenvalues also appear, while the bulk of the distribution resembles that of a random matrix. The eigenvector

---

[46] Yannick Malevergne and Didier Sornette, "Collective Origin of the Coexistence of Apparent RMT Noise and Factors in Large Sample Correlation Matrices," Cond-Mat 02/0115, 1, no. 4 (October 2002).

corresponding to the largest eigenvalue includes all components with all equal weights proportional to 1.

If we compute the distribution of the eigenvalues of the covariance matrix of the S&P 500 over a window of two years, we obtain a distribution of eigenvalues which is fairly close to the distribution of a random matrix. In particular, the empirical distribution of eigenvalues fits well the theoretical distribution, with the exception of a small number of eigenvalues that have significantly higher values. Following the reasoning of Malevergne and Sornette, the existence of a large eigenvalue with a corresponding eigenvector of 1s in a large variance-covariance matrix arises naturally in cases where correlations have a random distribution with a nonzero mean.

This analysis shows that there is little information in the sample covariance matrix of a large portfolio. Only a few eigenvalues carry information, while the others are simply the result of statistical fluctuations in the sample correlation.

Therefore, developing alternative techniques for modeling the covariance matrix of security returns is critical. One possibility is to filter out the small eigenvalues and their corresponding eigenvectors.[47] This procedure also appears to be promising in reducing the effect of estimation error in the covariance matrix in the portfolio optimization context. Another interesting technique, proposed by Higham, relies upon computing the nearest correlation or covariance matrix in the Frobenius matrix norm, without having to calculate all its eigenvalues or principal components.[48] In this chapter and in Chapter 8 we will discuss several other approaches, such as factor models and Bayesian shrinkage estimation.

ARBITRAGE PRICING THEORY AND FACTOR MODELS

In well-functioning capital markets, an investor should be rewarded for accepting the various risks associated with investing in a security. Throughout this chapter we have been discussing these risks and how, if possible, to quantify them. In this, and in the following two sections, we

---

[47] Laurent Laloux, Pierre Cizeau, Jean-Philippe Bouchaud, and Marc Potters, "Random Matrix Theory and Financial Correlations," *International Journal of Theoretical & Applied Finance* 3 (2000), pp. 391–397; and Vasiliki Plerou, Parameswaran Gopikrishnan, Bernd Rosenow, Luis A. Nunes Amaral, Thomas Guhr, and H. Eugene Stanley, "Random Matrix Approach to Cross Correlations in Financial Data," *Physical Review E* 65 (2002), pp. 1–18.
[48] Nicholas J. Higham, "Computing the Nearest Correlation Matrix—A Problem from Finance," *IMA Journal of Numerical Analysis* 22, no. 3 (2002), pp. 329–343.

consider the type of asset pricing models that practitioners refer to as *factor models*. These models are so-called because they attempt to model each exposure to risk as a separate factor. In this type of models, risks are also commonly referred to as "risk factors" or just "factors."

We begin with a general overview of the common characteristics of asset pricing models used in modern finance. Thereafter, we discuss the theoretical foundation for factor models laid by the *Arbitrage Pricing Theory* (APT). In the following two sections, we cover the practical usage of factor models and provide several real-world illustrations.

Characteristics of Asset Pricing Models

We can express an asset pricing model in general terms as

$$E(R_i) = f(F_1, F_2, F_3, \ldots, F_N)$$

where $E(R_i)$, F_k, and N denote the expected return on asset i, the k-th risk factor, and the number of risk factors, respectively.

By investing in an asset other than risk-free securities, investors will demand a premium over the risk-free rate. That is, the expected return that an investor will demand is

$$E(R_i) = R_f + \text{risk premium}$$

where R_f is the risk-free rate.

The "risk premium," or excess return expected over the risk-free rate, depends on the risk factors associated with investing in the asset. Thus, we can rewrite the general form of the asset pricing model given above as

$$E(R_i) = R_f + g(F_1, F_2, F_3, \ldots, F_N)$$

Risk factors can be divided into two general categories:

- *Systematic*, or nondiversifiable risk factors
- *Unsystematic*, or diversifiable risk factors

The first category refers to factors that cannot be diversified away via mean-variance techniques. The second category refers to risk factors that can be eliminated. These risk factors are not specific to any particular assets and can therefore be made to "cancel out" with other assets in the portfolio.

Example: The Capital Asset Pricing Model

The first asset pricing model derived from economic theory was developed by William Sharpe and is called the *capital asset pricing model* (CAPM)[49]

$$E(R_i) = R_f + \beta_i(E(R_M) - R_f)$$

where $E(R_M)$ is the expected return on the market portfolio and

$$\beta_i = \frac{\text{cov}(R_i, R_M)}{\text{var}(R_M)}$$

denotes the measure of systematic risk of asset i relative to the market portfolio.[50]

The CAPM has only one systematic risk factor, the risk of the overall movement of the market. This risk factor is referred to as "market risk." So, in the CAPM, the terms "market risk" and "systematic risk" are used interchangeably. By "market risk" it is meant the risk associated with holding a portfolio consisting of all assets, called the "market portfolio" introduced in Chapter 2.

Given the risk-free return, the expected return on the market portfolio, and an asset's β, we can use the CAPM to derive an estimate of the expected return on the asset. The β of each asset is typically estimated empirically from data for the return on the market portfolio and the return on the asset by econometric techniques such as those described in Chapter 7. The empirical analogue of the CAPM is given by

$$r_{it} - r_{ft} = \beta_i [r_{Mt} - r_{ft}] + e_{it}, \, t = 1, ..., T$$

where e_{it} is the error term, and T is the length of the sample used in the estimation.

Arbitrage Pricing Theory

As an alternative to the capital asset pricing model just discussed, Stephen Ross derived an asset pricing model based purely on arbitrage

---

[49] William F. Sharpe, "Capital Asset Prices," *Journal of Finance* 19, no. 3 (September 1964), pp. 425–442. See, also John Lintner, "The Valuation of Risk Assets and the Selection of Risky Investments in Stock Portfolio and Capital Budgets," *Review of Economics and Statistics* 47, no. 1 (February 1965), pp. 13–37; Jack L. Treynor, "Toward a Theory of Market Value of Risky Assets," Unpublished Paper, Arthur D. Little, Cambridge, MA, 1961; and, Jan Mossin, "Equilibrium in a Capital Asset Market," *Econometrica* 34, no. 4 (October 1966), pp. 768–783.

[50] We discussed the CAPM and its underlying assumptions in Chapter 5.

arguments called the *Arbitrage Pricing Theory* (APT).[51] This approach postulates that an asset's expected return is influenced by a variety of risk factors, as opposed to just market risk, as suggested by the CAPM. The APT states that the return on a security is linearly related to some K risk factors. However, the APT does *not* specify what these risk factors are, but it is assumed that the relationship between asset returns and the risk factors is linear. Moreover, unsystematic risk can be eliminated so that an investor is only compensated for accepting the systematic risk factors.

Arbitrage Principle

Since the APT relies on arbitrage arguments, we will digress at this point to define what is meant by arbitrage. In its simple form, arbitrage is the simultaneous buying and selling of an asset at two different prices in two different markets. The arbitrageur profits, without taking any risk, by buying at a cheaper price in one market and simultaneously selling at a higher price in the other market. Investors do not hold their breath waiting for such situations to occur because they are rare. In fact, a single arbitrageur with unlimited ability to sell short, could correct a mispricing condition by financing purchases in the underpriced market with the proceeds of short sales in the overpriced market. This means that in practice, riskless arbitrage opportunities are short lived.

Less obvious arbitrage opportunities exist in situations where a *portfolio of assets* can produce a payoff (expected return) identical to an asset that is priced differently. This arbitrage relies on a fundamental principle of finance called the *law of one price*, which states that a given asset must have the same price, regardless of the means by which one goes about creating that asset. The law of one price implies that if the payoff of an asset can be synthetically created by a portfolio of assets, the price of the portfolio, and the price of the asset whose payoff it replicates, must be equal.

When a situation is discovered whereby the price of the portfolio of assets differs from that of an asset with the same payoff, rational investors will trade these assets in such a way so as to restore price equilibrium. This market mechanism is assumed by the APT, and is founded on the fact that an arbitrage transaction does not expose the investor to any adverse movement in the market price of the assets in the transaction.

For example, let us consider how we can produce an arbitrage opportunity involving the three assets A, B, and C. These assets can be purchased today at the prices shown below, and can each produce only one of two payoffs (referred to as State 1 and State 2) a year from now:

---

[51] Stephen A. Ross, "The Arbitrage Theory of Capital Asset Pricing," *Journal of Economic Theory* 13, no. 3 (December 1976), pp. 343–362.

| Asset | Price | $ Payoff in | |
		State 1	State 2
A	70	50	100
B	60	30	120
C	80	38	112

While it is not obvious from the data presented above, an investor can construct a portfolio of assets A and B that will have the identical return as asset C in both State 1 or State 2. Let w_A and w_B be the proportion of assets A and B, respectively, in the portfolio. Then the payoff (i.e., the terminal value of the portfolio) under the two states can be expressed mathematically as follows:

If State 1 occurs: $\$50\ w_A + \$30\ w_B$
If State 2 occurs: $\$100\ w_A + \$120\ w_B$

We can now create a portfolio consisting of A and B that will reproduce the payoff of C, regardless of the state that occurs one year from now. For either condition (State 1 and State 2), we set the expected payoff of the portfolio equal to the expected payoff for C, as follows:

State 1: $\$50\ w_A + \$30\ w_B\quad = \$\ 38$
State 2: $\$100\ w_A + \$120\ w_B = \$112$

We also know that $w_A + w_B = 1$.

If we solved for the weights for w_A and w_B that would simultaneously satisfy the above equations, we would find that the portfolio should have 40% in asset A (i.e., $w_A = 0.4$) and 60% in asset B (i.e., $w_B = 0.6$). The cost of that portfolio will be equal to

$$(0.4)(\$70) + (0.6)(\$60) = \$64$$

Our portfolio comprised of assets A and B has the same payoff in State 1 and State 2 as the payoff of asset C. The cost of asset C is $80 while the cost of the portfolio is only $64. This is an arbitrage opportunity that can be exploited by buying assets A and B, in the proportions given above, and short-selling asset C.

For example, suppose that $1 million is invested to create the portfolio with assets A and B. The $1 million is obtained by selling short asset C. The proceeds from the short sale of asset C provide the funds to purchase assets A and B. Thus, there would be no cash outlay by the investor. The payoffs for States 1 and 2 are shown as follows:

Asset	Investment	$ Payoff in State 1	State 2
A	400,000	285,715	571,429
B	600,000	300,000	1,200,000
C	−1,000,000	−475,000	−1,400,000
Total	0	110,715	371,429

In either State 1 or 2, the investor profits without risk. The APT assumes that such an opportunity would be quickly eliminated by the marketplace.

APT Formulation

Let us now suppose that there are N securities and that each have a return distribution according to the factor structure

$$R_i = \alpha_i + \sum_{k=1}^{K} \beta_{ik} F_k + \varepsilon_i$$

where we also assume that

$$E(\varepsilon_i) = E(F_k) = 0$$

$$E(\varepsilon_i \varepsilon_j) = E(\varepsilon_i F_j) = E(F_i F_j) = 0$$

and

$$E(\varepsilon_j^2) = \sigma^2$$

for all $i \neq j$.[52] Here F_k, $k = 1, 2, ..., K$ are the K factors common to all the securities, β_{ik} is the sensitivity of the i-th security to the k-th factor, and ε_i is the nonsystematic (idiosyncratic) return for the i-th security. In vector form, we can write the above relationship as

---

[52] We choose to discuss a simplified version of the APT. Specifically, we assume that the nonsystematic errors are independent. In this case, returns are said to have a *strict factor structure*. Generalizations to an *approximate factor structure*, where the covariance matrix satisfies cov(ε) = Ω are possible, but technical. We also omit discussing approximate factor structures with infinitely many assets, which is the framework where the APT was originally established.

$$\mathbf{R} = \boldsymbol{\alpha} + \mathbf{B}\mathbf{F} + \boldsymbol{\varepsilon}$$

where

$$\mathbf{R} = \begin{bmatrix} R_1 \\ \vdots \\ R_N \end{bmatrix}, \boldsymbol{\alpha} = \begin{bmatrix} \alpha_1 \\ \vdots \\ \alpha_N \end{bmatrix}, \boldsymbol{\varepsilon} = \begin{bmatrix} \varepsilon_1 \\ \vdots \\ \varepsilon_N \end{bmatrix},$$

$$\mathbf{F} = \begin{bmatrix} F_1 \\ \vdots \\ F_K \end{bmatrix}$$

and

$$\mathbf{B} = \begin{pmatrix} \beta_{11} & \cdots & \beta_{1k} \\ \vdots & \ddots & \vdots \\ \beta_{k1} & \cdots & \beta_{kk} \end{pmatrix}$$

Ross showed that in the absence of arbitrage, the following relationship holds

$$E(R_i) = R_f + \sum_{k=1}^{K} \beta_{ik}(E(F_k) - R_f)$$

This is referred to as the APT.[53] The expression $E(F_k) - R_f$ is the excess return of the k-th systematic risk factor over the risk-free rate, and as such it can be thought of as the "price" (or risk premium) for the k-th systematic risk factor.

The APT asserts that investors want to be compensated for all the risk factors that *systematically* affect the return of a security. The compensation is the sum of the products of each risk factor's systematic risk

---

[53] Strictly speaking, this is not fully correct. In particular, the equality holds in the *mean-squared sense*, when the number of assets approaches infinity. That is, the APT states that in the absence of asymptotic arbitrage opportunities

$$\lim_{N \to \infty} \frac{1}{N} \sum_{k=1}^{K} \left(E(r_i) - R_f - \sum_{k=1}^{K} \beta_{ik}(E(F_k) - R_f) \right)^2 = 0$$

See, for example, Gur Huberman, "A Simple Approach to Arbitrage Pricing Theory," *Journal of Economic Theory* 28, no. 1 (1982), pp. 183–191.

β_{ik} and the risk premium assigned to it by the financial market, $E(F_k)$ – R_f. As in the case of the CAPM, an investor is *not* compensated for accepting nonsystematic risk.

As a matter of fact, it turns out that the CAPM is actually a special case of the APT. If the only risk factor in the APT is market risk, the APT reduces to the CAPM.[54] Both say that investors are compensated for accepting all systematic risk, but not nonsystematic risk. The CAPM states that systematic risk is market risk, while the APT does not specify what the systematic risk factors are.

How do the two different models differ? Supporters of the APT argue that it has several major advantages over the CAPM. First, it makes less restrictive assumptions about investor preferences toward risk and return. As explained in Chapter 5, the CAPM theory assumes investors trade-off between risk and return, solely on the basis of the expected returns and standard deviations of prospective investments. In contrast, the APT simply requires that some rather unobtrusive bounds be placed on potential investor utility functions. Second, the CAPM is a market equilibrium model, whereas APT relies upon the no-arbitrage condition. We note that while a market equilibrium implies no-arbitrage, no-arbitrage *does not* necessarily imply that the market is in equilibrium. Third, APT is a "relative" pricing model, in that it prices securities on the basis of the prices of other securities. Conversely, CAPM is an "absolute" pricing model that relates returns on the securities to the fundamental source of risk inherent in the portfolio of total wealth. Finally, in the APT, no assumptions are made about the distribution of asset returns besides the factor structure. Since the APT does not rely on the identification of the true market portfolio, the theory is potentially testable.[55]

---

[54] Two necessary conditions for the two models to be asymptotically equivalent are: (1) The one factor must be uncorrelated with the residuals so that factor risk and specific risk can be separated; and (2) any specific risk must be diversified away in the market portfolio.

[55] In a paper by Richard Roll, he demonstrates that the CAPM is not testable unless (1) the exact composition of the "true" market portfolio is known; and (2) the only valid test of the CAPM is to observe whether the ex ante true market portfolio is mean-variance efficient. (Richard R. Roll, "A Critique of the Asset Pricing Theory's Tests, Part I: On Past and Potential Testability of the Theory," *Journal of Financial Economics* 4, no. 2 (March 1977), pp. 129–176.) As a result of his findings, Roll states that he does not believe there ever will be an unambiguous test of the CAPM. He does not say that the CAPM is invalid, but rather that there is likely to be no unambiguous way to test the CAPM and its implications due to the nonobservability of the true market portfolio and its characteristics.

FACTOR MODELS IN PRACTICE

The APT provides theoretical support for an asset pricing model in which there is more than one risk factor. Consequently, models of this type are referred to as *multifactor risk models.* As we will see in the next section where these models are applied to equity portfolio management, they provide the tools for quantifying the risk profile of a portfolio relative to a benchmark, for constructing a portfolio relative to a benchmark, and controlling risk. Below, we provide a brief overview of the three different types of multifactor risk models used in equity portfolio management: statistical factor models, macroeconomic factor models, and fundamental factor models, and explain briefly how factor models can be estimated using linear regression.[56,57] The empirical estimation of factor models by linear regression and *maximum likelihood estimation* (MLE) is covered in detail in Fabozzi, Focardi, and Kolm.[58]

Statistical Factor Models

In a *statistical factor model,* historical and cross-sectional data on stock returns are tossed into a statistical model. The goal of the statistical model is to explain best the observed stock returns with "factors" that are linear return combinations and uncorrelated with each other. This is typically accomplished by *principal component analysis* (PCA). In statistical factor models the number of factors is normally much smaller than in macroeconomic and fundamental factor models.[59]

For example, suppose that monthly returns for 5,000 companies for ten years are computed. The goal of the statistical analysis is to produce factors that explain best the variance of the observed stock returns. For example, suppose that there are six factors that do this. These factors are statistical artifacts. The objective in a statistical factor model then becomes to determine the economic meaning of each of these statistically derived factors.

Because of the problem of interpretation, it is difficult to use the factors from a statistical factor model for valuation, portfolio construction, and risk control. Instead, practitioners prefer the two other models

---

[56] Gregory Connor, "The Three Types of Factor Models: A Comparison of Their Explanatory Power," *Financial Analysts Journal* 51, no. 3 (May–June 1995), pp. 42–57.
[57] Please refer to Chapter 7 for an introduction to linear regression.
[58] See Chapter 14 in Frank J. Fabozzi, Sergio M. Focardi, and Petter N. Kolm, *Financial Modeling of the Equity Market: From CAPM to Cointegration* (Hoboken, NJ: John Wiley & Sons, 2006).
[59] As a rule of thumb, practitioners often use 4 to 8 statistical factors. This is motivated by the results from random matrix theory.

described next, which allow them to prespecify meaningful factors, and thus produce more intuitive models.

Macroeconomic Factor Models

In a *macroeconomic factor model*, the inputs to the model are historical stock returns and observable macroeconomic variables. These variables are called *raw descriptors*. The goal is to determine which macroeconomic variables are persistent in explaining historical stock returns. Those variables that consistently explain the returns then become the factors and are included in the model. The responsiveness of a stock to these factors is estimated using historical time series data.

An example of a proprietary macroeconomic factor model is the *Burmeister, Ibbotson, Roll, and Ross* (BIRR) model.[60] In this model, there are five macroeconomic factors that reflect unanticipated changes in the following macroeconomic variables: investor confidence (confidence risk); interest rates (time horizon risk); inflation (inflation risk); real business activity (business cycle risk); and a market index (market risk). For each stock, the sensitivity of the stock to a factor risk is statistically estimated. In addition, for each factor risk, a market price for that risk is statistically estimated. Given these two estimates, the expected return can be projected.

Fundamental Factor Models

One of the most well-known fundamental factor models is the Fama-French three-factor model. Besides the market portfolio, the other two factors are the "size factor" and the "book-to-market factor."[61] The size factor is the return on a zero-cost portfolio that is long on small-cap stocks and short on large-cap stocks. The *book-to-market* (B/M) factor is the return on a zero-cost portfolio that is long on high B/M stocks and short on low B/M stocks. It turns out that the model explains the cross-sectional variation in stock returns fairly well.[62] However, the *forecasting power* of the model is less than satisfactory for most practical purposes. Therefore, it is common that practitioners extend the model with further factors.

Besides the three Fama-French factors, typical *fundamental factor models* use company and industry attributes and market data as raw descriptors. Examples are price/earnings ratios, estimated economic

---

[60] Edwin Burmeister, Roger Ibbotson, Richard Roll, and Stephen A. Ross, "Using Macroeconomic Factors to Control Portfolio Risk," Unpublished Paper.

[61] Eugene F. Fama and Kenneth R. French, "Common Risk Factors in the Returns on Stocks and Bonds," *Journal of Financial Economics* 33 (February 1993), pp. 3–56.

[62] Typical regressions have an R^2 of 0.6 or higher (see, for example, Eugene F. Fama and Kenneth R. French, "The Cross-Section of Expected Stock Returns," *Journal of Finance* 47, no. 2 (June 1992), pp. 427–465).

growth, trading activity, and liquidity. Other technical factors, such as volatility of total return and momentum, are also often included in modern factor models. The inputs into a fundamental factor model are stock returns and the raw descriptors about a company. Those fundamental variables about a company that are pervasive in explaining stock returns are then the raw descriptors retained in the model. Using cross-sectional analysis, the sensitivity of a stock's return to a raw descriptor is estimated.

Practical Issues and Estimation

Several considerations are important when developing factor models in practice. In particular, it should be verified that all the factors used in the model are both statistically and economically significant. Some factors may only prove to have explanatory power for certain periods, and although a factor has worked for the last 20 years, it is important to ask how well it has done for a more recent period, say the last three years. Persistent factors are often more desirable.

Selecting the "optimal" number of factors to use involves a trade-off between estimation error, bias, and ease of use.[63] On the one hand, single factor models, such as the so-called *market model* first proposed by Sharpe, can be estimated with less estimation error, but often tend to be severely biased and misspecified.[64] On the other hand, while multi-factor models are more flexible, resulting in reduced bias, the estimation error and the complexity of the model typically increases.

Simplistically speaking, there are two ways to estimate the factors' expected returns, either theoretically or from data. Both approaches have their own problems.

Theory is problematic to apply because we may not know what portfolio to use to represent a specific factor. In fact, as pointed out by Roll, we do not know what to use for the market portfolio in the CAPM, and we do not know what the factors are in the APT.[65] The market portfolio is unobservable and we have to use a proxy for it.

---

[63] For statistical factor models, some theory is available in the determination of the number of factors. See, for example, Jushan Bai and Serena Ng, "Determining The Number of Factors in Approximate Factor Models," *Econometrica* 70, no. 1 (2002), pp. 191–221; and George Kapetanios, "A New Method for Determining the Number of Factors in Factor Models with Large Datasets," Working Paper, Queen Mary, University of London, 2004.

[64] This approach is often referred to as the *single index model* or the *diagonal model*. See William Sharpe, "A Simplified Model for Portfolio Analysis," *Management Science* 9 (January 1963), pp. 277–293.

[65] Roll, "A Critique of the Asset Pricing Theory's Tests, Part I."

Nevertheless, in practice, the problem of not knowing or not being able to observe the true market portfolio is not as severe as one might think. Typical candidates for the market portfolio are often very highly correlated. It can also be argued that even human capital, which is unobservable, should be highly correlated with portfolios of traded assets.[66]

Estimation from data may be more problematic due to estimation error. Assuming that factors are stationary, we could mitigate this by using a long history to estimate the pricing of the factors. However, many typical factors used in practice are not stationary, but change significantly over time.[67]

There are many different factor models developed for the equity market, both commercially available and proprietary models used by large investment houses. A widely used fundamental multifactor risk model is MSCI Barra's model. Its "E3 model" version, for example, has 13 risk indices, such as volatility, momentum, size, and trading activity, and 55 industry groups, further classified into 13 sectors: basic materials, energy, consumer noncyclicals, consumer cyclicals, consumer services, industrials, utility, transport, health care, technology, telecommunications, commercial services, and financial services.[68] As an example, the energy sector comprises the following three industries: energy reserves and production, oil refining, and oil services.

Given the risk factors, information about the exposure of every stock to each risk factor $(\beta_{i,k})$ is estimated using statistical analysis. For a given time period, the expected rate of return for each risk factor (R_i) can also be estimated using statistical analysis as:

$$E(R_i) = R_f + \sum_{k=1}^{K} \beta_{ik}(E(F_k) - R_f)$$

The forecast for the expected return can then be obtained for any stock. The nonfactor return (e_i) is found by subtracting the actual return for the period for a stock from the return as predicted by the risk factors.

Moving from individual stocks to portfolios, the predicted return for a portfolio can be computed. The exposure to a given risk factor of a portfolio is simply the weighted average of the exposure of each stock in the portfolio to that risk factor. For example, suppose a portfolio has 42

[66] See Fischer Black, "Estimating Expected Return," *Financial Analysts Journal* 49, no. 5 (June 1993), pp. 36–38.
[67] This has led to the introduction of dynamic factor models in finance. This development is covered in Chapter 15 in Fabozzi, Focardi, and Kolm (2006).
[68] Barra, *Risk Model Handbook United States Equity: Version 3* (Berkeley, CA: Barra, 1998). Barra is now MSCI Barra.

stocks. Suppose further that stocks 1 through 40 are equally weighted in the portfolio at 2.2%, stock 41 is 5% of the portfolio, and stock 42 is 7% of the portfolio. Then the exposure of the portfolio to risk factor k is

$$0.022\,\beta_{1,k} + 0.022\,\beta_{2,k} + \ldots + 0.022\,\beta_{40,k} + 0.050\,\beta_{41,k} + 0.007\,\beta_{42,k}$$

The nonfactor error term is measured in the same way as in the case of an individual stock. However, in a well diversified portfolio, the nonfactor error term will be considerably less for the portfolio than for the individual stocks in the portfolio.

The same analysis can be applied to a stock market index because an index is nothing more than a portfolio of stocks.

The real usefulness of a linear multifactor model lies in the ease with which the risk of a portfolio with several assets can be estimated. Consider a portfolio with 100 assets. Risk is commonly defined as the variance of the portfolio's returns. So, in this case, we need to find the covariance matrix of the 100 assets. That would require us to estimate 100 variances (one for each of the 100 assets) and 4,950 covariances among the 100 assets. That is, in all we need to estimate 5,050 values, a very difficult undertaking. Suppose, instead, that we use a three-factor model to estimate risk. Then, we need to estimate (1) the three factor loadings for each of the 100 assets (i.e., 300 values); (2) the six values of the factor variance-covariance matrix; and (3) the 100 residual variances (one for each asset). That is, in all, we need to estimate only 406 values. This represents a nearly 90% reduction from having to estimate 5,050 values, a huge improvement. Thus, with well-chosen factors, we can substantially reduce the work involved in estimating a portfolio's risk. From a statistical estimation point of view, factor variance-covariance matrices also tend to be much more stable and reliable than asset covariance matrices.

In addition to making the estimation of total portfolio risk more robust, multifactor risk models have the benefit of enabling managers and clients to decompose risk in order to assess the performance, both potential and actual, of a portfolio relative to factors or a benchmark. This aids the portfolio construction and the performance attribution analysis of portfolio management models.

OTHER APPROACHES TO VOLATILITY ESTIMATION

There are several other estimation procedures for volatility that have received considerable interest in finance in general, but not necessarily in the area of portfolio management, in particular. We review implied volatility, clustering, GARCH, and stochastic volatility models next.

Implied Volatility

Another possibility to estimate the volatility of a stock is to solve for its implied volatility from the Black-Scholes option pricing formula. One can argue that volatility implied from option prices is more of a forward-looking measure than realized historical volatility. Since options on most stocks are available with different expirations, it makes sense to use the at-the-money option that has a maturity closest to the desired investment horizon. Alternatively, a weighted average of nearby in- and out-of-the-money options is a possibility.

Of course, there are not that many "correlation options" traded. Therefore, we can only expect to be able to gain insight about volatilities—not about correlations. This information can still be useful. For example, we may partition the covariance matrix according to

$$\Sigma = \Lambda C \Lambda'$$

where Λ is a diagonal matrix of the volatilities of returns and C is a correlation matrix. Hence, we see that the volatilities can be modified independently from the correlations.

A natural question is whether implied volatilities are better than historical volatilities in forecasting future volatility. Here, the results are mixed. Some studies conclude that implied volatilities provide an improved forecast, whereas others conclude the opposite.[69] Nevertheless, most of the available studies were done from the perspective of option pricing and these results can therefore not be directly extrapolated to portfolio management purposes.

Clustering

Focardi and Fabozzi discuss some of the uses of clustering in financial applications.[70] Clustering means forming groups that can be distinguished from each other by some rule, typically through a "distance

---

[69] See, for example, João Duque and Dean A. Paxson, "Empirical Evidence on Volatility Estimators," Working Paper, Universidade Técnica de Lisboa and University of Manchester, 1997; Linda Canina and Stephen Figlewski, "The Informational Content of Implied Volatility," Working Paper, New York University, Stern School of Business, 1991; and William K. H. Fung and David A. Hsieh, "Empirical Analysis of Implied Volatility Stocks, Bonds and Currencies," Proceedings of the 4th Annual Conference of the Financial Options Research Centre University of Warwick, Coventry, England, 19-20 July 1991.

[70] Sergio Focardi and Frank J. Fabozzi, "Clustering Economic and Financial Time Series: Exploring the Existence of Stable Correlation Conditions," *Finance Letters* 2, no. 3 (2004), pp. 1–9.

function."[71] In particular, objects within each group are "similar, while two objects from two different groups are "dissimilar." One of the proposed applications use the detection of stable long-term relationships such as long-term correlations (cointegrating relationships) between time series that are much more persistent than classical correlations.

ARCH/GARCH Models

Volatility exhibits persistence in terms of serial correlation. For example, periods of high (low) volatility tends to stay around for a while before volatility goes down (up) again. Engle introduced the so-called *autoregressive conditionally heteroskedastic* processes (ARCH) to capture this phenomenon.[72] Today, many different generalizations and extensions to these models exist. Probably the most well-known is the generalized ARCH (GARCH) model that first appeared in a paper by Bollerslev.[73] A univariate GARCH(p,q) is defined by

$$\sigma_{T+1}^2 = \omega + \sum_{i=1}^{p} \alpha_i (R_{T-i} - \mu)^2 + \sum_{j=1}^{q} \beta_j R_{T-j}^2$$

where ω, μ, α_i ($i = 1, ..., p$), and β_j ($j = 1, ..., q$) are parameters that need to be estimated.

ARCH/GARCH models noticeably depend on the sampling frequency: They are not invariant under time aggregation. This means that the results of the model will change if, for example, we use daily data as opposed to weekly or monthly data.

Several multivariate extensions of GARCH have been proposed where the entire variance-covariance matrix is time-dependent. In practice, however, estimates are difficult to obtain, given the exceedingly large number of parameters needed to estimate the entire variance-covariance matrix. A direct GARCH approach is therefore not practical, especially in a large portfolio context. One possible simplification that has been suggested is to assume that correlations are constant and model each individual variance with a univariate GARCH. The computational complexity of these models prevents all but the most sophisticated portfolio managers from using

---

[71] Clustering is a "data-mining" technique. An excellent reference to this very broad topic is Richard O. Duda, Peter E. Heart, and David G. Stork, *Pattern Classification* (New York: John Wiley & Sons, 2001).

[72] Robert F. Engle, "Autoregressive Conditional Heteroskedasticity with Estimates of the Variance of U.K. Inflation," *Econometrica* 50, no. 4 (1982), pp. 987–1008.

[73] Tim Bollerslev, "Generalized Autoregressive Conditional Heteroskedasticity," *Journal of Econometrics* 31, no. 3 (1986), pp. 307–327.

them. Different simplified approaches have been suggested, but there is yet no clear consensus about their effectiveness in portfolio management.

Stochastic Volatility Models

Recently, major developments have been achieved in so-called *structured stochastic volatility* (SV) models, by the introduction of dynamic factors and Bayesian analysis. Stochastic volatility models consider volatility as a variable term that should be forecasted. More generally, not only volatility but the entire covariance matrix can be regarded as a set of variable terms to forecast. As we know, estimates of the covariance matrix are not stable but vary with time. An early (and not entirely satisfactory) attempt to deal with this problem was covariance matrix discounting first introduced by Quintana and West.[74]

Covariance matrix discounting assumes that the covariance matrix changes with time. At any moment there is a "local" covariance matrix. The covariance matrix is estimated as a weighted average of past covariance matrices. Weighting factors typically decay exponentially with time. Since being introduced in the 1980s, covariance discounting has been used as a component of applied Bayesian forecasting models in financial applications.

Unfortunately, covariance matrix discounting methods do not have any real predictive power: simplistically speaking, they provide exponentially smoothed estimates of the local covariance structure (i.e., the covariance matrix which is supposed to hold at a given moment) within the Bayesian modeling framework. They estimate change rather than forecast change. As a consequence, these models tend to work reasonably well in slow-changing volatility environments, but do poorly in fast-moving markets or when structural change occurs.

Much greater flexibility is achieved by incorporating dynamic factor models or Bayesian dynamic factor models that can explicitly capture change through patterns of variation in process parameters throughout time.[75] In other words, the covariance matrix is assumed to be driven by a dynamic multifactor model. This approach has already shown significant improvement in short-term forecasting of multiple financial and

---

[74] Jose M. Quintana and Michael West, "An Analysis of International Exchange Rates Using Multivariate DLMs," *The Statistician* 36 (1987), pp. 275–281; and Jose M. Quintana and Michael West, "Time Series Analysis of Compositional Data," in J. M. Bernardo, M. H. De Groot, D. V. Lindley, and A. F. M. Smith (eds.), *Bayesian Statistics, 3rd ed.* (Oxford: Oxford University Press, 1988), pp. 747–756.
[75] Omar Aguilar and Mike West, "Bayesian Dynamic Factor Models and Variance Matrix Discounting for Portfolio Allocation," Working Paper, ISDS, Duke University, 1998.

economic time series, and appears to be a promising technique for intermediate and long-term horizons as well. Although Bayesian dynamic
factor models are computationally demanding and often require time-
consuming simulations, the availability of more powerful computers
and recent advances in Markov Chain Monte Carlo methods will contribute to the growing use of these models for forecasting purposes.

APPLICATION TO INVESTMENT STRATEGIES AND PROPRIETARY TRADING

After the meltdown of Long-Term Capital Management (LTCM) in September 1998, when many well-known investment banks lost significant
amounts of money, the view on the risk management of proprietary
trading functions and hedge funds drastically changed. For example, in
April 1999, the Clinton administration published a study on the LTCM
crisis and its implications for systemic risk in financial markets entitled
"Hedge Funds, Leverage, and the Lessons of Long-Term Capital Management."[76] This report describes the events around the LTCM crisis
and provides an analysis of some of the implications.

As a consequence, not only are hedge funds more regulated today,
but also hedge fund managers and proprietary traders themselves are
more aware and cautious of their different risk exposures.

A deeper discussion of hedge funds and their management is beyond
the scope of this book.[77] Nevertheless, the tools introduced in this book
can be applied to analyze many of the relevant questions regarding proprietary trading and hedge fund strategies. We highlight a few issues below.

Risk constraints are typically imposed upon each strategy. Such constraints include capital requirements, expected standard deviation of the
strategy, value at risk, liquidity constraints, and exposures to common
risk factors (for example, standard equity and fixed income indices). On
a second level, similar constraints are imposed upon the overall investment fund or hedge fund. These risk constraints are also used for risk
allocation purposes to determine what portion of the total fund should
be invested in or exposed to a specific strategy.[78]

---

[76] Report of The President's Working Group on Financial Markets, "Hedge Funds,
Leverage, and the Lessons of Long-Term Capital Management," April 1999.
[77] We refer the interested reader to Stuart A. McCrary, *How to Create and Manage a
Hedge Fund: A Professional's Guide* (Hoboken, NJ: John Wiley & Sons, 2002).
[78] For a good discussion on this topic see Kurt Winkelmann, "Risk Budgeting: Managing Active Risk at the Total Fund Level," Investment Management Division, Goldman Sachs, 2000.

When it comes to quantitative trading strategies, the consideration of model risk is a very important issue. Proprietary traders commonly use loss targets to minimize that risk. For example, if more money than a specific target is lost in a specific strategy, then that strategy is closed down and reevaluated.

One should exercise caution when using complex forecasting or estimation techniques, especially if only limited data are available for estimation and backtesting. When there are too many parameters or factors that have to be estimated, it is easy to end up with an over-parameterized model that leads to poor out-of-sample performance. In many instances simple models with few parameters tend to perform much better out-of-sample, confirming the merit of simple and robust estimators.

There is an ongoing debate on whether one should develop one or a few very good strategies, or combine many weaker strategies. Different portfolio managers, proprietary traders, and hedge fund managers diverge in opinion. The typical argument goes back to the correlation between the different strategies. From modern portfolio theory, we know that it is possible to combine several uncorrelated trading models, each with a moderate Sharpe ratio (say 1, for example), to obtain an overall portfolio with a higher Sharpe ratio (say 2, for example). The proponents of using just a few strategies argue that models are often more correlated than we really think. In particular, in downward markets—especially during crashes—correlations of individual securities tend to increase, which makes many trading strategies interrelated.[79] Proponents of this argument therefore believe in developing only a few good strategies that are significantly different from each other.

SUMMARY

- The value of one stock should equal the present value of all future dividends the owner of the stock expects to receive from that share. This is the essence behind *dividend discount models* (DDM).
- In order to apply the classical mean-variance framework, an investor has to provide estimates of expected returns and covariances.
- The sample means and covariances of financial return series are easy to calculate, but may exhibit significant estimation errors.
- Serial correlation or autocorrelation is the correlation of the return of a security with itself over successive time intervals. Heteroskedas-

---

[79] Peter Muller, "Proprietary Trading: Truth and Fiction," *Quantitative Finance* 1, no. 1 (January 2001), pp. 6–8.

ticity means that variances/covariances are not constant but changing over time.

- In practical applications, it is important to correct the covariance estimator for serial correlation and heteroskedasticity.
- The sample covariance estimator can be improved by increasing the
sampling frequency. This is not the case for the sample expected return
estimator, whose accuracy can only be improved by extending the
length of the sample.
- The Program Evaluation and Review Technique (PERT) is a simple
approach in which qualitative assessments of investment opportunities
can be translated into estimates of expected returns and risk.
- There is little information in the covariance matrix of a large portfolio.
Only a few eigenvalues or factors carry information while the others
are simply the result of statistical fluctuations.
- The *Arbitrage Pricing Theory* (APT) asserts that investors want to be
compensated for the risk factors that systematically affect the return of
a security.
- The compensation in the APT is the sum of the products of each risk
factor's systematic risk and the risk premium assigned to it by the
financial market.
- An investor is not compensated for accepting nonsystematic risk.
- Factor models can be used for estimating expected returns and covariances of securities.
- There are several other approaches to the estimation of the volatility of
a security: implied volatility, clustering, GARCH, and stochastic volatility models.

CHAPTER 7

Robust Estimation

In the previous chapter, we introduced the sample mean and covariance estimators for the purpose of estimating the expected returns and covariances among assets. However, one problem with the standard estimators is that they are sensitive to outliers. In some cases, even a single outlier—an extreme return—can significantly influence the resulting means and covariances. This is an undesirable property of many classical estimators. In this chapter, we discuss methods for *robust estimation*, with particular emphasis on the robust estimation of regressions. Robust estimation is a topic of robust statistics. Therefore, we first introduce the general concepts and methods of robust statistics and then apply them to regression analysis. In particular, we will introduce robust regression estimators and robust regression diagnostics.[1]

THE INTUITION BEHIND ROBUST STATISTICS

Broadly speaking, statistics is the science of describing and analyzing data and making inferences on a population based on a sample extracted from the same population. An important aspect of statistics is the compression of the data into numbers that are descriptive of some feature of the distribution. Classical statistics identified several single-number descriptors such as mean, variance, skewness, kurtosis, and higher moments. These numbers give a quantitative description of different properties of the population. For example, the mean describes the center of the population, the variance describes the spread, the skewness measures the symmetry, kurtosis measures if the data are peaked, and so on.

---

[1] Because in this book we focus on static models, we do not discuss robust methods for dynamic models such as Kalman filters and particle filters.

Classical statistics chooses single-number descriptors that have nice mathematical properties. For example, if we know all the moments of a distribution, we can reconstruct the same distribution. In a number of cases (but not always), the parameters that identify a closed-form representation of a distribution correspond to these descriptive concepts. For example, the parameters that identify a normal distribution correspond to the mean and to the variance. However, in classical statistics, most of these descriptive parameters are not robust in the sense that will be made precise in the following section. Intuitively, robustness means that small changes in the sample or small mistakes in identifying the distribution do not affect the descriptive parameters. Robust statistics entails a rethinking of statistical descriptive concepts; the objective is to find descriptive concepts that are little affected by the choice of the sample or by mistakes in distributional assumptions.

Robust statistics is not a technical adjustment of classical concepts but a profound rethinking of how to describe data. For example, robust statistics identifies parameters that represent the center or the spread of a distribution and that are robust with respect to outliers and to small changes in the distributions. Robust statistics seeks descriptive concepts that are optimal from the point of view of being insensitive to small errors in data or assumptions.

The notion of robust statistics carries over to statistical modeling. Statistical models such as regression models are theoretically elegant but not robust. That is, small errors in distributional assumptions or small data contamination might have unbounded effects on the overall model. This fact has important consequences in terms, for example, of asset allocation or risk management. Robust statistics is a technique to find models that are robust, that is, to find models that yield approximately the same results even if samples change or the assumptions are not correct. For example, robust regressions are not very sensitive to outliers.

Consider that statistical modeling involves some form of optimization insofar as any statistical model is the result of some form of optimization. Robust statistics changes the criteria of optimization with respect to classical statistics. Classical statistics seeks primarily mathematical convenience and elegance, robust statistics seeks robusteness.

Robust statistics can also be regarded as a method to separate the contribution of the bulk of data from the contribution of the extremes. This concept is particularly important in finance as many financial quantities are believed to follow fat-tailed distributions. Thus robust statistics allows one to discriminate between business-as-usual situations and extreme or catastrophic events.

ROBUST STATISTICS

Robust statistics addresses the problem of making estimates that are insensitive to small changes in the basic assumptions of the statistical models employed. The concepts and methods of robust statistics originated in the 1950s. The technical term "robust statistics" was coined by G. E. P. Box in 1953. However, the concepts of robust statistics had been used much earlier, for example by the physicist Arthur Eddington and the geophysicist Harold Jeffreys.

Statistical models are based on a set of assumptions; the most important include (1) the distribution of key variables, for example the normal distribution of errors, and (2) the model specification, for example model linearity or nonlinearity. Some of these assumptions are critical to the estimation process: if they are violated, the estimates become unreliable. Robust statistics (1) assesses the changes in estimates due to small changes in the basic assumptions and (2) creates new estimates that are insensitive to small changes in some of the assumptions. The focus of our exposition is to make estimates robust to small changes in the distribution of errors and, in particular, to the presence of outliers.

Robust statistics is also useful to separate the contribution of usual business situations from that of extreme events. We can say that robust statistics and classical nonrobust statistics are complementary. By conducting a robust analysis, one can better articulate important econometric findings.

As observed by Peter Huber, *robust*, *distribution-free*, and *nonparametrical* seem to be closely related properties but actually are not.[2] For

---

[2] Huber's book is a standard reference on robust statistics: Peter J. Huber, *Robust Statistics* (New York: John Wiley & Sons, Inc., 1981). See also, C. Goodall, "M-Estimators of Location: An Outline of the Theory," in David C. Hoaglin, Frederick Mosteller, and John W. Tukey (eds.), *Understanding Robust and Exploratory Data Analysis* (New York: John Wiley & Sons, 1983), pp. 339–403; F. R. Hampel, E. M. Ronchetti, P. J. Rousseeuw, and W. A. Stahel, *Robust Statistics: The Approach Based on Influence Functions* (New York: John Wiley & Sons, 1986); P. W. Holland and R. E. Welsch, "Robust Regression Using Iteratively Reweighted Least-Squares." *Communications in Statistics: Theory and Methods* A6, 9 (1977), pp. 813–827; L. A. Jaeckel, "Estimating Regression Coefficients by Minimizing the Dispersion of the Residuals," *Annals of Mathematical Statistics* 43, no. 5 (1972), pp. 1449–1458; R. Koenker and G. Basset Jr., "Regression Quantiles," *Econometrica* 46, no. 1 (1978), pp. 33–50; P. J. Rousseeuw and A. M. Leroy, *Robust Regression and Outlier Detection* (New York: John Wiley & Sons, 1987); R. A. Maronna, R. D. Martin, and V. J. Yohai, *Robust Statistics: Theory and Methods* (Hoboken, NJ: John Wiley & Sons, 2006); and J. W. Tukey, "A Survey of Sampling from Contaminated Distributions," in I. Olkin, S. G. Ghurye, W. Hoeffding, W. G. Madow, and H. B. Mann (eds.), *Contributions to Probability and Statistics, Essays in Honor of Harold Hotelling* (Stanford, CA: Stanford University Press, 1960), pp. 448–485.

example, the sample mean and the sample median are nonparametric estimates of the mean and the median but the mean is not robust to outliers.
In fact, changes of one single observation might have unbounded effects
on the mean while the median is insensitive to changes of up to half the
sample. Robust methods assume that there are indeed parameters in the
distributions under study and attempt to minimize the effects of outliers
as well as erroneous assumptions on the shape of the distribution.

A general definition of robustness is, by nature, quite technical. The
reason is that we need to define robustness with respect to changes in
distributions. That is, we need to make precise the concept that small
changes in the distribution, which is a function, result in small changes
in the estimate, which is a number.[3] Let us first give an intuitive, non-
technical overview of the modern concept of robustness and how to
measure robustness.

Robust statistics is starting to attract more attention in finance and
portfolio management. In particular, some studies report promising
results using robust statistical techniques in combination with portfolio
optimization.[4]

Qualitative and Quantitative Robustness

In this section we introduce the concepts of qualitative and quantitative
robustness of estimators. Estimators are functions of the sample data.
Given an N-sample of data $\mathbf{X} = (x_1, \ldots, x_N)'$ from a population with a
cdf $F(x)$, depending on parameter θ_∞, an estimator for θ_∞ is a function
$\hat{\vartheta} = \vartheta_N(x_1, \ldots, x_N)$. Consider those estimators that can be written as
functions of the cumulative empirical distribution function

$$F_N(x) = N^{-1} \sum_{i=1}^{N} I(x_i \le x)$$

where I is the indicator function. For these estimators we can write

$$\hat{\vartheta} = \vartheta_N(F_N)$$

---

[3] To this end, we need to define topological and metric concepts on the functional
space of distributions.
[4] See Victor DeMiguel and Francisco J. Nogales, "Portfolio Selection with Robust Estimates of Risk," working paper, London Business School and Universidad Carlos
III de Madrid, 2006.

Most estimators, in particular the ML estimators, can be written in this way with probability 1. In general, when $N \to \infty$ then $F_N(x) \to F(x)$ almost surely and $\hat{\vartheta}_N \to \vartheta_\infty$ in probability and almost surely. The estimator $\hat{\vartheta}_N$ is a random variable that depends on the sample. Under the distribution F, it will have a probability distribution $L_F(\vartheta_N)$. Intuitively, statistics defined as functionals of a distribution are robust if they are continuous with respect to the distribution. In 1968, Hampel introduced a technical definition of qualitative robustness based on metrics of the functional space of distributions.[5] The Hampel definition states that an estimator is robust for a given distribution F if small deviations from F in the given metric result in small deviations from $L_F(\vartheta_N)$ in the same metric or eventually in some other metric for any sequence of samples of increasing size. The definition of robustness can be made quantitative by assessing quantitatively how changes in the distribution F affect the distribution $L_F(\vartheta_N)$.

Resistant Estimators

An estimator is called *resistant* if it is insensitive to changes in one single observation.[6] Given an estimator $\hat{\vartheta} = \vartheta_N(F_N)$, we want to understand what happens if we add a new observation of value x to a large sample. To this end we define the *influence curve* (IC), also called *influence function*. The IC is a function of x given ϑ, and F is defined as follows:

$$ IC_{\vartheta, F}(x) = \lim_{s \to 0} \frac{\vartheta((1-s)F + s\delta_x) - \vartheta(F)}{s} $$

where δ_x denotes a point mass 1 at x (i.e., a probability distribution concentrated at the single point x). As we can see from its previous definition, the IC is a function of the size of the single observation that is added. In other words, the IC measures the influence of a single observation x on a statistics ϑ for a given distribution F. Mathematically, the IC is a Gateaux derivative of the functional θ. The Gateaux derivative is one of the several functional derivatives that have been defined. In practice, the influence curve is generated by plotting the value of the computed statistic with a single point of X added to Y against that X value. For example, the IC of the mean is a straight line. Several aspects of the influence curve are of particular interest:

---

[5] F. R. Hampel, "A General Qualitative Definition of Robustness," *Annals of Mathematical Statistics* 42, no. 6 (1971), pp. 1887–1896.

[6] For an application to the estimation of the estimation of beta, see R. Douglas Martin and Timothy T. Simin, "Outlier Resistant Estimates of Beta," *Financial Analysts Journal* 59, no. 5 (September–October 2003), pp. 56–58.

- Is the curve "bounded" as the X values become extreme? Robust statistics should be bounded. That is, a robust statistic should not be unduly influenced by a single extreme point.
- What is the general behavior as the X observation becomes extreme? For example, does it becomes smoothly down-weighted as the values become extreme?
- What is the influence if the X point is in the "center" of the Y points?

Let's now introduce concepts that are important in applied work. We then introduce the robust estimators.

Breakdown Bound

The *breakdown* (BD) *bound* or *point* is the largest possible fraction of observations for which there is a bound on the change of the estimate when that fraction of the sample is altered without restrictions. For example, we can change up to 50% of the sample points without provoking unbounded changes of the median. On the contrary, changes of one single observation might have unbounded effects on the mean.

Rejection Point

The *rejection point* is defined as the point beyond which the IC becomes zero. Note that observations beyond the rejection point make no contribution to the final estimate except, possibly, through the auxiliary scale estimate. Estimators that have a finite rejection point are said to be redescending and are well protected against very large outliers. However, a finite rejection point usually results in the underestimation of scale. This is because when the samples near the tails of a distribution are ignored, an insufficient fraction of the observations may remain for the estimation process. This in turn adversely affects the efficiency of the estimator.

Gross Error Sensitivity

The *gross error sensitivity* expresses asymptotically the maximum effect that a contaminated observation can have on the estimator. It is the maximum absolute value of the IC.

Local Shift Sensitivity

The *local shift sensitivity* measures the effect of the removal of a mass at y and its reintroduction at x. For continuous and differentiable IC, the local shift sensitivity is given by the maximum absolute value of the slope of IC at any point.

Winsor's Principle

Winsor's principle states that all distributions are normal in the middle.

M-Estimators

M-estimators are those estimators that are obtained by minimizing a function of the sample data. Suppose that we are given an N-sample of data $\mathbf{X} = (x_1, \ldots, x_N)'$. The estimator $T(x_1, \ldots, x_N)$ is called an M-estimator if it is obtained by solving the following minimum problem:

$$T = \arg\min_t \left\{ J = \sum_{i=1}^{N} \rho(x_i, t) \right\}$$

where $\rho(x_i, t)$ is an arbitrary function. Alternatively, if $\rho(x_i, t)$ is a smooth function, we can say that T is an M-estimator if it is determined by solving the equations:

$$\sum_{i=1}^{N} \psi(x_i, t) = 0$$

where

$$\psi(x_i, t) = \frac{\partial \rho(x_i, t)}{\partial t}$$

When the M-estimator is equivariant, that is $T(x_1 + a, \ldots, x_N + a) = T(x_1, \ldots, x_N) + a$, $\forall a \in R$, we can write ψ and ρ in terms of the residuals $x - t$. Also, in general, an auxiliary scale estimate, S, is used to obtain the scaled residuals $r = (x - t)/S$. If the estimator is also equivariant to changes of scale, we can write

$$\psi(x, t) = \psi\left(\frac{x - t}{S}\right) = \psi(r)$$

$$\rho(x, t) = \rho\left(\frac{x - t}{S}\right) = \rho(r)$$

ML estimators are M-estimators with $\rho = -\log f$, where f is the probability density. (Actually the name M-estimators means maximum likelihood-type estimators.) LS estimators are also M-estimators.

The IC of M-estimators has a particularly simple form. In fact, it can be demonstrated that the IC is proportional to the function ψ:

$$IC = \text{Constant} \times \psi$$

L-Estimators

Consider an N-sample $(x_1, \ldots, x_N)'$. Order the samples so that $x_{(1)} \leq x_{(2)} \leq \ldots \leq x_{(N)}$. The i-th element $X = x_{(i)}$ of the ordered sample is called the *i-th order statistic*. *L-estimators* are estimators obtained as a linear combination of order statistics:

$$L = \sum_{i=1}^{N} a_i x_{(i)}$$

where the a_i are fixed constants. Constants are typically normalized so that

$$\sum_{i=1}^{N} a_i = 1$$

An important example of an L-estimator is the *trimmed mean*. The trimmed mean is a mean formed excluding a fraction of the highest and/or lowest samples. In this way the mean, which is not a robust estimator, becomes less sensitive to outliers.

R-Estimators

R-estimators are obtained by minimizing the sum of residuals weighted by functions of the rank of each residual. The functional to be minimized is the following:

$$\arg \min \left\{ J = \sum_{i=1}^{N} a(R_i) r_i \right\}$$

where R_i is the rank of the i-th residual r_i and a is a nondecreasing score function that satisfies the condition

$$\sum_{i=1}^{N} a(R_i) = 0$$

The Least Median of Squares Estimator

Instead of minimizing the sum of squared residuals, as in LS, to estimate the parameter vector, Rousseuw[7] proposed minimizing the median of squared residuals, referred to as the *least median of squares* (LMedS) *estimator*. This estimator effectively trims the N/2 observations having the largest residuals, and uses the maximal residual value in the remaining set as the criterion to be minimized. It is hence equivalent to *assuming* that the noise proportion is 50%.

LMedS is unwieldy from a computational point of view because of its nondifferentiable form. This means that a quasi-exhaustive search on all possible parameter values needs to be done to find the global minimum.

The Least Trimmed of Squares Estimator

The *least trimmed of squares* (LTS) *estimator* offers an efficient way to find robust estimates by minimizing the objective function given by

$$\left\{ J = \sum_{i=1}^{h} r_{(i)}^2 \right\}$$

where $r_{(i)}^2$ is the i-th smallest residual or distance when the residuals are ordered in ascending order, that is: $r_{(1)}^2 \le r_{(2)}^2 \le \cdots \le r_{(N)}^2$ and h is the number of data points whose residuals we want to include in the sum. This estimator basically finds a robust estimate by identifying the $N - h$ points having the largest residuals as outliers, and discarding (trimming) them from the dataset. The resulting estimates are essentially LS estimates of the trimmed dataset. Note that h should be as close as possible to the number of points in the data set that we do not consider outliers.

Reweighted Least Squares Estimator

Some algorithms explicitly cast their objective functions in terms of a set of weights that distinguish between inliers and outliers. However, these weights usually depend on a scale measure that is also difficult to estimate. For example, the *reweighted least squares* (RLS) estimator uses the following objective function:

---

[7] P. Rousseuw, "Least Median of Squares Regression," *Journal of the American Statistical Association* 79, no. 388 (1984), pp. 871–890.

$$\arg\min\left\{ J = \sum_{i=1}^{N} \omega_i r_i^2 \right\}$$

where r_i are robust residuals resulting from an approximate LMedS or LTS procedure. Here the weights ω_i trim outliers from the data used in LS minimization, and can be computed after a preliminary approximate step of LMedS or LTS.

Robust Estimators of the Center and of the Scale

In this section we discuss robust estimators of the center and of the scale. The use of the term "estimator" in this context needs to be clarified. In statistics in general, an estimator is a function of sample data that assumes values close to that of a theoretical quantity. For example, the empirical average is an estimator of the mean. It is a function of the sample data while the mean is a theoretical quantity that depends on the distribution.

However, robust estimators of the center and of the scale imply a robust concept of center and scale; they are not robust estimators of the mean or of the standard deviation as they entail a concept of center and scale different from that of mean and standard deviation. We use the term estimator to signify a function of sample data that represents the center or the scale of a distribution. Its exact meaning, and the intuition behind it, depends on how each estimator is defined.

The first rigorous theory of robust estimators of the center and of the scale was developed by Peter Huber. Let's first consider estimation of the center. In Huber's theory, the center of a sample of data x_i is estimated as an M-estimator of location. That is, the center is that number t that solves the following minimization problem:

$$\min\left(\sum \rho(x_i - t) \right)$$

where ρ is a suitable function. Alternatively, the estimator solves the following equation:

$$\sum \psi(x_i - t) = 0, \ \psi = \rho'$$

As we saw in the previous section, these estimators are called M-estimators.

Huber's M-estimators solve a minimax problem. Consider the following contaminated normal distribution:[8]

---

[8] A contaminated normal distribution is a form of a mixture distribution. In this case, values observed can be from several normal distributions.

$$F(x) = (1 - \varepsilon)\Phi(x) + \varepsilon H(x)$$

where $\Phi(x)$ is the cumulative normal distribution and H is a "contaminating" symmetric distribution. That is, F is a normal distribution contaminated by an arbitrary symmetric distribution in function of a parameter ε. The distribution f is a mixture of two distributions: it yields a normal distribution with probability $1 - \varepsilon$ and the distribution H with (small) probability ε. The Huber estimator minimizes the asymptotic variance over all F distributions.

Huber also considers the estimates of scale. He shows that the solution of the minimax problem for scale is the solution of the following equation:

$$\sum \psi^2((x_i - t)/s) = n E_\Phi(\psi)$$

Estimators of center and scale can be analyzed in the framework of Hampel's *Influence Function*. It can be demonstrated that the Influence Function (IF) of M-estimators satisfies the following relationship:

$$IF(x, F, \psi) \propto \psi(x)$$

Estimators of the Center   Let us now introduce a number of estimators for the center. Resistant estimators of the center are:

- The trimmed mean
- The Winsorized mean
- The median

Suppose that we are given a sample of N data (x_i). The *trimmed mean* is obtained by "trimming" the data, which means excluding the smallest/largest data. Suppose $x_{(1)} \leq x_{(2)} \leq \cdots \leq x_{(N)}$ are the sample order statistics (i.e., the sample sorted). Let's define the lower and upper thresholds for trimming: L, U. The trimmed mean $T(L, U)$ is defined as follows:

$$T(L, U) = \frac{1}{U - L}\sum x_j$$

where the sum is extended to those indices j such that the $L \leq x_{(j)} \leq U$.

The *Winsorized mean* $\overline{X}_W$ is the mean of Winsorized data. Winsorizing data differs from trimming data. While trimming excludes a portion of the data, Winsorization means that data below and above given thresholds assume fixed values.

The *median*, Med(X), is defined as that value that occupies a central position in a sample order statistics:

$$\text{Med}(\mathbf{X}) = \begin{cases} x_{((n+1)/2)} & \text{if } n \text{ is odd} \\ (x_{(n/2)} + x_{(n/2+1)})/2 & \text{if } n \text{ is even} \end{cases}$$

Robust Estimators of the Spread   Robust estimators of the spread are:

- The median absolute deviation
- The interquartile range
- The mean absolute deviation
- The Winsorized standard deviation.

The *median absolute deviation* (MAD) is defined as the median of the difference between a variable and its median

$$\text{MAD} = \text{MED}|X - \text{MED}(X)|$$

The *interquartile range* (IQR) is defined as the difference between the highest and lowest quartile:

$$\text{IQR} = Q(0.75) - Q(0.25)$$

where $Q(0.75)$ and $Q(0.25)$ are the 75th and 25th percentiles of the data. The *mean absolute deviation* (MeanAD) is defined as follows:

$$\frac{1}{n} \sum_{j=1}^{n} |x_j - \text{MED}(\mathbf{X})|$$

The *Winsorized standard deviation* is the standard deviation of Winsorized data.

Illustration of Robust Statistics

To illustrate the effect of robust statistics, consider the series of daily returns of Nippon Oil in the period 1986 through 2005 depicted in Exhibit 7.1. If we compute the mean, the trimmed mean, and the median we obtain the following results:

Mean   = 3.8396e–005
Trimmed mean (20%)[9]   = –4.5636e–004
Median   = 0

---

[9] Trimmed mean (20%) means that we exclude the 20%/2 = 10% highest and lowest observations.

EXHIBIT 7.1   Daily Returns Nippon Oil, 1986–2005

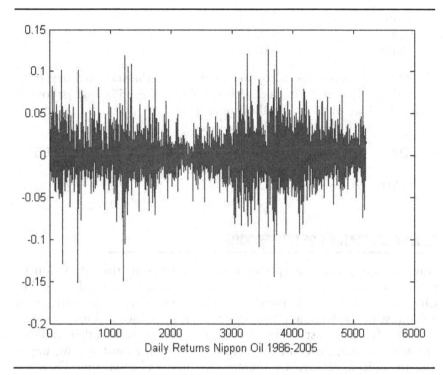

Daily Returns Nippon Oil 1986-2005

In order to show the robustness properties of these estimators, let's multiply the 10% highest/lowest returns by 2. If we compute again the same quantities we obtain:

Mean   = 4.4756e–004
Trimmed mean (20%)   = –4.4936e–004
Median   = 0

While the mean is largely affected, the median is not affected and the trimmed mean is only marginally affected by doubling the value of 20% of the points.

We can perform the same exercise for measures of the spread. If we compute the standard deviation, the IQR, and the MAD we obtain the following results:

Standard deviation = 0.0229
IQR   = 0.0237
MAD   = 0.0164

Let's multiply the 10% highest/lowest returns by 2. The new values are:

Standard deviation = 0.0415
IQR = 0.0237
MAD = 0.0248

The MAD are less affected by the change than the standard deviation while the IQR is not affected. If we multiply the 25% highest/lowest returns by 2 we obtain the following results:

Standard deviation = 0.0450
IQR = 0.0237 (but suddenly changes if we add/subtract one element)
MAD = 0.0299

ROBUST ESTIMATORS OF REGRESSIONS

Now we apply the concepts of robust statistics to the estimation of regression coefficients, which is sensitive to outliers. As we discussed in Chapter 6, a number of models for forecasting asset returns are based on regression analysis, and thus this topic is of particular importance.

Identifying robust estimators of regressions is a rather difficult problem. In fact, different choices of estimators, robust or not, might lead to radically different estimates of slopes and intercepts. Consider the following linear regression model:

$$Y = \beta_0 + \sum_{i=1}^{N} \beta_i X_i + \varepsilon$$

If data are organized in matrix form as usual,

$$\mathbf{Y} = \begin{pmatrix} Y_1 \\ \vdots \\ Y_T \end{pmatrix}, \mathbf{X} = \begin{pmatrix} 1 & X_{11} & \cdots & X_{N1} \\ \vdots & \vdots & \ddots & \vdots \\ 1 & X_{1T} & \cdots & X_{NT} \end{pmatrix}, \beta = \begin{pmatrix} \beta_1 \\ \vdots \\ \beta_N \end{pmatrix}, \varepsilon = \begin{pmatrix} \varepsilon_1 \\ \vdots \\ \varepsilon_T \end{pmatrix}$$

then the regression equation takes the form,

$$\mathbf{Y} = \mathbf{X}\beta + \varepsilon$$

The standard nonrobust LS estimation of regression parameters minimizes the sum of squared residuals,

$$\sum_{i=1}^{T} \varepsilon_t^2 = \sum_{i=1}^{T} \left(Y_i - \sum_{j=0}^{N} \beta_{ij} X_{ij} \right)^2$$

or, equivalently, solves the system of $N + 1$ equations,

$$\sum_{i=1}^{T} \left(Y_i - \sum_{j=0}^{N} \beta_{ij} X_{ij} \right) X_{ij} = 0$$

or, in matrix notation, $X'X\beta = X'Y$. The solution of this system is

$$\hat{\beta} = (X'X)^{-1} X'Y$$

The fitted values (i.e, the LS estimates of the expectations) of the Y are

$$\hat{Y} = X(X'X)^{-1} X'Y = HY$$

The H matrix is called the *hat matrix* because it puts a hat on, that is, it computes the expectation $\hat{Y}$ of the Y. The hat matrix H is a symmetric $T \times T$ projection matrix; that is, the following relationship holds: $HH = H$. The matrix H has N eigenvalues equal to 1 and $T - N$ eigenvalues equal to 0. Its diagonal elements, $h_i \equiv h_{ii}$ satisfy:

$$0 \le h_i \le 1$$

and its trace (i.e., the sum of its diagonal elements) is equal to N:

$$tr(H) = N$$

Under the assumption that the errors are independent and identically distributed with mean zero and variance σ^2, it can be demonstrated that the $\hat{Y}$ are consistent, that is, $\hat{Y} \to E(Y)$ in probability when the sample becomes infinite if and only if $h = \max(h_i) \to 0$. Points where the h_i have large values are called *leverage points*. It can be demonstrated that the presence of leverage points signals that there are observations that might have a decisive influence on the estimation of the regression parameters. A rule of thumb, reported in Huber,[10] suggests that values $h_i \le 0.2$ are safe, values $0.2 \le h_i \le 0.5$ require careful attention, and higher values are to be avoided.

---

[10] Huber, *Robust Statistics*.

Thus far we have discussed methods to ascertain regression robustness. Identifying robust estimators of regressions is a rather difficult problem. In fact, different choices of estimators, robust or not, might lead to radically different estimates of slopes and intercepts.

Robust Regressions Based on M-Estimators

Let us first discuss how to make *robust regressions* with Huber M-estimators. The LS estimators $\hat{\beta} = (X'X)^{-1}X'Y$ are M-estimators but are not robust. We can generalize LS seeking to minimize

$$J = \sum_{i=1}^{T} \rho\left(Y_i - \sum_{j=0}^{N} \beta_{ij}X_{ij}\right)$$

by solving the set of $N + 1$ simultaneous equations

$$\sum_{i=1}^{T} \psi\left(Y_i - \sum_{j=0}^{N} \beta_{ij}X_{ij}\right)X_{ij} = 0$$

where

$$\psi = \frac{\partial \rho}{\partial \beta}$$

Robust Regressions Based on W-Estimators

W-estimators offer an alternative form of M-estimators. They are obtained by rewriting M-estimators as follows:

$$\psi\left(Y_i - \sum_{j=0}^{N} \beta_{ij}X_{ij}\right) = w\left(Y_i - \sum_{j=0}^{N} \beta_{ij}X_{ij}\right)\left(Y_i - \sum_{j=0}^{N} \beta_{ij}X_{ij}\right)$$

Hence the $N + 1$ simultaneous equations become

$$w\left(Y_i - \sum_{j=0}^{N} \beta_{ij}X_{ij}\right)\left(Y_i - \sum_{j=0}^{N} \beta_{ij}X_{ij}\right) = 0$$

or in matrix form

$$\mathbf{X}'\mathbf{WX}\beta = \mathbf{X}'\mathbf{WY}$$

where $\mathbf{W}$ is a diagonal matrix.

The previous is not a linear system because the weighting function is in general a nonlinear function of the data. A typical approach is to determine iteratively the weights through an iterative *reweighted least squares* (RLS) procedure. Clearly the iterative procedure depends numerically on the choice of the weighting functions. Two commonly used choices are the *Huber weighting function* $w_H(e)$, defined as

$$w_H(e) = \begin{cases} 1 & \text{for } |e| \le k \\ k/|e| & \text{for } |e| > k \end{cases}$$

and the *Tukey bisquare weighting function* $w_T(e)$, defined as

$$w_T(e) = \begin{cases} \left(1 - (e/k)^2\right)^2 & \text{for } |e| \le k \\ 0 & \text{for } |e| > k \end{cases}$$

where k is a tuning constant often set at $1.345 \times$ (Standard deviation of errors) for the Huber function and $k = 4.6853 \times$ (Standard deviation of errors) for the Tukey function.

Illustration

Now we illustrate the robustness of regression with an example. Let's create an equally weighted index with the daily returns of 234 Japanese firms. Note that this index is created only for the sake of this illustration; no econometric meaning is attached to this index. The daily returns for the index for period 1986 to 2005 are shown in Exhibit 7.2.

Now suppose that we want to estimate the regression of Nippon Oil on this index; that is, we want to estimate the following regression:

$$R_{NO} = \beta_0 + \beta_1 R_{\text{Index}} + \text{Errors}$$

Estimation with the standard least squares method yields the following regression parameters:

R^2: 0.1349
Adjusted R^2: 0.1346
Standard deviation of errors: 0.0213

EXHIBIT 7.2   Daily Returns of the Japan Index, 1986–2005

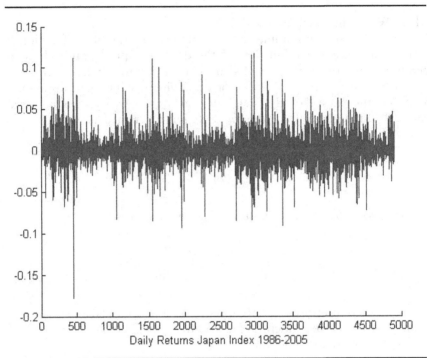

Daily Returns Japan Index 1986-2005

	beta	t-statistic	p-value
β_0	0.0000	0.1252	0.9003
β_1	0.4533	27.6487	0.0000

When we examined the diagonal of the hat matrix, we found the following results

Maximum leverage = 0.0189
Mean leverage   = $4.0783e{-}004$

suggesting that there is no dangerous point. Robust regression can be applied; that is, there is no need to change the regression design. We applied robust regression using the Huber and Tukey weighting functions with the following parameters:

Huber ($k = 1.345 \times$ Standard deviation)

and

$$\text{Tukey } (k = 4.685 \times \text{Standard deviation})$$

The robust regression estimate with Huber weighting functions yields the following results:

R^2 = 0.1324
Adjusted R^2 = 0.1322
Weight parameter = 0.0287
Number of iterations = 39

	beta	t-statistic	Change in p-value
β_0	−0.000706	−0.767860	0.442607
β_1	0.405633	7.128768	0.000000

The robust regression estimate with Tukey weighting functions yields the following results:

R^2 = 0.1315
Adjusted R^2 = 0.1313
Weight parameter = 0.0998
Number of iterations = 88

	beta	t-statistic	Change in p-value
β_0	−0.000879	−0.632619	0.527012
β_1	0.400825	4.852742	0.000001

We can conclude that all regression slope estimates are highly significant; the intercept estimates are insignificant in all cases. There is a considerable difference between the robust (0.40) and the nonrobust (0.45) regression coefficient.

Robust Estimation of Covariance and Correlation Matrices

Variance-covariance matrices are central to modern portfolio theory. In fact, the estimation of the variance-covariance matrices is critical for portfolio management and asset allocation. Suppose returns are a multivariate random vector written as

$$r_t = \mu + \varepsilon_t$$

The random disturbances ε_t is characterized by a covariance matrix Ω.

$$\begin{aligned} \rho_{X,Y} &= \mathrm{Corr}(X, Y) \\ &= \frac{\mathrm{Cov}(X, Y)}{\sqrt{\mathrm{Var}(X)\mathrm{Var}(Y)}} = \frac{\sigma_{X,Y}}{\sigma_X \sigma_Y} \end{aligned}$$

The correlation coefficient fully represents the dependence structure of multivariate normal distribution. More in general, the correlation coefficient is a valid measure of dependence for elliptical distributions (i.e., distributions that are constants on ellipsoids). In other cases, different measures of dependence are needed (e.g., copula functions).[11]

The empirical covariance between two variables is defined as

$$\hat{\sigma}_{X,Y} = \frac{1}{N-1} \sum_{i=1}^{N} (X_i - \bar{X})(Y_i - \bar{Y})$$

where

$$\bar{X} = \frac{1}{N} \sum_{i=1}^{N} X_i, \ \bar{Y} = \frac{1}{N} \sum_{i=1}^{N} Y_i$$

are the empirical means of the variables.

The empirical correlation coefficient is the empirical covariance normalized with the product of the respective empirical standard deviations:

$$\hat{\rho}_{X,Y} = \frac{\hat{\sigma}_{X,Y}}{\hat{\sigma}_X \hat{\sigma}_Y}$$

The empirical standard deviations are defined as

$$\hat{\sigma}_X = \frac{1}{N}\sqrt{\sum_{i=1}^{N} (X_i - \bar{X})^2}, \ \hat{\sigma}_Y = \frac{1}{N}\sqrt{\sum_{i=1}^{N} (Y_i - \bar{Y})^2}$$

---

[11] Paul Embrechts, Filip Lindskog, and Alexander McNeil, "Modelling Dependence with Copulas and Applications to Risk Management," in S. T. Rachev (ed.), *Handbook of Heavy Tailed Distributions in Finance* (Amsterdam: Elsevier/North-Holland, 2003), pp. 329–384.

Empirical covariances and correlations are not robust as they are highly sensitive to tails or outliers. Robust estimators of covariances and/or correlations are insensitive to the tails. However, it does not make sense to robustify correlations if dependence is not linear.[12]

Different strategies for robust estimation of covariances exist; among them are:

- Robust estimation of pairwise covariances
- Robust estimation of elliptic distributions

Here we discuss only the robust estimation of pairwise covariances. As detailed in Huber,[13] the following identity holds:

$$cov(X, Y) = \frac{1}{4ab}[var(aX + bY) - var(aX - bY)]$$

Assume S is a robust scale functional:

$$S(aX + b) = |a|S(X)$$

A robust covariance is defined as

$$C(X, Y) = \frac{1}{4ab}[S(aX + bY)^2 - S(aX - bY)^2]$$

Choose

$$a = \frac{1}{S(X)}, b = \frac{1}{S(Y)}$$

A robust correlation coefficient is defined as

$$c = \frac{1}{4}[S(aX + bY)^2 - S(aX - bY)^2]$$

---

[12] There are several related concepts of robustness of covariance matrices. In particular, as large covariance matrices are very noisy, we need to reduce their dimensionality in order to separate information from noise. In this chapter, we do not discuss methods for dimensionality reduction such as factor models.

[13] Huber, *Robust Statistics*.

The robust correlation coefficient thus defined is not confined to stay in the interval $[-1,+1]$. For this reason the following alternative definition is often used:

$$r = \frac{S(aX+bY)^2 - S(aX-bY)^2}{S(aX+bY)^2 + S(aX-bY)^2}$$

CONFIDENCE INTERVALS

In this section, we introduce a concept widely used in robust optimization: confidence intervals. *Confidence intervals* are intervals around estimates; they evaluate the level of reliability of statistical estimates. Confidence intervals contain the true level of a parameter with a given probability (the confidence level), assuming certain distributional assumptions. The latter statement is critical: We cannot construct the confidence interval for an estimate if we do not have an idea of the distribution from which the sample is drawn. For example, if data is normally distributed, we can easily compute a confidence interval for the mean but if the data follows an α-stable distribution with $\alpha < 1$, for example, the confidence interval of the mean would be infinite.

The reasoning behind confidence intervals lends itself to many misconceptions. We have already pointed out that establishing confidence intervals entails the knowledge of the underlying distribution of the data. If we cannot make a reasonable prior guess about the distribution of the population, we cannot establish a confidence interval for our estimates. Another important point is that a confidence interval is not an event with an associated probability. For example, the statement that a given parameter ϑ will fall in the interval $(\vartheta_1,\vartheta_2)$ at a 95% confidence level *does not mean* that there is a 0.95 probability that ϑ will fall in a *given* interval $(\vartheta_1,\vartheta_2)$. In fact, ϑ is not a random variable but it is the true parameter of the population. It means that there is an interval $(\vartheta_1,\vartheta_2)$ around any estimate that contains the true value of the parameter with probability 95%. It is also easy to confuse confidence intervals with Bayesian concepts. Let's now introduce the precise notion of confidence intervals step by step.

First, consider a population with a given distribution and a population parameter ϑ. Consider now an estimator $\hat{\vartheta}$ of ϑ. For example, given a sample X_i, $i = 1, 2, \ldots, N$ consider the empirical average $\overline{X}$ as an estimator of the population mean μ. The parameter ϑ is not a random variable but a well-defined, fixed number. Any estimator $\hat{\vartheta}$ of ϑ is a function of the sample data. As such, it is a random variable characterized by a distribution. If we know the population distribution we can establish, for samples of any size, the probability that $\hat{\vartheta}$ falls in any given interval. For instance, if we know the population distribution we can establish the probability that the empirical average $\overline{X}$ of an arbitrary sample of size N falls in a given interval around the population's mean μ. That is, when a distribution is given, we know the true value of all parameters and it is meaningful to consider the probability that an estimator of a parameter falls in a specific confidence interval.

However, in general we know neither the distribution nor the correct value of the parameter of interest ϑ; if we did, the estimation process would be a futile exercise. We can only observe an estimated value $\hat{\vartheta}$ of the parameter ϑ. For example, we observe the empirical average $\overline{X}$ of a sample as an estimator of the population's mean μ. If we do not have any additional information on the population, we cannot draw any conclusion. For example, we cannot even determine if the true population mean is finite.

Suppose now that we know the general form of the population distribution in function of the parameter ϑ. Given ϑ, an estimate $\hat{\vartheta}$ is a random variable and, for any number a, the interval $(\hat{\vartheta} - a, \hat{\vartheta} + a)$ is a random interval. It is therefore meaningful to compute the probability that any given interval $(\hat{\vartheta} - a, \hat{\vartheta} + a)$ includes ϑ.

Suppose that this probability $P(\hat{\vartheta} - a < \vartheta < \hat{\vartheta} + a | \vartheta)$ does not depend on ϑ but only on a. Functions of sample data and parameters whose distribution is independent of population parameters are called *pivotal quantities* or, simply, *pivotals*. We can then determine a value a independent of ϑ such that $P(\hat{\vartheta} - a < \vartheta < \hat{\vartheta} + a | \vartheta)$ equals a given value p. We say that the interval $(\hat{\vartheta} - a < \vartheta < \hat{\vartheta} + a)$ is a *confidence interval at the confidence level p* (or $100p\%$). Note that the confidence interval is a random interval around an estimate. We do not say that the true value ϑ falls in a given interval but that a specific interval around any estimate will include the true value ϑ with a fixed probability p.

For example, suppose we know that a population is normally distributed with unknown mean μ and known standard deviation σ. The assumption that the mean is unknown but the standard deviation is known is very unrealistic but it is helpful to explain the concepts. The standard deviation of an independent sample of N elements is $\sigma/\sqrt{N}$. Let us express the number a in terms of number of standard deviations: $a = k(\sigma/\sqrt{N})$. Given μ, we can determine the probability that any interval $\overline{X} - a < \mu < \overline{X} + a$ includes μ. This is the probability that the true value of the mean falls within a number of standard deviations from the estimate

$$P\left(\overline{X} - k(\sigma/\sqrt{N}) < \mu < \overline{X} + k(\sigma/\sqrt{N})|\mu\right)$$

For a normal distribution, this probability depends only on k and not on μ. For $k = 2$, the probability P is approximately 95%, that is, there is a 95% probability that the true mean falls within two standard deviations from any estimate.

The concept of confidence intervals can perhaps be better understood in terms of relative frequencies. Suppose we want to estimate a population parameter ϑ with an estimator $\hat{\vartheta}$. Suppose that we have been able to determine that the true parameter ϑ will fall in the confidence interval $(\hat{\vartheta} - a < \vartheta < \hat{\vartheta} + a)$ at a 95% confidence level. This means that if we repeat the estimation process many times, in approximately 95% of the experiments the true parameter ϑ will fall in the interval $(\hat{\vartheta} - a < \vartheta < \hat{\vartheta} + a)$ around each estimator. Obviously we cannot identify the 95% of cases where the true parameters fall within the confidence interval since we do not know the true parameter value. Nevertheless, this idea helps get a better intuitive understanding of the concept.

The assumption that the probability $P(\hat{\vartheta} - a < \vartheta < \hat{\vartheta} + a|\vartheta)$ does not depend on ϑ but only on a is not necessarily true but must be verified for each distribution. In other words, we cannot establish confidence intervals for every distribution. We now illustrate the above concepts computing the confidence intervals for the mean and for the correlation coefficients assuming normally distributed variables.

Confidence intervals for the Mean

Suppose X_i, $i = 1, 2, \ldots, N$ are N independent samples from a population which is normally distributed with mean μ and standard deviation σ. Suppose that both μ and σ are unknown. Therefore, both the mean and the standard deviation have to be estimated. Suppose that we estimate the mean and the standard deviation with the empirical average and the empirical standard deviation

$$\hat{\mu} = \overline{X} = \frac{\sum\limits_{i=1}^{N} X_i}{N}$$

$$\hat{\sigma}^2 = S^2 - \frac{\sum\limits_{i=1}^{N} (X_i - \overline{X})^2}{N-1}$$

The mean of N independent samples is normally distributed with standard deviation $S/\sqrt{N}$. Given μ, we have to evaluate the probability

$$P\left(\overline{X} - k(S/\sqrt{N}) < \mu < \overline{X} + k(S/\sqrt{N})\,|\,\mu\right)$$

We can replace the variable X with the standardized variable

$$Z = \frac{\overline{X} - \mu}{S\sqrt{N}}$$

The variable Z is a pivotal quantity which has a Student's t distribution with $N - 1$ degrees of freedom. The distribution of Z does not depend on the population mean and standard deviation. We can determine the values a such that

$$P(-a < Z < a) = 1 - \alpha$$

or equivalently,

$$P\left(\overline{X} - k(S/\sqrt{N}) < \mu < \overline{X} + k(S/\sqrt{N})\,|\,\mu\right) = 1 - \alpha$$

Confidence Interval for the Mean and the Variance of a Gaussian Distribution

Suppose X_i, $i = 1, 2, \ldots, N$ are N independent samples extracted from the Gaussian law $N(\mu,\sigma)$ with mean μ and variance σ^2. We want to establish a bidimensional confidence interval for the bidimensional parameter (μ,σ). The Theorem of Fisher establishes that the empirical mean and the empirical average are independent variables. The empirical mean

$$\hat{\mu} = \overline{X} = \frac{\sum\limits_{i=1}^{N} X_i}{N}$$

is distributed as a normal variable

$$N\left(\mu, \frac{\sigma}{\sqrt{N}}\right)$$

while the quantity

$$(N-1)\frac{S^2}{\hat{\sigma}^2}$$

where S is the empirical variance, is distributed as chi-square variable $\chi^2(N-1)$. The joint interval of confidence of level $1-\alpha$ for the two quantities μ, σ is given by

$$\frac{\displaystyle\sum_{i=1}^{N}(X_i-\mu)^2}{\chi^2_{1-\frac{\alpha}{2}}(N-1)} \leq \sigma^2 \leq \frac{\displaystyle\sum_{i=1}^{N}(X_i-\mu)^2}{\chi^2_{\frac{\alpha}{2}}(N-1)}$$

$$\frac{N(\overline{X}-\mu)^2}{\sigma^2} \leq u^2$$

where u is the quantile $1-\alpha/2$ of the standard normal distribution. We established the latter confidence interval in the previous section.

Confidence Intervals for the Correlation Coefficients

Given two random variables X and Y, the correlation coefficient ρ is a measure of the strength of their linear dependence. If the joint distribution of the random variables X and Y is normal or at least elliptical, then the two variables are linearly dependent and the correlation coefficient captures their dependency. However, if the dependency of the two variables is not linear, the correlation coefficient may mathematically not be meaningful. The correlation coefficient is defined as follows:

$$\rho_{XY} = \rho_{YX} = \frac{E[(X-E(X))(Y-E(Y))]}{\sqrt{E(X-E(X))^2 E(Y-E(Y))^2}}$$

The well-known estimator $\hat{\rho}$ of the correlation coefficient is given by the following formula:

$$\hat{\rho}_{XY} = \hat{\rho}_{YX} = r = \frac{\sum\limits_{i=1}^{N}\left(X_i - \sum\limits_{j=1}^{N}X_j\right)\left(Y_i - \sum\limits_{j=1}^{N}Y_j\right)}{\sqrt{\sum\limits_{i=1}^{N}\left(X_i - \sum\limits_{j=1}^{N}X_j\right)^2\sum\limits_{i=1}^{N}\left(Y_i - \sum\limits_{j=1}^{N}Y_j\right)^2}}$$

The estimated correlation coefficient depends on the sample. Given the number of observations N, the distribution of r for a small sample is not known. However, Fisher has demonstrated that the distribution of the following *Fisher z transform* rapidly becomes normal as the sample size N increases

$$z = \frac{1}{2}\log\left(\frac{1+r}{1-r}\right)$$

The approximate variance of z is independent of r and is given by

$$\sigma_z^2 = \frac{1}{N-3}$$

In order to compute a confidence interval for r, we must first compute a confidence interval for z,

$$\zeta_L = z - z_{\left(1-\frac{\alpha}{2}\right)}\sqrt{\frac{1}{N-3}}$$

$$\zeta_U = z + z_{\left(1-\frac{\alpha}{2}\right)}\sqrt{\frac{1}{N-3}}$$

and then recover the confidence interval for r,

$$r_L = \tanh(\zeta_L) = \frac{\exp(2\zeta_L) - 1}{\exp(2\zeta_L) + 1}$$

$$r_U = \tanh(\zeta_U) = \frac{\exp(2\zeta_U) - 1}{\exp(2\zeta_U) + 1}$$

SUMMARY

- Robust statistics addresses the problem of obtaining estimates that are less sensitive to small changes in the basic assumptions of the statistical models used. It is also useful for separating the contribution of the tails from the contribution of the body of the data.
- An estimator is said to be resistant if it is insensitive to changes in one single observation. An indifference curve or indifference functions allows us to understand what happens if we add a new observation to a large sample.
- Important concepts in applying robust statistics are the breakdown bound (or breakdown point), the rejection point, the gross error sensitivity, the local shift sensitivity measure, M-estimators, L-estimators, R-estimators, least median of squares, least trimmed of squares estimator, and reweighted least squares estimator
- Resistant estimators of the center include the trimmed mean, the Winsorized mean, and the median. Robust estimators of the spread include the median absolute deviation, the interquartile range, the mean absolute deviation, and the Winsorized standard deviation.
- Identifying robust estimators of regressions is a rather difficult problem. Different choices of estimators, robust or not, might lead to radically different estimates of slopes and intercepts. Different strategies for robust estimation of covariances include robust estimation of pairwise covariances and robust estimation of elliptic distributions.

Robust Frameworks for Estimation: Shrinkage, Bayesian Approaches, and the Black-Litterman Model

I n Chapter 6, we discussed the estimation of expected returns and covariances of stock returns and saw that they are subject to estimation error. Investment policies constructed using inferior estimates, such as sample means and sample covariance matrices, typically perform very poorly in practice. Besides introducing spurious changes in portfolio weights each time the portfolio is rebalanced, this undesirable property also results in unnecessary turnover and increased transaction costs. These phenomena are not necessarily a sign that portfolio optimization does not work, but rather that the modern portfolio theory framework is very sensitive to the accuracy of inputs.

There are different ways to address this issue. On the estimation side, one can try to produce robust estimates of the input parameters for the optimization problems. This is most often achieved by using estimators that are less sensitive to outliers, and possibly, other sampling errors, such as Bayesian and shrinkage estimators. On the modeling side, one can constrain portfolio weights, use portfolio resampling, or apply robust or stochastic optimization techniques to specify scenarios or ranges of values for parameters estimated from data, thus incorporating uncertainty into the optimization process itself.[1] While this chapter

---

[1] Interestingly, some new results suggest that the two approaches are not necessarily disjoint, and in some cases may lead to the same end result; see Bernd Scherer, "How Different Is Robust Optimization Really?" forthcoming in the *Journal of Asset Management*.

will provide a brief review of all approaches, it will focus on robust estimation techniques. Resampling and robust optimization are covered in more detail in Chapter 12.

The outline of the chapter is as follows. First, we provide a general overview of some of the common problems encountered in mean-variance optimization before we turn our attention to shrinkage estimators for expected returns and the covariance matrix. Within the context of Bayesian estimation, we focus on the Black-Litterman model. We derive the model using so-called "mixed estimation" from classical econometrics. Introducing a simple cross-sectional momentum strategy, we then show how we can combine this strategy with market equilibrium using the Black-Litterman model in the mean-variance framework to rebalance the portfolio on a monthly basis. Finally, we discuss methods for calculating confidence intervals for estimates.

PRACTICAL PROBLEMS ENCOUNTERED IN MEAN-VARIANCE OPTIMIZATION

The simplicity and the intuitive appeal of portfolio construction using modern portfolio theory have attracted significant attention both in academia and in practice. Yet, despite considerable effort, it took many years until portfolio managers started using modern portfolio theory for managing real money. Unfortunately, in real world applications there are many problems with it, and portfolio optimization is still considered by many practitioners to be difficult to apply. In this section we consider some of the typical problems encountered in mean-variance optimization. In particular, we elaborate on: (1) the sensitivity to estimation error; (2) the effects of uncertainty in the inputs in the optimization process; and (3) the large data requirement necessary for accurately estimating the inputs for the portfolio optimization framework. We start by considering an example illustrating the effect of estimation error.

Example: The True, Estimated, and Actual Efficient Frontiers

Broadie introduced the terms *true frontier*, *estimated frontier*, and *actual frontier* to refer to the efficient frontiers computed using the true expected returns (unobservable), estimated expected returns, and true expected returns of the portfolios on the estimated frontier, respectively.[2] In this example, we refer to the frontier computed using the true, but unknown,

---

[2] Mark Broadie, "Computing Efficient Frontiers Using Estimated Parameters," *Annals of Operations Research: Special Issue on Financial Engineering* 45, nos. 1–4 (December 1993), pp. 21–58.

expected returns as the true frontier. Similarly, we refer to the frontier computed using estimates of the expected returns and the true covariance matrix as the estimated frontier. Finally, we define the actual frontier as follows: We take the portfolios on the estimated frontier and then calculate their expected returns using the true expected returns. Since we are using the true covariance matrix, the variance of a portfolio on the estimated frontier is the same as the variance on the actual frontier.

From these definitions, we observe that the actual frontier will always lie below the true frontier. The estimated frontier can lie anywhere with respect to the other frontiers. However, if the errors in the expected return estimates have a mean of zero, then the estimated frontier will lie above the true frontier with extremely high probability, particularly when the investment universe is large. We look at two cases considered by Ceria and Stubbs:[3]

1. Using the covariance matrix and expected return vector from Idzorek,[4] they randomly generate a time series of normally distributed returns and computed the average to use as estimates of expected returns. Using the expected-return estimate calculated in this fashion and the true covariance matrix, they generate an estimated efficient frontier of risk versus expected return where the portfolios were subject to no-shorting constraints and the standard budget constraint that the sum of portfolio weights is one. Similarly, Ceria and Stubbs compute the true efficient frontier using the *original* covariance matrix and expected return vector. Finally, they construct the actual frontier by computing the expected return and risk of the portfolios on the estimated frontier with the true covariance and expected return values. These three frontiers are illustrated in Exhibit 8.1.

2. Using the same estimate of expected returns, Ceria and Stubbs also generate risk versus expected return where active holdings of the assets are constrained to be ±3% of the benchmark holding of each asset. These frontiers are illustrated in Exhibit 8.2.

We observe that the estimated frontiers significantly overestimate the expected return for any risk level in both types of frontiers. More importantly, we note that the actual frontier lies far below the true frontier in

---

[3] We are grateful to Axioma Inc. for providing us with this example. Previously, it has appeared in Sebastian Ceria and Robert A. Stubbs, "Incorporating Estimation Errors into Portfolio Selection: Robust Portfolio Construction," Axioma, Inc., 2005.
[4] Thomas M. Idzorek, "A Step-By-Step Guide to the Black-Litterman Model: Incorporating User-Specified Confidence Levels," Research Paper, Ibbotson Associates, Chicago, 2005.

EXHIBIT 8.1 Markowitz Efficient Frontiers

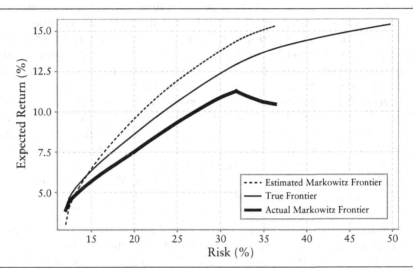

Source: Figure 2 in Sebastian Ceria and Robert A. Stubbs, "Incorporating Estimation Errors into Portfolio Selection: Robust Portfolio Construction," Axioma, Inc., 2005, p. 6. This figure is reprinted with the permission of Axioma, Inc.

EXHIBIT 8.2 Markowitz Benchmark-Relative Efficient Frontiers

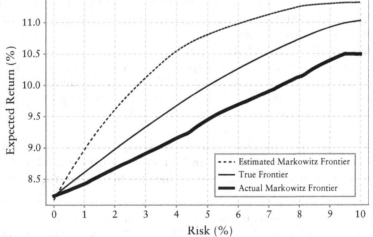

Source: Figure 3 in Sebastian Ceria and Robert A. Stubbs, "Incorporating Estimation Errors into Portfolio Selection: Robust Portfolio Construction," Axioma, Inc., 2005, p. 7. This figure is reprinted with the permission of Axioma, Inc.

both cases. This shows that the "optimal" mean-variance portfolio is not necessarily a good portfolio, that is, it is not "mean-variance efficient." Since the true expected return is not observable, we do not know how far the actual expected return may be from the expected return of the mean-variance optimal portfolio, and we end up holding an inferior portfolio.

Sensitivity to Estimation Error

In a portfolio optimization context, securities with large expected returns and low standard deviations will be overweighted and conversely, securities with low expected returns and high standard deviations will be underweighted. Therefore, large estimation errors in expected returns and/or variances/covariances introduce errors in the optimized portfolio weights. For this reason, people often cynically refer to optimizers as "error maximizers."

Uncertainty from estimation error in expected returns tends to have more influence than in the covariance matrix in a mean-variance optimization.[5] The relative importance depends on the investor's risk aversion, but as a general rule of thumb, errors in the expected returns are about 10 times more important than errors in the covariance matrix, and errors in the variances are about twice as important as errors in the covariances.[6] As the risk tolerance increases, the relative impact of estimation errors in the expected returns becomes even more important. Conversely, as the risk tolerance decreases, the impact of errors in expected returns relative to errors in the covariance matrix becomes smaller. From this simple "rule," it follows that the major focus should be on providing good estimates for the expected returns, followed by the variances.

Constraining Portfolio Weights

Several studies have shown that the inclusion of constraints in the mean-variance optimization problem leads to better out-of-sample per-

---

[5] See, Michael J. Best and Robert R. Grauer, "The Analytics of Sensitivity Analysis for Mean-Variance Portfolio Problems," *International Review of Financial Analysis* 1, no. 1 (1992), pp. 17–37; and Michael J. Best and Robert R. Grauer, "On the Sensitivity of Mean-Variance-Efficient Portfolios to Changes in Assets Means: Some Analytical and Computational Results," *Review of Financial Studies* 4, no. 2 (1991), pp. 315–342.

[6] Vijay K. Chopra and William T. Ziemba, "The Effect of Errors in Means, Variances, and Covariances on Optimal Portfolio Choice," *Journal of Portfolio Management* 19, no. 2 (1993), pp. 6–11; and Jarl G. Kallberg and William T. Ziemba, "Misspecification in Portfolio Selection Problems," in G. Bamberg and K. Spremann (eds.), *Risk and Capital: Lecture Notes in Economics and Mathematical Systems* (New York: Springer, 1984).

formance.[7] Practitioners often use no short-selling constraints or upper and lower bounds for each security to avoid overconcentration in a few assets. Gupta and Eichhorn suggest that constraining portfolio weights may also assist in containing volatility, increase realized efficiency, and decrease downside risk or shortfall probability.[8]

Jagannathan and Ma provide a theoretical justification for these observations.[9] Specifically, they show that the no short-selling constraints are equivalent to reducing the estimated asset covariances, whereas upper bounds are equivalent to increasing the corresponding covariances. For example, stocks that have high covariance with other stocks tend to receive negative portfolio weights. Therefore, when their covariance is decreased (which is equivalent to the effect of imposing no short-selling constraints), these negative weights disappear. Similarly, stocks that have low covariances with other stocks tend to get overweighted. Hence, by increasing the corresponding covariances the impact of these overweighted stocks decrease.

Furthermore, Monte Carlo experiments performed by Jagannathan and Ma indicate that when no-short-sell constraints are imposed, the sample covariance matrix has about the same performance (as measured by the global minimum variance portfolio) as a covariance matrix estimator constructed from a factor structure.

Care needs to be taken when imposing constraints for robustness and stability purposes. For example, if the constraints used are too "tight," they will completely determine the portfolio allocation—not the forecasts.

Instead of providing ad hoc upper and lower bounds on each security, as proposed by Bouchaud, Potters, and Aguilar one can use so-called "diversification indicators" that measure the concentration of the portfolio.[10] These diversification indicators can be used as constraints in the portfolio construction phase to limit the concentration to individual

---

[7] See, for example, Peter A. Frost and James E. Savarino, "For Better Performance: Constrain Portfolio Weights," *Journal of Portfolio Management* 15, no. 1 (1988), pp. 29–34; Vijay K. Chopra, "Mean-Variance Revisited: Near-Optimal Portfolios and Sensitivity to Input Variations," Russell Research Commentary, December 1991; and Robert R. Grauer, and Frederick C. Shen, "Do Constraints Improve Portfolio Performance?" *Journal of Banking and Finance* 24, no. 8 (August 2000), pp. 1253–1274.
[8] Francis Gupta and David Eichhorn, "Mean-Variance Optimization for Practitioners of Asset Allocation," Chapter 4 in Frank J. Fabozzi (ed.), *Handbook of Portfolio Management* (Hoboken, NJ: John Wiley & Sons, 1998).
[9] Ravi Jagannathan and Tongshu Ma, "Risk Reduction in Large Portfolios: Why Imposing the Wrong Constraints Helps," *Journal of Finance* 58, no. 4 (2003), pp. 1651–1683.
[10] Jean-Philippe Bouchaud, Marc Potters, and Jean-Pierre Aguilar, "Missing Information and Asset Allocation," working paper, Science & Finance, Capital Fund Management, 1997.

securities. The authors demonstrate that these indicators are related to the information content of the portfolio in the sense of information theory.[11] For example, a very concentrated portfolio corresponds to a large information content (as we would only choose a very concentrated allocation if our information about future price fluctuations is "perfect"), whereas an equally weighted portfolio would indicate low information content (as we would not put "all the eggs in one basket" if our information about future price fluctuations is poor).

Importance of Sensitivity Analysis

In practice, in order to minimize dramatic changes due to estimation error, it is advisable to perform sensitivity analysis. For example, one can study the results of small changes or perturbations to the inputs from an efficient portfolio selected from a mean-variance optimization. If the portfolio calculated from the perturbed inputs drastically differ from the first one, this might indicate a problem. The perturbation can also be performed on a security by security basis in order to identify those securities that are the most sensitive. The objective of this sensitivity analysis is to identify a set of security weights that will be close to efficient under several different sets of plausible inputs.

Issues with Highly Correlated Assets

The inclusion of highly correlated securities (0.7 or higher) is another major cause for instability in the mean-variance optimization framework. For example, high correlation coefficients among common asset classes are one reason why real estate is popular in "optimized" portfolios. Real estate is one of the few asset classes that has a low correlation with other common asset classes. But real estate does in general not have the liquidity necessary in order to implement these portfolios and may therefore fail to deliver the return promised by the real estate indices.

The problem of high correlations typically becomes worse when the correlation matrix is estimated from historical data. Specifically, when the correlation matrix is estimated over a slightly different period, correlations may change, but the impact on the new portfolio weights may be drastic. In these situations, it may be a good idea to resort to a shrinkage estimator or a factor model to model covariances and correlations.

---

[11] The relationship to information theory is based upon the premise that the diversification indicators are generalized entropies. See, Evaldo M.F. Curado and Constantino Tsallis, "Generalized Statistical Mechanics: Connection with Thermodynamics," *Journal of Physics A: Mathematical and General* 24, no. 2 (January 1991), pp. L69–L72, 1991.

Incorporating Uncertainty in the Inputs into the Portfolio Allocation Process

In the classical mean-variance optimization problem, the expected returns and the covariance matrix of returns are uncertain and have to be estimated. After the estimation of these quantities, the portfolio optimization problem is solved as a deterministic problem—completely ignoring the uncertainty in the inputs. However, it makes sense for the uncertainty of expected returns and risk to enter into the optimization process, thus creating a more realistic model. Using point estimates of the expected returns and the covariance matrix of returns, and treating them as error-free in portfolio allocation, does not necessarily correspond to prudent investor behavior.

The investor would probably be more comfortable choosing a portfolio that would perform well under a number of different scenarios, thereby also attaining some protection from estimation risk and model risk. Obviously, to have some insurance in the event of less likely but more extreme cases (e.g., scenarios that are highly unlikely under the assumption that returns are normally distributed), the investor must be willing to give up some of the upside that would result under the more likely scenarios. Such an investor seeks a "robust" portfolio, that is, a portfolio that is assured against some worst-case model misspecification. The estimation process can be improved through robust statistical techniques such as shrinkage and Bayesian estimators discussed later in this chapter. However, jointly considering estimation risk and model risk in the financial decision-making process is becoming more important.

The estimation process frequently does not deliver a point forecast (that is, one single number), but a full distribution of expected returns. Recent approaches attempt to integrate estimation risk into the mean-variance framework by using the expected return distribution in the optimization. A simple approach is to sample from the return distribution and average the resulting portfolios (Monte Carlo approach). However, as a mean-variance problem has to be solved for each draw, this is computationally intensive for larger portfolios. In addition, the averaging does not guarantee that the resulting portfolio weights will satisfy all constraints.

Introduced in the late 1990s by Ben-Tal and Nemirovski[12] and El Ghaoui and Lebret,[13] the robust optimization framework is computa-

---

[12] Aharon Ben-Tal and Arkadi S. Nemirovski, "Robust Convex Optimization," *Mathematics of Operations Research* 23, no. 4 (1998), pp. 769–805; and Aharon Ben-Tal and Arkadi S. Nemirovski, "Robust Solutions to Uncertain Linear Programs," *Operations Research Letters* 25, no. 1 (1999), pp. 1–13.

[13] Laurent El Ghaoui and Herve Lebret, "Robust Solutions to Least-Squares Problems with Uncertain Data," *SIAM Journal Matrix Analysis with Applications* 18, no. 4 (1997), pp. 1035–1064.

tionally more efficient than the Monte Carlo approach. This development in optimization technology allows for efficiently solving the robust version of the mean-variance optimization problem in about the same time as the classical mean-variance optimization problem. The technique explicitly uses the distribution from the estimation process to find a robust portfolio in one single optimization. It thereby incorporates uncertainties of inputs into a deterministic framework. The classical portfolio optimization formulations such as the mean-variance portfolio selection problem, the maximum Sharpe ratio portfolio problem, and the value-at-risk (VaR) portfolio problem all have robust counterparts that can be solved in roughly the same amount of time as the original problem.[14] We describe Monte Carlo simulation techniques in Chapter 12, and the robust optimization frameworks in Chapters 10, 12, and 13.

Large Data Requirements

In classical mean-variance optimization, we need to provide estimates of the expected returns and covariances of all the securities in the investment universe considered. Typically, however, portfolio managers have reliable return forecasts for only a small subset of these assets. This is probably one of the major reasons why the mean-variance framework has not been adopted by practitioners in general. It is simply unreasonable for the portfolio manager to produce good estimates of all the inputs required in classical portfolio theory.

We will see later in this chapter that the Black-Litterman model provides a remedy in that it "blends" any views (this could be a forecast on just one or a few securities, or all them) the investor might have with the market equilibrium. When no views are present, the resulting Black-Litterman expected returns are just the expected returns consistent with the market equilibrium. Conversely, when the investor has views on some of the assets, the resulting expected returns deviate from market equilibrium.

SHRINKAGE ESTIMATION

It is well known since Stein's seminal work that biased estimators often yield better parameter estimates than their generally preferred unbiased counterparts.[15] In particular, it can be shown that if we consider the

---

[14] See, for example, Donald Goldfarb and Garud Iyengar, "Robust Portfolio Selection Problems," *Mathematics of Operations Research* 28, no. 1 (February 2003), pp. 1–38.
[15] Charles Stein, "Inadmissibility of the Usual Estimator for the Mean of Multivariate Normal Distribution," *Proceedings of the Third Berkeley Symposium on Mathematical Statistics and Probability* 1 (1956), pp. 197–206.

problem of estimating the mean of an N-dimensional multivariate normal variable $(N > 2)$, $\mathbf{X} \in N(\mu, \Sigma)$ with known covariance matrix Σ, the sample mean $\hat{\mu}$ is not the best estimator of the population mean μ in terms of the quadratic loss function

$$L(\mu, \hat{\mu}) = (\mu - \hat{\mu})'\Sigma^{-1}(\mu - \hat{\mu})$$

For example, the so-called *James-Stein shrinkage estimator*

$$\hat{\mu}_{JS} = (1 - w)\hat{\mu} + w\mu_0\iota$$

has a lower quadratic loss than the sample mean, where

$$w = \min\left(1, \frac{N - 2}{T(\hat{\mu} - \mu_0\iota)'\Sigma^{-1}(\hat{\mu} - \mu_0\iota)}\right)$$

and $\iota = [1, 1, \ldots, 1]'$. Moreover, T is the number of observations, and μ_0 is an *arbitrary* number. The vector $\mu_0\iota$ and the weight w are referred to as the shrinkage target and the shrinkage intensity (or shrinkage factor), respectively. Although there are some choices of μ_0 that are better than others, what is surprising with this result is that it could be *any* number! This fact is referred to as the *Stein paradox*.

In effect, shrinkage is a form of averaging different estimators. The shrinkage estimator typically consists of three components: (1) an estimator with little or no structure (like the sample mean above); (2) an estimator with a lot of structure (the shrinkage target); and (3) the shrinkage intensity. The shrinkage target is chosen with the following two requirements in mind. First, it should have only a small number of free parameters (robust and with a lot of structure). Second, it should have some of the basic properties in common with the unknown quantity being estimated. The shrinkage intensity can be chosen based on theoretical properties or simply by numerical simulation.

Probably the most well-known shrinkage estimator[16] used to estimate expected returns in the financial literature is the one proposed by Jorion,[17] where the shrinkage target is given by $\mu_g\iota$ with

---

[16] Many similar approaches have been proposed. For example, see Jobson and Korkie, "Putting Markowitz Theory to Work" and Frost and Savarino, "An Empirical Bayes Approach to Efficient Portfolio Selection."

[17] Philippe Jorion, "Bayes-Stein Estimation for Portfolio Analysis," *Journal of Financial and Quantitative Analysis* 21, no. 3 (September 1986), pp. 279–292.

$$\mu_g = \frac{\iota'\Sigma^{-1}\hat{\mu}}{\iota'\Sigma^{-1}\iota}$$

and

$$w = \frac{N+2}{N+2+T(\hat{\mu}-\mu_g\iota)'\Sigma^{-1}(\hat{\mu}-\mu_g\iota)}$$

We note that μ_g is the return on the minimum variance portfolio discussed in Chapter 2. Several studies document that for the mean-variance framework: (1) the variability in the portfolio weights from one period to the next decrease; and (2) the out-of-sample risk-adjusted performance improves significantly when using a shrinkage estimator as compared to the sample mean.[18]

We can also apply the shrinkage technique for covariance matrix estimation. This involves shrinking an unstructured covariance estimator toward a more structured covariance estimator. Typically the structured covariance estimator only has a few degrees of freedom (only a few nonzero eigenvalues) as motivated by Random Matrix Theory (see Chapter 6).

For example, as shrinkage targets, Ledoit and Wolf[19] suggest using the covariance matrix that follows from the single-factor model developed by Sharpe[20] or the constant correlation covariance matrix. In prac-

---

[18] See, for example, Michaud, "The Markowitz Optimization Enigma: Is 'Optimized' Optimal?" Jorion, "Bayesian and CAPM Estimators of the Means: Implications for Portfolio Selection," and Glen Larsen, Jr. and Bruce Resnick, "Parameter Estimation Techniques, Optimization Frequency, and Portfolio Return Enhancement," *Journal of Portfolio Management* 27, no. 4 (Summer 2001), pp. 27–34.

[19] Olivier Ledoit and Michael Wolf, "Improved Estimation of the Covariance Matrix of Stock Returns with an Application to Portfolio Selection," *Journal of Empirical Finance* 10, no. 5 (2003), pp. 603–621; and Olivier Ledoit and Michael Wolf, "Honey, I Shrunk the Sample Covariance Matrix," *Journal of Portfolio Management* 30, no. 4 (2004), pp. 110–119.

[20] William F. Sharpe, "A Simplified Model for Portfolio Analysis," *Management Science* 9, no. 2 (January 1963), pp. 277–293. Elton, Gruber, and Urich proposed the single factor model for purposes of covariance estimation in 1978. They show that this approach leads to: (1) better forecasts of the covariance matrix; (2) more stable portfolio allocations over time; and (3) more diversified portfolios. They also find that the average correlation coefficient is a good forecast of the future correlation matrix. See, Edwin J. Elton, Martin J. Gruber, and Thomas J. Urich, "Are Betas Best?" *Journal of Finance* 33, no. 5 (December 1978), pp. 1375–1384.

tice the single-factor model and the constant correlation model yield similar results, but the constant correlation model is much easier to implement. In the case of the constant correlation model, the shrinkage estimator for the covariance matrix takes the form

$$\hat{\Sigma}_{LW} = w\hat{\Sigma}_{CC} + (1 - w)\hat{\Sigma}$$

where $\hat{\Sigma}$ is the sample covariance matrix, and $\hat{\Sigma}_{CC}$ is the sample covariance matrix with constant correlation. The sample covariance matrix with constant correlation is computed as follows.

First, we decompose the sample covariance matrix according to

$$\hat{\Sigma} = \Lambda C \Lambda'$$

where Λ is a diagonal matrix of the volatilities of returns and C is the sample correlation matrix, that is,

$$C = \begin{bmatrix} 1 & \hat{\rho}_{12} & \cdots & & \hat{\rho}_{1N} \\ \hat{\rho}_{21} & \ddots & & \ddots & \vdots \\ \vdots & \ddots & & \ddots & \hat{\rho}_{N-1N} \\ \hat{\rho}_{N1} & \cdots & \hat{\rho}_{NN-1} & & 1 \end{bmatrix}$$

Second, we replace the sample correlation matrix with the constant correlation matrix

$$C_{CC} = \begin{bmatrix} 1 & \hat{\rho} & \cdots & \hat{\rho} \\ \hat{\rho} & \ddots & \ddots & \vdots \\ \vdots & \ddots & \ddots & \hat{\rho} \\ \hat{\rho} & \cdots & \hat{\rho} & 1 \end{bmatrix}$$

where $\hat{\rho}$ is the average of all the sample correlations, in other words

$$\hat{\rho} = \frac{2}{(N-1)N} \sum_{i=1}^{N} \sum_{j=i+1}^{N} \hat{\rho}_{ij}$$

The optimal shrinkage intensity can be shown to be proportional to a constant divided by the length of the history, T.[21]

In their two articles, Ledoit and Wolf compare the empirical out-of-sample performance of their shrinkage covariance matrix estimators with other covariance matrix estimators, such as the sample covariance

---

[21] Although straightforward to implement, the optimal shrinkage intensity, w, is a bit tedious to write down mathematically. Let us denote by $r_{i,t}$ the return on security i during period t, $1 \leq i \leq N$, $1 \leq t \leq T$,

$$\bar{r}_i = \frac{1}{T} \sum_{t=1}^{T} r_{i,t} \text{ and } \hat{\sigma}_{ij} = \frac{1}{T-1} \sum_{t=1}^{T} (r_{i,t} - \bar{r}_i)(r_{j,t} - \bar{r}_j)$$

Then the optimal shrinkage intensity is given by the formula

$$w = \max\left\{0, \min\left\{\frac{\hat{\kappa}}{T}, 1\right\}\right\}$$

where

$$\hat{\kappa} = \frac{\hat{\pi} - \hat{c}}{\hat{\gamma}}$$

and the parameters $\hat{\pi}$, $\hat{c}$, $\hat{\gamma}$ are computed as follows. First, $\hat{\pi}$ is given by

$$\hat{\pi} = \sum_{i,j=1}^{N} \hat{\pi}_{ij}$$

where

$$\hat{\pi}_{ij} = \frac{1}{T} \sum_{t=1}^{T} \left((r_{i,t} - \bar{r}_i)(r_{j,t} - \bar{r}_j) - \hat{\sigma}_{ij}\right)^2$$

Second, $\hat{c}$ is given by

$$\hat{c} = \sum_{i=1}^{N} \hat{\pi}_{ii} + \sum_{\substack{i=1 \\ i \neq j}}^{N} \frac{\hat{\rho}}{2}\left(\sqrt{\hat{\rho}_{jj}/\hat{\rho}_{ii}}\,\hat{\vartheta}_{ii,ij} + \sqrt{\hat{\rho}_{ii}/\hat{\rho}_{jj}}\,\hat{\vartheta}_{jj,ij}\right)$$

where

$$\hat{\vartheta}_{ii,ij} = \frac{1}{T} \sum_{t=1}^{T} [((r_{i,t} - \bar{r}_i)^2 - \hat{\sigma}_{ii})((r_{i,t} - \bar{r}_i)(r_{j,t} - \bar{r}_j) - \hat{\sigma}_{ij})]$$

Finally, $\hat{\gamma}$ is given by

$$\hat{\gamma} = \|C - C_{CC}\|_F^2$$

where $\|\cdot\|_F$ denotes the Frobenius norm defined by

$$\|A\|_F = \sqrt{\sum_{i,j=1}^{N} a_{ij}^2}$$

matrix, a statistical factor model based on the first five principal components, and a factor model based on the 48 industry factors[22] as defined by Fama and French.[23] The results indicate that when it comes to computing a global minimum variance portfolio, their shrinkage estimators are superior compared to the others tested, with the constant correlation shrinkage estimator coming out slightly ahead. Interestingly enough, it turns out that the shrinkage intensity for the single-factor model (the shrinkage intensity for the constant coefficient model is not reported) is fairly constant throughout time with a value around 0.8. This suggests that there is about four times as much estimation error present in the sample covariance matrix as there is bias in the single-factor covariance matrix.

In the following two examples we illustrate the effect of different estimators for the expected return on a portfolio of the country indices in the MSCI World Index.

Example: Rebalancing the MSCI World Index Portfolio, Part 1

In this and in the following example, we construct portfolios using the individual country indices from the MSCI World Index over the period January 1980 through May 2004.[24] First, we compare three simple approaches of monthly rebalancing of a portfolio containing the different country indices with the overall index:

1. Hold an equal proportion of each asset throughout the whole sample.
2. Rebalance the portfolio on a monthly basis by calculating the global minimum variance portfolio, not allowing for short-selling.
3. Rebalance the portfolio on a monthly basis using the risk aversion formulation of the mean-variance optimization problem with a risk aversion coefficient, λ, equal to 2, not allowing for short-selling.

For convenience, we refer to these three approaches as "Equal," "GMV," and "RiskAver." We will simply refer to the MSCI World Index as the "Index." Each time we rebalance the portfolios, we need a forecast of the monthly covariance matrix for GMV, and a forecast of the monthly expected returns and of the covariance matrix for RiskAver. Here, we use the historical sample means and covariances calculated from five years of daily data. In other words, at the beginning of each

---

[22] Besides some other proprietary and nonindustry-based factors, MSCI Barra's factor model discussed in the previous chapter uses these factors.

[23] Eugene F. Fama and Kenneth R. French, "Industry Costs of Equity," *Journal of Financial Economics* 43, no. 2 (February 1997), pp. 153–193.

[24] A description and basic statistical properties of this data set are provided in Appendix A.

month, we use the last five years of available daily data to compute our estimates. For example, the first five years of the sample, from January 1980 to December 1984, are used to construct the first estimates used in the simulation in January 1985. Before rebalancing at the end of each month, we calculate the realized portfolio return and its volatility. The results are depicted in Exhibits 8.3 and 8.4, and portfolio summary statistics of the different approaches and of the index itself are presented in Exhibits 8.5 to 8.8.

We observe that the three approaches outperform the index. In particular, the full period alphas range from 4.1% to 4.7% and the Sharpe ratios are 0.82 (GMV), 0.78 (Equal), 0.59 (RiskAver), and 0.45 (Index). However, only the index has a significant positive return (6.1%) during the last quarter of the simulation. All portfolios and the index have negative skew, where the largest full period skew of –0.34 is achieved by

EXHIBIT 8.3   Growth of Equity Invested on January 1985 in Each of the Different Portfolios and in the MSCI World Index

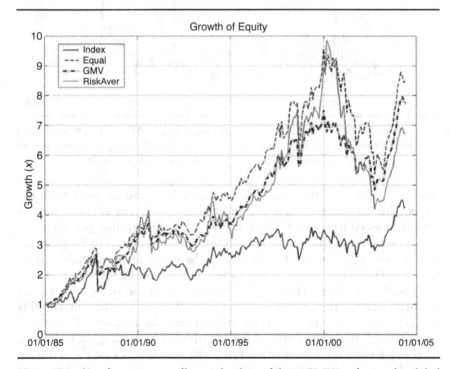

Note: "Equal" refers to an equally weighted portfolio; "GMV" refers to the global minimum variance portfolio; "RiskAver" refers to the risk aversion formulation of the mean-variance optimization problem with risk aversion coefficient $\lambda = 2$.

EXHIBIT 8.4 Portfolio Volatility of the Different Portfolios and the MSCI World
Index

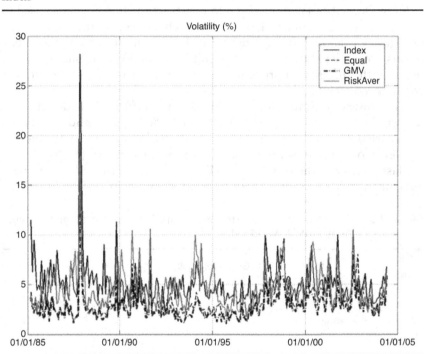

Note: "Equal" refers to an equally weighted portfolio; "GMV" refers to the global
minimum variance portfolio; "RiskAver" refers to the risk aversion formulation of
the mean-variance optimization problem with risk aversion coefficient $\lambda = 2$.

RiskAver. The portfolios all have smaller full period kurtosis than the
index, due to the fact that the most negative return of the index is
almost a devastating –45%! It is, however, somewhat disappointing and
discouraging that the portfolios relying upon mean-variance optimization do not perform much better than the portfolio using naïve equal
weights. The risk aversion optimization actually performs worse.

Should not the portfolios relying on optimization be "optimal"? As
we discussed in the introduction to this chapter, the reason for this
problem is in the inputs to the optimization, the forecast of expected
returns, and the covariance matrix. Intuitively speaking, when these
forecasts have a large estimation error, the performance of the resulting
portfolios will be anything less than desired. Optimizers are often cynically referred to as "error maximizers" as they overweight the estimation error in the inputs. In particular, assets with large expected returns

EXHIBIT 8.5 Portfolio Summary Statistics of the Equally Weighted Portfolio

	Start Date	End Date	Mean	Volatility	Sharpe Ratio	Skew	Kurtosis	Min	Max	Alpha	Beta
1st Qtr	Feb-85	Dec-89	27.8%	16.5%	1.69	−2.14	12.14	−21.7%	9.8%	15.3%	0.30
2nd Qtr	Jan-90	Dec-94	5.8%	14.6%	0.40	−0.25	3.64	−12.1%	9.6%	0.5%	0.45
3rd Qtr	Jan-95	Dec-99	15.8%	14.0%	1.12	−0.87	6.65	−14.9%	11.7%	9.6%	0.61
4th Qtr	Jan-00	May-04	−1.2%	17.1%	−0.07	−0.44	3.02	−12.2%	10.5%	−6.5%	0.72
1st Half	Feb-85	Dec-94	16.7%	15.8%	1.06	−1.21	7.60	−21.7%	9.8%	7.5%	0.34
2nd Half	Jan-95	May-04	7.8%	15.7%	0.50	−0.68	4.33	−14.9%	11.7%	2.1%	0.67
Full	Feb-85	May-04	12.4%	15.8%	0.78	−0.94	5.91	−21.7%	11.7%	4.7%	0.44

Note: The columns Mean, Volatility, Sharpe Ratio, and Alpha are the annualized mean returns, volatilities, Sharpe ratios, and alphas of the portfolio over the different periods. Min and Max are the daily minimum and maximum portfolio returns, respectively. Skew and Kurtosis are calculated as the third and fourth normalized centered moments. Alphas and betas are calculated using one-month LIBOR.

EXHIBIT 8.6 Portfolio Summary Statistics of the Global Minimum Variance Portfolio Rebalanced Monthly

	Start Date	End Date	Mean	Volatility	Sharpe Ratio	Skew	Kurtosis	Min	Max	Alpha	Beta
1st Qtr	Feb-85	Dec-89	26.4%	16.2%	1.63	-3.03	18.82	-24.4%	9.6%	13.7%	0.31
2nd Qtr	Jan-90	Dec-94	2.9%	13.2%	0.22	-0.35	3.60	-10.4%	9.1%	-2.4%	0.46
3rd Qtr	Jan-95	Dec-99	14.8%	12.4%	1.19	-1.25	6.25	-13.1%	8.6%	8.7%	0.53
4th Qtr	Jan-00	May-04	1.7%	14.1%	0.12	-0.45	2.66	-9.4%	7.1%	-3.2%	0.62
1st Half	Feb-85	Dec-94	14.6%	15.1%	0.97	-1.83	11.98	-24.4%	9.6%	5.3%	0.36
2nd Half	Jan-95	May-04	8.7%	13.3%	0.65	-0.83	4.00	-13.1%	8.6%	3.1%	0.57
Full	Feb-85	May-04	11.7%	14.2%	0.82	-1.41	8.99	-24.4%	9.6%	4.1%	0.42

Note: The columns Mean, Volatility, Sharpe Ratio, and Alpha are the annualized mean returns, volatilities, Sharpe ratios, and alphas of the portfolio over the different periods. Min and Max are the daily minimum and maximum portfolio returns, respectively. Skew and Kurtosis are calculated as the third and fourth normalized centered moments. Alphas and betas are calculated using one-month LIBOR.

EXHIBIT 8.7 Portfolio Summary Statistics of the Risk Aversion Formulation of the Mean-Variance Portfolio Rebalanced Monthly with Risk Aversion Coefficient $\lambda = 2$

	Start Date	End Date	Mean	Volatility	Sharpe Ratio	Skew	Kurtosis	Min	Max	Alpha	Beta
1st Qtr	Feb-85	Dec-89	25.4%	20.5%	1.24	-0.35	3.25	-16.1%	14.0%	13.9%	0.24
2nd Qtr	Jan-90	Dec-94	5.3%	24.4%	0.22	-0.18	4.35	-22.4%	19.4%	0.0%	0.57
3rd Qtr	Jan-95	Dec-99	20.3%	16.7%	1.21	-0.82	5.30	-16.7%	11.2%	14.2%	0.52
4th Qtr	Jan-00	May-04	-4.8%	17.6%	-0.27	-0.23	3.11	-11.1%	13.2%	-9.8%	0.63
1st Half	Feb-85	Dec-94	15.3%	22.7%	0.67	-0.30	4.06	-22.4%	19.4%	6.2%	0.32
2nd Half	Jan-95	May-04	8.5%	17.4%	0.49	-0.52	3.87	-16.7%	13.2%	3.0%	0.57
Full	Feb-85	May-04	12.0%	20.3%	0.59	-0.34	4.26	-22.4%	19.4%	4.5%	0.40

Note: The columns Mean, Volatility, Sharpe Ratio, and Alpha are the annualized mean returns, volatilities, Sharpe ratios, and alphas of the portfolio over the different periods. Min and Max are the daily minimum and maximum portfolio returns, respectively. Skew and Kurtosis are calculated as the third and fourth normalized centered moments. Alphas and betas are calculated using one-month LIBOR.

EXHIBIT 8.8 Summary Statistics of the MSCI World Index

	Start Date	End Date	Mean	Volatility	Sharpe Ratio	Skew	Kurtosis	Min	Max
1st Qtr	Feb-85	Dec-89	23.1%	33.0%	0.70	-2.02	11.05	-44.7%	17.6%
2nd Qtr	Jan-90	Dec-94	5.4%	18.6%	0.29	0.20	2.12	-9.6%	11.1%
3rd Qtr	Jan-95	Dec-99	6.4%	16.9%	0.38	-0.67	3.81	-13.7%	10.1%
4th Qtr	Jan-00	May-04	6.1%	18.6%	0.33	0.01	3.22	-12.9%	14.1%
1st Half	Feb-85	Dec-94	14.1%	26.7%	0.53	-1.68	12.10	-44.7%	17.6%
2nd Half	Jan-95	May-04	6.3%	17.6%	0.36	-0.30	3.50	-13.7%	14.1%
Full	Feb-85	May-04	10.3%	22.7%	0.45	-1.40	12.12	-44.7%	17.6%

Note: The columns Mean, Volatility, and Sharpe Ratio are the annualized mean returns, volatilities, and Sharpe ratios of the index over the different periods. Min and Max are the daily minimum and maximum Index returns, respectively. Skew and Kurtosis are calculated as the third and fourth normalized centered moments.

and low standard deviations will be overweighted and, conversely, assets with low expected returns and high standard deviations will be underweighted. Therefore, estimation errors both in expected returns and variances/covariances will introduce errors in the optimal portfolio weights.

It is well known that equally weighted portfolios often outperform mean-variance optimized portfolios over time.[25] The uncertainty and estimation error in the expected returns have more influence than the ones in the covariance matrix in the mean-variance optimization.[26] This is consistent with the finding in this example that the GMV portfolio performs better than the risk aversion portfolio: The GMV portfolio only relies upon the covariance matrix, not on the expected returns. To see what happens when we use more robust estimators for the expected returns, we now turn to the next example.

Example: Rebalancing the MSCI World Index Portfolio, Part 2

In this example we use two robust estimators for the construction of expected returns: (1) the James-Stein shrinkage estimator with the global minimum variance portfolio as the shrinkage target; and (2) the Black-Litterman model (introduced in the next section) using historical means as the views. For comparison, as in the previous example, we use the global minimum variance portfolio (GMV).

For convenience we will refer to these three approaches as "Shrinkage GMV," "BL," and "GMV." For the Shrinkage GMV and BL simulations, the optimal portfolios were calculated using the risk aversion formulation of the mean-variance optimization problem with risk aversion coefficient $\lambda = 2$.[27] The results are presented in Exhibits 8.9 through 8.12.

We observe that the full sample Sharpe ratios of the Shrinkage GMV and BL portfolios are very similar, at 0.71 and 0.72, respectively. Recall that the full sample Sharpe ratios of the other approaches presented in the previous example were 0.82 (GMV), 0.78 (Equal), 0.59 (RiskAver),

---

[25] John D. Jobson and Robert M. Korkie, "Putting Markowitz Theory to Work," *Journal of Portfolio Management* 7, no. 4 (Summer 1981), pp. 70–74.

[26] Vijay K. Chopra and William T. Ziemba, "The Effect of Errors in Means, Variances, and Covariances on Optimal Portfolio Choice," *Journal of Portfolio Management* 19, no. 2 (1993), pp. 6–11.

[27] We chose not to calibrate the risk aversion parameter but left it the same for both approaches. One could for example, calibrate this parameter such that both the Shrinkage GMV and BL portfolios have about the same realized volatility. Because we perform the comparison on a Sharpe ratio basis, this has no influence on the results.

EXHIBIT 8.9   Growth of Equity Invested on January 1985 in the GMV, Shrinkage GMV, and BL Portfolios

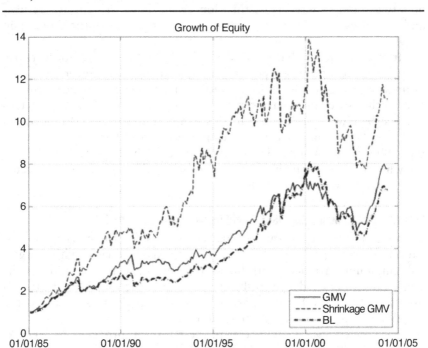

Note: GMV refers to the global minimum variance portfolio; Shrinkage GMV refers to the portfolio where the expected returns are estimated with the James-Stein shrinkage estimator with the global minimum variance portfolio as the shrinkage target; and BL refers to the portfolio where the expected returns are estimated with the Black-Litterman model using historical means as the views. In the last two cases, we use the risk aversion formulation of the mean-variance optimization problem with risk aversion coefficient $\lambda = 2$.

and 0.45 (Index). In other words, the new estimators clearly perform better than the risk aversion formulation using historical means, yet perform worse than both the global minimum variance portfolio and the equally weighted portfolio. These results are consistent with the findings by Jorion,[28] who used monthly returns on the stocks listed on the NYSE over the period January 1926 through December 1987.

---

[28] Jorion, "Bayesian and CAPM Estimators of the Means: Implications for Portfolio Selection."

EXHIBIT 8.10   Portfolio Volatility of the GMV, Shrinkage GMV, and BL Portfolios

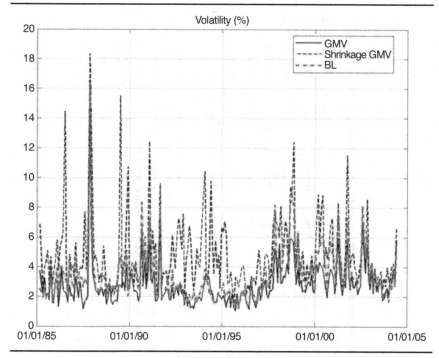

Note: GMV refers to the global minimum variance portfolio; Shrinkage GMV refers to the portfolio where the expected returns are estimated with the James-Stein shrinkage estimator and the global minimum variance portfolio as the shrinkage target; and BL refers to the portfolio where the expected returns are estimated with the Black-Litterman model using historical means as the views. In the last two cases, we use the risk aversion formulation of the mean-variance optimization problem with risk aversion coefficient $\lambda = 2$.

BAYESIAN APPROACHES

The classical approach to estimating future expected returns assumes that the "true" expected returns and covariances of returns are unknown and *fixed*. A point estimate (i.e., an estimate of the most likely return represented by a single number) is obtained using forecasting models of observed market data and proprietary data. However, it is difficult to make accurate estimates and the mean-variance portfolio allocation decision is influenced by the estimation error of the forecasts.

EXHIBIT 8.11 Portfolio Summary Statistics of the Portfolio Where the Expected Returns Are Estimated with the James-Stein Shrinkage Estimator with the Global Minimum Variance Portfolio as the Shrinkage Target

	Start Date	End Date	Mean	Volatility	Sharpe Ratio	Skew	Kurtosis	Min	Max	Alpha	Beta
1st Qtr	Feb-85	Dec-89	34.9%	21.9%	1.59	−0.94	5.16	−21.3%	15.3%	21.0%	0.39
2nd Qtr	Jan-90	Dec-94	12.0%	21.1%	0.57	1.21	7.02	−10.8%	27.3%	6.7%	0.45
3rd Qtr	Jan-95	Dec-99	9.4%	17.9%	0.53	−1.10	6.66	−20.6%	12.5%	3.2%	0.68
4th Qtr	Jan-00	May-04	0.7%	19.6%	0.03	0.63	6.96	−15.2%	22.8%	−4.4%	0.63
1st Half	Feb-85	Dec-94	23.3%	21.7%	1.08	0.10	5.27	−21.3%	27.3%	13.6%	0.41
2nd Half	Jan-95	May-04	5.3%	18.7%	0.28	−0.19	6.62	−20.6%	22.8%	−0.3%	0.65
Full	Feb-85	May-04	14.6%	20.4%	0.71	0.05	5.83	−21.3%	27.3%	6.7%	0.49

Note: The columns Mean, Volatility, Sharpe Ratio, and Alpha are the annualized mean returns, volatilities, Sharpe ratios, and alphas of the portfolio over the different periods. Min and Max are the daily minimum and maximum portfolio returns, respectively. Skew and Kurtosis are calculated as the third and fourth normalized centered moments. Alphas and betas are calculated using one-month LIBOR.

EXHIBIT 8.12 Portfolio Summary Statistics of the Portfolio Where the Expected Returns Are Estimated with the Black-Litterman Model Using Historical Means As the Views.

	Start Date	End Date	Mean	Volatility	Sharpe Ratio	Skew	Kurtosis	Min	Max	Alpha	Beta
1st Qtr	Feb-85	Dec-89	22.6%	16.6%	1.36	-0.85	5.10	-16.5%	10.4%	11.7%	0.19
2nd Qtr	Jan-90	Dec-94	3.2%	15.0%	0.21	-0.33	4.20	-13.8%	9.8%	-2.1%	0.43
3rd Qtr	Jan-95	Dec-99	19.4%	14.4%	1.35	-1.07	6.79	-15.5%	10.3%	13.4%	0.53
4th Qtr	Jan-00	May-04	-2.0%	15.0%	-0.14	-0.39	2.39	-9.1%	6.9%	-7.0%	0.61
1st Half	Feb-85	Dec-94	12.8%	16.0%	0.80	-0.55	4.44	-16.5%	10.4%	4.3%	0.26
2nd Half	Jan-95	May-04	9.4%	14.9%	0.63	-0.71	4.20	-15.5%	10.3%	3.8%	0.57
Full	Feb-85	May-04	11.1%	15.5%	0.72	-0.61	4.36	-16.5%	10.4%	3.9%	0.35

Note: The columns Mean, Volatility, Sharpe Ratio, and Alpha are the annualized mean returns, volatilities, Sharpe ratios, and alphas of the portfolio over the different periods. Min and Max are the daily minimum and maximum portfolio returns, respectively. Skew and Kurtosis are calculated as the third and fourth normalized centered moments. Alphas and betas are calculated using one-month LIBOR.

The Bayesian approach, in contrast, assumes that the "true" expected returns are unknown and *random*. Named after the English mathematician Thomas Bayes, the Bayesian approach is based on the *subjective* interpretation of probability. A probability distribution is used to represent an investor's belief on the probability that a specific event will actually occur. This probability distribution, called the "prior distribution," reflects an investor's knowledge about the probability before any data are observed. After more information is provided (e.g., data observed), the investor's opinions about the probability might change. Bayes' rule is the formula for computing the new probability distribution, called the "posterior distribution". The posterior distribution is based on knowledge of the prior probability distribution plus the new data.

A posterior distribution of expected return is derived by combining the forecast from the empirical data with a prior distribution. For example, in the Black-Litterman model, which we will introduce later in this section, an estimate of future expected returns is based on combining market equilibrium (e.g., the CAPM equilibrium) with an investor's views. Such views are expressed as absolute or relative deviations from equilibrium together with confidence levels of the views (as measured by the standard deviation of the views).

The Black-Litterman expected return is calculated as a weighted average of the market equilibrium and the investor's views. The weights depend on (1) the volatility of each asset and its correlations with the other assets and (2) the degree of confidence in each forecast. The resulting expected return, which is the mean of the posterior distribution, is then used as input in the portfolio optimization process. Portfolio weights computed in this fashion tend to be more intuitive and less sensitive to small changes in the original inputs (i.e., forecasts of market equilibrium, investor's views, and the covariance matrix).

The ability to incorporate exogenous insight, such as a portfolio manager's judgment, into formal models is important: such insight might be the most valuable input used by the model. The Bayesian framework allows forecasting systems to use such external information sources and subjective interventions (i.e., modification of the model due to judgment) in addition to traditional information sources such as market data and proprietary data.

Because portfolio managers might not be willing to give up control to a "black box," incorporating exogenous insights into formal models through Bayesian techniques is one way of giving the portfolio manager better control in a quantitative framework. Forecasts are represented through probability distributions that can be modified or adjusted to incorporate other sources of information deemed relevant. The only restriction is that such additional information (i.e., the investor's "views") be combined with the existing model through the laws of probability. In effect, incorporating Bayesian views into a model allows one to "rationalize" subjectivity within a formal, quantitative framework. "[T]he rational investor is a Bayesian," as Markowitz noted.[29]

Interventions can be either feed-forward (anticipatory actions) or feed-back (corrective actions).[30] The Bayesian framework also allows for mixing, selecting, and switching among dynamic models in a common framework. In the first half of the last decade, progress in Bayesian modeling has put these general and powerful computational techniques within reach of practitioners in the financial markets.[31]

The Black-Litterman Model

The basic feature of the Black-Litterman model that we discuss in this and the following sections is that it combines an investor's views with the market equilibrium. Let us understand what this statement implies. In the classical mean-variance optimization framework an investor is required to provide estimates of the expected returns and covariances of all the securities in the investment universe considered. This is of course a humongous task, given the number of securities available today. Portfolio and investment managers are very unlikely to have a detailed understanding of all the securities, companies, industries, and sectors that they have at their disposal. Typically, most of them have a specific area of expertise that they focus on in order to achieve superior returns.

This is probably one of the major reasons why the mean-variance framework has not been adopted among practitioners in general. It is simply unrealistic for the portfolio manager to produce reasonable estimates (besides the additional problems of estimation error) of the inputs required in classical portfolio theory.

Furthermore, many trading strategies used today cannot easily be turned into forecasts of expected returns and covariances. In particular, not all trading strategies produce views on *absolute* return, but rather just provide *relative* rankings of securities that are predicted to outper-

---

[29] See page 57 in Harry M. Markowitz, *Mean-Variance Analysis in Portfolio Choice and Capital Markets*, (Cambridge, MA: Basil Blackwell, 1987).

[30] See, for example, Michael West and P. Jeff Harrison, *Bayesian Forecasting and Dynamic Models*, (New York: Springer, 1989).

[31] See, for example, Bradley P. Carlin, Nicholas G. Polson, and David S. Stoffer, "A Monte Carlo Approach to Nonnormal and Nonlinear State-Space Modeling," *Journal of the American Statistical Association* 87, no. 418 (1992), pp. 493–500; C. K. Carter and R. Kohn, "On Gibbs Sampling for State Space Models," *Biometrica* 81, no. 3 (1994), pp. 541–553; and Sylvia Fruhwirth-Schnatter, "Data Augmentation and Dynamic Linear Models," *Journal of Time Series Analysis* 15, no. 2 (1994), pp. 183–202.

form/underperform other securities. For example, considering two stocks, A and B, instead of the *absolute view*, "the one-month expected return on A and B are 1.2% and 1.7% with a standard deviation of 5% and 5.5%, respectively," while a *relative view* may be of the form "B will outperform A with half a percent over the next month" or simply "B will outperform A over the next month." Clearly, it is not an easy task to translate any of these relative views into the inputs required for the modern portfolio theoretical framework. We now walk through and illustrate the usage of the Black-Litterman model in three simple steps.

Step 1: Basic Assumptions and Starting Point

One of the basic assumptions underlying the Black-Litterman model is that the expected return of a security should be consistent with market equilibrium *unless* the investor has a specific view on the security.[32] In other words, an investor who does not have any views on the market should hold the market.[33]

Our starting point is the CAPM model:[34]

$$E(R_i) - R_f = \beta_i(E(R_M) - R_f)$$

where $E(R_i)$, $E(R_M)$, and R_f are the expected return on security i, the expected return on the market portfolio, and the risk-free rate, respectively. Furthermore,

$$\beta_i = \frac{\text{cov}(R_i, R_M)}{\sigma_M^2}$$

where σ_M^2 is the variance of the market portfolio. Let us denote by $\mathbf{w}_b = (w_{b1}, ..., w_{bN})'$ the market capitalization or benchmark weights, so that

---

[32] Fischer Black and Robert Litterman, *Asset Allocation: Combining Investor Views with Market Equilibrium*, Goldman, Sachs & Co., Fixed Income Research, September 1990.

[33] A "predecessor" to the Black-Litterman model is the so-called Treynor-Black model. In this model, an investor's portfolio is shown to consist of two parts (1) a passive portfolio/positions held purely for the purpose of mimicking the market portfolio, and (2) an active portfolio/positions based on the investor's return/risk expectations. This somewhat simpler model relies on the assumption that returns of all securities are related only through the variation of the market portfolio (Sharpe's Diagonal Model). See, Jack L. Treynor and Fischer Black, "How to Use Security Analysis to Improve Portfolio Selection," *Journal of Business* 46, no. 2 (January 1973) pp. 66–86.

[34] See Chapters 5 and 6 for a review of this model.

with an asset universe of N securities[35] the return on the market can be written as

$$R_M = \sum_{j=1}^{N} w_{bj} R_j$$

Then by the CAPM, the expected excess return on asset i, $\Pi_i = E(R_i) - R_f$, becomes

$$\Pi_i = \beta_i (E(R_i) - R_f)$$

$$= \frac{\text{cov}(R_i, R_M)}{\sigma_M^2} (E(R_i) - R_f)$$

$$= \frac{E(R_M) - R_f}{\sigma_M^2} \sum_{j=1}^{N} \text{cov}(R_i, R_j) w_{bj}$$

We can also express this in matrix-vector form as[36]

---

[35] For simplicity, we consider only equity securities. Extending this model to other assets classes such as bonds and currencies is fairly straightforward.

[36] Two comments about the following two relationships are of importance:

1. As it may be difficult to accurately estimate expected returns practitioners use other techniques. One is that of *reverse optimization* also referred to as the technique of *implied expected returns*. The technique simply uses the expression $\Pi = \delta \Sigma w$ to calculate the expected return vector given the market price of risk δ, the covariance matrix Σ, and the market capitalization weights w. The technique was first introduced by Sharpe (1974) and Fisher (1975); see, William F. Sharpe, "Imputing Expected Returns from Portfolio Composition," *Journal of Financial and Quantitative Analysis* 9, no. 3 (June 1974), pp. 463–472; and Lawrence Fisher, "Using Modern Portfolio Theory to Maintain an Efficiently Diversified Portfolio," *Financial Analysts Journal* 31, no. 3 (May–June 1975), pp. 73–85; and is an important component of the Black-Litterman model.
2. We note that $E(R_M) - R_f$ is the market risk premium (or the equity premium) of the universe of assets considered. As pointed out in Herold (2005) and Idzorek (2005); see, Ulf Herold, "Computing Implied Returns in a Meaningful Way," *Journal of Asset Management* 6 (June 2005) pp. 53–64, and Thomas M. Idzorek, "A Step-By-Step Guide to the Black-Litterman Model: Incorporating User-Specified Confidence Levels"; using a market proxy with different risk-return characteristics than the market capitalization weighted portfolio for determining the market risk premium may lead to nonintuitive expected returns. For example, using a market risk premium based on the S&P 500 for calculating the implied equilibrium return vector for the NASDAQ 100 should be avoided.

$$\Pi = \delta\Sigma w$$

where we define the market price of risk as

$$\delta = \frac{E(R_M) - R_f}{\sigma_M^2},$$

the expected excess return vector

$$\Pi = \begin{bmatrix} \Pi_1 \\ \vdots \\ \Pi_N \end{bmatrix},$$

and the covariance matrix of returns

$$\Sigma = \begin{bmatrix} \mathrm{cov}(R_1, R_1) & \cdots & \mathrm{cov}(R_1, R_N) \\ \vdots & & \vdots \\ \mathrm{cov}(R_N, R_1) & \cdots & \mathrm{cov}(R_N, R_N) \end{bmatrix}$$

The true expected returns μ of the securities are unknown. However, we assume that our equilibrium model above serves as a reasonable estimate of the true expected returns in the sense that

$$\Pi = \mu + \varepsilon_\Pi, \ \varepsilon_\Pi \sim N(0, \tau\Sigma)$$

for some small parameter $\tau \ll 1$. We can think about $\tau\Sigma$ as our confidence in how well we can estimate the equilibrium expected returns. In other words, a small τ implies a high confidence in our equilibrium estimates and vice versa.

Because the market portfolio is on the efficient frontier, as we saw in Chapter 2, as a consequence of the CAPM an investor will be holding a portfolio consisting of the market portfolio and a risk-free instrument earning the risk-free rate. But let us now see what happens if an investor has a particular view on some of the securities.

Step 2: Expressing an Investor's Views

Formally, K views in the Black-Litterman model are expressed as a K-dimensional vector q with

$$q = P\mu + \varepsilon_q, \ \varepsilon_q \sim N(0, \Omega)$$

where P is a $K \times N$ matrix (explained in the following example) and Ω is a $K \times K$ matrix expressing the confidence in the views. In order to understand this mathematical specification better, let us take a look at an example.

Let us assume that the asset universe that we consider has five stocks ($N = 5$) and that an investor has the following two views:

1. Stock 1 will have a return of 1.5%.
2. Stock 3 will outperform Stock 2 by 4%.

We recognize that the first view is an absolute view where as the second one is a relative view. Mathematically, we express the two views together as

$$\begin{bmatrix} 1.5\% \\ 4\% \end{bmatrix} = \begin{bmatrix} 1 & 0 & 0 & 0 & 0 \\ 0 & -1 & 1 & 0 & 0 \end{bmatrix} \begin{bmatrix} \mu_1 \\ \mu_2 \\ \mu_3 \\ \mu_4 \\ \mu_5 \end{bmatrix} + \begin{bmatrix} \varepsilon_1 \\ \varepsilon_2 \end{bmatrix}$$

The first row of the P matrix represents the first view, and similarly, the second row describes the second view. In this example, we chose the weights of the second view such that they add up to zero, but other weighting schemes are also possible. For instance, the weights could also be chosen as some scaling factor times one over the market capitalizations of the stock, some scaling factor times one over the stock price, or other variations thereof. We come back to these issues later in this section when we discuss how to incorporate time-series based strategies and cross-sectional ranking strategies.

We also remark at this point that the error terms ε_1, ε_2 do not explicitly enter into the Black-Litterman model—but their variances do. Quite simply, these are just the variances of the different views. Although in some instances they are directly available as a byproduct of the view or the strategy, in other cases they need to be estimated separately. For example,

$$\Omega = \begin{bmatrix} 1\%^2 & 0 \\ 0 & 1\%^2 \end{bmatrix}$$

corresponds to a higher confidence in the views, and conversely,

$$\Omega = \begin{bmatrix} 5\%^2 & 0 \\ 0 & 7\%^2 \end{bmatrix}$$

represents a much lower confidence in the views. We discuss a few different approaches in choosing the confidence levels below. The off diagonal elements of Ω are typically set to zero. The reason for this is that the error terms of the individual views are most often assumed to be independent of one another.

Step 3: Combining an Investor's Views with Market Equilibrium

Having specified the market equilibrium and an investor's views separately, we are now ready to combine the two together. There are two different, but equivalent, approaches that can be used to arrive to the Black-Litterman model. We will describe a derivation that relies upon standard econometrical techniques, in particular, the so-called *mixed estimation technique* described by Theil.[37] The approach based on Bayesian statistics has been explained in some detail by Satchell and Scowcroft.[38]

Let us first recall the specification of market equilibrium

$$\Pi = \mu + \varepsilon_\Pi, \; \varepsilon_\Pi \sim N(0, \tau\Sigma)$$

and the one for the investor's views

$$q = P\mu + \varepsilon_q, \; \varepsilon_q \sim N(0, \Omega)$$

We can "stack" these two equations together in the form

$$y = X\mu + \varepsilon, \; \varepsilon \sim N(0, V)$$

where

$$y = \begin{bmatrix} \Pi \\ q \end{bmatrix}, \; X = \begin{bmatrix} I \\ P \end{bmatrix}, \; V = \begin{bmatrix} \tau\Sigma & \\ & \Omega \end{bmatrix}$$

with I denoting the $N \times N$ identity matrix. We observe that this is just a standard linear model for the expected returns μ. Calculating the Generalized Least Squares (GLS) estimator for μ, we obtain

---

[37] Henri Theil, *Principles of Econometrics* (New York: Wiley and Sons, 1971).

[38] Stephen Satchell and Alan Scowcroft, "A Demystification of the Black-Litterman Model: Managing Quantitative and Traditional Portfolio Construction," *Journal of Asset Management* 1, no. 2 (2000), pp. 138–150.

$$\hat{\mu}_{BL} = (X'V^{-1}X)^{-1}X'V^{-1}y$$

$$= \left(\begin{bmatrix} I & P' \end{bmatrix} \begin{bmatrix} (\tau\Sigma)^{-1} & \\ & \Omega^{-1} \end{bmatrix} \begin{bmatrix} I \\ P \end{bmatrix} \right)^{-1} \begin{bmatrix} I & P' \end{bmatrix} \begin{bmatrix} (\tau\Sigma)^{-1} & \\ & \Omega^{-1} \end{bmatrix} \begin{bmatrix} \Pi \\ q \end{bmatrix}$$

$$= \left(\begin{bmatrix} I & P' \end{bmatrix} \begin{bmatrix} (\tau\Sigma)^{-1} \\ \Omega^{-1}P \end{bmatrix} \right)^{-1} \begin{bmatrix} I & P' \end{bmatrix} \begin{bmatrix} (\tau\Sigma)^{-1}\Pi \\ \Omega^{-1}q \end{bmatrix}$$

$$= [(\tau\Sigma)^{-1} + P'\Omega^{-1}P]^{-1}[(\tau\Sigma)^{-1}\Pi + P'\Omega^{-1}q]$$

The last line in the above formula is the Black-Litterman expected returns that "blend" the market equilibrium with the investor's views.

Some Remarks and Observations

Following are some comments are in order to provide a better intuitive understanding of the formula. We see that if the investor has no views (that is, $q = \Omega = 0$) or the confidence in the views is zero, then the Black-Litterman expected return becomes $\hat{\mu}_{BL} = \Pi$. Consequently, the investor will end up holding the market portfolio as predicted by the CAPM. In other words, the optimal portfolio in the absence of views is the defined market.

If we were to plug return targets of zero or use the available cash rates, for example, into an optimizer to represent the absence of views, the result would be an optimal portfolio that looks very much different from the market. The equilibrium returns are those forecasts that in the absence of any other views will produce an optimal portfolio equal to the market portfolio. Intuitively speaking, the equilibrium returns in the Black-Litterman model are used to "center" the optimal portfolio around the market portfolio.

By using $q = P\mu + \varepsilon_q$, we have that the investor's views alone imply the estimate of expected returns $\hat{\mu} = (P'P)^{-1}P'q$. Since $P(P'P)^{-1}P' = I$ where I is the identity matrix, we can rewrite the Black-Litterman expected returns in the form

$$\hat{\mu}_{BL} = [(\tau\Sigma)^{-1} + P'\Omega^{-1}P]^{-1}[(\tau\Sigma)^{-1}\Pi + P'\Omega^{-1}P\hat{\mu}]$$

Now we see that the Black-Litterman expected return is a "confidence weighted" linear combination of market equilibrium Π and the expected return $\hat{\mu}$ implied by the investor's views. The two weighting matrices are given by

$$w_\Pi = [(\tau\Sigma)^{-1} + P'\Omega^{-1}P]^{-1}(\tau\Sigma)^{-1}$$

$$w_q = [(\tau\Sigma)^{-1} + P'\Omega^{-1}P]^{-1}P'\Omega^{-1}P$$

where

$$w_\Pi + w_q = I$$

In particular, $(\tau\Sigma)^{-1}$ and $P'\Omega^{-1}P$ represent the confidence we have in our estimates of the market equilibrium and the views, respectively. Therefore, if we have low confidence in the views, the resulting expected returns will be close to the ones implied by market equilibrium. Conversely, with higher confidence in the views, the resulting expected returns will deviate from the market equilibrium implied expected returns. We say that we "tilt" away from market equilibrium.

It is straightforward to show that the Black-Litterman expected returns can also be written in the form

$$\hat{\mu}_{BL} = \Pi + \tau\Sigma P'(\Omega + \tau P\Sigma P')^{-1}(q - P\Pi)$$

where we now immediately see that we tilt away from the equilibrium with a vector proportional to $\Sigma P'(\Omega + \tau P\Sigma P')^{-1}(q - P\Pi)$.

We also mention that the Black-Litterman model can be derived as a solution to the following optimization problem:

$$\hat{\mu}_{BL} = \arg\min_{\mu} \{(\Pi - \mu)'\Sigma^{-1}(\Pi - \mu) + \tau(q - P\mu)'\Omega^{-1}(q - P\mu)\}$$

From this formulation we see that $\hat{\mu}_{BL}$ is chosen such that it is *simultaneously* as close to Π, and $P\mu$ is as close to q as possible. The distances are determined by Σ^{-1} and Ω^{-1}. Furthermore, the relative importance of the equilibrium versus the views is determined by τ. For example, for τ large the weight of the views is increased, whereas for τ small the weight of the equilibrium is higher. Moreover, we also see that τ is a "redundant" parameter as it can be absorbed into Ω.

It is straightforward to calculate the variance of the Black-Litterman combined estimator of the expected returns by the standard "sandwich formula," that is,

$$\text{var}(\hat{\mu}_{BL}) = (X'V^{-1}X)^{-1}$$

$$= [(\tau\Sigma)^{-1} + P'\Omega^{-1}P]^{-1}$$

The most important feature of the Black-Litterman model is that it uses the mixed estimation procedure to adjust the *entire* market equilibrium implied expected return vector with an investor's views. Because security returns are correlated, views on just a few assets will, due to these correlations, imply changes to the expected returns on *all* assets. Mathematically speaking, this follows from the fact that although the vector q can have dimension $K \ll N$, $P'\Omega^{-1}$ is an $N \times K$ matrix that "propagates" the K views into N components, $P'\Omega^{-1}q$. This effect is stronger the more correlated the different securities are. In the absence of this adjustment of the expected return vector, the differences between the equilibrium expected return and an investor's forecasts will be interpreted as an arbitrage opportunity by a mean-variance optimizer and result in portfolios concentrated in just a few assets ("corner solutions"). Intuitively, any estimation errors are spread out over all assets, making the Black-Litterman expected return vector less sensitive to errors in individual views. This effect contributes to the mitigation of estimation risk and error maximization in the optimization process.

Practical Considerations and Extensions

In this subsection we discuss a few practical issues in using the Black-Litterman model. Specifically, we discuss how to incorporate factor models and cross-sectional rankings in this framework. Furthermore, we also provide some ideas on how the confidences in the views can be estimated in cases where these are not directly available.

It is straightforward to incorporate factor models in the Black-Litterman framework. Let us assume we have a factor representation of the returns of some of the assets. We use the same notation introduced in Chapter 6, and assume we have a factor model of the form

$$R_i = \alpha_i + F\beta_i + \varepsilon_i, \, i \in I$$

where $I \subset \{1, 2, ..., N\}$. Typically, from a factor model it is easy to obtain an estimate of the residual variance, $\text{var}(\varepsilon_i)$. In this case, we set

$$q_i = \begin{cases} \alpha + F\beta_i, & i \in I \\ 0, & \text{otherwise} \end{cases}$$

and the corresponding confidence

$$\omega_{ii}^2 = \begin{cases} \text{var}(\varepsilon_i), \, i \in I \\ 0, \text{ otherwise} \end{cases}$$

The **P** matrix is defined by

$$p_{ii} = \begin{cases} 1, \, i \in I \\ 0, \text{ otherwise} \end{cases}$$

$$p_{ij} = 0, \, i \neq j$$

Of course in a practical implementation we would omit rows with zeros.

Many quantitative investment strategies do not *a priori* produce expected returns, but rather just a simple ranking of the securities. Let us consider a ranking of securities from "best to worst" (from an outperforming to an underperforming perspective, etc.). For example, a value manager might consider ranking securities in terms of increasing book-to-price ratio (B/P), where a low B/P would indicate an undervalued stock (potential to increase in value) and high B/P an overvalued stock (potential to decrease in value). From this ranking we form a long-short portfolio where we purchase the top half of the stocks (the group that is expected to outperform) and we sell short the second half of stocks (the group that is expected to underperform). The view q in this case becomes a scalar, equal to the expected return on the long-short portfolio. The confidence of the view can be decided from backtests, as we describe below. Further, here the **P** matrix is a $1 \times N$ matrix of ones and minus ones. The corresponding column component is set to one if the security belongs to the outperforming group, or minus one if it belongs to the underperforming group.

In many cases we may not have a direct estimate of the expected return and confidence (variance) of the view. There are several different ways to determine the confidence level.

One of the advantages of a quantitative strategy is that it can be backtested. In the case of the long-short portfolio strategy discussed above, we could estimate its historical variance through simulation with historical data. Of course, we cannot completely judge the performance of a strategy going forward from our backtests. Nevertheless, the backtest methodology allows us to obtain an estimate of the Black-Litterman view and confidence for a particular view/strategy.

Another approach of deriving estimates of the confidence of the view is through simple statistical assumptions. To illustrate, let us consider the second view in the example above: "Stock 3 will outperform

Stock 2 by 4%." If we don't know its confidence, we can come up with an estimate for it from the answers to a few simple questions. We start asking ourselves with what certainty we believe the strategy will deliver a return between 3% and 5% (4% $\pm \alpha$ where α is some constant, in this case $\alpha = 1\%$). Let us say that we believe there is a chance of two out of three that this will happen, $\frac{2}{3} \approx 67\%$. If we assume normality, we can interpret this as a 67% confidence interval for the future return to be in the interval [3%, 5%]. From this confidence interval we calculate that the implied standard deviation is equal to about 0.66%. Therefore, we would set the Black-Litterman confidence equal to $(0.66\%)^2 = 0.43\%$.

Some extensions to the Black-Litterman model have been derived. For example, Satchel and Scowcroft propose a model where an investor's view on global volatility is incorporated in the prior views by assuming that τ is unknown and stochastic.[39] Idzorek introduces a new idea for determining the confidence level of a view.[40] He proposes that the investor derives his confidence level indirectly by first specifying his confidence in the tilt away from equilibrium (the difference between the market capitalization weights and the weights implied by the view alone). Qian and Gorman describe a technique based on conditional distribution theory that allows an investor to incorporate his views on *any* or *all* variances.[41]

Of course other asset classes beyond equities and bonds can be incorporated into the Black-Litterman framework.[42] Some practical experiences and implementation details have been described by Bevan and Winkelman[43] and He and Litterman.[44] A Bayesian approach, with some similarity to the Black-Litterman model, to portfolio selection using higher moments has been proposed by Harvey, et al.[45]

---

[39] Satchel and Scowcroft, "A Demystification of the Black-Litterman Model: Managing Quantitative and Traditional Portfolio Construction."

[40] Idzorek, "A Step-By-Step Guide to the Black-Litterman Model: Incorporating User-Specified Confidence Levels."

[41] Edward Qian and Stephen Gorman, "Conditional Distribution in Portfolio Theory," *Financial Analysts Journal* 57, no. 2 (March–April 2001), pp. 44–51.

[42] See, for example, Fischer Black and Robert Litterman, "Global Asset Allocation with Equities, Bonds, and Currencies," Fixed Income Research, Goldman Sachs 1991 and Robert Litterman, *Modern Investment Management: An Equilibrium Approach* (Hoboken, NJ: John Wiley & Sons, 2003).

[43] Andrew Bevan and Kurt Winkelmann, "Using the Black-Litterman Global Asset Allocation Model: Three Years of Practical Experience," *Fixed Income Research*, Goldman Sachs, 1998.

[44] Guangliang He and Robert Litterman, "The Intuition Behind Black-Litterman Model Portfolios," *Investment Management Division*, Goldman Sachs, 1999.

[45] Campbell R. Harvey, John C. Liechty, Merril W. Liechty, and Peter Mueller, "Portfolio Selection with Higher Moments," Duke University, Working Paper, 2003.

The Black-Litterman Model: An Example

In this section we provide an illustration of the Black-Litterman model by combining a cross-sectional momentum strategy with market equilibrium. The resulting Black-Litterman expected returns are subsequently fed into a mean-variance optimizer. We start by describing the momentum strategy before we turn to the optimized strategy.

A Cross-Sectional Momentum Strategy

Practitioners and researchers alike have identified several ways to successfully predict security returns based on the past history returns. Among these findings, perhaps the most popular ones are those of momentum and reversal strategies.

The basic idea of a momentum strategy is to buy stocks that have performed well and to sell the stocks that have performed poorly with the hope that the same trend will continue in the near future. This effect was first documented in academic literature by Jegadeesh and Titman[46] in 1993 for the U.S. stock market and has thereafter been shown to be present in many other international equity markets.[47] The empirical findings show that stocks that outperformed (underperformed) over a horizon of 6 to 12 months will continue to perform well (poorly) on a horizon of 3 to 12 months to follow. Typical backtests of these strategies have historically earned about 1% per month over the following 12 months.

Many practitioners rely on momentum strategies—both on shorter as well as longer horizons. Short-term strategies tend to capitalize on intraday buy and sell pressures, whereas more intermediate and long-term strategies can be attributed to over- and underreaction of prices relative to their fundamental value as new information becomes available.[48]

Momentum portfolios tend to have high turnover so transaction and trading costs become an issue. Most studies show that the resulting profits of momentum strategies decrease if transaction costs are taken into account. For example, Korajczyk and Sadka, taking into account the different costs of buying and short-selling stocks, report that depending on the method of measurement and the particular strategy,

---

[46] Narasimhan Jegadeesh and Sheridan Titman, "Returns to Buying Winners and Selling Losers: Implications for Stock Market Efficiency," *Journal of Finance* 48, no. 1 (1993), pp. 65–91.
[47] K. Geert Rouwenhorst, "International Momentum Strategies," *Journal of Finance* 53, no. 1 (1998), pp. 267–283.
[48] Kent D. Daniel, David Hirshleifer, and Avanidhar Subrahmanyam, "Investor Psychology and Security Market Under- and Overreactions," *Journal of Finance* 53, no. 5 (1998), pp. 1839–1885.

profits between 17 to 35 basis points per month (after transaction costs) are achievable.[49]

While researchers seem to be in somewhat of an agreement on the robustness and pervasiveness of the momentum phenomenon, the debate is still ongoing on whether the empirical evidence indicates market inefficiency or if it can be explained by rational asset pricing theories. This discussion is beyond the scope of this book. Instead, we provide an illustration of a simple cross-sectional momentum strategy using the country indices from the MSCI World Index.[50]

The cross-sectional momentum portfolio is constructed at a point in time t ("today") and held for one month. We sort the countries based on their "one-day lagged" past nine-month return normalized by their individual volatilities. In other words, the ranking is based on the quantity

$$z_{t,i} = \frac{P_{t-1 \text{ day}, i} - P_{t-1 \text{ day} - 9 \text{ months}, i}}{P_{t-1 \text{ day} - 9 \text{ months}, i} \cdot \sigma_i}$$

where $P_{t-1 \text{ day}, i}$, $P_{t-1 \text{ day} - 9 \text{ months}, i}$ and σ_i denote the prices of security i at one day before t, one day and nine months before t, and the volatility of security i, respectively. After the ranking, the securities in the top half are assigned a weight of

$$w_i = \frac{1}{\sigma_i \cdot \kappa}$$

where κ is a scaling factor chosen such that the resulting annual portfolio volatility is at a desirable level. In this example, we set it equal to 20%.[51] Similarly, the securities in the bottom half are assigned a weight of

$$w_i = -\frac{1}{\sigma_i \cdot \kappa}$$

We make the portfolio weights a function of the individual volatilities in order not to overweight the most volatile assets. This is not a zero cost long-short portfolio as the portfolio weights do not sum up to zero. It is straightforward to modify the weighting scheme to achieve a zero

---

[49] Robert A. Korajczyk and Ronnie Sadka, "Are Momentum Profits Robust to Trading Costs?" *Journal of Finance* 59, no. 3 (June 2004), pp. 1039–1082.

[50] A more detailed description of the data is provided in Appendix A.

[51] κ can be estimated from past portfolio returns at each time of rebalancing. Typically, it's value does not change significantly from period to period.

cost portfolio, but for our purposes this does not matter and will not significantly change the results. The results from this simple momentum strategy are given in Exhibits 8.13 through 8.16.[52]

The momentum strategy outperforms the index on both an "alpha" and a Sharpe ratio basis. The Sharpe ratio of the strategy over the full period is 0.88 versus 0.62 for the index. The full period-annualized alpha is 11.7%, consistent with the standard results in the momentum literature. We also see that the beta of the strategy is very low, only 0.05 for the full sample. The realized correlation between the momentum strategy and the index is 3.5%. In other words, this momentum strategy is more or less market neutral.

It turns out that this particular implementation has an average monthly portfolio turnover of 23.7% with a cross-sectional standard deviation of 9.3%. The United Kingdom has the highest average turnover (40.6%) and New Zealand has the lowest (10.8%). For a "real-

EXHIBIT 8.13   Growth of Equity for the Momentum Strategy and the MSCI World Index

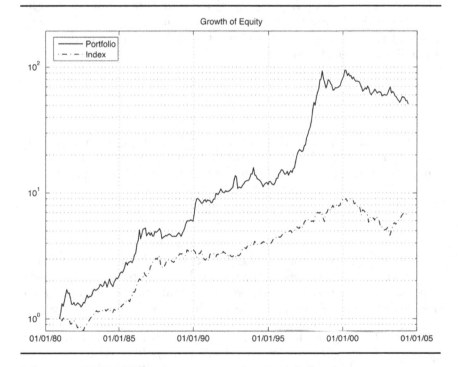

---

[52] The first portfolio is constructed in January 1981, as we need the previous nine-month return in order to perform the ranking.

EXHIBIT 8.14   A Comparison of the Annualized Volatility of the Momentum
Strategy and the Index

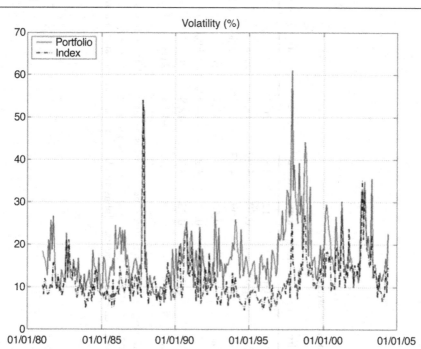

Volatility (%)

world" implementation it would therefore be important to consider the
impact of transaction costs.

An Optimized Cross-Sectional Momentum Strategy

In the previous section we introduced a simple cross-sectional momentum strategy. In this section we demonstrate how it can be combined
with market equilibrium in a portfolio optimization framework by
using the Black-Litterman model.

In this case, we only have one view—the momentum strategy. We
use the approach described earlier where we discussed the "practical
considerations and extensions" to specify the parameters for the Black-
Litterman view.

The covariance matrices needed for the portfolio optimization are calculated from daily historical data with weighting (monthly decay parameter of $d = 0.95$) and with the correction for autocorrelation of Newey and
West (2 lags).[53] We choose $\tau = 0.1$ for the Black-Litterman model.

---

[53] This particular covariance matrix estimator is described in Chapter 6.

EXHIBIT 8.15 REF15—Summary Statistics of the Momentum Strategy

	Start Date	End Date	Mean	Volatility	Sharpe Ratio	Skew	Kurtosis	Min	Max	Alpha	Beta
1st Qtr	Jan-81	Dec-85	23.0%	19.4%	1.18	0.12	2.82	-10.4%	17.1%	11.7%	0.25
2nd Qtr	Jan-86	Dec-91	22.1%	21.7%	1.02	0.50	4.90	-14.9%	21.8%	14.3%	0.06
3rd Qtr	Jan-92	Dec-97	26.9%	20.9%	1.29	-0.09	4.87	-18.8%	20.2%	22.3%	-0.02
4th Qtr	Jan-98	May-04	3.7%	20.8%	0.18	0.54	3.33	-13.1%	16.9%	-0.1%	-0.05
1st Half	Jan-81	Dec-91	22.5%	20.6%	1.09	0.36	4.23	-14.9%	21.8%	12.9%	0.12
2nd Half	Jan-92	May-04	14.8%	21.1%	0.70	0.23	3.82	-18.8%	20.2%	10.7%	-0.03
Full	Jan-81	May-04	18.4%	20.9%	0.88	0.29	4.01	-18.8%	21.8%	11.7%	0.05

Note: The columns Mean, Volatility, Sharpe Ratio, and Alpha are the annualized mean returns, volatilities, Sharpe ratios, and alphas of the portfolio over the different periods. Min and Max are the daily minimum and maximum portfolio returns, respectively. Skew and Kurtosis are calculated as the third and fourth normalized centered moments. Alphas and betas are calculated using one-month LIBOR.

EXHIBIT 8.16   REF16—Summary Statistics of the MSCI World Index

	Start Date	End Date	Mean	Volatility	Sharpe Ratio	Skew	Kurtosis	Min	Max
1st Qtr	Jan-81	Dec-85	10.2%	11.5%	0.88	−0.29	2.70	−7.6%	7.7%
2nd Qtr	Jan-86	Dec-91	13.2%	16.4%	0.81	−0.21	4.05	−14.6%	12.8%
3rd Qtr	Jan-92	Dec-97	9.6%	9.8%	0.98	0.62	3.28	−3.9%	9.5%
4th Qtr	Jan-98	May-04	2.9%	17.2%	0.17	0.17	3.49	−12.3%	16.0%
1st Half	Jan-81	Dec-91	11.8%	14.3%	0.83	−0.21	4.22	−14.6%	12.8%
2nd Half	Jan-92	May-04	6.1%	14.1%	0.43	0.15	4.32	−12.3%	16.0%
Full	Jan-81	May-04	8.8%	14.2%	0.62	−0.02	4.22	−14.6%	16.0%

Note: The columns Mean, Volatility, and Sharpe Ratio are the annualized mean returns, volatilities, and Sharpe ratios of the index over the different periods. Min and Max are the daily minimum and maximum Index returns, respectively. Skew and Kurtosis are calculated as the third and fourth normalized centered moments.

After computing the implied Black-Litterman expected returns, we use the risk aversion formulation introduced in Chapter 2 of the mean-variance optimization problem with a risk aversion coefficient of $\lambda = 2$ (calibrated to achieve about the same volatility as the index) to calculate the optimal portfolio weights and rebalance the portfolio monthly. Before rebalancing at the end of each month, we calculate the realized portfolio return and its volatility. Results and summary statistics are presented in Exhibits 8.17 through 8.19. A comparison with the MSCI World Index is given in Exhibit 8.16.

The optimized strategy has a full sample Sharpe ratio of 0.92 versus 0.62 for the index and an "alpha" of 8.3%. We observe that in the last quarter the Sharpe ratio and the "alpha" of the strategy were negative, largely due to the general downturn in the market during that period. In contrast to the standalone momentum strategy that we discussed in the previous section, since the optimized strategy is a blend of momentum and market equilibrium, its resulting correlation with the index is signif-

EXHIBIT 8.17   Growth of Equity of the Optimized Strategy and the MSCI World Index

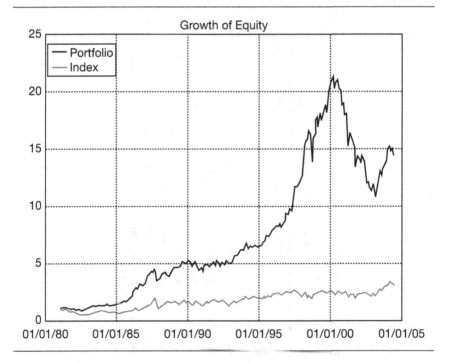

EXHIBIT 8.18 Monthly Portfolio Volatility of the Optimized Strategy Compared to Monthly Volatility of the MSCI World Index

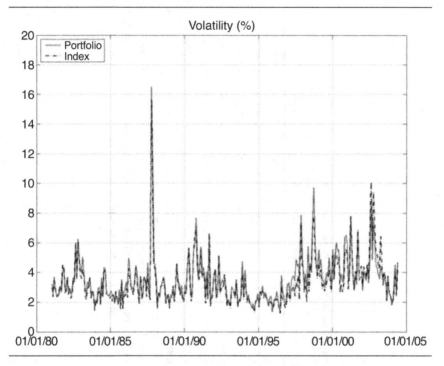

icantly different from zero. For example, the full sample correlation with the index in this case is 0.36.[54]

Albeit rudimentary, this illustration shows that it is possible to use portfolio theory and mean-variance optimization in the design of profitable investment strategies. We recall that in the illustrations presented earlier in this chapter, the standard textbook version of the mean-variance optimization always underperformed an equally weighted portfolio and the global minimum variance portfolio. There we argued that the problem of the classical mean-variance approach is in the estimation of the expected returns of the securities. The mixed estimation procedure used in the computation of the Black-Litterman implied expected returns by blending an investor's views with market equilibrium is, in practice, an effective way to mitigate estimation errors. Simply speaking, the Black-Litterman model manages to spread out any estimation

---

[54] One possibility to decrease the correlation of the strategy with the index is to impose zero β constraints.

EXHIBIT 8.19 Portfolio Summary Statistics of the Optimized Strategy Rebalanced Monthly

	Start Date	End Date	Mean	Volatility	Sharpe Ratio	Skew	Kurtosis	Min	Max	Alpha	Beta
1st Qtr	Jan-81	Dec-89	18.9%	15.0%	1.26	−0.33	4.39	−15.1%	13.2%	9.2%	0.28
2nd Qtr	Jan-90	Dec-94	13.8%	13.7%	1.01	0.35	3.92	−9.4%	12.8%	11.23%	0.40
3rd Qtr	Jan-95	Dec-99	23.8%	14.0%	1.70	0.19	4.12	−9.1%	14.4%	18.1%	0.39
4th Qtr	Jan-00	May-04	−2.9%	15.3%	−0.19	−0.28	2.82	−11.9%	8.5%	−5.0%	0.65
1st Half	Jan-81	Dec-94	16.5%	14.6%	1.13	−0.09	4.08	−15.1%	13.2%	11.4%	0.31
2nd Half	Jan-95	May-04	11.4%	15.2%	0.75	−0.13	3.60	−11.9%	14.4%	6.3%	0.37
Full	Jan-81	May-04	13.6%	14.9%	0.92	−0.11	3.88	−15.1%	14.4%	8.3%	0.36

Note: The columns Mean, Volatility, Sharpe Ratio, and Alpha are the annualized mean returns, volatilities, Sharpe ratios, and alphas of the portfolio over the different periods. Min and Max are the daily minimum and maximum portfolio returns, respectively. Skew and Kurtosis are calculated as the third and fourth normalized centered moments. Alphas and betas are calculated using one-month LIBOR.

errors in individual views over all assets and thereby makes the resulting expected returns more robust to estimation risk.

SUMMARY

- Classical mean-variance optimization is sensitive to estimation error and small changes in the inputs.
- We pointed out four different approaches to make the classical mean-variance framework more robust: (1) improve the accuracy of the inputs; (2) use constraints for the portfolio weights; (3) use portfolio resampling to calculate the portfolio weights; and (4) apply the robust optimization framework to the portfolio allocation process. This chapter focused on (1) and (2). Approaches (3) and (4) will be discussed in detail in Chapter 12.
- Typically, errors in the expected returns are about 10 times more important than errors in the covariance matrix, and errors in the variances are about twice as important as errors in the covariances.
- Estimates of expected return and covariances can be improved by using shrinkage estimation. Shrinkage is a form of averaging different estimators. The shrinkage estimator typically consists of three components: (1) an estimator with little or no structure; (2) an estimator with a lot of structure (the shrinkage target); and (3) the shrinkage intensity.
- Jorion's shrinkage estimator for the expected return shrinks towards the return of the global minimum variance portfolio.
- The sample covariance matrix should not be used as an input to the mean-variance problem. By shrinking it towards the covariance matrix with constant correlations, its quality will be improved.
- The Black-Litterman model combines an investor's views with the market equilibrium.
- The Black-Litterman expected return is a "confidence" weighted linear combination of market equilibrium and the investor's views. The confidence in the views and in market equilibrium determines the relative weighting.
- Factor models as well as simple ranking models can be simultaneously incorporated into the Black-Litterman model.

Optimization Techniques

CHAPTER 9

Mathematical and Numerical Optimization

The concept of optimization is fundamental to finance theory. The seminal work of Harry Markowitz demonstrated that financial decision making for a rational agent is essentially a question of achieving an optimal trade-off between risk and return.

From an application perspective, mathematical programming allows the rationalization of many business or technological decisions. Nevertheless, in practice, the computational tractability of the resulting analytical models is a key issue. It does not make much sense to formulate models that we are not able to solve in a reasonable timeframe. The simplex algorithm, developed in 1947 by George Dantzig, was the first tractable mathematical programming algorithms to be developed for linear optimization. Its subsequent successful implementation contributed to the acceptance of optimization as a scientific approach to decision making, and initiated the field known today as operations research.

As we showed in Chapter 4, today's portfolio allocation models often involve more complicated functional forms and constraints than the classical mean-variance optimization problem. The inclusion of transaction cost models such as those discussed in Chapters 4 and 13 has added yet another level of complexity. The asset universe available today is also much larger than what it was when Markowitz originally developed his theory.

All these factors make the resulting optimization problems more difficult to solve. Until recently, complicated large-scale portfolio optimization problems could only be solved on supercomputers. However, due to the increased computational power and the tremendous algorithmic development by researchers in operations research during the last 15 to

20 years, today many of these problems are solved routinely on desktop computers.

The area of optimization is highly technical and we do not aspire to provide a full theoretical treatment in this chapter.[1] Instead, our purpose is to provide a general understanding of the field, develop intuition for how some of the most common algorithms work, and show how they can be used in practice.

This chapter is structured as follows. We start off with a general discussion of mathematical optimization and provide a standard classification of different subclasses of optimization problems. Since today's optimization software is highly specialized and relies on specific features of a particular problem, a thorough understanding of this standard taxonomy is important for the successful use of optimization software. Thereafter, we outline the necessary conditions for optimality: the standard gradient condition in the unconstrained case and the so-called Karush-Kuhn-Tucker conditions in the constrained case. We also review optimization duality theory, a theory that plays an important role in many optimization algorithms, and is critical for understanding the idea behind robust optimization and the optimal portfolio allocation problems we will see in Chapters 12 and 13. We provide a discussion of the basic workings of different types of optimization algorithms, attempting to develop a more intuitive understanding rather than provide a full theoretical treatment. In particular, we discuss the simplex algorithm, line search methods, Newton-type methods, barrier and interior-point methods, sequential quadratic programming, and combinatorial and integer programming approaches. In Chapter 11, we review optimization software and will discuss practical issues when considering the adoption of optimization software.

MATHEMATICAL PROGRAMMING

An optimization problem consists of three basic components:

1. An objective function, denoted by f.
2. A set of unknown variables, denoted by the vector $\mathbf{x}$.
3. A set of constraints.

---

[1] For a more complete treatment of mathematical programming, see David G. Luenberger, *Linear and Nonlinear Programming* (Reading, MA: Addison-Wesley, 1984) and Jorge Nocedal and Stephen J. Wright, *Numerical Optimization* (New York: Springer Verlag, 1999).

The objective function is a mathematical expression of what we want to optimize (minimize or maximize) that depends upon the unknown variables. Constraints are sometimes provided for all or a subset of the unknown variables. For example, in the risk aversion formulation of the classical mean-variance optimization problem, the objective function is given by

$$f(\mathbf{w}) = \mathbf{w}'\boldsymbol{\mu} - \lambda\mathbf{w}'\boldsymbol{\Sigma}\mathbf{w}$$

where $\boldsymbol{\Sigma}$ is the covariance matrix, $\boldsymbol{\mu}$ is the expected return vector, λ is the risk aversion coefficient, and the unknown variables are the portfolio weights $\mathbf{w}$. If we do not allow for short-selling, we would express this constraint on the portfolio weights by the long-only constraint $\mathbf{w} \geq 0$. We discussed some of the most commonly used constraints in portfolio management in Chapter 4.

The area of mathematical and numerical optimization is devoted to the study of both theoretical properties and practical solution techniques for optimization problems of various forms. The starting point for the subject is the *nonlinear programming* (NLP) problem:

$$\min_{\mathbf{x}} f(\mathbf{x})$$
$$s.t. \quad g_i(\mathbf{x}) \leq 0 \quad i = 1, ..., I$$
$$\quad\quad h_j(\mathbf{x}) = 0 \quad j = 1, ..., J$$

where f, g_i, and h_j are smooth functions of the N-dimensional variable $\mathbf{x}$ and referred to as the *objective function*, the *inequality constraints*, and the *equality constraints*, respectively. We note that a problem that involves finding the maximum of a function f can be recast in this form simply by minimizing $-f$.

In practice, situations are encountered where it might be desirable to optimize several objectives simultaneously. For example, in Chapter 3, where we discussed portfolio optimization with higher moments, we argued that a portfolio manager might want to maximize the mean and the skew, and at the same time minimize the variance and the kurtosis. Optimization problems with multiple objectives are typically reformulated as single objective problems and then transformed into a standard optimization problems.

The nonlinear programming formulation above encompasses a large class of optimization problems. In subsequent sections, we take a closer look at some subclasses that are important in real-world modeling.

When there are no constraints, the problem is referred to as an *unconstrained optimization problem*. In this case, we would search for candidates to the solution over the whole N–dimensional space, where N is the number of decision variables. However, in the presence of constraints, not all points in the N–dimensional space are possible candidates. We say that a point x is *feasible* if it satisfies all the constraints of the optimization problem.

In mathematical programming, we distinguish between two different types of solutions, global and local solutions. We say that a feasible point x^* is a *global solution* to the optimization problem above if $f(x^*) \leq f(x)$ for all feasible points x. Further, we say that a feasible point x^* is a *local solution* to the optimization problem above if $f(x^*) \leq f(x)$ for all feasible points x in a small neighborhood of (points close to) x^*.

One could, with good reason, argue that in most situations we are interested in the global solution. So why do we make this distinction? To see that this distinction is important, let us take a look at the objective function depicted in Exhibit 9.1. The minimization problem has three local solutions indicated by A, B, and C. The global optimal solution is located at A. If we constrain solutions to be within the interval

EXHIBIT 9.1   Local versus Global Solutions

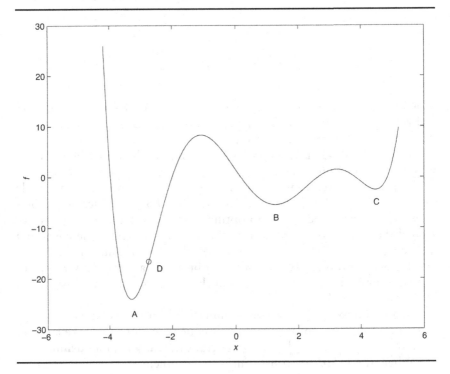

[0, 5] the global solution is located at B. However, if we change the feasible region of x to be the interval [–2.75, 5], the global optimal solution will be located at D, which is the left-end point of the interval. This simple illustration shows that locating and distinguishing the local and global solutions even for a relatively simple objective function requires some care.

Most optimization algorithms available today attempt to find only a local solution. In general, finding the global optimal solution can be very difficult, and it requires an exhaustive search that first locates all local optimal solutions and then chooses the best one among those. There is no general efficient algorithm for the global optimization problem currently available, but rather there are specialized algorithms that rely upon unique properties of the objective function and constraints. Global optimization is an active research area, but it is outside the scope of this book.[2]

Although a vast set of problems can be formulated as nonlinear programs, in practice many problems possess further structure and have properties that if, taken into account, will deliver stronger mathematical results as well as more efficient algorithms. Therefore, it makes sense to categorize optimization problems based upon their properties. Typically, problems are classified according to the form of the objective function and the functions defining the constraints. A mathematical program can be formulated in many different but equivalent ways. Thus, it is reasonable to introduce standardized formulations, *standard forms*, in which a particular class of optimization problems can be expressed. The nonlinear program introduced above is one such standard form. We discuss some of the more common classes and their standard forms next.

Linear Programming

Linear programming (LP) refers to the problem of minimizing a linear function subject to linear equality and inequality constraints. The standard form of a linear program is given by

$$\min_{\mathbf{x}} \mathbf{c}'\mathbf{x}$$
$$s.t. \ \ A\mathbf{x} = b$$
$$\mathbf{x} \geq 0$$

---

[2] We refer the interested reader to Christodoulos A. Floudas and Panos M. Pardalos, *Recent Advances in Global Optimization* (Princeton: Princeton University Press, 1992) and Panos M. Pardalos and H. Edwin Romeijn, *Handbook of Global Optimization* (Dordrecht: Kluwer, 2002).

where c is an N-dimensional vector, A is a $J \times N$ matrix, and b is a J-dimensional vector.

The linear programming problem is maybe the best known and the most frequently solved optimization problem in the real world. Some examples of when linear programming arises in financial applications include determining whether there exist static arbitrage opportunities in current market prices,[3] calculating the smallest cost hedging portfolio, pricing American options,[4] and solving portfolio optimization problems with linear risk measures such as *mean-absolute deviation* (MAD), CVaR or portfolio shortfall.[5]

Quadratic Programming

Minimizing a quadratic objective function subject to linear equality and inequality constraints is referred to as *quadratic programming* (QP). This problem is represented in standard form as

$$\min_{x} \ (\tfrac{1}{2}x'Qx + c'x)$$
$$s.t. \quad Ax = b$$
$$x \geq 0$$

where Q is an $N \times N$ matrix, c is an N-dimensional vector, A is a $J \times N$ matrix, and b is a J-dimensional vector.

We can assume that Q is symmetric. If this is not the case, we can replace Q by $\tfrac{1}{2}(Q + Q')$ without changing the value of the objective function since $x'Qx = x'Q'x$. If the matrix Q is positive semidefinite or positive definite, then this becomes a convex programming problem. In this case, *any local optimum is a global optimum*, and the problem can be solved by many of the standard algorithms for convex quadratic programming. When the matrix Q is indefinite (i.e., has both positive and negative eigenvalues), the problem can have several stationary points and local solutions and therefore becomes more difficult to solve.

---

[3] Stefano Herzel, "Arbitrage Opportunities on Derivatives: A Linear Programming Approach," Technical Report, Department of Economics, University of Perugia, 2000.

[4] Michael A. H. Dempster, James P. Hutton, and Darren G. Richards, "LP valuation of Exotic American Options Exploiting Structure," *Computational Finance* 2, no. 1 (1998), pp. 61–84.

[5] Dimitris Bertsimas, Geoffrey J. Lauprete, and Alexander Samarov, "Shortfall As Risk Measure: Properties, Optimization, and Applications," *Journal of Economic Dynamics and Control* 28, no. 7 (2004), pp. 1353–1381; and Chapter 3 in this book.

In finance, quadratic programs are a very important class of problems encountered in, for example, portfolio allocation problems (mean-variance optimization, Sharpe ratio maximization), model estimation through *ordinary least squares* (OLS) and *generalized least squares* (GLS), as well as subproblems when solving more general nonlinear programming problems through *sequential quadratic programming*, which is discussed later in this chapter.

Convex Programming

Convex programming is a large class of optimization problems that contains subclasses such as *semidefinite programs* (SPD), *second-order cones programs* (SOCP), *geometric programs* (GP), *least squares* (LS), *convex quadratic programming* (QS), and *linear programming* (LP). A convex program in standard form is given by

$$\min_{\mathbf{x}} f(\mathbf{x})$$
$$s.t. \quad g_i(\mathbf{x}) \le 0, \quad i = 1, \dots, I$$
$$\mathbf{Ax} = \mathbf{b}$$

where f and g_i are convex[6] functions, $\mathbf{A}$ is a $J \times N$ matrix, and $\mathbf{b}$ is a J-dimensional vector. Furthermore, we require that the set of all feasible points is convex.

The most fundamental property of convex programs (unlike general nonlinear programs) is that *local optimal solutions are also global optimal solutions*. Unfortunately, checking that a given optimization problem is convex is in general far from straightforward and might even be more difficult than solving the problem itself.

However, many problems in financial applications are convex by design. Some examples of convex programs that occur in finance include robust linear and quadratic programming, mean-variance optimization with quadratic constraints or loss risk constraints,[7] and some portfolio allocation problems with trading cost models.

Many efficient algorithms for these types of problems are available. In particular, during the last decade or so the development of so-called

---

[6] A subset D of the N-dimensional space is said to be convex if for every $\mathbf{x}, \mathbf{y} \in D$, all convex combinations $\alpha\mathbf{x} + (1 - \alpha)\mathbf{y}$, where $0 < \alpha < 1$, are in D. A function $f: R^N \to R$ defined on a convex set D is said to be convex if for every $\mathbf{x}, \mathbf{y} \in D$ it holds that $f(\alpha\mathbf{x} + (1 - \alpha)\mathbf{y}) \le \alpha f(\mathbf{x}) + (1 - \alpha)f(\mathbf{y})$ where $0 \le \alpha \le 1$.

[7] Loss risk constraints are of the form $\Pr(r_p \le r_0) \le \varepsilon$ where r_p is the return on a portfolio (assumed to be normally distributed), r_0 is a given undesired return level (for example, for a loss of 10% we would set $r_0 = -0.1$), and ε is the maximum probability for the undesired return.

interior-point methods for convex programming has been tremendous.[8] The name of this family of algorithms comes from the fact that they operate strictly in the interior of the feasible region. The first interior-point algorithm for solving linear programs was developed by Karmarkar.[9] Interior-point methods made the logical tie between linear and nonlinear programs clearer and now provide for a more systematic treatment of these classes of problems. We provide an introduction to some of these algorithms below.

Conic Optimization

By replacing the nonnegativity constraints in the standard form of a linear program with so-called *conic inclusion constraints*, we obtain the conic optimization problem

$$\min_{\mathbf{x}} \mathbf{c}'\mathbf{x}$$
$$s.t. \ \mathbf{Ax} = \mathbf{b}$$
$$\mathbf{x} \in C$$

where $\mathbf{c}$ is an N-dimensional vector, $\mathbf{A}$ is a $J \times N$ matrix, $\mathbf{b}$ is a J-dimensional vector, and C is a closed convex cone.[10]

Virtually any convex program can be represented as a conic optimization problem by specifying C appropriately. When $C = R_+^N$, the problem reduces to the linear programming problem in standard form with which we are familiar from above. One important class of cones is the so-called *second-order cones* ("ice cream cones")

$$C = \left\{ (x_1, \dots, x_N) \in R^N : \left(x_1 \geq \sqrt{\sum_{i=2}^{N} x_i^2} \right) \right\}$$

and Cartesian products of second-order cones. The resulting *second-order cone program* (SOCP) occurs frequently in practice and takes the form

---

[8] For a thorough treatment of interior-point algorithms, see for example, Yinyu Ye, *Interior Point Algorithms: Theory and Practice* (New York: John Wiley & Sons, 1997); Stephen J. Wright. *Primal Dual Interior Point Methods* (Philadelphia: Society of Industrial and Applied Mathematics Publications, 1999); and James Renegar, *A Mathematical View of Interior-Point Methods in Convex Optimization* (Philadelphia: Society of Industrial and Applied Mathematics Publications, 2001).
[9] Narendra Karmarkar, "A New Polynomial-Time Algorithm for Linear Programming," *Combinatorica* 4, no. 4 (December 1984), pp. 373–395.
[10] A set C is a cone if for all $\mathbf{x} \in C$ it follows that $\alpha\mathbf{x} \in C$ for all $\alpha \geq 0$. A convex cone is a cone with the property that $\mathbf{x} + \mathbf{y} \in C$ for all $\mathbf{x}, \mathbf{y} \in C$.

$$\min_{\mathbf{x}} \mathbf{c}'\mathbf{x}$$

$$s.t. \ \mathbf{A}\mathbf{x} = \mathbf{b}$$

$$\|\mathbf{C}_i\mathbf{x} + \mathbf{d}_i\| \leq \mathbf{c}_i'\mathbf{x} + e_i \ , \ i = 1, \ldots, I$$

where $\mathbf{c}$ is an N-dimensional vector, $\mathbf{A}$ is a $J{\times}N$ matrix, $\mathbf{b}$ is a J-dimensional vector, $\mathbf{C}_i$ are $I_i{\times}N$ matrices, $\mathbf{d}_i$ are I_i-dimensional vectors, and e_i are scalars.

This class of problems is general enough to encompass linear programs, convex quadratic programs, and quadratically constrained convex quadratic programs. At the same time, the problems in this class share many of the properties of linear programs, so the optimization algorithms used for solving these problems are very efficient and highly scalable. Many robust portfolio allocation problems can be formulated as SOCPs.

Several primal-dual interior-point methods have been developed in the last few years for SOCPs.[11] For example, Lobo et al. show theoretically that the number of iterations required to solve a SOCP grows at most as the square root of the problem size, while their practical numerical experiments indicate that the typical number of iterations ranges between 5 and 50—more or less independent of the problem size.[12]

Another important type of cone is the cone of semidefinite matrices.[13] An optimization problem of the kind

$$\min_{\mathbf{x}} \mathbf{C} \bullet \mathbf{X}$$

$$s.t. \ \mathbf{A}_i \bullet \mathbf{X} = b_i, i = 1, \ldots, J$$

$$\mathbf{X} \succeq 0$$

where $\mathbf{C}$, $\mathbf{A}_i$, and $\mathbf{X}$ are matrices, is called a *semidefinite program* (SDP). $\mathbf{C}$ and $\mathbf{X}$ are symmetric matrices ($\mathbf{C}$ can be converted to a symmetric

---

[11] Details on the theory and applications of SOCP can be found in Farid Alizadeh and Donald Goldfarb, "Second Order Cone Programming," Technical Report 51-2001, RUTCOR, Rutgers University, 2001; Miguel Sousa Lobo, Lieven Vandenberghe, Stephen Boyd and Hervé Lebret, "Applications of Second-Order Cone Programming," *Linear Algebra and its Applications* 284 (1998), pp. 193–222; and Yurii E. Nesterov and Arkadii Nemirovski, "Interior Point Polynomial Methods in Convex Programming," *Studies in Applied Mathematics* 13 (Philadelphia: SIAM, 1994).

[12] Miguel Sousa Lobo, Lieven Vandenberghe, Stephen Boyd, and Hervé Lebret, "Applications of Second-order Cone Programming," Technical Report, Information Systems Laboratory and the Electrical Engineering Department, Stanford University, 1998.

[13] A matrix $\mathbf{X}$ is called positive semidefinite (denoted $\mathbf{X} \succeq 0$) if $\mathbf{z}'\mathbf{X}\mathbf{z} \succeq 0$ for every real vector $\mathbf{z}$.

matrix without loss of generality). The symbol "$\bullet$" is used to denote component-wise multiplication, that is,

$$C \bullet X = \sum_{i=1}^{n} \sum_{j=1}^{n} C_{ij}X_{ij}$$

SDPs appear as robust portfolio risk minimization formulations, in particular when one models robustness with respect to errors in the estimate of the correlation matrix of asset returns. In such cases, it is natural to think of a matrix as a variable in a portfolio optimization problem. We will discuss such formulations in Chapter 12.

Despite the complicated notation, the variables in the problem are simply arrays of numbers reminiscent of vectors in linear programming. In fact, LP is a special case of SDP: just imagine that the matrix X is diagonal, with off-diagonal entries equal to 0 and diagonal entries equal to the vector of decision variables x in a linear programming formulation. Many important results and optimization algorithms such as interior point methods from linear programming have counterparts in semidefinite programming.[14]

Semidefinite programming also includes second order cone programming as a special case. Specifically, the SOCP in the form described earlier can be written as an SDP in the following way:

$$\min_{x} c'x$$
$$s.t. \ Ax = b$$
$$\begin{bmatrix} (c_i'x + e_i)I & C_ix + d_i \\ (C_ix + d_i)' & c_i'x + e_i \end{bmatrix} \succeq 0$$

where I denotes the identity matrix.

It is important to keep in mind, however, that SDPs are more computationally intensive than SOCPs, and significantly harder than LPs.[15]

---

[14] For excellent introductions to semidefinite programming, see Linden Vandenberghe and Stephen Boyd, "Semidefinite Programming," *SIAM Review* 38 (March 1996), pp. 49–95 and Robert Freund and Brian Anthony, "Introduction to Semidefinite Programming," unpublished paper, May 2004, available from http://ocw.mit.edu.

[15] Complexity results on interior point methods for semidefinite programming are described in Yurii Nestorov and Arkadi Nemirovski, "Interior-Point Polynomial Methods in Convex Programming," *Studies in Applied Mathematics* 13 (Philadelphia, PA: SIAM, 1994).

Therefore, whenever possible, it is better to formulate an optimization problem as an LP or an SOCP rather than an SDP.

Integer and Combinatorial Programming

So far our discussion has focused on optimization problems where the variables are continuous. When they are only allowed to take on discrete values such as binary values (0, 1) or integer values (..., –2, –1, 0, –1, 2, ...), we refer to the resulting mathematical programming problem as a *combinatorial, discrete,* or *integer programming* (IP) *problem.* If some variables are continuous and others are discrete, the resulting optimization problem is called a *mixed-integer programming* (MIP) *problem.*

As shown in Chapter 4, some common extensions to the classical portfolio problems may include formulations where some variables are allowed to take on only discrete values. For example, round lot and cardinality constraints are combinatorial in nature, and the resulting mean-variance problem is a mixed-integer quadratic program. Furthermore, portfolio optimization problems with transaction cost models with both fixed and proportional costs are often formulated as mixed-integer programs.

Integer and combinatorial programs are solved by branch and bound, branch and cut, disjunctive programming, special-purpose heuristics, and cutting planes algorithms. Due to the computational complexity of general combinatorial and integer programs, problem-specific algorithms are often used. Later in this chapter, we briefly discuss the general ideas behind the branch and bound, and the branch and cut methods.

NECESSARY CONDITIONS FOR OPTIMALITY FOR CONTINUOUS OPTIMIZATION PROBLEMS

In calculus we learn that optimal points of a smooth function have a simple derivative characterization: the derivative of the function must be zero at every optimal point. This result is easy to understand in the one-dimensional case. Let us assume that x^* is a local minimum and $f'(x) > 0$ for some point $x > x^*$. By moving a small amount to the left, $x - \varepsilon$, where $\varepsilon > 0$, we would be able to decrease the value of f until we reach $f(x^*)$.

In the general case of the unconstrained optimization problem

$$\min_{\mathbf{x}} f(\mathbf{x})$$

where f is an N-dimensional function, the necessary condition for a local optimal solution is given by the *gradient condition*

$$\nabla f(\mathbf{x}^*) = \left(\frac{\partial}{\partial x_1}f(\mathbf{x}^*), ..., \frac{\partial}{\partial x_N}f(\mathbf{x}^*)\right) = 0$$

If equality constraints $h_i(\mathbf{x}) = 0$, $i = 1, ..., I$ are present, then we can convert the resulting optimization problem into an unconstrained problem by using Lagrange multipliers λ_i, $i = 1, ..., I$ with a resulting objective function of the form

$$\min_{\mathbf{x}} f(\mathbf{x}) + \sum_{i=1}^{I} \lambda_i h_i(\mathbf{x})$$

The gradient condition can then be applied to this unconstrained problem for each of the vectors $\mathbf{x}$ and $\boldsymbol{\lambda}$.

In the presence of both equality and inequality constraints, $h_j(\mathbf{x}) = 0$, $j = 1, ..., J$ and $g_i(\mathbf{x}) \le 0$, $i = 1, ..., I$, the extension of the gradient condition is given by the so-called Karush-Kuhn-Tucker (KKT) conditions:

Karush-Kuhn-Tucker Conditions: Suppose that $\mathbf{x}^*$ is a local minimum of the nonlinear programming problem and that the gradient vectors $\nabla h_j(\mathbf{x}^*)$ for all j and $\nabla g_i(\mathbf{x}^*)$ for all indices i for which $g_i(\mathbf{x}^*) = 0$ are linearly independent. Then there exist vectors $\boldsymbol{\lambda} \in \mathbb{R}^J$ and $\boldsymbol{\mu} \in \mathbb{R}^I$ such that

$$\nabla f(\mathbf{x}^*) + \sum_{j=1}^{J} \lambda_j \nabla h_j(\mathbf{x}^*) + \sum_{i=1}^{I} \mu_i \nabla g_i(\mathbf{x}^*) = 0$$

$$h_j(\mathbf{x}^*) = 0, j = 1, ..., J$$
$$g_i(\mathbf{x}^*) \le 0, i = 1, ..., I$$
$$\mu_i \ge 0, i = 1, ..., I$$
$$\mu_i g_i(\mathbf{x}^*) = 0, i = 1, ..., I$$

The vectors $\boldsymbol{\lambda}$ and $\boldsymbol{\mu}$ are called *Lagrange multipliers.*

Any point that satisfies the KKT conditions is called a *KKT point.* It can be shown that if $\mathbf{x}^*$ is an optimal solution of the nonlinear programming problem, then it must be a KKT point. However, the converse is not true in general. In other words, the KKT conditions are necessary for optimality in nonlinear programming problems, but not sufficient. However, for the subclass of convex nonlinear programs, the KKT conditions are also sufficient.

We observe that the KKT conditions for general nonlinear programs take the form of a system of nonlinear equations. Many optimization algorithms are based upon solving this set of nonlinear equations.

OPTIMIZATION DUALITY THEORY

The Lagrange multipliers λ and μ from the KKT conditions have a special role in optimization theory and practice. They are in fact variables in a certain *dual* optimization problem that is related to the *primal* optimization problem in particular ways. If the primal problem is a minimization problem, then the dual problem is a maximization problem, and vice versa. The number of variables in the dual problem is equal to the number of constraints in the primal problem, and vice versa. Moreover, there is a relationship between the optimal objective function values of the primal and the dual problem that can frequently be exploited. Optimization duality theory has numerous critical applications, including, but not restricted to the following:

- Often, the dual problem has better mathematical or computational structure that can be used to compute optimal solutions to both the primal and the dual optimization problems. In addition, computing dual variables is part of a number of efficient optimization algorithms. We describe one such algorithm, the *Primal-Dual Interior Point Method*, later in this chapter.
- For some types of convex optimization problems, one can prove that an optimal solution to the primal problem has been found by constructing a dual problem solution with the same objective function value. Along the same lines, a good dual problem optimal solution can be used to bound the primal objective function value, and so can be used to identify when a primal solution is near-optimal.
- One can use dual variables to perform sensitivity analysis on the primal optimization problem. The dual variable corresponding to a particular constraint in the primal problem represents the incremental change in the optimal function value per unit increase in the value on the right hand side of the constraint equality or inequality.

Duality theory plays a major part in the methodology for deriving robust optimization problem formulations for portfolio optimization problems. We discuss such applications in Chapters 10, 12 and 13. It is therefore important to explain how dual problems are constructed and interpreted for some classes of optimization problems relevant in portfolio management.

Consider a general optimization problem (the primal problem):

$$P: \quad \begin{array}{l} \min_{\mathbf{x}} f(\mathbf{x}) \\ s.t. \ g_i(\mathbf{x}) \le 0, i = 1, ..., I \end{array}$$

The dual problem D is constructed in three steps:

1. Place the constraints in the objective function by using I nonnegative multipliers u_i to form the so-called *Lagrangian* function:

$$L(\mathbf{x}, \mathbf{u}) = f(\mathbf{x}) + \mathbf{u}'g(\mathbf{x}) = f(\mathbf{x}) + \sum_{i=1}^{I} u_i g(\mathbf{x})$$

2. Create the dual function:

$$L^*(\mathbf{u}) = \min_{\mathbf{x}} f(\mathbf{x}) + \mathbf{u}'g(\mathbf{x})$$

3. Write the dual problem:

$$D: \quad \begin{array}{l} \max_{\mathbf{u}} L^*(\mathbf{u}) \\ s.t. \ \mathbf{u} \ge 0 \end{array}$$

Usually, we construct the dual problem in the hope that computing the optimal solution will be an easy task.

Some important examples of primal and dual problems are summarized in the following table:

	Primal Problem	Dual Problem
General Conic Problems	$\min_{\mathbf{x}} c'\mathbf{x}$ $s.t. \ A\mathbf{x} = b$ $\mathbf{x} \in C$ where C is a closed convex cone.	$\max_{\mathbf{u}} \mathbf{u}'b$ $s.t. \ c - A'\mathbf{u} \in C^*$ where C^* is the dual cone of C.
Linear Problems	$\min_{\mathbf{x}} c'\mathbf{x}$ $s.t. \ A\mathbf{x} = b$ $\mathbf{x} \ge 0$	$\max_{\mathbf{u}} \mathbf{u}'b$ $s.t. \ A'\mathbf{u} \le c'$

	Primal Problem	Dual Problem
Linear Problems	$\min\limits_{x} c'x$ $s.t.\ \ Ax \geq b$	$\max\limits_{u} u'b$ $s.t.\ \ A'u = c'$ $\qquad u \geq 0$
Quadratic Problems	$\min\limits_{x} \tfrac{1}{2}x'Qx + c'x$ $s.t.\ \ Ax \geq b$	$\max\limits_{u} u'b - \tfrac{1}{2}(c - A'u)'Q^{-1}(c - A'u)$ $s.t.\ \ u \geq 0$
SOCPs	$\min\limits_{x} c'x$ $s.t.\ \ \|C_i x + d_i\| \leq c_i'x + e_i ,$ $\qquad i = 1, ..., I$	$\max\limits_{u,\,v} -\sum\limits_{i=1}^{I} u_i'd_i + v_i e_i$ $s.t.\ \ \sum\limits_{i=1}^{I} u_i C_i + v_i c_i = c$ $\qquad \|u_i\| \leq v_i, i = 1, ..., I$
SDPs	$\min\limits_{x} C \bullet X$ $s.t.\ \ A_i \bullet X = b_i, i = 1, ..., J$ $\qquad X \succeq 0$	$\max\limits_{u,\,S} \sum\limits_{i=1}^{J} u_i b_i$ $s.t.\ \ \sum\limits_{i=1}^{J} u_i A_i + S = C$ $\qquad S \succeq 0$

Note that the type of problem (LP, SOCP, SDP) in the primal is preserved in the dual problem for all of these examples (this is not the case in general nonlinear optimization). Moreover, it can be shown that for all of these types of convex problems, the objective function value of the primal problem for a feasible primal problem solution is at least as large as the objective function value of the dual problem for a feasible dual problem. In fact, for all examples of convex cone optimization problems in the table with the exception of SDPs, it is guaranteed that if the primal problem has an optimal solution, then so does the dual, and the respective objective function values are the same.[16] This has important implications for optimization algorithm applications. We will come back to this result in Chapters 10 and 12, as it is extensively used as a tool to incorporate uncertainty in estimated parameters in optimal port-

---

[16] The case of SDP duality is more complicated since the existence of solutions in one does not guarantee existence of solutions in the other problem. It is also possible that both the primal and the dual problems are feasible, but their optimal values are not equal. However, it still holds true that if one can find a feasible solution to the primal and a feasible solution to the dual, and the solutions found produce equal values for the objective functions of the two problems, then these solutions are optimal.

folio allocation models without increasing the computational complexity of the resulting robust models.

HOW DO OPTIMIZATION ALGORITHMS WORK?

Today, optimization packages are built upon rather sophisticated algorithms. It is hard for the nonexpert to learn and understand in detail how particular algorithms work. However, frequently a basic level of understanding is sufficient for making efficient use of optimization software.

In this section, we provide an intuitive overview of some of the basic principles underlying numerical optimization techniques. For further details, we refer the reader to some of the many references quoted in the text.

Optimization algorithms are of an iterative nature. That is, the algorithm or the "solver" generates a sequence of approximate solutions x_0, x_1, x_2, ... that gets closer and closer to the true solution x^*. We say that the sequence of approximate solutions converges to the true solution if

$$\|x_k - x^*\| \to 0 \text{ as } k \to \infty$$

However, since the true solution is not known and the solver cannot go on indefinitely, the iterative process is ended when a *termination criterion* or *convergence criterion* is satisfied. One of the more common convergence criteria is to stop when progress is not being made any longer; that is when

$$\|x_k - x_{k+1}\| < TOL$$

where *TOL* is a user-defined tolerance (typically a small number).

Linear Programming

Linear problems with tens or hundreds of thousands of continuous variables can today be solved efficiently. The tractable size of linear integer programs is significantly smaller but, as a general rule hundreds or thousands of variables and constraints can normally be handled without a problem.

There are two basic approaches to solving linear problems: *simplex methods* and *interior-point methods*. Both visit a progressively improving series of approximate solutions, until a solution that satisfies some convergence criteria is reached.

Simplex methods, introduced by Dantzig in the 1940s, visit so-called basic feasible solutions computed by fixing enough of the variables at their bounds to reduce the constraints $Ax = b$, where A is a $J \times N$ matrix, to a square system. This square system can then be uniquely solved for the remaining variables. Basic feasible solutions represent extreme boundary points of the feasible region, defined by $Ax = b$, $x \geq 0$, and the simplex method can be viewed as moving from one corner to another along the edges of this boundary. We give a more detailed description of the simplex method next.

The simplex method is highly efficient for most practical problems. Typically, the method requires about $2N$ to $3N$ (where N is the number of variables in the problem) iterations until the solution is found. However, theoretically speaking, the simplex method has exponential complexity (i.e., the computational time is proportional to an exponential function of the size of the problem). Therefore, it is possible to encounter problems that can be very difficult to solve computationally.[17]

It was not until the end of the 1970s when Khachiyan first discovered a method with polynomial complexity for the linear programming problem. Karmarkar described the first practical algorithm in 1984. In contrast to the simplex method, which moves along the edges of the boundary of the feasible region, Karmarkar's algorithm approaches the solution from within the interior of the feasible region and is therefore called an *interior-point method*. We give a more detailed description of interior-point methods when we discuss nonlinear problems in the next section.

The Simplex Method

The *feasible set* of a linear programming problem is the set C of points that satisfies the constraints; that is $C = \{x: Ax = b, x \geq 0\}$. We assume that the $J \times N$ matrix A defining the linear constraints has full rank. If this is not the case, we can use standard linear algebra techniques to reduce the matrix into a new matrix that satisfies this assumption.

The geometric shape of the feasible set is that of a *polytope*. The simplex method searches for optima on the vertices of the polytope.

Suppose that $x = (x_1, ..., x_N) \in C$, with at most J nonzero components. We denote by $I(x)$ the set of nonzero components of x. In other words, for $i \in I(x)$ it holds that $x_i > 0$, and for $j \notin I(x)$ it follows that $x_j = 0$. We say that x is a *basic feasible solution* if the $J \times J$ matrix made up of the columns of A corresponding to the nonzero components of x, that is

---

[17] A classical example is the one constructed by Victor Klee and George J. Minty, "How Good Is the Simplex Algorithm?" in Oved Shisha (ed.), *Inequalities* (New York: Academic Press, 1972), pp. 159–175, where the simplex method has to visit every single vertex of a polytope with 2^N vertices, N being the number of unknowns.

$$\mathbf{B} = [\mathbf{A}_i]_{i \in I(\mathbf{x})}$$

is nonsingular.

So how are the basic feasible solutions related to the solution of the linear programming problem? In fact, it is possible to demonstrate the following important results, which are often referred to as the *fundamental theorem of linear programming*:

- If the linear program is feasible and bounded, then there is at least one optimal solution. Furthermore, at least one of the optimal solution corresponds to one of the vertices of the feasible set.
- If the linear program is feasible, then there is a basic feasible solution.
- If the linear program has solutions, then at least one of these solutions is a basic feasible solution.

The first result implies that in order to obtain an optimal solution of the linear program, we can limit our search to the set of points corresponding to the vertices of the feasible polytope. The last two results imply that each of these points is determined by selecting a set of basic variables, with cardinality equal to the number of the constraints of the linear program and the additional requirement that the (uniquely determined) values of these variables are nonnegative. This further implies that the set of extreme points for a linear program in standard form, with N variables and J constraints can have only a finite number of extreme points.

A naïve approach in solving the problem would be to enumerate the entire set of extreme points and select the one that minimizes the objective function over this set. However, since there are

$$\binom{N}{J} = \frac{N!}{J!(N-J)!}$$

vertices, this approach would be very inefficient even for relatively small problem sizes. Hence a more systematic method to organize the search is needed. The simplex algorithm provides such systematic approach.

At the *k-th* iteration of the simplex method, the basic feasible solution $\mathbf{x}_k$ is known. We can partition this vector into the two subvectors

$$\mathbf{x}_B = [x_{ki}]_{i \in I(\mathbf{x}_k)} \quad \text{and} \quad \mathbf{x}_N = [x_{ki}]_{i \in I^c(\mathbf{x}_k)}$$

where $I^c(\mathbf{x}_k) = \{1, 2, ..., N\} \setminus I(\mathbf{x}_k)$ and where, for simplicity, we have dropped the superscript. Similarly, we also partition the vector $\mathbf{c}$ in the objective function and the constraint matrix $\mathbf{A}$ such that

$$\mathbf{B} = [\mathbf{A}_i]_{i \in I(\mathbf{x}_k)}, \mathbf{N} = [\mathbf{A}_i]_{i \in I(\mathbf{x}_k)}, \mathbf{c}_B = [c_i]_{i \in I(\mathbf{x}_k)}, \text{and } \mathbf{c}_N = [c_i]_{i \in I^c(\mathbf{x}_k)}$$

To construct the next basic feasible solution $\mathbf{x}_{k+1}$ we exchange one component from $\mathbf{x}_B$ and $\mathbf{x}_N$ and vice versa. What happens geometrically during this swapping process is that we move from one vertex of the feasible set to an adjacent one. However, there are many components that we could pick, so which one should be chosen?

We observe that with the notation introduced above, $\mathbf{A}\mathbf{x} = \mathbf{b}$ implies that

$$\mathbf{B}\mathbf{x}_B + \mathbf{N}\mathbf{x}_N = \mathbf{b}$$

so that

$$\mathbf{x}_B = \mathbf{B}^{-1}(\mathbf{b} - \mathbf{N}\mathbf{x}_N)$$

By writing

$$\mathbf{c}'\mathbf{x} = \mathbf{c}_B'\mathbf{x}_B + \mathbf{c}_N'\mathbf{x}_N$$

and substituting the expression for x_B above into this expression, we have

$$\mathbf{c}'\mathbf{x} = \mathbf{c}_B'\mathbf{B}^{-1}\mathbf{b} + (\mathbf{c}_N' - \mathbf{c}_B'\mathbf{B}^{-1}\mathbf{N})\mathbf{x}_N = \mathbf{c}_B'\mathbf{B}^{-1}\mathbf{b} + \mathbf{d}_B'\mathbf{x}_N$$

where $\mathbf{d}_N = \mathbf{c}_N - \mathbf{N}'(\mathbf{B}^{-1})'\mathbf{c}_B$ is referred to as the *reduced cost vector*.

From this decomposition we see that if some component, say i, of $\mathbf{d}_N$ is negative, we decrease the value of the objective function, $\mathbf{c}'\mathbf{x}$, by allowing the i-th component of $\mathbf{x}_N$ to become positive and simultaneously adjusting $\mathbf{x}_B$ to make sure that $\mathbf{x}$ stays feasible. If there is more than one negative component of $\mathbf{d}_N$, we would typically choose the one that leads to the largest decrease in the objective function. This approach is referred to as *Dantzig's rule*. However, several other strategies have been devised. When there are no negative entries in the reduced cost vector, the current basic feasible solution is the optimal solution.

From the description above it is clear that the algorithm will terminate in a finite number of steps. There are a few special pathological cases when convergence problems can occur, but well-designed solvers are normally able to overcome these difficulties.

Nonlinear Programming

Earlier in this chapter we saw that the general Karush-Kuhn-Tucker optimality conditions for a nonlinear program take the form of a system of nonlinear equations. For that reason, in order to solve the optimization problem, the majority of algorithms apply either some variant of the Newton method to this system of equations or solve a sequence of approximations of this system.

In this section, we first take a look at *line-search* and *Newton-type* methods as they provide some of the foundation for unconstrained nonlinear programming. Thereafter, we discuss two very important classes of methods for constrained nonlinear programming: *interior-point methods* and *sequential quadratic programming*.

Line-Search and Newton-Type Methods

We first describe the Newton method for the one-dimensional unconstrained optimization problem

$$\min_{x} f(x)$$

where we assume that the first and second order derivatives of f exist. Further, let us assume that we have an approximation x_k of the optimal solution x^* and we want to compute a "better" approximation x_{k+1}. The Taylor series expansion around x_k is given by

$$f(x_k + h) = f(x_k) + f'(x_k)h + \tfrac{1}{2}f''(x_k)h^2 + O(h^3)$$

where h is some small number.

If we assume h is small enough, we can ignore third and higher order terms in h. Since x_k is known, we can rewrite the original optimization problem as

$$\min_{h} f(x_k) + f'(x_k)h + \tfrac{1}{2}f''(x_k)h^2$$

This is a simple quadratic optimization problem in h, so by taking derivatives with respect to h, we have that

$$f'(x_k) + f''(x_k)h = 0$$

Solving for h we then obtain

$$h = -\frac{f'(x_k)}{f''(x_k)}$$

Therefore, we define the new approximation x_{k+1} by

$$x_{k+1} = x_k + h = x_k - \frac{f'(x_k)}{f''(x_k)}$$

This is the Newton method for the one-dimensional unconstrained optimization problem above. Given a starting value x_0, we can calculate x_1 and so forth by iteration.

The Newton method is easily extended to N-dimensional problems and then takes the form

$$\mathbf{x}_{k+1} = \mathbf{x}_k - [\nabla^2 f(\mathbf{x}_k)]^{-1} \nabla f(\mathbf{x}_k)$$

where $\mathbf{x}_{k+1}$, $\mathbf{x}_k$ are N-dimensional vectors, and $\nabla f(\mathbf{x}_k)$ and $\nabla^2 f(\mathbf{x}_k)$ are the gradient and the Hessian of f at x_k, respectively. We emphasize that $[\nabla^2 f(\mathbf{x}_k)]^{-1} \nabla f(\mathbf{x}_k)$ is shorthand for solving the linear system

$$\nabla^2 f(\mathbf{x}_k)\mathbf{h} = \nabla f(\mathbf{x}_k)$$

The Newton method is a so-called *line search strategy*: After the k-th step, $\mathbf{x}_k$ is given and the $(k+1)$-st approximation is calculated according to the iterative scheme

$$\mathbf{x}_{k+1} = \mathbf{x}_k + \gamma \mathbf{p}_k$$

where $\mathbf{p}_k \in R^N$ is the *search direction* chosen by the algorithm. Of course, in the case of the Newton method, the search direction is chosen to be $\mathbf{p}_k = -[\nabla^2 f(\mathbf{x}_k)]^{-1} \nabla f(\mathbf{x}_k)$ and $\gamma = 1$. Other search directions lead to algorithms with different properties.

For example, in the *method of steepest descent* the search direction is chosen to be $\mathbf{p}_k = -\nabla f(\mathbf{x}_k)$. The name of this method comes from the fact that at point $\mathbf{x}_k$ the direction given by $-\nabla f(\mathbf{x}_k)$ is the direction in which the function f decreases most rapidly. The step size γ can be chosen in a variety of ways.

One advantage of steepest descent is that it only requires the first-order derivatives of the function f, and not second-order derivatives as the Newton method does. Therefore, a steepest descent iteration is computationally less burdensome to perform than a Newton iteration.

However, it turns out that steepest descent and the Newton method have different convergence properties. The rate of convergence to a solution is faster for the Newton method. In particular, the Newton method has *second-order convergence* (or *quadratic convergence*) in a local neighborhood of the solution x^*, such that for all k sufficiently large it holds that

$$\left\| \mathbf{x}_{k+1} - \mathbf{x}^* \right\| \leq C \left\| \mathbf{x}_k - \mathbf{x}^* \right\|^2$$

for some constant $C > 0$. Steepest descent, in contrast, has *first-order convergence* (or *linear convergence*) in a local neighborhood of the solution x^*, which means that for all k sufficiently large it holds that

$$\left\| \mathbf{x}_{k+1} - \mathbf{x}^* \right\| \leq c \left\| \mathbf{x}_k - \mathbf{x}^* \right\|$$

for some constant $0 < c < 1$.

The main advantage of the standard Newton method is its fast local convergence. *Local convergence* means that if we are sufficiently close to a solution, the method guarantees finding it. Although the method of steepest descent converges slower than the Newton method, it always guarantees to decrease the value of the objective function.[18] Therefore, steepest descent and Newton-type methods are sometimes combined in the same optimization routine creating more efficient tools for smooth unconstrained minimization.

The main drawback of the Newton-type methods is their relatively high computational cost. At each iteration, we have to compute the Hessian of the objective function and solve an $N \times N$ linear system. If the objective function is computationally costly to evaluate or the dimension of the problem, N, is large, then the Newton method might no longer be competitive. Although the method might have fast conver-

---

[18] The Newton method can be shown to always guarantee that the value of the objective function decreases with each iteration when the Hessian matrices $\nabla^2 f(x_k)$ are positive definite and have condition numbers that can be uniformly bounded. For the method of steepest descent, these requirements do not have to be valid for the same property to hold.

gence, in this situation each iteration takes time to calculate. The method also requires that the Hessian be stored, which can be an issue for large problems. Modified Newton, quasi-Newton, and conjugate gradient methods are often computationally more efficient for large problems and converge faster than the method of steepest descent. Simplistically, modified and quasi-Newton methods use a search direction given by

$$\mathbf{p}_k = -\mathbf{B}_k^{-1}\nabla f_k$$

where $\mathbf{B}_k$ is a positive definite approximation of the true Hessian. In one of the most successful and widely used general-purpose quasi-Newton methods known as *BFGS* (Broyden, Fletcher, Goldfarb, and Shanno), the approximations are calculated according to

$$\mathbf{B}_{k+1} = \mathbf{B}_k + \frac{\mathbf{q}_k \mathbf{q}_k'}{\mathbf{q}_k' \mathbf{s}_k} - \frac{\mathbf{B}_k' \mathbf{s}_k' \mathbf{s}_k \mathbf{B}_k}{\mathbf{s}_k' \mathbf{B}_k \mathbf{s}_k}, \mathbf{B}_0 = \mathbf{I}$$

where $\mathbf{I}$ is the $N \times N$ identity matrix, and

$$\mathbf{s}_k = \mathbf{x}_{k+1} - \mathbf{x}_k$$
$$\mathbf{q}_k = \nabla f(\mathbf{x}_{k+1}) - \nabla f(\mathbf{x}_k)$$

Modern nonlinear optimization methods mimic the performance of the Newton method even though they calculate and store only a small fraction of the derivative information required by the original approach. Several other improvements have also been made for constrained problems, such as a better use of the Lagrange multipliers (often referred to as the *dual variables*) in order to speed up and improve the performance of the algorithm.

Barrier and Interior-Point Methods

In this section we describe the idea behind interior-point methods for the solution of the convex optimization problem in standard form:

$$\min_{\mathbf{x}} f(\mathbf{x})$$
$$s.t. \ g_i(\mathbf{x}) \le 0, \quad i = 1, ..., I$$
$$\mathbf{A}\mathbf{x} = \mathbf{b}$$

where f and g_i are convex functions, $\mathbf{A}$ is a $J \times N$ matrix, and $\mathbf{b}$ is a J-dimensional vector.[19]

We assume that the problem is (strictly) feasible so that a unique solution $\mathbf{x}^*$ exists. Then the KKT conditions for this problem guarantee that there exist vectors $\boldsymbol{\lambda}$ (J-dimensional) and $\boldsymbol{\mu}$ (I-dimensional) such that

$$\nabla f(\mathbf{x}^*) + \sum_{i=1}^{I} \mu_i \nabla g_i(\mathbf{x}^*) + \mathbf{A}'\boldsymbol{\lambda} = 0$$

$$\mathbf{A}\mathbf{x}^* = \mathbf{b}$$
$$g_i(\mathbf{x}^*) \leq 0, i = 1, ..., I$$
$$\mu_i \geq 0, i = 1, ..., I$$
$$\mu_i g_i(\mathbf{x}^*) = 0, i = 1, ..., I$$

In a nutshell, interior-point methods solve the optimization problem by either applying the Newton method to a sequence of equality-constrained approximations of the original problem or to a sequence of slightly modified versions of these KKT conditions. First, we will describe one type of interior-point method called the *barrier method*. Thereafter, we briefly outline the so-called primal-dual interior-point method.

A Barrier Method   In the barrier method, the idea is to convert the general problem with both equality and inequality constraints into a sequence of equality constrained approximations, which then can be solved by the Newton method.

By introducing the indicator function

$$\chi_{R_-}(x) = \begin{cases} 0, x \leq 0 \\ \infty, x > 0 \end{cases}$$

we can rewrite the original problem as

---

[19] Interior-point algorithms that follow the logic of the methods we will present in this section are also widely used for solving SDPs (recall that the decision variables in SDPs are positive semidefinite matrices instead of vectors). However, the derivation of interior-point methods for SDPs is much more involved, so we omit it here. We refer interested readers to Linden Vanderberge and Stephen Boyd, "Semidefinite Programming"; Robert Freund, "Introduction to Semidefinite Programming," Manuscript, available from http://ocw.mit.edu; and Yuri Nesterov and Arkadi Nemirovski, Interior Point Polynomial Methods in Convex Programming: Theory and Applications, SIAM, Philadelphia, PA, 1994.

$$\min_{\mathbf{x}} f(\mathbf{x}) + \sum_{i=1}^{I} \chi_{R_-}(g_i(\mathbf{x}))$$

$$s.t. \ \mathbf{Ax} = \mathbf{b}$$

In particular, we see that the domain of the function

$$\Phi(\mathbf{x}) = \sum_{i=1}^{I} \chi_{R_-}(g_i(\mathbf{x}))$$

coincides with the interior of $G = \{\mathbf{x} \in R^N : g_i(\mathbf{x}) \le 0, i = 1, ..., I\}$. However, the problem with this formulation is that the new objective function is in general *not* differentiable. The reason for this is that the indicator function χ_{R_-} is neither smooth nor differentiable at zero. The "trick" is therefore to approximate the indicator function with a smooth and differentiable function.

A common choice is to use the approximation

$$\Phi^{\varepsilon}(\mathbf{x}) = -\varepsilon \sum_{i=1}^{I} \log(-g_i(\mathbf{x})) = \varepsilon \cdot \Psi_{\log}(\mathbf{x})$$

where

$$\Psi_{\log}(\mathbf{x}) = -\sum_{i=1}^{I} \log(-g_i(\mathbf{x}))$$

is referred to as the *logarithmic barrier function*. We note that the logarithmic barrier function has the following important properties:

- It is convex and differentiable.
- Its domain is the set of points that *strictly* satisfy the inequality constraints.
- $\Psi\log(\mathbf{x}) \to \infty$ when $g_i(\mathbf{x}) \to 0$ for any i.

The resulting nonlinear programming problem with equality constraints

$$\min_{\mathbf{x}} f(\mathbf{x}) + \varepsilon \cdot \Psi_{\log}(\mathbf{x})$$

$$s.t. \ \mathbf{Ax} = \mathbf{b}$$

turns out to be a good approximation of the original problem and can be solved by the Newton method. In fact, one can show that the approximation improves incrementally as ε gets closer to zero. However, when ε is small, the resulting Hessian changes drastically when **x** takes on values such that $g_i(\mathbf{x})$ is close to zero. This behavior makes it difficult to minimize the objective function with the Newton method. The way to circumvent this problem is by solving a sequence of approximations and steadily decreasing the value of ε for each new step. At each step, the starting point for the Newton iteration is the solution of the approximation for the previous value of ε. We will see how this works below.

To apply the Newton method, we first form the Lagrangian

$$F(\mathbf{x}, \boldsymbol{\lambda}) = \frac{1}{\varepsilon} f(\mathbf{x}) + \Psi_{\log}(\mathbf{x}) + \boldsymbol{\lambda}'(\mathbf{A}\mathbf{x} - \mathbf{b})$$

where, for mathematical convenience, we first divide the objective function by ε. The gradient and the Hessian of F are easily calculated at the point $(\mathbf{x}_k, \boldsymbol{\lambda}_k)$

$$\nabla F(\mathbf{x}_k, \boldsymbol{\lambda}_k) = \begin{bmatrix} \dfrac{1}{\varepsilon} \nabla f(\mathbf{x}_k) + \nabla \Psi_{\log}(\mathbf{x}_k) + \boldsymbol{\lambda}' \mathbf{A} \\ \mathbf{A}\mathbf{x}_k - \mathbf{b} \end{bmatrix}$$

and

$$\nabla^2 F(\mathbf{x}_k, \boldsymbol{\lambda}_k) = \begin{bmatrix} \dfrac{1}{\varepsilon} \nabla^2 f(\mathbf{x}_k) + \nabla^2 \Psi_{\log}(\mathbf{x}_k) & \mathbf{A}' \\ \mathbf{A} & 0 \end{bmatrix}$$

If we already have $(\mathbf{x}_k, \boldsymbol{\lambda}_k)$ and we now want to calculate $(\mathbf{x}_{k+1}, \boldsymbol{\lambda}_{k+1})$, using the Newton method we would proceed as follows:

1. Solve the linear system

$$\nabla^2 F(\mathbf{x}_k, \boldsymbol{\lambda}_k) \begin{bmatrix} \Delta \mathbf{x} \\ \Delta \boldsymbol{\lambda} \end{bmatrix} = \nabla F(\mathbf{x}_k, \boldsymbol{\lambda}_k)$$

for the search direction $(\Delta \mathbf{x}, \Delta \boldsymbol{\lambda})'$.
2. Update

$$\begin{bmatrix} \mathbf{x}_{k+1} \\ \lambda_{k+1} \end{bmatrix} = \begin{bmatrix} \mathbf{x}_k \\ \lambda_k \end{bmatrix} - \begin{bmatrix} \Delta \mathbf{x} \\ \Delta \lambda \end{bmatrix}$$

3. If convergence criteria is not satisfied, decrease ε and go back to step 1.

The direction $(\Delta \mathbf{x}, \Delta \lambda)'$ is often referred to as the *barrier method search direction*.

A Primal-Dual Interior-Point Method It is not difficult to show that the method derived above is equivalent to applying the Newton method directly to the modified KKT equations

$$\nabla f(\mathbf{x}) + \sum_{i=1}^{I} \mu_i \nabla g_i(\mathbf{x}) + \mathbf{A}'\lambda = 0$$
$$\mathbf{A}\mathbf{x} = \mathbf{b}$$
$$-\mu_i g_i(\mathbf{x}) = \varepsilon, i = 1, \ldots, I$$

Nevertheless, the method used above is not the only approach to solve this system of nonlinear equations.

Another possibility is to apply the Newton method directly on the nonlinear system of equations with the unknown the vector $(\mathbf{x}, \mu, \lambda)$ where $\mathbf{x} \in R^N$, $\mu \in R^I$, and $\lambda \in R^J$. Written in a somewhat more compact form, the Newton method would be used on the nonlinear system

$$H(\mathbf{x}, \lambda, \mu) = \begin{bmatrix} \nabla f(\mathbf{x}) + J_g(\mathbf{x})'\mu + \mathbf{A}'\lambda \\ -\Lambda g(\mathbf{x}) - \varepsilon \mathbf{I} \\ \mathbf{A}\mathbf{x} - \mathbf{b} \end{bmatrix} = 0$$

where $\mathbf{I}$ is the $J \times J$ identity matrix and

$$\Lambda = \begin{bmatrix} \lambda_1 & & \\ & \ddots & \\ & & \lambda_J \end{bmatrix}$$

This is referred to as a primal-dual interior-point method. We see that both this and the barrier method are very closely related. The resulting search direction, $(\Delta \mathbf{x}, \Delta \mu, \Delta \lambda)$ is called the *primal-dual search direction*. It is common in the primal-dual interior-point method to take a modified Newton step

$$
\begin{bmatrix} \mathbf{x}_{k+1} \\ \mathbf{\mu}_{k+1} \\ \mathbf{\lambda}_{k+1} \end{bmatrix} = \begin{bmatrix} \mathbf{x}_k \\ \mathbf{\mu}_k \\ \mathbf{\lambda}_k \end{bmatrix} + \gamma \begin{bmatrix} \Delta\mathbf{x} \\ \Delta\mathbf{\mu} \\ \Delta\mathbf{\lambda} \end{bmatrix}
$$

where γ is chosen via a line search.

General Nonlinear Programming Problems: The Sequential Quadratic Programming Approach

In this section we provide an intuitive introduction of the *sequential quadratic programming* (SQP) approach (also referred to as *recursive quadratic programming*) for solving general nonlinear programming problems. In this approach, a sequence of approximate solutions to the original problem are generated by solving a series of quadratic programming problems. SQP methods can handle small and large optimization problems with significant nonlinearities.

We start by considering the nonlinear programming problem

$$
\min_{\mathbf{x}} f(\mathbf{x})
$$
$$
s.t. \ g_i(\mathbf{x}) \le 0 \quad i = 1, ..., I
$$
$$
h_j(\mathbf{x}) = 0 \quad j = 1, ..., J
$$

where f, g_i, and h_j are smooth functions of the N-dimensional variable $\mathbf{x}$. However, frequently a basic level of understanding is sufficient for making efficient use of optimization software. As we did for the Newton method above, let us assume that we have calculated an approximate solution $\mathbf{x}_k$ to the nonlinear programming problem. We now define a subproblem by approximating the objective function with a quadratic function and linearizing the inequality and equality constraints[20]

---

[20] We obtain the approximations through the second and first-order Taylor expansions

$$
f(\mathbf{x}_k + \mathbf{d}) = f(\mathbf{x}_k) + \nabla f(\mathbf{x}_k)\mathbf{d} + \frac{1}{2}\mathbf{d}'\nabla^2 f(\mathbf{x}_k)\mathbf{d} + O(\|\mathbf{d}\|^3)
$$

$$
h_i(\mathbf{x}_k + \mathbf{d}) = h_i(\mathbf{x}_k) + \nabla h_i(\mathbf{x}_k)\mathbf{d} + O(\|\mathbf{d}\|^2), i = 1, ..., I
$$

$$
g_j(\mathbf{x}_k + \mathbf{d}) = g_j(\mathbf{x}_k) + \nabla g_j(\mathbf{x}_k)\mathbf{d} + O(\|\mathbf{d}\|^2), j = 1, ..., J
$$

We note that by using a first-order Taylor expansion of the objective function we would get a linear approximation to the nonlinear programming problem. This is the basic idea behind *sequential linear programming* (SLP), in which a sequence of linear approximations are each solved by linear programming to produce a final solution of the nonlinear programming problem.

$$\min_{\mathbf{d}} \frac{1}{2}\mathbf{d}'\mathbf{B}_k\mathbf{d} + \nabla f(\mathbf{x}_k)\mathbf{d}$$

$$s.t. \quad \nabla h_i(\mathbf{x}_k)\mathbf{d} + h_i(\mathbf{x}_k) = 0 \quad i = 1, ..., I$$

$$\nabla g_j(\mathbf{x}_k)\mathbf{d} + g_j(\mathbf{x}_k) \leq 0 \quad j = 1, ..., J$$

where $\mathbf{B}_k = \nabla^2 f(\mathbf{x}_k)$ is the Hessian of the objective function at $\mathbf{x}_k$.

In principle, any quadratic programming algorithm can be used to solve this quadratic subproblem. However, the particular method chosen is important for large problems where otherwise the lack of computational efficiency and numerical robustness quickly becomes noticeable. Today, many SQP implementations are based on fast interior-point methods for the quadratic subproblem.

One complication that might arise is that $\mathbf{B}_k = \nabla^2 f(\mathbf{x}_k)$ may not be positive definite unless $\mathbf{x}_k$ is sufficiently close to the solution. In this case, the quadratic programming problem is no longer convex and a unique solution of the subproblem may no longer exist. One possibility is to modify the Hessian to make it positive definite at each iteration as is done in Han and Powell's version of the quasi-Newton method.[21]

Combinatorial and Integer Programming

Integer models come essentially in two different flavors: pure integer programs or mixed integer programs. In pure integer programs, the variables are restricted to either binary values, 0 or 1, or the integers ..., –2, –1, 0, 1, 2, ... Mixed-integer programs are problems that require only some of the variables to take integer values whereas others can be continuous.

Integer problem with many variables can be very difficult to solve. In contrast to continuous programs, for an integer program it can be hard to prove that a particular solution is indeed the optimal one. Therefore, in many cases, the user might have to be satisfied with an approximate solution with a provable upper bound on its distance from optimality.

In this section we make the somewhat simplifying assumption that we are dealing with a pure integer program. Our purpose is to give general ideas and provide intuition for how integer programs are solved.

The nonlinear discrete or integer programming problem has the same form as the nonlinear programming problem with the additional requirement that variables can only take on discrete or integer values

---

[21] See, for example, Luenberger, *Linear and Nonlinear Programming.*

$$\min_{\mathbf{z}} f(\mathbf{z})$$
$$s.t. \ \ g_i(\mathbf{z}) \leq 0 \quad i = 1, ..., I$$
$$\qquad h_j(\mathbf{z}) = 0 \quad j = 1, ..., J$$
$$\mathbf{z}: \text{integer}$$

Many integer problems that occur in practice are either linear or convex quadratic problems. To simplify the discussion, we drop the equality constraints and therefore consider the problem

$$\min_{\mathbf{z}} f(\mathbf{z})$$
$$s.t. \ \ g_i(\mathbf{z}) \leq 0 \quad i = 1, ..., I$$
$$\mathbf{z}: \text{integer}$$

One approach for solving these problems is by exhaustive search. For example, if for simplicity we assume that we are dealing with a 0–1 program with N variables, then we could calculate the value of the objective function for all feasible combinations of the binary 0–1 vector. Possibly, we would then have to compare 2^N candidates and choose the one that has the smallest value. Clearly, this is only possible for very small problems.

Branch and Bound

Typically, general-purpose integer programming routines are based on a procedure called "branch-and-bound." The optimal integer solution is reached by solving a sequence of so-called *continuous relaxations* organized in an *enumeration tree* with two branches at each node.

Starting at the root, we would solve the optimization problem removing the requirement that variables take on integer values

$$\min_{\mathbf{z}} f(\mathbf{z})$$
$$s.t. \ \ g_i(\mathbf{z}) \leq 0 \quad i = 1, ..., I$$

This can be done with a suitable continuous optimization algorithm. In general, the solution to the root problem, $\mathbf{x}$, will not have all integer components.

In the next step we will perform a branching in which we partition the problem (the "parent") into two mutually exclusive problems. First, we choose some noninteger component x_j of $\mathbf{x}$ and round this to the closest integer, $I_j = \lfloor x_j \rfloor$. Then, we define the two subproblems, also referred to as the "children,"

1. $\min_{\mathbf{z}} f(\mathbf{z})$

   $s.t.\ g_i(\mathbf{z}) \leq 0 \quad i = 1, \ldots, I$

   $\qquad z_j \leq I_j$

2. $\min_{\mathbf{z}} f(\mathbf{z})$

   $s.t.\ g_i(\mathbf{z}) \leq 0 \quad i = 1, \ldots, I$

   $\qquad z_j \geq I_j + 1$

These two subproblems with the additional constraints are now solved and a new branching is performed. In this way, each of the subproblems leads to two new children. If we repeat this process, sooner or later, when enough bounds have been introduced, integer solutions to the different subproblems are obtained.

At this point, we need to keep track of the best integer solution, $\mathbf{z}^*$, that so far has given the smallest value of the objective function. Doing so allows us to "prune" the binary enumeration tree. For example, if another subproblem at another branch has been solved and its final objective value is greater than $f(\mathbf{z}^*)$, then all its children will also be greater than $f(\mathbf{z}^*)$. This is because at each iteration we are making the feasible set smaller by adding more constraints, so the minimum we can find over the reduced set can be only worse than the minimum at the parent node. As we will not obtain any improvements along that particular branch, we can prune it (i.e., get rid of it).

The branching and the pruning are the two basic components in branch and bound. Implementations differ in how the branching components are selected.[22] In a worst-case situation we might, however, end up solving all of the subproblems. Therefore, branch and bound is usually combined with other techniques such as cutting planes.[23]

Cutting Planes

The branch and bound technique is often used in conjunction with cutting plane algorithms that introduce further linear constraints to the relaxed continuous problem. These linear constraints, also referred to as

---

[22] See, for example, Brian Borchers and John E. Mitchell, "An Improved Branch and Bound Algorithm for Mixed Integer Nonlinear Programs," *Computers and Operations Research* 21, no. 4 (1994), pp. 359–367.

[23] See, for example, Daniel Bienstock, "Computational Study of a Family of Mixed-Integer Quadratic Programming Problems," *Mathematical Programming* 74, no. 2 (1996), pp. 121–140.

cutting planes, are constructed based upon the underlying structure of the problem in such a way that the set of continuous feasible points, but not the set of integer feasible points, is reduced.[24] In effect, these linear constraints "cut off" part of the continuous feasible set without affecting the integer feasible set.

SUMMARY

- An optimization problem consists of three basic components: (1) an objective function; (2) a set of unknown (decision) variables; and (3) a set of constraints.
- A point is feasible if it satisfies all the constraints of the optimization problem. Otherwise, it is unfeasible.
- We distinguish between local and global solutions. If there is more than one local solution, most optimization algorithms will find one local solution that is not necessarily the global solution.
- Optimization problems are categorized according to the form of the objective function and the functions defining the constraints. Some examples of common optimization problems are linear programming, quadratic programming, convex programming, and nonlinear programming.
- For convex programs, a local optimal solution is also the global optimal solution.
- When the decision variables are not continuous but allowed to take on discrete values, the resulting optimization problem is referred to as a combinatorial, discrete or integer programming problem.
- The gradient condition is a necessary condition for a local optimal solution for continuous unconstrained optimization problems. The Karush-Kuhn-Tucker conditions are necessary conditions for a local optimal solution for continuous constrained optimization problems.
- Using optimization duality theory, one can construct a dual problem for a given optimization problem. The dual problem may have better computational properties, and may help solve the primal problem or bound the optimal objective function value of the primal problem.

---

[24] The interested reader might want to consult one of the following standard references: Laurence A. Wolsey, *Integer Programming* (New York: Wiley-Interscience, 1998); Laurence A. Wolsey and George L. Nemhauser, *Integer and Combinatorial Optimization* (New York: Wiley-Interscience, 1999); and, Christos H. Papadimitriou and Kenneth Steiglitz, *Combinatorial Optimization: Algorithms and Complexity* (Mineola, NY: Dover, 1998).

- Most optimization algorithms are iterative in nature. The number of iterations taken by an algorithm is determined by the convergence or stopping criteria.
- Today, linear problems with tens or hundreds of thousands of continuous variables can be solved efficiently. The tractable size of linear integer programs is around hundreds or thousands of variables.
- There are two basic approaches to solving linear problems: simplex methods and interior-point methods.
- Newton-type methods are common for solving unconstrained nonlinear problems. For constrained nonlinear problems, modern interior-point methods and sequential quadratic programming can be used.
- Combinatorial and integer programs are solved by branch and bound, branch and cut, disjunctive programming, special-purpose heuristics, and cutting planes techniques.

CHAPTER 10

Optimization Under Uncertainty

While optimization algorithms and software today allow a user to handle a wide variety of very complex optimization problems, the optimal solutions produced by optimization solvers can be very sensitive to small fluctuations in the problem inputs. Since real-world data are rarely certain or accurate, a number of optimization methods have been suggested for treating parameter uncertainty. The oldest such method, *sensitivity analysis*, deals with uncertainty after an optimal solution is obtained. It enables the user to determine the parameter ranges over which the current solution remains optimal, assuming that only one parameter at a time deviates from its nominal value.

Other methods incorporate uncertainty directly into the computation of the optimal solution. *Stochastic programming* methods, for example, represent the uncertain data by scenarios generated in advance: traditional stochastic linear programming finds an optimal solution that produces the best average objective function value over all scenarios. More advanced stochastic programming methods include risk considerations such as penalties for constraint violation and probabilistic guarantees.

Dynamic programming methods are designed to deal with stochastic uncertain systems over multiple stages. The optimization problem is solved recursively, going backwards from the last state, and computing the optimal solution for each possible state of the system at a particular stage. Unfortunately, they suffer from the *curse of dimensionality*: The problem size increases exponentially as new scenarios or states are added.

Robust optimization methods have emerged as a computationally attractive alternative to stochastic and dynamic programming methods. They treat uncertainty as deterministic, but do not limit parameter values to point estimates. Robust optimization requires problems to remain feasible for any values of the uncertain parameters within pre-specified uncertainty sets. Those sets are typically based on statistical estimates and probabilistic guarantees on the solution. When the uncertainty sets have special shapes, the resulting robust optimization problem can be solved efficiently.

Although the fields of stochastic programming, dynamic programming, and robust optimization overlap, historically they have evolved independently of one another. This chapter provides an intuitive overview of these techniques for optimization under uncertainty, and attempts to show the links between the three areas. We discuss applications of these techniques in Chapters 12 and 13.

The chapter is structured as follows. First, we discuss the stochastic programming methodology. We review the three most common types of stochastic programming problems (multistage, mean-risk, and chance-constrained) in the context of financial models for asset management. We then briefly introduce dynamic programming, and proceed with a more detailed review of the robust optimization field. We discuss the idea and the actual implementation of robust optimization, show some common ways of defining the uncertainty in the optimization problem, and conclude with a list of types of optimization problems that are relevant in financial management, and for which robust optimization is computationally tractable.

The material presented in this chapter is dense, so readers who are encountering problems of this type for the first time may want to focus on issues of importance to them and omit details. Portfolio managers who deal with asset allocation over longer horizons and use models which involve complicated dependencies among multiple factors may find the sections on multistage stochastic programming useful. The key idea of such stochastic programming models is to represent the realizations of important parameters in the problem via scenarios, and to solve an optimization problem that incorporates information about these scenarios. Multistage stochastic programming models have been successfully applied in asset-liability management, bond portfolio management, and pension fund management. Mean-risk and chance-constrained stochastic problems are related to different risk measures in portfolio optimization, and provide the setup for some of the advanced robust modeling topics in Chapter 13.

As we mentioned earlier, dynamic programming is a technique for solving optimization problems with uncertain coefficients over multiple periods. However, it is more widely used in financial derivative pricing than it is in asset management, so we provide only a cursory description of the technique.

The robust optimization section is particularly useful for portfolio managers interested in computationally efficient ways to incorporate uncertainty in statistical estimates of parameters in traditional portfolio optimization. The main idea behind the technique is to allow for multiple possible values of the uncertain parameters to be taken into consideration during the optimization procedure. The robust optimization section provides the background for the robust portfolio modeling applications described in Chapters 12 and 13.

STOCHASTIC PROGRAMMING

The term *stochastic programming* refers to a class of methods for incorporating stochastic components into the traditional mathematical programming framework. Typically, stochastic programming models imply optimization over scenarios of possible realizations for the random inputs. Stochastic programming theory is generally used to address the presence of random data in three types of problems:

1. Expected value two- and multistage models.
2. Models involving risk measures.
3. Chance-constrained models.

Consider a general stochastic optimization (say, maximization) problem, in which the objective function $F(\mathbf{x}, \xi)$ depends on a decision vector $\mathbf{x}$ of dimension N and a vector of uncertain parameters ξ of dimension d. Such problems are not well-defined since the objective depends on the unknown value of ξ. The simplest way to make the objective well-defined is to optimize it on average:

$$\max_{\mathbf{x}} f(\mathbf{x}) = \max_{\mathbf{x}} E[F(\mathbf{x}, \xi)]$$

where the expectation is taken over ξ.

What if uncertainty is present in the constraints? In some cases, one can formulate such problems similarly by introducing penalties for violating the constraints, thus defining a mean-risk objective function.[1] An alternative approach is to require that the constraints be satisfied for all possible (in particular, the worst-case) values of the uncertain parameters. This is a stochastic programming method whose philosophy over-

---

[1] See, for example, John Mulvey, Robert Vanderbei, and Stavros Zenios, "Robust Optimization of Large-Scale Systems," *Operations Research* 43, no. 2 (March–April 1995), pp. 264–280 and Andrzej Ruszczynski and Alexander Shapiro, "Optimization of Risk Measures," *Mathematics of Operations Research* 31, no. 3 (2006), pp. 433–452.

laps with the philosophy of *robust optimization*. Finally, one may impose the requirement that the constraints be satisfied with a high probability. This leads to a stochastic programming formulation with *chance constraints*. Recent work in robust optimization has provided methods for specifying uncertainty sets that ensure that chance constraints are satisfied with a desired probability, thus providing another link between the areas of stochastic programming and robust optimization.[2] We will come back to this point when we discuss optimization of portfolio Value-at-Risk in Chapter 13.

Multistage Stochastic Models

In *multistage stochastic programming models*, decision variables, and constraints are divided into groups corresponding to time periods, or stages $t = 1,...,T$. It is important to specify the information structure in such models in advance (i.e., what is known at each stage). A large number of financial applications—asset-liability management, index tracking, investment management—can be represented as a sequence of decisions and observations. For instance, consider the following investment example: Suppose there are $N + 1$ assets with random returns $\tilde{r}_t = (\tilde{r}_{0t}, \tilde{r}_{1t}, ..., \tilde{r}_{Nt})$ in time periods $t = 1,...,T$.[3] We assume that the 0th asset is cash. Our objective is to invest a given amount W_0 at time 0 in such a way as to maximize the expected utility of our wealth W_T at the last time period T. The utility of wealth is represented by a concave function $u(W_T)$. While we can rebalance the portfolio at each time period, we do not withdraw or add cash to it.

The situation can be described by a stochastic data process $\xi = \{\xi_1,...,\xi_T\}$ representing the realizations of asset returns $\tilde{r} = (\tilde{r}_1, ..., \tilde{r}_T)$, and decision processes

$$w(\xi) = \left\{ w_0, w_1^{\xi_1}, ..., w_T^{\xi_T} \right\}, \quad y(\xi) = \left\{ y_0, y_1^{\xi_1}, ..., y_{T-1}^{\xi_{T-1}} \right\}$$

and

$$z(\xi) = \left\{ z_0, z_1^{\xi_1}, ..., z_{T-1}^{\xi_{T-1}} \right\}$$

---

[2] Xin Chen, Melvyn Sim, and Peng Sun, "A Robust Optimization Perspective of Stochastic Programming," Working Paper, National University of Singapore Business School, June 2005.

[3] In general, we use "~" to denote random variables.

where the vectors w, y, and z at each stage correspond to the holdings, amounts sold and amounts bought for each asset in the portfolio, respectively.[4] The investor makes an investment decision at time 0 before observing the outcome of the random parameters: He (or she) buys an amount $z_{0,i}$ or sells an amount $y_{0,i}$ of a particular asset i, and incurs linear trading costs of c_{buy} or c_{sell}, respectively. Then he waits until the outcomes of the first stage ($t = 1$) random parameters are realized. In the next step, the decision is made based on the knowledge of the realization of the random parameters from the previous stage, but without observing the outcomes of the random parameters from following stages. The latter condition is called *nonanticipativity*.

Suppose that at the end of the time horizon, there are a total of S distinct scenarios for asset returns. One possible formulation of the investor's stochastic problem for a utility function $U(W_T)$ of the final wealth W_T is

$$\max_{w(\xi), y(\xi), z(\xi)} \sum_{s=1}^{S} p_s \cdot u(W_T^s)$$

$$s.t. \quad \sum_{i=1}^{N} w_{i,0}^s = W_0, \quad s = 1, \ldots, S$$

$$\sum_{i=1}^{N} w_{i,T}^s = W_T^s, \quad s = 1, \ldots, S$$

$$w_{i,t}^s = (1 + r_{i,t}^s)(w_{i,t-1}^s - y_{i,t-1}^s + z_{i,t-1}^s), s = 1, \ldots, S, t = 1, \ldots, T$$

$$w_{0,t}^s = (1 + r_{0,t}^s)\left(w_{0,t-1}^s + \sum_{i=1}^{N}(1 - c_{sell})y_{i,t-1}^s - \sum_{i=1}^{N}(1 + c_{buy})z_{i,t-1}^s \right)$$

$$s = 1, \ldots, S, t = 1, \ldots, T$$

$$w_{i,t}^s = w_{i,t}^{s'} \quad \text{for all scenarios } s \text{ and } s' \text{ with identical past up to}$$

$$\text{time } t, t = 1, \ldots, T$$

$$w_{i,t}^s, y_{i,t}^s, z_{i,t}^s \geq 0, \quad s = 1, \ldots, S, \quad t = 1, \ldots, T, \quad i = 0, \ldots, N$$

Here p_s is the probability of scenario s occurring. $p_s = 1/S$ if each scenario is equally likely.

The constraints

---

[4] The superscripts in the expressions for w(ξ), y(ξ), and z(ξ) do not mean exponents; they are used to denote the fact that the variables w, y, and z at each stage depend on the specific realizations of the random process ξ.

$$w_{i,t}^{s} = (1 + r_{i,t}^{s})(w_{i,t-1}^{s} - y_{i,t-1}^{s} + z_{i,t-1}^{s})$$

are the balance equations, reflecting the asset holdings at each time period after updating the number based on the amounts sold and bought of each asset.

The constraints

$$w_{0,t}^{s} = (1 + r_{0,t}^{s})\left(w_{0,t-1}^{s} + \sum_{i=1}^{N}(1 - c_{\text{sell}})y_{i,t-1}^{s} - \sum_{i=1}^{N}(1 + c_{\text{buy}})z_{i,t-1}^{s}\right)$$

represent the updates to the cash account based on proceeds from sales and expenses for purchases.

The constraints

$$w_{i,t}^{s} = w_{i,t}^{s'}$$

for all scenarios s and s' with identical past up to time t, $t = 1, ..., T$, represent the nonanticipativity condition.

This model can be enhanced further by, for example, requiring that the portfolio weights do not deviate too much from the weights of a benchmark portfolio in every scenario and at every stage.[5]

If one assumes a linear (or linearized) utility function, one can formulate the multistage portfolio optimization problem as a special case of the following standard-form *multistage stochastic linear program*:[6]

$$\max_{\mathbf{x}} c_0' \mathbf{x}_0 + E_{\xi_1}\left[\left(c_1^{\xi_1}\right)' \mathbf{x}_1^{\xi_1} + \ldots \right.$$

$$\left. + E_{\xi_{T-1}|\xi_{T-2}}\left[\left(c_{T-1}^{\xi_1,\ldots,\xi_{T-1}}\right)' \mathbf{x}_{T-1}^{\xi_1,\ldots,\xi_{T-1}} + E_{\xi_T|\xi_{T-1}}\left[\left(c_T^{\xi_1,\ldots,\xi_T}\right)' \mathbf{x}_T^{\xi_1,\ldots,\xi_T}\right]\right]\right]$$

s.t.

---

[5] See, for example, Nalan Gulpinar, Berc Rustem and Reuben Settergren, "Multistage Stochastic Mean-Variance Portfolio Analysis with Transaction Costs," *Innovations in Financial and Economic Networks* 3 (2003), pp. 46–63.

[6] The notation $E_{\xi_t|\xi_{t-1}}[.]$ means "expectation of the expression inside the brackets over realizations of the uncertain variable ξ_t at time t conditional on the realizations of ξ_{t-1} at time $t-1$."

$$
\begin{aligned}
A_0 x_0 &= b_0 \\
B_0^{\xi_1} x_0 \;+\; A_1^{\xi_1} x_1^{\xi_1} &= b_1^{\xi_1} \\
&\;\;\vdots \\
B_{T-1}^{\xi_T} x_{T-1}^{\xi_1, \dots, \xi_{T-1}} \;+\; A_T^{\xi_T} x_T^{\xi_1, \dots, \xi_T} &= b_T^{\xi_T} \\
x_0,\, x_1^{\xi_1},\, \dots,\, x_{T-1}^{\xi_1, \dots, \xi_{T-1}},\, x_T^{\xi_1, \dots, \xi_T} &\geq 0
\end{aligned}
$$

This block-matrix formulation of the stochastic optimization problem is frequently preferable, because specialized software (stochastic optimization packages in particular) can take advantage of the structure when applying decomposition algorithms for solving the problem. To see the equivalence of the formulations, note that the vector x_t in the above formulation can be defined to be the vector of all decision variables (holdings, amount to be bought or sold) at time period t. The diagonal elements of the matrices B_{t-1} can be defined to be the negative of the single period returns $r_{i,t-1}$, i.e., the negative of the product $B_{t-1} x_{t-1}$ is the vector of holdings of each asset and cash available at time period t. Thus, the matrices B_t "link" the information in the optimization formulation across stages. The entries for matrix A_t can be defined to represent the balance equations accounting for the change in holdings from one time period to the next, as they get updated based on the realizations of the returns over the previous time period. In our example, these matrices do not depend on the particular realizations of the uncertain parameters, but they could in a more general setting. The right hand side vector b_0 equals the initial holdings of each asset and cash, and $b_1^{\xi_1},\dots,b_T^{\xi_T}$ equal 0. The nonanticipativity constraints can substituted into the balance equations, and thus become part of the matrices B_t and A_t. Most of the objective function coefficients (namely, $c_0,\dots, c_{T-1}$) are zero. The objective function is in fact a re-formulation of the generalized stochastic programming objective[7]

$$
\max_{x}\left\{ f_0(x_0) + E_{\xi_1}\left[\max_{x_1^{\xi_1}} \left\{ f_1\!\left(x_0^{\xi_1}\right) + \dots + E_{\xi_T \mid \xi_{T-1}}\left[\max_{x_1^{\xi_1, \dots, \xi_T}} f_T\!\left(x_T^{\xi_1, \dots, \xi_T}\right) \right] \right\} \right] \right\}.
$$

In this general stochastic programming formulation, the matrices B_t and A_t, as well as the vectors b_t and c_t may all be uncertain (although

---

[7] The standard form is frequently written as a minimization problem in the literature. Note, however, that one can easily switch between maximization or minimization objectives, since maximization of a function $f(x)$ is equivalent to minimization of $-f(x)$, and the negative sign can be absorbed in the coefficients of the objective function.

EXHIBIT 10.1 Sequence of actions in the stochastic programming approach.

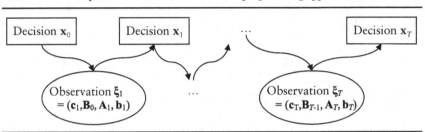

this is not the case for the particular portfolio optimization example above), and the sequence of actions is shown in Exhibit 10.1.

Scenarios and Event Trees

In order to complete the multistage stochastic programming model, one needs to specify the structure of the random process for the asset returns, which is typically reduced to a set of scenarios. The scenarios are organized in an event tree which at each stage describes the unfolding of the uncertainties with respect to possible values of the uncertain parameters (the asset returns in our example). The values of these realizations (denoted $r_{i,t}^s$ above) are then plugged into the problem formulation.

Exhibit 10.2 shows an example of such a tree if only one uncertain parameter is modeled, e.g., the price of a single factor, which is then used to compute the realized returns for the different assets in the portfolio. There are three time periods, and two optimization stages. The nodes represent points in time at which the information about the realizations of the uncertain parameter is updated. They are numbered for each stage t. The numbers in bold above the nodes denote the specific realizations of the uncertain parameter. At time 0, its value is known and unique (it is 33). At that time, there is only one node (node 0), which is called the *root* of the tree. At the last stage, there are $S_T = 5$ possible scenarios, represented by the paths from the root to the *leaves* of the tree. The numbers above the arcs of the tree represent the probabilities of moving to the next node *conditional* on having reached its ancestor node. Note that the probabilities on all branches emanating from the same node add up to 1.

Given this scenario tree, one can create the block stochastic programming formulation as follows:

1. Define decision variables $x_t^{(j)}$ for each possible scenario j at each time period t. There are different ways to define a set of decision variables, but one possibility is to have eight of them: $x_0^{(0)}$ for stage 0; $x_1^{(1)}$ and $x_1^{(2)}$ for stage 1; and $x_2^{(1)}$, $x_2^{(2)}$, $x_2^{(3)}$, $x_2^{(4)}$, $x_2^{(5)}$ for stage 2. In this

EXHIBIT 10.2   A simplified example of a scenario tree.

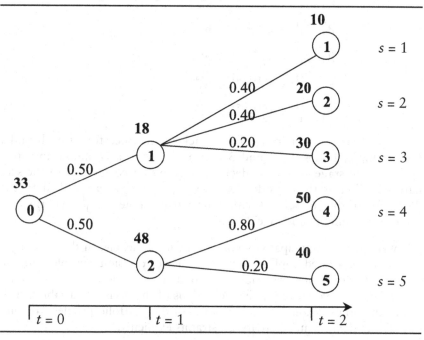

example, the number of scenarios at each stage is equal to the number of nodes at that stage, because the tree does not recombine.

2. Write out the objective as a function of these decision variables and the uncertain data:

$$\max_{\mathbf{x}} \; (\mathbf{c}_0)'\mathbf{x}_0 + p_1^{(1)}\left(\mathbf{c}_1^{(1)}\right)'\mathbf{x}_1^{(1)} + p_1^{(2)}\left(\mathbf{c}_1^{(2)}\right)'\mathbf{x}_1^{(2)} + p_2^{(1)}\left(\mathbf{c}_2^{(1)}\right)'\mathbf{x}_2^{(1)} + p_2^{(2)}\left(\mathbf{c}_2^{(2)}\right)'\mathbf{x}_2^{(2)}$$

$$+ p_2^{(3)}\left(\mathbf{c}_2^{(3)}\right)'\mathbf{x}_2^{(3)} + p_2^{(4)}\left(\mathbf{c}_2^{(4)}\right)'\mathbf{x}_2^{(4)} + p_2^{(5)}\left(\mathbf{c}_2^{(5)}\right)'\mathbf{x}_2^{(5)}$$

In the expression above, $p_t^{(j)}$ denotes the probability of scenario j at time t. For example, $p_1^{(1)} = 0.50$ and $p_2^{(4)} = (0.50)(0.80) = 0.40$.

3. Write a set of constraints for each stage and each scenario:

Stage 0: $\mathbf{A}_0^{(0)}\mathbf{x}_0^{(0)} = \mathbf{b}_0^{(0)}$

Stage 1: $\mathbf{B}_0^{(1)}\mathbf{x}_0^{(0)} + \mathbf{A}_1^{(1)}\mathbf{x}_1^{(1)} = \mathbf{b}_1^{(1)}$

$\mathbf{B}_0^{(2)}\mathbf{x}_0^{(0)} + \mathbf{A}_1^{(2)}\mathbf{x}_1^{(2)} = \mathbf{b}_1^{(2)}$

Stage 2:
$$B_1^{(1)}x_1^{(1)} + A_2^{(1)}x_2^{(1)} = b_2^{(1)}$$

$$B_1^{(2)}x_1^{(1)} + A_2^{(2)}x_2^{(2)} = b_2^{(2)}$$

$$B_1^{(3)}x_1^{(1)} + A_2^{(3)}x_2^{(3)} = b_2^{(3)}$$

$$B_1^{(4)}x_1^{(2)} + A_2^{(4)}x_2^{(4)} = b_2^{(4)}$$

$$B_1^{(5)}x_1^{(2)} + A_2^{(5)}x_2^{(5)} = b_2^{(5)}$$

Note that the constraints keep track of the ancestor of each node. For example, nodes 1, 2, and 3 at stage 2 have a common ancestor: node 1 from stage 1. So, the decision variables associated with the scenarios ending at those nodes ($x_2^{(1)}$, $x_2^{(2)}$, and $x_2^{(3)}$) are linked to the decision variable associated with node 1 from stage 1 ($x_1^{(1)}$) via the first three constraints from Stage 2.

4. Write the nonanticipativity conditions, if applicable. In this case, they are incorporated implicitly by our choice of decision variables and the fact that only one scenario corresponds to each node. Some formulations that involve alternative definitions of the decision variables, such as the original nonblock formulation of the portfolio problem, require stating the nonanticipativity constraints explicitly.[8]

Common ways to create scenario trees for the uncertain parameters include bootstrapping historical data, using parametric models in which one assumes specific probability distributions and then estimates their parameters from data, generating simple discrete distributions whose

---

[8] For example, in an alternative formulation one could associate two variables with every given node: one variable at stage t, and a copy of that decision variable for each particular "child" of that node. This kind of representation may be convenient for formulating the problem in a modeling language, depending on how the scenario data are stored. For instance, in the scenario tree in Exhibit 10.2, we could have two copies of the variable $x_1^{(2)}$ (associated with node 2 at stage 1): $x_1^{(2, 4)}$ for its "child" node 4 at stage 2, and $x_1^{(2, 5)}$ for its "child" node 5 at stage 2. Then, the constraints

$$B_1^{(4)}x_1^{(2)} + A_2^{(4)}x_2^{(4)} = b_2^{(4)} \text{ and } B_1^{(5)}x_1^{(2)} + A_2^{(5)}x_2^{(5)} = b_2^{(5)}$$

should be written as

$$B_1^{(4)}x_1^{(2, 4)} + A_2^{(4)}x_2^{(4)} = b_2^{(4)} \text{ and } B_1^{(5)}x_1^{(2, 5)} + A_2^{(5)}x_2^{(5)} = b_2^{(5)}$$

We would have to specify explicitly that $x_1^{(2, 4)} = x_1^{(2, 5)}$ to make sure that the nonanticipativity condition is satisfied. For further details, see, for example, Emmanuel Fragniere and Jacek Gondzio, "Stochastic Programming from Modeling Languages," in Stein Wallace and William Ziemba (eds.), *Applications of Stochastic Programming* (Philadelphia: Cambridge University Press, 2005).

moments are then matched to moments of real data distributions, or constructing vector autoregressive models.[9] One has to use caution when creating the tree. Its dimension becomes unmanageable very quickly, and, as the simple example above illustrated, the number of decision variables and constraints in the optimization problem is directly related to the number of scenarios. If, for example, at every stage the random returns for N assets are allowed to have just two possible realizations, the total number of scenarios at the last stage is 2^{NT}. For a portfolio of 10 assets rebalanced monthly over one year, one would have to work with 2^{120} scenarios—a number larger than the number of atoms in the universe.

Needless to say, optimization problems of such dimension are impossible to solve. Since the size of the problem tends to grow exponentially with the number of nodes, it is important to represent the underlying stochastic process with as few nodes as possible. However, it is also important to take into consideration the trade-off between the dimension of the problem and the accuracy of approximation of the underlying stochastic process, otherwise little insight is gained from solving the optimization problem.

Practical Considerations

Multistage stochastic models have been successfully applied in a variety of financial contexts, such as management of portfolios of mortgage-backed securities and asset/liability management for pension funds and insurance companies.[10] They are particularly useful in situations in which modeling complicated dependencies in a number of uncertain parameters over multiple time periods is essential. This kind of situations arise, for

---

[9] For a survey of stochastic programming applications in financial optimization and scenario generation techniques, see Li-Yong Yu, Xiao-Dong Ji and Shou-Yang Wang, "Stochastic Programming Models in Financial Optimization: A Survey," *Advanced Modeling and Optimization 5*, no. 1 (2003), pp. 1–26 and Nalan Gulpinar, Berc Rustem, Reuben Settergren, "Simulation and Optimization Approaches to Scenario Tree Generation," *Journal of Economic Dynamics and Control 28*, no. 7 (2004), pp. 1291–1315. For a description of the different econometric techniques used in scenario generation, see Frank J. Fabozzi, Sergio M. Focardi, and Petter N. Kolm, *Financial Modeling of the Equity Market* (Hoboken, New Jersey: John Wiley & Sons, 2006).

[10] See, for example, William Ziemba and John Mulvey, (eds.), *Worldwide Asset and Liability Modeling* (Cambridge: Cambridge University Press, 1998); G. Consigli and M.A.H. Dempster, "Dynamic Stochastic Programming for Asset-Liability Management," *Annals of Operations Research 81* (1998), pp. 131–161; Stavros Zenios and Pan Kang, "Mean-Absolute Deviation Portfolio Optimization for Mortgage-Backed Securities," *Annals of Operations Research 45* (1993), pp. 433–450; David Carino and William Ziemba, "Formulation of the Russell-Yasuda Kasai Financial Planning Model," *Operations Research 46*, no. 4 (July-August 1998), pp. 433–449; and Erik Bogentoft, H. Edwin Romeijn, and Stanislav Uryasev, "Asset/Liability Management for Pension Funds Using CVaR Constraints," *Journal of Risk Finance 3*, no. 1 (Fall 2001), pp. 57–71.

example, in managing callable bond portfolios or international asset portfolios, where the callable feature of the bonds, interest rate risk, default risk, or currency risk have to be taken into consideration.[11] Unfortunately, the dimension of realistic stochastic programming problems is usually very large, and optimization is challenging even with today's advanced technology. For certain types of stochastic problems, and linear optimization problems in particular, techniques such as *nested Benders decomposition*[12] and *importance sampling* can be used.[13]

The idea behind Benders decomposition is to split the multistage problem into a series of two-stage relations that are connected overall by *nesting*. Subproblems of much smaller size than the original problem are solved at each stage and scenario—these subproblems receive a trial solution from their ancestors, and communicate a trial solution to their successors. Some stochastic programming software packages, such as, OSL/SE by IBM and SPInE by the CHARISMA research center at Brunel University, contain subroutines for decomposition of large stochastic programming problems that can be called directly.[14] However, if standard optimization solvers are used, one has to implement the decomposition by calling the optimization solver repeatedly for each different subproblem.[15]

A substantial amount of research has been dedicated also to developing methodologies for effective scenario generation. The main idea is

---

[11] One of the first references to dynamic bond portfolio management is the paper by Stephen Bradley and Dwight Crane, "A Dynamic Model for Bond Portfolio Management," *Management Science* 19, no. 3 (1992). See also Andrea Beltratti, Andrea Consiglio and Stavros A. Zenios, "Scenario Modeling for the Management of International Bond Portfolios," forthcoming in *Annals of Operations Research*, and Christiana Vassiadou-Zeniou and Stavros Zenios, "Robust Optimization Models for Managing Bond Portfolios," *European Journal of Operations Research* 91 (1996), pp. 264–273.

[12] See Erwin Kalvelagen, "Benders Decomposition with GAMS," available from http://www.gams.com/~erwin/benders/benders.pdf; John Birge, "Decomposition and Partitioning Methods for Multistage Stochastic Linear Programs," *Operations Research* 33, no. 5 (1985), pp. 989–1007; George Dantzig and Gerd Infanger, "Multistage Stochastic Linear Programs for Portfolio Optimization," *Annals of Operations Research* 45 (1993), pp. 59–76; and H. I. Gassmann, "An Algorithm for the Multistage Stochastic Linear Programming Problem," *Ph.D. Thesis*, Faculty of Commerce, University of British Columbia, Vancouver.

[13] Gerd Infanger, "Monte Carlo (Importance) Sampling within a Benders Decomposition Algorithm for Stochastic Linear Programs," *Annals of Operations Research* 39 (1992), pp. 69–95.

[14] See Wallace and Ziemba (eds.), *Applications of Stochastic Programming*.

[15] For example, the optimization modeling language AMPL contains syntax for loops that can be used to generate and solve multiple subproblems. In general, however, traditional optimization modeling languages do not provide the best environment for implementing the complicated algorithms needed to solve stochastic programming problems. See Chapter 11 for description of optimization solvers and languages.

that scenario generation should not try to approximate the probability distributions of the uncertain parameters, but rather the optimal value of the optimization problem.[16] It has been shown that stochastic programming problems with two stages can be solved very efficiently, and with proven accuracy, by Monte Carlo sampling methods. However, little is known about the computational complexity and the quality of approximation of Monte Carlo sampling methods for multistage problems. In the financial modeling context, factor models and bundling of similar sample paths (as opposed to building entire scenario trees) have been used in order to reduce the dimension of such multistage problems.[17]

Mean-Risk Stochastic Models

Mean-risk stochastic models use an objective that is composed of two parts: the expectation and some measure of risk.[18] Their main idea derives from Markowitz's work on the trade-off between portfolio risk and return, described in Chapter 2. For example, suppose there are N assets with random returns $\tilde{r}_1, \tilde{r}_2, ..., \tilde{r}_N$ in the next period. We would like to invest percentages $w_1, w_2, ..., w_N$ of our capital so as to maximize our expected return and penalize for risk. We can achieve that by subtracting a multiple κ of a risk measure

$$\rho\left(\sum_{i=1}^{N} \tilde{r}_i w_i \right)$$

from the objective function. The problem then becomes[19]

$$\max_{\mathbf{w}} \sum_{i=1}^{N} \mu_i w_i - \kappa\rho\left(\sum_{i=1}^{N} \tilde{r}_i w_i \right)$$

---

[16] A good overview of recent developments in stochastic programming and importance sampling in particular is available in Andrej Ruszczynki and Alexander Shapiro (eds.), *Handbooks in Operations Research and Management Science, Volume 10: Stochastic Programming* (Amsterdam: Elsevier Science, 2003).

[17] Bogentoft, Romeijn, and Uryasev, "Asset/Liability Management for Pension Funds Using CVaR Constraints." See also John Mulvey, Robert Rush, John Mitchell, and Tom Willemain, "Stratified Filtered Sampling in Stochastic Optimization," *Journal of Applied Mathematics and Decision Sciences* 4, no. 1 (2000), pp. 17–38.

[18] For a discussion of alternative risk measures, see Chapter 3.

[19] The notation in this formulation is the same as the one used in Chapter 2 and throughout the book: μ_i are the expected returns of the individual assets, and ι is a vector of ones.

$$\text{s.t.} \quad \mathbf{w}'\iota = 1$$
$$\mathbf{w} \geq 0$$

For example, the risk measure can be defined as the portfolio variance

$$\rho \equiv E\left[\left(\tilde{\mathbf{r}}'\mathbf{w} - E\left[\tilde{\mathbf{r}}'\mathbf{w}\right]\right)^2\right]$$

which can be equivalently written as

$$\rho \equiv E\left[\left(\tilde{\mathbf{r}}'\mathbf{w}\right)^2\right] - \left(E\left[\tilde{\mathbf{r}}'\mathbf{w}\right]\right)^2$$

Suppose we are given a set of S possible scenarios for returns at stage 1, and μ_i are the average returns for assets $i = 1,\ldots,N$ over the scenarios. Let r_i^s be the realization of the return of security i in scenario s. Denote the probabilities of the scenarios by $p_1,\ldots,p_s$, where

$$\sum_{s=1}^{S} p_s = 1$$

Then, the objective in the mean-variance stochastic problem can be written as

$$\max_{\mathbf{w}} \sum_{i=1}^{N} \mu_i w_i - \kappa\left[\sum_{s=1}^{S}\left[p_s\left(\sum_{i=1}^{N} r_i^s w_i\right)^2\right] - \left(\sum_{s=1}^{S} p_s \sum_{i=1}^{N} r_i^s w_i\right)^2\right]$$

Alternatively, suppose that risk is defined as semideviation, which only looks at the shortfall below the mean:

$$\rho \equiv E\left[\max\left(E\left[\tilde{\mathbf{r}}'\mathbf{w}\right] - \tilde{\mathbf{r}}'\mathbf{w}, 0\right)\right]$$

Then the problem can be formulated as[20]

---

[20] Note that

$$\sum_{i=1}^{N} \mu_i w_i - \kappa\rho\left(\sum_{i=1}^{N} r_i w_i\right) = \sum_{i=1}^{N} \mu_i w_i - \kappa E\left[\max\left(\sum_{i=1}^{N} \mu_i w_i - \sum_{i=1}^{N} \tilde{r}_i w_i, 0\right)\right]$$

which is equal to

$$\sum_{i=1}^{N} \mu_i w_i - \kappa\sum_{i=1}^{N} \mu_i w_i - \kappa E\left[\max\left(\sum_{i=1}^{N} \mu_i w_i, \sum_{i=1}^{N} \tilde{r}_i w_i\right)\right]$$

which in turn is equal to the expression in the objective function.

$$\max_{\mathbf{w}} \; (1 - \kappa) \sum_{i=1}^{N} \mu_i w_i + \kappa E\left[\min\left(\sum_{i=1}^{N} \mu_i w_i, \; \sum_{i=1}^{N} \tilde{r}_i w_i \right) \right]$$

Given a set of S possible scenarios for returns, the above mean-risk problem can be converted into a linear programming problem. This allows for computational efficiency and becomes important in large-scale practical portfolio optimization problems. As before, let r_i^s be the realization of the return of security i in scenario s, and let us denote the probabilities of the scenarios by $p_1, ..., p_S$. We can introduce auxiliary variables R_s, $s = 1, ..., S$, to keep track of the smaller of the mean return and the realized return in each scenario, and can formulate the problem as

$$\max_{\mathbf{w}, \mathbf{R}} \; (1 - \kappa) \sum_{i=1}^{N} \mu_i w_i + \kappa \sum_{s=1}^{S} p_s R_s$$

$$s.t. \quad R_s \le \sum_{i=1}^{N} \mu_i w_i, \quad s = 1, ..., S$$

$$R_s \le \sum_{i=1}^{N} r_i^s w_i, \quad s = 1, ..., S$$

$$\mathbf{w}'\iota = 1$$

$$\mathbf{w} \ge 0$$

This problem can be handled by any linear optimization solver.

In recent years, significant progress has been made in understanding the relationship between the selected risk measures and the complexity of stochastic programming problems. For example, it is now known that other risk measures, such as Conditional Value-at-Risk (CVaR), also have the desirable property that the single-stage optimization of a portfolio subject to constraints on risk are linear optimization problems when parameter uncertainty is presented in the form of *scenarios*.[21]

At first glance, multistage mean-risk stochastic optimization should not be too much harder than single-period mean-risk optimization. However, multistage mean-risk models present challenges on both the theoretical and the computational side. Only particular classes of risk measures preserve coherence[22] and computational tractability across

---

[21] See Chapter 3 for a formulation of the sample CVaR portfolio optimization problem.

[22] See Chapter 3 for a discussion of coherent risk measures.

multiple stages of optimization, and some popular risk measures such as the variance do not have that property.[23]

Chance-Constrained Models

Chance-constrained stochastic optimization problems contain requirements on the probability of satisfying particular constraints. An important example of a chance-constrained stochastic programming problem in the portfolio management context is portfolio Value-at-Risk (VaR) optimization.[24] As before, suppose there are N assets with random returns $\tilde{r}_1, \tilde{r}_2, ..., \tilde{r}_N$ in the next year. We would like to invest percentages $w_1, w_2, ..., w_N$ of our capital in such a way that the chance of losing more than some fixed amount γ_0 (to be determined) is at most ε, where ε is in $(0,1)$, and is selected by the portfolio manager (typical values for ε include 1% and 5%).

The problem can be formulated mathematically as

$$\min_{\gamma_0, \mathbf{w}} \quad \gamma_0$$
$$s.t. \quad P(W_0 - \tilde{r}'\mathbf{w} \geq \gamma_0) \leq \varepsilon$$
$$\mathbf{w}'\iota = 1$$

where W_0 is the value of the portfolio today, and P denotes "probability."[25] The expression $W_0 - \tilde{r}'\mathbf{w}$ is the change in the portfolio value over the time period under consideration. By using a change of variables to eliminate dependence on the initial value of the portfolio ($\gamma = \gamma_0 - W_0$), the problem can be re-written as

$$\min_{\gamma, \mathbf{w}} \quad \gamma$$
$$s.t. \quad P(-\tilde{r}'\mathbf{w} \geq \gamma) \leq \varepsilon$$
$$\mathbf{w}'\iota = 1$$

---

[23] Presentation of the mathematical theory behind such risk measures is beyond the scope of this book, but the interested reader is referred to Ruszczynki and Shapiro, *Handbooks in Operations Research and Management Science, Volume 10: Stochastic Programming* for a discussion of some of the important issues. See also Philippe Artzner, Freddy Delbaen, Jean-Marc Eber, David Heath, and Hyejin Ku, "Coherent Multiperiod Risk Measurement," Working Paper, Department of Mathematics, ETH-Zurich, 2002.

[24] Recall that we introduced Value-at-Risk when we discussed advanced portfolio risk measures in Chapter 3.

[25] When the distribution of future portfolio returns is not continuous, as is the case when the optimization is performed on a set of scenarios, the "≥" inequality sign is replaced by a strict inequality.

Chance-constrained problems are very difficult to handle computationally. For example, in order to solve the problem above over a set of scenarios for the uncertain returns, one would have to introduce additional integer variables, and formulate it as a mixed-integer programming problem.[26] The first problem with the scenario formulation is that formulations with integer variables are relatively hard to solve in the general case, especially if the number of decision variables (in this case, the number of portfolio weights to be determined) is large. The second problem is that the formulation is nonconvex, which means that we do not have a guarantee that the optimization solver will find the global optimum. In fact, for practical purposes, assumptions frequently need to be made about the probability distribution of uncertain components in a chance-constrained optimization problem, so that the probabilistic constraint can be expressed in closed form. In the case of the VaR problem above, such closed form expression for the constraint is available, for example, if one assumes that future asset returns are multivariate normal. Then the future portfolio return is also normally distributed. The value of γ so that $P(-\tilde{r}'w \geq \gamma)$ (i.e., the probability that a normal random variable $\tilde{r}'w$ is less than or equal to $-\gamma$) is at most ε is actually equal to the negative of the value for the ε-quantile of the normal distribution of $\tilde{r}'w$. The value of the ε-quantile for this general normal distribution can be computed as

$$E[\tilde{r}'w] + \Phi^{-1}(\varepsilon)\sqrt{w'\Sigma w}$$

where Σ denotes the covariance matrix of the future returns (so $\sqrt{w'\Sigma w}$ is the standard deviation of the future portfolio returns) and $\Phi^{-1}(\varepsilon)$ denotes the ε-quantile of a standard normal distribution.[27] The negative of the above expression equals γ. Thus, the VaR optimization problem under the assumption of multivariate normal asset returns becomes

$$\min_{\gamma, w} \quad \gamma$$
$$s.t. \quad -E[\tilde{r}'w] - \Phi^{-1}(\varepsilon)\sqrt{w'\Sigma w} \leq \gamma$$
$$w'\iota = 1$$

---

[26] See, for example, Karthik Natarajan, Dessislava Pachamanova, and Melvyn Sim, "A Tractable Parametric Approach to Value-at-Risk Optimization," *Technical Report*, University of Singapore, July 2005.

[27] Note that in VaR optimization ε is a small number, such as 1% or 5%, so $\Phi^{-1}(\varepsilon)$ is a negative number, as it is below the mean (which is 0) of the standard normal distribution. For example, for $\varepsilon = 5\%$, $\Phi^{-1}(\varepsilon) = -1.65$. Note also that $-\Phi^{-1}(\varepsilon) = \Phi^{-1}(1 - \varepsilon)$, so that the value of the ε-quantile can be equivalently written as

$$E[\tilde{r}'w] - \Phi^{-1}(1 - \varepsilon)\sqrt{w'\Sigma w}$$

Note that to get the actual value of the VaR, we would have to add the original portfolio value, W_0, to the optimal value of γ. This is in fact the formulation that is used in practice most frequently—practitioners approximate the $(1 - \varepsilon)$-VaR of the portfolio by adding $(-\Phi^{-1}(\varepsilon))$ portfolio standard deviations to the expected portfolio loss. This approach works quite well in the case of large portfolios of stocks whose return distributions are fairly close to normal, but can grossly underestimate the VaR of portfolios of assets with skewed return distributions, such as portfolios containing financial derivatives or credit-risky securities.

Recently, robust optimization techniques have been successfully applied for approximating the optimal solutions of problems with chance constraints in stochastic programming. We will come back to the problem of VaR optimization in Chapter 13.

DYNAMIC PROGRAMMING

Dynamic programming, sometimes also called *stochastic control*, is an optimization technique for dealing with decision problems under stochastic uncertainty over multiple stages.[28] It can be used to address similar types of problems as multistage stochastic programming, but the philosophy of solving the problems is different. Most generally, instead of considering one large optimization problem, in dynamic programming one solves multiple optimization problems sequentially, starting at the last stage and proceeding backwards, thus keeping track only of the optimal paths from any given time period onwards. The differences between the dynamic programming and the stochastic programming methodologies are not clear cut, however, because dynamic programming-type methods are used in some decomposition algorithms for solving stochastic programming problems.

The basic dynamic programming model has an underlying dynamic system and an objective function (called a *reward* or a *cost* function depending on whether the problem is a maximization or a minimiza-

---

[28] The technique dates back to Bellman (see Richard Bellman, *Dynamic Programming* (Princeton, NJ: Princeton University Press, 1957)). Modern treatment of the area with applications in engineering, finance, and operations research is provided in Dimitri Bertsekas, *Dynamic Programming and Optimal Control*, vols. 1 and 2 (Belmont, MA: Athena Scientific, 1995). Applications of dynamic programming to optimal consumption and portfolio selection are discussed, for example, in Robert Merton, *Continuous-Time Finance: Revised Edition* (Cambridge, MA: Blackwell, 1995), and in Jonathan Ingersoll, Jr., *Theory of Financial Decision Making* (Savage, MD: Rowman and Littlefield, 1987).

tion) that is additive over time. The dynamic system at any point in time t is described by a vector of *state* variables $\mathbf{x}_t$ that summarizes all past information about the system, and evolves according to a relationship

$$\mathbf{x}_{t+1} = g_t(\mathbf{x}_t, \mathbf{u}_t, \boldsymbol{\xi}_t)$$

where $\mathbf{u}_t$ is a vector of *control,* or *policy,* variables to be selected by the decision-maker, and $\boldsymbol{\xi}_t$ is a vector of *random parameters* (also called disturbance or noise depending on the context). The reward at time t, which we will denote by

$$f_t(\mathbf{x}_t, \mathbf{u}_t, \boldsymbol{\xi}_t)$$

accumulates over time. Dynamic programming problems can be defined over a *finite horizon*, e.g., over a period of time T, or over an *infinite horizon*. We will assume that the horizon is finite and time is discrete. The total reward can then be written as

$$\sum_{t=0}^{T} f_t(\mathbf{x}_t, \mathbf{u}_t, \boldsymbol{\xi}_t)$$

Consider the simple multiperiod investment example we discussed when we introduced multistage stochastic programming problems. The investor has wealth W_0 at time 0, and a time horizon of T. Recall that in the previous section we formulated his problem as the following stochastic program:

$$\max_{\mathbf{x}} \left\{ f_0(\mathbf{x}_0) + E_{\boldsymbol{\xi}_1}\left[\max_{\mathbf{x}_1^{\boldsymbol{\xi}_1}} \left\{ f_1\left(\mathbf{x}_1^{\boldsymbol{\xi}_1}\right) + \ldots + E_{\boldsymbol{\xi}_T|\boldsymbol{\xi}_{T-1}}\left[\max_{\mathbf{x}_T^{\boldsymbol{\xi}_1,\ldots,\boldsymbol{\xi}_T}} f_T\left(\mathbf{x}_T^{\boldsymbol{\xi}_1,\ldots,\boldsymbol{\xi}_T}\right) \right] \right\} \right] \right\}$$

s.t.

$$
\begin{array}{lllll}
\mathbf{A}_0\mathbf{x}_0 & & & = & \mathbf{b}_0 \\
\mathbf{B}_0^{\boldsymbol{\xi}_1}\mathbf{x}_0 & + & \mathbf{A}_1^{\boldsymbol{\xi}_1}\mathbf{x}_1^{\boldsymbol{\xi}_1} & = & \mathbf{b}_1^{\boldsymbol{\xi}_1} \\
& \ddots & & \vdots & \\
& & \mathbf{B}_{T-1}^{\boldsymbol{\xi}_T}\mathbf{x}_{T-1}^{\boldsymbol{\xi}_1,\ldots,\boldsymbol{\xi}_{T-1}} + \mathbf{A}_T^{\boldsymbol{\xi}_T}\mathbf{x}_T^{\boldsymbol{\xi}_1,\ldots,\boldsymbol{\xi}_T} & = & \mathbf{b}_T^{\boldsymbol{\xi}_T}
\end{array}
$$

$$\mathbf{x}_0, \mathbf{x}_1^{\boldsymbol{\xi}_1}, \ldots, \mathbf{x}_{T-1}^{\boldsymbol{\xi}_1,\ldots,\boldsymbol{\xi}_{T-1}}, \mathbf{x}_T^{\boldsymbol{\xi}_1,\ldots,\boldsymbol{\xi}_T} \geq 0$$

In the above problem, x_t were defined to be vectors of the form $[w_t, y_t, z_t]$, i.e., consisting of all decision variables at time t—amounts invested in each available asset (w_t), amounts sold from each asset (y_t), and amounts bought from each asset (z_t). All $f_t(x_t)$ are 0 except for $f_T(x_T)$, which equals the investor's utility of final wealth.

The dynamic programming representation of the same problem is

$$\max_{u_0, u_1, \dots, u_T} \left\{ f_0(x_0) + E_{\xi_1} \left[\max_{x_1} \left\{ f_1(w_1, u_1, \xi_1) + \dots + E_{\xi_T | \xi_{T-1}} [\max_{x_T} f_T(w_T, u_T, \xi_T)] \right\} \right] \right\}$$

s.t. $B_{t-1} x_{t-1} + A_t x_t = b_t$, $\quad t = 1, \dots, T$

$\quad\quad u_t = [y_t, z_t]$, $\quad t = 1, \dots, T$

$\quad\quad x_t = [w_t, y_t, z_t]$, $\quad t = 1, \dots, T$

$\quad\quad x_0, x_1, \dots, x_{T-1}, x_T \geq 0$

The state variable for this problem is w_t, the vector of amounts invested in each asset at the start of period t. It contains all relevant past information at time t. The policy variables (u_t in our general notation) are y_t and z_t, the amounts sold and bought in time period t. The investor controls those variables. The evolution of the system is described by the relationship

$$B_{t-1} x_{t-1} + A_t x_t = b_t$$

in which the matrices B_{t-1} and A_t may be random (in our example, B_{t-1} contains information about the realizations of the uncertain parameters).

At a fundamental level, the dynamic programming algorithm for solving the problem is based on estimating the *value function* V_t in each state of the system. The value function assigns a numerical value to how good it is for the system to be in that state in terms of future rewards that can be expected. Thus, at time t in state w_t, the investor solves the problem

$$\max_{u_t} \left\{ f_t(w_t, u_t, \xi_t) + V_{t+1}(w, u, \xi) \right\}$$

s.t. $B_t x_t + A_{t+1} x_{t+1} = b_{t+1}$

$\quad\quad u_t = [y_t, z_t]$

$\quad\quad x_t = [w_t, y_t, z_t]$

$\quad\quad x_t \geq 0$

where

$$V_{t+1}(\mathbf{w}, \mathbf{u}, \boldsymbol{\xi})$$

$$= E_{\boldsymbol{\xi}_{t+1}|\boldsymbol{\xi}_t}\left[\max_{\mathbf{x}_{t+1}}\left\{f_{t+1}(\mathbf{w}_{t+1}, \mathbf{u}_{t+1}, \boldsymbol{\xi}_{t+1}) + \ldots + E_{\boldsymbol{\xi}_T|\boldsymbol{\xi}_{T-1}}[\max_{\mathbf{x}_T} f_T(\mathbf{w}_T, \mathbf{u}_T, \boldsymbol{\xi}_T)]\right\}\right]$$

Each of the maximization problems in the above expression are constrained by the equation describing the evolution of the system and all other constraints.

The procedure for finding the optimal solution $\{\mathbf{u}_0^*, \mathbf{u}_1^*, \ldots, \mathbf{u}_{T-1}^*\}$ (which is the *optimal policy* or *control* at each stage) is based on Bellman's *principle of optimality*, which states that for any intermediate time period t, the subsequence $\{\mathbf{u}_t^*, \mathbf{u}_{t+1}^*, \ldots, \mathbf{u}_{T-1}^*\}$ is optimal for the investor's problem from time t onwards. This implies that the optimal strategy can be constructed in a piecemeal fashion. First, the investor computes the optimal policy for the last stage of the problem, then he uses the solution from that problem to compute the optimal policy for the second-to-last stage, and the like.

For example, suppose the randomness in the system can be represented by the simple scenario tree in Exhibit 10.2. The investor would start by computing the optimal value of the function $f_T(\mathbf{w}_T, \boldsymbol{\xi}_T)$ at each node in stage 2. She (or he) will end up with values $f_2^{(1)}, f_2^{(2)}, f_2^{(3)}, f_2^{(4)}, f_2^{(5)}$ for nodes 1, 2, 3, 4 and 5, respectively. Then, he would look at the nodes at the previous stage (stage 1), and solve a single-period optimization problem using the optimal values for f he already computed for stage 2. At node 1 in stage 1, she would solve the following problem:

$$f_1^{(1)} = \max_{\mathbf{u}_1^{(1)}}\left\{f_1\left(\mathbf{w}_1^{(1)}, \mathbf{u}_1^{(1)}, \boldsymbol{\xi}_1^{(1)}\right) + 0.40 * f_2^{(1)} + 0.40 * f_2^{(2)} + 0.20 * f_2^{(3)}\right\}$$

$$s.t. \quad \mathbf{B}_1^{(1)}\mathbf{x}_1^{(1)} + \mathbf{A}_2\mathbf{x}_2 = \mathbf{b}_2$$

$$\mathbf{u}_1^{(1)} = [\mathbf{y}_1^{(1)}, \mathbf{z}_1^{(1)}]$$

$$\mathbf{x}_1^{(1)} = [\mathbf{w}_1^{(1)}, \mathbf{y}_1^{(1)}, \mathbf{z}_1^{(1)}]$$

$$\mathbf{x}_1^{(1)} \geq 0$$

Similarly, at node 2 in stage 1, the investor would look only at the successors of that node, and optimize

$$f_1^{(2)} = \max_{\mathbf{u}_1^{(2)}}\left\{f_1\left(\mathbf{w}_1^{(2)}, \mathbf{u}_1^{(2)}, \boldsymbol{\xi}_1^{(2)}\right) + 0.80 * f_2^{(4)} + 0.20 * f_2^{(5)}\right\}$$

subject to similar constraints. The outcome will be the optimal values of the objective function at each node in stage 2 (the values $f_1^{(1)}$ and $f_1^{(2)}$) and the optimal policy ($\mathbf{u}_1^{(1)}$ and $\mathbf{u}_1^{(2)}$) for each of these nodes. The investor will then solve another single-period problem at node 0 in stage 0.

The point of this example was only to illustrate the dynamic programming procedure. The example is overly simplified, because the number of possible states at stage t could actually be infinite.[29] It is impossible to evaluate the optimal policy an infinite number of times. In order to obtain a solution in practice, one would try to come up with a good estimate of the form of the optimal policy as a function of the state of the world at every stage instead of evaluating the exact optimal policy in every state of the world. Chryssikou[30] describes approaches for characterizing the optimal policy, and for using *approximate dynamic programming* methods to solve the investor's problem with a quadratic or exponential utility function of final wealth. In fact, approximate dynamic programming approaches are widely used in practice, since one can rarely obtain closed-form solutions to dynamic programming problems,[31] and real world problems are too large to evaluate exactly. Such approaches usually rely on *value function approximation* methods, in which an approximation of the expression for V_t is based on guesses about the structure of the optimal reward-to-go function at each stage. There is no recipe for how to construct such approximations—one usually employs the approximation that works best from experience. For example, Chryssikou bases her approximation of the value function at all stages on observations about the structure of the single-period value function. Approximate optimal policies can then be derived for each stage of the problem.

ROBUST OPTIMIZATION

A major problem with dynamic and stochastic programming formulations is that in practice it is often difficult to obtain detailed information about

---

[29] Recall that the state at stage t is defined by the current holdings $\mathbf{w}_t$. There will be an infinite number of possible values for wt if the asset holdings are represented by non-discrete numbers.

[30] Efthalia Chryssikou, "Multiperiod Portfolio Optimization in the Presence of Transaction Costs," *Ph.D. Thesis*, MIT, 1998.

[31] Sometimes this is possible, however, if particular assumptions on the evolution of the stochastic system and investor behavior are made (see, for example, Merton, *Continuous-Time Finance*).

the probability distributions of the uncertainties in the model. At the same time, depending on the number of scenarios involved, dynamic and stochastic programming methods can be prohibitively costly computationally. Thus, the dynamic and stochastic programming methodologies have not become as widely spread in practice as their tremendous modeling potential would suggest. Robust optimization is a recently developed technique that addresses the same type of problems as stochastic programming does; however, it typically makes relatively general assumptions on the probability distributions of the uncertain parameters in order to work with problem formulations that are more tractable computationally.

In the optimization literature, the term "robust optimization" has been used to describe several different concepts, and is therefore a little confusing.[32] Usually, however, *robust optimization* refers to an area of optimization whose roots are in the robust control engineering literature. It deals with making optimization models robust with respect to constraint violations by solving so-called robust counterparts of these problems for appropriately defined uncertainty sets for the uncertain parameters. These robust counterparts are in fact worst-case formulations of the original problem in terms of deviations of the parameters from their nominal values; however, typically the worst-case scenarios are defined in smart ways that do not lead to overly conservative formulations.

Consider the portfolio optimization problem we discussed earlier: there are N assets with random returns $\tilde{r} = (\tilde{r}_1, \tilde{r}_2, ..., \tilde{r}_N)$ in the next period. We would like to invest percentages $w_1, w_2, ..., w_N$ of our capital in each asset so as to maximize return. The problem can be formulated as

$$\max_{\mathbf{w}} \sum_{i=1}^{N} \tilde{r}_i w_i$$
$$s.t. \quad \mathbf{w}'\iota = 1$$
$$\mathbf{w} \geq 0$$

As before, the returns $\tilde{r}_1, \tilde{r}_2, ..., \tilde{r}_N$ can be viewed as uncertain parameters in an optimization problem. The problem, however, is not well-defined, because the objective as it is currently stated is to maxi-

---

[32] For example, "robust optimization" was used as a term by Mulvey, Vanderbei, and Zenios in their paper "Robust Optimization of Large-Scale Systems." They introduced the concepts of *solution robustness* and *model robustness*. The former holds when a solution remains "close" to optimal for all scenarios of the input data, and the latter holds if a solution remains "almost" feasible for all realizations of the input data. The authors used a penalty function to control the robustness of the solution. Their approach is based on ideas from stochastic programming, and is related to mean-risk models.

mize a random variable. In robust optimization, one makes the problem well-defined by assuming that the uncertain parameters vary in a particular set defined by one's knowledge about their probability distributions, and then takes a worst-case (max-min) approach: find portfolio weights such that the portfolio return is maximized even when the vector of realizations for the asset returns takes its "worst" value over the uncertainty set. For example, if one has information about the first and the second moments of the distribution of uncertain parameters, one can specify the following uncertainty set for the uncertain returns:

$$\sqrt{(\tilde{r} - \mu_r)'\Sigma_r^{-1}(\tilde{r} - \mu_r)} \leq \kappa$$

where μ_r is the vector of expected returns, and Σ_r is the covariance matrix of returns.

The intuition behind this uncertainty set is as follows. Random coefficient realizations are assumed to be close to the forecasts μ_r, but they may deviate. They are more likely to deviate from their means if their variability (measured by their standard deviation) is higher, so deviations from the mean are scaled by the inverse of the covariance matrix of the uncertain coefficients. The parameter κ corresponds to the overall amount of scaled deviations of the realized returns from the forecasts against which the investor would like to be protected.

The *robust counterpart* of the problem above is a *deterministic* problem, that is, a problem with no random parameters, and has the form

$$\max_{\mathbf{w}} \sum_{i=1}^{N} r_i w_i$$
$$s.t. \quad \mathbf{w}'\iota = 1$$

for every r such that $\sqrt{(r - \mu_r)'\Sigma_r^{-1}(r - \mu_r)} \leq \kappa$

$$\mathbf{w} \geq 0$$

The optimal solution of this optimization problem results in a portfolio return that will be optimal if the overall amount of scaled deviations of the realized returns from the forecasts is up to κ.

It is not immediately obvious how such a problem can be solved, as the formulation is not one that can be input directly into an optimization solver.[33] The methodology for rewriting this problem into a form that is

---

[33] Note that we cannot simply input the problem in a solver, and specify both the returns $\tilde{r}$ and the weights w as variables, since the optimization solver will return values for $\tilde{r}$ that achieve the best value of the objective function. Our goal, however, is to solve the problem for *all* values of $\tilde{r}$ in the uncertainty set.

acceptable by a solver is based on a trick from optimization duality. Namely, we first formulate a problem in which the original variables **w** are treated as fixed, and we try to find the worst-case value for the expression containing the vector of uncertain parameters $\tilde{\mathbf{r}}$. We then use optimization duality[34] to convert the expression into an optimization problem that does not contain uncertain parameters, and plug it into the original optimization problem. Finally, we solve the modified original problem with **w** as decision variables. While a certain amount of pre-processing is involved in formulating the robust problem, there is only one call to an optimization solver once the robust problem is formulated correctly.

We illustrate in more detail how the robust counterpart of the above problem can be found.

First, we write the optimization problem of finding the worst-case value of the expression containing the vector of uncertain coefficients $\tilde{\mathbf{r}}$. In this case, this expression is the objective function, and the worst-case value of the expression is the minimum portfolio return that would result from the uncertain parameters $\tilde{\mathbf{r}}$ deviating from their forecasted (nominal) values:[35]

$$\min_{\mathbf{r}} \ \sum_{i=1}^{N} r_i w_i$$

$$s.t. \quad \left\| \Sigma_r^{-1/2} (\mathbf{r} - \mu_r) \right\| \leq \kappa$$

This is an SOCP, and its dual problem is[36]

$$\max_{\mathbf{u}, v} \ -(-\mathbf{u}'\Sigma_r^{-1/2}\mu_r) - \kappa v$$

$$s.t. \quad \Sigma_r^{-1/2}\mathbf{u} + 0 \cdot v = \mathbf{w}$$

$$\|\mathbf{u}\| \leq v$$

---

[34] See Chapter 9 for a brief introduction to optimization duality theory.

[35] We use the fact that the expression

$$\sqrt{(\mathbf{r} - \mu_r)'\Sigma_r^{-1}(\mathbf{r} - \mu_r)}$$

is equivalent to $\left\| \Sigma_r^{-1/2}(\mathbf{r} - \mu_r) \right\|$, where $\|.\|$ is the l_2 (Euclidean, elliptic) norm, defined as

$$\sqrt{x_1^2 + \ldots + x_N^2}$$

for a vector **x** of dimension N.

[36] See the introduction to second order cone problems and optimization duality in Chapter 9.

Note that one of the constraints allows us to express **u** in terms of v and **w**, that is,

$$\mathbf{u} = \Sigma_r^{1/2}\mathbf{w}$$

Therefore, the dual problem is equivalent to

$$\max_{v} \; \mathbf{w}'\Sigma_r^{1/2}\Sigma_r^{-1/2}\boldsymbol{\mu}_r - \kappa v$$
$$s.t. \quad \left\|\Sigma_r^{1/2}\mathbf{w}\right\| \leq v$$

which can be rewritten as

$$\max_{v} \; \mathbf{w}'\boldsymbol{\mu}_r - \kappa v$$
$$s.t. \quad \left\|\Sigma_r^{1/2}\mathbf{w}\right\| \leq v$$

Since this is an SOCP, duality theory states that the optimal objective function value is the same as the value of the primal (minimization) problem. Therefore, the worst-case value for the portfolio return will be given by the expression

$$\mathbf{w}'\boldsymbol{\mu}_r - \kappa\left\|\Sigma_r^{1/2}\mathbf{w}\right\| = \mathbf{w}'\boldsymbol{\mu}_r - \kappa\sqrt{\mathbf{w}'\Sigma_r\mathbf{w}}$$

for any fixed set of weights **w**. Note that this expression does not contain the uncertain coefficients $\tilde{\mathbf{r}}$. So, we can replace the expression in the objective function of the original portfolio optimization problem, and optimize over **w**:

$$\max_{\mathbf{w}} \; \mathbf{w}'\boldsymbol{\mu}_r - \kappa\sqrt{\mathbf{w}'\Sigma_r\mathbf{w}}$$
$$s.t. \quad \mathbf{w}'\iota = 1$$
$$\mathbf{w} \geq 0$$

This optimization formulation is equivalent to the optimization problem we wanted to solve. However, now the formulation is in a form that can be passed to an optimization solver. Nonlinear solvers such as MINOS can handle it. Alternatively, since it is an SOCP, a solver such as SeDuMi or SDPT3 would be able to take advantage of its structure and solve it more efficiently.

Note that this robust formulation is reminiscent of Markowitz's portfolio problem, except that we penalize for the standard deviation (instead of the variance) of the portfolio return. In fact, it can be shown that by defining different types of uncertainty sets for the uncertain returns, one defines different risk measures on the future portfolio return, so there is a natural link between the robust optimization philosophy and mean-risk portfolio optimization or mean-risk stochastic programming models.[37] We presented this simple example only to illustrate the main idea behind finding robust counterparts. Chapter 12 contains a number of illustrations of applications of robust optimization in incorporating estimation errors from parameter estimation in portfolio allocation formulations. More recently, robust optimization has also been successfully applied to multiperiod portfolio optimization problems that previously were considered intractable computationally. We will discuss such applications in Chapter 13.

Only particular types of optimization problems paired with particular types of uncertainty sets are known to allow for closed-form robust formulations that are computationally tractable. Before we present some general results on robust formulations for common portfolio optimization problems, we provide guidance as to how uncertainty sets can be selected in practice.

Selecting Uncertainty Sets

A simple way to model uncertainty is to generate scenarios for the possible values of the uncertain parameters using, for example, future asset returns. As we mentioned earlier in this chapter, scenario optimization can be incorporated in the robust optimization framework by specifying an uncertainty set that is a collection of scenarios for the uncertain parameters. The robust formulation of the original problem would then contain a set of constraints—one for each scenario in the uncertainty set—and the optimization would make sure that the original constraint is satisfied for the worst-case scenario in the set. How many scenarios from the underlying distribution for the uncertain parameters should be included in the uncertainty set in order to guarantee that the probability that the constraint will be violated in reality will be at most ε? For a convex constraint of the kind $f(x, \tilde{z}) \geq 0$, where x is an N-dimensional vector of decision variables, Calafiore and Campi[38] showed that if the number of scenarios n is selected so that

---

[37] Karthik Natarajan, Dessislava Pachamanova, and Melvyn Sim, "Constructing Risk Measures from Uncertainty Sets," Working Paper, July 2005.

[38] Giuseppe Calafiore and M. Campi, "Uncertain Convex Programs: Randomized Solutions and Confidence Levels," *Mathematical Programming* (Ser. A) 102, no. 1 (January 2005), pp. 25–46.

$$n \geq \frac{N}{\varepsilon\beta} - 1$$

then with probability $1 - \beta$, the probability of violating the constraint is at most ε.[39] This bound, however, can be conservative. For example, if one has a portfolio of $N = 100$ stocks and would like to be sure that the probability that a constraint on the future portfolio return of the kind

$$\sum_{i=1}^{N = 100} \tilde{r}_i w_i \geq r_{\text{target}}$$

is violated is less than $\varepsilon = 1\%$ with probability $1 - \beta = 99\%$, one has to draw

$$n \geq \frac{100}{0.01 \cdot 0.01} - 1 = 999{,}999$$

scenarios, and solve an optimization problem with 999,999 constraints, one for each scenario for the set of N asset returns.

In practice, uncertainty sets are usually extended to richer sets ranging from polytopes to more advanced conic-representable sets derived from statistical procedures. For example, one can frequently obtain confidence intervals for the uncertain parameters. The uncertainty set then is *polytopic*, and looks like a "box". For a vector of uncertain coefficients $\tilde{a}$ of dimension N, the "box" uncertainty set can be defined as

$$S_{\tilde{a}} = \{\tilde{a} : \tilde{a} = \hat{a} + \zeta, |\zeta_i| \leq \gamma_i, i = 1, ..., N\}$$

or, equivalently, as

$$S_{\tilde{a}} = \{\tilde{a} : |\tilde{a}_i - \hat{a}_i| \leq \gamma_i, i = 1, ..., N\}$$

where $\hat{a}$ are some nominal (typically, average) estimates for $\tilde{a}$.

Ellipsoidal uncertainty sets allow for including second moment information about the distributions of uncertain parameters, and have been used extensively. There are several ways to formulate them, but most generally, they can be written in the form

---

[39] β can be selected to be very small, so that we only have to be concerned about the probability of violating the constraint, ε.

$$S_{\tilde{a}} = \{\tilde{a} : \tilde{a} = \hat{a} + P^{1/2}u, \|u\| \le 1\}$$

where P is an appropriately selected matrix.

Polyhedral and ellipsoidal sets appear naturally if one uses regression techniques to estimate the uncertain parameters, and can be related to probabilistic guarantees. We illustrate this with an example from Goldfarb and Iyengar.[40] We will see additional examples of definitions of uncertainty sets and discuss related probabilistic guarantees in the context of robust mean-variance portfolio optimization in Chapter 12.

Example: Uncertainty Sets for Regression-Based Factor Model Estimates of Parameters

Suppose that the single-period vector of returns is modeled using a factor model[41]

$$r = \mu + V'f + \varepsilon$$

where

μ = an N-dimensional vector of mean returns.

f = an M-dimensional vector of factors (assumed to be normally distributed with mean 0 and covariance matrix F).

V = an $M \times N$ matrix of factor loadings of the N assets.

ε = the N-dimensional vector of residuals (assumed to be normally distributed with mean 0 and covariance matrix Σ).

As is standard in factor models, we assume that the vector of residual returns ε is independent of the vector of factor returns f, and that the variance of μ is zero.

All parameters in the model are subject to estimation error, since they are typically estimated from historical or simulated data. Assuming that the factor covariance matrix F is constant, one can specify the following uncertainty sets for the other parameters:

$$S_m = \{\mu : \mu = \mu_0 + \zeta, |\zeta_i| \le \gamma_i, i = 1, ..., N\}$$
$$S_v = \{V : V = V_0 + W, \|W_i\|_G \le \rho_i, i = 1, ..., N\}$$

---

[40] Donald Goldfarb and Garud Iyengar, "Robust Portfolio Selection Problems," *Mathematics of Operations Research* 28, no. 1 (February 2003), pp. 495–515.

[41] Here we use the notation from Goldfarb and Iyengar's paper. Note that it is different from the notation for factor models in Chapter 7, where we followed the standard statistics literature.

This definition for the uncertainty sets implies that the components of the vector of mean returns lie within intervals, and the factor loadings matrix $\mathbf{V}$ belongs to an ellipsoid. $\mathbf{W}_i$ in the expression above denotes the i-th column of $\mathbf{W}$, and $\|\mathbf{w}\|_G = \sqrt{\mathbf{w}'\mathbf{G}\mathbf{w}}$ is the Euclidean (l_2 or elliptic)[42] norm of $\mathbf{w}$ with respect to a symmetric positive definite matrix $\mathbf{G}$.[43] We discuss how to select the parameters ρ_i and γ_i next.

Suppose there are T historical (or simulated) observations for the asset returns and the factor returns. Let

$\mathbf{S} = [\mathbf{r}^1, \mathbf{r}^2, ..., \mathbf{r}^T]$ = the $N \times T$ matrix of asset returns.
$\mathbf{B} = [\mathbf{f}^1, \mathbf{f}^2, ..., \mathbf{f}^T]$ = the $M \times T$ matrix of factor returns.

For every asset return i, one can estimate the factor loadings by running a linear regression of the form

$$\mathbf{y}_i = \mathbf{A}\mathbf{x}_i + \boldsymbol{\varepsilon}_i$$

where

$\mathbf{y}_i = \left[r_i^1, r_i^2, ..., r_i^T \right]'$ = the vector of asset i's observed returns.

$\mathbf{A} = \left[\boldsymbol{\iota} \; \mathbf{B}' \right]$, where $\boldsymbol{\iota}$ denotes a vector of 1's.

$\mathbf{x}_i = \left[\mu_i \; \mathbf{V}_{1i} \; \mathbf{V}_{2i} \; ... \; \mathbf{V}_{Mi} \right]'.$

$\boldsymbol{\varepsilon}_i$ = the vector of residual returns corresponding to asset i.

Let

$\hat{\mathbf{x}}_i = \left[\hat{\mu}_i \; \hat{\mathbf{V}}_{1i} \; \hat{\mathbf{V}}_{2i} \; ... \; \hat{\mathbf{V}}_{Mi} \right]'$ denote the least-squares estimate of $\mathbf{x}_i$.

$s_i^2 = \dfrac{\|\mathbf{y}_i - \mathbf{A}\hat{\mathbf{x}}_i\|}{T - M - 1}$ denote the standard error in the regression for asset i.

$c(\omega)$ denote the ω-critical value for an F-distribution with $M+1$ degrees of freedom in the numerator and $T{-}M{-}1$ degrees of freedom in the denominator.

Then, if one sets

$$\mu_{0,i} = \hat{\mu}_i, \gamma_i = \sqrt{(M+1)(\mathbf{A}'\mathbf{A})_{11}^{-1} c(\omega) s_i^2}$$

---

[42] Defined as $\|\mathbf{x}\|_2 = \sqrt{x_1^2 + ... + x_N^2}$ for a vector $\mathbf{x}$ of dimension N.
[43] A real matrix $\mathbf{G}$ is positive definite if for every vector $\mathbf{x}$, $\mathbf{x}'\mathbf{G}\mathbf{x} > 0$.

$$V_0 = \begin{bmatrix} \hat{V}_1 & \hat{V}_2 & \dots & \hat{V}_N \end{bmatrix}$$

$$G = BB' - \frac{1}{T}[B\iota][B\iota]'$$

$$\rho_i = \sqrt{(M+1)c(\omega)s_i^2}$$

one can obtain a joint confidence set for μ and V. In other words, the probability that the actual values for μ and V fall in the specified uncertainty sets S_m and S_v is ω^N. Thus, if there are $T = 1{,}000$ observations, $M = 10$ factors, $N = 30$ assets, and the confidence level ω is 99% for each of the 30 assets, then $c(\omega) = 2.2657$, and the probability that the actual realizations for μ and V fall in the specified uncertainty sets S_m and S_v is $0.99^N = 74.97\%$.

The latter confidence regions for the parameters can be used to derive probabilistic guarantees on the quality of the solution. For example, if S_m and S_v are selected based on confidence level ω, then one can guarantee with confidence ω that the actual Sharpe ratio[44] of the portfolio will be at least as large as the optimal Sharpe ratio resulting from solving the optimization problem. It follows that one can interpret the level of confidence ω as the level of risk an investor is willing to take, or the tolerance the investor has to inaccuracies in the estimation of uncertain parameters.

While ellipsoidal uncertainty sets such as the set S_v appear naturally, they can be replaced by polytopic uncertainty sets that incorporate second-moment information about the distribution of uncertain parameters but preserve some attractive computational properties of the original optimization problem in its robust counterpart. For example, if the norm in the definition of S_v is not the Euclidean norm, but the l_1[45] or the l_∞[46] norm, the resulting uncertainty set is polytopic. Uncertainty sets defined by polyhedral norms tend to be more conservative than ellipsoidal sets in the sense that they require a bigger trade-off in the optimality of the optimization problem solution, but computational studies suggest that the difference is not too big.[47]

Confidence regions can be derived also by using the posterior distribution in a Bayesian setting. We discussed Bayesian estimators in Chap-

---

[44] William F. Sharpe, "Capital Asset Prices: A Theory of Market Equilibrium under Conditions of Risk," *Journal of Finance* 19, no. 3 (1963) pp. 425–442. We provided a definition of the Sharpe ratio in Chapter 2.

[45] Defined as $|x_1| + \dots + |x_N|$ for a vector x of dimension N.

[46] Defined as $\max\{|x_1|, \dots, |x_N|\}$ for a vector x of dimension N.

[47] Dimitris Bertsimas, Dessislava Pachamanova, and Melvyn Sim, "Robust Linear Optimization Under General Norms," *Operations Research Letters* 32, no. 6 (November 2004), pp. 510–516.

ter 8, and will return to such uncertainty sets in the context of mean-variance optimization in Chapter 12.

Ellipsoidal and other uncertainty sets defined by general norms that incorporate second moment information about the distribution are convenient computationally and generally work well when one can assume that the uncertainties are symmetrically distributed. However, they may not be appropriate, or be too conservative, if the actual distributions are asymmetric. Recently, Chen, Sim, and Sun[48] suggested a new family of uncertainty sets that can take into consideration asymmetry in the distribution of uncertain parameters, and results in computationally tractable robust problems. For a general constraint of the form

$$f(\mathbf{x}, \tilde{\mathbf{z}}) \geq 0$$

where $\tilde{\mathbf{z}}$ is the vector of uncertain parameters (assumed to be uncorrelated with zero mean, which can be achieved by suitable scaling), and $\mathbf{x}$ is the vector of decision variables,[49] the asymmetric uncertainty set for $\tilde{\mathbf{z}}$ can be formulated as

$$U(\tilde{\mathbf{z}}) = \left\{ \begin{array}{l} \tilde{\mathbf{z}} : \ \exists \mathbf{v}, \mathbf{y} \in \mathfrak{R}^N_+, \\ \tilde{\mathbf{z}} = \mathbf{v} - \mathbf{y}, \\ \left\| \mathbf{P}^{-1}\mathbf{v} + \mathbf{Q}^{-1}\mathbf{y} \right\| \leq \Delta, \\ -\underline{\mathbf{z}} \leq \tilde{\mathbf{z}} \leq \bar{\mathbf{z}} \end{array} \right\}$$

where $[-z_i, \bar{z}_i]$ is the minimal set that contains $\tilde{z}_i$, and $\mathbf{P} = \text{diag}(p_1, \ldots, p_N)$ and $\mathbf{Q} = \text{diag}(q_1, \ldots, q_N)$ are diagonal matrices that contain the "forward" and the "backward" deviations of the random variables $\tilde{z}_i$.[50]

---

[48] Xin Chen, Melvyn Sim, and Peng Sun, "A Robust Optimization Perspective of Stochastic Programming," Working Paper, NVS Business School, 2005.

[49] In the context of portfolio optimization, $\mathbf{x}$, for example, could be the vector of portfolio weights.

[50] The "forward" and "backward" deviations p and q are the deviations to the right and the left of the mean of the distribution, respectively. They are generalizations of the standard deviation, and equal the standard deviation if the underlying distribution is normal. More precisely, for a random variable $\tilde{z}$ and a constant Ω, p and q are defined by the following probabilistic inequalities:

$$P(\tilde{z} \leq \Omega p) \leq e^{-\Omega^2/2} \ \text{ and } \ P(\tilde{z} \leq -\Omega q) \leq e^{-\Omega^2/2}$$

Details on computing p and q from data can be found in Chen, Sim, and Sun, "A Robust Optimization Perspective of Stochastic Programming," or in Natarajan, Pachamanova, and Sim, "A Tractable Parametric Approach to Value-at-Risk Optimization."

Intuitively speaking, the uncertain factors $\tilde{z}$ are decomposed into two random variables, $\tilde{v} = \max\{\tilde{z}, 0\}$ and $\tilde{y} = \max\{-\tilde{z}, 0\}$, so that $\tilde{z} = \tilde{v} - \tilde{y}$. The multipliers $1/p_i$ and $1/q_i$ are used to scale the deviations, so that the total scaled deviation falls within the tolerance level Δ.

This uncertainty set is more general than the ellipsoidal sets based on second moments. If $P = Q = I$, where I is the identity matrix, and $z_i = \bar{z}_i = \infty$, it reduced to an ellipsoidal uncertainty set. Using the concept of left and right deviation (as opposed to standard deviation) is particularly useful when dealing with quantile-based risk measures in portfolio optimization and with portfolios involving assets with highly skewed return distributions, such as, assets with credit risk. As Natarajan, Pachamanova, and Sim[51] show, the optimal asset allocation using this risk measure (and this uncertainty set) as opposed to the standard deviation (which corresponds to an ellipsoidal uncertainty set) assigns lower weights to assets with negatively skewed distributions, even when their standard deviations are the same as those of assets with positively skewed distributions. We revisit this topic in the context of robust portfolio Value-at-Risk optimization in Chapter 13.

Recently, there has been a substantial interest in developing "structured" uncertainty sets, that is, uncertainty sets that are constructed for a specific purpose, frequently by using intersections of elementary uncertainty sets in order to minimize the "conservatism" in traditional ellipsoidal or "box" uncertainty sets. For example, in Chapter 12 we will elaborate more on the so-called zero net alpha adjustment method for robust portfolio expected return modeling.[52] The main idea is to slice an ellipsoidal uncertainty set which is defined by considering possible scaled deviations of the estimates of expected asset returns from their actual values with a hyperplane that ensures that that the sum of all deviations from these nominal values is zero. This makes the robust portfolio optimization problem less conservative when expected returns are modeled using robust optimization—in effect, instead of protecting against the possible worst-case deviations of all of the asset expected return estimates from their nominal values, the investor assumes that some of the actual returns may be below the estimates, while some may be above.

---

[51] Natarajan, Pachamanova, and Sim, "A Tractable Parametric Approach to Value-at-Risk Optimization."

[52] Sebastian Ceria and Robert Stubbs, "Incorporating Estimation Errors into Portfolio Selection: Robust Portfolio Construction," *Journal of Asset Management* 7, no. 2 (July 2006), pp. 109–127.

Bertsimas and Sim[53] developed a framework that links the *number* of uncertain parameter realizations that go "against" the modeler to probabilistic guarantees on satisfying the constraint. In their framework, the estimates of uncertain parameters are assumed to come from a symmetric and bounded distribution. By formulating uncertainty sets this way, the modeler can specify against how many of the deviations of the estimates from their actual values he would like to be protected. This idea is related to specifying uncertainty sets in robust optimization by using advanced polyhedral norms such as the d-norm that only consider the sum of the maximum k (out of N) possible deviations of realizations of uncertainty parameters from their expected values.[54]

Other structured uncertainty sets include "tiered" uncertainty sets in which some of the uncertain parameters are modeled as "well-behaved," while others are modeled as "misbehaving," and the modeler can require protection against a prespecified number of parameters which he believes will "misbehave," that is, which will deviate significantly from their expected values.[55] In the context of portfolio optimization, one can imagine that one would want to specify "misbehaving" parameters as those realizations of expected asset returns that are likely to be lower than their estimates.

There have also been attempts to link the construction of uncertainty sets to investor preferences, alternative portfolio risk measures, and the concept of coherence in risk measures in particular.[56]

While appropriate representation of the uncertainties in the problem is important, it is also important to keep in mind that not all uncertainty sets result in robust optimization problems that are easy to solve. The uncertainty sets we discussed in this section, however, result in computationally tractable robust counterparts for important types of optimization problems. We list some well-known complexity results in the following section. The section is quite technical, and is recommended only for readers interested in the general theory behind robust optimization formulations, or presented with complex nontraditional portfolio

---

[53] Dimitris Bertsimas and Melvyn Sim, "The Price of Robustness," *Operations Research* 52, no. 1 (2004), pp. 35–53.

[54] See Dimitris Bertsimas, Dessislava Pachamanova, and Melvyn Sim, "Robust Linear Optimization Under General Norms."

[55] Daniel Bienstock, "Experiments with Robust Optimization," Presentation at ISMP 2006, Rio de Janeiro, Brazil.

[56] See Karthik Natarajan, Dessislava Pachamanova, and Melvyn Sim, "Constructing Risk Measures from Uncertainty Sets," Manuscript, National University of Singapore, 2005, and Dimitris Bertsimas and David Brown, "Constructing Uncertainty Sets for Robust Linear Optimization," Manuscript, 2006. See Chapter 3 for an introduction to coherent risk measures.

management problems, for which they need to derive the robust formulations themselves. In Chapter 12, we will present the actual robust formulations for traditional portfolio optimization problems, in particular, mean-variance optimization and Sharpe ratio optimization, under a variety of assumptions for the uncertain inputs. Thus, most readers can find all the information they need for defining robust formulations for typical situations in Chapter 12. Some readers may find it easier to read Chapter 12 first, and then come back to the last section of this chapter.

Robust Counterparts for Some Important Types of Optimization Problems

We note that in discussing robustness, it is sufficient to talk about robustness with respect to satisfying constraints. If there are uncertain parameters in the objective function of an optimization problem, the problem can be easily reformulated as one in which uncertain parameters are present only in the constraints. For example,

$$
\min_{\mathbf{x}} \ f(\mathbf{x}, \tilde{\mathbf{z}})
$$
$$
s.t. \quad f_i(\mathbf{x}, \tilde{\mathbf{z}}) \geq 0
$$
$$
\mathbf{x} \in X
$$

is equivalent to

$$
\min_{\mathbf{x}, v} \ v
$$
$$
s.t. \quad f(\mathbf{x}, \tilde{\mathbf{z}}) \leq v
$$
$$
f_i(\mathbf{x}, \tilde{\mathbf{z}}) \geq 0
$$
$$
\mathbf{x} \in X
$$

In most financial applications, one has to work with linear and quadratic constraints. We showed a number of examples of such constraints in Chapter 4. Below, we discuss in detail important results on the tractability of the robust counterparts of such constraints.

Linear Constraints

An uncertain linear constraint can be written as $\tilde{\mathbf{a}}'\mathbf{x} \leq b$, where $\tilde{\mathbf{a}}$ is a vector of uncertain parameters. Constraints of this kind in portfolio optimization include the constraint on minimum expected portfolio return, or risk exposure constraints.[57] For example, the portfolio expected return constraint

---

[57] See Chapter 4.

$$\hat{r}'w \geq r_{target}$$

can be formulated in the standard form by setting $x = w$, $\tilde{a} = -\hat{r}$, and $b = -r_{target}$.

When the uncertainty set for $\tilde{a}$ is a polyhedron[58] (e.g., a collection of confidence intervals), the robust counterpart is also a linear constraint. When the uncertainty set is an ellipsoid, the robust counterpart is an SOCP. When the uncertainty set is a conic constraint expressed by a linear matrix inequality,[59] the resulting robust counterpart is an SDP.[60]

For example, suppose that $\tilde{a}$ varies in an uncertainty set formulated as the total scaled distance from an estimate $\hat{a}$ according to a general norm,[61]

$$U_a = \{\tilde{a} : \|M(\tilde{a} - \hat{a})\| \leq \Delta\}$$

To find the robust counterpart of this constraint, we need to compute

$$\max_{\tilde{a} \in U_a} \{\tilde{a}'x \leq b\}$$

Let

$$y = \frac{M(\tilde{a} - \hat{a})}{\Delta}$$

Then,

---

[58] A polyhedron can be thought of as an intersection of half-spaces. A polytope is a bounded polyhedron.

[59] A linear matrix inequality (LMI) is an inequality of the kind

$$A_0 + x_1 A_1 + \ldots + x_N A_N \succeq 0$$

where $x_1, \ldots, x_N$ are decision variables (scalars), and $A_0, A_1, \ldots, A_N$ are symmetric matrices. The notation "$\succeq$" means "positive semi-definite." A real matrix Q is positive semi-definite if for every vector x, $x'Qx \geq 0$.

[60] See Chapter 9 for definitions of linear optimization problems, SOCPs and SDPs.

[61] As mentioned before, the scaling matrix M is typically selected to be related to the inverse of the covariance matrix of the uncertain coefficients.

$$\max_{\tilde{a} \in U_a} \{\tilde{a}'x\} = \max_{y:|y| \leq 1} \left\{ \hat{a}'x + \Delta \left(M^{-1}y \right)'x \right\}$$

$$= \hat{a}'x + \Delta \max_{y:\|y\| \leq 1} \left\{ y' \left(M^{-1} \right)'x \right\}$$

$$= \hat{a}'x + \Delta \left\| \left(M^{-1} \right)'x \right\|^*$$

where $\|.\|^*$ denotes "dual norm."

The dual norm of the Euclidean norm is the Euclidean norm itself; that is why the robust counterpart of a linear constraint can be formulated as a second-order cone constraint if an ellipsoidal uncertainty set is used. Namely,

$$\max_{\tilde{a} \in U_a = \{\tilde{a} : \|M(\tilde{a}-a)\|_2 \leq \Delta\}} \{\tilde{a}'x\} = \hat{a}'x + \Delta \left\| \left(M^{-1} \right)'x \right\|_2$$

We will see this expression again in Chapter 12, as it defines the robust counterpart of the classical mean-variance optimization problem when expected returns are assumed to vary in a specific ellipsoidal uncertainty set. In particular, the vector of estimated expected returns $\hat{\mu}$ in the classical mean-variance formulation is replaced by

$$\hat{\mu} - \Delta \left\| \Sigma_\mu^{1/2} w \right\|_2$$

in the robust formulation. Here Σ_μ is the covariance matrix of expected return estimation errors.[62]

As we mentioned earlier, other norms that have been used to define uncertainty sets include the l_1 norm and the l_∞ norm. The l_1 norm is the dual of the l_∞ norm, and vice versa. The l_1 and the l_∞ norms are special cases of the d-norm, introduced in Bertsimas et al.,[63] which can loosely

---

[62] The negative sign in front of the norm in the expression

$$\hat{\mu} - \Delta \left\| \Sigma_\mu^{1/2} w \right\|_2$$

comes from the fact that the vector of uncertain parameters $\tilde{a}$ in the general expression corresponds to the negative of the expected returns vector $\hat{\mu}$ in the expected return constraint.

[63] Bertsimas, Pachamanova, and Sim, "Robust Linear Optimization Under General Norms."

be defined as the sum of the d largest absolute values of the entries of a vector $\mathbf{x}$. When $d = \sqrt{N}$, the d-norm approximates the Euclidean norm most closely. Robust constraints defined using d-norms can be formulated as linear constraints. The resulting optimization problems can be solved with any optimization solver.[64]

Quadratic Constraints

Most generally, an uncertain quadratic constraint has the form

$$\|\tilde{\mathbf{A}}\mathbf{x}\|_2^2 + 2\tilde{\mathbf{b}}'\mathbf{x} + \tilde{c} \leq 0 \text{ (equivalently, } \mathbf{x}'\tilde{\mathbf{A}}\mathbf{x} + 2\tilde{\mathbf{b}}'\mathbf{x} + \tilde{c} \leq 0 \text{)},$$

where the matrix $\tilde{\mathbf{A}}$, the vector $\tilde{\mathbf{b}}$, and the scalar $\tilde{c}$ can be subject to data uncertainty.

We saw examples of use of quadratic constraints in portfolio optimization in Chapter 4—they include tracking error constraints and minimum portfolio variance constraints. In order to limit portfolio tracking error to a predetermined level of σ_{TE}^2, for example, one would write the constraint

$$(\mathbf{w} - \mathbf{w}_b)'\Sigma(\mathbf{w} - \mathbf{w}_b) \leq \sigma_{\text{TE}}^2$$

Suppose that the covariance matrix of returns Σ is inaccurately estimated, and is thus assumed uncertain. Then we can establish a correspondence between the portfolio tracking error constraint and a general uncertain quadratic constraint by setting $\tilde{\mathbf{A}} = \Sigma$, $\mathbf{x} = \mathbf{w} - \mathbf{w}_b$, $\tilde{\mathbf{b}} = 0$, and $\tilde{c} = -\sigma_{\text{TE}}^2$ (in this example, $\tilde{c}$ is certain since we know σ_{TE}^2 in advance).

If the matrix $\tilde{\mathbf{A}}$ is positive semi-definite, the quadratic constraint is convex. The constraint is then equivalent to the second order cone constraint

$$\left\| \begin{bmatrix} 2\tilde{\mathbf{V}}\mathbf{x} \\ (1 + c + 2\tilde{\mathbf{b}}'\mathbf{x}) \end{bmatrix} \right\| \leq 1 - c - 2\tilde{\mathbf{b}}'\mathbf{x}$$

where $\tilde{\mathbf{A}} = \tilde{\mathbf{V}}'\tilde{\mathbf{V}}$. As discussed in Chapter 9, SOCP constraints are harder to handle than linear constraints, but are still tractable computationally.

---

[64] See Bertsimas, Pachamanova, and Sim, "Robust Linear Optimization Under General Norms," and Dimitris Bertsimas and Dessislava Pachamanova, "Robust Multiperiod Portfolio Management in the Presence of Transaction Costs," Special Issue of *Computers and Operations Research* on *Applications of Operations Research in Finance*, 2006.

The results we describe in this section are based on work by Goldfarb and Iyengar.[65] The robust counterpart of a quadratic constraint for a positive semidefinite $\tilde{A}$ is most generally an SDP if the uncertainty set is a simple ellipsoid, and NP-hard[66] if the set is polyhedral. SDPs include SOCPs as a special case, but a general SDP is an order of magnitude harder to solve than an SOCP. Goldfarb and Iyengar derived several types of uncertainty sets for which the robust counterpart of a quadratically constrained problem is an SOCP. These types of uncertainty sets are useful in the financial modeling context.

For example, *discrete and polytopic uncertainty sets* of the kind

$$U = \left\{ (\mathbf{A}, \mathbf{b}, c) : (\mathbf{A}, \mathbf{b}, c) = \sum_{j=1}^{k} \lambda_j (\mathbf{A}_j, \mathbf{b}_j, c_j), \mathbf{A}_j \succeq 0, \lambda_j \geq 0, \forall j, \sum_{j=1}^{k} \lambda_j = 1 \right\}$$

result in the equivalent set of robust quadratic constraints

$$\left\| \tilde{\mathbf{A}}_j x \right\|_2^2 + 2\tilde{\mathbf{b}}_j' x + \tilde{c}_j \leq 0$$

The latter constraints can in turn be cast as SOCP constraints, and solved with an efficient SOCP solver. These uncertainty sets arise when one would like to incorporate scenarios in portfolio optimization—each $(\mathbf{A}_j, \mathbf{b}_j, c_j)$ then corresponds to a particular scenario for the uncertain data. *Affine[67] uncertainty sets* of the form

$$U = \left\{ (\mathbf{A}, \mathbf{b}, c) : \begin{array}{c} (\mathbf{A}, \mathbf{b}, c) = (\mathbf{A}_0, \mathbf{b}_0, c_0) + \sum_{j=1}^{k} u_j (\mathbf{A}_j, \mathbf{b}_j, c_j) \\ \mathbf{A}_j \succeq 0, j = 0, \ldots, k, \mathbf{u} \geq 0, \|\mathbf{u}\| \leq 1 \end{array} \right\}$$

lead to robust counterparts of the kind

---

[65] Donald Goldfarb and Garud Iyengar, "Robust Convex Quadratically Constrained Problems," *Mathematical Programming* 97, no. 3 (2003), pp. 495–515.

[66] A formal definition of NP-completeness is technical and outside the scope of this book. However, for our purposes, it suffices to loosely define it as algorithms of exponential complexity, that is, algorithms for which the time required to solve the problem grow exponentially with the size of the problem. For a formal definition, refer to Michael Garey, *Computers and Intractability: A Guide to NP-completeness* (New York: W. H. Freeman, 1979).

[67] The term *affine* most generally refers to a linear function of variables plus a constant term. For example, $y = 2x + 5$ is an affine function of x.

$$\left\| \begin{bmatrix} 2V_j x \\ 1 - f_j + c_j + 2b_j' x \end{bmatrix} \right\| \le 1 + f_j - c_j - 2b_j' x, \quad j = 1, \dots, k$$

$$\left\| \begin{bmatrix} 2V_0 x \\ 1 - v \end{bmatrix} \right\| \le 1 + v$$

$$\|\mathbf{f}\| \le -v - 2b_0' x - c_0$$

where $\mathbf{f}$, a k-dimensional nonnegative vector, and v, a nonnegative scalar, are auxiliary variables. The above constraints are SOCPs. These uncertainty sets are restricted versions of more general ellipsoidal uncertainty sets for the data. As we mentioned earlier, ellipsoidal uncertainty sets are frequently useful when the modeler has first and second moment information about the distributions of the uncertain parameters.

Finally, *factorized uncertainty sets* of the form

$$U = \left\{ (A, b, c) : \begin{array}{l} A = V'FV, F = F_0 + \Delta \succ 0, \Delta = \Delta', \left\| N^{-1/2} \Delta N^{-1/2} \right\| \le \eta, N \succ 0 \\ V = V_0 + W \in \Re^{M \times N}, \|W_i\|_G = \sqrt{W_i' G W_i} \le \rho_i, \forall i, G \succ 0 \\ b = b_0 + \zeta, \|\zeta\|_s = \sqrt{\zeta' S \zeta} \le \delta, S \succ 0 \end{array} \right\}$$

where the norm $\|Q\|$ of a symmetric matrix Q can be either the Euclidean (l_2) norm, or the Frobenius norm,[68] also result in SOCP robust counterparts. The above uncertainty structure is suitable for capturing confidence regions around the maximum likelihood estimates of uncertain parameters. These uncertainty sets are present in the derivation of the robust portfolio formulations where parameter estimates come from regression models. They are implicit in some of the robust formulations of traditional mean-variance portfolio optimization we will present in Chapter 12, but the derivations of the robust problems are too technical to be a part of this book.[69] The robust counterpart (equivalent) of quadratic constraints in which the uncertain parameters vary in the above factorized uncertainty sets is a set of linear and SOCP constraints:

---

[68] The Euclidean, or *spectral* norm for a symmetric positive semi-definite matrix Q is equal to the absolute value of the largest eigenvalue of Q. The Frobenius norm or a symmetric matrix Q is defined as

$$\sqrt{\sum_{i=1}^{N} \lambda_i^2(Q)}$$

where $\lambda_i(Q)$ are the eigenvalues of the matrix Q.
[69] For more information, see Goldfarb and Iyengar, "Robust Portfolio Selection Problems."

$$\tau \geq 0$$
$$v \geq \tau + \iota't$$
$$\sigma \leq \lambda_{\min}(H)$$
$$r \geq \sum_{i=1}^{N} \rho_i u_i$$
$$u_j \geq x_j, \quad j = 1, \ldots, N$$
$$u_j \geq -x_j, \quad j = 1, \ldots, N$$
$$\left\| \begin{bmatrix} 2r \\ \sigma - \tau \end{bmatrix} \right\| \leq \sigma + \tau$$
$$\left\| \begin{bmatrix} 2q_i \\ \lambda_i - \sigma - t_i \end{bmatrix} \right\| \leq \lambda_i - \sigma + t_i, \quad i = 1, \ldots, M$$
$$2\delta \|S^{-1/2} x\| \leq -v - 2b_0' x - c_0$$

where

$H = G^{-1/2}(F_0 + \eta N)G^{-1/2}$, $H = A'\Lambda A$, is the spectral decomposition of H.
$\Lambda = \text{diag}(\lambda_i)$.
$q = A'H^{1/2}G^{1/2}V_0$.

The constraints involve a number of auxiliary variables, that is, variables whose only purpose is to help the user to formulate the optimization problem in a computationally tractable way, but have no other meaning: u, q, t, τ, v, σ, and r. Those variables are simply stated as decision variables when the problem is passed to an optimization solver. u is an N-dimensional vector; q and t are M-dimensional vectors; and τ, v, σ, and r are scalars.

Theoretical results on the complexity of the robust counterparts are available for some additional types of constraints encountered in practice, e.g., SOCP constraints and SDP constraints. For example, SOCP constraints in the case of ellipsoidal uncertainty sets for the parameters can be solved as SDPs. SDP constraints in the case of ellipsoidal uncertainty sets for the parameters or some special conditions can be *approximated* by SDPs. These results are very involved to derive and present, and are not as relevant to our discussion. We refer interested readers to Ben-Tal and Nemirovski[70] for further information.

---

[70] Aharon Ben-Tal and Arkadii Nemirovski, *Lectures on Modern Convex Optimization*, SIAM Series on Optimization, 2001.

SUMMARY

- Popular methods for dealing with uncertainty in the parameters of optimization problems include stochastic programming, dynamic programming, and robust optimization. Although there is overlap among the three approaches, historically they have evolved independently of each other.
- The stochastic programming approach most generally deals with optimization problems in which scenarios are generated for the values of the uncertain parameters. The optimization may be performed so that the value of the objective function is optimized on average, or may include penalties for constraint violation and risk considerations. It can also be performed over a single stage or multiple stages.
- Multistage stochastic programming models have been particularly useful in index tracking, bond portfolio management, and investment planning—areas, in which complex interactions of multiple random parameters over time can be incorporated into a scenario framework.
- In most real-world applications, the dimensions of stochastic programming problems are very large, and decomposition methods need to be used to break up the problems into smaller pieces that can be handled by optimization solvers.
- The dynamic programming approach is used for optimization over multiple time periods. Its main idea is to break up solving a large multi-period problem into solving smaller problems, starting from the last stage and proceeding backwards.
- The robust optimization approach deals with making optimization models robust with respect to constraint violations due to uncertainty in problem parameters by solving so-called robust counterparts of these problems. Robust counterparts solve for the worst-case realization of the uncertain parameters within prespecified uncertainty sets for the random parameters.
- The robust methodology can be applied in both single-stage and multi-stage optimization, and is a computationally attractive alternative to the stochastic and the dynamic programming methodology.

CHAPTER 11

Implementing and Solving Optimization Problems in Practice

Significant progress has been made in the area of computational optimization. Today, one can find efficient solvers to handle a wide variety of optimization problems. Selecting and purchasing optimization software, however, can be both very costly and time-consuming. It is important to evaluate different optimization software packages with the particular applications in mind. Unfortunately, often the only way to find out how well a piece of software works for a particular problem is through extensive testing.

The increased sophistication in optimization tools can make optimization software intimidating and difficult for the nonexpert. The goal of this chapter is to provide some guidelines for approaching the problem of implementing and solving optimization problems in practice.

We start by surveying the most recent advances in optimization software and reviewing the most widely used solvers and optimization languages. Then we provide a discussion of the implementation process, and provide examples and code for actual implementation of important portfolio optimization formulations with widely used optimization software.

OPTIMIZATION SOFTWARE

Where do we find software for a particular optimization problem?

Before settling on specific software, we recommend studying several of the optimization software guides that are available.[1] Hans Mittelmann has made his Decision Tree for Optimization Software[2] available online. Also very useful is Stephen Nash's nonlinear programming software survey[3] from 1998. Arnold Neumaier maintains a summary of public domain and commercially available software for both local and global optimization.[4] We note that while noncommercial optimization packages may be slower than the best commercial optimization packages, the former often show a much greater degree of flexibility and extendibility as the source code can usually be obtained. This is of special interest to users who want to develop customized software. For some noncommercial libraries, the documentation is sparse at best. However, many users will be fully satisfied with noncommercial optimization packages.

It is important to differentiate between *optimization solvers* (optimizers) and *optimization modeling languages*. An optimization solver is software that implements numerical routines for finding the optimal solution of an optimization problem. Optimization modeling languages have emerged as user-friendly platforms that allow the user to specify optimization problems in a more intuitive generic fashion, independently of the specific algorithmic and input requirements of optimization routines. Typically, optimization language software automates the underlying mathematical details of the optimization model formulation, but does not actually solve the problem. It passes the formulation to a solver the user deems appropriate and retrieves the results from the solver in a convenient format. Two popular modeling languages are AMPL[5] and GAMS.[6] They communicate with a wide range of solvers. Open-source modeling languages such as ZIMPL[7] and the GNU LP Kit (whose GNU MathProg language is a subset of AMPL)[8] provide useful, albeit some-

[1] Jorge J. Moré and Stephen J. Wright, *Optimization Software Guide, Frontiers in Applied Mathematics*, vol. 14 (Philadelphia: Society of Industrial and Applied Mathematics Publications, 1993).

[2] The guide can be accessed online at http://plato.asu.edu/guide.html.

[3] Stephen G. Nash, "Software Survey: NLP," *OR/MS Today* 25, no. 3 (1998).

[4] For global optimization, http://www.mat.univie.ac.at/~neum/glopt/software_g.html; for local optimization, http://www.mat.univie.ac.at/~neum/glopt/software_l.html.

[5] See http://www.ampl.com and Robert Fourer, David M. Gay, Brian W. Kernighan, *AMPL: A Modeling Language for Mathematical Programming* (Belmont, CA: Duxbury Press, 2002).

[6] See http://www.gams.com and Enrique Castillo, Antonio J. Conejo, Pablo Pedregal, Ricardo García, and Natalia Alguacil, *Building and Solving Mathematical Programming Models in Engineering and Science* (New York: John Wiley & Sons, 2001).

[7] See http://www.zib.de/koch/zimpl/.

[8] See http://www.gnu.org/software/glpk/glpk.html.

times limited, alternatives to the latter commercial packages. There is also a number of languages that provide modeling interfaces for particular types of optimization problems or solvers. For example, YALMIP[9] allows Matlab users to preprocess SDPs and SOCPs which are then passed to semidefinite solvers such as SeDuMi and SDPT3. Some of these languages are discussed in more detail later in this chapter.

Optimization solvers and modeling languages are frequently part of *modeling environments* that handle not only the optimization, but also the input and output processing, statistical analysis, and perform other functions a user may need for a comprehensive analysis of a situation. For example, ILOG's OPL Studio[10] allows the user to build optimization models that are then accessed from a subroutine library using Visual Basic, Java, or C/C++. Thus, a user can connect optimization systems directly to data sources, and make calls to the optimization subroutines repeatedly. MATLAB[11] is another example of a high-level technical computing and interactive environment for model development that also enables data visualization, data analysis, and numerical simulation. The Optimization Toolbox for MATLAB can solve a variety of constrained and unconstrained optimization problems for linear programming, quadratic programming, nonlinear optimization, nonlinear equations, multiobjective optimization, and binary integer programming.

Both OPL Studio and MATLAB are commercial packages, but one can create one's own modeling environment using freeware and open-source software. A useful source of free software is the Comprehensive Perl Archive Network (http://www.cpan.org). CPAN is a large collection of software modules and documentation that add extra functionality to the open-source programming language Perl. Perl modules can be used to access spreadsheets and databases, to download stock price data directly from websites, or to do statistical analysis on data. Perl modules have been developed also for interfacing with AMPL, MATLAB, and a number of free optimization solvers.[12]

The Network Enabled Optimization System (NEOS) at the Optimization Technology Center at Argonne National Laboratory and Northwestern University is an excellent resource for both experienced and inexperienced users of optimization software. NEOS consists of the NEOS

---

[9] See http://control.ee.ethz.ch/~joloef/yalmip.php.

[10] See http://www.ilog.com/products/oplstudio/.

[11] Trademarked and copyrighted by The MathWorks, Inc.

[12] See, for example, Christian Hicks and Dessislava Pachamanova, "Metamodeling with Perl and AMPL," *Dr. Dobb's Journal: Software Tools for the Professional Programmer* 30, no. 1 (January 2005), pp. 16–22.

Guide[13] and the NEOS Server.[14] The NEOS Guide is a comprehensive guide to public and commercial optimization algorithms and software covering more than 100 software packages for linear programming, quadratic programming, nonlinear programming, and integer programming with or without constraints.

The NEOS server provides free Internet access to over 50 optimization solvers that can handle a large class of unconstrained and nonlinearly constrained optimization problems. Optimization problems can be submitted online in programming languages such as Fortran and C, modeling languages such as AMPL and GAMS, or a wide variety of low-level data formats.

We review some of the most widely used optimization solvers. For further details, we refer the reader to the optimization guides provided earlier in this section.

Spreadsheet programs such as Microsoft Excel and Corel Quattro Pro are equipped with general-purpose optimization algorithms for linear, integer, and nonlinear programming problems. These routines work well for small-scale problems, up to about a few hundred decision variables. Premium Solver Platform,[15] also a spreadsheet-based optimization tool, can handle linear, integer, and quadratic problems of up to 2000 decision variables, as well as arbitrary Excel models with spreadsheet functions such as IF, INDEX, COUNTIF, and others that are not recognized by traditional solvers.[16]

---

[13] The NEOS Guide can be accessed online at http://www-fp.mcs.anl.gov/otc/Guide/index.html.

[14] The NEOS Server can be accessed online at http://www-neos.mcs.anl.gov and is described in the following references: Joseph Czyzyk, Michael P. Mesnier, and Jorge J. Moré, "The NEOS Server," *IEEE Journal on Computational Science and Engineering 5*, no. 3 (July 1998), pp. 68–75; William Gropp and Jorge J. Moré, "Optimization Environments and the NEOS Server," in Martin D. Buhmann and Arieh Iserles (eds.), *Approximation Theory and Optimization* (Cambridge: Cambridge University Press, 1997), pp. 167–182; and Elizabeth D. Dolan, *The NEOS Server 4.0 Administrative Guide*, Technical Memorandum ANL/MCS-TM-250, Mathematics and Computer Science Division, Argonne National Laboratory, May 2001.

[15] Premium Solver Platform is created by the developers of Excel Solver, the standard optimization solver that comes with Microsoft Excel. See http://www.solver.com/ for more information.

[16] Premium Solver Platform implements efficient interior point (barrier) methods for solving standard linear, quadratic and SOCP problems, and uses *genetic* algorithms for solving arbitrary Excel models involving spreadsheet functions that are not recognized by traditional solvers. The latter type of algorithms is used also by spreadsheet optimization solvers such as Evolver and RiskOptimizer (http://www.palisade.com/). Genetic algorithms employ randomization in the search for the optimal solution. There is no guarantee that the solution found by a genetic algorithm solver will be the optimal solution, but most of the time such algorithms get reasonably close given sufficient amount of time.

CPLEX,[17] LINDO,[18] and XPRESS[19] are robust and efficient commercial optimizers for large linear and convex quadratic programming. Both simplex and primal-dual interior-point methods are available. The software packages handle integer problems through a variety of branching and node selection techniques such as cuts, branch-and-cut algorithms, or heuristics. CBC is a noncommercial mixed-integer linear programming package that provides support for different kinds of branching.[20]

MOSEK is a commercial optimizer for linear, quadratic, and convex quadratically constrained optimization problems well-known for speed and numerical stability.[21] The subroutine library is based upon an interior-point implementation that is capable of exploiting sparsity and special structure, which yields accurate and efficient results in many applications, from small to large scale.

The optimizer LOQO for smooth constrained optimization problems is based on an infeasible, primal-dual interior-point method applied to a sequence of quadratic approximations to the given problem.[22]

MINOS[23] is a commercial solver designed to handle large-scale linear and nonlinear optimization problems efficiently. It takes advantage of sparsity in the constraint matrix, and uses fast-converging methods for nonlinear optimization such as the *reduced gradient method* combined with a *quasi-Newton method* for problems with nonlinear objective and linear constraints, and the *projected Lagrangian method* for problems with nonlinear constraints.

SeDuMi[24] and SDPT3[25] are publicly available Matlab libraries for solving optimization problems over symmetric cones. In other words, these software packages can handle not only linear constraints, but also

---

[17] See http://www.ilog.com/products/cplex.

[18] See http://www.lindo.com.

[19] See http://www.dashopt.com.

[20] See http://www.coin-or.org.

[21] See http://www.mosek.com.

[22] Robert J. Vanderbei, "LOQO: An Interior Point Code for Quadratic Programming," *Optimization Methods and Software* 12 (1999), pp. 451–484; and Robert J. Vanderbei and D.F. Shanno, "An Interior-Point Algorithm for Nonconvex Nonlinear Programming," *Computational Optimization and Applications* 13 (1999), pp. 231–252.

[23] See http://www.sbsi-sol-optimize.com/asp/sol_product_minos.htm and http://tomlab.biz/docs/minosref/tomlab_minos007.htm.

[24] Jos F. Sturm, "Using SeDuMi 1.02, A MATLAB Toolbox for Optimization over Symmetric Cones," *Optimization Methods and Software* 11–12 (1999), pp. 625–653. SeDuMi is available online at http://sedumi.mcmaster.ca.

[25] Reha H. Tütüncü, Kim C. Toh, and Michael J. Todd, "SDPT3—A Matlab Software Package for Semidefinite-Quadratic-Linear Programming," Version 3.0, 2001. SDPT3 is available online at http://www.math.nus.edu.sg/~mattohkc/sdpt3.html.

quasi-convex-quadratic constraints and positive semidefinite constraints. Both are built upon a primal-dual interior-point method referred to as the *centering-predictor-corrector method,* and can exploit sparse matrix structure, making them very efficient.[26] Generating the inputs for these semidefinite programming solvers can be very time consuming, and may require substantial background in optimization modeling. Fortunately, as we mentioned earlier, languages such as YALMIP[27] and PROF[28] that are built as layers on top of these solvers in Matlab allow for intuitive formulation of SDPs and SOCPs, and help the user retrieve the results from the solvers with very little effort.

TOMLAB is a general purpose development environment in MAT-LAB for the practical solution of optimization problems.[29] TOMLAB supplies MATLAB solver algorithms, and interacts with state-of-the-art optimization software packages for mixed-integer linear and quadratic programming, nonlinear programming, semidefinite programming, and global optimization, such as CGO, CPLEX, MINLP, MINOS, PENOPT, SNOPT, Xpress, and so on.

The "Numerical Recipes" books are useful for anyone developing computer models and running simulations.[30] They provide simple to use algorithms in languages such as Basic, C, C++, Fortran, and Pascal for a large range of numerical analysis problems such as linear algebra, interpolation, special functions, random numbers, nonlinear sets of equations, optimization, eigenvalue problems, Fourier methods and wavelets, statistical tests, ordinary and partial differential equations, integral equations, and inverse problems.

The Netlib repository contains freely available software, documents, and databases of interest to the numerical, scientific computing, and other communities.[31] The repository is maintained by AT&T Bell Laboratories, the University of Tennessee, Oak Ridge National Laboratory, and colleagues worldwide. The collection is replicated at several

---

[26] Jos F. Sturm, "Primal-Dual Interior Point Approach to Semidefinite Programming," Vol. 156 of Tinbergen Institute Research Series, Thesis Publishers, The Netherlands, 1997.

[27] See http://control.ee.ethz.ch/~joloef/yalmip.php.

[28] Currently being developed by Melvyn Sim at the National University of Singapore, http://www.nus.edu.sg/.

[29] See http://tomlab.biz.

[30] See for example, William H. Press, Saul A. Teukolsky, William T. Vetterling, and Brian P. Flannery, *Numerical Recipes in C++: The Art of Scientific Computing* (Cambridge: Cambridge University Press, 2002). Numerical recipes are also freely available online at http://www.nr.com.

[31] Netlib can be accessed online at http://www.netlib.org.

sites around the world, and is automatically synchronized to provide reliable and network-efficient service to the global community.

Financial Optimization Software

There are numerous optimization software packages that target portfolio management applications in particular. Most generally, such software packages can be divided into *security level* optimizers and *asset-class* optimizers.

Security level optimizers are developed specifically for security allocation. This type of software is built to handle an asset universe of several thousand securities and does in some cases also provide customized risk models. Some of the most established vendors are Axioma,[32] Barra,[33] ITG,[34] and Northfield Information Services.[35] Portfolio managers who seek an optimizer to perform portfolio allocation for a (potentially large) set of securities will typically find this category of optimizers, which does not require the use of any programming language, to fully satisfy their needs.

Asset-class optimizers are a class of commercially available portfolio optimizers that are "stripped down." This means that they do not have the flexibility or power to handle large numbers of securities but

---

[32] See http://www.axiomainc.com. Axioma's Portfolio Precision 3.1™ is a highly specialized portfolio optimizer that allows for investment models to include market impact, transaction costs, tax implications, minimum/maximum holdings, sector and industry bets, and many other common business and investment restrictions. The software combines proprietary linear and quadratic programming solvers for both continuous and integer problems. A preprocessor automatically routes the problem to the appropriate solver based on the characteristics of the portfolio and the investment strategy. A branch-and-bound method along with specialized heuristics has been incorporated to handle common integer and combinatorial restrictions such as limits on the number of securities traded, limits on the total number of holdings, and round lots. The latest version also includes support for robust optimization in order to take estimation error into account. We discuss robust optimization in Chapters 10 and 12.

[33] See http://www.barra.com. The Barra Aegis System™ is a comprehensive portfolio management software package for risk decomposition, portfolio optimization, and performance attribution that is integrated with Barra's multifactor risk models.

[34] See http://www.itginc.com. ITG/Opt is a portfolio optimization platform that enables users to construct portfolios with optimal risk by taking transaction costs, taxes, and a wide variety of business and investment constraints into account. The optimization engine is based on the CPLEX mixed-integer programming solver.

[35] See http://www.northinfo.com. The Northfield Optimizer is a sophisticated portfolio optimizer that has the ability to use any user provided risk factor model, perform tax sensitive optimization and round lotting, choose tracking error targets, integrate transaction costs for all securities, and deal with many common portfolio constraints.

they can optimize across a limited number of asset classes. These optimizers are typically less expensive (and also easier to use) than security-level optimizers. Asset-class optimizers are provided by, for example, APT, Efficient Solutions, Ibbotson Associates, Insightful Corporation, AIG SunAmerica (Polaris), Wagner Math Finance, and Sungard (WealthStation). New Frontier Advisors' ROM Optimizer uses resampling[36] to reduce the impact of estimation error on outputs, and one version of the Ibbotson optimizer uses a different resampling technique to accomplish a similar objective. The Ibbotson optimizer also has a module that allows the user to apply the Black-Litterman model.[37] WealthStation, which is Web-based software for financial advisors serving high-net-worth clients, offers tools for viewing and managing investors' diverse assets and for generating client specific reports.

PRACTICAL CONSIDERATIONS WHEN USING OPTIMIZATION SOFTWARE

Today numerical software for different kinds of problems is widely available both freely and commercially. This makes modeling and problem solving easier and more convenient. We can create financial models with modeling languages and software packages such as Matlab, Mathematica, SPlus, and SAS, or by using numerical subroutine libraries from the development environment at hand. However, we have to be careful when using numerical routines as "black boxes." Despite available documentation, it is often very hard to understand exactly what methods and techniques sophisticated numerical subroutines may use. The incorrect usage of numerical software may lead to reduced efficiency, lack of robustness, and loss in accuracy.

We provide some general guidelines and rules of thumb in solving a mathematical programming problem with optimization software.

The Solution Process
The solution process for solving an optimization problem can be divided into three parts:

- Formulating the problem.
- Choosing an optimizer.
- Solving the problem with the optimizer.

---

[36] We discuss portfolio resampling techniques in Chapter 12.
[37] The Black-Litterman model is discussed in Chapter 8.

Formulating the Problem

The first step in solving an optimization problem with numerical software is to formulate it mathematically. This is sometimes harder than it sounds. There is an art to expressing one's objective and constraints into a form that optimization software can understand. Some solvers also require that one identifies the optimization problem's type. Sometimes this is straightforward, because the problem might already be given in some standard form. However, more often than not this is not the case, and the original problem has to be transformed into one of the standard forms.

Choosing an Optimizer

When it comes to the choice of optimization algorithms, unfortunately, there may be no single technique that is better or outperforms all the others. It is also unrealistic to expect to find one software package that will solve all optimization problems—software packages are frequently better suited for some types of problems than others. In practice, it is often recommendable to try different algorithms on the same problem to see which one performs best as far as speed, accuracy, and stability are concerned.

Although it is possible to solve a simple linear program with a nonlinear programming algorithm, this is not necessarily advisable. In general, we can expect more specialized algorithms to solve the problem not just faster but also more accurately.

Constraints Whether a problem is constrained or unconstrained affects the choice of algorithm or technique that is used for its solution. In general, unconstrained optimization is somewhat simpler than constrained optimization. However, the type of constraints also matter. Problems with equality constraints are in general easier to deal with than inequality constraints, as are linear compared to nonlinear constraints.

Derivatives Many optimization routines use derivative information. Thus, it is best if some or all of the first-order derivatives (and sometimes also second-order derivatives) of the objective function and constraints are available analytically. If they are not available, but all the functions involved are differentiable, then the algorithm will have to calculate these derivatives numerically. As a general rule of thumb, if analytic derivatives can be supplied by the user, this greatly speeds up each iteration. In most instances, analytic derivatives will also increase the numerical stability and accuracy of the algorithm.

Dense versus Sparse and Medium- versus Large-Size Problems When many decision variables are involved (for nonlinear problems more than thousand or tens of thousand, and for linear problems more than a hundred thousand), we refer to the problem as a *large-scale optimization problem*. For efficiency reasons, large-scale numerical algorithms try to take advantage of the specific structure in a particular problem. For example, so-called *sparse matrix techniques* are often used if possible, in order to improve the efficiency of the linear algebra type of computations inside the routines.

User Interface and Settings   By using optimization modeling languages, an optimization problem can be specified on a higher level (much closer to the original mathematical formulation) than by using a lower level programming language such as C, C++, and Fortran, and the like. Furthermore, by making the user interface and the mathematical programming formulation independent of a particular optimizer, we obtain greater flexibility and portability of our model. Portability will make it easier to test the model with different solvers.

Good optimization software allows the user to specify different options and settings of the algorithms such as the maximum number of iterations or function evaluations allowed, the convergence criteria and tolerances, and the like.

Many optimization platforms also provide a preoptimization phase. During this phase, the problem at hand is analyzed in order to select the best and most suitable algorithm. Normally, there is also software support for checking the correctness of the analytically supplied derivatives by comparing them with numerical approximations.

Solving the Problem with the Optimizer

The final step is solving the problem with the optimizer.

The Starting Vector   Some optimizers expect a starting solution. The latter should preferably be a good guess for the optimal solution. For some problems it is easy to find a natural candidate for a good starting point (for example, sometimes the analytical solution of a simplified problem works well), although in general it can be difficult. For optimizers that provide support in generating a good starting point (often a feasible point is generated), it is in general advisable to let the algorithm choose, unless the user knows that his information is superior. Numerical testing should confirm this.

Monitor Progress   Valuable information can be obtained if we monitor the progress of the optimization process. In particular, the number of iterations and the number of function evaluations tell us how quickly the problem is converging. The magnitude of constraint and first-order optimality condition violations to some extent conveys how far away we are from reaching the optimal point. The values of the Lagrange multipliers provide information on which constraints are most binding as well as on the sensitivity of the value of the objective function to the different constraints.

Analyze Results Even if the optimizer converges and produces a solution, we should not blindly believe that the output is correct. The best way to understand how a particular software behaves is through experimentation. Indeed, understanding the behavior of software is necessary in order to make practical decisions regarding algorithm selection and to confirm that the results are valid. It is often a good idea to rerun the optimization with more stringent settings (e.g., smaller tolerances) and evaluate whether the problem still converges. By performing a few reruns, we also should be able to confirm if the optimization converges according to what we expect from theory. If we have several optimizers available, we can compare the results we get from each one. Any discrepancy needs to be fully understood. To make sure that the software is used and is working correctly, it is good practice to begin by solving a simplified problem that has a known analytical solution.

Sometimes we do not know whether our problem has a single or multiple local optimal points. A simple way of checking if there is more than one optimal point is to rerun the optimizer with a number of different starting values. If they all converge to the same solution, then it is likely that we have found the one unique solution.

By having a computer model of our problem, we can test how sensitive the outputs are to changes in the inputs. In the case of mean-variance portfolio optimization, we can study how the solution (the optimal solution) changes as we slightly perturb expected return and covariance forecasts. A simple experiment of this kind will show how sensitive our model is to measurement errors in the forecasts.

On a computer, real numbers can only be represented up to a certain level of precision. Beyond a certain point, real numbers have to be rounded. Therefore, a certain amount of information (or precision) is lost when operations are performed with real numbers. In most practical circumstances, rounding errors are not an issue. When dealing with poorly scaled and ill-conditioned problems, however, we need to keep in mind that errors due to rounding may have an effect.

Some Important Numerical Issues

In this section we elaborate more on some common pitfalls in the use of numerical software. In particular, we discuss (1) scaling and ill-conditioning, and (2) the importance of smoothness and differentiability of the objective and constraint functions for optimization routines that rely upon derivative information.

Scaling and Ill-Conditioning

In numerical computations, the performance and accuracy of an algorithm may be affected by how the particular problem formulation is *scaled*. An optimization problem is poorly scaled if changes in the decision variable produce large changes in the objective or constraint functions for some components and not for others. For example, in the case of the function

$$f(\mathbf{x}) = (x_1 \ x_2) \begin{pmatrix} 10^2 & 10^{-9} \\ 10^{-9} & 10^{-8} \end{pmatrix} \begin{pmatrix} x_1 \\ x_2 \end{pmatrix}$$

changes in x_1 have a much larger effect than changes in x_2. Some optimization techniques such as steepest descent are very sensitive to poor scaling, whereas Newton-based methods normally handle poor scaling better. Well-designed algorithms and software will automatically rescale the original problem if scaling has an effect upon the method used.

Another problem that can be encountered in numerical computations is that of *ill-conditioning*. An optimization problem is well-conditioned if small changes in the in-data (the data that define the problem) only lead to small or minor changes in the out-data (the solution). If this is not the case, the problem is said to be ill-conditioned.

A First Example of Ill-Conditioning   The problem

$$\min_{\mathbf{x}} \frac{1}{2}\mathbf{x}'\mathbf{A}\mathbf{x} - \mathbf{x}'\mathbf{b}$$

with

$$\mathbf{A} = \begin{pmatrix} 1 & 1 \\ 1 & 1.0001 \end{pmatrix} \quad \text{and} \quad \mathbf{b} = \begin{pmatrix} 0.5 \\ 0.5 \end{pmatrix}$$

has the solution $\mathbf{x} = (0.5 \ 0)'$. However, if we instead take

$$\mathbf{b} = \begin{pmatrix} 0.5 \\ 0.5001 \end{pmatrix}$$

(i.e., if we change the second component of the original **b** by only 0.02%), then the solution is **x** = $(-0.5 \ 1)'$. The reason for this is that the matrix **A** is ill-conditioned (its condition number is about 40,000—the condition number of a symmetric matrix is defined as the ratio of the largest to the smallest eigenvalue) and close to being singular. Although this example is highly simplified, this type of situation is not uncommon in portfolio optimization with highly correlated assets.

A Second Example of Ill-Conditioning   Optimization problems with equality constraints can be recast as unconstrained problems by augmenting the objective function with a penalty function that includes the constraints. For example, the optimization problem

$$\min_{\mathbf{x}} f(\mathbf{x})$$
$$s.t. \ h_i(\mathbf{x}) = 0, \quad i = 1, ..., I$$

can be rewritten as a constrained problem using the *quadratic penalty approach*

$$\min_{\mathbf{x}} F_\lambda(\mathbf{x}) = f(\mathbf{x}) + \frac{1}{2\lambda}\sum_i h_i^2(\mathbf{x})$$

where $\lambda > 0$ is the *penalty parameter*. As λ is chosen smaller and smaller, the penalty from unsatisfied constraints becomes larger and larger. Some problems can be treated efficiently in this manner by solving a sequence of problems $F_{\lambda_k}(\mathbf{x})$, where each λ_k is chosen such that $\lambda_k \leq \lambda_{k-1}$. However, unless special techniques are used, often this type of approach runs into ill-conditioning problems when λ_k becomes small. Specifically, the Hessian $\nabla^2 F_{\lambda_k}(\mathbf{x})$ becomes ill-conditioned near the optimal solution, which might result in poor convergence or no convergence at all. In these cases, it is usually better to treat the constraints explicitly and not through the penalty approach.

Smoothness and Differentiability
Many optimization routines use derivative information, such as first and sometimes also second order derivatives of the objective and constraint functions. If some function in the problem is nondifferentiable at a particular point, we might no longer be able to use a derivative-based routine.

In theory, there is nothing that prevents a nonsmooth convex program from being solved as efficiently as a smooth one, for example, with interior-point techniques.[38] However, the performance of many standard optimization packages decreases for nonsmooth and nondifferentiable problems. Some very common nondifferentiable functions are the absolute value and the many different kinds of norms. If possible, it is recommended that points of nondifferentiability be eliminated by using Boolean variables.

Transformations of this sort are problem-specific and not always straightforward. For example, the function

$$f(x) = \begin{cases} cx + d, & \text{if } x > 0 \\ 0, & \text{if } x = 0 \end{cases}$$

where $c, d > 0$, sometimes occurs in transaction cost models incorporating both fixed and proportional costs. The minimization of this function can be replaced by a mixed-integer linear program (MILP) by the introduction of the integer variable z, $0 \leq z \leq 1$, where z is equal to 1 whenever $x > 0$. The MILP would take the form

$$\min_{x} cx + dz$$
$$s.t. \ x \leq Uz$$
$$0 \leq z \leq 1, \ \text{integer}$$

where U is some upper bound on x.

IMPLEMENTATION EXAMPLES

We provide a few simple examples of how one would implement portfolio optimization problems with the widely used modeling language AMPL and MATLAB's Optimization Toolbox. While the input formats vary across solvers and modeling environments, AMPL and MATLAB's syntax illustrates two main ways in which an optimization problem can be formulated for a solver. In AMPL, the user describes the problem mathematically in a relatively free form, and AMPL converts it into an array format that is understood by the solver. In MATLAB, the user manipulates the data himself in order to create inputs that are used as specific arguments in a function call to a solver.

---

[38] Iu E. Nesterov, Arkadii Nemirovsky, and Yurii Nesterov, *Interior-Point Polynomial Algorithms in Convex Programming: Theory and Algorithms*, vol. 13 of *Studies in Applied Mathematics* (Philadelphia: Society of Industrial and Applied Mathematics Publications, 1993).

Classical Mean-Variance Optimization

We use the portfolio example from in Chapter 2. Consider a portfolio of four assets representing four country equity indices: Australia, Austria, Belgium, and Canada. We formulate the problem of minimizing the portfolio variance subject to the constraint that the target return should be at least μ_0 as follows:

$$\min_{\mathbf{w}} \ \mathbf{w}'\Sigma\mathbf{w}$$
$$s.t. \ \ \mathbf{w}'\mathbf{\mu} \geq \mu_0$$
$$\mathbf{w}'\iota = 1$$
$$\mathbf{w} \geq 0$$

Suppose we would like to find the optimal allocation so that the target return is at least 8%.

While all commands can be entered directly at the AMPL prompt, it is typically more convenient to create a *model file* (with suffix .mod) and an input *data file* (with suffix .dat) that can then be easily modified if necessary.[39] The minvar.mod file below contains an example of the optimization problem formulation in AMPL (code line numbers are provided for ease of reference). Lines 3 to 6 contain declarations of the data that AMPL will expect to obtain from the user. NumAssets is an input variable (a *parameter*) that specifies the number of assets under consideration. Its dimension is one. ExpectedReturns is a list of expected returns for all assets under consideration. Its dimension is $1 \times N$, where N is the number of assets. The information about the dimension of the array is specified directly after the declaration of the variable; in this case by writing ExpectedReturns{1..NumAssets}. The covariance matrix is a square array of dimension $N \times N$, which is declared as CovarianceMatrix{1..NumAssets, 1..NumAssets}.

Line 10 contains a declaration of the decision variables the solver is allowed to change in order to come up with an optimal solution. In this case, the decision variable is a row vector of weights for the assets in the portfolios. We require them to be nonnegative, and such bounds on the decision variables can be imposed directly after the declaration. Alternatively, the bounds can be expressed explicitly as part of the constraints in the formulation. The constraints are declared in lines 20 to 25. Every constraint starts with "subject to" and has a name (e.g., the constraint

---

[39] One of the main advantages of mod and dat files is that they can be called from within larger scripts, and altered dynamically. Thus, for example, one can link a process of updating statistical estimates of parameters directly to updating values in the model and data files for performing the optimization.

on lines 20 to 22 is called "portfolio_target_return"), which can then be used for obtaining additional diagnostic information, such as, whether the constraint is binding in the optimal solution, and what the value of the dual variable associated with that constraint is.

The objective function (lines 14 to 16) is declared similarly to the constraints: one specifies whether it is minimization ("minimize") or maximization ("maximize"), names it (e.g., "portfolio_variance"), and writes out an expression in terms of the decision variables and the parameters in the problem.

minvar.mod

```
1   #DECLARE INPUT PARAMETERS TO BE READ FROM DAT FILE
2
3   param NumAssets;
4   param ExpectedReturns{1..NumAssets};
5   param CovarianceMatrix{1..NumAssets, 1..NumAssets};
6   param TargetReturn;
7
8   #DECLARE DECISION VARIABLES
9
10  var weights{1..NumAssets} >= 0;
11
12  #DECLARE OBJECTIVE FUNCTION
13
14  minimize portfolio_variance:
15  sum{i in 1..NumAssets} ( sum{j in 1..NumAssets}
16  (weights[i]*CovarianceMatrix[i,j]*weights[j]) );
17
18  #DECLARE CONSTRAINTS
19
20  subject to portfolio_target_return:
21  sum{i in 1..NumAssets} (ExpectedReturns[i]*weights[i]) >= TargetReturn;
22
23  subject to portfolio_total:
24  sum{i in 1..NumAssets} (weights[i]) = 1;
25
```

Note that the decision variables, the objective function, and the constraints in minvar.mod appear virtually in the same way in which they appear in the mathematical formulation of the portfolio variance minimization problem.

The actual values for the parameters are stored in the data file minvar.dat:

minvar.dat

```
1   param NumAssets := 4;
2   param ExpectedReturns :=
3                    1      0.079
4                    2      0.079
5                    3      0.09
6                    4      0.071;
7
8   param CovarianceMatrix:
9                    1           2           3           4      :=
10       1    0.038025    0.008518    0.008921    0.007079
11       2    0.008518    0.033124    0.015654    0.004204
12       3    0.008921    0.015654    0.033489    0.007549
13       4    0.007079    0.004204    0.007549    0.027225;
14
15  param TargetReturn := 0.08;
```

There are several ways to specify the data file, some of which are easier to generate automatically. For example, instead of the table format used above, the covariance matrix can be formulated as a "flat" list of indexed elements.[40] This kind of indexing allows for specifying more complex data structures, such as three-dimensional arrays.

Once the model and the data file are created, we specify which solver AMPL should call (e.g., CPLEX) by entering the following command at the AMPL prompt:[41]

```
ampl: option solver cplex;
```

To solve the problem, we enter

```
ampl: model minvar.mod;
ampl: data minvar.dat;
ampl: solve;
```

We can then browse through the results by using the display command. For example, if we enter

```
ampl: display portfolio_variance;
```

AMPL returns the optimal value of the objective function:

---

[40] Robert Fourer, David M. Gay, and Brian W. Kernighan, *AMPL: A Modeling Language for Mathematical Programming*, 2nd ed. (Pacific Grove, CA: Duxbury Press, 2002).

[41] The exact name of the solver to be used will depend on the specifics of the installation and the version of the solver. For example, most recent versions of the CPLEX solver for AMPL are called cplexamp, but older versions are called cplex.

```
portfolio_variance = 0.0146963
```

Similarly, if we enter

```
ampl: display weights;
```

AMPL returns the optimal weights for the four assets:

```
weights [*] :=
1   0.210604
2   0.204162
3   0.299046
4   0.286188
;
```

It is easy to automate this solution process by writing sequences of commands in AMPL *scripts*, to solve the optimization problem and then save the output to a file, etc. Scripts can be run directly from the AMPL command prompt or from within another programming language such as C/C++.

The procedure for solving the same problem with MATLAB's Optimization Toolbox is different. The Optimization Toolbox has a number of functions that can be called to solve particular types of optimization problems. One has to transform the problem into one of the standard forms supported, and then call the appropriate function with the correct arguments.[42] For example, the mean-variance portfolio allocation problem is a quadratic optimization problem with linear constraints. The quadprog function in MATLAB solves exactly problems of this kind:

$$\min_{x} \frac{1}{2} x'Hx + f'x$$

$$s.t. \quad Ax \le b$$
$$Aeq \cdot x = beq$$
$$lb \le b \le ub$$

and is called with the command quadprog(H,f,A,b,Aeq,beq,lb,ub).

A MATLAB script that generates the input data and then calls the optimization solver may take the following form (saved as a file with suffix .m):

---

[42] For detailed information on the available functions, please refer to the *Optimization Toolbox User's Guide*, The MathWorks, Inc., 2005.

minvar.m

```
1   NumAssets = 4;
2   ExpectedReturns = [0.079; 0.079; 0.09; 0.071];
3   CovarianceMatrix =  [0.038025   0.0085176   0.00892125  0.0070785;
4                        0.0085176  0.033124    0.01565382  0.0042042;
5                        0.00892125 0.01565382  0.033489    0.00754875;
6                        0.0070785  0.0042042   0.00754875  0.027225];
7
8   TargetReturn = 0.08;
9
10  %GENERATE INPUT DATA
11
12  %create the matrix H
13  H = 2*CovarianceMatrix;
14
15  %create a vector of length NumAssets with zeros as entries
16  f = zeros(NumAssets,1);
17
18  %create right hand and left hand side of inequality constraints
19  A = -transpose(ExpectedReturns);
20  b = -TargetReturn;
21
22  %require that all weights are nonnegative
23  lb = zeros(NumAssets,1);
24
25  %specify an infinite upper bound on asset weights
26  ub = inf*ones(NumAssets,1);
27
28  %create right hand and left hand side of equality constraints
29  beq = [1];
30  Aeq = transpose(ones(NumAssets,1));
31
32  %CALL OPTIMIZATION SUBROUTINE
33
34  [weights,objective] = quadprog(H,f,A,b,Aeq,beq,lb,ub);
35
36  %print output to screen
37  weights
38  objective
```

Note that the function arguments are specified in terms of the available data. For example, to map the objective function

$$\min_{w} w'\Sigma w$$

into the expression

$$\min_{x} \frac{1}{2} x'Hx + f'x$$

we set $H = 2\Sigma$ and create an input vector f whose entries are all zeros (lines 13 and 16 in the file minvar.m).

Manipulating matrix and vector arrays in MATLAB is easy and efficient. However, one has to be careful in specifying the dimensions of the arrays when calling the quadprog function in order for the matrix and vector operations to work out correctly. Additionally, one has to be careful in specifying the inequalities in the optimization formulation in the correct way. For example, the mean-variance optimization problem has an inequality constraint of the kind

$$w'\mu \geq \mu_0$$

However, the inequality constraint assumed by the quadprog function is of the general form

$$Ax \leq b$$

that is, the inequality sign points the opposite way. Therefore, we need to specify the required target return constraint in MATLAB as

$$-w'\mu \leq -\mu_0$$

Lines 19 and 20 in minvar.m create a matrix A of dimension equal to the negative of the transpose of the column vector of weights w, and a scalar b equal to the negative of the target return μ_0 so that the above constraint can be passed to the solver.

The command

```
[weights,objective] = quadprog(H,f,A,b,Aeq,beq,lb,ub);
```

on line 34 ensures that the optimal solution to the optimization problem will be stored in a vector called weights, and the optimal objective function value (the minimum portfolio variance) will be stored in the scalar objective. Lines 37 and 38 print the values of these arrays to screen.

The MATLAB output from minvar.m is as follows:

```
weights =
   0.2106
   0.2042
   0.2990
   0.2862
```

objective =

0.0147

AMPL and MATLAB compute and keep a double-precision 16 digits results, but have different default settings for precision in reporting the output. As we saw earlier, the default precision level in AMPL's output is 6 digits after the decimal point, while MATLAB's output default precision level is 4 digits after the decimal point. These options can be changed.[43] For example, if we increase the precision level to 14 digits after the decimal point, we get the following results (the commands in line 1 specify the precision for AMPL and MATLAB, respectively):

Line	AMPL	MATLAB
1	ampl: option display_precision 14;	>> format long
2	ampl: display weights;	>> minvar
3		
4	weights [*] :=	weights =
5		
6	1 0.21081812452415	0.21060564405841
7	2 0.20388671930507	0.20416106641646
8	3 0.29907172497489	0.29904559558953
9	4 0.28622343119590	0.28618769393560
10	;	
11		
12	ampl: display portfolio_variance;	objective =
13		
14	portfolio_variance = 0.01469866028242	0.01469624397728

We observe that the results produced by MATLAB's Optimization Toolbox and AMPL are not exactly identical. As explained earlier, optimization software solves problems in an iterative fashion and terminates when a specified termination criterion has been satisfied. Also, multiple different algorithms exist for solving the same type of optimization problems. Therefore, it is to be expected that different optimization routines may not give exactly the same results. Nevertheless, we note that the first few digits in the solutions provided by AMPL and MATLAB are the same.

---

[43] While the default settings typically provide satisfactory levels of accuracy of the solution, users may want to change some of the defaults and to interact with the solver, especially if they have knowledge about a specific structure of the optimization problem or if they desire a higher accuracy. In general, solvers allow users to specify options such as tolerance level, number of iterations, number of function evaluations, etc. We note that by increasing the desired accuracy the time for solving a particular problem will increase, sometimes dramatically. Changing the default settings may be particularly useful in integer and mixed-integer problems, which we will discuss later in this chapter.

In Chapter 12, we will see extensions of the formulations presented in this section that incorporate a user-defined level of robustness with respect to estimation errors in the input parameters.

Mean-Variance Optimization with Integer Variables

As explained in Chapter 4, portfolio managers in practice frequently have to deal with portfolio constraints that require integer variables. Consider again the problem of solving for the minimum variance of the portfolio with four assets for a target return μ_0 that is at least 8%, with the additional constraint that only a prespecified number of assets can be included in the portfolio. The constraint can be expressed as

$$\sum_{i=1}^{N} \delta_i = K$$

where K is a positive integer significantly less than the number of assets in the investment universe, N, and δ_i are binary variables defined by

$$\delta_i = 1, \text{ if } w_i \neq 0;$$
$$\delta_i = 0, \text{ if } w_i = 0.$$

The minimum portfolio variance formulation then becomes

$$\min_{\mathbf{w}} \mathbf{w}'\Sigma\mathbf{w}$$
$$s.t. \quad \mathbf{w}'\mu \geq \mu_0$$
$$\mathbf{w}'\iota = 1$$
$$\sum_{i=1}^{N} \delta_i = K$$
$$0 \leq w_i \leq \delta_i, i = 1, ..., N$$
$$\delta_i \text{ binary}$$

In the formulation above, the constraint

$$0 \leq w_i \leq \delta_i$$

ensures that the weight of asset i is equal to 0 in the optimal solution if δ_i is equal to 0. If $\delta_i = 1$, then the constraint is irrelevant (redundant), because all asset weights are at most 1.

MATLAB's Optimization Toolbox has a subroutine for solving problems with binary variables, but cannot handle mixed-integer programs in which some of the variables are binary and others are continuous.[44] The Optimization Toolbox does not have a subroutine for handling problems with general integer variables. One can solve discrete problems by first solving the equivalent continuous problem, and then progressively eliminating discrete variables by rounding them up or down to the nearest discrete value.[45] Alternatively, TOMLAB, the general purpose development environment in MATLAB, provides interfaces to solvers that can handle integer optimization. As we mentioned before, CPLEX is one of the most widely used solvers for handling large-scale mixed-integer linear and quadratic optimization problems, and it can be called from within TOMLAB.

The modeling language AMPL allows for specifying integer variables directly. To specify that variables are integer (or binary) in AMPL, one just has to add "integer" (respectively, "binary") after the declaration of the variable. An AMPL model file for the mixed integer optimization problem above can be formulated as follows:

minvarint.mod

```
1   #DECLARE INPUT PARAMETERS TO BE READ FROM DAT FILE
2
3   param NumAssets;
4   param ExpectedReturns{1..NumAssets};
5   param CovarianceMatrix{1..NumAssets, 1..NumAssets};
6   param TargetReturn;
7   param K; #number of assets to be included in the portfolio
8
9   #DECLARE DECISION VARIABLES
10
11  var weights{1..NumAssets} >= 0;
12  var delta{1..NumAssets} binary;
13
14  #DECLARE OBJECTIVE FUNCTION
15
16  minimize portfolio_variance:
17  sum{i in 1..NumAssets} ( sum{j in 1..NumAssets}
18  (weights[i]* CovarianceMatrix[i,j]*weights[j]) );
19
20  #DECLARE CONSTRAINTS
```

[44] The portfolio optimization problem formulation with a cardinality constraint is a mixed-integer program, because the weights w are continuous, while the variables δ_i are binary.

[45] See explanation of the branch-and-bound method in Chapter 9.

```
21
22  subject to portfolio_target_return:
23  sum{i in 1..NumAssets} (ExpectedReturns[i]*weights[i]) >= Tar-
24  getReturn;
25
26  subject to portfolio_total:
27  sum{i in 1..NumAssets} (weights[i]) = 1;
28
29  subject to num_assets_to_include:
30  sum{i in 1..NumAssets} (delta[i]) = K;
31
32  subject to dependency_constraints {i in 1..NumAssets} :
33  weights[i] <= delta[i];
```

Line 12 contains the declaration of the binary variables. Lines 29 to 33 describe the set of constraints in the formulation that involve the binary variables, namely

$$\sum_{i=1}^{N} \delta_i = K$$
$$w_i \le \delta_i, i = 1, ..., N$$

Suppose $K = 2$, that is, we would like to restrict the number of assets in the portfolio to two. We add the declaration of the parameter K to the file minvar.dat as follows:

```
param K:= 2;
```

We call AMPL; AMPL passes the problem to the CPLEX solver, and returns the following output:

```
ILOG CPLEX 9.100, options: e m b q
CPLEX 9.1.0: optimal integer solution; objective 0.01881578947
16 MIP simplex iterations
2 branch-and-bound nodes
```

Therefore, the minimum variance for a portfolio of two assets out of the universe of four in our example is 0.0188. The optimal solution can be retrieved by using the display command:

```
ampl: display delta;
delta [*] :=
1  0
2  0
```

```
3  1
4  1
;

ampl: display weights;
weights [*] :=
1  0
2  0
3  0.473684
4  0.526316
;
```

It is therefore optimal to invest only in the third and the fourth asset (Belgium and Canada). The AMPL output shows that $\delta_3 = \delta_4 = 1$ and the weights are, respectively, $w_3 = 0.473684$ for Belgium and $w_4 = 0.526316$ for Canada.

This problem instance is small, and the solver finds the solution very quickly. However, as discussed earlier, larger integer programs in general are hard, computationally intensive, and time consuming. Frequently, because of memory limitations or in the interest of time, it may be preferable to settle for a relatively good intermediate solution even if it is not the optimal one. Most solvers that can handle optimization problems with integer variables have options that can be prespecified to set limits on the time, the number of iterations of the algorithm, the level of tolerance with respect to closeness to the optimal solution, and the like. Using these options requires familiarity with the optimization algorithms involved. It is also difficult to know in advance which combination of options works best, and some level of experimentation is typically necessary. Sometimes, one's knowledge of the particular problem structure may provide ideas for using particular branch-and-bound strategies. It is usually a good idea to obtain informative output and save intermediate results, so that the search for the optimal solution can proceed from the current point if necessary.

To specify CPLEX options for optimization (also called *directives*) from within AMPL, one can use the command

```
ampl: option cplex_options '...';
```

The CPLEX directive is given in single quotation marks. For example, CPLEX uses the branch-and-bound algorithm for problems with integer variables, and at each node, the value of the objective function is bounded on the one side by the best integer value found so far, and on the other side by a value deduced from all the node subproblems solved so far. CPLEX terminates the search when the difference is zero. One can relax the optimality of the result in the interest of time by the increasing the required value for the difference, i.e., by specifying a higher value for the directive 'absmipgap' than 0.[46]

SPECIALIZED SOFTWARE FOR OPTIMIZATION UNDER UNCERTAINTY

While the optimization community has been aware of the importance of incorporating uncertainty in optimization algorithms, actual optimization software for optimization under uncertainty is difficult to find. Instead, users need to use modeling environments to create their own optimization models. The sheer variety in optimization under uncertainty problem formulations presents a big part of the challenge.

As discussed in Chapter 10, the data for stochastic programming problems are in the form of scenario trees, and scenario generation is specific to the application at hand. The most frequently encountered stochastic programming formulation in financial applications is the multistage stochastic programming problem, which is typically solved by some form of the Benders decomposition method.[47] One commercial solver for this kind of problems is OSL/SE.[48] In many cases, practitioners apply selective reduction techniques to provide model instances that are sufficiently representative of the underlying uncertainty structure, but at the same time can be solved in a reasonable time. SPInE[49] is a stochastic programming package that attempts to integrate data generation and optimization models and to facilitate the formulation of multistage stochastic programming problems. SLP-IOR[50] is another sto-

---

[46] A good review of CPLEX options with respect to linear and mixed-integer optimization algorithms, as well as instructions on how to call them from within AMPL are available from *ILOG AMPL CPLEX System Version 8.0 User's Guide*, http://cm.bell-labs.com/netlib/ampl/solvers/cplex/ampl80.pdf, September 2002.

[47] See Chapter 10 for a description of common types of stochastic programming problems.

[48] See, for example, http://www.gams.com/dd/docs/solvers/oslse.pdf.

[49] See http://carisma.brunel.ac.uk/ and the report by Nico Di Domenica, George Birbilis, Gautam Mitra, and Patrick Valente, "Stochastic Programming and Scenario Generation within a Simulation Framework: An Information Systems Perspective," available from http://hera.rz.hu-berlin.de/speps/artikel/CTR-26-Nico.pdf.

[50] P. Kall and J. Meyer, "SLP-IOR: A Model Management System for Stochastic Linear Programming," *Mathematical Programming* 75, no. 2 (1996), pp. 221–240, also available from www.unizh.ch/ior/Pages/Deutsch/Mitglieder/Kall/bib/ka-may-92a.pdf and P. Kall and J. Meyer, "Building and solving stochastic linear programming models with SLP-IOR," Chapter 6 in S. W. Wallace and W. T. Ziemba (eds.), *Applications of Stochastic Programming* (Cambridge: Cambridge University Press, 2005), pp. 79–94.

chastic modeling environment whose goal is to provide modeling support for all stages of a stochastic modeling formulation. The NEOS server supports some stochastic programming solvers. Optimization modeling languages such as AMPL and GAMS contain subroutines for looping and writing general scripts, and can be used to implement decomposition methods for large stochastic programming problems whose dimension does not allow them to be handled directly.[51] Generally, however, the complexity of implementing stochastic programming algorithms with standard optimization modeling languages is highly problem-specific, and standard optimization modeling languages are not thought of as the best environment for such implementation.[52]

As we discussed in Chapter 10 and will illustrate in Chapter 12, robust optimization formulations can be handled with standard optimization software. While no specialized robust optimization software exists at this time, Melvyn Sim and his research team at the National University of Singapore Business School[53] are currently developing an interface for MATLAB that would allow for user-friendly formulations of robust optimization problems with the most commonly used uncertainty sets that can then be passed to SOCP and SDP solvers. This interface will simplify significantly the process of making important classes of optimization problems robust. In addition, some modeling languages such as YALMIP are now adding the capability of specifying confidence intervals as uncertainty sets for uncertain parameters in optimization problems. As mentioned earlier, Axioma's software also supports robust optimization formulations in the specific context of optimal portfolio allocation.

There is no all-encompassing dynamic programming software package. However, as explained in Chapter 10, solving a dynamic programming problem over many stages actually reduces to solving multiple single-period optimization problems. Thus, in order to solve dynamic programming problems, one can create dynamic models that include repeated calls to optimization solvers in some of the optimization modeling environments mentioned earlier (OPL Studio, AMPL Studio,

---

[51] See Horand Gassmann and David Gay, "An Integrated Modeling Environment for Stochastic Programming," Chapter 10 in *Applications of Stochastic Programming*. They show an example of the AMPL implementation of a debt management problem formulated as a stochastic program. See also Erwin Kalvelagen, "Benders Decomposition with GAMS," available from http://www.gams.com/~erwin/benders/benders.pdf, for an example of Benders decomposition with the modeling language GAMS.

[52] A good source for information on stochastic programming software is the website of the stochastic programming community, http://www.stoprog.org.

[53] See http://www.bschool.nus.edu/STAFF/dscsimm/.

MATLAB, etc.). When implementing such problems, one has to be aware of memory and time limitations, as dynamic programming tends to be computationally intensive, and may become prohibitively costly after very small increases in model parameters such as the number of stages.

SUMMARY

- Selecting and purchasing optimization software is a costly and time-consuming process. While some solvers work better for certain types of problems than others, often the only way to find out how well a solver works for a particular problem is through testing.
- The process for solving an optimization problem has three parts: (1) formulating the problem; (2) choosing a solver; and (3) solving the problem with the solver. Optimization modeling languages and environments can frequently facilitate formulating the problem, as well as handling the output from the solver.
- In numerical calculations, it is important to be aware of issues with poor scaling and ill-conditioning.
- Software for linear optimization is well developed and the user rarely needs to change the defaults or interfere with the solver. However, some user intervention may be necessary for efficient handling of non-linear, integer, and mixed-integer problems. The effectiveness of the intervention depends on the user's familiarity with optimization algorithms and solvers, as well as on the user's knowledge of a particular special structure of the problem at hand.
- Software for optimization under uncertainty is still scarce. One can use regular optimization solvers for robust optimization problems, and modeling environments for creating advanced multistage stochastic and dynamic programming models.

Four

Robust Portfolio
Optimization

Robust Modeling of Uncertain Parameters in Classical Mean-Variance Portfolio Optimization

Harry Markowitz was the first to model the trade-off between risk and return in portfolio selection as an optimization problem.[1] His idea laid ground for the Capital Asset Pricing Model (CAPM), the most fundamental General Equilibrium Theory, and initiated a substantial amount of research in the theory and practice of portfolio risk management. However, more than 50 years after Markowitz's seminal work, it appears that full risk-return optimization at the portfolio level is only done at the more quantitative firms, where processes for automated forecast generation and risk control are already in place. Although advanced optimization software is widely available, many asset managers have problems applying optimization methodology or avoid it altogether. One reason is that in practical applications portfolio optimization is very sensitive to the inputs (e.g., expected returns of assets and their covariances), and "optimal" portfolios frequently have extreme or non-intuitive weights for some assets. Generally, the practitioner's solution to this problem has been to add constraints to the original optimization problem in order to limit nonintuitive results. However, as a result, the constraints—instead of forecasts—often determine the portfolio, making the risk-return optimization process pointless.

---

[1] Harry M. Markowitz, "Portfolio Selection," *Journal of Finance* 7, no. 1 (March 1952), pp. 77–91.

From a practical point of view, it is important to make the portfolio selection process robust to different sources of risk—including estimation risk and model risk. In Chapter 8, we discussed several techniques through which one can obtain robust statistical estimates of the parameters in the model. In this chapter, we explain different ways in which an increased level of robustness can be achieved in the modeling (optimization and allocation) procedures. We discuss *portfolio resampling* techniques, and illustrate how the *robust optimization* methodology is used to make portfolio management robust with respect to errors in the estimation of the input parameters to the optimization problem. Interestingly, the computational cost of making portfolio optimization robust is minimal—the robust counterparts of the classical portfolio allocation problems can be frequently cast in a form that has comparable computational complexity to the original optimization problems. We discuss applications to variations on Markowitz's mean-variance portfolio optimization formulation, and show explicitly how to make the problem robust with respect to errors in expected return and covariances estimates. Finally, we address some practical considerations and caveats in using the robust optimization framework.

PORTFOLIO RESAMPLING TECHNIQUES

One way in which estimation errors can be incorporated in the portfolio allocation process is through Monte Carlo simulation.[2] The technique is based on resampling from the estimated inputs of the portfolio optimization process, and is therefore often referred to as *portfolio resampling*.

We start from our original estimates for the expected returns, $\hat{\mu}$, and the covariance matrix, $\hat{\Sigma}$, and first solve for the global minimum variance portfolio (GMV) and the maximum return portfolio (MR). Let us assume that the standard deviations of these portfolios are σ_{GMV} and σ_{MR} where per construction $\sigma_{GMV} < \sigma_{MR}$. Further, we define an equally spaced partition of the interval $[\sigma_{GMV}, \sigma_{MR}]$ in M points ($m = 1,...,M$), so that $\sigma_{GMV} = \sigma_1 < \sigma_2 < ... < \sigma_M = \sigma_{MR}$. For each one of these standard deviations, we solve for the corresponding maximum return portfolio, and thereby obtain a representation of the efficient frontier with M portfolios. Let us denote the corresponding vectors of portfolio weights by $w_1, ..., w_M$. So

---

[2] See, for example, Richard O. Michaud, *Efficient Asset Management: A Practical Guide to Stock Portfolio Optimization and Asset Allocation* (Oxford: Oxford University Press, 1998); Philippe Jorion, "Portfolio Optimization in Practice," *Financial Analysts Journal* 48, no. 1 (January 1992), pp. 68–74, and; Bernd Scherer, "Portfolio Resampling: Review and Critique," *Financial Analysts Journal* 58, no. 6 (November–December 2002), pp. 98–109.

far we have just been following the standard recipe for constructing the efficient frontier. Next, we perform the portfolio resampling:

Step 1: We draw T random samples from the multivariate distribution $N(\hat{\mu}, \hat{\Sigma})$ and use these to estimate a new expected return vector, $\hat{\mu}_i$, and covariance matrix, $\hat{\Sigma}_i$.

Step 2: Using $\hat{\mu}_i$ and $\hat{\Sigma}_i$ we solve for the corresponding global minimum variance and maximum return portfolios, $\sigma_{GMV,i}$ and $\sigma_{MR,i}$. Then, as before, we partition the interval $[\sigma_{GMV,i}, \sigma_{MR,i}]$ into M equally spaced points $(m = 1, ..., M)$. For each standard deviation in the partition, we calculate the corresponding maximum return portfolios, $w_{1,i}, ..., w_{M,i}$.

Step 3: We repeat steps 1 and 2 a total of I times.

Typically the parameter I is large, say around 100 or 500. After the portfolio resampling has been completed for each point in the partition, we calculate the *resampled portfolio weights* as the average

$$\overline{w}_M = \frac{1}{I} \sum_{i=1}^{I} w_{M,i}$$

If we recompute the efficient frontier using our original inputs, $\hat{\mu}$ and $\hat{\Sigma}$, and the new resampled portfolio weights, the new resampled efficient frontier would appear below the original one. This is because the weights $w_{1,i}, ..., w_{M,i}$ are efficient relative to $\hat{\mu}_i$ and $\hat{\Sigma}_i$ but inefficient relative to the original estimates $\hat{\mu}$ and $\hat{\Sigma}$. Therefore, the resampled portfolio weights are also inefficient relative to $\hat{\mu}$ and $\hat{\Sigma}$. By the sampling and reestimation that occur at each step in the portfolio resampling process, the effect of estimation error is incorporated into the determination of the resampled portfolio weights.

Moreover, for each security in the asset universe, a distribution of the portfolio weight can be calculated from the simulated data. For example, a large standard deviation of a portfolio weight is an indication that the original portfolio weight is not very precise due to estimation error. This type of diagnostic can be generalized in the following manner.

By introducing a test statistic, we can determine whether two portfolios are statistically different or not. For example, two natural test statistics are given by

$$d_1(w^*, w) = (w^* - w)' V_w^{-1} (w^* - w)$$

and

$$d_2(\mathbf{w}^*, \mathbf{w}) = (\mathbf{w}^* - \mathbf{w})'\mathbf{\Sigma}^{-1}(\mathbf{w}^* - \mathbf{w})$$

where $\mathbf{w}^*$, $\mathbf{w}$ are two different portfolios, and $\mathbf{V_w}$ and $\mathbf{\Sigma}$ are the covariance matrix of the resampled portfolio weights and the covariance matrix of returns, respectively. These test statistics follow chi-square (χ^2)-distributions with degrees of freedom equal to the number of securities considered. Using one of these test statistics, we can determine which portfolio vectors calculated in the resampling process are statistically equivalent to the original one. An important application of this idea is in the rebalancing of portfolios.

Let us assume that we are considering rebalancing our current holdings. Given our forecasts of expected returns and risk, we could calculate a set of new portfolios through the resampling procedure given above. We can now determine whether these new portfolios are statistically different from our current holdings and, therefore, whether it would be worthwhile to rebalance or not. If we find the need to rebalance, we could do so using any of the statistically equivalent portfolios that are different from our current portfolio. Which one should we choose? A natural choice is to select the portfolio that would lead to the lowest transaction costs. We note that although we have described this idea in the context of portfolio resampling, it has much wider application.

Some drawbacks have been identified with the resampled portfolio approach. We discuss some of them here.

Since the resampled portfolio is calculated through a simulation procedure in which, at each step, a portfolio optimization problem has to be solved, this approach can be computationally cumbersome—especially for large portfolios. It is important to find a good trade-off between the number of resampling steps to perform in a reasonable time; and at the same time achieve the necessary accuracy in order to measure the effects of estimation error on the optimized portfolios.

Due to the averaging in the calculation of the resampled portfolio, all assets will most likely obtain a nonzero weight. One possibility is to include constraints that would limit both the turnover as well as the number of assets with nonzero weights. Again however, due to the averaging process used in calculating the resampled portfolio, the resulting portfolio weights may no longer satisfy the imposed constraints. In general, only *convex* (e.g., linear) constraints imposed on each optimization will still be satisfied for the resampled portfolio. This is a serious limitation of the resampled portfolio approach for practical applications.

The resampled portfolio approach is suboptimal in terms of expected utility maximization, and is therefore inconsistent with Von Neumann and Morgenstern[3] expected utility axioms and the behavior of a "rational investor."[4]

Markowitz and Usmen present a comparison between the resampled efficient frontier and classical mean-variance with forecasts derived from diffuse Bayesian priors.[5] In their simulation study based on returns drawn from a multivariate normal distribution, both methods overestimate the portfolio expected return. For example, for a risk aversion parameter $\lambda =$ 0.5, the mean-variance approach forecasted an average annual growth rate of 18.05%, whereas the actual portfolios it chose had an average realized growth rate of 10.89%. The resampled efficient frontier forecasted an average annual growth rate of 15.09%, and the average realized growth rate was 11.46%. Nevertheless, in this study the resampled efficient frontier showed an improvement over the mean-variance approach.

ROBUST PORTFOLIO ALLOCATION

Another way in which uncertainty in the inputs can be modeled is by taking it into consideration directly in the optimization process. Robust optimization, the technique described in Chapter 10, is an intuitive and efficient way to model this form of uncertainty. We can only speculate as to why robust portfolio modeling is not more widely used by practitioners in the financial community. Probably, a major reason for this is that the technique is relatively new and is considered too technical. The implementation, however, is frequently straightforward, and has a comparable level of complexity to that of the original, nonrobust formulation. In this section, we show explicitly how the technique can be applied.

First, we discuss the robust versions of the mean-variance portfolio optimization problem when uncertainty is assumed to be present only in the expected return estimates. We show several ways of modeling the uncertainty, based on factor models and Bayesian statistics. We then extend the model to include uncertainty in the asset return covariance matrix. We conclude this section with a discussion of important considerations when using robust modeling techniques in practice, and present an example of a robust version of the mean-variance optimization problem.

---

[3] John Von Neumann and Oscar Morgenstern, *Theory of Games and Economic Behavior*, 3rd ed. (Princeton: Princeton University Press, 1953).

[4] Campbell R. Harvey, John C. Liechty, Merril W. Liechty, and Peter Mueller, "Portfolio Selection with Higher Moments," Working Paper, Duke University, 2003.

[5] Harry M. Markowitz and Nilufer Usmen, "Resampled Frontiers versus Diffuse Bayes: An Experiment," *Journal of Investment Management* 1, no. 4 (2003), pp. 9–25.

Robust Mean-Variance Formulations

We recall that the classical mean-variance problem introduced in Chapter 2 is

$$\max_{w} \quad \mu'w - \lambda w'\Sigma w$$

$$s.t. \quad w'\iota = 1$$

where $\iota = [1,1, . . ., 1]'$. In this optimization problem μ, Σ, λ, and w denote the expected return, asset return covariance matrix, risk aversion coefficient, and portfolio weights, respectively.

As discussed in more detail in Chapters 8 and 10, the estimation error in the forecasts may significantly influence the resulting optimized portfolio weights. A study by Black and Litterman[6] demonstrated that small changes in the expected returns, in particular, had a substantial impact. It follows that if the estimation errors in expected returns are large—which is often the case in practice—they will significantly influence the optimal allocation. For practical applications, it is therefore crucial to incorporate the uncertainty about the accuracy of estimates in the portfolio optimization process.

Uncertainty in Expected Return Estimates

An easy way to incorporate uncertainty caused by estimation errors is to require that the investor be protected if the estimated expected return $\hat{\mu}_i$ for each asset is "around" the true expected return μ_i. The error from the estimation can be assumed to be not larger than some small number $\delta_i > 0$. The simplest possible choice for the *uncertainty set* for μ is the "box"

$$U_\delta(\hat{\mu}) = \{\mu \,|\, |\mu_i - \hat{\mu}_i| \le \delta_i, i = 1, ..., N\}$$

The δ_i's could be specified by assuming some confidence interval around the estimated expected return. For example, if expected returns are estimated using simulation (in which case the Central Limit Theorem applies)[7] or if asset returns are assumed to follow a normal distribution,

---

[6] Fischer Black and Robert Litterman, "Global Portfolio Optimization," *Financial Analysts Journal* 48, no. 5 (September–October 1992), pp. 28–43.

[7] The Central Limit Theorem states that under mild assumptions, the mean of a sample of independent and identically distributed observations from any distribution follows an approximately normal distribution with mean equal to the actual mean of the original distribution and standard deviation equal to the standard deviation of the original distribution divided by the square root of the sample size.

then a 95% confidence interval for μ_i can be obtained by setting $\delta_i = 1.96\sigma_i/\sqrt{T}$, where T is the sample size used in the estimation.

The robust formulation of the mean-variance problem under the assumption on $\hat{\mu}_i$ above is

$$\max_{\mathbf{w}} \quad \hat{\mu}'\mathbf{w} - \delta'|\mathbf{w}| - \lambda\mathbf{w}'\Sigma\mathbf{w}$$
$$s.t. \quad \mathbf{w}'\iota = 1$$

This formulation is in fact obvious without any involved mathematics. If the weight of asset i in the portfolio is negative, the worst-case expected return for asset i is $\mu_i + \delta_i$ (we lose the largest amount possible). If the weight of asset i in the portfolio is positive, then the worst-case expected return for asset i is $\mu_i - \delta_i$ (we gain the smallest amount possible). Note that $\mu_i w_i - \delta_i|w_i|$ equals $(\mu_i - \delta_i)w_i$ if the weight w_i is positive and $(\mu_i + \delta_i)w_i$ if the weight w_i is negative. Therefore, the mathematical expression in the objective agrees with our intuition: it tries to minimize the worst-case expected portfolio return. In this robust version of the mean-variance formulation, assets whose mean return estimates are less accurate (have a larger estimation error δ_i) are penalized in the objective function, and will tend to have smaller weights in the optimal portfolio allocation. We note that this problem has the same computational complexity as the nonrobust mean-variance formulation.[8]

---

[8] There are two well-known techniques for making this optimization problem solver-friendly by getting rid of the absolute value of the vector of weights $\mathbf{w}$, and thus converting it into a standard quadratic optimization problem. One is to introduce a new variable, ψ, to replace the absolute value. The problem can be then rewritten as

$$\max_{\mathbf{w},\,\psi} \quad \hat{\mu}'\mathbf{w} - \delta'\psi - \lambda\mathbf{w}'\Sigma\mathbf{w}$$
$$s.t. \quad \mathbf{w}'\iota = 1$$
$$\psi_i \geq w_i;\ \psi_i \geq -w_i,\ i = 1, \ldots, N$$

Another way is to write $\mathbf{w}$ as a difference of two nonnegative variables $\mathbf{w}_+$ and $\mathbf{w}_-$, and replace occurrences of $|\mathbf{w}|$ by $\mathbf{w}_+ + \mathbf{w}_-$. The optimization problem becomes

$$\max_{\mathbf{w},\,\mathbf{w}_+,\,\mathbf{w}_-} \quad \hat{\mu}'\mathbf{w} - \delta'(\mathbf{w}_+ + \mathbf{w}_-) - \lambda\mathbf{w}'\Sigma\mathbf{w}$$
$$s.t. \quad \mathbf{w}'\iota = 1$$
$$\mathbf{w} = \mathbf{w}_+ - \mathbf{w}_-,\ \mathbf{w}_+ \geq 0,\ \mathbf{w}_- \geq 0.$$

We will be using this change of variables in many of the following robust formulations. This is particularly helpful in formulations that would otherwise be SOCPs (see Chapter 9). An SOCP cannot contain absolute values for the variables, and this kind of transformation allows us to formulate robust mean-variance and Sharpe ratio problems in a way that can be handled efficiently computationally.

To gain some additional insight, let us rewrite the robust formulation as

$$\max_{\mathbf{w}} \; (\hat{\boldsymbol{\mu}} - \boldsymbol{\mu}_{\delta, \, \mathbf{w}})' \mathbf{w} - \lambda \mathbf{w}' \boldsymbol{\Sigma} \mathbf{w}$$
$$s.t. \quad \mathbf{w}' \boldsymbol{\iota} = 1$$

where

$$\boldsymbol{\mu}_{\delta, \, \mathbf{w}} = \begin{bmatrix} \mathrm{sign}(w_1)\delta_1 \\ \vdots \\ \mathrm{sign}(w_N)\delta_N \end{bmatrix}$$

Here sign(.) is the sign function (that is, $\mathrm{sign}(x) = 1$ when $x \geq 0$ and $\mathrm{sign}(x) = -1$ when $x < 0$). In this re-formulation of the problem we see that robust optimization is related to statistical shrinkage, and the original expected return vector is shrunk to $\hat{\boldsymbol{\mu}} - \boldsymbol{\mu}_{\delta, \, \mathbf{w}}$.

By using the equality

$$w_i \mathrm{sign}(w_i)\delta_i = w_i \frac{w_i}{|w_i|}\delta_i = \frac{w_i}{\sqrt{|w_i|}} \delta_i \frac{w_i}{\sqrt{|w_i|}}$$

we can rewrite the problem as

$$\max_{\mathbf{w}} \; \boldsymbol{\mu}' \mathbf{w} - \lambda \mathbf{w}' \boldsymbol{\Sigma} \mathbf{w} - \hat{\mathbf{w}}' \boldsymbol{\Delta} \hat{\mathbf{w}}$$
$$s.t. \quad \mathbf{w}' \boldsymbol{\iota} = 1$$

where

$$\hat{\mathbf{w}} = \begin{bmatrix} \dfrac{w_1}{\sqrt{|w_1|}} \\ \vdots \\ \dfrac{w_N}{\sqrt{|w_N|}} \end{bmatrix}$$

and

$$\boldsymbol{\Delta} = \begin{bmatrix} \delta_1 & & \\ & \ddots & \\ & & \delta_N \end{bmatrix}$$

Observe that this problem is yet another modification of the classical mean-variance problem. In particular, a "risk-like" term $\hat{w}'\Delta\hat{w}$ has been added to the classical formulation. This term can be interpreted as a risk adjustment performed by an investor who is averse to estimation error. The exact form of the investor's estimation error aversion is specified by the magnitude of the deltas.

One can define many other uncertainty sets for the expected returns vector μ. While more general uncertainty sets lead to more complicated optimization problems, the basic intuition and interpretation remain the same. For instance, consider the uncertainty set

$$U_\delta(\hat{\mu}) = \left\{ \mu \,|\, (\mu - \hat{\mu})'\Sigma_\mu^{-1}(\mu - \hat{\mu}) \leq \delta^2 \right\}$$

It captures the idea that the investor would like to be protected in instances in which the total scaled deviation of the realized average returns from the estimated returns is within δ.[9] The derivation of the robust formulation with this uncertainty set is a bit more involved, but we show it below for illustrative purposes.

Similarly to the first example of modeling uncertainty in expected return estimates, we ask ourselves what the "worst" estimates of the expected returns would be, and how we would allocate the portfolio in this case. Mathematically, this can be expressed as

$$\max_{w} \quad \min_{\mu \in \{\mu | (\mu - \hat{\mu})'\Sigma_\mu^{-1}(\mu - \hat{\mu}) \leq \delta^2\}} \mu'w - \lambda w'\Sigma w$$
$$s.t. \qquad w'\iota = 1$$

As we explained in Chapter 10, this problem is called the *robust counterpart*, or the "max-min" problem, and is not in a form that can be input into a standard optimization solver. We need to solve the "inner" problem first while holding the vector of weights w fixed, and compute the worst expected portfolio return over the set of possible values for μ:

---

[9] Recall from the discussion in Chapter 10 that this kind of uncertainty set scales the distances between the estimated and the possible values for the expected returns by the variability (standard deviation) in the estimates. This uncertainty set ensures that the total "budget" of tolerance to uncertainty, δ, is distributed evenly among expected return estimates that have different variability.

$$\min_{\mu} \; \mu'w - \lambda w'\Sigma w$$

$$s.t. \;\; (\mu - \hat{\mu})'\Sigma_{\mu}^{-1}(\mu - \hat{\mu}) \le \delta^2$$

The Lagrangian of this problem takes the form

$$L(\mu, \gamma) = \mu'w - \lambda w'\Sigma w - \gamma(\delta^2 - (\mu - \hat{\mu})'\Sigma_{\mu}^{-1}(\mu - \hat{\mu}))$$

Differentiating this with respect to μ, we obtain the first-order condition

$$w + 2\gamma\Sigma_{\mu}^{-1}(\mu - \hat{\mu}) = 0$$

and therefore the optimal value of μ is

$$\mu^* = \hat{\mu} - \frac{1}{2\gamma}\Sigma_{\mu}w$$

The optimal value of γ can be found by maximizing the Lagrangian after substituting the expression for the worst-case μ, that is,

$$\max_{\gamma \ge 0} L(\mu, \gamma) = \mu'w - \lambda w'\Sigma w - \frac{1}{4\gamma}w'\Sigma_{\mu}w - \gamma\delta^2$$

After solving the first-order condition, we obtain

$$\gamma^* = \frac{1}{2\delta}\sqrt{w'\Sigma_{\mu}w}$$

Finally, by substituting the expression for γ^* in the Lagrangian, we obtain the robust problem

$$\max_{w} \; \mu'w - \lambda w'\Sigma w - \delta\sqrt{w'\Sigma_{\mu}w}$$

$$s.t. \;\; w'\iota = 1$$

Just as in the previous problem, we interpret the term $\delta\sqrt{w'\Sigma_{\mu}w}$ as the penalty for estimation risk, where δ reflects the degree of the investor's aversion to estimation risk. We remark that the uncertainty set used here can be interpreted as an N-dimensional confidence region for the parameter vector $\hat{\mu}$, defined by the estimation error covariance matrix Σ_μ.[10]

It is not immediately obvious how one can estimate Σ_μ. Note that Σ_μ is the covariance matrix of the errors in the estimation of the *expected* (average) returns. Thus, if a portfolio manager forecasts 5% active return over the next time period, but gets 1%, he cannot argue that there was a 4% error in his *expected* return—the actual error would consist of both an estimation error in the expected return and the inherent volatility in actual realized returns. In fact, critics of the approach have argued that the *realized* returns typically have large stochastic components that dwarf the *expected* returns, and hence estimating Σ_μ accurately from historical data is very hard, if not impossible.[11]

In theory, if returns in a given sample of size T are independent and identically distributed, then Σ_μ equals $(1/T) \cdot \Sigma$, where Σ is the covariance matrix of asset returns as before. However, experience seems to suggest that this may not be the best method in practice. One issue is that this approach applies only in a world in which returns are stationary. Another important issue is whether the estimate of the asset covariance matrix Σ itself is reliable if it is estimated from a sample of historical data. As we explained in Chapter 6, computing a meaningful asset return covariance matrix requires a large number of observations—many more observations than the number of assets in the portfolio—and even then the sample covariance matrix may contain large estimation errors that may produce poor results in the mean-variance optimization. One approach when sufficient data are not available for computing the covariance matrix for all securities in the portfolio is to compute the estimation errors in expected returns at a factor (e.g., industry, country, sector)

---

[10] In some references, the term $\sqrt{w'\Sigma_\mu w}$ is replaced by $\left\| \Sigma_\mu^{1/2} w \right\|$, where $\|.\|$ denotes the l_2 (Euclidean, elliptic) norm of a vector. The two expressions are equivalent, but $\sqrt{w'\Sigma_\mu w}$ makes it evident that the new penalty term involves the standard error of the estimate, and is therefore easier to interpret. When implementing an SOCP problem in an optimization modeling language, it may be helpful to use the equivalence of these expressions. Most general optimization modeling languages, such as AMPL (see Chapter 11), understand the notation $\sqrt{w'\Sigma_\mu w}$, while specialized SOCP and SDP modeling interfaces may only accept the notation $\left\| \Sigma_\mu^{1/2} w \right\|$. In most modeling languages (including AMPL and GAMS), one can include the term $\sqrt{w'\Sigma_\mu w}$ in the formulation easily by using the sqrt command. Once the optimization problem formulation is passed to a solver, some advanced solvers such as CPLEX are capable of automatically detecting SOCP problems and taking advantage of terms involving square roots.

[11] Jyh-Huei Lee, Dan Stefek and Alexander Zhelenyak, "Robust Portfolio Optimization—A Closer Look," *MSCI Barra Research Insights* report, June 2006.

level, and use their variances and covariances in the estimation error covariance matrix for the individual asset returns.

Several approximate methods for estimating Σ_μ have been found to work well in practice.[12] For example, it has been observed that simpler estimation approaches, such as using just the diagonal matrix containing the variances of the estimates (as opposed to the complete error covariance matrix), frequently provide most of the benefit in robust portfolio optimization. In addition, standard approaches for estimating expected returns, such as Bayesian statistics and regression-based methods,[13] can produce estimates for the estimation error covariance matrix in the process of generating the estimates themselves. Practical ways to compute an effective estimation error covariance matrix include least squares regression models, the James-Stein estimator, and the Black-Litterman model.[14] We describe some of these techniques next.

Least-Squares Regression Models If expected returns are estimated based on linear regression, then one can calculate an estimate of the error covariance matrix from the regression errors. As explained in Chapters 6 and 10, factor models for returns are typically estimated by linear regression, and have the form

$$r = \mu + V'f + \varepsilon$$

which can be rewritten as[15]

$$y_i = Ax_i + \varepsilon_i$$

for every asset i or, more generally, as

$$Y = AX + \varepsilon$$

where

---

[12] Robert Stubbs and Pamela Vance, "Computing Return Estimation Error Matrices for Robust Optimization," Report, Axioma, April 2005.

[13] See introduction to Bayesian statistics and regression in Chapters 6 and 8.

[14] For more details, refer to Stubbs and Vance, "Computing Return Estimation Error Matrices for Robust Optimization."

[15] Here we use the notation from Chapter 10, which is also the notation used in Goldfarb and Iyengar's paper "Robust Portfolio Selection Problems." Please note that the notation in the introduction to linear regression models in Chapter 7, which is the standard notation in statistics references, is different.

$\mathbf{Y} = [\mathbf{y}_1,\dots,\mathbf{y}_N]$ is a $T \times N$ matrix of T return data observations for N assets,

$\mathbf{A} = [\mathbf{1},\mathbf{f}_1,\dots,\mathbf{f}_M]$ is a $T \times (M + 1)$ matrix of factor realizations, and

$\mathbf{X} = [\boldsymbol{\mu},\mathbf{x}_1, \dots,\mathbf{x}_M]'$ is an $(M + 1) \times N$ matrix of regression coefficients.

If a portfolio manager decomposes the expected return forecast into factor-specific and asset-specific return, then he is concerned about the standard error covariance matrix for the intercept term $\boldsymbol{\mu}$. This covariance matrix can be used as an estimate for $\boldsymbol{\Sigma}_\mu$. The matrix of estimation errors for the mean response corresponding to the vector of intercept terms can be estimated by

$$\boldsymbol{\mu}'(\mathbf{A}'\mathbf{A})^{-1}\boldsymbol{\mu}\left(\frac{1}{T}(\mathbf{Y} - \mathbf{A}'\mathbf{X})(\mathbf{Y} - \mathbf{A}'\mathbf{X})\right)$$

The James-Stein Estimator   In Chapter 8, we introduced the James-Stein estimator of expected returns. The estimator is computed as a weighted average of the sample average returns (computed from a sample of size T) and a *shrinkage target* of $\boldsymbol{\mu}_0$:

$$\hat{\boldsymbol{\mu}}_{JS} = (1 - w)\hat{\boldsymbol{\mu}} + w\boldsymbol{\mu}_0$$

The special form of the James-Stein shrinkage estimator proposed by Jorion[16] (named the Bayes-Stein estimator) is based on Bayesian methodology. The shrinkage target $\boldsymbol{\mu}_0$ for the Bayes-Stein estimator is computed as

$$\boldsymbol{\mu}_0 = \frac{\iota'\boldsymbol{\Sigma}^{-1}}{\iota'\boldsymbol{\Sigma}^{-1}\iota}\hat{\boldsymbol{\mu}}$$

where $\boldsymbol{\Sigma}$ is the "real" covariance matrix of the N returns. This matrix is unknown in practice, but one can replace $\boldsymbol{\Sigma}$ in the above equation by

$$\hat{\boldsymbol{\Sigma}} = \frac{T-1}{T-N-3}\mathbf{S}$$

---

[16] Philippe Jorion, "Bayes-Stein Estimation for Portfolio Analysis," *Journal of Financial and Quantitative Analysis* 21, no. 3 (September 1986), pp. 279–292.

and S is the usual sample covariance matrix. The variance of the Bayes-Stein estimator for the expected returns is given by[17]

$$\text{var}(\hat{\mu}_{BS}) = \Sigma + \frac{1}{T+\tau}\Sigma + \frac{\tau}{T(T+\tau+1)}\frac{\iota\iota'}{\iota'\Sigma\iota}$$

and can be used as an estimate for the error covariance matrix Σ_{μ}. The parameter τ is a scalar that describes the confidence in the precision of estimation of the covariance matrix Σ. Namely, the Bayes-Stein estimator assumes that the prior of the expected returns is the normal distribution with mean μ_0 and covariance matrix $(1/\tau)\Sigma$.

The Black-Litterman Model   As we explained in Chapter 8, the Black-Litterman model for estimating expected returns combines the market equilibrium with an investor's views. The formula for the estimate is a weighted sum of the two estimates of expected returns

$$\hat{\mu}_{BL} = [(\tau\Sigma)^{-1} + P'\Omega^{-1}P]^{-1}(\tau\Sigma)^{-1}\Pi + [(\tau\Sigma)^{-1} + P'\Omega^{-1}P]^{-1}[P'\Omega^{-1}P]\mu,$$

or, equivalently,

$$\hat{\mu}_{BL} = [(\tau\Sigma)^{-1} + P'\Omega^{-1}P]^{-1}[(\tau\Sigma)^{-1}\Pi + P'\Omega^{-1}q]$$

where

Σ is the $N \times N$ covariance matrix of returns.
$\Pi = [\Pi_1,...,\Pi_N]'$ is the vector of expected excess returns, computed from an equilibrium model such as the CAPM.
τ is a scalar that represents the confidence in the estimation of the market prior.
q is a K-dimensional vector of K investor views.
P is a $K \times N$ matrix of investor views.
Ω is a $K \times K$ matrix expressing the confidence in the investor's views. Frequently, the matrix Ω is assumed to be diagonal, i.e., investor views are assumed to be independent.

As we showed in Chapter 8, the covariance of the Black-Litterman estimator of expected returns is

$$[(\tau\Sigma)^{-1} + P'\Omega^{-1}P]^{-1}$$

---

[17] See Philippe Jorion, "Bayes-Stein Estimation for Portfolio Analysis."

This covariance matrix can be used as an approximation for the estimation error covariance matrix Σ_μ.

Uncertainty in Return Covariance Matrix Estimates

Mean-variance portfolio optimization is less sensitive to inaccuracies in the estimate of the covariance matrix Σ than it is to estimation errors in expected returns. Nonetheless, insurance against uncertainty in these estimates can be incorporated at not too large a cost. Most generally, the robust mean-variance portfolio optimization problem can then be formulated as

$$\max_{w} \left\{ \min_{\mu \in U_\mu} \{\mu' w\} - \lambda \max_{\Sigma \in U_\Sigma} \{w' \Sigma w\} \right\}$$

$$s.t. \quad w' \iota = 1$$

where U_μ and U_Σ denote the uncertainty sets of expected returns and covariances, respectively.

A few different methods for modeling uncertainty in the covariance matrix are used in practice. Some are superimposed on top of factor models for returns, while others consider confidence intervals for the individual covariance matrix entries. Benefits for portfolio performance have been observed even when the uncertainty set U_Σ is defined simply as a collection of several possible scenarios for the covariance matrix.[18] As we explained in Chapter 10, the latter definition of uncertainty set results in the introduction of several constraints in the optimization problem, each of which corresponds to a scenario for the covariance matrix, that is, the size of the optimization problem does not increase significantly.

Factor Models   If we assume a standard factor model for returns

$$r = \mu + V'f + \varepsilon$$

then the covariance matrix of returns Σ can be expressed as

$$\Sigma = V'FV + D$$

where

---

[18] Eranda Dragoti-Cela, Peter Haumer, and Raimund Kovacevic, "Applying Robust Optimization to Account for Estimation Risk in Dynamic Portfolio Selection," Manuscript, FSC (Financial Soft Computing), Siemens AG, Vienna, Austria, 2006.

$\mathbf{V}$ = the matrix of factor loadings.

$\mathbf{F}$ = the covariance matrix of factor returns.

$\mathbf{D}$ = the diagonal matrix of error term variances.

It is assumed that the vector of residual returns $\boldsymbol{\varepsilon}$ is independent of the vector of factor returns $\mathbf{f}$, and that the variance of $\boldsymbol{\mu}$ is zero.

As we discussed in Chapter 10, the statistical properties of the estimate of $\mathbf{V}$ naturally lead to an uncertainty set of the kind

$$S_\nu = \{\mathbf{V} : \mathbf{V} = \mathbf{V}_0 + \mathbf{W}, \|\mathbf{W}_i\|_G \leq \rho_i, i = 1, ..., N\}$$

where $\mathbf{W}_i$ denotes the i-th column of $\mathbf{W}$, and

$$\|\mathbf{w}\|_G = \sqrt{\mathbf{w}'\mathbf{G}\mathbf{w}}$$

is the Euclidean (elliptic) norm of $\mathbf{w}$ with respect to a symmetric positive definite matrix $\mathbf{G}$.[19] If we assume also that the estimates of expected returns belong to an interval uncertainty set

$$U_\delta(\hat{\boldsymbol{\mu}}) = \{\boldsymbol{\mu} | |\mu_i - \hat{\mu}_i| \leq \delta_i, i = 1, ..., N\}$$

we can formulate the resulting robust optimization problem as the SOCP[20]

$$\max_{\mathbf{w}, \boldsymbol{\psi}, \upsilon, \kappa, \tau, \eta, t, s} \boldsymbol{\mu}'\mathbf{w} - \boldsymbol{\delta}'\boldsymbol{\psi} - \lambda(\upsilon + \kappa)$$

$$s.t. \quad \left\| \begin{bmatrix} 2\mathbf{D}^{1/2}\mathbf{w} \\ 1 - \kappa \end{bmatrix} \right\| \leq 1 + \kappa$$

$$\mathbf{w}'\boldsymbol{\iota} = 1$$

$$\psi_i \geq w_i; \ \psi_i \geq -w_i, i = 1, ..., N$$

$$\tau + t'\boldsymbol{\iota} \leq \upsilon - \kappa$$

$$\eta \leq \frac{1}{l_{\max}(\mathbf{H})}$$

---

[19] As we pointed out in section "Selecting Uncertainty Sets" in Chapter 10, there is a natural way to define the matrix $\mathbf{G}$ that is related to probabilistic guarantees on the likelihood that the actual realization of the uncertain coefficients will lie in the ellipsoidal uncertainty set S_ν. Specifically, the definition of the matrix $\mathbf{G}$ can be based on the data used to produce the estimates of the regression coefficients of the factor model.

[20] Donald Goldfarb and Garud Iyengar, "Robust Portfolio Selection Problems," *Mathematics of Operations Research* 28, no. 1 (2003), pp. 1–38.

$$\left\| \begin{bmatrix} 2\rho'\psi \\ \eta - \tau \end{bmatrix} \right\| \le \eta + \tau$$

$$\left\| \begin{bmatrix} 2s_i \\ 1 - nl_i - t_i \end{bmatrix} \right\| \le 1 - \eta l_i + t_i, \; i = 1, \dots, M$$

where

M = the number of factors in the factor model.

QLQ' = the spectral decomposition of $H = G^{-1/2}FG^{-1/2}$ (recall that G was the matrix used for defining the norm in the uncertainty set for the factor loadings matrix V).

L = a diagonal matrix with elements $l_1, \dots, l_M$ (l_{max} is the maximum of these elements).

s = $Q'H^{1/2}G^{1/2}V_0w$.

Even though the mathematical formulation appears complicated at first sight, it is straightforward and computationally efficient to solve it with an SOCP solver or general nonlinear software. As we mentioned before, constraints such as

$$\left\| \begin{bmatrix} 2D^{1/2}w \\ 1 - \kappa \end{bmatrix} \right\| \le 1 + \kappa$$

are SOCP constraints. The norm $\|.\|$ simply requires taking a square root of the sum of the squared terms of the elements of the vector

$$\begin{bmatrix} 2D^{1/2}w \\ 1 - \kappa \end{bmatrix}$$

Some specialized SOCP software may require the constraint to be input in this form, and will be more efficient if the SOCP structure is explicitly stated. However, if a general-purpose modeling language or nonlinear solver is used, this constraint can be rewritten as a general nonlinear constraint, namely,[21]

---

[21] In some circumstances, one can raise both sides of an SOCP constraint to the second power, and obtain an equivalent quadratic constraint. This is the case here: the SOCP constraint

$$\sqrt{4w'(D^{1/2})'D^{1/2}w + (1 - \kappa)^2} \le 1 + \kappa$$

is equivalent to the convex quadratic constraint $w'Dw \le \kappa$. However, in general, quadratic and SOCP constraints are not automatically equivalent. It is therefore usually safer to input SOCP constraints directly into a nonlinear solver, without trying to convert them to quadratic constraints first. As we mentioned earlier, modeling languages such as AMPL and GAMS have commands for specifying square roots of expressions.

$$\sqrt{4w'(D^{1/2})'D^{1/2}w + (1-\kappa)^2} \le 1+\kappa$$

Confidence Intervals for the Entries of the Covariance Matrix   Instead of using uncertainty sets based on estimates from a factor model, one can specify intervals for the individual elements of the covariance matrix of the kind

$$\underline{\Sigma} \le \Sigma \le \bar{\Sigma}$$

If we assume that the estimates of expected returns vary in intervals

$$U_\delta(\hat{\mu}) = \{\mu \,|\, |\mu_i - \hat{\mu}_i| \le \delta_i, i = 1, ..., N\}$$

short sales are not allowed (i.e., $w \ge 0$), and the matrix $\bar{\Sigma}$ is positive semidefinite (which means that the upper bound matrix derived from data is a well-defined covariance matrix), the resulting optimization problem is very simple to formulate. We just need to replace μ by $\hat{\mu}+\delta$ and Σ by $\bar{\Sigma}$ in the mean-variance formulation, as the expression

$$\max_{w} (\hat{\mu}+\delta)'w - \lambda w'\bar{\Sigma}w$$

in fact equals

$$\max_{w} \left\{ \min_{\mu \in U_\mu} \{\mu'w\} - \lambda \max_{\Sigma \in U_\Sigma} \{w'\Sigma w\} \right\}$$

under the above conditions.[22]

     In the general case, the formulation of the robust counterpart is not as trivial, but remains a convex problem. The resulting optimization problem is in fact a semidefinite program (SDP). More precisely, assuming as before that the estimates of expected returns vary in intervals

$$U_\delta(\hat{\mu}) = \{\mu \,|\, |\mu_i - \hat{\mu}_i| \le \delta_i, i = 1, ..., N\}$$

the robust formulation of the mean-variance optimization problem is

---

[22] See R. Tutuncu and M. Koenig, "Robust Asset Allocation," *Annals of Operations Research* 132, no. 1 (2004), pp. 157–187.

$$\max_{\mathbf{w},\,\mathbf{w}_+,\,\mathbf{w}_-,\,\underline{\boldsymbol{\Lambda}},\,\overline{\boldsymbol{\Lambda}}} \hat{\boldsymbol{\mu}}'\mathbf{w} - \boldsymbol{\delta}'(\mathbf{w}_+ + \mathbf{w}_-) - \lambda(\langle \overline{\boldsymbol{\Lambda}}, \overline{\boldsymbol{\Sigma}} \rangle - \langle \underline{\boldsymbol{\Lambda}}, \underline{\boldsymbol{\Sigma}} \rangle)$$

$$s.t. \quad \mathbf{w}'\boldsymbol{\iota} = 1$$

$$\mathbf{w} = \mathbf{w}_+ - \mathbf{w}_-,\, \mathbf{w}_+ \geq 0,\, \mathbf{w}_- \geq 0$$

$$\overline{\boldsymbol{\Lambda}} \geq 0,\, \underline{\boldsymbol{\Lambda}} \geq 0$$

$$\begin{bmatrix} \overline{\boldsymbol{\Lambda}} - \underline{\boldsymbol{\Lambda}} & \mathbf{w} \\ \mathbf{w}' & 1 \end{bmatrix} \succeq 0$$

where the notation $\langle \mathbf{A}, \mathbf{B} \rangle$ for two symmetric matrices $\mathbf{A}$, $\mathbf{B}$ stands for "Tr(AB)," the trace of the matrix product $\mathbf{AB}$. Tr(AB) is equal to the sum of the diagonal elements of the matrix product $\mathbf{AB}$.[23]

We explained earlier the part of the robust formulation that is related to uncertainty in expected returns. In order to demystify the derivation of robust counterparts of optimization problems that are SDPs, we show how one would derive the terms related to the uncertainty in the covariance matrix.

As before, we start by asking ourselves what the worst-case value for the portfolio variance $\mathbf{w}'\boldsymbol{\Sigma}\mathbf{w}$ would be if the estimates of the covariance matrix $\boldsymbol{\Sigma}$ vary in intervals $\underline{\boldsymbol{\Sigma}} \leq \boldsymbol{\Sigma} \leq \overline{\boldsymbol{\Sigma}}$. For any fixed vector of portfolio weights $\mathbf{w}$, we can find it by solving the optimization problem

$$\max_{\boldsymbol{\Sigma}} \mathbf{w}'\boldsymbol{\Sigma}\mathbf{w}$$

$$s.t. \quad \underline{\boldsymbol{\Sigma}} \leq \boldsymbol{\Sigma} \leq \overline{\boldsymbol{\Sigma}}$$

$$\boldsymbol{\Sigma} \succeq 0$$

---

[23] The notation $\langle \mathbf{A}, \mathbf{B} \rangle$ is typically used to denote the inner product of $\mathbf{A}$ and $\mathbf{B}$. In this case, we are dealing with an inner product on the space of symmetric matrices, defined as the trace of the product of two matrices $\mathbf{A}$ and $\mathbf{B}$. The trace of a symmetric matrix $\mathbf{X}$ with N rows and N columns is mathematically defined as

$$\sum_{i=1}^{N} X_{ii}$$

that is, it is the sum of the elements of the main diagonal (left to right). It is easy to see that the trace of the product of two matrices $\mathbf{A}$ and $\mathbf{B}$ can be expressed as

$$\text{Tr}(\mathbf{AB}) = \sum_{i=1}^{N} (\mathbf{AB})_{ii} = \sum_{i=1}^{N}\sum_{j=1}^{N} (\mathbf{A})_{ij}(\mathbf{B})_{ji}$$

Some optimization modeling languages (e.g., YALMIP) contain direct syntax for the trace of a matrix, which makes formulating an optimization problem easier. See Chapter 11 for an introduction to optimization languages and software.

We use "$\geq$, $\leq$" to denote component-wise inequality, and "$\succeq$" to denote positive semidefiniteness of a matrix.[24]

The above problem is a semidefinite program (SDP). As explained in Chapter 9, the dual problem of this semidefinite program can be found to be

$$\min_{\mathbf{w}, \underline{\Lambda}, \overline{\Lambda}} \langle \overline{\Lambda}, \overline{\Sigma} \rangle - \langle \underline{\Lambda}, \underline{\Sigma} \rangle$$
$$s.t. \quad -\mathbf{Z} + \overline{\Lambda} - \underline{\Lambda} = \mathbf{ww}'$$
$$\mathbf{Z} \succeq 0, \overline{\Lambda} \geq 0, \underline{\Lambda} \geq 0$$

where $\underline{\Lambda}$ and $\overline{\Lambda}$ are the dual variables associated with the constraints $\underline{\Sigma} \leq \Sigma$ and $\Sigma \leq \overline{\Sigma}$, respectively, and $\mathbf{Z}$ is the explicit dual slack variable. This problem can be rewritten as

$$\min_{\mathbf{w}, \underline{\Lambda}, \overline{\Lambda}} \langle \overline{\Lambda}, \overline{\Sigma} \rangle - \langle \underline{\Lambda}, \underline{\Sigma} \rangle$$
$$s.t. \quad \overline{\Lambda} - \underline{\Lambda} - \mathbf{ww}' \succeq 0$$
$$\overline{\Lambda} \geq 0, \underline{\Lambda} \geq 0$$

The constraint $\overline{\Lambda} - \underline{\Lambda} + \mathbf{ww}' \succeq 0$ can be recast into a so-called linear matrix inequality (LMI) form which is understood by SDP solvers by using *Schur complements*[25] resulting in

---

[24] A matrix $\mathbf{X}$ is positive semidefinite, i.e., $\mathbf{X} \succeq 0$, if and only if $\mathbf{z}'\mathbf{Xz} \geq 0$ for every real vector $\mathbf{z}$.

[25] In linear algebra, the Schur complement of a block of a square matrix $\mathbf{D}$ in a larger square matrix $\mathbf{M}$,

$$\mathbf{M} = \begin{bmatrix} \mathbf{A} & \mathbf{B} \\ \mathbf{C} & \mathbf{D} \end{bmatrix}$$

is defined as the expression $\mathbf{A} - \mathbf{BD}^{-1}\mathbf{C}$. Recognizing Schur complements in nonlinear expressions is frequently a key to formulating difficult nonlinear optimization problems as computationally tractable SDPs. In particular, if we have a constraint of the kind $\mathbf{Q}(\mathbf{x}) - \mathbf{S}(\mathbf{x})\mathbf{R}(\mathbf{x})^{-1}\mathbf{S}(\mathbf{x})' \succeq 0$ where $\mathbf{x}$ is a vector of variables, and if both $\mathbf{Q}(\mathbf{x}) - \mathbf{S}(\mathbf{x})\mathbf{R}(\mathbf{x})^{-1}\mathbf{S}(\mathbf{x})' \succeq 0$ and $\mathbf{R}(\mathbf{x}) \succeq 0$, then we can express the constraint as the LMI

$$\begin{bmatrix} \mathbf{Q}(\mathbf{x}) & \mathbf{S}(\mathbf{x}) \\ \mathbf{S}(\mathbf{x})' & \mathbf{R}(\mathbf{x}) \end{bmatrix} \succeq 0$$

Note that if $\mathbf{Q}(\mathbf{x})$ is a scalar, then we have the nonlinear constraint $\mathbf{Q}(\mathbf{x}) - \mathbf{S}(\mathbf{x})\mathbf{R}(\mathbf{x})^{-1}\mathbf{S}(\mathbf{x})' \geq 0$ in which the positive semidefiniteness sign $\succeq$ is replaced by an inequality sign $\geq$.

$$\min_{w,\,\underline{\Lambda},\,\overline{\Lambda}} \langle \overline{\Lambda}, \overline{\Sigma} \rangle - \langle \underline{\Lambda}, \underline{\Sigma} \rangle$$

$$s.t. \quad \begin{bmatrix} \overline{\Lambda} - \underline{\Lambda} & w \\ w' & 1 \end{bmatrix} \succeq 0$$

$$\overline{\Lambda} \geq 0, \underline{\Lambda} \geq 0$$

Notice that the variable Σ is not present in the above optimization problem. However, the optimal values of the dual problem will be at least as large as the optimal value of the primal problem (see the discussion in Chapter 9). Therefore, one can use the expression

$$\min_{w,\,\underline{\Lambda},\,\overline{\Lambda}} \langle \overline{\Lambda}, \overline{\Sigma} \rangle - \langle \underline{\Lambda}, \underline{\Sigma} \rangle$$

instead of the expression

$$\max_{\Sigma} w'\Sigma w$$

in the robust mean-variance problem formulation (all of the constraints, of course, will have to be preserved in the formulation as well). This leads to the robust SDP formulation we provided above.

As discussed in Chapter 9, SDPs are more difficult to solve than SOCPs, but are still convex problems for which interior point methods and bundle methods for large-scale (sparse) problems have been developed. Efficient SDP routines such as SeDuMi[26] (for use with MATLAB) are now available, and modeling languages such as YALMIP make it easy to describe an SDP problem to SDP solvers and retrieve the solution.[27] Moreover, because of the increasing popularity of robust optimization methods in practice, several modeling languages (PROF and YALMIP in particular) have incorporated some support for robustness in their syntax. YALMIP, for example, now offers an interface for specifying which parameters in an optimization problem are uncertain, formulates the robust counterpart of such problems if the uncertain

---

[26] Jos F. Sturm, "Using SeDuMi 1.02, A MATLAB Toolbox for Optimization over Symmetric Cones," *Optimization Methods and Software* 11–12 (1999), pp. 625–653; see also SeDuMi's official site at http://sedumi.mcmaster.ca/ for tutorials and free downloads.

[27] The description of the SDP problem in YALMIP, for example, is no longer than a few lines of code. While a complete introduction to modeling languages is beyond the scope of this book, YALMIP's home page, http://control.ee.ethz.ch/~joloef/wiki/pmwiki.php, contains a number of examples of implementations of SDP problems.

parameters are assumed to vary in interval uncertainty sets, and returns the robust solution directly to the user.[28]

Robust Sharpe Ratio Optimization

A problem closely related to the mean-variance problem is the Sharpe ratio optimization problem

$$\max_{\mathbf{w}} \ \frac{\boldsymbol{\mu}'\mathbf{w} - r_f}{\sqrt{\mathbf{w}'\Sigma\mathbf{w}}}$$

$$s.t. \quad \mathbf{w}'\boldsymbol{\iota} = 1$$

where r_f denotes the risk-free rate of return. We recall from Chapter 2 that the Sharpe ratio is a performance measure that evaluates the excess return per unit of risk. If we assume a factor structure of returns with the corresponding uncertainty sets for the expected returns and the covariance matrix as above, the robust counterpart of the Sharpe ratio problem is[29]

$$\max_{\mathbf{w}, \boldsymbol{\psi}, \upsilon, \kappa, \tau, \eta, t, s} \ \upsilon + \kappa$$

$$s.t. \quad \left\| \begin{bmatrix} 2\mathbf{D}^{1/2}\mathbf{w} \\ 1 - \kappa \end{bmatrix} \right\| \leq 1 + \kappa$$

$$\mathbf{w}'\boldsymbol{\iota} = 1$$

$$\boldsymbol{\mu}'\mathbf{w} - \boldsymbol{\delta}'\boldsymbol{\psi} \geq 1$$

$$\psi_i \geq w_i; \ \psi_i \geq -w_i, \ i = 1, \ldots, N$$

$$\tau + t'\boldsymbol{\iota} \leq \upsilon$$

$$\eta \leq \frac{1}{l_{\max}(\mathbf{H})}$$

$$\left\| \begin{bmatrix} 2\boldsymbol{\rho}'\boldsymbol{\psi} \\ \eta - \tau \end{bmatrix} \right\| \leq \eta + \tau$$

$$\left\| \begin{bmatrix} 2s_i \\ 1 - \eta l_i - t_i \end{bmatrix} \right\| \leq 1 - \eta l_i + t_i, \ i = 1, \ldots, M$$

---

[28] At the time of writing of this book, such features were still at the beta (testing) stage. See http://control.ee.ethz.ch/~joloef/wiki/pmwiki.php for more information.

[29] Emre Erdogan, Donald Goldfarb, and Garud Iyengar, "Robust Portfolio Management," *CORC Technical Report TR-2004-11*, available from http://www.corc.ieor.columbia.edu/reports/techreports.html.

where we use the same notation as introduced earlier in this chapter. As in the case of the robust mean-variance formulation, while this problem may look complicated, it really is not. It is straightforward to solve it with any SOCP solver.

Goldfarb and Iyengar[30] studied the effect of "robustification" on portfolio return and turnover. Their results show that for low levels of confidence, the classical and the robust portfolios have very similar performance, as expected. It is not until the confidence is more than 80% that the robust strategy outperforms the classical one—at least for their data sample. In particular, for the 95% and 99% confidence levels, the final wealth of the robust portfolios is 40% and 50% higher than that of the classical portfolio, respectively.

These results are similar to the ones reported by Ceria.[31] His simulation experiments show an improvement in realized Sharpe ratios of portfolios rebalanced with robust mean-variance versus classical mean-variance of between 20% and 45% dependent on the aversion to estimation error (confidence level).

Let us now take a look at the difference in average turnover between the two portfolios over the investment horizon defined by

$$\frac{\frac{1}{10}\sum_{t=1}^{10}\left\|\mathbf{w}_{r,\,t}-\mathbf{w}_{r,\,t-1}\right\|_1}{\frac{1}{10}\sum_{t=1}^{10}\left\|\mathbf{w}_{c,\,t}-\mathbf{w}_{c,\,t-1}\right\|_1}$$

where the subscripts r and c are used to denote the robust and the classical portfolio weights, respectively, and

$$\|\mathbf{w}\|_1 = \sum_{i=1}^{N} |w_i|$$

The ratio of the average turnover of the robust and the classical portfolios is more or less constant (between about 1.005 to 1.015) up to the 90% confidence level. This means that the turnover of the robust portfolios is around 0.5% to 1.5% higher than the classical portfolio. However, for confidence levels greater than 90%, the turnover decreases monotonically. For example, at the 95% and 99% confidence levels, the

---

[30] Goldfarb and Iyengar, "Robust Portfolio Selection Problems."

[31] Sebastian Ceria, "Overcoming Estimation Error in Portfolio Construction," Presentation at the Chicago Quantitative Alliance Las Vegas Conference, 2003.

turnover of the robust portfolios is 4% and 7% lower than the classical portfolio, respectively.

Note that if the confidence level is chosen too high, the robust portfolio becomes very conservative. Typically, in this case, the portfolio weights will be close to those of the global minimum variance portfolio and not change much from period to period, thereby reducing turnover.

Using Robust Mean-Variance Portfolio Optimization in Practice

As we saw in the examples earlier in this section, the computational complexity of the robust formulations of the classical portfolio optimization problems is not a real issue. Robust optimization does, however, come at the cost of additional modeling effort. The important question is whether this effort is worthwhile. In other words, what are the benefits of incorporating uncertainty in the optimization process?

Critics have argued that robust optimization does not provide more benefit than, for instance, shrinkage estimators that combine the minimum variance portfolio with a speculative investment portfolio. Indeed, under certain conditions (short sales allowed, ellipsoidal uncertainty model for expected return estimates, error covariance matrix estimated as $(1/T)\Sigma$), it can be shown that the optimal portfolio weights using robust optimization are a linear combination of the weights of the minimum variance portfolio[32] and a mean-variance efficient portfolio with speculative demand, and thus the implied expected return is equivalent to the expected return obtained using a shrinkage estimator with certain weights.[33] Robust optimization thus appears to offer a less transparent way to express investor preferences and tolerance to uncertainty than other approaches, such as Bayesian methods, in which the shrinkage weights can be defined explicitly. In the general case, however, robust optimization is not necessarily equivalent to shrinkage estimation. They are particularly different in the presence of additional portfolio constraints. Furthermore, as we illustrated in this chapter, robust optimization can be used to account for uncertainty in parameters other than expected asset returns, making its relationship with Bayesian methods difficult to establish.

It can be argued that a difficulty with assessing the benefits of the robust optimization approach is that its performance is highly dependent on the choice (or calibration) of the model parameters, such as the aversion to the estimation error δ. However, this issue is no different

---

[32] The minimum variance portfolio is independent of investor preferences or expected returns, see Chapter 2.

[33] See, for example, Bernd Scherer, "How Different is Robust Optimization Really?" Deutsche Asset Management, New York, 2005.

from the calibration of standard parameters in the classical portfolio optimization framework, such as the length of the estimation period and the risk aversion coefficient. These and other parameters need to be determined subjectively.

We remark that other modeling devices such as Bayesian estimation (for example, James-Stein shrinkage estimators and the Black-Litterman model) have similar issues. In particular, for shrinkage estimators, the portfolio manager needs to determine which shrinkage target to use and the size of the shrinkage parameter. In the Black-Litterman model, he needs to provide his confidence in equilibrium as well as his confidence in each individual view. These quantities are most often derived from subjective assumptions—or from the experience of the portfolio manager.

As we argued in Chapter 10, an advantage of the robust optimization approach is that the parameter values in the robust formulation can be matched to probabilistic guarantees. For example, if the estimates of the expected asset returns are assumed to be normally distributed, then there is an $\omega\%$ chance that the true expected returns will fall in the ellipsoidal set around the manager's estimates $\hat{\mu}$,

$$U_{\delta}(\hat{\mu}) = \{\mu | (\mu - \hat{\mu})' \Sigma_{\mu}^{-1} (\mu - \hat{\mu}) \leq \delta^2\}$$

if δ^2 is assigned the value of the ωth percentile of a χ^2 distribution with degrees of freedom equal to the number of assets in the portfolio. More generally, if the expected returns are assumed to belong to any possible probability distribution, then assigning

$$\delta = \sqrt{\frac{1 - \omega}{\omega}}$$

guarantees that the estimates fall in the uncertainty set $U_{\delta}(\hat{\mu})$ with probability at least $\omega\%$.[34, 35]

Dealing with Conservatism: The Zero Net Alpha-Adjustment

Traditional uncertainty sets are frequently modified so that they can serve a particular purpose, or so that they deliver increased robustness

---

[34] Laurent El Ghaoui, Maksim Oks, and Francois Oustry, "Worst-Case Value-at-Risk and Robust Portfolio Optimization: A Conic Optimization Approach," *Operations Research* 51, no. 4 (2003), pp. 543–556.

[35] We note that in practice sometimes these theoretical estimates may be too conservative. Often, however, this can be detected and adjusted by explicit calibration of model parameters to historical data.

over classical portfolio optimization without being too conservative.[36] It has been observed in practice that the standard robust mean-variance formulation with ellipsoidal uncertainty specification for expected return estimates sometimes results in portfolio allocations that are too pessimistic. Of course, we can always make a formulation less pessimistic by considering a smaller uncertainty set. For the ellipsoidal uncertainty set, we can achieve this by decreasing the radius of the ellipsoid. However, there is a recent trend among practitioners to apply more structured restrictions. Here we discuss a technique that has been observed to work particularly well in the practice of robust portfolio expected return modeling. The idea is to incorporate a *zero net alpha-adjustment* into the robust optimization problem.[37]

Recall that the traditional robust counterpart tries to find the optimal solution so that constraints containing uncertain coefficients are satisfied for the worst-case realization of the uncertain parameters. In particular, when trying to make a portfolio optimization problem robust with respect to errors in expected return estimates, we make the assumption that all of the actual realizations of expected returns could be worse than their expected values. Thus, the net adjustment in the expected portfolio return will always be downwards. While this leads to a more robust problem than the original one, in many instances it may be too pessimistic to assume that all estimation errors go against us. It may therefore be more reasonable, in practice, to assume that at least some of the true realizations may be above their expected values. For example, we may make the assumption that there are approximately as many realizations above the estimated values as there are realizations below the estimated values. This condition can be incorporated in the portfolio optimization problem by adding a constraint to, say, the ellipsoidal uncertainty set used for the expected returns. Namely, instead of the uncertainty set

$$U_\delta(\hat{\mu}) = \{\mu | (\mu - \hat{\mu})' \Sigma_\mu^{-1} (\mu - \hat{\mu}) \leq \delta^2\}$$

we can consider

---

[36] See section "Selecting Uncertainty Sets" in Chapter 10 for a taxonomy of advanced specifications of uncertainty sets.
[37] Sebastian Ceria and Robert Stubbs, "Incorporating Estimation Errors into Portfolio Selection: Robust Portfolio Construction," *Journal of Asset Management* 7, no. 2 (July 2006), pp. 109–127.

$$U_\delta(\hat{\mu}) = \left\{ \mu \left| \begin{array}{l} (\mu - \hat{\mu})'\Sigma_\mu^{-1}(\mu - \hat{\mu}) \le \delta^2 \\ \iota'D(\mu - \hat{\mu}) = 0 \end{array} \right. \right\}$$

for some invertible matrix **D**. When **D** = **I**, where **I** is the identity matrix, the total net adjustment to the expected returns is zero, that is, the adjustment in the expected portfolio return is zero.

It can be shown then—by using the procedure that involves optimization duality as we did earlier, but with somewhat more complicated uncertainty set restrictions—that the expected return vector in the portfolio optimization problem, $\mu'w$, should be replaced by

$$\mu'w - \delta \left\| \left(\Sigma_\mu - \frac{1}{\iota'D\Sigma_\mu D'\iota} \Sigma_\mu D'\iota\iota'D\Sigma_\mu \right)^{1/2} w \right\|$$

instead of

$$\mu'w - \delta \left\| \Sigma_\mu^{1/2} w \right\|$$

as was the case with the simple ellipsoidal uncertainty set. Therefore, the zero net alpha-adjustment can be thought of as the standard robust mean-variance formulation with a modified covariance matrix of estimation errors.

There can be further variations on the zero net adjustment idea. For example, instead of restricting the adjustment of the expected return estimates, we can restrict their standard deviations. Namely, we can impose the requirement that every standard deviation of upward adjustment in the expected returns is offset by an equal downward adjustment of one standard deviation. To do this, it suffices to choose

$$D = L^{-1}$$

where $LL' = \Sigma_\mu$ is the Cholesky decomposition of the covariance matrix of expected return estimates.

Similarly, if we would like to achieve a zero net adjustment in the variance of the expected return estimates, we can select

$$D = \Sigma_\mu^{-1}$$

It can be shown that the zero net adjustment has the desired effect on portfolio weights—that is, it does not make the portfolio unnecessarily conservative in terms of expected return. If an asset's portfolio weight is above the weight that asset would have in the portfolio that simply minimizes the estimation error in expected returns, that asset's expected return (alpha) gets adjusted downwards. Conversely, if an asset's portfolio weight is below the weight that asset would have in the portfolio that simply minimizes the estimation error in expected returns, that asset's expected return (alpha) gets adjusted upwards. This type of adjustment has proven to be very effective in practice.

In Exhibit 8.1, we reported results from Ceria and Stubbs[38] that showed how different the true, the estimated, and the actual Markowitz efficient frontiers can be. Exhibit 12.1 shows their results on the effect of making expected returns robust with respect to estimation error on

EXHIBIT 12.1 Robust Efficient Frontiers

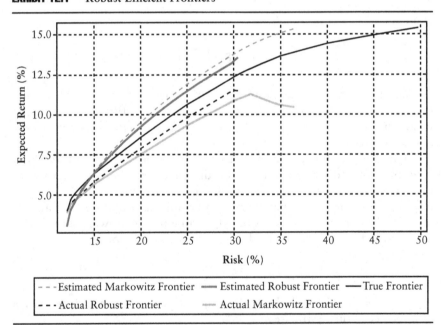

Source: Figure 4 in Sebastian Ceria and Robert Stubbs, "Incorporating Estimation Errors into Portfolio Selection: Robust Portfolio Construction," Axioma, Inc., 2005, p. 14. This copyrighted material is reprinted with permission from the authors.

---

[38] Sebastian Ceria and Robert Stubbs, "Incorporating Estimation Errors into Portfolio Selection: Robust Portfolio Construction."

the efficient portfolio frontiers, where the robust efficient frontier is generated by using the zero net alpha adjustment with $D = I$. The estimated Markowitz and the estimated robust frontier both overestimate the true frontier. However, both the estimated and the actual realized robust efficient frontiers are closer to the true efficient frontier.

Robust optimization is, unfortunately, not a panacea. From a behavioral and decision-making point of view, few individuals have max-min preferences. Indeed, max-min preferences describe the behavior of decision makers who face great ambiguity and thus make choices consistent with the belief that the worst possible outcomes are highly likely.

By using robust portfolio optimization formulations, investors are likely to trade off the optimality of their portfolio allocation in cases in which nature behaves as they predicted for protection against the risk of inaccurate estimation. Therefore, investors using the technique should not expect to do better than classical optimization when estimation errors have little impact, or when typical scenarios occur. They should, however, expect insurance in scenarios in which their estimates deviate from the actual realized values by up to the amount they have pre-specified in the modeling process. Some tests with simulated and real market data indicate that robust optimization, when inaccuracy is assumed in the expected return estimates, outperforms classical mean-variance optimization in terms of total excess return a large percentage (70% to 80%) of the time.[39] Other tests have not been as conclusive.[40] The factor that accounts for much of the difference is how the uncertainty in parameters is modeled. Therefore, finding a suitable degree of robustness and an appropriate definition of uncertainty set can have a significant impact on portfolio performance.

Independent tests by practitioners and academics using both simulated and market data appear to confirm that robust optimization generally results in more stable portfolio weights; that is, that it eliminates the extreme corner solutions resulting from traditional mean-variance optimization. This fact has implications for portfolio rebalancing in the presence of transaction costs and taxes, as transaction costs and taxes can add substantial expenses when the portfolio is rebalanced. Depending on the particular robust formulations employed, robust mean-variance optimization also appears to improve worst-case portfolio performance, and results in smoother and more consistent portfolio returns. Finally, by preventing large swings in positions, robust optimization frequently makes better use of the turnover budget and risk constraints.

---

[39] Sebastian Ceria and Robert Stubbs, "Incorporating Estimation Errors into Portfolio Selection: Robust Portfolio Construction."
[40] Lee, Stefek, and Zhelenyak, "Robust Portfolio Optimization—A Closer Look."

SOME PRACTICAL REMARKS ON ROBUST PORTFOLIO ALLOCATION MODELS

The discussion in the previous sections leads to the question: So which approach is best for modeling financial portfolios? The short answer is: it depends. It depends on the size of the portfolio, the type of assets and their distributional characteristics, the portfolio strategies and trading styles involved, and existing technical and intellectual infrastructure, among others. Sometimes it makes sense to consider a combination of several techniques, such as a blend of Bayesian estimation *and* robust portfolio optimization. This is an empirical question; indeed, the only way to find out is through extensive research and testing. To offer some guidance in this regard, we provide a simple step-by-step checklist for "robust quantitative portfolio management"[41]:

1. Risk forecasting: develop an accurate risk model.
2. Return forecasting: construct robust expected return estimates.
3. Classical portfolio optimization: start with a simple framework.
4. Mitigate model risk:
    a. Minimize estimation risk through the use of robust estimators.
    b. Improve the stability of the optimization framework through robust optimization.
5. Extensions.

In general, the most difficult item in this list is to calculate robust expected return estimates. Developing profitable trading strategies ("α generation") is notoriously hard, but not impossible.[42] It is important to remember that modern portfolio optimization techniques and fancy mathematics are not going to help much if the underlying trading strategies are subpar.

Implicit in this list is that for *each step* it is important to perform thorough testing in order to understand the effect of changes and new additions to the model. It is not unusual that quantitative analysts and portfolio managers will have to revisit previous steps as part of the

---

[41] By no means do we claim that this list is complete or that it has to be followed religiously. It is simply provided as a starting point and general guidance for the quantitative portfolio manager.

[42] We review some of the most common trading strategies in Chapter 14. For a survey of equity return forecasting models conducted during the summer of 2005 among 21 large quantitatively oriented money managers in North America and Europe, we refer the reader to Frank J. Fabozzi, Sergio M. Focardi, and Petter N. Kolm, *Trends in Quantitative Finance* (Charlottesville, VA: Research Foundation of CFA Institute, 2006).

research and development process. For example, it is important to understand the interplay between forecast generation and the reliability of optimized portfolio weights. Introducing a robust optimizer may lead to more reliable, and often more stable, portfolio weights. However, how to make the optimization framework more robust depends on how expected return and risk forecasts are produced. Therefore, one may have to refine or modify basic forecast generation. Identifying the individual and the combined contribution of different techniques is crucial in the development of a successful quantitative framework.

Minimizing estimation risk and improving the robustness of the optimization framework can be done in either order, or sometimes at the same time. The goal of both approaches is of course to improve the overall reliability and performance of the portfolio allocation framework. Some important questions to consider here are: When/why does the framework perform well (poorly)? How sensitive is it to changes in inputs? How does it behave when constraints change? Are portfolio weights intuitive—do they make sense? How high is the turnover of the portfolio?

Many extensions are possible, starting from the simple framework of portfolio optimization. Such extensions include—the introduction of transaction costs models, complex constraints (for example, integer constraints such as round lotting), different risk measures (e.g. downside risk measures, higher moments), dynamic and stochastic programming for incorporating intertemporal dependencies. Often these are problem specific and have to be dealt with on a case-by-case basis. We provide some examples in Chapter 13.

SUMMARY

- Classical mean-variance optimization is very sensitive to estimation errors and small changes in the inputs. Two ways in which the portfolio allocation process can be made more robust with respect to uncertainty in the input parameters are resampling and robust optimization.
- The idea behind portfolio resampling is to compute the optimal portfolio allocations for a sample of possible values for the expected values and covariance matrix of asset returns, and average the optimal portfolio weights found with each sampled data point. Some drawbacks of this approach include the fact that resampling is computationally cumbersome for large portfolios, and that it does not provide guarantees that the optimal portfolio allocation will satisfy all constraints in the original optimization problem. However, there is evidence that resam-

pling methods lead to more diversified portfolios in the case of long-only portfolios, and thus they may outperform the classical mean-variance portfolios out-of-sample.

- Robust portfolio optimization incorporates uncertainty directly into the optimization process. The uncertain parameters in the optimization problem are assumed to vary in pre-specified uncertainty sets that are selected based on statistical techniques and probabilistic guarantees.

- Making the portfolio optimization process robust with respect to uncertainty in the parameters is not very expensive in terms of computational cost, but it may result in a worse objective value. This can be corrected by using "smart" uncertainty sets for parameters that do not make the expected portfolio return too conservative.

- There is evidence that robust optimization may reduce portfolio turnover and transaction costs, improve worst-case performance, and lead to increased and more stable returns in the long run.

- A simple step-by-step checklist for "robust quantitative portfolio management":
  1. Risk forecasting: develop an accurate risk model.
  2. Return forecasting: construct robust expected return estimates.
  3. Classical portfolio optimization: start with a simple framework.
  4. Mitigate model risk:
     a. Minimize estimation risk through the use of robust estimators.
     b. Improve the stability of the optimization framework through robust optimization.
  5. Extensions.

CHAPTER 13

The Practice of Robust Portfolio Management: Recent Trends and New Directions

In the previous chapters, we reviewed a number of techniques for making the estimation of model parameters and portfolio optimization robust with respect to inevitable errors in the data and subjective guesses about market behavior. The concept of robustness, however, extends beyond statistical and modeling methods. It defines a particular way of thinking about asset allocation, portfolio management, and trading. As we explained in the introduction to this book, a robust quantitative investment framework consists of four stages: (1) developing reliable forecasts for future asset behavior; (2) selecting an informed model for portfolio allocation; (3) managing the portfolio rebalancing and execution of trades as market conditions change, and (4) monitoring and managing the entire investment process. Specifically, a portfolio manager employing a robust portfolio strategy should be guided by a checklist that includes, but is not limited to, the questions below, as well as considerations for the trade-offs between the different goals the manager might want to achieve:

- Are the statistical estimates produced by forecasting models reliable?
- Do actual probability distributions follow the shapes assumed in the estimates, and if not, how far away are they from the assumptions?
- Is the measure of risk used the right one given the particular circumstances? Is the risk estimated correctly based on the available information?
- How much do rebalancing strategies cost in terms of transaction and trading costs? Is the turnover of the portfolio at a desirable level?
- What are the costs of execution of trades? What is the portfolio liquidity risk exposure?

■ Is the portfolio rebalancing time horizon well defined? Is long-term performance sacrificed for short-term gains? Are tax implications for investors taken into consideration in the long-term portfolio management strategy?

In this chapter, we address several of these questions in more detail, and discuss recent trends and new directions in the area of robust portfolio management. In particular, we elaborate on extensions and refinements of some of the techniques described elsewhere in the book, and provide an overview of more advanced topics such as handling risk underestimation in factor models for asset returns, robust applications of different risk measures depending on the distributions involved, portfolio rebalancing, transaction and trading cost optimization, and multiperiod portfolio optimization models.

SOME ISSUES IN ROBUST ASSET ALLOCATION

Markowitz's idea that investors should aim to minimize the portfolio variance for any given expected return does not necessarily work under all market conditions. However, it did make a substantial contribution to finance theory and practice by defining optimal portfolio allocation as a trade-off between risk and return, introducing the concept of minimizing risk through diversification, and setting the stage for more advanced risk-return modeling. In this section, we discuss several practical issues in strategic portfolio allocation. First, we take a look at problems in the implementation of factor models in portfolio optimization, and discuss the Axioma Alpha Factor™ Method. We then discuss important issues to keep in mind when optimizing portfolio allocation using a sample of returns, and introduce some new developments in the area of quantile-based portfolio risk minimization that are based on ideas from the robust optimization field.

Robustness in Factor Model Estimation: The Axioma Alpha Factor™ Method[1]

Portfolio optimization procedures, whether automated or human-managed, typically try to minimize risk for a given level of expected return. In the process, they have to decide between portfolio allocations that fall into one of four categories, as illustrated in Exhibit 13.1. On the one hand, portfolio

---

[1] "Axioma Alpha Factor" is a trademark of Axioma, Inc. It first appeared in "Axioma's Alpha Factor Method: Improving Risk Estimation by Reducing Risk Model Portfolio Selection Bias," White Paper, Axioma, Inc., 2005.

EXHIBIT 13.1   Risk Model Performance Decomposed by Risk Model Accuracy and the Forecasted Risk Level

		Low	High
Forecasted Risk Level	High	False Negatives	True Negatives
	Low	False Positives	True Positives

Risk Model Accuracy

Source: "Axioma's Alpha Factor Method: Improving Risk Estimation by Reducing Risk Model Portfolio Selection Bias," White Paper, Axioma, Inc., 2005, p. 2. This copyrighted material is reprinted with permission from Axioma, Inc., 17 State Street, Suite 800, New York, NY 10004.

risk models may forecast Low (Positive) or High (Negative) risk, marked on the y-axis on the graph. However, depending on the accuracy of the forecasts (Low or High, as marked on the x-axis of the graph), this classification may result in either True or False prediction of portfolio risk.

Portfolio managers create risk models by using algorithms and data-sampling procedures that generate as accurate and unbiased risk models as possible, thus attempting to select portfolios in the right two boxes of Exhibit 13.1. An additional layer of risk modeling can be incorporated in the portfolio optimization procedures themselves. As discussed in Chapter 12, resampling and robust optimization are two techniques that allow for doing just that. In the case of risk minimization optimization models, these robust modeling methods protect against underestimation of risk, and in effect make sure that the selected portfolio lies in one of the two top categories in Exhibit 13.1.

The most difficult category is the combination of low model accuracy and low forecasted risk, which is the box in the lower left corner of Exhibit 13.1, and it is frequently not addressed satisfactorily in the portfolio allocation process. To illustrate this, we consider the following simple example based on a factor model for returns.

Single-Factor Model Example

Consider a portfolio of 5 stocks: A, B, C, D, and E, with true asset-asset covariance matrix[2]

---
[2] We thank Axioma, Inc. for providing us with this numerical example.

$$\Sigma = \begin{bmatrix} 0.2000 & 0.0650 & 0.0150 & -0.0550 & -0.1700 \\ 0.0650 & 0.0450 & 0.0075 & -0.0175 & -0.0550 \\ 0.0150 & 0.0075 & 0.0450 & 0.0075 & 0.0150 \\ -0.0550 & -0.0175 & 0.0075 & 0.0289 & 0.0650 \\ -0.1700 & -0.0550 & 0.0150 & 0.0650 & 0.1936 \end{bmatrix}$$

Suppose the vector of weights of assets A, B, C, D, and E in the portfolio is

$$\mathbf{w} = [0\%, 23.82\%, 22.47\%, 13.10\%, 40.61\%].$$

The true variance of the portfolio is therefore

$$\mathbf{w}'\Sigma\mathbf{w} = 0.03641$$

which corresponds to a volatility of 19.08%.

Suppose that returns are forecasted based on a one-factor model, with factor exposure for each asset $\mathbf{V}$, factor-factor covariance $\mathbf{F}$, and error covariance matrix Δ^2, where

$\mathbf{V} = [-3, -1, 0, 1, 3]'$
$\mathbf{F} = [0.021]$, and
$\Delta^2 = \mathrm{diag}(0.010404, 0.023409, 0.044100, 0.007396, 0.004096)$

The asset-asset covariance matrix based on this factor model can be computed as

$$\hat{\Sigma} = \mathbf{VFV}' + \Delta^2 = \begin{bmatrix} 0.1994 & 0.0630 & 0.0000 & -0.0630 & -0.1890 \\ 0.0630 & 0.0444 & 0.0000 & -0.0210 & -0.0630 \\ 0.0000 & 0.0000 & 0.0441 & 0.0000 & 0.0000 \\ -0.0630 & -0.0210 & 0.0000 & 0.0284 & 0.0630 \\ -0.1890 & -0.0630 & 0.0000 & 0.0630 & 0.1931 \end{bmatrix}$$

It is easy to see that the two asset-asset covariance matrices are not identical. There is an especially large difference in their third row and column. If the variance of the portfolio is computed with the estimate of Σ based on the one-factor model, we would obtain

$$\mathbf{w}'\hat{\Sigma}\mathbf{w} = 0.03028$$

which corresponds to a volatility of 17.40%, and clearly underestimates the true portfolio volatility of 19.08%.

The Alpha Factor™ Method

A method recently developed by Axioma, Inc., suggests a technique to make portfolios with such underestimated risk less desirable by optimization procedures. Namely, the estimate of the portfolio variance gets inflated by introducing an extra factor, f, and measuring how far the weights of the current portfolio are from the null space of the factor loadings matrix.[3]

The main observation is that portfolio allocations whose goal it is to eliminate factor risk (and be left only with specific risk) tend to underestimate the specific risk. Thus, one could attempt to introduce an artificial factor in order to capture some of the risk not captured by the specific asset risks as measured from the estimated factor model. In order to be more specific, we reintroduce the factor model for asset returns we discussed in Chapters 10 and 12,

$$r = \mu + V'f + \varepsilon$$

where

μ = an N-dimensional vector of mean returns.

f = an M-dimensional vector of factors with mean 0 and covariance matrix F.

V = an $M \times N$ matrix of factor loadings of the N assets.

ε = the N-dimensional vector of residuals (assumed to be normally distributed with mean 0 and diagonal covariance matrix Δ^2).

The estimated covariance matrix of asset returns based on this factor model is

$$\hat{\Sigma} = V'FV + \Delta^2$$

Typically, the estimate of the portfolio risk (as measured by standard deviation) would be

$$\sigma_p = \sqrt{w'V'FVw + w'\Delta^2 w}$$

and, for portfolio allocations for which the factor risk is neutralized (i.e., $Vw = 0$), the estimated portfolio risk is reduced to

$$\sigma_p = \sqrt{w'\Delta^2 w}$$

---

[3] The null space of a matrix A is the set of all vectors x such that $Ax = 0$.

The problem is, during the estimation of the factor model, the matrix Δ^2 is constructed to be unbiased for all possible portfolios. However, it is not necessarily true that it remains unbiased for portfolios lying in the null space of the factor loadings matrix V. Thus, the risk of such portfolios may be underestimated.

Axioma's methodology assumes that the extent to which risk is underestimated is related to the extent to which a portfolio has exposure to (i.e., is "close to") the null space of V. Thus, it uses the "projection matrix" P into the null space of V, computed as

$$P = I - V'(VV')^{+}V$$

to adjust estimates accordingly. In the expression for P, I is the identity matrix, and V^{+} denotes the pseudo-inverse of the matrix V.[4]

The adjustment is based on introducing a new, unspecified factor to the original factor risk model. This factor is chosen from the null space of V. The modified estimate of the covariance matrix of the assets is then

$$\hat{\Sigma}_{adj} = \begin{bmatrix} V' & g \end{bmatrix} \begin{bmatrix} F & 0 \\ 0 & 1 \end{bmatrix} \begin{bmatrix} V' & g \end{bmatrix}' + \Delta^2$$

where g is an N-dimensional column vector of unspecified factor exposures. One way of specifying the new factor is by computing the factor exposures as

$$g = \kappa \frac{Pw}{\|Pw\|}$$

for some constant κ prespecified by the portfolio manager.[5] The standard deviation of the portfolio then gets inflated to

$$\sigma_p^{adj} = \sqrt{w'V'FVw + \kappa^2 \frac{(w'Pw)^2}{w'P'Pw} + w'\Delta^2 w}$$

---

[4] The definition of the pseudo-inverse of a matrix is quite technical, but when VV' has full rank, the pseudo-inverse is just the inverse, that is, $(VV')^{+} = (VV')^{-1}$.

[5] The selection of κ is subjective, and if the purpose of the risk model is to create an actual correction to portfolio optimization procedures, the value of κ should be chosen carefully by back-testing. However, if the goal is simply to identify portfolios with potentially underestimated risk, then the choice of κ is not critical. Most generally, κ can be thought of as the magnitude of the volatility of the unknown factor g.

in order to compensate for the risk underestimation. The resulting portfolio optimization problem can be stated as an SOCP.[6] Observe that when **w** is close to the null space of **V**,

$$\sigma_p^{adj} \approx \sqrt{\kappa^2 \frac{(\mathbf{w}'\mathbf{Pw})^2}{\mathbf{w}'\mathbf{P}'\mathbf{Pw}} + \mathbf{w}'\Delta^2\mathbf{w}}$$

which is an increasing function in κ. In other words, by adjusting κ, we can penalize portfolio weights that are close to the null space of **V**. This is exactly the type of portfolios that factor models would underestimate.

Single-Factor Model Example, Continued

Let us go back to the simple example of a single-factor model we introduced earlier in this section. The vector of current portfolio weights is not in the null space of the factor loadings matrix **V**, as **Vw** = 1.111. However, the Alpha Factor™ Method can still be used to inflate the current estimate of risk. Suppose $\kappa = 0.15$. Then, the new factor exposures can be computed as

$$\mathbf{g} = \kappa \frac{\mathbf{Pw}}{\|\mathbf{Pw}\|}$$

and equal [0.052404, 0.092362, 0.070659, 0.02371, 0.075288]. The adjusted estimate for the covariance matrix based on the factor model therefore becomes

$$\hat{\Sigma}_{adj} = \begin{bmatrix} \mathbf{V}' & \mathbf{g} \end{bmatrix} \begin{bmatrix} \mathbf{F} & 0 \\ 0 & 1 \end{bmatrix} \begin{bmatrix} \mathbf{V}' & \mathbf{g} \end{bmatrix}' + \Delta^2$$

$$= \begin{bmatrix} 0.19984 & 0.06377 & 0.00059 & -0.06280 & -0.18837 \\ 0.06377 & 0.04577 & 0.00104 & -0.02065 & -0.06189 \\ 0.00059 & 0.00104 & 0.04490 & 0.00027 & 0.00085 \\ -0.06280 & -0.02065 & 0.00027 & 0.02849 & 0.06329 \\ -0.18837 & -0.06189 & 0.00085 & 0.06329 & 0.19400 \end{bmatrix}$$

This estimate is closer to the actual covariance matrix, and the variance of the portfolio can be computed to be 0.0354, that is, the portfo-

---

[6] See Chapter 9 for a definition of second order cone problems (SOCPs), Chapter 11 for a discussion of optimization software for such problems, and Chapter 12 for other examples of formulating robust portfolio optimization problems as SOCPs.

lio volatility is 18.82% which is much closer to the true value of 19.08%.

Robustness with Respect to Assumptions on the Underlying Asset Probability Distributions

A number of techniques described in this book rely on making assumptions about the probability distributions of uncertain parameters in the underlying models. In fact, as it is by now well known, the fundamental mean-variance model of Markowitz in theory should only be applied if one can assume that the portfolio asset returns follow a normal distribution (more precisely, a distribution from the elliptical family, of which the normal distribution is a member), or that investors have quadratic utility. In practice, it has been shown that mean-variance approximations work well even if investors have more realistic power utility functions,[7] or the underlying asset distributions deviate from normal. However, mean-variance approximations are not useful if investors have more complex S-shape or bilinear utility functions, or when asset return distributions are far from normal, as is the case with portfolios containing, for example, hedge funds, equity options, emerging market equity, or credit risky securities.

There are several approaches for dealing with portfolio optimization in such cases. For example, as we mentioned in Chapter 3, given the computational power available today, one can perform *full-scale optimization*, in which the optimal portfolio (at least for a not-too-large collection of assets) can be identified for a given set of asset return distributions and for any description of investor preferences.[8] The idea is to use smart search optimization algorithms to find the portfolio weights that maximize the assumed investor utility function over a sample of asset returns drawn from the assumed distribution.

In practice, however, this approach is still very computationally expensive, especially for large portfolios. Moreover, portfolio managers rarely know the *exact* distribution of future asset returns, so they may not be able to generate a representative collection of scenarios. Their forecasts and subjective "gut feeling" frequently tell them about the *expected* returns, the *spread* and the *shape* of their future distributions (i.e., are they more likely to go up or down) than about the specific outcomes they can expect.

---

[7] Haim Levy and Harry M. Markowitz, "Approximating Expected Utility by a Function of Mean and Variance," *American Economic Review* 69, no. 3 (1979), pp. 308–317.

[8] Timothy Adler and Mark Kritzman, "Mean-Variance versus Full-Scale Optimization: In and Out of Sample," Revere Street Working Paper Series, May 2006.

It follows that mean-risk optimization models may still be the method of choice in some circumstances. Mean-risk models capture some characteristics of the underlying distributions, but without necessarily requiring exact specification of these distributions. As we mentioned in Chapter 3, the theory of advanced risk measures has made significant progress in recent years. More sophisticated dispersion measures, as well as risk measures dealing only with downside risk, such as semi-deviation, CVaR and VaR, are widely used in the financial industry today. There is no unique answer to which risk measure is "best." The question the investment manager needs to ask himself is what his objectives are. On the one hand, a portfolio manager tracking an index may be interested in limiting the tracking error. On the other hand, a portfolio manager in charge of a portfolio containing sophisticated financial derivatives may be more concerned about downside risk such as the likelihood of losing a certain amount of money.

The Inherent Risks of Sampling

While advanced risk measures may allow for specifying investor preferences different from the classical mean-variance framework, one still has to use caution when applying such measures to determine the optimal portfolio based on samples of data. There is an inherent error in sampling that may result in widely varying portfolio weights.

For example, in Chapter 3 we introduced Conditional Value-at-Risk (CVaR), and explained its attractiveness both in terms of its computational tractability, and its theoretical properties (it is a coherent risk measure, see Chapter 3). Recall, however, that only the CVaR *sample* optimization formulation is computationally tractable; the general CVaR optimization is actually very hard, as it involves the calculation of a multidimensional integral. Thus, in order to take advantage of the computational tractability of CVaR, one would have to produce a sample of realizations for possible future asset returns.

Exhibit 13.2 illustrates how dangerous it can be to rely on sample optimization to determine a unique set of optimal portfolio weights. It graphs the range of optimal weights for a portfolio of 24 assets obtained with sample CVaR optimization. The returns for all 24 assets are simulated from independent simple two-point probability distributions with the same means and standard deviations, but with an increasing degree of skewness. Asset 1's distribution is symmetric, while asset 24's distribution is most negatively skewed. Since CVaR optimization aims to reduce the negative skewness of the portfolio return distribution, the optimal allocation should contain higher weights for the assets with smaller indices (such as assets 1, 2, 3), and lower weights for the assets with larger

EXHIBIT 13.2　　Ranges of Optimal Asset Weights (as Proportions) Obtained with 99% CVaR Sample Optimization

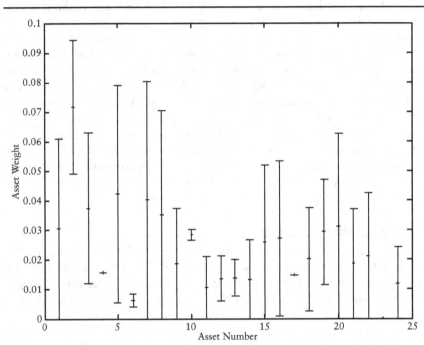

Source: Karthik Natarajan, Dessislava Pachamanova, and Melvyn Sim, "A Tractable Parametric Approach to Value-at-Risk Optimization," Working Paper, National University of Singapore Business School, July 2006, p. 26. This copyrighted material is reprinted with permission from the authors.

indices (assets 22, 23, 24). A sample of 1,000 realizations of asset returns is used to solve the CVaR optimization problem and compute the optimal weight for each asset. This is repeated 1,000 times to obtain the range in weights. We observe that while the median weight for the assets with smaller indices are larger in general, this relationship is not monotonic. More importantly, however, the range of the weights for most assets is quite large, suggesting that they are very sensitive to sampling errors. The two-point discrete probability distribution used to generate the asset returns in each sample of 1,000 returns is much simpler than the asset return distributions one would observe in practice. The variability in asset weights despite the simplified forecasting model for asset returns is a sign that in practice, one could expect much wider swings.

This example suggests that in certain circumstances it may be preferable to use parametric, as opposed to sample-based, risk measure optimization. Namely, if the parameters of the asset return distributions can be estimated robustly,[9] then the resulting optimization problem should produce more stable optimal allocations.

We discuss an example of such a robust parametric approximation to portfolio VaR optimization based on the approach of Natarajan, Pachamanova, and Sim.[10] It illustrates (1) how downside risk can be taken into consideration by using a quantile-based risk measure such as VaR; (2) how the problem with sample optimization we observed in the CVaR example can be reduced by estimating distribution parameters from data, and using them in a parametric, yet data-driven approach to VaR optimization; and (3) how the risk measure can be made coherent, thus ensuring robustness with respect to assumptions. The "glue" that holds all aspects of the example together is a robust optimization-based approach for approximating chance constraints in stochastic optimization.[11]

Example: Robust Parametric Value-at-Risk (VaR) Approximation

As we explained in Chapters 3 and 10, VaR is a quantile-based risk measure that provides information about the amount of losses that will not be exceeded with certain probability. Mathematically, $(1 - \varepsilon)$-VaR is defined as the minimum level γ_0 such that the probability that the portfolio loss exceeds γ_0 is less than ε, where ε is specified by the portfolio manager. Typically, ε equals 1% or 5%. Thus, the portfolio VaR optimization problem can be formulated as

$$\min_{\gamma_0,\, \mathbf{w}} \gamma_0$$
$$s.t. \quad P(W_0 - \tilde{\mathbf{r}}'\mathbf{w} > \gamma_0) \leq \varepsilon$$
$$\mathbf{w}'\iota = 1$$

where W_0 is the value of the portfolio today, and the symbol "~" is used to denote the variability in asset returns, that is $\tilde{\mathbf{r}}$ is a vector of random variables representing future asset returns. By using a change of variables ($\gamma_0 = \gamma_0 - W_0$), the problem can be formulated as

---

[9] See Chapter 7 for an introduction to robust statistical estimation, and Chapters 6 and 8 for a discussion of robust estimation methods for the parameters in classical mean-variance optimization, such as expected returns and covariances of assets.

[10] Karthik Natarajan, Dessislava Pachamanova, and Melvyn Sim, "A Tractable Parametric Approach to Value-at-Risk Optimization," Working Paper, National University of Singapore Business School, July 2006, p. 26.

[11] See Chapter 10 for an introduction to robust optimization and stochastic programming with chance constraints.

$$\min_{\gamma, \, w} \gamma$$

$$s.t. \quad P(-\tilde{r}'w > \gamma) \le \varepsilon$$

$$w'\iota = 1$$

As discussed in Chapter 10, the constraint $P(-\tilde{r}'w > \gamma) \le \varepsilon$ is a chance constraint of the kind encountered in stochastic programming, and as such is very difficult to handle computationally. In practice, in order to make the problem manageable, managers frequently assume that asset returns are normally distributed, in which case there is a closed-form expression for the probability term in the constraint. We will refer to the latter formulation as the *Normal VaR*. Goldfarb and Iyengar[12] derive the robust counterpart of the Normal VaR formulation when future returns are computed using a factor model and it is assumed that there is some error in the estimation of their alphas and covariance matrix. In terms of the resulting portfolio composition, the effect of Normal VaR optimization is virtually the same as Markowitz's problem: assets are selected based on the trade-off between their expected returns and their contribution to portfolio risk as measured by the portfolio standard deviation.[13]

As we mentioned earlier, there is significant evidence that some asset returns are not normal, and that in fact their distributions are skewed or exhibit *fat tails*.[14] There is also some support for the belief that the variances of some asset returns are not bounded (that is, they are infinite and therefore do not exist). This unfortunately means that portfolio allocations obtained by using the Normal VaR tend to underestimate losses. When one thinks of robustness with respect to estimation of VaR, it is therefore more natural to think of robustness with respect to possible *probability distributions* of uncertain returns. There are a number of results in probability theory that allow one to specify the level of one's tolerance to errors in the probability distribution assumptions in terms of probabilistic guarantees on the reliability of the solution. For

---

[12] Donald Goldfarb and Garud Iyengar, "Robust Portfolio Selection Problems," *Mathematics of Operations Research* 28, no. 1 (February 2003), pp. 1–38.

[13] See Gordon J. Alexander and Alexandre M. Baptista, "Economic Implications of Using a Mean-VaR Model for Portfolio Selection: A Comparison with Mean-Variance Analysis," *Journal of Economic Dynamics and Control* 26, nos. 7–8 (July 2002), pp. 1159–1193.

[14] The first study in this area is by Benoit Mandelbrot, "The Variation of Certain Speculative Prices," *Journal of Business* 36, no. 3 (1963), pp. 394–419. For a discussion of the empirical evidence for equity and fixed income returns, see Chapter 11 in Svetlozar T. Rachev, Christian Menn, and Frank J. Fabozzi, *Fat-Tailed and Skewed Return Distributions: Implications for Risk Management, Portfolio Selection, and Option Pricing* (Hoboken, NJ: John Wiley & Sons, 2005).

example, an approximation to the problem of minimizing the worst-case VaR over all possible probability distributions for future returns takes the form[15]

$$\min_{\gamma,\, w} \gamma$$
$$s.t. \quad \kappa\sqrt{w'\Sigma w} - \mu'w \leq \gamma$$
$$w'\iota = 1$$

where $\kappa = \sqrt{(1-\varepsilon)/\varepsilon}$. We will refer to the above formulation as *Worst-Case VaR*. Note that the Worst-Case VaR portfolio allocation is still selected on the basis of the first and second moment of portfolio returns.

As usual, the important question is how conservative is conservative enough. Overprotecting may result in worse overall portfolio performance than not making portfolio allocation robust. Computational studies seem to indicate that Worst-Case VaR does not necessarily perform better than Normal VaR and other approaches for approximating VaR at the same level of ε.[16]

Several other approaches to VaR optimization are used in practice. Because of the computationally unfriendly VaR problem formulations, one usually has to make specific assumptions, or use approximation algorithms. Many of these approximations algorithms rely on optimizing portfolio CVaR, as it can be shown that minimizing portfolio CVaR also minimizes portfolio VaR.[17] Recently, Natarajan, Pachamanova, and Sim suggested a data-driven approach for solving the portfolio VaR optimization problem that uses ideas from robust optimization.[18] Their main idea was to define an "appropriate" uncertainty set for the random parameters (asset returns) in the chance constraint for VaR, and use robust optimization to derive the robust counterpart of the portfolio VaR minimization problem, thus producing a computationally tractable approximate formulation. The "appropriateness" of the uncertainty set is defined by how well it represents the

---

[15] Laurent El Ghaoui, Maksim Oks, and Francois Oustry, "Worst-Case Value-at-Risk and Robust Portfolio Optimization: A Conic Programming Approach," *Operations Research* 51, no. 4 (2003), pp. 543–556. This result is based on a multi-dimensional version of the Tschebycheff bound in probability theory, which specifically computes the probability that an observation from a probability distribution will be more than a certain number of standard deviations away from the mean of the distribution for any type of distribution. Because of its generality, this bound is frequently too conservative.

[16] Natarajan, Pachamanova, and Sim, "A Tractable Parametric Approach to Value-at-Risk Optimization."

[17] See Chapter 3.

[18] Natarajan, Pachamanova, and Sim, "A Tractable Parametric Approach to Value-at-Risk Optimization."

tails of the probability distributions for asset returns. They achieved a close representation by incorporating a measure of distribution variability similar to standard deviation, but one that treats downside risk differently from upside risk. Namely, they used measures of downside and upside deviation p and q such that for a random variable $\tilde{z}$ with zero mean

$$P(\tilde{z} \geq \Omega p) \leq e^{(-\Omega^2/2)} \quad \text{and} \quad P(\tilde{z} \leq -\Omega q) \leq e^{(-\Omega^2/2)}$$

for a fixed constant Ω. When $\tilde{z}$ is normally distributed, p and q equal $\tilde{z}$'s standard deviation. In general, p and q can be estimated from historical or simulated data on asset returns using an iterative procedure described in Natarajan, Pachamanova, and Sim[19] and Chen, Sim, and Sun.[20,21]

Having defined an uncertainty set for the parameters in the chance-constrained VaR stochastic problem formulation, one can find the robust counterpart by using the duality technique explained in detail in Chapter 10.[22] The robust counterpart formulation does not compute the *exact* optimal portfolio VaR, but it provides a conservative approximation to it. Specifically, if a *minimum* confidence level of $(1 - \varepsilon)$ is desired for the

---

[19] Natarajan, Pachamanova, and Sim, "A Tractable Parametric Approach to Value-at-Risk Optimization."

[20] Chen, Sim, and Sun, "A Robust Optimization Perspective of Stochastic Programming," forthcoming in *Operations Research*. Available also from http://www.bschool.nus.edu/STAFF/dscsimm/research.htm.

[21] The concept of correlation matrix is not directly applicable to this measure of variability. Instead, the authors used a statistical factor model for returns of the kind $r = \mu + A'z$ where z is assumed to be an M-dimensional vector of *uncorrelated* factors with zero mean. This can almost be achieved through principal component analysis (PCA). For a review of principal component analysis see, for example, Frank J. Fabozzi, Sergio M. Focardi, and Petter N. Kolm, *Financial Modeling of the Equity Market: From CAPM to Cointegration* (Hoboken, NJ: John Wiley & Sons, 2006).

The vector of factors z is assumed to vary in the uncertainty set

$$U_{\tilde{z}} = \{z \mid \exists v, x \in R_+^N, \; z = v - x, \; \|P^{-1}v + Q^{-1}x\| \leq \Omega, \; -\underline{z} \leq z \leq \bar{z}\}$$

We already saw this uncertainty set in Chapter 10. It defines a region for the uncertain parameters in the problem that is associated with their variability, as expressed by the information in $P = \text{diag}(p_1, \ldots, p_N)$ and $Q = \text{diag}(q_1, \ldots, q_N)$, in some sense similar to the information contained in a covariance matrix. $\bar{z}$ and $\underline{z}$ represent upper and lower bounds on the values the vector of factors z can take (they can be infinity). The only difference between this uncertainty set and the symmetric uncertainty sets defined by the inverse of the covariance matrix with which we worked in Chapter 12 is that the variability is defined in a direction-dependent way.

portfolio VaR, then the constant Ω should be selected to be $\sqrt{-2\ln\varepsilon}$. For example, for $\varepsilon = 5\%$, $\Omega = 2.4477$.

The robust parametric VaR (RPVaR) formulation is an SOCP and is therefore computationally tractable, but more importantly from a financial point of view, it results in the optimization of a coherent portfolio risk measure, which is not the case in traditional approaches for portfolio VaR optimization.[23] This means that a portfolio manager who uses the optimal portfolio allocations produced by this optimization formulation can be confident that the overall risk of the portfolio does not increase with the number of assets, but rather stays the same or decreases.

Natarajan, Pachamanova, and Sim compared the performance of several different methods for VaR optimization, namely, (1) Worst-Case VaR (WVaR); (2) Robust Parametric VaR (RPVaR); (3) Sample CVaR; (4) Normal VaR (NVaR); and (5) Exact sample VaR (EVaR), obtained by solving a mixed-integer optimization problem over discrete sample data for returns. The computational results with simulated and real market data indicate that portfolio allocations obtained using the RPVaR approach demonstrate a more robust performance (lower realized VaR, more consistent average portfolio returns) than portfolios obtained with the Normal VaR, the Worst-Case VaR or the sample CVaR approaches, especially in out-of-sample experiments with skewed distributions for asset returns. Exhibit 13.3 shows typical *realized* efficient frontiers for the five approaches for minimizing VaR. The data set used to generate these efficient frontiers contained returns on 24 stocks from different industry categories of the S&P SmallCap 600 Index for the period April 1998 to June 2006.

---

[22] The robust counterpart turns out to be the optimization problem

$$\min_{\gamma,\, w,\, u,\, y,\, t,\, s} \gamma$$

$$\text{s.t.} \quad \gamma + \mu'w \geq \Omega\|u\| + t'z + s'\bar{z}$$

$$y = A'w$$

$$u_j \geq -p_j(y_j + t_j - s_j), \quad u_j \geq q_j(y_j + t_j - s_j), \quad j = 1, \ldots, M$$

$$w'\iota = 1$$

The variables u, t, s, and y are auxiliary variables that have no other meaning but to help formulate the VaR problem as an SOCP.

[23] Recall from Chapter 3 that coherent risk measures have four desirable properties, the most important of which is *subadditivity*: the risk of a portfolio of two funds should not be more than the risk of the individual portfolios. The traditional VaR risk measure does not have this property.

EXHIBIT 13.3   Realized Out-of-Sample Efficient Frontiers

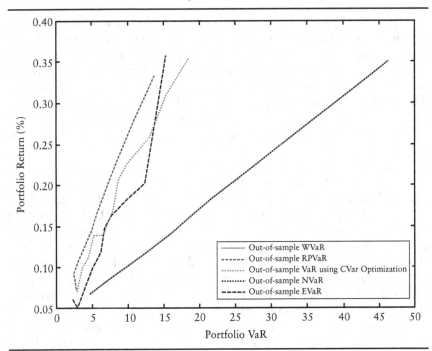

Source: Karthik Natarajan, Dessislava Pachamanova, and Melvyn Sim, "A Tractable Parametric Approach to Value-at-Risk Optimization," Working Paper, National University of Singapore Business School, July 2006, p. 29. This copyrighted material is reprinted with permission from the authors.

PORTFOLIO REBALANCING

If the statistical properties of asset returns were constant over multiple time periods, myopic portfolio optimization would always result in the optimal allocation. However, this assumption rarely holds in practice, especially for long time horizons. As we can see from Appendix A, where we provide some basic statistical properties of the MSCI World Index and its constituents, asset return distributions change—albeit not necessarily drastically—over time.

Consider, for example, an investor who maximizes the Sharpe ratio of his portfolio over one month. We saw in Chapter 2 that the optimal portfolio for this investor is equal to the market portfolio. One month later, this investor revisits his portfolio decision. If the statistical properties of the asset returns for the new period are the same as those in the previous one, and returns in the new and the previous periods are uncorrelated, then the new portfolio weights will be the same as in the previous period. However, if prices have moved during the month, the market capitalization weights (the weights of the market portfolio) may no longer be the same. Therefore, the investor's portfolio will no longer correspond to the market portfolio.

Portfolios, therefore, need to be rebalanced. In practice, they are rebalanced as new information becomes available that changes forecasts of risk and returns, as the investment choices change, or as the prices of the assets in the portfolio move, thus changing the constitution of the portfolio. Unfortunately, while substantial analysis goes into making the "optimal" asset allocation decision in terms of portfolio risk and expected return (which is a strategic decision), typically there is relatively little understanding of how to achieve the selected target portfolio in a cost-efficient manner. Prudent rebalancing strategies, however, can have a substantial impact on portfolio performance. A study by Arnott and Lovell suggests that disciplined rebalancing can improve returns as much as a fairly large shift in the investment policy mix can.[24] For example, in their study the choice between 60% or 50% in equities is less important than the decision of how and when to rebalance. Elton, et al. find that active managers with low turnover outperform managers with high turnover.[25] They provide evidence that the difference in performance is due to the increased transaction costs for the managers with high turnover. They also show that the same results apply to individual investors. A study by Barber and Odean suggests that individual investors who trade the most (in their study defined by the investors who trade more than 48 times per year) have the lowest gross return as well as the lowest net return.[26]

So, how often should a portfolio be rebalanced? The answer to this question is determined by factors such as the type of investment strategy, targeted tracking error, transaction costs, and simply the amount of work required by portfolio managers in the rebalancing process.[27] Finding a balance between tracking error on the one hand and transaction costs on the

---

[24] Robert D. Arnott and Robert M. Lovell, "Rebalancing: Why? When? How Often?" *Journal of Investing* 2, no. 1 (Spring 1993), pp. 5–10.

[25] Edwin J. Elton, Martin J. Gruber, Sanjiv Das, and Matthew Hlavka, "Efficiency with Costly Information: A Reinterpretation of Evidence from Managed Portfolios," *Review of Financial Studies* 6, no. 1 (1993), pp. 1–22.

[26] Brad Barber and Terrance Odean, "The Common Stock Investment Performance of Individual Investors," Working Paper, Graduate School of Management, University of California, Davis, 1998.

[27] We discussed transaction costs modeling in Chapter 4, and will come back to the topic later in this chapter.

other is very important: Portfolios targeting lower tracking error require more frequent rebalancing, which in turn increases transaction costs.

In general, we can distinguish the following three different approaches to portfolio rebalancing:

1. *Calendar rebalancing.* Rebalance the portfolio back to the optimal allocation at a certain frequency such as weekly, monthly, quarterly, and so on.
2. *Threshold rebalancing.* Rebalance the portfolio back to its optimal composition once it is outside a certain range. For example, the portfolio could be rebalanced when the portfolio weights differ more than, say, 10% from its optimal weight. Another type of threshold rebalancing is based upon the rebalancing of the portfolio when the expected tracking error exceeds a predetermined target.
3. *Range rebalancing.* Rebalance the portfolio back to a predetermined range once it has deviated from it. For example, suppose that an optimal mix of 60/40 equities and bonds is established as the target. A 10% tolerance would imply an allowed range of 54% through 66% for equities. In this case, if an equity investment drifts away to, say, 68%, then it should be rebalanced to bring it back within the allowed range.

The range rebalancing approach in fact assumes that portfolios within a certain range are statistically equivalent. This idea is related to the concepts of measurement errors, portfolio resampling, and robust portfolio optimization we discussed in Chapters 7, 10, and 12.

Trading and transaction costs can have a significant effect on the rebalancing decision, and we will come back to the important problem of "optimal" trading later. Recent research on dynamic trading strategies for asset allocation has shown that when transaction costs are taken into account, there is a so-called no-trade region around the optimal target portfolio weights.[28] If the portfolio weights lie inside this region, no trade is necessary. When the portfolio weights lie outside, Leland has demonstrated that it is optimal to trade, but only to the extent of bringing the portfolio weights back to the nearest edge of the no-trade region rather than to the optimal allocation. Theoretically, it has been shown that this strategy reduces transaction costs by about 50%. Nonetheless, the calculation of the optimal allocation involves solving a high-dimensional partial differential equation, making this

---

[28] Hayne E. Leland, "Optimal Portfolio Management with Transaction Costs and Capital Gains Taxes," Haas School of Business Technical Report, University of California–Berkeley, December 1999.

technique of limited use for practical applications. As we mentioned in Chapter 12, robust mean-variance optimization has been observed to reduce the turnover of a portfolio as well, although the effect cannot be described in precise terms.

Rebalancing using an optimizer opens up new opportunities. If dynamic forecasting models are used, the portfolio holdings will be adjusted over time depending on changes in the market and the economy. The allocation decision will rely on current forecasts, as well as on the optimal blend of investments, such that risk and return targets are met.

There are different ways in which optimizers are used to improve the portfolio rebalancing process in practice. One approach is to split the process in stages. The "optimal" target portfolio is identified in the first stage, and the optimal way to achieve the target portfolio is identified at the second stage. A second approach is to incorporate penalties for the costs of rebalancing, such as execution costs, transaction costs, and potential tax implications, in the portfolio allocation model itself. We showed a possible formulation for the portfolio allocation problem in this case in Chapter 4. Yet a third approach is to develop a full multiperiod model that allows for rebalancing. While unquestionably the most comprehensive and potentially the most prudent, the latter approach is very computationally intensive, and up until recently was considered too intractable to implement in practice. Recent improvements in computer speed and advances in stochastic and robust optimization have made this approach much more appealing today. We will discuss each of the three approaches in more detail in subsequent sections.

Another layer of complexity to the problem is created by the need to execute the trades optimally once the optimal allocation is known. The latter problem should in fact be interwoven into the portfolio allocation and rebalancing decision, as it has an effect on the transaction costs. Unfortunately, matters can get very complicated when all of these considerations are incorporated into portfolio rebalancing models simultaneously. We start out by reviewing some developments in the area of transaction cost modeling, and proceed with a discussion of optimizer-based portfolio rebalancing models.

UNDERSTANDING AND MODELING TRANSACTION COSTS

Portfolio optimization and rebalancing routines are only as good as the quality of the parameters that go into them. Transaction costs in particular can have a substantial influence on the portfolio allocation decision, so they need to be estimated carefully.

Transaction costs most generally can be divided into two categories: explicit (such as bid-ask spreads, commissions and fees), and implicit (such as market impact costs and price movement risk costs). Of those, the implicit costs, especially market impact costs, are much more difficult to measure and model. We briefly discussed market impact costs in the context of multiaccount optimization in Chapter 3. The main problem with measuring them is that the true measure, which is the difference between the price of the stock in the absence of a money manager's trade and the execution price, is not observable, because the security price in the absence of a trade cannot be known with accuracy. Furthermore, the execution price is dependent on supply and demand conditions on the margin. It may be influenced by competitive traders who demand immediate execution, or by other investors with similar motives for trading. This means that the execution price realized by an investor is the consequence of the structure of the market mechanism, the demand for liquidity by the marginal investor, and the competitive forces of investors with similar motivations for trading.

In practice, implicit transaction costs are instead evaluated as the difference between the execution price and some appropriate benchmark, a so-called *fair market benchmark*. Practitioners have identified three different basic approaches for measuring the market impact:[29]

- *Pretrade measures* use prices occurring before or at the decision to trade as the benchmark, such as the opening price on the same-day or the closing price on the previous day.
- *Posttrade measures* use prices occurring after the decision to trade as the benchmark, such as the closing price of the trading day or the opening price on the next day.
- *Same-day* or *average measures* use average prices of a large number of trades during the day of the decision to trade, such as the *volume-weighted average price* (VWAP) calculated over all transactions in the security on the trade day.[30]

The volume-weighted average price is calculated as follows. Suppose that it was a trader's objective to purchase 10,000 shares of stock

---

[29] Bruce M. Collins and Frank J. Fabozzi, "A Methodology for Measuring Transaction Costs," *Financial Analysts Journal* 47, no. 2 (March–April 1991), pp. 27–36; Louis K. C. Chan and Joseph Lakonishok, "Institutional Trades and Intraday Stock Price Behavior," *Journal of Financial Economics* 33, no. 2 (April 1993), pp. 173–199; and, Chapter 11 in Frank J. Fabozzi and James L. Grant, *Equity Portfolio Management* (Hoboken, NJ: John Wiley & Sons, 1999).

[30] Strictly speaking, VWAP is not the benchmark here but rather the transaction type.

XYZ. After completion of the trade, the trade sheet showed that 4,000 shares were purchased at \$80, another 4,000 at \$81, and finally 2,000 at \$82. In this case, the resulting VWAP is $(4,000 \times 80 + 4,000 \times 81 + 2,000 \times 82)/10,000 = \$80.80$.

We denote by χ the indicator function that takes on the value 1 or -1 if an order is a buy or sell order, respectively. Formally, we now express the three types of measures of *market impact* (MI) as follows

$$MI_{pre} = \left(\frac{p^{ex}}{p^{pre}} - 1 \right) \chi$$

$$MI_{post} = \left(\frac{p^{ex}}{p^{post}} - 1 \right) \chi$$

$$MI_{VWAP} = \left(\frac{\sum_{i=1}^{k} V_i \cdot p_i^{ex}}{\sum_{i=1}^{k} V_i} \Big/ p^{pre} - 1 \right) \chi$$

where p^{ex}, p^{pre}, and p^{post} denote the execution price, pretrade price, and posttrade price of the stock, and k denotes the number of transactions in a particular security on the trade date. Using this definition, for a stock with market impact MI the resulting *market impact cost* for a trade of size V, MIC, is given by

$$MIC = MI \cdot V$$

It is also common to adjust market impact for general market movements. For example, the pretrade market impact with market adjustment would take the form

$$MI_{pre} = \left(\frac{p^{ex}}{p^{pre}} - \frac{p_M^{ex}}{p_M^{pre}} \right) \chi$$

where p_M^{ex} represent the value of the index at the time of the execution, and p_M^{pre} the price of the index at the time before the trade. Market-adjusted market impact for the posttrade and same-day trade benchmarks are calculated in an analogous fashion.

The above three approaches for measuring market impact are based upon measuring the fair market benchmark of a stock at a point in time. Clearly, different definitions of market impact lead to different results. Which one should be used is a matter of preference and is dependent on the application at hand. For example, Elkins/McSherry, a financial consulting firm that provides customized trading costs and execution analysis, calculates a same-day benchmark price for each stock by taking the mean of the day's open, close, high and low prices. The market impact is then computed as the percentage difference between the transaction price and this benchmark. However, in most cases VWAP and the Elkins/McSherry approach lead to similar measurements.[31]

For the purposes of portfolio allocation and rebalancing, transaction costs are frequently modeled as nonlinear (or piecewise-linear) functions calibrated to fit reasonable estimates from historical data. More sophisticated approaches for modeling transaction costs are sometimes used, especially for the purposes of optimal trading. We next describe a methodology for modeling implicit transaction costs, and specifically, market impact costs. The methodology is a linear-factor-based approach, in which market impact is the dependent variable. We distinguish between trade-based and asset-based independent variables or forecasting factors.

Trade-Based Factors

Some examples of trade-based factors include:

- Trade size
- Relative trade size
- Price of market liquidity
- Type of trade (information or noninformation trade)
- Efficiency and trading style of the investor
- Specific characteristics of the market or the exchange
- Time of trade submission and trade timing
- Order type

Probably the most important market impact forecasting variables are based on absolute or relative trade size. Absolute trade size is often measured in terms of the number of shares traded, or the dollar value of the trade. Relative trade size, on the other hand, can be calculated as number of shares traded divided by average daily volume, or number of shares

---

[31] John Willoughby, "Executions Song," *Institutional Investor* 32, no. 11 (1998), pp. 51–56; and Richard McSherry, "Global Trading Cost Analysis," mimeo, Elkins/McSherry Co., Inc., 1998.

traded divided by the total number of shares outstanding. Note that the former can be seen as an explanatory variable for the temporary price impact and the latter for the permanent price impact. In particular, we expect the temporary price impact to increase as the ratio of the trade size to the average daily volume increases because a larger trade demands more liquidity.

Each type of investment style requires a different need for immediacy.[32] Technical trades often have to be traded at a faster pace in order to capitalize on some short-term signal and therefore exhibit higher market impact costs. In contrast, more traditional long-term value strategies can be traded more slowly. These types of strategies can in many cases even be liquidity providing, which might result in negative market impact costs.

Several studies show that there is a wide variation in equity transaction costs across different countries.[33] Markets and exchanges in each country are different, and so are the resulting market microstructures. Forecasting variables can be used to capture specific market characteristics such as liquidity, efficiency, and institutional features.

The particular timing of a trade can affect the market impact costs. For example, it appears that market impact costs are generally higher at the beginning of the month than at the end of the month.[34] One of the reasons for this phenomenon is that many institutional investors tend to rebalance their portfolios at the beginning of the month. Because it is likely that many of these trades will be executed in the same stocks, this rebalancing pattern induces an increase in market impact costs. The particular time of the day a trade takes place also has an effect. Many informed institutional traders tend to trade at the market open as they want to capitalize on new information that appeared after the market close the day before.

Market impact costs are asymmetric. In other words, buy and sell orders have significantly different market impact costs. Separate models for buy and sell orders can therefore be estimated. However, it is now

---

[32] Donald B. Keim, and Ananth Madhavan, "Transaction Costs and Investment Style: An Inter-Exchange Analysis of Institutional Equity Trades," *Journal of Financial Economics* 46, no. 3 (October 1997), pp. 265–292.

[33] See Ian Domowitz, Jack Glen, and Ananth Madhavan, "Liquidity, Volatility, and Equity Trading Costs Across Countries and Over Time," *International Finance* 4, no. 2, pp. 221–255; and Chiraphol N. Chiyachantana, Pankaj K. Jain, Christine Jian, and Robert A. Wood, "International Evidence on Institutional Trading Behavior and Price Impact," *Journal of Finance* 59, no. 2 (2004), pp. 869–898.

[34] F. Douglas Foster and S. Viswanathan, "A Theory of the Interday Variations in Volume, Variance, and Trading Costs in Securities Markets," *Review of Financial Studies* 3, no. 4 (1990), pp. 593–624.

more common to construct a model that includes dummy variables for different types of orders such as buy/sell orders, market orders, limit orders, and the like.

Asset-Based Factors

Some examples of asset-based factors are:

- Price momentum
- Price volatility
- Market capitalization
- Growth versus value
- Specific industry or sector characteristics

For a stock that is exhibiting positive price momentum, a buy order is liquidity demanding and it is, therefore, likely that it will have higher price impact cost than a sell order.

Generally, trades in high volatility stocks result in higher permanent price effects. It has been suggested by Chan and Lakonishok[35] and Smith et al.[36] that this is because trades have a tendency to contain more information when volatility is high. Another possibility is that higher volatility increases the probability of hitting and being able to execute at the liquidity providers' price. Consequently, liquidity suppliers display fewer shares at the best prices to mitigate adverse selection costs.

Large-cap stocks are more actively traded and therefore more liquid than small-cap stocks. As a result, the market impact cost is normally lower for large-caps.[37] However, if we measure market impact costs with respect to relative trade size (normalized by average daily volume, for instance), they are generally higher. Similarly, growth and value stocks have different market impact costs. One reason for that is related to the trading style. Growth stocks typically exhibit momentum and high volatility. This attracts technical traders who are interested in capitalizing on short-term price swings. Value stocks are traded at a slower pace, and holding periods tend to be slightly longer.

---

[35] Louis K. C. Chan and Joseph Lakonishok, "Institutional Equity Trading Costs: NYSE versus Nasdaq," *Journal of Finance* 52, no. 2 (June 1997), pp. 713–735.

[36] Brian F. Smith, D. Alasdair S. Turnbull, and Robert W. White, "Upstairs Market for Principal and Agency Trades: Analysis of Adverse Information and Price Effects," *Journal of Finance* 56, no. 5 (October 2001), pp. 1723–1746.

[37] Keim and Madhavan, "Transaction Costs and Investment Style," and Laura Spierdijk, Theo Nijman, and Arthur van Soest, "Temporary and Persistent Price Effects of Trades in Infrequently Traded Stocks," Working Paper, Tilburg University and Center, 2003.

Different market sectors show different trading behaviors. For instance, Bikker and Spierdijk show that equity trades in the energy sector exhibit higher market impact costs than other comparable equities trades in nonenergy sectors.[38]

A Factor-Based Market Impact Model

One of the most common approaches in practice and in the literature in modeling market impact is through a linear factor model of the form

$$MI_t = \alpha + \sum_{i=1}^{I} \beta_i x_i + \varepsilon_t$$

where α, β_i are the factor loadings, and x_i are the factors. Frequently, the error term ε_t is assumed to be independently and identically distributed. Recall that the resulting market impact cost of a trade of (dollar) size V is then given by $MIC_t = MI_t \cdot V$. However, extensions of this model that include conditional volatility specifications are also possible. By analyzing both the mean and the volatility of the market impact, we can better understand and manage the trade-off between the two. For example, Bikker and Spierdijk use a specification where the error terms are jointly and serially uncorrelated with mean zero, satisfying

$$Var(\varepsilon_t) = \exp\left(\gamma + \sum_{j=1}^{J} \delta_j z_j\right)$$

where γ, δ_j, and z_j are the volatility, factor loadings, and factors, respectively.

The fact that the price impact function is linear does not of course mean that the dependent variables have to be. In particular, the factors in the specification above can be nonlinear transformations of the descriptive variables.

Consider, for example, factors related to trade size (e.g., trade size and trade size to daily volume). It is well known that market impact is nonlinear in these trade size measures. One of the earliest studies in this regard was performed by Loeb,[39] who showed that for a large set of

---

[38] Jacob A. Bikker, Laura Spierdijk, and Pieter Jelle van der Sluis, "Market Impact Costs of Institutional Equity Trades," Memorandum 1725, Department of Applied Mathematics, University of Twente, Enschede.

[39] Thomas F. Loeb, "Trading Costs: The Critical Link between Investment Information and Results," *Financial Analysts Journal* 39, no. 3 (1983), pp. 39–44.

stocks the market impact is proportional to the square root of the trade size, resulting in a market impact cost proportional to $V^{3/2}$. Typically, a price impact function that is linear in trade size will underestimate the price impact of small to medium-sized trades, and overestimate the price impact of larger trades.

Chen, Stanzl, and Watanabe suggest to model the nonlinear effects of trade size (dollar trade size V) in a price impact model by using the Box-Cox transformation;[40] that is,

$$\mathrm{MI}(V_t) = \alpha_b + \beta_b \frac{V_t^{\lambda_b} - 1}{\lambda_b} + \varepsilon_t$$

$$\mathrm{MI}(V_\tau) = \alpha_s + \beta_s \frac{V_\tau^{\lambda_s} - 1}{\lambda_s} + \varepsilon_\tau$$

where t and τ represent the time of transaction for the buys and the sells, respectively. In their specification, they assumed that ε_t and ε_τ are independent and identically distributed with mean zero and variance σ^2. The parameters α_b, β_b, λ_b, α_s, β_s, and λ_s are then estimated from market data by nonlinear least squares for each individual stock. We remark that λ_b, $\lambda_s \in [0,1]$ in order for the market impact for buys to be concave and for sells to be convex.

In their data sample (NYSE and Nasdaq trades between January 1993 and June 1993), Chen, et al. report that for small companies the curvature parameters λ_b, λ_s are close to zero, whereas for larger companies they are not far away from 0.5. Observe that for $\lambda_b = \lambda_s = 1$ market impact is linear in the dollar-trade size. Moreover, when $\lambda_b = \lambda_s = 0$, the impact function is logarithmic by virtue of

$$\lim_{\lambda \to 0} \frac{V^\lambda - 1}{\lambda} = \ln(\lambda)$$

As just mentioned, market impact is also a function of the characteristics of the particular exchange, where the securities are traded as well as of the trading style of the investor. These characteristics can also be included

---

[40] Zhiwu Chen, Werner Stanzl, and Masahiro Watanabe, "Price Impact Costs and the Limit of Arbitrage," Yale School of Management, International Center for Finance, 2002.

in the general specification outlined above. For example, Keim and Madhavan proposed the following two different market impact specifications:[41]

1. $MI = \alpha + \beta_1 \chi_{OTC} + \beta_2 \frac{1}{p} + \beta_3 |q| + \beta_4 |q|^2 + \beta_5 |q|^3 + \beta_6 \chi_{Up} + \varepsilon$

    where

    χ_{OTC} is a dummy variable equal to one if the stock is an OTC traded stock, and zero otherwise.

    p is the trade price.

    q is the number of shares traded over the number of shares outstanding.

    χ_{Up} is a dummy variable equal to one if the trade is done in the upstairs[42] market, and zero otherwise.

2. $MI = \alpha + \beta_1 \chi_{Nasdaq} + \beta_2 q + \beta_3 \ln(MCap) + \beta_4 \frac{1}{p} + \beta_5 \chi_{Tech} + \beta_6 \chi_{Index} + \varepsilon$

    where

    χ_{NASDAQ} is a dummy variable equal to one if the stock is traded on NASDAQ, and zero otherwise.

    q is the number of shares traded over the number of shares outstanding, MCap is the market capitalization of the stock.

    p is the trade price.

    χ_{Tech} is a dummy variable equal to one if the trade is a short-term technical trade, and zero otherwise.

    χ_{Index} is a dummy variable equal to one if the trade is done for a portfolio that attempts to closely mimic the behavior of the underlying index, and zero otherwise.

These two models provide good examples for how nonlinear transformations of the underlying dependent variables can be used along with dummy variables that describe specific market or trade characteristics.[43]

---

[41] Donald B. Keim and Ananth Madhavan, "Transactions Costs and Investment Style: An Inter-Exchange Analysis of Institutional Equity Trades," *Journal of Financial Economics* 46, no. 3 (1997), pp. 265–292; and Donald B. Keim and Ananth Madhavan, "The Upstairs Market for Large-Block Transactions: Analysis and Measurement of Price Effects," *Review of Financial Studies* 9, no. 1 (1996), pp. 1–36.

[42] A securities transaction not executed on the exchange but completed directly by a broker in house is referred to an upstairs market transaction. Typically, the upstairs market consists of a network of trading desks of the major brokerages and institutional investors. The major purpose of the upstairs market is to facilitate large block and program trades.

[43] Some practitioners feel that the χ_{OTC} and χ_{NASDAQ} factors may become less relevant in the modern trading era of ECNs and proliferating trading destinations.

Several vendors and broker/dealers such as MSCI Barra[44] and ITG[45] have developed commercially available market impact models. These are sophisticated multimarket models that rely upon specialized estimation techniques using intraday data or tick-by-tick transaction based data. However, the general characteristics of these models are similar to the ones described in this section.

REBALANCING USING AN OPTIMIZER

Transaction cost models such as the models reviewed in the previous section are frequently incorporated into larger automated platforms for optimal portfolio rebalancing. As we mentioned earlier, there are three general approaches to modeling portfolio rebalancing as an optimization problem that can then be solved with an optimizer. In this section, we discuss each of them in detail.

Approach I: Consider Portfolio Allocation and Portfolio Rebalancing as Separate Stages, and Perform Optimization at Each Stage

Bertsimas, Darnell, and Soucy[46] described in detail an approach to portfolio rebalancing at Grantham, Mayo, Van Otterloo and Company (GMO) that is similar in spirit to those employed by other asset management companies. The target investment portfolio of N stocks with weights represented by a vector w_{target} is selected by solving a variant of a mean-variance portfolio optimization problem, in which the securities' alphas are generated according to a multifactor forecasting model. A final portfolio with weights represented by an N-dimensional vector w_{final} that is "as close as possible" to the target portfolio is determined by using a separate optimization procedure. The objective function for the latter procedure is to minimize the sum of the absolute differences

$$\sum_{i=1}^{N} \left| w_{target}(i) - w_{final}(i) \right|$$

---

[44] Nicolo G. Torre and Mark J. Ferrari, "The Market Impact Model," Barra Research Insights.

[45] "ITG ACE—Agency Cost Estimator: A Model Description," 2003, www.itginc.com.

[46] Dimitris Bertsimas, Christopher Darnell, and Robert Soucy, "Portfolio Construction through Mixed-Integer Programming at Grantham, Mayo, Van Otterloo and Company," *Interfaces* 29, no. 1 (January–February 1999), pp. 49–66.

subject to additional constraints, such as exposure to different sectors similar to that of the target portfolio, a small number of trades, a small number of transactions, high return, high liquidity, and low transaction costs.[47] Bertsimas, et al. modeled liquidity and transaction costs as piecewise-linear functions of the trade size, but other transaction costs models can be implemented as well.[48] The model is flexible enough to allow for incorporating multiaccount optimization for trades.[49] The latter is modeled simply by considering the sum of the holdings of each asset across all portfolios in the trading costs, liquidity, and risk constraints.

One may ask why the second optimization step is necessary. As we mentioned in Chapter 4, after computing an optimal target portfolio, practitioners frequently simply eliminate positions that they deem too small or that may incur too much in terms of transaction costs to acquire. The answer is that the second-stage optimization does this elimination in a more disciplined way, and makes sure that some key constraints, such as attaining a particular target return, remain satisfied. This cannot always be achieved by eliminating positions *ad hoc*.

The two-stage optimization approach allows for separating the possibly subjective or qualitative asset allocation decision from the actual rebalancing decision. From a financial point of view, it is always preferable to execute the portfolio re-allocation strategy so that the costs of rebalancing are minimized. In addition, there are some numerical and strategic advantages to using this two-stage optimization approach relative to the other two approaches for rebalancing (single-step and multiperiod optimization) that we explain later. If the first stage of the process is based on using quantitative techniques to determine a portfolio that attains a particular risk/reward target, decoupling the allocation decision from the rebalancing step ensures that each of the two stages

---

[47] We note that this objective function can be stated as a linear objective function (which is more solver-friendly) if one uses the trick described in Chapter 12: Introduce a new vector of decision variables ψ of dimension equal to the number of assets N and rewrite the minimization problem as

$$\min_{\psi,\ w_{\text{final}}} \sum_{i=1}^{N} \psi_i$$

$$s.t. \quad \psi_i \geq w_{\text{target}}(i) - w_{\text{final}}(i), \ i = 1, ..., N$$

$$\psi_i \geq -(w_{\text{target}}(i) - w_{\text{final}}(i)), \ i = 1, ..., N$$

[48] See Chapter 4 for information about quadratic and piecewise-linear approximations to transaction cost functions.

[49] See Chapter 4 for a discussion of the advantages of taking into consideration the impact of trading for multiple accounts.

involves solving a relatively "easy" optimization problem. The first stage is typically a quadratic problem, for which very efficient numerical routines exist. The second stage can be formulated as a mixed-integer linear optimization problem, which is much easier to solve (and for which more software solvers are available) than general mixed-integer nonlinear problems. The optimal portfolio allocation obtained through the two-stage approach, however, may in theory be suboptimal relative to an optimal portfolio allocation obtained with a fully integrated portfolio allocation and rebalancing optimization approaches, such as the approaches we discuss next.

Approach II: Incorporate Considerations for Market Frictions Directly into the Optimal Portfolio Allocation Decision

As we discussed in Chapter 4, practitioners frequently attempt to incorporate considerations for transaction costs and taxes by including penalty terms in the objective function of single-period portfolio allocation problems.[50] Transaction cost functions are typically assumed to be quadratic or piecewise linear, so as to incorporate the effect of the market impact of trading large volumes of a particular asset. The parameters of the transaction cost function are calibrated so that the transaction costs have observed typical (in other words, "average") behavior in the market.

Engle and Ferstenberg[51] pointed out that the *risk* in transaction cost behavior should be taken in consideration as well, and developed a generalized Markowitz model for optimal portfolio allocation that incorporates this consideration. Their model is a recent addition to the optimal trading literature,[52] and captures important aspects of robust portfolio allocation modeling. We describe the main idea next.

Consider a version of the classical portfolio optimization problem, as it was introduced in Chapter 2:[53]

---

[50] See, for example, Arlen Khodadadi, Reha Tutuncu, and Peter Zangari, "Optimization and Quantitative Investment Management," *Journal of Asset Management* 7, no. 2 (August 2006), pp. 83–92; or Roberto Apelfeld, Gordon Fowler, Jr., and James Gordon, Jr., "Tax-Aware Portfolio Optimization," *Journal of Portfolio Management* 22, no. 2 (Winter 1996), pp. 18–29.

[51] Robert Engle and Robert Ferstenberg, "Execution Risk," NBER Working Paper 12165, April 2006.

[52] See, for example, Robert Almgren and Neil Chriss, "Optimal Execution of Portfolio Transactions," *Journal of Risk* 3 (Winter 2000), pp. 5–39, and Dimitris Bertsimas and Andrew Lo, "Optimal Execution of Transaction Costs," *Journal of Financial Markets* 1, no. 1 (April 1998), pp. 1–50, among others.

[53] In Chapter 2, we introduced the Markowitz problem formulation in terms of returns. Here we formulate it in terms of wealth, so that transaction costs can be measured in dollar amounts.

$$\max_{\mathbf{w}_T} E[\,W_T] - \lambda \cdot \mathrm{var}(\,W_T)$$

Here the investor is assumed to have an investment horizon of T, and his portfolio value at time T, W_T, is a function of the N-dimensional vector of portfolio holdings $\mathbf{w}_T$ during that time period. The investor tries to find the optimal portfolio allocation so that the optimal balance of risk (as defined by the portfolio variance) and expected return is achieved.[54]

In practice, trade orders are frequently not executed immediately, but, rather, gradually over the time, and each piece of a large order may potentially trade at a different price. Let us divide the time from 0 to T into smaller time periods, indexed $t = 1, \ldots, T$, and let the vector of N original asset prices at the time the order is submitted be $\mathbf{p}_0$. At each of the next time periods, the vector of transaction prices $\tilde{\mathbf{p}}_t$ may be different from $\mathbf{p}_0$.[55] The transaction costs of order execution (let us denote them by TC) between the initial date and time T until the portfolio is rebalanced will then equal

$$\mathrm{TC} = \sum_{t=1}^{T} (\Delta \mathbf{w}_t)'(\tilde{\mathbf{p}}_t - \mathbf{p}_0)$$

where $\Delta \mathbf{w}_t$ is the vector of trades (equivalently, the vector of changes in portfolio holdings) at time period t. To gain some intuition, note that if the trades are purchases, then the transaction costs will be positive when the price of execution rises relative to the original price at which the order was placed. Similarly, if the trades are sales, then the transaction costs will be positive when the price of execution is lower than the original price at which the order was placed.

While a "pure" version of the classical Markowitz portfolio allocation optimization problem can be stated as

$$\max_{\mathbf{w}_T} E[(\mathbf{w}_T)'(\tilde{\mathbf{p}}_T - \mathbf{p}_0)] - \lambda \cdot \mathrm{var}((\mathbf{w}_T)'(\tilde{\mathbf{p}}_T - \mathbf{p}_0))$$

a "cost-adjusted" version would be written as

---

[54] This problem can also be formulated relative to a given benchmark, that is, the value of the portfolio and the asset holdings can be stated relative to a benchmark portfolio. The mathematical core of the risk/return analysis, however, remains the same with or without a benchmark.

[55] Recall that we use the symbol "tilde" to denote randomness—in this case, the randomness in the future behavior of market prices.

$$\max_{\mathbf{w}_T} E[(\mathbf{w}_T)'(\tilde{\mathbf{p}}_T - \mathbf{p}_0) - \mathrm{TC}] - \lambda \cdot \mathrm{var}((\mathbf{w}_T)'(\tilde{\mathbf{p}}_T - \mathbf{p}_0))$$

i.e., the transaction costs (but not risks) are taken into account. Engle and Ferstenberg argued that the most realistic or "true" version of the problem should in fact be stated as

$$\max_{\mathbf{w}_T} E[(\mathbf{w}_T)'(\tilde{\mathbf{p}}_T - \mathbf{p}_0) - \mathrm{TC}] - \lambda \cdot \mathrm{var}((\mathbf{w}_T)'(\tilde{\mathbf{p}}_T - \mathbf{p}_0) - \mathrm{TC})$$

Notice that transaction costs enter not only the expectation term, but also the risk term. The "pure Markowitz" efficient frontier will be the highest, followed by the "cost-adjusted Markowitz" and the "true Markowitz." An optimal portfolio on the pure or cost-adjusted efficient frontier will not necessarily lie on the true efficient frontier, and thus may not be a prudent choice in practice.

The expression for the "true" portfolio allocation problem formulation is intuitive, but deceptively simple. In practice, the transactions $\Delta \mathbf{w}_t$ at each time period may affect the evolution of prices, and the term TC in the expression should not be treated separately from the term involving $\tilde{\mathbf{p}}_T$ and $\mathbf{p}_0$. Engle and Ferstenberg studied characteristics of the joint optimization of positions and trades under different assumptions on the asset price processes and market impact of trades. While their results are rather technical to be presented here in detail, they provide several important insights. First, Engle and Ferstenberg show conditions under which the optimal execution of trades does not depend upon the holdings of the portfolio. That means that the generalized problem under these conditions reduces to the two separate problems that are more familiar: the optimal allocation and the optimal execution problem. Second, they show that in order to hedge trading risks, sometimes it may be optimal to execute trades in assets that may not have been in the trading order. This depends on how the transitory impact and the asset covariance matrices are structured.[56] Finally, they point out that taking trade execution risk into account leads to a natural measure of liquidity risk. Namely, typically the value of a portfolio is marked to market, that is, it is computed as $(\mathbf{w}_0)'\mathbf{p}_0$. Instead, Engle and Ferstenberg suggest looking at the portfolio liquidation value,

$$(\mathbf{w}_T)'(\tilde{\mathbf{p}}_T - \mathbf{p}_0) - \mathrm{TC}$$

---

[56] The transitory impact matrix measures how the size of the trade impacts the change in asset price.

because it represents correctly the fact that the assets in the portfolio cannot necessarily be liquidated at their current market prices. In the same way in which the portfolio market risk is estimated by looking at a prespecified percentile of the distribution of portfolio losses after a fixed time period, such as 10 days,[57] the portfolio liquidity risk can be estimated by computing a percentile of the possible distribution of portfolio liquidation values. There is in fact a range of possible distributions for future portfolio liquidation values, depending on how the trade execution is accomplished, but the specific liquidity risk measure can be defined relative to the distribution of portfolio values obtained with the *optimal* execution policy according to the integrated asset allocation and trading model Engle and Ferstenberg suggest. This risk measure will incorporate both market and liquidity risk, and will be more general than the VaR and CVaR portfolio risk measures defined in Chapter 3.

Engle and Ferstenberg's approach is an interesting combination of single-period ideas for portfolio allocation and multiperiod views of the market. In the next section, we focus explicitly on multiperiod portfolio allocation and rebalancing models.

Approach III: Develop a Multiperiod Portfolio Allocation Model

The models discussed so far have an advantage over simple mean-risk formulations, because they take into consideration the costs involved in rebalancing the portfolio to reach a desired optimal portfolio. However, there is one aspect of portfolio management—the fact that it is inherently a multiperiod problem—that is not handled perfectly in these models. By incorporating long-term views on asset behavior in rebalancing models, portfolio managers can implicitly reduce their transaction costs, as the portfolio will not get rebalanced unnecessarily often. As a simple example, if a portfolio manager expects asset returns to dip at the next time period, but then recover, he may choose to hold on to the assets in his portfolio in order to minimize transaction costs. On the other hand, if the net gain from realizing the loss for tax purposes is higher than the expense of the transactions, he may choose to trade despite believing that the portfolio value will recover after two trading periods. These trade-offs can be incredibly complex to evaluate and model. Nevertheless, several approaches employing stochastic programming, dynamic programming, and robust optimization techniques have been used to extend and break away from the inherently myopic nature of traditional mean-risk portfolio optimization.

One possibility for developing a full multiperiod approach that takes transaction and trading costs into consideration is to optimize the portfo-

---

[57] See Chapter 3 for a review of quantile-based risk measures of portfolio market risk, such as VaR and CVaR.

lio over scenarios. The scenarios are generated to represent possible real-izations of the returns of the assets in the portfolio over multiple periods. As we explained in Chapter 10, such formulations have a tremendous modeling potential, and can be approached with tools from stochastic programming.[58] Unfortunately, even with the computational power avail-able today, the dimension of stochastic programming problems is typi-cally too large to allow for constructing meaningful portfolio strategies. Frequently, one has to compromise on the quality of the representation of reality by reducing the number of scenarios substantially, which in turn may lead to portfolio allocation recommendations of dubious value.

Recently, Sun, et al.[59] proposed a different framework based on *dynamic programming*[60] that minimizes the cost of rebalancing in terms of risk-adjusted returns net of transaction costs. They suggested that the deci-sion of whether to rebalance or not should be based on a consideration of three costs: (1) the tracking error associated with the deviation of the port-folio from an "optimal" portfolio; (2) the trading costs associated with buying or selling assets during rebalancing; and (3) the expected future cost from the next time period onwards given our current actions. The units of measurement of tracking error costs are not necessarily the same as the units of measurement of the other two types of costs, so one of the authors' contributions was to define a unified way of measuring all three types of costs. They applied the concept of *certainty equivalents* to trans-late the risk preferences embedded in a specific utility function into an equivalent certain return.[61] The basic idea is that, given a specific inves-tor's utility function, it is possible to find a risk-adjusted rate of return r_{CE} (referred to as *certainty equivalent return*) that produces the same expected utility. If the investment portfolio with value W is suboptimal, then its utility $U(W)$ will be lower than the utility of the optimal portfolio $U(W^*)$. In particular, for the certainty equivalent returns it holds that

$$r_{CE}(W) \leq r_{CE}(W^*)$$

---

[58] See the Stochastic Programming section in Chapter 10 for a number of references on such implementations.

[59] Walther Sun, Ayres Fan, Li-Wei Chen, Tom Schouwenaars, and Marius Albota, "Optimal Rebalancing for Institutional Portfolios," *Journal of Portfolio Manage-ment* 32, no. 2 (Winter 2005), pp. 33–43.

[60] See Chapter 10 for a brief introduction to dynamic programming.

[61] Given an investor's utility function $U(\tilde{r})$, the certainty equivalent of the invest-ment return $\tilde{r}$ is defined as the certain return that makes an investor indifferent be-tween taking that return and making the risky investment. The certainty equivalent can be expressed mathematically as

$$C(\tilde{r}) = U^{-1}(E[U(\tilde{r})])$$

Consequently, the difference

$$D(W) = r_{CE}(W^*) - r_{CE}(W)$$

can be interpreted as an adjusted risk-free return that is given up for not holding the optimal portfolio.[62] It is now a straightforward matter to translate this difference into the dollar numeraire. This allows for computing the tracking error in dollar terms and calculating the total cost of rebalancing in dollars in each time period.[63]

The next step is to formulate a dynamic programming problem, in which the cost function to be minimized is the sum of the three types of costs. At each point in time, the decision of whether to rebalance, and how much to trade, is determined based on the cost-to-go estimate at that point. In practice, one needs to simulate scenarios for the possible paths of the asset returns in the portfolio, and optimize over these scenarios. The difference between this approach and stochastic programming approaches is the way in which the optimization problem is actually solved.[64] Furthermore, one needs to present discrete choices for the possible asset weights, and select among those options.[65]

In simulation experiments, Sun, et al.'s method performs between 25% and 35% more efficiently (in terms of expected transaction costs) than heuristic rebalancing methods, such as calendar, threshold and range rebalancing. Despite its innovative idea and great promise, however, in practice the approach suffers from similar problems as the stochastic programming models we described earlier: it is difficult to implement it for large portfolios because of the curse of dimensionality. The authors mention that for five assets, they allowed about 15 discrete values as possible weights for each asset, and had an observation space

---

[62] We note that the choice of whether or not to hold the optimal portfolio in terms of expected utility is influenced by the costs of rebalancing, which is why this difference exists in practice, and should be taken into consideration.

[63] Of course, this approach requires knowing the exact form of the certainty equivalent of the investor's utility function. However, the certainty equivalent can be computed approximately to a satisfactory degree after computing the expected utility function by expanding the utility function around the expected return using a Taylor series. See Chapter 3 for more details.

[64] See Chapter 10 for an explanation of the difference between the dynamic programming and the stochastic programming approach to solving multistage problems over scenarios.

[65] Recall from our discussion on dynamic programming in Chapter 10 that allowing continuous ranges for asset weights in the multistage portfolio allocation problem results in an infinite number of states at which the optimal strategy should be evaluated.

of about 750,000 points (i.e., the computations for optimal policy had to be performed at each of these points), which took 75 minutes on their PC. The optimization can be parallelized, so the total processing time can be reduced by using multiple machines, but for portfolios consisting of thousands of assets, dynamic programming methods for portfolio allocation and rebalancing may still present a challenge to apply in practice.

Recently, more computationally tractable multiperiod models that are based on robust optimization techniques have been suggested, and have been included in one way or another as part of robust portfolio allocation systems.[66] While a large part of the success of such systems is determined by how well the models are calibrated, they represent a new direction in multistage portfolio management that is worth noting. Such systems are, of course, proprietary, but some of the main ideas can be traced back to the academic literature.

An article by Ben-Tal, Margalit, and Nemirovski[67] was the first to suggest a generalization of mean-standard deviation optimization for multiple time periods as a robust optimization problem[68] that can be written as a second order cone problem of small dimension, thus reducing substantially the computational difficulties in solving the portfolio allocation problem over multiple stages. They also studied the performance of the new method versus stochastic programming methods for multistage portfolio management, and found that the method was not only preferable in terms of computational tractability, but also in terms of realized portfolio performance according to a variety of measures. Subsequent

---

[66] A natural application of such techniques is in providing guidance for appropriate asset allocations over an investor's lifetime. For example, a couple of years ago Ameriprise Financial (formerly American Express Financial Advisors) launched Lifetime Optimizer, a comprehensive proprietary platform that uses robust optimization as one of its optimal multiperiod portfolio allocation tools. The Lifetime Optimizer software uses the CPLEX optimization solver engine to help financial advisors identify good investment strategies for clients with diverse investment goals, time schedules, risk tolerance levels, and tax circumstances. The lifetime asset allocation problem is inherently multiperiod and incredibly complex. Using robust optimization to handle uncertainty in the future realizations of different market variables helps keep the dimension of the problem manageable, yet allows for incorporating taxes and other realistic market frictions considerations.

[67] Aharon Ben-Tal, Tamar Margalit, and Arkadi Nemirovski, "Robust Modeling of Multi-Stage Portfolio Problems," in H. Frenk, K. Roos, T. Terlaky, S. Zhang (eds), *High-Performance Optimization* (Dordrecht: Kluwer Academic Publishers, 2000, pp. 303–328).

[68] See Chapter 10 for an introduction to robust optimization, and Chapter 9 for a description of second order cone problems.

studies[69] explored other aspects of the approach, such as introducing different uncertainty sets to make the resulting optimization problem linear,[70] and comparing the approach to single-period mean-standard deviation optimization under variety of assumptions for the stochastic behavior of the asset returns. The general conclusion from these computational studies is that incorporating views on the direction of asset prices in the future through multiperiod robust optimization models tends to reduce transaction costs, and improve overall portfolio performance characteristics such as realized average and median returns, probability of loss, and others.

The main idea of Ben-Tal, et al.'s approach is actually related to a technique for modeling dynamic programming problems, the *Certainty Equivalent Controller* (CEC), that has been well-known in engineering applications for many years. The CEC technique applied at stage t of a particular dynamic programming problem finds the optimal policy by assuming that all uncertain parameters for subsequent stages are fixed at their expected values, that is, it eliminates uncertainty from the optimization problems. An obvious drawback of this approach is that risk is not taken into consideration in the solution of the problem. Ben-Tal, et al. extend the CEC and incorporate risk by considering ellipsoidal uncertainty sets around the random parameters at all subsequent time periods (the random parameters in the case of the multiperiod portfolio optimization problem are future asset returns). Consequently, if there are T time periods, they end up solving simultaneously T mean-standard deviation portfolio problems that are linked across time.[71]

---

[69] See Dimitris Bertsimas and Dessislava Pachamanova, "Robust Multiperiod Portfolio Management in the Presence of Transaction Costs," to appear in the special issue of *Computers and Operations Research* on *Applications of Operations Research in Finance.*

[70] Although second order cone problems are convex optimization problems, for which efficient solvers exist, they are still nonlinear problems. The aspect of linearizing the multiperiod portfolio allocation problem is important, because, as we explained in Chapter 4, in practice portfolio managers frequently face constraints that require using integer variables to model. The availability of efficient optimization software for mixed-integer linear problems is much greater than for mixed-integer nonlinear problems, as the latter type of problems tend to be computationally challenging.

[71] Recall from the simple robust optimization example in Chapter 10 that when uncertain parameters (asset returns in the portfolio optimization context) are assumed to vary in ellipsoidal uncertainty sets involving the inverse of the asset return covariance matrix, the problem of maximizing the uncertain single-period portfolio return (equivalently, maximizing the expected utility of an investor with a linear utility function) is equivalent to maximizing an objective function that contains the expected portfolio return and the portfolio standard deviation, that is, it is reminiscent of standard portfolio allocation schemes. The extension of this result to multiple time periods is intuitive and straightforward.

Using the robust optimization method, the multistage robust portfolio allocation problem can be formulated as a single optimization problem with a small number of variables and constraints. We illustrate how this can be done. For simplicity, we assume linear transaction costs, i.e., if the size of the trade is t, then transactions costs are $c_{buy} \cdot t$ and $c_{sell} \cdot t$ for purchases and sales, respectively. Recall from Chapter 10 that the multistage portfolio optimization problem for a portfolio of N assets over T stages can be stated as

$$\max_{w, y, z} E[u(W_T)]$$

$s.t.$

$$\sum_{i=1}^{N} w_{i,0} = W_0$$

$$\sum_{i=1}^{N} w_{i,T} = W_T$$

$$w_{i,t} = (1 + \tilde{r}_{i,t})(w_{i,t-1} - y_{i,t-1} + z_{i,t-1}), \quad t = 1, \ldots, T,$$
$$i = 1, \ldots, N$$

$$w_{0,t} = (1 + \tilde{r}_{0,t})\left(w_{0,t-1} + \sum_{i=1}^{N} (1 - c_{\text{sell}})y_{i,t-1} - \sum_{i=1}^{N} (1 + c_{\text{buy}})z_{i,t-1} \right)$$
$$t = 1, \ldots, T$$

$$w_{i,t}, y_{i,t}, z_{i,t} \geq 0, \quad t = 1, \ldots, T, \quad i = 0, \ldots, N$$

Here $w_{i,t}$, $y_{i,t}$, and $z_{i,t}$ denote the holdings, amount sold and amount bought of asset i at trading period t, respectively. The asset returns at each time period are unknown, and can be treated as uncertain parameters in the optimization problem. As explained in Chapter 10, the stochastic programming approach is to generate scenarios for their possible realizations at each time period, and find the portfolio allocation that maximizes the average objective function value over these scenarios. Ben-Tal, et al.'s approach, based on the robust optimization idea, instead allows the unknown future asset returns to vary in prespecified uncertainty sets (in their example, these uncertainty sets are ellipsoids defined by the asset returns' means and covariance matrices at each time period), and solves the problem so that the constraints are satisfied for the worst-case realizations of the asset returns within those uncertainty sets.[72] We need to mention here that while the

---

[72] There are some technical conditions associated with re-stating the constraints so that feasible solutions to the problem exist if returns are modeled this way. See Ben-Tal, Margalit, and Nemirovski, "Robust Modeling of Multi-Stage Portfolio Problems," for further details.

solution to this optimization problem prescribes an optimal portfolio allocation for all time periods ahead, in practice, an investment manager would approach the problem as a *rolling horizon* problem. In other words, the investment manager would solve the problem at time period t, implement the optimal strategy over time period $t + 1$, but then re-solve the problem again at time $t + 1$ as new market information becomes available.

Ben-Tal, et al. noticed that the problem becomes too conservative if all constraints involving single-period returns,[73]

$$w_{i,t} = (1 + \tilde{r}_{i,t})(w_{i,t-1} - y_{i,t-1} + z_{i,t-1}), \quad t = 1, \ldots, T, \quad i = 1, \ldots, N$$

are replaced by their robust counterparts.[74] They made a change of variables, so that the number of constraints containing uncertain coefficients (single-period returns) is reduced, and *cumulative* returns (instead of simple returns) are used in the problem formulation. The new decision variables $\xi_{i,t}$, $\eta_{i,t}$, and $\zeta_{i,t}$ that replace the original decision variables $w_{i,t}$, $y_{i,t}$, and $z_{i,t}$ have similar interpretations, but are scaled by the realized cumulative returns up to that time period.[75] Let us denote the cumulative return of asset i up to time period t by $\tilde{R}_{i,t}$, that is,

$$\tilde{R}_{i,t} = (1 + \tilde{r}_{i,1})(1 + \tilde{r}_{i,2})\ldots(1 + \tilde{r}_{i,t})$$

Then the scaled decision variables for holdings, amount sold and amount bought are computed as

$$\xi_{i,t} = \frac{w_{i,t}}{\tilde{R}_{i,t}}, \eta_{i,t} = \frac{y_{i,t}}{\tilde{R}_{i,t}}, \zeta_{i,t} = \frac{z_{i,t}}{\tilde{R}_{i,t}}$$

The multiperiod portfolio optimization problem can then be written as

---

[73] There are $T \cdot N$ of them. For simplicity, we assume that the returns on the riskless asset, $\tilde{r}_{0,t}$, are known in advance for all time periods (it is trivial to extend the problem if they are not).

[74] Recall from Chapter 10 that the robust counterpart of a constraint that contains uncertain coefficients is a constraint which is reformulated in such a way that the solution to the optimization problem satisfies it even if the uncertain parameters take their worst possible values in a pre-specified uncertainty set.

[75] Since the investor in practice uses a rolling horizon, that is, he implements only the first stage policy, and resolves the problem again at the next time period, this change of variables is mostly for computational convenience (the new decision variables for the first time period are equivalent to the old decision variables).

$$\max_{\xi_t, \eta_t, \zeta_t} \xi_T' E[\tilde{R}_T] + \xi_{0,T} R_{0,T}$$

$$s.t.$$

$$\xi_{i,t+1} \leq \xi_{i,t} + (1 - c_{\text{sell}}) \sum_{i=1}^{N} \frac{\tilde{R}_{i,t}}{R_{0,t}} \eta_{i,t} - (1 + c_{\text{buy}}) \sum_{i=1}^{N} \frac{\tilde{R}_{i,t}}{R_{0,t}} \zeta_{i,t}$$

$$\xi_{i,t+1} = \xi_{i,t} - \eta_{i,t} + \zeta_{i,t}, \quad i = 1, \ldots, N, \quad t = 1, \ldots, T-1$$

Assuming that the investor would like his portfolio allocation to remain optimal even if the joint realizations of future returns at each time period t are away from their expected values by up to a certain number of standard deviations, we can define ellipsoidal uncertainty sets for these future returns by using the inverse of the covariance matrix of cumulative returns at time t, as we did in Chapter 10:

$$U_{\tilde{R}_t} = \left\{ \tilde{R}_t : \left\| \Sigma^{-1/2} \left(\tilde{R}_t - E[\tilde{R}_t] \right) \right\|_2 \leq \lambda_t \right\}$$

The robust counterpart of the multiperiod portfolio allocation problem for this definition of uncertainty sets is

$$\max_{\xi_t, \eta_t, \zeta_t} \xi_T' E[\tilde{R}_T] + \xi_{0,T} R_{0,T} - \lambda_T \sqrt{\xi_T' \Sigma_T \xi_T'}$$

$$s.t.$$

$$\xi_{i,t+1} \leq \xi_{i,t} + (1 - c_{\text{sell}}) \sum_{i=1}^{N} E\left[\frac{\tilde{R}_{i,t}}{R_{0,t}} \right] \eta_{i,t} - (1 + c_{\text{buy}}) \sum_{i=1}^{N} E\left[\frac{\tilde{R}_{i,t}}{R_{0,t}} \right] \zeta_{i,t}$$

$$- \lambda_T \sqrt{\binom{\eta_t}{\zeta_t}' \Xi_t \binom{\eta_t}{\zeta_t}}$$

$$\xi_{i,t+1} = \xi_{i,t} - \eta_{i,t} + \zeta_{i,t}, \quad i = 1, \ldots, N, \quad t = 1, \ldots, T-1$$

In the formulation above, Σ_T is the covariance matrix of the cumulative returns $\tilde{R}_T$ at the last time period T, and Ξ_t is the covariance matrix at time t of the vector

$$\left((1 - c_{\text{sell}}) \frac{\tilde{R}_t}{R_{0,t}}, -(1 + c_{\text{buy}}) \frac{\tilde{R}_t}{R_{0,t}} \right)'$$

which contains a transformation of the cumulative returns $\tilde{R}_t$ of the N assets at time t.

Note that the objective function in this portfolio allocation formulation is similar to traditional mean-risk optimization in that it involves the expected return and the standard deviation of the portfolio at the last time period. However, it includes similar expressions for the intermediate time periods as well. The robust optimization nature of this formulation is visible in the presence of the penalty term

$$\lambda_t \sqrt{\binom{\eta_t}{\zeta_t}' \Xi_t \binom{\eta_t}{\zeta_t}}$$

in each constraint that contained uncertain coefficients in the original problem. The interpretation for the parameters $\lambda_1, ..., \lambda_T$ is similar to the interpretation for the penalty parameter for risk λ in the objective function of traditional mean-risk models.

The optimal solution of this optimization problem consists of a trading policy for all time periods ahead, but, as we mentioned earlier, only the first step is of practical interest. Because of the small size of the problem and its convex formulation, re-solving the problem periodically is easy and fast.[76] The advantage of solving a multiperiod problem instead of standard single-period rebalancing formulations is that the weights today will be selected with a view of future movements of the asset prices, so unnecessary rebalancing will be avoided.

SUMMARY

- A robust investment strategy extends beyond statistical and modeling methods. It involves (1) developing reliable forecasts for future asset behavior; (2) selecting an informed model for portfolio allocation; (3) managing the portfolio rebalancing and execution of trades as market conditions change, and (4) monitoring and managing the entire investment process.
- Traditional factor models for forecasting asset returns may underestimate portfolio risk. The Axioma Alpha Factor™ Method can be used to adjust risk estimates and to make portfolios with underestimated risk less desirable by optimization procedures.

---

[76] As a point of comparison, note that the robust multiperiod optimization problem contains of the order of $N \times T$ constraints and variables, and thus its size does not grow exponentially with the number of time periods under consideration, or the number of assets in the portfolio. This is not the case for stochastic and dynamic programming formulations of the multiperiod allocation problem.

- One has to exercise caution when using sampling methods for estimation and portfolio allocation. While the sampling of possible future realizations of returns has been extremely useful for evaluating portfolio risk, there is an inherent error in sampling that may result in widely divergent recommendations for optimal asset weights. When a reliable sample is not available, one can avoid the dependency on the particular sample by estimating parameters from the distribution of returns robustly, and using those in portfolio allocation procedures.

- While portfolio allocation is an important strategic decision, the decision of how to attain a desired portfolio allocation in a cost-effective manner is also critical for superior performance. Portfolio rebalancing is additionally necessitated by changes in return and risk forecasts, in security prices, and in the investment universe available to a portfolio manager.

- Standard portfolio rebalancing schemes include (1) calendar rebalancing, (2) threshold rebalancing, and (3) range rebalancing. Using optimizers for portfolio rebalancing has opened up new opportunities.

- Trading and transaction costs can have a significant impact on performance, and should enter the portfolio allocation and rebalancing decisions. Transaction costs can be categorized as explicit or implicit. Explicit costs include commissions, fees, bid-ask spreads, and taxes. Implicit costs include market impact costs and price movement risk.

- In general, implicit trading costs are measured as the difference between the execution price and some appropriate fair market benchmark. The latter is the price that would have prevailed had the trade not taken place.

- Typical forecasting models for market impact costs are based on statistical factor methods. Some common trade-based factors are trade size, relative trade size, price of market liquidity, type of trade, efficiency and trading style of the investor, specific characteristics of the market or the exchange, time of trade submission, trade timing, and order type. Some common asset-based factors include price momentum, price volatility, market capitalization, growth versus value, and specific industry/sector characteristics.

- Transaction cost models can be incorporated into portfolio allocation and rebalancing algorithms. Optimizers can be used to improve such algorithms, which include (1) splitting the process into two stages—identifying the "optimal" target portfolio in the first stage, and the finding the optimal way to attain it in the second stage; (2) incorporating penalties for the costs of rebalancing in the portfolio allocation model itself; and (3) developing a full multiperiod portfolio allocation model that takes the costs of rebalancing into consideration.

■ There are numerous benefits to taking a long-term view of investment. While unquestionably the most comprehensive and potentially the most prudent, the third approach to portfolio rebalancing—developing a full multiperiod portfolio allocation model—is the most computationally intensive, and up until recently was considered too intractable to implement in practice. Recent improvements in computer speed and advances in robust optimization have made this approach much more appealing today.

CHAPTER 14

Quantitative Investment Management Today and Tomorrow

Modern finance theory, quantitative models, and econometric techniques provide the foundation that has revolutionized the investment management industry over the last several decades. The earliest use of quantitative methods in the industry was primarily for measuring risk, with models assessing exposure to a number of risk factors. Today, quantitative and econometric techniques have found their way into all the major areas of investment management. They range from the pricing of structured products and derivatives, market forecasting, trading strategies and execution, customer account management, performance attribution and measurement, to client advisory. Nevertheless, the industry as a whole has not reached this point, and incorporated the full multitude of quantitative techniques. Many challenges remain to be resolved and it goes without saying that the development of quantitative investment management platforms is time-consuming and resource-intensive. For some larger investment management firms and hedge funds, quantitative investment management is still a niche that offers a competitive advantage. It constitutes a framework for informed investment analysis, continues to be a source of new products, and is starting to provide increased economies of scale to the asset management business as a whole.

Future success for the industry will depend on its ability not only to provide excess returns in a risk-controlled fashion to investors, but also to integrate further modern financial innovation and process automation. In this world, quantitative approaches and techniques play an increasingly important role as they now influence all major aspects of a disciplined investment management process:

1. Setting the investment objectives.
2. Developing and defining the investment policy.
3. Selecting allocation and investment strategies.
4. Constructing the portfolio and implementing the investment plan.
5. Monitoring, measuring, and evaluating investment performance and risk.

In this book, we have focused primarily on presenting a robust quantitative framework for the last two points. This last chapter provides an overview of modern techniques used in some of the other areas, as well as an outlook on some of the current trends in the quantitative investment management industry as a whole. First, we discuss the use of derivatives in portfolio management, currency management in international portfolios, and benchmark selection. Then we review the most common quantitative and model-based trading strategies used by investment management companies and hedge funds today. We address model risk, data snooping and overfitting. We conclude the chapter with an introduction to optimal execution and algorithmic trading.

USING DERIVATIVES IN PORTFOLIO MANAGEMENT

Derivatives serve the following four main roles in portfolio management:[1]

- Modify the risk characteristics of a portfolio (risk management).
- Enhance the expected return of a portfolio (return management).
- Reduce transaction costs associated with managing a portfolio (cost management).
- Achieve efficiency in the presence of legal, tax, or regulatory obstacles (regulatory management).

Derivatives are used primarily to manage risk or to buy and sell risk at a favorable price, whether it is for regulatory, cost management, or return enhancing purposes. Broadly speaking, risk management is a dynamic process that allows a portfolio manager to identify, measure, and assess the current risk attributes of a portfolio as well as to analyze the potential benefits from taking those risks. In fact, risk management involves understanding and managing any and all of the factors that can have an adverse impact on the targeted rate of return and thus on the

---

[1] For a more detailed discussion of many of the different aspects of these roles, see Bruce M. Collins and Frank J. Fabozzi, "Equity Derivatives I: Features and Valuation," in Frank J. Fabozzi and Harry M. Markowitz (eds.), *The Theory and Practice of Investment Management* (Hoboken, NJ: John Wiley & Sons, 2002).

performance of the portfolio. The main objective is to attain a desired return for a given level of corresponding risk after costs have been taken into account. This is consistent with modern portfolio theory. The role of derivative products in this process is to shift the efficient frontier in favor of the investor by implementing a strategy at a lower cost, lower risk and higher return, or to gain access to investments that are otherwise not available due to some regulatory or other restrictions.

Undoubtedly, derivative products give investors more degrees of freedom. In the past, the implementation and management of investment strategies for pension funds, for example, was a function of management style and was carried out in the cash market. Pension funds managed risk by diversifying among management styles. Prior to the advent of the over-the-counter (OTC) derivatives market in the late 1980s, the first risk management tools available to investors were limited to the listed futures and options markets. Although providing a valuable addition to an investor's risk management toolkit, listed derivatives were limited in application due to their standardized features, limited size, and liquidity constraints. The OTC derivatives market gave investors access to longer term products that better match their investment horizon and flexible structures to meet their exact risk/reward requirements.[2] We now turn our attention to options, contracts which allow buyers the right to enter into a transaction with the sellers to either buy or sell an underlying asset at a specified price on or before an expiration date.

The real value of options in portfolio management regardless of the motivation for their use is that they allow the investor a means of modifying the risk and return characteristics of their investment portfolio. Adding options to an existing portfolio or using options as an investment vehicle creates asymmetric skewed return distributions that reflect different risks as opposed to an investment in the underlying asset. For example, the purchase of a call option rather than the stock itself changes the payout profile of the investment by capping the losses. It thereby truncates the probability distribution associated with possible outcomes and changes the risk-return profile of the investment.[3] The

---

[2] For further discussion of the impact of the OTC market on risk and portfolio management, see Bruce M. Collins, and Frank J. Fabozzi, "Equity Derivatives II: Portfolio Management Applications," in *The Theory and Practice of Investment Management*.
[3] From the perspective of performance measurement and the use of derivatives, some caution is warranted when evaluating different investment funds. Specifically, many standard performance measures used in the industry can be "gamed" by using option-like strategies. For example, the Sharpe ratio of a portfolio can easily be increased just by selling out-of-the-money calls and puts according to a simple strategy, see William Goetzmann, Jonathan Ingersoll, Matthew Spiegel, and Ivo Welch, "Sharpening Sharpe Ratios," Yale ICF Working Paper, Yale School of Management, 2004.

degree of the volatility affects the peakedness or kurtosis of the distributions as well. High volatility conditions, for example, correspond to distributions with thicker tails and low volatility conditions correspond to distributions with higher peaks.

The probability distribution of returns for an option is not normally distributed. The lognormal distribution assumption in the Black-Scholes option pricing model for the underlying physical asset allows the mapping to a skewed distribution. For example, the expected returns can be estimated directly from a Taylor expansion, through the use of a factor model or through the use of Monte Carlo simulation. Nonetheless, if the resulting portfolio return distribution is far away from normal, portfolio construction based upon expected returns and covariances alone can give a very distorted picture. A simple way to extend portfolio optimization to incorporate for some nonnormality is to add to, for example, a standard mean-variance optimization one or more threshold constraints that take higher moments or different forms of "event risk" or "tail risk" into account.[4] In Chapter 3 we discussed several extensions of the classical portfolio allocation framework using other risk measures that incorporate higher moments or various forms of "tail risk" in a more rigorous fashion.

CURRENCY MANAGEMENT

A portfolio manager can further diversify his portfolio by investing in assets beyond those available domestically. The benefit from international diversification is that by adding low correlated assets from other countries, the overall portfolio variance decreases and the risk-adjusted performance increases.

Nonetheless, the portfolio manager encounters several challenges with an international portfolio. We can think about international asset returns as consisting of two basic sources of risk: asset-specific risk and currency risk. One way in which these risks can manifest themselves is that a portfolio manager's investment decision was correct (for example, he picked a foreign stock that increased in value–asset-specific risk), but there was a decline in the foreign currency (currency risk). Therefore, when he sells the stock and converts the proceeds back to dollars, the gain is zero.

Academic studies suggest that international asset returns can be modeled by multifactor models where excess returns are explained by

---

[4] For an example of an extension of this kind, see Gerhard Scheuenstuhl nd Rudi Zagst, "Integrated Portfolio Management with Options," to appear in *European Journal of Operations Research*.

several risk factors.[5] Among others, these risks include a "market risk" and the local currency risks. The market risk component of an asset is typically measured by the covariance of its return with a chosen world market index. Currency risks, on the other hand, are measured by the covariances between asset returns and returns of the local currencies. Just like for the asset pricing theory (APT),[6] for each one of these sources of risk there is an associated price of risk—a risk premium—which can be interpreted as the compensation for bearing that specific risk. The risk premium associated with a local currency is referred to as its *currency risk premium.*

While it can be argued that in the long run currencies follow a mean-reverting process and are subject to the Purchasing Power Parity (PPP),[7] the short-term dynamics often result in significant deviations from equilibrium and are therefore very important to consider when managing an international portfolio's currency exposure. For example, a simple carry trade in which the investor borrows the currency with low interest rate and buys the currency with a high interest rate is on average profitable.[8] If the portfolio manager is concerned only with the long-term returns and risk of the portfolio, it may not be necessary to hedge the currency proportion of the risk in the portfolio. However, more often than not, short-term portfolio performance is important, and therefore it becomes necessary to hedge against currency risk. For countries with very volatile currencies, the return of a foreign stock may even be completely dominated by the currency return.

---

[5] The first *international asset pricing models* (IAPM) were proposed in Robert C. Merton, "An International Capital Asset Pricing Model," *Econometrica* 41, no. 5 (September 1973), pp. 867–887; Bruno H. Solnik, "An Equilibrium Model of the International Capital Market," *Journal of Economic Theory* 8, no. 4 (August 1974), pp. 500–524; Patrick Sercu, "A Generalization of International Asset Pricing Model," *Revue de l'Association Française de Finance* 1, no. 4 (June 1980), pp. 91–135; and Michael Adler and Bernard Dumas, "International Portfolio Selection and Corporate Finance: A Synthesis," *Journal of Finance* 46, no. 3 (June 1983), pp. 925–984.

[6] See Chapter 6.

[7] PPP states that exchange rates between two different currencies are in equilibrium when their purchasing power is the same in each of the two countries. This implies that the exchange rate between two countries should equal the ratio of the price levels in the two countries (as measured by a fixed basket of goods and services). PPP is based on the *law of one price*, that is, in an efficient market identical goods must have the same price.

[8] See, for example, Kenneth A. Froot and Richard H. Thaler, "Anomalies: Foreign Exchange," *Journal of Economic Perspectives* 4, no. 2 (1990), pp. 179–192; and Charles Engel, "The Forward Discount Anomaly and the Risk Premium: A Survey of Recent Evidence," *Journal of Empirical Finance* 3, no. 2 (1996), pp. 123–192.

In practice, currency forecasting and hedging are considered separately from asset selection. Specifically, forecasting models for foreign assets are most often developed for so-called *hedged returns*, and currency forecasts are performed separately. For example, in the case of a U.S.-based fund, on the one hand, the portfolio manager makes portfolio allocation decisions based on all asset returns converted into dollar returns using the prevalent exchange rates. These returns—based on the assets' dollar value—are the hedged returns and not directly subject to currency risk. On the other hand, the currency manager makes decisions about how much currency risk the fund is going to be exposed to at given point in time. He might decide to hedge anything from 100% down to 0%. In this sense, each currency is treated as a separate asset. The hedging decisions of different asset classes in a foreign country (such as stocks and bonds) have to be treated separately, although they are denominated in the same currency. Needless to say, hedging is subject to transaction costs, which depend on the liquidity of the currencies and the term of the hedging instruments used (typically, currency forward contracts).

We point out that stock index futures are a viable and important alternative in obtaining foreign equity exposure compared to investing in the foreign stocks themselves. In particular, the use of stock index futures for implementing a global equity investment strategy can reduce currency risk. The reason for this is that the currency risk is limited to the initial margin payments and the variation margin. These margin payments are typically much smaller than the initial value of the equity portfolio.[9]

Currency risk management is consistent with the portfolio optimization framework—one can use mean-variance optimization methods to determine optimal hedge ratios in practice. Grubel provided the first extension of modern portfolio selection to the international environment.[10] Probably the most common approach today is to formulate a portfolio optimization problem where the unknown weights consist of asset class weights (one for each asset, as usual) and hedge ratios (one

---

[9] Some other advantages of stock index futures include: high liquidity, rapid execution, low transaction costs, broad market exposure, no tracking error, and no custodial costs. Particularly applicable to foreign investment is that cash settlement avoids the risk of delivery; using stock index futures for country allocation gets around the problem of different settlement periods that may exist between two or more countries; and using futures may circumvent withholding taxes. In some countries the use of stock index futures allows foreign investors to avoid restrictions on capital movements.

[10] Herbert G. Grubel, "Internationally Diversified Portfolios," *American Economic Review* 58, no. 5 (1968), pp. 1299–1314.

for each foreign currency).[11] The resulting model can then be solved by the same portfolio optimization engines as in the domestic case. Note that the same caveats as in standard mean-variance optimization apply also in this case. Optimization methods are sensitive to small changes in the input parameters. However, many of the techniques described throughout this book—including robust estimation and optimization techniques—have proven to be beneficial in improving upon portfolio optimization approaches for making currency exposure and hedging decisions.[12]

BENCHMARKS

A benchmark is a hypothetical portfolio of assets.[13] Most common purposes of benchmarks are to (1) provide passive exposure to certain segments of the market; (2) serve as proxies for broad asset classes; and (3) function as performance standards against which active portfolio management can be measured. Some concrete examples include the following:

■ Investors who seek specific exposure to a sector, industry group, or industry segment can achieve this by holding investments that track a sector, industry group, or industry benchmark. Today, there are many ETFs (exchange traded funds) and futures contract that provide this opportunity;

---

[11] Bapi Maitra and Emmanuel Acar, *Optimal Portfolio Selection and the Impact of Currency Hedging* (London: Citibank FX Engineering, 2006); and Glen A. Larsen Jr. and Bruce G. Resnick, "The Optimal Construction of Internationally Diversified Equity Portfolios Hedged Against Exchange Rate Uncertainty," *European Financial Management* 6, no. 4 (December 2000), pp. 479–514.

[12] As we have discussed in other parts of this book, among the estimated inputs needed for mean-variance optimization, expected returns have the most impact on the sensitivity of optimal portfolio weights. Therefore, it is a good idea to try to avoid using historical average currency returns in determining long-term optimal currency allocations. As an alternative, one can use long run equilibrium or parity relations such as *uncovered interest-rate parity* (UIP) for this purpose. UIP states that the interest differential between two countries should equal the expected exchange rate change. Many other techniques, beyond the scope of this book, have been developed for forecasting short-term currency returns.

[13] For an in-depth discussion of benchmarks and their usages, see Laurence B. Siegel, *Benchmarks and Investment Management* (Charlottesville, VA: The Research Foundation of AIMR, 2003).

■ In defining the investment objective and formulating the policy statement of the fund, the fund sponsor can use various benchmarks to estimate the hypothetical long-term historical performance of different fund compositions. Specifically, the performance of a fund of funds with exposure to long-short equity, convertible arbitrage, and fixed income arbitrage strategies can be approximated by combining the appropriate hedge fund benchmarks.

■ To evaluate the skill of an active manager, investors can compare his performance relative to the benchmark (or a set of benchmarks). If he outperforms the benchmark, he is said to generate "alpha" relative to this benchmark.[14]

Choosing an appropriate performance benchmark is foremost a function of investment objectives and policy, but also of pure practicality. The choice of benchmark is normally specified in the investment policy statement. In this case, the benchmark serves as a reference point from which the performance of any active portfolio is measured and should represent the portfolio manager's investment philosophy. Typically, the amount of risk a portfolio manager can take is specified relative to the benchmark in terms of the portfolio's tracking error.[15] For example, a quantitative portfolio manager allowed to have a tracking error of no more than 200 basis points relative to the benchmark on an annual basis may therefore choose to use a tracking error constraint (see Chapter 4) in managing his risk. In defining investment objectives one should try to avoid benchmarks that are hard to replicate, have high turnover, or contain many illiquid assets.[16]

In the last decade there has been an enormous boom—an index and benchmark revolution—in the number of financial market benchmarks. Today, there is virtually a benchmark for every industry, sector or market segment imaginable, including ethical and environmentally friendly stock market indexes, such as the Dow Jones Sustainability Index and Wilderhill Clean Energy Index, comprised of only those companies that satisfy ecological or social criteria.

---

[14] This analysis is typically done by regressing the excess returns of the portfolio manager on the excess returns of the benchmark. The "alpha" is then the constant term and the "beta" is the slope coefficient in this regression. A positive (negative) alpha corresponds to outperforming (underperforming) the benchmark. See Chapters 6 and 7 for more information on applications of regression analysis.

[15] As we explained in Chapter 3, a portfolio's tracking error is the standard deviation of the difference between the portfolio's return and that of the benchmark.

[16] David Blitzer, "Talking Indexes," *Journal of Indexes* (November–December 2006).

QUANTITATIVE RETURN-FORECASTING TECHNIQUES AND MODEL-BASED TRADING STRATEGIES

Throughout this book we have discussed many of the standard techniques for estimating return and risk forecasts for a set of assets (see, for example, Chapters 6, 7, and 8). The basis of these forecasts is the past historical returns of each asset considered. While these approaches are widely used to estimate strategic (long-term equilibrium) target returns and in performing asset-class allocation, in practice, tactical decisions (short and intermediate term) are most often based on more involved trading strategies. A reason for this is that long-term returns tend to be close to market equilibrium returns, but that short-term returns can deviate substantially. Investment managers often make the simplifying assumption that long-term returns are close to stationary (or just slowly varying), whereas short-term returns are not. One purpose of tactical trading strategies is therefore to capture these short-run departures from the long-run equilibrium.

Broadly speaking, one can distinguish two categories of trading strategies: quantitative and nonquantitative. Quantitative strategies are based on models that take numerical data as inputs. Over the last decade there has been a dramatic increase in this form of trading. A major reason for this is that during the downturn of the general economy at the turn of the century, quantitative trading models with low correlation to traditional asset classes offered investors a new source of "alpha." Certainly, also the success of the hedge fund industry and its ability to outperform traditional markets during the bear market has increased the interest in the advanced trading strategies that they employ. Nonquantitative strategies have traditionally been referred to as "stock picking," but are in a wider sense simply just strategies that rely on qualitative as opposed to quantitative assessments.

In this section we provide a brief overview of some of the most common types of quantitative trading strategies used by practitioners today. Specifically, we address strategies based on momentum, reversals, exogenous factor prediction models, and econometric techniques.[17]

Before we turn to reviewing some of the most common strategies, we ask: what are the major characteristics of successful quantitative trading approaches? First, they are consistent. That is, using the same inputs they always produce the same signals. Second, models enforce a disciplined framework, circumventing decisions based on emotions or other subjective

---

[17] For a recent survey of quantitative methods used in the asset management industry in North America and Europe, see Frank J. Fabozzi, Sergio M. Focardi, and Petter N. Kolm, *Trends in Quantitative Finance* (Charlottesville, VA: The Research Foundation of CFA Institute, 2006).

criteria. Third, they can be fully automated. This allows an investment manager to scale up the size of a successful strategy. Automated models tend to be fairly portable to similar and related markets. Fourth, they can be fully tested on past historical data as well as on simulated scenarios, offering means to study and tune them to different market environments.

Momentum and Reversal Strategies

Momentum and reversal models are probably the most widely used quantitative trading techniques used today. Momentum strategies are intended to capture the *persistence of local trends*, such as continuous price rises or price declines. Reversal models, on the other hand, attempt to identify a *change of direction of local trends*. We gave a brief overview of momentum strategies in Chapter 8 and discussed a simple cross-sectional momentum strategy using the country indices in the MSCI World Index. Although most academic studies agree about the existence and duration of these effects, there is no general consensus on what is driving them.[18]

Momentum and reversal are coupled phenomena: If momentum exists, so does reversal. However, complex time dynamics exist in momentum and reversals that give rise to different patterns of momentum and reversal at different time horizons. While in the equity market, momentum is a short and intermediate term phenomenon over a 3 to 12 month period, reversals tend to occur over the very short-term as well as over longer horizons such as 3 to 5 years.

The long-term reversal effect was first documented by DeBondt and Thaler.[19] They constructed a simple long-short trading strategy formed by a combination of two different types of portfolios. The first portfolio consisted of the 35 stocks that had the lowest returns over the past three-to-five-year period ("the past loser portfolio"), and the second contained the 35 stocks that had the highest returns over the same period ("the past winner portfolio"). They showed that the differences in returns between the past loser and a past winner portfolios averaged about 8% annually over their sample period.

Over the very short-term, Jegadeesh[20] and Lehmann[21] showed that weekly and monthly stock returns tend to have negative autocorrelation.

---

[18] Alan Scowcroft and James Sefton, "Understanding Momentum," *Financial Analysts Journal* 61, no. 2 (March–April 2005), pp. 64–82.

[19] Werner F.M. DeBondt and Richard H. Thaler, "Does the Stock Market Overreact?" *Journal of Finance* 40, no. 3 (1985), pp. 793–808.

[20] Narasimhan Jegadeesh, "Evidence of Predictable Behavior of Security Returns," *Journal of Finance* 45, no. 3 (1990), pp. 881–898.

[21] Bruce N. Lehmann, "Fads, Martingales and Market Efficiency," *Quarterly Journal of Economics* 105, no. 1 (1990), pp. 1–28.

In other words, the best performing stocks over the previous week (month) are more likely to perform poorly during the following week (month), and vice versa for the worst performing stocks, generating almost 30% annual returns excluding trading costs. Nevertheless, it is often argued that this short-term reversal effect is due to the *"bid-ask" bounce effect*. Bid-ask bounce occurs in high-frequency transaction prices as consecutive quotes tend to bounce between buy and sell prices. Using these bid and ask prices as proxies for the midprice gives the illusion that markets are moving more than they actually are, inducing short-term return reversals.

These types of strategies generate high turnover, which results in significant transaction costs. Some academic evidence shows that momentum strategies are profitable after taking transaction costs into account.[22] However, the costs involved in short-selling stocks are often substantial, especially for small-cap stocks, and have so far been ignored in academic studies of momentum and reversal strategies. Nonetheless, many practitioners report successful implementations, pointing out that constructing a successful momentum or reversal strategy requires balancing pure strategy returns and implementation costs by using liquidity-adjusted weighting schemes and turnover penalty functions during the portfolio construction.

Models Based on Exogenous Predictors

Regression models based on exogenous predictors are a very common forecasting technique among quantitatively oriented investment management firms—and sometimes the core of their return-forecasting effort.[23] As we explained in Chapter 6, this technique is based upon running forecasting regressions of returns on one or more explanatory variables. A typical such model is returns regressed on scaled price ratios such as price/dividend (P/D), price/book (P/B), and price/earnings (P/E).[24] A stock with a high (low) scaled price ratio (for example, P/E ratio) is referred to as a growth (value) stock. It is well known that, on average, portfolios of value stocks have historically outperformed portfolios of growth stocks over the long term.

[22] Robert A. Korajczyk and Ronnie Sadka, "Are Momentum Profits Robust to Trading Costs?" *Journal of Finance* 59, no. 3 (2004), pp. 1039–1082.

[23] Based upon the survey results presented in Fabozzi, Focardi, and Kolm, *Trends in Quantitative Finance*.

[24] See, for example, Eugene Fama and Kenneth French, "The Cross-Section of Expected Stock Returns," *Journal of Finance* 47, no. 2 (1992), pp. 427–465. The P/B ratio is often also referred to as the market-to-book (M/B) ratio; and John H. Cochrane, "Where Is the Market Going? Uncertain Facts and Novel Theories," *Federal Reserve Bank of Chicago Economic Perspectives* 21, no. 6 (November–December 1997), pp. 3–37.

The basic idea behind these relationships is easy to understand. Let us take the P/D ratio as an example. For a stock with price P that pays a dividend of D next period, we have by the *Gordon formula*[25]

$$P = \frac{D}{R - G}$$

where R is the constant discount rate and G is the constant dividend growth rate.[26] Rearranging, we have

$$\frac{P}{D} = \frac{1}{R - G}$$

From this relationship we observe that when P/D increases it must be that the difference between the discount and the dividend growth rate decreases. In fact, as Campbell and Shiller[27] have shown empirically, changes in the P/D ratio are not explained by changes in the growth rate. Therefore, it follows that an increasing (decreasing) P/D ratio implies decreasing (increasing) future returns. In a similar fashion, other scaled price ratios are negatively correlated with future returns.

In addition to accounting measures, another common variable that occurs in forecasting regressions is market capitalization. In his classical book from 1962, Gordon[28] demonstrated that stock returns are inversely related to the firm size. Later, many academic studies have confirmed this result. For example, Fama and French[29] show that over the period 1963 to 1990, the average difference in annual return between the smallest and largest deciles of NYSE, AMEX, and NASDAQ stocks grouped based on market capitalization is almost 9%.

---

[25] Myron J. Gordon, *The Investment, Financing and Valuation of the Corporation* (Homewood, IL: Richard D. Irwin, 1962).

[26] We remark that the same argument can be generalized by using the standard present value formula

$$P_t = \sum_{\tau = 1}^{\infty} \frac{D_{t+\tau}}{\prod_{i=1}^{\tau} (1 + R_{t+i})}$$

that holds for any dividend paying stock.

[27] John Y. Campbell and Robert J. Shiller, "Valuation Ratios and the Long-Run Stock Market Outlook," *Journal of Portfolio Management* 24, no. 2 (1998), pp. 11–26.

[28] Gordon, *The Investment, Financing and Valuation of the Corporation.*

[29] Fama and French, "The Cross-Section of Expected Stock Returns."

More Sophisticated Econometric Models

More sophisticated econometric and time series models such as autoregressive models, dynamic factor approaches, and cointegration techniques are starting to be more widely used for forecasting purposes in the investment management industry.[30]

In an autoregressive model, a variable is regressed on its own lagged values—that is, on its own past. If the model involves only one variable, it is called an *autoregressive* (AR) *model*. If more than one variable is regressed contemporaneously in the model, it is referred to as a *vector-autoregressive* (VAR) *model*. An intuitive way of thinking about an AR model with lag k is that it prescribes that the forecast at time $t + 1$ ("tomorrow") is a weighted average of the values of the same variable at times $t, t - 1, \ldots, t - k$ plus an error term. The weighting coefficients are the model parameters and have to be estimated. In a VAR model with lag k each forecast is expressed as a weighted average over its own lagged values plus the lagged values of the other variables. For example, if we consider a VAR model with two forecasting variables with a lag of k, then each variable is regressed on $2k$ lagged values, and therefore, the model includes $4k$ parameters. This reasoning can be extended to any number of variables. VAR models offer a rich modeling framework as they can capture cross-autocorrelations. In other words, they can describe how a forecasting variable is linked to its own past values as well as the other variables at other times.

Although used in the investment management industry, autoregressive models have not been widely evaluated. Being able to incorporate time series dynamics at different horizons simultaneously, they generalize the momentum and reversal approaches discussed in the previous section. However, they require much more resources in terms of data requirements and econometric modeling. In particular, the number of model parameters grows very quickly in a VAR model as the number of forecasting variables and lags increases. Unfortunately, there are no symmetry considerations that can reduce the number of these parameters. Therefore, in applying VAR models to financial time series, we can only expect to model a small number of assets. For many assets, such as the stocks in the S&P 500 Index, the number of parameters that need to be estimated becomes too large. In these situations it is hard (often impossible) to produce reliable estimates with small enough estimation error. For example, a VAR model of the stocks in the S&P 500 index

---

[30] For a more detailed mathematical exposition of the models presented in this section, see Frank J. Fabozzi, Sergio M. Focardi, and Petter N. Kolm, *Financial Modeling of the Equity Market: From CAPM to Cointegration* (Hoboken, NJ: John Wiley & Sons, 2006).

that includes two lags requires the estimation of $500 \times 500 \times 2 = 500,000$ parameters. This is clearly a daunting task. Nevertheless, VAR models can be very useful in modeling the relationship between different asset classes. Today, VAR models are commonly used to describe the dynamic relationships between different macroeconomic variables.

Dynamic factor and *state-space models* are extensions of VAR models for the purpose of reducing model dimensionality. For a model to be useful, the number of model parameters to be estimated needs to be small; otherwise, it is difficult to estimate all parameters and estimation errors become too large. A dynamic factor model fulfills this requirement by mapping the dynamics of a larger number of assets to a small number of dynamic factors. Simply put, instead of modeling individual asset dynamics, these approaches focus on the factors that are common among all assets. For example, for the S&P 500 Index, an analyst might use three dynamic factors modeled by a VAR model with, say, four lags, which results in a model with only 12 state variables rather than all of the individual assets required in the standard VAR framework.

Cointegration models, models that simultaneously incorporate short-term dynamics and long-run equilibrium, are still at an infant stage as a forecasting tool in the investment management industry. Two or more nonstationary time series that are *integrated*[31] are said to be *cointegrated* if they stay close together even if, individually, they behave as random walks. A pictorial illustration of cointegration is that of a drunken man walking his dog. Both of them wander aimlessly about, but the distance between the man and the dog fluctuates in a stationary way.

Cointegrating relationships express long-run equilibrium relationships between time series and their existence in asset prices implies that a small number of common trends are at work in financial markets. If cointegration is present, price processes can be expressed as regressions on a restricted number of common trends. Trading strategies can be devised based on extracting and forecasting these trends.

Cointegration is related to mean reversion and trend reversal. In fact, between two cointegrated time series, one process reverts to the other. A classical question about the behavior of stock price processes is the existence of mean reversion: Do stock prices fluctuate in the long-run around some deterministic trend, or do they behave as random

---

[31] A nonstationary process $x_1, x_2, \ldots, x_t, \ldots$ is said to be *integrated of order one* (often abbreviated as $I(1)$) if the difference process $x_2 - x_1, x_3 - x_4, \ldots, x_t - x_{t-1}, \ldots$ is stationary. An integrated process of order one is also referred to as a *unit root process*. The level of an integrated process is the sum of all past shocks; in other words, any shock to the system is permanent and never decays away. The random walk process is an example of an $I(1)$ process.

walks? In his famous book, Malkiel argued in favor of the random walk theory.[32] Empirical studies have shown mixed evidence of random walk behavior and no strong evidence in favor of mean reversion.[33]

From a practical point of view, the key question may not be whether cointegration exists in financial prices or not, but whether there is sufficient cointegration for a trading strategy to yield economically significant profits. Cointegrating relationships are notoriously difficult to identify in large sets of data, such as among stocks composing the S&P 500. The standard methodologies for testing and estimating cointegrating relationships are applicable only to a small number (in the range of 10 to 20) of processes. For this reason, cointegration has mostly been exploited in a limited fashion, primarily at the level of *pairs trading*. Here, the idea is to identify a pair of stocks that historically have moved in tandem. Then, if the price spread between them significantly widens, by short-selling the winner and buying the loser there is a potential for profit if the pair subsequently returns to its previous relationship. Needless to say, pairs trading does not take advantage of the full potential of cointegration.

Another important implication of cointegration is that meaningful linear regressions between integrated time series are possible. In general, a meaningful linear regression of one integrated time series on another integrated time series is not possible, because they are both random. Such regressions are *spurious*, although they might have a high R^2. However, if the series are cointegrated, the linear regressions are meaningful. In the previous section, we discussed how financial ratios and other variables are used as predictors of returns. A problem with these regressions is that financial ratios are often close to being integrated of order one (that is, they are unit root processes). Therefore, regressing returns that are close to stationary variables on financial ratios may yield spurious predictive relationships.[34] In general, the problem of spurious regressions is one of the major difficulties in performing predictive regressions.

Model Selection and Testing

In practice, model selection often involves an interplay between business requirements, financial theory and experience. Business needs can be of various kinds, including the need to build or modify a suite of models; or

---

[32] Burton Malkiel, *A Random Walk Down Wall Street* (New York: Norton, 1973).

[33] See John Y. Campbell, Andrew A. Lo, and Craig A. MacKinlay, *The Econometrics of Financial Markets* (Princeton, NJ: Princeton University Press, Princeton, 1996).

[34] When running predictive regressions it is important to test the data for unit roots. This is typically done with the so-called Dickey-Fuller test. See, for example, G.S. Maddala and In-Moo Kim, *Unit Roots, Cointegration, and Structural Change* (Cambridge: Cambridge University Press, 1998).

to model specific markets, market segments, or market regimes. Given broad business needs, the starting point of the analyst is most often theoretical knowledge and economic intuition. Pure data-mining approaches, in which the analyst probes data automatically in a search for patterns, are not feasible. The possibility of feeding computers data and news in an attempt to find profitable strategies is a far cry from reality. Although computers can perform repetitive operations at a speed that is billions of times that of human capabilities, we are far from being able to replace human intuition and judgment. For example, intuition will suggest whether to use an explanatory model, which is based on exogenous factors, or an autoregressive model, which makes predictions on the basis of its own past. Or the process may be the reverse: Financial theory and economic intuition may suggest a new trading strategy.

Suppose, for example, that the objective is to model the economic intuition that a set of company financial ratios are good predictors of stock returns. The first step is to formulate the econometric hypothesis that embodies this intuition. Among the decisions that have to be made are the choice of regressions (that is, linear or nonlinear), the number and type of predictors, and the number of lags. Perhaps the analyst wants to use functions (modifications) of financial ratios, such as logarithms, or to extract special predictors formed as combinations of returns and/or exogenous variables.

Next, the model has to be implemented as a software program, and its parameters estimated with sample data. During this part of the model building process, the analyst can rely upon standard econometric techniques. After estimating the model, it must be thoroughly tested. For example, in a linear regression framework, one can use sample data to test the relative importance of regressors, statistical significance and model fit. The real issue, however, is whether a forecasting model performs well when applied to new data—*out-of-sample data*. For this reason, the model has to be tested on data that is *different* from the data used during the estimation.

Interestingly enough, despite many efforts in problem solving, no general "recipe" for model design exists. Each step requires knowledge, experience, and hard work. The testing and analysis of models, however, is a well-defined step-by-step methodology with a sound scientific foundation. The most important part of the discipline required in model selection is the implementation of a rigorous testing methodology in order to avoid model overfitting and data snooping.

A good starting point for limiting data snooping is to be prudent and diligent in the modeling process. It is particularly important to choose the framework, defining how the model will be specified before beginning to analyze the actual data. Model hypotheses that make financial or economic sense should be formulated in the initial stage of model building rather than trying to find a good fit for the data and then creating an ex post explanation or story for the model.[35]

Calibrating models on some data set ("training set") and testing them on another data set ("test set") is essential. Needless to say, the test set must be large and must cover all possible patterns, at least in some approximate sense. For example, to test a trading strategy, one needs test data in as many varied market conditions as possible, such as those with high and low volatility, in expansionary and recessionary periods, in various correlation situations, and so on. In some special cases, the impact of systematic parameter searches can be computed explicitly by correcting the statistical distributions used for inference.[36] In more general settings, sampling, bootstrapping, and randomization techniques[37] can be used to evaluate whether a given model has predictive power over a benchmark model after taking into consideration the effects of data snooping.[38]

A model is overfitted when it captures the underlying structure or the dynamics in the data as well as random noise. The use of too many model parameters that restrict the degrees of freedom relative to the size of the sample data is a common cause for overfitting. Typically, the result is good in-sample fit but poor out-of-sample behavior. By systematically searching the parameter space, even an incorrect or a misspecified model can be made to fit the available data. Obviously, this apparent fit is due to chance, and therefore does not have any descriptive or predictive power. In many cases, it is hard to distinguish spurious phenomena that are the result of overfitting or data mining from a valid empirical finding and a truly good model. As an example, the *Super Bowl theory* is probably one of the better known and longer-lasting spurious market predictions. Its remarkable record and lack of any rational connection contribute to its popularity. According to the theory, the U.S. stock market will end the year up over the previous year if a National Football Conference team wins the Super Bowl.

---

[35] When Peter Bernstein was working on his book *Capital Ideas* and interviewed Fischer Black, he learned that Black always expressed a new idea in words first, before he started writing it down in mathematical form. If he could not put it in words, he discarded the equations.

[36] See Andrew W. Lo and Craig A. MacKinlay, "Data-Snooping Biases in Tests of Financial Asset Pricing Models," *Review of Financial Studies* 3, no. 3 (1990), pp. 431–468.

[37] Sampling methods define the strategy to be followed in sampling a data set. Bootstrap methods create additional samples from a given sample through computer simulation.

[38] See Halbert White, "A Reality Check for Data Snooping," *Econometrica* 68, no. 5 (September 2000), pp. 1097–1127.

An important lesson in the theory of learning is that a key virtue for models is simplicity. Complex models require large amounts of data for estimation and testing. In practice, there is a trade-off between model complexity, explanatory power, and the size of available data sets. Despite their apparent superabundance, economic and financial data are actually scarce relative to what is needed to estimate many kinds of models. As we discussed in Chapter 6, the 125,000 individual possible pairwise correlations in the S&P 500 need to be reduced. Only a tiny fraction of the potential correlation structure is revealing—the rest is pure noise. Financial econometrics ignores the details and attempts to determine probabilistic laws. Discovering probabilistic laws with confidence, however, requires working with large samples. The samples available for financial econometric analysis are too small to allow for a safe estimate of probability laws; small changes in the sample therefore induce changes in the laws. As a result of this scarcity of economic data, many different statistical models, even simple ones, can be compatible with the same data with roughly the same level of statistical confidence. Therefore, simplicity is a fundamental requirement. If two models have roughly the same explanatory power, the simpler model—that is, the one with a smaller number of parameters to estimate—is most often preferable. As Albert Einstein once said: "Make everything as simple as possible, but not simpler."

Finally, forecasting models should be monitored and reviewed on a regular basis. Deteriorating results from a model or predictive variable should be investigated and understood. Well-designed and thoroughly tested models should not have to be changed often, but structural shifts and major alterations in underlying market conditions due to changes in exogenous factors such as economic policy, political climate, and shocks caused by unforeseeable events sometimes trigger model revisions or recalibrations.

TRADE EXECUTION AND ALGORITHMIC TRADING

Trade execution is an integral components of the investment process. A poorly executed trade can eat directly into portfolio returns. Costs are incurred when buying or selling securities in the form of, for example, brokerage commissions, bid-ask spreads, taxes, and market impact costs. As we explained in Chapter 13, the first four costs are referred to as explicit costs and are more or less known before a security is bought or sold. Market impact costs, however, are implicit and dependent on factors such as general market conditions, liquidity of the security being traded, trade size, and trading style.

The decisions of the portfolio manager and the trader are based on different objectives. The portfolio manager constructs the optimal portfolio to reflect the best trade-off between expected returns and risk, given his assessment of the prevailing trading costs. The trader decides on the timing of the execution of the trades based on the trade-off between opportunity costs and market impact costs. Opportunity cost is the cost suffered when a trade is not executed quickly enough, or not executed at all. On the one hand, market impact cost *declines* with time as it is positively related to the *immediacy of execution*. In other words, if a trader can "work an order" over time, the resulting transaction costs are expected to be lower. On the other hand, opportunity cost *increases* over time as it is positively related to the *delay in execution*. This means that if a trader waits too long, a part of the "alpha" of the investment opportunity might disappear. Taken together, these two basic mechanisms give a total cost that is shaped like a parabola. Minimizing the total cost for a trade (or a series of trades) becomes a problem of finding the optimal trade-off between market impact costs and opportunity costs.

In general, this problem results in a complicated stochastic and dynamic optimization problem. The first models of this kind appeared towards the end of the 1990s. For example, Bertsimas, Hummel, and Lo[39] and Almgren and Chriss[40] developed continuous-time models for optimal execution that minimize average transaction costs over a specific time horizon. Almgren and Chriss assumed that securities prices evolve according to a random-walk process, and solved the resulting continuous time problem. Given that most empirical studies have rejected the random-walk hypothesis, this assumption is sometimes too restrictive for real-world applications. Nevertheless, the article is an important contribution as it is one of the first of its kind to consider a dynamic model with market impact costs in which transactions occur over time.[41]

These earlier models along with the growth of Electronic Communications Networks (ECNs)[42] and automatic trade routing provided the foundation for advanced trade execution services known as *algorithmic trading*. In a nutshell, algorithmic trading is a combination of smart

---

[39] Dimitris Bertsimas, Paul Hummel, and Andrew W. Lo, "Optimal Control of Execution Costs for Portfolios," MIT Sloan School of Management, 1999.

[40] Robert Almgren and Neil Chriss, "Optimal Execution of Portfolio Transactions," Courant Institute of Mathematical Sciences, 2000; and Robert F. Almgren, "Optimal Execution with Nonlinear Impact Functions and Trading-Enhanced Risk," University of Toronto, 2001.

[41] Some models of this kind have been described in "ITG ACE—Agency Cost Estimator: A Model Description," 2003, www.itginc.com.

[42] Electronic Communications Networks are electronic trading systems that automatically match buy and sell orders at specified prices.

trade routing, program trading, and rules-based trading to perform automated computer-based execution of trade orders via direct market-access channels.[43]

Today, algorithmic trading is a widespread tool throughout the investment management industry to the extent that it is next to every major broker, and many technology providers offer these services in one form or another. For instance, a study by Tabb[44] shows that 61% of U.S. buy-side firms employ some form of model-based execution vehicles. Based on his survey evidence, Tabb forecasts a 144% growth in the use of algorithmic trading by the end of 2006. In another study of European investment managers, 58% of the surveyed firms perform up to 50% of their trades using algorithmic trading programs.[45] This suggests that algorithmic trading underlies more than a quarter of the trades among European investment managers. This naturally gives rise to the question: Besides the productivity enhancement of automation, how cost-effective is algorithmic trading?

Domowitz and Yegerman[46] conducted one of the first studies to analyze the performance of algorithmic trading engines. They compared about one million algorithmic-based orders spread across a subset of model-based trading service providers, consisting of about 2.6 billion shares with a value of $82 billion traded from January through December of 2004 by over 40 institutions, against a control sample of about 1.5 million orders (totaling around 7.3 billion shares) executed by non-algorithmic means. Not only does their data sample permit a comparison of algorithmic executions of a broad universe of trades, but it also allows one to study the performance across providers of model-based trading services. They show that in aggregate, algorithmic trading is less

---

[43] See Randy Grossman, "The Search for the Ultimate Trade: Market Players in Algorithmic Trading," *Financial Insights* (2005); and Ian Domowitz and Henry Yegerman, "The Cost of Algorithmic Trading: A First Look at Comparative Performance," ITG Inc. (2005) for a more detailed discussion of the definition of algorithmic trading. Robert Kissell and Roberto Malamut, "Algorithmic Decision Making Framework," JP Morgan, Global Execution Services (2005) outlines a decision-making framework for selecting appropriate algorithmic trading strategies based on pretrade goals and objectives. This approach is based on a simple three step methodology: (1) choosing the price benchmark; (2) specifying the trading style (from passive to aggressive); and (3) selecting the dynamic adaptation tactic.

[44] Larry Tabb, "Institutional Equity Trading in America: A Buy-Side Perspective," The Tabb Group (2004).

[45] Jean-Ren Giraud, 2004, "Best Execution for Buy-Side Firms: A Challenging Issue, A Promising Debate, A Regulatory Challenge," Edhec-Risk Advisory (2004).

[46] Ian Domowitz and Henry Yegerman, "The Cost of Algorithmic Trading: A First Look at Comparative Performance," ITG Inc (2005).

expensive than the nonalgorithmic means, even after taking into account trade difficulty, differences in market, side of trade, and volatility regime. Nonetheless, the study demonstrates that the superiority of algorithmic trading performance applies only for order sizes up to 10% of average daily volume.[47]

A popular product offered by many brokers is *guaranteed VWAP* (volume weighted average price). In a guaranteed VWAP order the client provides a trade list to the broker-dealer who charges a fixed commission per share and guarantees the day's VWAP for each stock traded. The guaranteed VWAP price removes any trade execution uncertainty on an order for the client. The volume weighted average price is calculated by an average weighting of all transactions during trading hours and displayed after the markets have closed.

Although algorithmic trading is still a relatively recent technology, it offers great benefits in increasing productivity and in managing trades in a cost-effective manner. A challenge from the modeling perspective is that trading algorithms have to be highly flexible and adaptive in order to account for changing market conditions and various trading styles. In particular, algorithms need to incorporate trade dynamic characteristics such as whether a trade is liquidity providing or demanding,[48] crossable[49] or not, and large relative to the average volume.[50] One of the issues in this regard is to construct algorithmic trading strategies that adapt to changes in market behavior such as varying volume, market

---

[47] The following article offers a critical analysis of the results presented by Domowitz and Yegerman: Richard Rosenblatt and Joseph Gawronski, "Sell-Side Algorithmic Offerings: Don't Believe the Hype (at Least not Yet)—A Quick Review of the Anecdotal and Empirical Evidence to Date," *Journal of Trading* 2, no. 1 (Winter 2006), pp. 43–45. The major critique is that of the reliability of the data and sample selection bias.

[48] The timing of the purchase or sale of a position has a significant impact. The determining question here is whether the trader trades with or against the market. A momentum trade, for example, occurs in the same direction as the market. Several managers may be trading the same security in the same direction—at the same time. The price impact of these multiple trades can make momentum trades expensive. Trades that must be filled as quickly as possible by traders are often considered to be most difficult. For example, when a portfolio manager has received bad news about a particular stock he is holding, he might decide to get out of his position immediately by liquidating his total holdings in the stock in order to avoid major losses.

[49] Crossing networks (such as Posit and Liquidnet) are attractive, as they by-pass the middleman in situations where he is not needed, and thus help lowering trade execution costs. These networks match a buyer and a seller, and allow them to execute a direct trade between themselves. However, most crossing networks today still have relatively low hit rates.

[50] For a stock, 10% of daily volume is commonly used as a rule of thumb.

volatility, and liquidity. In fact, time-varying liquidity is a major factor, especially for smallcap stocks.[51] These and related topics will be the focus of future research in this area.

SUMMARY

- Quantitative approaches and techniques will play an increasingly important role throughout the whole investment management process.
- Derivatives serve four main roles in portfolio management: modify the risk characteristics of a portfolio, enhance the expected return of a portfolio, reduce transaction costs, and efficiently manage regulatory requirements.
- Currency risk has to be managed in international portfolios.
- Optimal hedge ratios for each currency can be determined by mean-variance optimization methods.
- The most common uses of benchmarks are to: provide passive exposure to certain segments of the market, serve as proxies for broad asset classes, and function as performance standards against which active portfolio management can be evaluated.
- Long-term and short-term return forecasts are typically very different. Long-term returns tend to be close to market equilibrium returns, whereas short-term returns may deviate substantially.
- Investment managers often make the simplifying assumption that long-term returns are close to stationary (or just slowly varying), and therefore estimate them by simple statistical techniques. Short-term returns can vary significantly, and tactical trading strategies are used to capture these departures from long-run equilibrium.
- Some of the most common types of quantitative trading strategies are based on: momentum, reversals, exogenous factor regressions, and other econometric techniques.
- When developing models, care has to be taken in choosing an appropriate specification. Some of the most common modeling pitfalls include overfitting and data snooping biases.
- Optimal trading systems rely on mathematical models that determine the timing of the trade execution by balancing the trade-off between opportunity cost and market impact cost.

---

[51] See, for example, Robert Almgren, "New Directions in Optimal Trading," CQA/SQA Quantitative Trading Seminar (2006); Ian Domowitz, and Xiaoxin Wang, "Liquidity, Liquidity Commonality and Its Impact on Portfolio Theory," Department of Finance, Smeal College of Business Administration, Pennsylvania State University, University Park (2002).

■ Algorithmic trading is a combination of smart trade routing, program trading, and rules-based trading to perform automated computer-based execution of trade orders via direct market-access channels.

Data Description:
The MSCI World Index

In some of the examples throughout this book, we use the MSCI World Index and its individual constituents (developed market country indices) in some examples. In this appendix we provide some basic statistics and properties of this data set.

We obtained daily levels and returns of the MSCI World Index and all its constituents along with market capitalization weights over the period 1/1/1980 through 5/31/2004 directly from Morgan Stanley Capital International, Inc.[1] The levels and returns are given from the perspective of an investor in the United States.

The MSCI World Index is a free float-adjusted market capitalization index that is designed to measure global developed market equity performance. As of December 2004, the MSCI World Index consisted of the following 23 constituents (developed market country indices): Australia, Austria, Belgium, Canada, Denmark, Finland, France, Germany, Greece, Hong Kong, Ireland, Italy, Japan, the Netherlands, New Zealand, Norway, Portugal, Singapore, Spain, Sweden, Switzerland, the United Kingdom, and the United States. Other constituents that were part of the index at some point throughout the time period January 1980 through May 2004 were Malaysia, Mexico, and South African Gold Mines.

The different constituents of the index as of January in the years 1985, 1995, and 2004 along with their market capitalization in billions of U.S. dollars and percentage weight, and their ranking (in terms of market capitalization) are displayed in Exhibit A.1. We observe that the relative rank-

---

[1] We would like to thank Morgan Stanley Capital International, Inc., http://www.msci.com, for providing us with the data set. In particular, we thank Nicholas G. Keyes for preparing and for answering all our questions in regards to the data set.

EXHIBIT A.1 Market Capitalization Weights of the MSCI World Index and its Constituents as of the First Business Day in January in the Years 1985, 1995, and 2004

	1985			1995			2004		
	$US (billion)	Percent	Rank	$US (billion)	Percent	Rank	$US (billion)	Percent	Rank
World	1,765.1	100.00%		7,650.8	100.00%		17,416.4	100.00%	
Australia	27.8	1.57%	6	125.1	1.63%	10	373.6	2.15%	9
Austria	0.8	0.05%	20	18.0	0.23%	20	16.0	0.09%	22
Belgium	7.6	0.43%	15	49.3	0.64%	16	77.5	0.45%	15
Canada	71.7	4.06%	4	171.1	2.24%	7	463.9	2.66%	7
Denmark	3.6	0.20%	17	35.3	0.46%	17	55.5	0.32%	17
Finland	26.7	0.35%	18	122.8	0.71%	13			
France	23.1	1.31%	9	265.6	3.47%	5	727.6	4.18%	4
Germany	49.1	2.78%	5	300.1	3.92%	4	530.8	3.05%	6
Greece							33.3	0.19%	20
Hong Kong	14.7	0.83%	12	136.5	1.78%	9	118.5	0.68%	14
Ireland	12.5	0.16%	23	54.1	0.31%	18			
Italy	15.1	0.85%	10	102.9	1.34%	12	285.3	1.64%	10
Japan	367.5	20.82%	2	2,145.7	28.04%	2	1,576.7	9.05%	3
Malaysia				105.6	1.38%	11			
Mexico	1.7	0.10%	19						
Netherlands	25.7	1.46%	8	167.9	2.19%	8	380.8	2.19%	8

EXHIBIT A.1 (Continued)

	1985			1995			2004		
	$US (billion)	Percent	Rank	$US (billion)	Percent	Rank	$US (billion)	Percent	Rank
New Zealand				17.3	0.23%	21	15.8	0.09%	23
Norway	2.7	0.15%	18	19.9	0.26%	19	35.7	0.20%	19
Portugal							26.5	0.15%	21
Singapore	14.7	0.84%	11	56.8	0.74%	15	60.4	0.35%	16
South African Gold Mines	12.4	0.70%	13	13.6	0.18%	22			
Spain	7.0	0.40%	16	74.3	0.97%	14	271.3	1.56%	11
Sweden	11.8	0.67%	14	76.1	1.00%	13	167.7	0.96%	12
Switzerland	26.4	1.49%	7	215.0	2.81%	6	545.0	3.13%	5
United Kingdom	131.2	7.43%	3	731.1	9.56%	3	1,906.4	10.95%	2
United States	950.4	53.85%	1	2,784.6	36.40%	1	9,571.3	54.96%	1

ings among the different countries have been relatively stable throughout time. Nevertheless, the total market capitalization of the MSCI World Index has grown from about $1.8 trillion as of January 1985 to $17.4 trillion as of May 2004. Details about how the country indices are constructed are available in the *MSCI Standard Methodology Book*.[2]

In Exhibits A.2, A.3, and A.4, we display some basic statistical properties of the data set. For simplicity, as all of the constituents that were part of the index as of May 2004 also were part of the index in January 1988, we only display statistics calculated over this period. The statistics are calculated over the full period as well as over each half; the

EXHIBIT A.2 Statistics of Daily Returns over the Period January 1988 through May 2004

	Mean	Volatility	Sharpe Ratio	Rank	Skew	Kurtosis	Min	Max
World	6.4%	12.9%	0.49	6	−0.06	6.19	−5.1%	4.9%
Australia	7.3%	17.6%	0.42	15	−0.20	6.02	−8.5%	7.7%
Austria	7.7%	19.1%	0.41	17	−0.17	9.68	−12.6%	9.7%
Belgium	8.3%	18.1%	0.46	8	0.31	9.19	−8.6%	9.1%
Canada	7.2%	16.0%	0.45	9	−0.54	9.73	−9.3%	5.4%
Denmark	11.9%	18.1%	0.65	1	−0.25	6.16	−9.0%	7.0%
Finland	13.7%	33.2%	0.41	16	−0.14	9.76	−18.2%	17.3%
France	10.5%	19.9%	0.53	5	−0.13	5.89	−9.7%	7.6%
Germany	9.4%	22.5%	0.42	14	−0.29	7.87	−12.9%	7.3%
Greece	12.7%	29.9%	0.43	13	0.30	8.54	−11.1%	17.3%
Hong Kong	11.5%	26.3%	0.44	11	−0.47	20.42	−23.0%	17.4%
Ireland	8.7%	19.3%	0.45	10	−0.14	6.94	−7.5%	7.2%
Italy	6.4%	22.3%	0.29	21	−0.12	5.88	−10.5%	6.9%
Japan	1.1%	23.2%	0.05	24	0.41	7.41	−8.1%	13.1%
Netherlands	9.2%	18.7%	0.49	7	−0.14	7.20	−8.1%	6.8%
New Zealand	2.8%	22.1%	0.13	23	−0.14	10.16	−14.6%	11.7%
Norway	9.2%	21.3%	0.43	12	−0.26	8.23	−11.6%	10.3%
Portugal	2.8%	18.6%	0.15	22	−0.03	8.63	−9.6%	9.2%
Singapore	7.6%	21.0%	0.36	20	0.21	11.76	−10.2%	12.6%
Spain	8.4%	21.1%	0.40	19	−0.05	7.02	−10.6%	9.6%
Sweden	13.5%	25.0%	0.54	4	0.07	7.00	−9.3%	12.1%
Switzerland	11.6%	17.9%	0.65	2	−0.14	7.08	−9.0%	7.0%
United Kingdom	6.8%	16.9%	0.40	18	−0.04	5.52	−5.2%	7.5%
United States	10.1%	16.1%	0.62	3	−0.14	7.24	−6.7%	5.8%

Note: The columns Mean, Volatility, and Sharpe Ratio are the annualized mean returns, volatilities, and Sharpe ratios of each country index. Rank is the numerical rank based on each country's Sharpe ratio. Min and Max are the daily minimum and maximum returns, respectively. Skew and Kurtosis are calculated as the third and fourth normalized centered moments.

---

[2] *MSCI Standard Methodology Book*, Morgan Stanley Capital International Inc., May 11 version, 2004.

EXHIBIT A.3 Statistics of Daily Returns over the Period January 1988 through December 1994

	Mean	Volatility	Sharpe Ratio	Rank	Skew	Kurtosis	Min	Max
World	6.4%	11.1%	0.57	12	0.04	7.70	−5.1%	4.9%
Australia	9.0%	17.4%	0.51	14	−0.43	5.98	−8.5%	4.5%
Austria	11.2%	21.2%	0.53	13	−0.08	11.80	−12.6%	9.7%
Belgium	10.2%	15.8%	0.64	7	0.32	12.84	−8.6%	8.5%
Canada	2.7%	10.6%	0.25	19	−0.35	5.08	−3.8%	3.2%
Denmark	13.2%	17.4%	0.76	5	−0.28	7.97	−9.0%	7.0%
Finland	5.7%	21.7%	0.26	18	0.08	5.86	−7.9%	7.3%
France	11.4%	17.8%	0.64	8	−0.30	7.93	−9.7%	7.6%
Germany	12.1%	20.1%	0.61	10	−0.77	14.54	−12.9%	7.3%
Greece	15.7%	31.9%	0.49	16	0.51	10.29	−11.1%	17.3%
Hong Kong	20.3%	24.1%	0.84	3	−2.28	37.08	−23.0%	8.6%
Ireland	10.1%	19.8%	0.51	15	0.01	7.49	−7.5%	7.2%
Italy	3.0%	22.2%	0.14	21	−0.29	7.12	−10.5%	6.9%
Japan	4.3%	22.6%	0.19	20	0.47	8.53	−8.1%	11.4%
Netherlands	11.7%	13.6%	0.87	2	−0.46	6.11	−6.4%	3.4%
New Zealand	2.2%	22.7%	0.10	22	0.02	7.83	−10.0%	8.4%
Norway	13.1%	22.4%	0.59	11	−0.15	9.09	−11.6%	10.3%
Portugal	−3.1%	19.3%	−0.16	24	0.06	12.10	−9.6%	9.2%
Singapore	18.8%	16.2%	1.16	1	−0.52	11.49	−9.1%	5.5%
Spain	1.2%	19.1%	0.06	23	−0.20	11.16	−10.6%	9.6%
Sweden	13.2%	21.0%	0.63	9	0.05	7.59	−9.3%	8.3%
Switzerland	13.4%	17.0%	0.79	4	−0.41	8.47	−9.0%	6.5%
United Kingdom	6.8%	16.1%	0.42	17	0.09	6.13	−5.2%	7.5%
United States	9.0%	12.6%	0.71	6	−0.55	9.30	−6.5%	3.8%

Note: The columns Mean, Volatility, and Sharpe Ratio are the annualized mean re turns, volatilities, and Sharpe ratios of each country index. Rank is the numerica rank based on each country's Sharpe ratio. Min and Max are the daily minimum anc maximum returns, respectively. Skew and Kurtosis are calculated as the third anc fourth normalized centered moments.

first half is January 1988 through December 1994, and the second half is January 1995 through May 2004.

We report the mean returns, return volatilities, and Sharpe ratios in annual terms. The minimum return (Min) and the maximum return (Max) are all in daily terms. The skew and kurtosis are calculated as the third and fourth normalized centered moments. The definition of the Sharpe ratio used in this book is the annualized mean return divided by the annualized volatility for the period under consideration.

We observe that the performance of the MSCI World Index as well as for most of its constituents was very good over the period considered. The

EXHIBIT A.4 Statistics of Daily Returns over the Period January 1995 through May 2004

	Mean	Volatility	Sharpe Ratio	Rank	Skew	Kurtosis	Min	Max
World	6.3%	14.0%	0.45	9	−0.09	5.39	−4.4%	4.7%
Australia	6.1%	17.7%	0.35	16	−0.03	6.05	−6.8%	7.7%
Austria	5.2%	17.3%	0.30	20	−0.29	5.11	−6.1%	4.0%
Belgium	6.9%	19.7%	0.35	15	0.30	7.57	−6.2%	9.1%
Canada	10.6%	19.0%	0.56	4	−0.54	8.11	−9.3%	5.4%
Denmark	10.9%	18.7%	0.58	3	−0.22	5.10	−6.1%	5.7%
Finland	19.7%	39.7%	0.50	7	−0.17	7.99	−18.2%	17.3%
France	9.8%	21.3%	0.46	8	−0.06	4.93	−6.1%	6.1%
Germany	7.4%	24.1%	0.31	18	−0.08	5.18	−7.5%	7.1%
Greece	10.5%	28.2%	0.37	14	0.07	6.11	−9.4%	8.8%
Hong Kong	4.9%	27.8%	0.18	21	0.42	13.03	−12.9%	17.4%
Ireland	7.6%	19.0%	0.40	11	−0.28	6.44	−7.5%	6.1%
Italy	8.9%	22.3%	0.40	10	0.01	4.97	−6.9%	6.9%
Japan	−1.3%	23.7%	−0.06	24	0.38	6.70	−6.9%	13.1%
Netherlands	7.2%	21.7%	0.33	17	−0.06	6.18	−8.1%	6.8%
New Zealand	3.2%	21.7%	0.15	22	−0.28	12.18	−14.6%	11.7%
Norway	6.3%	20.5%	0.31	19	−0.37	7.20	−9.0%	7.5%
Portugal	7.1%	18.1%	0.39	12	−0.10	5.23	−6.3%	5.2%
Singapore	−0.7%	24.0%	−0.03	23	0.41	10.40	−10.2%	12.6%
Spain	13.7%	22.5%	0.61	1	0.01	5.18	−6.2%	7.3%
Sweden	13.7%	27.6%	0.50	6	0.07	6.32	−9.2%	12.1%
Switzerland	10.2%	18.5%	0.55	5	0.02	6.29	−6.9%	7.0%
United Kingdom	6.8%	17.5%	0.39	13	−0.11	5.15	−5.1%	5.4%
United States	10.8%	18.3%	0.59	2	−0.03	6.05	−6.7%	5.8%

Note: The columns Mean, Volatility, and Sharpe Ratio are the annualized mean returns, volatilities, and Sharpe ratios of each country index. Rank is the numerical rank based on each country's Sharpe ratio. Min and Max are the daily minimum and maximum returns, respectively. Skew and Kurtosis are calculated as the third and fourth normalized centered moments.

average annual mean return for the index over the full period was 6.4% with an annual volatility of 12.9%. The average mean return in the first and the second halves were virtually the same (6.4% versus 6.3%), but the volatility increased from 11.1% to 14.0%. The individual country returns over the full sample range from 1.1% (Japan) to 13.7% (Finland), whereas volatilities range from 16.0% (Canada) to 33.2% (Finland).

If we rank the performance of individual countries in terms of their Sharpe ratio, Denmark and Switzerland (both with 0.65) come out ahead followed by the United States (0.62). Interestingly enough, comparing the rankings between the two periods based on the Sharpe ratio, we see that there is virtually no persistence at all. Indeed, the Spearman rank correlation coefficient (the correlation between the rankings of the two periods) is –0.07.

There is significant time-variation in volatilities. Exhibit A.5 demonstrates this fact for some of the countries in the sample, showing the one-year rolling standard deviation for the MSCI World Index, Singapore, Spain, Sweden, Switzerland, the United Kingdom, and the United States.

The correlation matrix for the full period is given in Exhibit A.6. Correlations between the different countries range from 0.01 (United States and Italy) to 0.76 (Canada and the Netherlands). We would therefore expect there to be some benefits of diversification.

Also the correlations exhibit time-variation. For example, in Exhibit A.7 the two year rolling correlations of United States with Germany, Hong Kong, Italy, Japan, and the Netherlands are depicted. Note that while some correlations have increased (United States versus Germany) others have decreased (United States versus Hong Kong). In fact, a further analysis of this data set shows that the correlations between the dif-

EXHIBIT A.5   One-Year Rolling Volatility (Standard Deviation) of the MSCI World Index, Singapore, Spain, Sweden, Switzerland, United Kingdom, and the United States

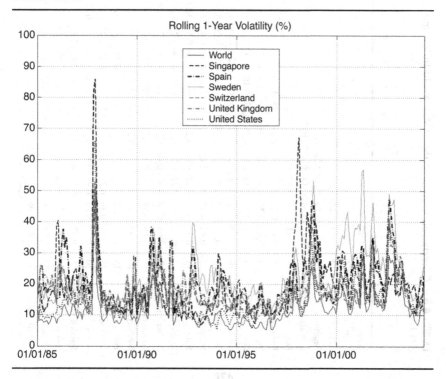

EXHIBIT A.6 Correlation Matrix of the MSCI World Index and the Individual Constituents over the Period 1/5/1988 through 5/31/2004

		1	2	3	4	5	6	7	8	9	10	11	12	13	14	15	16	17	18	19	20	21	22	23	24
World	1	1.00																							
Australia	2	0.29	1.00																						
Austria	3	0.34	0.24	1.00																					
Belgium	4	0.53	0.24	0.48	1.00																				
Canada	5	0.61	0.20	0.14	0.25	1.00																			
Denmark	6	0.41	0.24	0.45	0.53	0.21	1.00																		
Finland	7	0.46	0.22	0.26	0.37	0.33	0.38	1.00																	
France	8	0.65	0.23	0.41	0.62	0.38	0.50	0.51	1.00																
Germany	9	0.65	0.26	0.49	0.63	0.38	0.53	0.48	0.71	1.00															
Greece	10	0.24	0.16	0.28	0.30	0.12	0.29	0.20	0.27	0.29	1.00														
Hong Kong	11	0.31	0.37	0.21	0.18	0.18	0.21	0.24	0.23	0.26	0.15	1.00													
Ireland	12	0.42	0.30	0.42	0.48	0.20	0.46	0.33	0.48	0.49	0.31	0.23	1.00												
Italy	13	0.50	0.22	0.37	0.50	0.28	0.44	0.40	0.60	0.56	0.22	0.19	0.39	1.00											
Japan	14	0.53	0.31	0.26	0.25	0.15	0.23	0.19	0.23	0.23	0.19	0.29	0.26	0.19	1.00										
Netherlands	15	0.64	0.26	0.40	0.65	0.37	0.50	0.50	0.76	0.71	0.26	0.25	0.49	0.56	0.23	1.00									
New Zealand	16	0.19	0.51	0.22	0.18	0.10	0.17	0.16	0.16	0.20	0.14	0.25	0.23	0.16	0.22	0.19	1.00								
Norway	17	0.42	0.31	0.40	0.42	0.25	0.47	0.37	0.48	0.48	0.26	0.25	0.43	0.38	0.24	0.51	0.22	1.00							
Portugal	18	0.37	0.21	0.41	0.47	0.20	0.45	0.34	0.45	0.47	0.30	0.17	0.40	0.39	0.22	0.43	0.18	0.36	1.00						
Singapore	19	0.34	0.36	0.24	0.23	0.18	0.23	0.24	0.25	0.27	0.20	0.54	0.26	0.21	0.35	0.26	0.28	0.29	0.20	1.00					
Spain	20	0.59	0.25	0.43	0.57	0.34	0.49	0.45	0.71	0.64	0.28	0.23	0.44	0.60	0.24	0.65	0.18	0.45	0.48	0.26	1.00				
Sweden	21	0.57	0.29	0.35	0.47	0.36	0.47	0.61	0.63	0.59	0.25	0.27	0.42	0.51	0.26	0.59	0.20	0.49	0.40	0.30	0.58	1.00			
Switzerland	22	0.58	0.24	0.46	0.63	0.29	0.52	0.41	0.68	0.68	0.30	0.21	0.49	0.53	0.25	0.70	0.17	0.48	0.46	0.24	0.62	0.55	1.00		
United Kingdom	23	0.64	0.24	0.34	0.51	0.36	0.43	0.44	0.68	0.58	0.21	0.24	0.50	0.50	0.24	0.70	0.16	0.43	0.36	0.25	0.57	0.54	0.60	1.00	
United States	24	0.78	0.06	0.08	0.24	0.62	0.14	0.24	0.34	0.35	0.07	0.11	0.14	0.24	0.08	0.33	0.01	0.17	0.12	0.13	0.30	0.29	0.26	0.34	1.00

EXHIBIT A.7   Two-Year Rolling Correlations of United States with Germany,
Hong Kong, Italy, Japan, and the Netherlands

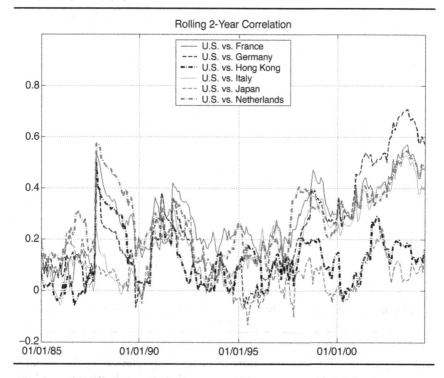

ferent countries have actually *decreased* over time whereas the
volatilities have *increased*. This result is consistent with several academic studies.[3] If we perform a decomposition of the correlation
throughout the sample, we find that about half the benefits of diversification available today to the international investor are due to the
increasing number of available markets, and the other half is due to the
lower average correlation among the different markets.

   In some examples in this book we use one-month LIBOR.[4] LIBOR,
which stands for the London Interbank Offered Rate, is one of the most

----

[3] See, for example, Richard O. Michaud, Gary L. Bergstrom, Ronald D. Frashure,
and Brian K. Wolahan, "Twenty Years of International Equity Investing," *Journal
of Portfolio Management* 23, no. 1 (Fall 1996), pp. 9–22; and William N. Goetzmann, Lingfeng Li, and K. Geert Rouwenhorst, "Long-Term Global Market Correlations," Yale ICF Working Paper No. 00-60, Yale International Center for Finance
(2002).

[4] British Bankers' Association, http://www.bba.org.uk/bba/jsp/polopoly.jsp?d=103.

EXHIBIT A.8   One-Month LIBOR

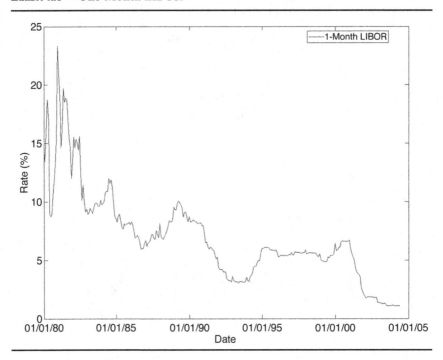

widely used benchmarks for short-term interest rates. It is the variable interest rate at which banks can borrow funds from each other in the London interbank market. The one-month LIBOR is depicted in Exhibit A.8.

Index

473